D1224922

IN PURSUIT OF WISDOM
The Scope of Philosophy

Other books by the same author:

Power and Society (with H. D. Lasswell)
The New World of Philosophy
American Ethics and Public Policy
The Conduct of Inquiry
Individuality and the New Society (editor)
Love . . . And Death

IN PURSUIT OF WISDOM
The Scope of Philosophy

ABRAHAM KAPLAN
The University of Haifa

GLENCOE PRESS

A division of Benziger Bruce & Glencoe, Inc.
Beverly Hills

Collier Macmillan Publishers
London

Printed in the United States of America

GLENCOE PRESS
A division of Benziger Bruce & Glencoe, Inc.
8701 Wilshire Boulevard
Beverly Hills, California 90211
Collier Macmillan Canada, Ltd.

Library of Congress catalog card number: 76-4017

First printing, 1977

ACKNOWLEDGMENTS

Acknowledgment is gratefully made to the following agents and publishers who have granted permission to use selections from their publications.

George Allen & Unwin Ltd., for: "On the Birth of His Son" by Su Tung-p'o, from *Translations from the Chinese*, translated by Arthur Waley. Copyright 1919 and renewed 1947 by Arthur Waley. Reprinted also by permission of Alfred A. Knopf, Inc.

Jonathan Cape Ltd., for: "Fire and Ice" by Robert Frost, from *The Poetry of Robert Frost*, edited by Edward Connery Lathem. Copyright 1923, ©1969 by Holt, Rinehart and Winston. Copyright 1951 by Robert Frost. Reprinted also by permission of the Estate of Robert Frost and Holt, Rinehart and Winston, Publishers.

Faber & Faber (Publishers), Ltd., for: Excerpts from *Fragment of an Agon* from *Collected Poems 1909–1962* by T. S. Eliot. Copyright 1936 by Harcourt Brace Jovanovich, Inc.; copyright, 1963, 1964 by T. S. Eliot. Reprinted also by permission of Harcourt Brace Jovanovich, Inc.

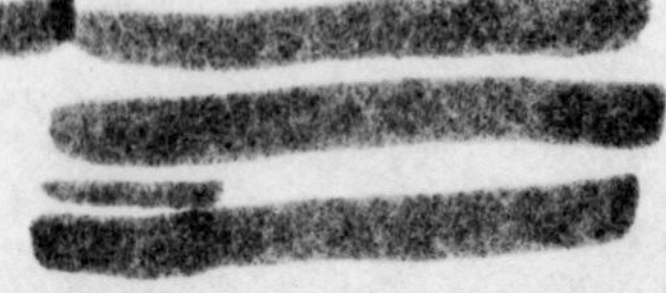

Harcourt Brace Jovanovich, Inc., for: Excerpt from "what if a much of a which of a wind" and "all ignorance toboggans into know" in *Complete Poems 1913–1962* by E. E. Cummings. Excerpt from "since feeling is first" in *Complete Poems 1913–1962* by E. E. Cummings. Copyright, 1926, by Horace Liveright; copyright, 1954, by E. E. Cummings. "a politician is an arse upon," copyright, 1944, by E. E. Cummings; copyright, 1972, by Nancy T. Andrews. Reprinted from *Complete Poems 1913–1962* by E. E. Cummings. Excerpts from *Fragment of an Agon* from *Collected Poems 1909–1962* by T. S. Eliot, copyright, 1936, by Harcourt Brace Jovanovich, Inc.; copyright 1963, 1964 by T. S. Eliot. Reprinted also by permission of Faber & Faber (Publishers), Ltd.

Holt, Rinehart and Winston, Publishers, for: "With rue my heart is laden" and excerpt from "Terrence, this is stupid stuff" from "A Shropshire Lad"—Authorized Edition—from *The Collected Poems of A. E. Housman.* Copyright 1939, 1940, ©1965 by Holt, Rinehart and Winston. Copyright ©1967, 1968 by Robert E. Symons. Excerpt from "The laws of God, the laws of man" from *The Collected Poems of A. E. Housman.* Copyright 1922 by Holt, Rinehart and Winston. Copyright 1950 by Barclays Bank, Ltd. Reprinted also by permission of The Society of Authors. "Fire and Ice" by Robert Frost, from *The Poetry of Robert Frost,* edited by Edward Connery Lathern. Copyright 1923, ©1969 by Holt, Rinehart and Winston. Copyright 1951 by Robert Frost. Reprinted also by permission of Jonathan Cape Ltd.

Jeffers Literary Properties, for: "Promise of Peace" from *Roan Stallion, Tamar, and Other Poems* by Robinson Jeffers, The Modern Library, Inc. Copyright 1935.

Alfred A. Knopf, Inc., for: "On the Birth of His Son" by Su Tung-p'o, from *Translations from the Chinese,* translated by Arthur Waley. Copyright 1919 and renewed 1947 by Arthur Waley. Reprinted also by permission of George Allen & Unwin Ltd.

Macmillan Publishing Co., Inc., for: Excerpt from "Mr. Flood's Party" from *Collected Poems* by Edwin Arlington Robinson. Copyright 1921 by Edwin Arlington Robinson, renewed 1949 by Ruth Nivison.

Mrs. Edgar Lee Masters, for: Excerpts from "Silence" by Edgar Lee Masters from *Songs and Satires,* published by Macmillan Publishing Co.

Charles Scribner's Sons, for: Excerpt from "To think that two and two are four" by A. E. Housman, from *My Brother, A. E. Housman* by Laurence Housman. Copyright 1937, 1938 Laurence Housman.

Martin Secker & Warburg, Limited, for: Excerpt from "The Crying Water" from *Collected Works of Arthur Symons.*

The Society of Authors (as the literary representative of the Estate of A. E. Housman and Jonathan Cape Ltd.), for: "With rue my heart is laden" and excerpt from "Terrence, this is stupid stuff" from "A Shropshire Lad"—Authorized Edition—from *The Collected Poems of A. E. Housman.* Copyright 1939, 1940, ©1967, 1968 by Robert E. Symons. Excerpt from "The laws of God, the laws of man" from *The Collected Poems of A. E. Housman.* Copyright 1922 by Holt, Rinehart and Winston. Copyright 1950 by Barclays Bank, Ltd. Reprinted also by permission of Holt, Rinehart and Winston, Publishers.

Twayne Publishers, A Division of G. K. Hall & Co., Boston, for: four-line poem by D. H. Lawrence from *Sex, Literature and Censorship,* copyright by Twayne Publishers, Inc.

Frederick Ungar Publishing Co., for: "Ode" from *History of Chinese Literature,* translated by Herbert Giles.

For
Martin, David, and Mayer
a time to remember

Contents

Preface

This book is a survey of the main ideas in philosophy as they have crystallized in our time. My aim is to present philosophy as something that matters to everyone. Technicalities and abstractions which are needed for the work of philosophy have inevitably been condemned as the hairsplitting jargon of a coterie of professionals, speaking only to one another. For a time the condemnation was, I think, deserved. Today, philosophers, by and large, are not content with cultivating an activity (called "doing" philosophy) which, however intellectually challenging, is of no use to anyone save those studying it so as to be able to teach it to others. We teach philosophy in the conviction that thinking about these things may make a difference, even an important difference, in how men deal with their problems and predicaments. Philosophy matters because it is occupied with what matters, in every domain of human action and experience. If, at times, the ideas appear remote, it is because only distance can provide perspective.

I have tried, therefore, to present philosophy as an integral part of human culture, intimately interwoven with every other form of thought and expression. Philosophy is one of the humanities, after all, and to my mind should be central in every curriculum of humanistic and social studies. Because culture, in its essence, is a heritage of the past as well as a product of the emerging present, I have presented contemporary philosophical ideas in continuity with the great ideas of the past. The more fundamental our concerns, the more they have in common with those of other times and with other cultures. I have tried to heighten awareness of this kinship, especially with the classical cultures of India, China, and Japan.

Philosophy is no place for parochialism, but there is no such thing as a universal background to thought, nor is there a universal language in which thought can be expressed. Both art and mathematics, each in its own way as nearly universal a language as men have devised, are nevertheless decidedly shaped by the culture and period in which they are produced. My own standpoint is unmistakably, I suppose, that of an American and an Israeli, facing the last quarter of the twentieth century. My background is in science and the philosophies of scientific empiricism and logical positivism; but in the course of time, politics, religion, art, and psychodynamics have increasingly invited my attention. I hope that both sorts of interests have found expression in these pages, in both philosophic content and method. If any single aim has dominated my thinking, so far as I am aware, it is to reinstate the claims of reason in what I feel to be an age of madness, the claims of intelligence in an era of unthinking violence, the claims of moral decency in this time of base and contemptible self-seeking among the nations. To those who share this aim, from whatever standpoint, this book is meant to say, "Be strong, and let us strengthen one another."

I have aimed at an introduction to the whole scope of philosophy. There is a chapter, or at least a section, on each of the fields of philosophy conventionally discriminated—semantics (though only the nonformal discipline), logic (both deductive and inductive), foundations of mathematics, epistemology, philosophy of science, metaphysics, philosophy of mind, theory of value, normative ethics, social philosophy, philosophy of education, philosophy of history, political philosophy, philosophy of law, aesthetics, and philosophy of religion.

An introduction can do no more than introduce; I have made no attempt to present every variant opinion, nor to explore any position down to its ultimate foundations. Seeking breadth, I am aware of having paid the necessary price in depth. An alternative strategy, followed by many introductions to philosophy, is to probe deeply here and there in the philosophical domain, leaving most of the terrain unexplored. An overview also has its uses, especially in philosophy. Frequent citations and the appended reading list may guide the student to his own deeper reflections.

Philosophy finds expression in a variety of forms, not always in explicitly philosophical treatises. I have, therefore, often turned to literature, not as an embellishment but because men other than professional philosophers have also been profoundly occupied with the same concerns, and it may be, to better effect. Felicity of expression does not necessarily preclude significance of content. Apropos, "the Master" who is so often quoted in these pages is not a single individual, but a generic label I have adopted for the various spokesmen of Hassidism, the Jewish mystical movement of the last two centuries or so. Most of the references are sayings attributed to the Baal Shem Tov, the founder of the movement; Schneuer Zalman; Simcha Bunam; Mendel of Kotzk; Levi Yitzchak of Berditchev; Naftali of Ropshitz; and Nachman of Bratslav. I have similarly used the generic term *roshi* in place of the names of a number of Zen masters, especially as cited in the various writings of Daisetz Suzuki.

My thanks are due to John Gallagher, who conceived the idea for this book, and persisted till it was brought to birth; to Ruth Glushanok, who worked to make it readable; and most of all to Iona, who listened to every word with an unfailing warmth of acceptance.

Mount Carmel
Sivan 5735

Chapter One

Philosophy

1. The Love of Wisdom

Still vivid in the memories of my childhood in northern Minnesota are the clear wintry nights and the brilliance of the stars. Nights were darker then, I think; cities were not so well lit, and the air may have been clearer, too. With my biblical upbringing, the words of the Psalms often came to mind, "The heavens declare the glory of God, the skies show forth the work of his hands." Though I had not then so much as heard of Immanuel Kant, in retrospect his words (in the conclusion of *The Critique of Practical Reason*) may have fit my experience more closely than the Psalmist's words, for they confined themselves to the quality of the experience itself: "Two things fill the mind with ever-increasing wonder and awe the more often and the more intensely the mind is drawn to them: the starry heavens above me and the moral law within me." As to the moral law within me, I do not know if it ever filled me with a sense of the sublime. But the starry heavens above certainly did. Aristotle says in his *Metaphysics* that it is owing to their wonder that men first began to philosophize; they wondered about the moon and the sun and the stars, and about the genesis of the universe. At any rate this was true for me.

I have another vivid memory of those days—or nights, rather—which evoked philosophical reflections of a sort very common in childhood, I venture to say. Often, as I lay wakefully or just falling asleep, I heard the chimes of the clock in the tower of the school near which we lived. The melody—called, I think, Westminster Quarters—seemed to me unutterably melancholy, and the reverberation of the deep tones engulfed me in their sadness. I felt much more awe than wonder. The muted, slow, and measured bells inevitably brought thoughts of funerals and death. I never sent to know for whom the bells tolled; I knew they tolled for me, that they would sound inexorably as the hours moved on, quarter by quarter, and that they would continue to sound long after I was dead, on and on, long after anyone remained who knew or cared that I had lived, on and on to eternity. They were Platonic Ideas of bells, not subject to change and decay, to be cracked by use and struck down by lightning, but the voice of Time itself, in mourning for me.

This experience of awe—perhaps "anxiety" would be a more accurate word—I did not pursue till many years later. My wonder about the starry heavens above was nurtured by a series of books of speculative astronomy, popular in the 1920s and 30s, by James Jeans and Arthur Eddington. For some reason, I devoted my serious studies to chemistry rather than to astronomy. It was both a shock and a relief when, in my first course in philosophy, I heard the opening statement of Aristotle's *Metaphysics*, that all men by nature desire to know. In later years, I often had occasion to doubt the universality of his dictum as did, surely, every teacher from Aristotle's day to our own; there are always some natures in whom there seems to be no such desire. It was reassuring, then, to learn that though speculation may be unscientific, it is not for that reason unnatural.

Why I left science to devote myself to speculation is not quite clear to me now. I think it was because my religious background and a burgeoning interest in politics and art found science insufficient; perhaps, too, the bells still tolled. Maybe, after all, it was simply more inviting to occupy myself with the kind of questions which engaged me in the laboratory while waiting for some reagent to dissolve or be distilled.

The details of this personal history may be idiosyncratic; its substance, I am sure, is not. The love of wisdom (which is the root meaning of "philosophy") is not as universal as Aristotle thought. There are not many who devote their lives to the pursuit of wisdom, as did Spinoza and Bertrand Russell; and fewer still who, like Socrates and Giordano Bruno, give up their lives for their philosophy. But all men, in some measure, share in the life of the mind; this sharing must surely be included in any list of characteristically human traits.

Aristotle defined man as the rational animal. Irrationality seems to be even more characteristic of the species, especially for each of us as judged on the basis of what we ourselves conceive to be rational (§49). Yet, a capacity for rationality is there, although it would be irrational to demand more of a man than he is capable of. In any case, though a man's thought be misguided or foolish, he *is* thinking. Though he may act thoughtlessly, his action, as long as it is identifiably that of a human being, is not altogether mindless and unknowing. A man who seems to be indifferent to truth may, in reality, only care nothing for *my* truth—because he sees it as falsehood or, at best, as trivial or irrelevant. *His* truth remains central to his being; it is in coming to know that truth that he becomes the man he is.

People enjoy the use of their intellectual capacities, apart from any other considerations, simply because they have them, as a strong person rejoices in his strength. They have a need to provide themselves with the occasion for the exercise of their mental powers if no other needs provide it for them. There is no culture without its intellectual games, puzzles, and riddles. What has been disparaged as "idle" curiosity has absorbed the energies of many men who apparently had more pressing concerns. The satisfaction of such curiosity has been prized beyond many other attainments.

Whatever else it may be, philosophy is an expression of intellectual curiosity. Socrates maintained that the unexamined life is not worth living; his own life reveals his conviction that the examination itself is worth living for. Hebrew *chachamim*, Greek Sophists, Indian *rishis*, and Chinese literati had at least this in common, that they desired to know—whatever their reasons. The sense of wonder, Socrates said (as reported by Plato in his dialogue *Theaetetus*), is the mark of the philosopher; for Socrates, as for Aristotle, the love of wisdom has no other origin.

Curiosity, however intense, implies a certain impersonality; and wonder, however compelling, connotes a certain detachment. Such selflessness may characterize the attainment of wisdom, but not the pursuit. Man desires to know, not only because he is by his nature drawn to knowledge, but also because he is driven to find out what he can lest the world destroy him, or lest it thwart his less disinterested wants than the desire to know. If it is wise to seek wisdom, the search may after all be folly, for only those who are already wise would embark upon the search; and, as Zen has it, why should the rider on the donkey seek the donkey?

Toward the end of the eighteenth century, Kant formulated a number of questions which, he maintained, the human mind irresistibly poses to itself, although it is powerless to answer them. Has the universe lasted forever, or did it have a beginning? Is it infinite in extent, or does space come to an end? An unqualified yes or no to each question appears to be quite unacceptable (§37), yet there is no middle ground. (To the counter question, what God might have been doing *before* He created the world, Augustine refers us to the reply that He was preparing Hell for pryers into mysteries.) Such questions are indeed disinterested. It cannot matter, save for the love of truth for its own sake, whether space and time are strictly infinite or finite but so vast as to be infinite *to all intents and purposes.*

There are other philosophical questions which are not, in this sense, disinterested. Differences in philosophies can make a difference and do have a bearing on intents and purposes other than those expressed in the pursuit of truth. Kant also asked whether man has free will or is governed by causal necessity; whether there is a God; and whether man has an immortal soul. How a philosophy answers these questions—or indeed, whether it regards them as answerable—would surely matter to those who live by the philosophy. Basic questions such as Kant's: What am I? What ought I to do? What may I hope for? undeniably have a practical bearing on the conduct of life.

It is because of its practical bearing as well as its theoretical interest that philosophic reflection has commanded so much attention, even in periods when philosophy was attacked as "purely academic" or "scholastic." "The philosophers," Marx declared in his *Theses on Feuerbach*, "have only *interpreted* the world, in various ways; the point, however, is to *change* it." To which John Dewey replies that the point of interpretation is precisely to give impulse and direction to change. From a properly pragmatic point of view, theory is only the form that practice takes when action encounters blocks or conflicts which prevent its consummation. We think because we must; I am, but might not be—therefore, I think.

On this score American pragmatism is at one with European currents of thought—Marxism itself, which contains a strong element of pragmatism, as Sidney Hook has made explicit; existentialism, especially in the form which Friedrich Nietzsche gave it; and the evolutionism of Henri Bergson. After Darwin, how else are we to explain the growth of mental capacity in humans if not by reference to the serviceability of thought in the struggle for survival? Why animals sleep is still something of a mystery; some time ago, it was suggested that the more fruitful question is, why do they ever wake up? The answer is that our troubles do not let us sleep: we must waken or die. Magic and religion, science and art, and philosophy as well, are the cries of wakefulness.

2. Puzzles and Problems

There are troubles and troubles. Some of those with which the mind is occupied are of its own making. I do not mean neurotic guilts and anxieties, psychotic delusions of persecution, and the like. There is a reality within as without, and *thinking* so does not *make* it so for the facts of the inner life any more than for the facts of the outer life. Mental illness cannot be cured just by setting the patient straight and explaining something to him—though many purported therapies (not all of them quackery) amount to just that.

Those troubles that can be ended merely by straightening out our thinking I call *puzzles*, as contrasted with *quandaries*, which have an objective locus. Confronted by a puzzle, we find ourselves in a quandary, but one which on solving the puzzle we see to have been unreal. We may be in a real quandary if failure to solve the puzzle will bring down other troubles on our heads. The riddle of the Sphinx of Thebes was only a puzzle: "What has one voice, but four legs, two legs, and three?" (Answer: Man, as he moves from crawling infancy to the cane of old age.) The quandary was that whoever failed to give the answer to the riddle was devoured by the sphinx; when Oedipus guessed it, the monster killed herself. If a puzzle illuminates a real quandary, its contribution is subtle and indirect—in a word, symbolic—like the contribution of mythology (to which, not incidentally, the sphinx belongs), or wit, or perhaps art in general (§81). Similarly, Samson's riddle was a puzzle: "Out of the eater something to eat; out of the strong, sweetness." (Answer: Honey in the carcass of the lion he had killed with his bare hands.) The quandary was that failure to guess the riddle would result in the forfeit of thirty festive robes (though the riddle was guessed, thirty men lost their lives because of it).

So-called "philosophical" questions are often only puzzles. Take the question of whether a tree that falls in a remote forest makes a sound. Yes, if the question is whether it sets up sound waves in the air (a meteorite crashing onto the airless moon does *not* make a sound). The answer is no, if by "sound" we mean something heard: obviously, there is no hearing without a hearer. Is the grass green at night? Certainly, though not on a night in February—if we are asking what pigment is in the grass. Certainly not, if "green" refers to light of a certain wavelength: grass reflects no light at all, if no light is shining on it. There are no mysteries here, only confusions. William James gives a similar example of a hunter who sees a squirrel on a tree trunk. As the hunter circles, the squirrel moves always to the opposite side of the tree; has the hunter gone round the squirrel? It depends on whether "going round" means moving successively through the four points of the compass while the squirrel remains in the space thus enclosed, or whether it means moving from a position in front of the squirrel to one behind it, then around its other side to its front again. We know all we need to know about the movements of both the hunter and the squirrel; there is no uncertainty about the facts, only about what we should say.

We also do not know what to say in cases where we cannot determine the facts. We might then experience puzzlement. If our uncertainty stems from the extremely hypothetical character of the question raised, the question is sometimes called a "philosophical" one in reference to its being wholly and hopelessly academic, in the pejorative sense of that word. A suitor at a loss for topics of conversation is advised to discuss tastes, family, or philosophy. Accordingly, he asks the young lady, "Do you like noodles?" "No." "Do you have a brother?" "No." "Well, if you had a brother, would *he* like noodles?" The same dig at philosophy is in this passage from Oscar Wilde's *The Importance of Being Earnest:*

> JACK. You don't really mean to say that you couldn't love me if my name wasn't Ernest?
>
> GWENDOLEN. But your name is Ernest.
>
> JACK. Yes, I know it is. But supposing it was something else? Do you mean to say you couldn't love me then?
>
> GWENDOLEN (glibly). Ah! that is clearly a metaphysical speculation, and like most metaphysical speculations has very little reference at all to the actual facts of real life, as we know them.

The question is only hypothetical, not metaphysical. Scientific questions often pose conditions we know to be false to fact so that we may formulate and test alternative hypotheses.

Puzzles have philosophic import only if the uncertainty they express has its locus, not in facts, but in meanings, especially when one meaning gets in the way of another. Gilbert Ryle calls such puzzles "dilemmas" (in a book with that title). He describes them as "tangles brought about in our lines of thought when we treat one subject with a conceptual apparatus appropriate to another, or when we express one interest in idioms appropriate to another. Disparate systems or contexts of thinking have been knotted together. The dilemma is resolved when each line of thought or manner of speaking is put back into its proper place; the conflict is in the tangle and not in the lines themselves." Many puzzles—for instance, the puzzle concerning the relations between "the mind" and "the body"—have been dealt with in this way (§43).

Puzzles, in short, are only amusing or, at best, therapeutic. Their solution does not advance knowledge, and contributes to understanding only in the sense of removing misunderstandings, as medicine does not nourish the organism, making for vigor and growth, but only combats disease.

Puzzles are of our own making, but it is life that puts us into quandaries. There are some quandaries in which we might not have found ourselves if we had pursued other interests or acted otherwise in the pursuit. But that we *are* in the quandary is not altogether our own doing. Though crime, war, and disease can be prevented, doing so demands considerably more than "putting a line of thought or manner of speaking back into its proper place." Philosophy, as I conceive it, is not engaged solely (or even most significantly) in solving puzzles; it deals with quandaries but of a special kind, which are therefore to be dealt with in a special way. We do not philosophize primarily because we have misused language or been misguided in our thinking, but because we find ourselves in real quandaries.

Most quandaries are what I call *problems:* it is possible, at least in principle, to extricate oneself from them. Problems have solutions, though not in the way that puzzles do. When we have solved a puzzle we are done with it; the solution of a problem usually confronts us with new problems. We do not dispose of problems but, at best, deal with them in such a way as to be able to confront the new problems which emerge from our handling of the old. Crime, war, and disease—the examples of the last paragraph—are problems; there can be no thought—save in a wholly utopian vein—of settling them once for all. But problems need not—as these examples might misleadingly suggest—relate to what are called "practical" concerns in contrast to "purely theoretical" interests. The origins of the solar system or the distribution of the prime numbers also presents us with problems. What is essential to my presentation here is that problems can be solved.

A quandary might more accurately be described as a *problematic situation,* rather than a problem. In a strict sense, a problem is a formulation of the difficulty with which the problematic situation confronts us. As John Dewey has emphasized, often a correct formulation of the difficulty points the way to the solution, while an incorrect formulation may delay the solution. (A correct formulation of the problem may very well call for just such a flash of insight as solves a puzzle.) The history of science provides many examples of problems which, because of improper formulation, appeared to be insoluble.

Sometimes it can be demonstrated that what was thought to be a problem is in fact insoluble, and therefore only a "pseudoproblem." In the nineteenth century, mathematicians were able to prove, for instance, that there simply cannot be any way to "square the circle," to trisect an angle with only a straightedge and compass, or to derive the axiom of parallels from the other axioms of Euclidean geometry. In disposing of these pseudoproblems, mathematicians uncovered whole nests of genuine problems. As new problems were formulated, the problematic situations in mathematics were themselves transformed. In somewhat this spirit Rudolf Carnap has spoken of pseudoproblems in philosophy—for instance, those arising when problems about kinds of words and sentences are mistakenly formulated as though they concerned objects and facts. More careful formulations have generated whole new disciplines in logic, semantics, and related fields (Chapters Two and Three). This is not to say that all distinctively philosophical questions relate to pseudoproblems and so have been disposed of definitively—though Carnap and some of his followers espoused this view for a short time.

3. Quandaries: Predicaments

In addition to problems—pseudo- or genuine—there are quandaries of quite another kind. To deal with quandaries is the task of science, technology, and the inquiries in which we engage in the conduct of all the affairs of life. There remain other quandaries which I call *predicaments*, with which philosophy is distinctively concerned. These are quandaries which do not allow for solutions, not because of any deficiencies in either knowledge or power, but simply because of the nature of things. We can only learn to live with them, cope, manage somehow. Every position in the game of chess presents the players with certain *problems:* problems of attack or defense, of establishing control over certain squares, gaining tempi, or winning material. Such problems are capable of solution, or can be shown to be impossible to solve. The *predicament* in which the chess player finds himself is that he alone is not free to determine what the future course of the game will be but must face an opponent whose aims are the opposite of his own; that the pieces with which he must play are limited in number and can move only in certain preestablished ways; that once a man is captured he is removed from the board till the game has ended (although once in its lifetime a pawn may be promoted to a queen); and that the king cannot be replaced and his capture ends the game. It is easy enough to imagine other rules, but in that case the game would no longer be chess; what is more to the point, the new rules would define new predicaments.

Problems are in a certain sense unnecessary, that is, any particular problem is unnecessary, but not the circumstance that we must face problems. Problems have to do with the facts of the situation, rather than with the laws which govern it. The world would still be recognizably *this* world even though our problems were solved; but without our predicaments it would no longer be the world we know. When Tevya asks (in *Fiddler on the Roof*),

> *Would it spoil some vast, eternal plan—*
> *If I were a wealthy man?*

he is expressing the conviction that his poverty is only a problem, not a predicament. It could have happened—or might yet happen, God willing!—that he would be a rich man. "I realize, of course, that it's no shame to be poor," he says, "but it's no great honor either." The question is whether, in his case, it would be a violation of the order of nature.

Problems are contingent, dependent upon the circumstances obtaining in particular cases; not so predicaments, which are universal. One man is poor, another rich; one suffers the pangs of unrequited love, while another rejoices in endearments; one is sick, while another glows with health; and so for all our problems—or, at any rate, so it might be. No man is exempt from the predicaments which define the human condition. By the same token, problems are temporary, even though in their passage one problem only gives way to another. But as to predicaments, each of us serves a life sentence—with no time off for good behavior and no parole.

Typical of our predicaments is the very nature of objectivity—that facts are what they are whether we like them or not. Wishes are not horses, and the sad truth is that beggars do not ride. A world in which all our wishes are fulfilled belongs to the domain of fantasy as does, indeed, a world in which *any* wish may be fulfilled merely by wishing. In fairy tales, wishes are "granted"; in reality, effort must be expended for any fulfillment. If, as in infancy, we are in the care of another, the effort need not be our own; but effort there must be. God can say, "Let there be light!" and there *is* light; when man contents himself with the mere proclamation, he remains in darkness.

One of the most influential twentieth-century philosophers, Ludwig Wittgenstein, puts it: "The world is independent of my will. Even if everything we wished were to happen, this would only be, so to speak, a favor of fate, for there is no *logical* connection between will and the world which would guarantee this, and the assumed physical connection we could not again will." The outcome of the logical analysis coincides with the findings of psychoanalysis at about the same period. The infant is swaddled in the delusion of omnipotence: that every wish brings its own fulfillment. The mind of the infant—perhaps better, his will, and at bottom, his voice—is, indeed, to paraphrase Kant, the lawgiver to nature as the infant experiences it. There is, in reality, a world of causal determination which is not to be wheedled or cajoled. The predicament of maturity is that the world, as Freud has remarked, is not, after all, a nursery.

To fulfill our wishes it is not enough to make them known; we must act on the world. Our actions must be based on the recognition that materials are recalcitrant, that they have a will of their own. An object, Dewey says somewhere, is that which objects. Nature, to be commanded, must be obeyed, as Francis Bacon admonishes. But Nature signs no contracts; our obedience carries no guarantee that we shall command in turn. It is from this perspective that Arthur Schopenhauer, in his *Studies in Pessimism,* speaks of the long battle which forms the history of life, where every effort is checked by difficulties and stopped until they are overcome.

The optimism of the age of science which Bacon heralded is expressed in another aphorism of his, that knowledge is power. The predicament is that we so seldom know enough to deal with our problems, or, having the knowledge, so seldom also have the power to put the knowledge into practice. To see knowledge as power is to mistake potentiality for its own actualization. If there are no limits to what can be known, there are at any rate limits to what we can do with our knowledge. "There is no man who has power over the wind or over the day of death; and there is no discharge from war" (Ecclesiastes). One may quarrel over specifics; but there is no denying the general point that action—and, therefore, the fulfillment of our wishes—is limited always by physical, biological, and social constraints. The lack of either knowledge or power or both paves the road to Hell with even the best of intentions.

Action is often enmeshed in another predicament: not merely that knowledge is limited, but that what we *do* know is not to the point, while what is relevant lies outside our knowledge. In particular, we cannot foretell the future. "The evil of man is great upon him," says the Preacher, "for he does not know that which is to be." The time of his death falls suddenly upon him, as the fish, all unknowing, is taken in the net and the bird caught in the snare. "Who can tell a man what shall be after him under the sun?"—"under the sun," which is to say, not in some heaven, but here on earth, where what we have done in life moves to an unknown sequel after our death.

Expectations are continually thwarted because human affairs are governed by chance. "The race is not to the swift, nor the battle to the strong, nor bread to the wise, nor riches to men of understanding, nor yet favor to men of skill; but time and chance happens to them all." The race may not be to the swift, a Damon Runyon character advises, but that's the way to bet; yet as Sam the Gonoph points out, in human affairs the odds are never better than 6 to 5 against. Often they are much worse: the most unlikely eventualities keep coming about. I propose a new word I believe should prove useful: *agathonic,* from the name of the tragic poet to whom Aristotle attributes the view that it is very probable that the improbable should happen. We may call an event agathonic to convey that, though it itself was highly unlikely, we might have known that something of that sort was bound to happen. If only we could know beforehand just which it would be! This is what we cannot know, and that is our predicament.

Our ignorance of the future is a special form of a more general predicament—that we are creatures bound by time. The occurrence of events not only follows a definite order, but also a fixed direction. The movement from past to future is irreversible; we cannot go home again, and the past cannot be recaptured. Among twentieth-century philosophers, Bergson especially has emphasized the significance for human experience of the difference in this respect between space and time: that we can move freely in space in any direction, and not at all in time (§37).

I remember returning after the passing of many years to the scenes of my childhood. The journey was of several thousand miles (from California to Minnesota), but space was quite unresisting to the jet plane, and I sat eagerly awaiting the journey's end. When I had arrived, however, the intervening years still confronted me, neither mocking nor compassionate, but wholly unyielding. The past remained only a memory, and I had not returned at all. A time machine is no more than a fantasy.

The Moving Finger writes; and, having writ,
Moves on: nor all your Piety nor Wit
Shall lure it back to cancel half a Line,
Nor all your Tears wash out a Word of it.

It is not only remorse or regret which makes so poignant the irreversibility of time. The inexorable flow means that even our fulfillments are ephemeral. Another quatrain from the *Rubaiyat* runs:

The Worldly Hope men set their Hearts upon
Turns Ashes—or it prospers; and anon,
Like Snow upon the Desert's dusty Face,
Lighting a little Hour or two—is gone.

In his pact with Mephistopheles, Faust agrees that the Devil may cast him into chains "if ever I should tell the moment: O stay! You are so beautiful!" Much good would it do him to tell the moment to stay, pact or no! A recurrent theme in the wisdom literatures of many peoples is this evanescence of all things beautiful and good as of all things ugly and evil, of the mighty as of the weak, of the greatest emperors as of their meanest subjects. The apocryphal Ben Sira in declaring, "Everything made will decay and disappear, and the man who made it will vanish with it," is at one with the pagan Emperor Marcus Aurelius, who writes in his *Meditations,* "View the other epochs of time and of whole nations, and see how many, after great efforts, soon fell and were resolved into the elements."

Above all, man's subjection to time is manifested in his mortality. In our Western tradition, man's fate was sealed from the very beginning: "You shall surely die! Dust thou art, and to dust thou shalt return." A classical Japanese poem, in a translation by Arthur Waley, reads:

High mountains and the sea—
The one goes on being a mountain,
Always just as solid;
The other goes on being the sea,
And will never be anything else.
But man is a flower-like thing,
Man of this fleeting world.

The flower as an image of the fragile and ephemeral character of man's life is a widespread symbol. In the Book of Job we have, "Man that is born of woman is of few days, and full of trouble. He comes forth like a flower, and withers; he flees like a shadow." Isaiah proclaims, "All flesh is grass, and all its grace is as the flower of the field. The grass withers, the flower fades." A contemporary folk song, popular with the counterculture because of its political content, is nevertheless deeply rooted in tradition when it asks, referring to the young men killed in battle, "Where have all the flowers gone?" Death is the universal destiny; there is a touch of gallows humor in Sholom Aleichem's folkwitticism that if the rich could hire others to die in their place, a poor man could make a living.

The sheer passage of time, and so the impermanence of all things, has been thought by many to rob everything in experience of significance. Time, says Schopenhauer, is that agent by which at every moment all things in our hands become as nothing, and lose any real value they possess. This is a cardinal tenet of Buddhism: that all is impermanence, *anitya,* and so is worthy only of renunciation. It is central to the idealism of the Hindus and of Plato, who both look to a reality outside time for the ground of value. Aristotle criticized Plato with the realistic observation that something eternally white is not for that reason any whiter. Yet the fact is that, in time, the white always darkens. Lovers, apparently, are intuitive Platonists, with their recurrent question, "Will you love me always?" We may take as sufficient unto the day the evil thereof, but for some it seems that even the good thereof partakes of evil if it is for the day only.

Bertrand Russell urges that both in thought and in feeling, to realize the unimportance of time is the gate of wisdom (*Our Knowledge of the External World*). But, as he himself adds, "unimportance is not unreality." In reality, all that we cherish passes away; it is difficult to view this circumstance as unimportant. A. E. Housman surely does not stand outside the gate of wisdom because of the thought and feeling he expresses in "A Shropshire Lad":

With rue my heart is laden
For golden friends I had,
For many a rose-lipt maiden
And many a lightfoot lad.

By brooks too broad for leaping
The lightfoot boys are laid;
The rose-lipt girls are sleeping
In fields where roses fade.

To grieve endlessly no doubt *is* folly; but is it folly to live in the realization that no man lives forever? For my part, I must say, with Andrew Marvell,

At my back I always hear
Time's winged chariot hurrying near,
And yonder all before us lie
Deserts of vast eternity.

—"To His Coy Mistress"

The predicament of mortality is made the more bitter by the circumstance that a man's death is so often encompassed by other men. This in itself is a predicament—that though human we are subject to man's inhumanity. "Master, I marvel how the fishes live in the sea." To which one of Shakespeare's philosophical fools replies, "Why, as men do a land; the great ones eat up the little ones." The victim is given neither succor nor sympathy. "I saw all the oppressions that are done under the sun," says the Preacher. "Behold the tears of the oppressed, and they had no one to comfort them! On the side of their oppressors there was power." Job is expressing not only his own experience but a very nearly universal one when he laments, "I cry aloud, but there is no justice."

What makes injustice a predicament rather than a problem—which, though frequent and widespread, would still allow for redress—is that the very institutions for such redress are themselves implicated in the injustice, or even responsible for it. When the salt loses its savor, with what shall it be salted? One of the great political cartoons of our time stems from the Nazi period, though each age no doubt can draw its own version: A thug in uniform is beating a helpless little man; the caption reads, "Ya want da police? *I'm* da police!" Charges of "police brutality" are not peculiar to our time (it by no means follows that such charges are therefore without substance). What is unusual is that today the charges are so freely voiced.

The sense of helplessness in the face of injustice has no doubt been felt continuously from Job's day to our own. I believe it is this, more than anything else, which underlies the worldwide repudiation by the young of "the Establishment"—the sense that nothing significant can be done by "working within the system." (What marks the quandary as a predicament is the ineluctable fact that if revolutionary efforts succeed, what they establish is—an Establishment.) This is the alienation expressed for my generation a half-century ago by A. E. Housman in his *Last Poems:*

The laws of God, the laws of man,
He may keep that will and can;
Not I: let God and man decree
Laws for themselves and not for me.

The predicament is that while we ourselves do not want to be bound by laws, we want all others to be law-abiding, so that we may know what to expect of them. The thief would like to be free to take what he likes, but it would do him no good to make it his own if others will not respect what has become *his* property.

There is a predicament, too, in the nature of law, and of all the institutions embodying the norms of a society. As circumstances change, norms must also change if they are to serve the needs and interests of the members of the society. If changes are made arbitrarily, without regard to the values sustained by the patterns being discarded, the fabric of society disintegrates, and pattern disappears. The danger in simply thrusting precedent aside is that this might establish a precedent: the Mogul emperors who deposed their fathers were in turn deposed by their sons. In short, societies need both conservation and change, for the new pattern is introduced in the hope that *it* will be conserved. Here may be the basis of the "generation gap": unless a society is altogether stagnant, conflict is inevitable between the Old Guard and the Young Turks. It is true that conservatives face extinction—deservedly so, for they are looking only to the past. But radicals face a fate worse than death: their future is to become the Old Guard.

Whatever the nature of society, it confronts its members with another predicament: they are members of society, but they also have their *own* lives to lead. Man is a social animal, but he is also an individual. Though there is enormous variation in how individuality is conceived, no matter how others are related to, they remain *other.* Though I may want you, need you, even live only for you, the inescapable fact is that I am I, and you remain always you. The self embraces the other in the act of love, then rises renewed and enriched—but still a self. The experience is still "*I* love *you,* and *you* love *me,*" not "*It* loves." Even if it is "*We* love," we love "one another." To care for our children means to provide the conditions under which they can grow up to lead their own lives. Friends must eventually drift apart unless they are linked so tightly that neither is any longer an unfettered personality capable of freely giving friendship or anything else.

More closely bound up with the individual psyche is the predicament in which we are placed by the circumstance that desire is limitless; as Freud would say, the id knows no restraint. The Talmud tells a story about Alexander the Great: Alexander was once presented with a marvelous eye which, being placed on one pan of a scale, could not be overbalanced by any amount of gold or silver put on the other pan; it was outweighed at last—by a handful of dust. "All the labor of man is for his mouth," says the Preacher, "yet his appetite is not satisfied." "What does a man gain by all his labor? It is all a striving after wind, a man's rivalry with his neighbor." Whether the appetite be for pleasure, profit, or prestige, it grows by what it feeds on and so never has enough.

Even the attainment of the heart's desire is often unfulfilling. Our present action is for future fulfillment, but when the future becomes the present we are already other than we were, and perhaps can scarcely even understand what impelled us to such efforts for something which means so little to us now. If, on the contrary, the attainment does bring the consummation so devoutly wished for, then without new aspirations—and so, new frustrations, or at least, unfulfillments—life becomes impoverished and even empty. Thus Oscar Wilde, in *Lady Windermere's Fan:* "In this world there are only two tragedies. One is not getting what one wants, and the other is getting it. The last is much the worst." Such paradoxes, by the way, are often the mark of predicaments; what makes them predicaments is precisely this element of you're damned if you do and damned if you don't. From a recent comic strip: "Some people say there are intelligent creatures on planets around every one of those stars. . . . Others think that we're the only ones. . . . Either way, it's a sobering thought!"

There is a certain futility in action. This does not entail the conclusion that life is therefore without meaning but only that such meaning cannot be found in action itself. After all has been done, in essentials all is just as it was before. "As a man came from his mother's womb, he shall go back again, naked as he came, and shall carry away in his hand nothing of all his labor." There is a fable of a fox who lived near an enclosed vineyard which he repeatedly tried to enter. At last he found a hole in the fence, but it was too small for him to slip through, till hunger made him lean enough. In the vineyard he ate his fill, but he was now too fat again to leave by the hole; only by starving himself until he was as thin as before could he escape.

In perspective, and looking to the realities underlying appearances, the more the world changes the more it is the same. "That which has been is that which shall be, and that which has been done is that which shall be done; and there is nothing new under the sun." Once more the Roman emperor and the Hebrew Preacher echo one another: "They who come after us will see nothing new," says Marcus Aurelius, "and they who went before us saw nothing more than we have seen." When a man has children, he waits for grandchildren so as to have someone to tell about his own childhood. But the child hears nothing he could not know for himself; that he does not know it already is the quintessence of his childishness.

The question is how we can find meaning and value in a life so caught up in predicaments. To human eyes—and how else shall we look out upon it?—the world leaves much to be desired. Commentators have noted that on each of the days of Creation God saw that the world was good—save only on the day He made man, as though to say that here final judgment cannot be rendered, and that if now the world falls short of the good, it is man's doing. Undeniably, not everything in the world, even in untouched nature, is of human significance and worth. Undeniably, what *is* worthy is not so in every respect. Our sense of value gives us always an image of a better future, an image, however, which makes us the more painfully aware of the worst in the present. And, undeniably, even were the present all that we might wish, it cannot last. In short, perfection is not of this world.

It would be easy enough, or so we imagine, to accommodate to an imperfect world if only its imperfections answered exactly to our own. For in that case we would know nothing but the good if only we ourselves were good. Alas, the world seems quite indifferent to the moral quality of conduct. "All things come alike to all," says the Preacher; "as to the good man, so to the sinner." The difference between fantasy and fact is just this. In her three-volume novel, Oscar Wilde's Miss Prism says, "The good ended happily, and the bad unhappily. That is what Fiction means." In reality, we are not the heroes of our own life stories; the unfolding of events is not shaped to the development of our purposes and character; we do not win the prince or princess and half the kingdom; and we die in the end.

The image of man adrift on the boundless seas of space, infirm and impotent in an indifferent world—movingly depicted in Russell's essay *A Free Man's Worship*—is not a discovery (or invention) of this age. What is characteristic of modern times (though the notion is neither uniquely ours nor uniquely modern) is the faith that man's capacity and desire to know somehow frees him from his fate. This is Russell's view; it is the view also of Blaise Pascal, who was, unlike Russell, a religious thinker as well as a scientist and a mathematician. "Man is but a reed," said Pascal, "the weakest in nature, but a thinking reed." This means that he can think about the past and the future as well as the present, about the death that awaits him, and about the failures in life behind him. In short, he can suffer both anxiety and guilt. Hamlet addresses himself more directly to our predicament: "I could be bounded in a nutshell, and count myself a king of infinite space, were it not that I have bad dreams."

It is these quandaries—over and above the awakening of intellectual curiosity—which give urgency to the philosophic impulse. I turn once more to A. E. Housman, whose question is that asked by philosophers the world over, from earliest times:

And how am I to face the odds
Of man's bedevilment and God's?
I, a stranger and afraid
In a world I never made.

4. Religion, Science, and Philosophy

To be able to face those odds—to be able to cope with our predicaments, to see them as opportunities, and to do what we can with our chances—that is wisdom. Cultures differ in what they perceive as significant predicaments and opportunities; all agree that wisdom is making the most of whatever life affords. The word "wisdom" is in some disrepute nowadays, probably because of its association with the widespread religiosity and moralization of our time (quite different from religion and morality). Psychology and politics provide substitutes for "wisdom," like "maturity" and "normality" and the various labels for ideological correctness and revolutionary fervor. All come to the same thing: to live as befits a man, in the light of his universal humanity as well as of the particular circumstances of his life.

To aspire to wisdom is all very well; the question is how to fulfill the aspiration. "Where is wisdom to be found?" Job asks; not in the sea nor the sky, not in the land of the living. "I said, 'I will get me wisdom,' " the Preacher records, "but it was far from me. That which is far off and very deep, who can find it out?" Who indeed? For one to suppose that he alone of all men had found it out would mark him as a fool. "Beware lest you say, 'We have found wisdom!' " (Job).

In many cultures, including our own, there is a widespread view that the task exceeds merely human powers. Wisdom comes from God, and is to be found in the sacred writings which record the word of God. Quite often, wisdom has been personified as the divine power and purpose. Wisdom is the first of God's works: by Wisdom was all the rest created.

Philosophy might be described as the secular alternative to, or component of, divine wisdom. It is the use of merely human powers in the pursuit of wisdom, though these powers may, in turn, be God-given. Several major religions venerate and even deify sages acknowledged to be of purely human birth who promulgated wisdom and embodied it in their own persons—Zoroaster, Mahavira, Buddha, Confucius. Perhaps after some centuries (if not already), the figures of Marx, Lenin, and Mao will also be central in cults devoted to what will be presented as their teachings. The philosopher-god is not necessarily a philosopher-king: none of the ancients mentioned above were heads of state. The converse is more nearly true: through the agency of divine wisdom, the king is the epiphany of the god. "By me," says Wisdom (in the biblical Book of Proverbs), "kings reign, and princes decree justice. By me princes rule, and nobles, and all the governors of the earth."

If religion is seen as philosophy in practice—as several Asian religions see themselves—philosophy, in turn, may be viewed as the theoretical aspect of religion. Buddhism, though institutionally a religion, might well be considered a philosophy; Stoicism, though unquestionably a philosophy, served its adherents as a religion (for some centuries the great Stoics were regarded by many as having been crypto-Christians); while Confucianism is quite explicitly both a religion and a philosophy. The philosophical foundations of religion will concern us later (Chapter Thirteen); philosophy as the pursuit of wisdom makes do with the powers of the *human* mind—though it may hold, as many philosophers have held, that the mind of man is a fragment of the infinite mind of God.

The ancient Hebrews distinguished the tasks and corresponding capacities of priest, prophet, and sage (*chacham*)—for instance, in the Books of Jeremiah and Ezekiel. The priest expounds and applies the Word brought by the prophet; the sage gives counsel grounded in reason and experience. What is enjoined by priest, prophet, and sage may be one and the same; the prohibition of removing landmarks, for example, can be found in the Books of Deuteronomy, Hosea, and Proverbs. Only the last, however, belongs to the "wisdom literature." A sense of the divine may be the beginning of wisdom, but it is only the beginning, after all.

Whatever else wisdom may be, it is in some sense an *understanding* of life. It is not a purely cerebral attainment; wisdom is as much a matter of what we do and feel as it is of how we think. But thought is central to it or, at any rate, to that species of wisdom which philosophy pursues. Wisdom may not lie in "plain living and high thinking," as Wordsworth has it, but it certainly calls for *right* thinking. Matthew Arnold was closer to the mark, at least for philosophy, when in "To a Friend," he spoke of that "even-balanced soul who saw life steadily and saw it whole." He was speaking of a tragic poet, Sophocles, but there is scarcely a philosopher who would not aspire to deserve such a characterization. Wisdom is a matter of *seeing* things—but as they are, not subjectively. The imagery of Ecclesiastes is quite common: "Wisdom excels folly as far as light excels darkness." "Now we see through a glass, darkly," says Paul; "now I know in part; then I shall understand fully." What William James said about metaphysics applies, I think, to all branches of philosophy: it is "nothing but an unusually obstinate effort to think clearly."

One of the tasks of philosophy (some say, the *only* task) is to *clarify* our ideas. In this connection, philosophy addresses itself to the puzzles which stand in the way of our coming to grips with real problems. John Locke thought, in the seventeenth century, that "in an age that produces such masters as the incomparable Mr. Newton it is ambition enough to be employed as an under-laborer in clearing the ground a little and removing some of the rubbish that lies in the way of knowledge." Locke demonstrated, for instance, that "essences" belong to the words we apply to things rather than to things themselves, and so brought definition to the forefront of scientific attention. A few decades later, another British empiricist, Bishop Berkeley, showed the crucial dependence on observation of our idea of "matter." His younger contemporary, David Hume, made clear that in the notion of "cause" what is central is regularity of concurrence, rather than a mysterious impulsion, and so paved the way for later application of statistical methods to problems of causal connection. This British empiricist tradition of clarifying our thinking was continued by such influential philosophers as John Stuart Mill in the nineteenth century and Bertrand Russell in the twentieth.

Clarification is often inseparable from criticism. Kant characterized his time as the Age of Criticism, and his own thought as Critical Philosophy. Through *analysis,* laying out the components of complex ideas or lines of thought, we can arrive at the presuppositions of our thinking, what Aristotle called "first principles" and Russell, the "foundations" of knowledge. Analysis makes explicit what, in our thinking, is implicit. Socrates, for instance, devoted himself to the analysis of familiar ideas like "justice" and "virtue" with the aim of disclosing what we know of these matters without realizing it. He described himself, therefore, as practicing the art of the midwife. "Those who frequent my company at first appear, some of them, quite unintelligent, but as we go further with our discussions, all who are favored by heaven make progress at a rate that seems surprising to others as well as to themselves, although it is clear that they have never learned anything from me. The many admirable truths they bring to birth have been discovered by themselves from within."

The assumption implicit in Socrates' thinking is that most men already know what is essential to these ideas; the task is only to make them aware of what they know. Many philosophers make the same assumption and so devote themselves to the analysis of what they call "ordinary language." The assumption is valid, I believe, insofar as puzzles are concerned, as well as certain problems like some in psychopathology, where unconscious and preconscious processes play an important part. There are other problems, however, like those we characteristically face in science and society, where analysis discloses only our ignorance or confusion. Whether dealing with predicaments calls only for analysis—so that wisdom is independent of the acquisition or growth of knowledge but demands only the realization and integration of what we know—is another question.

To uncover ignorance and confusion is, in itself, no small contribution, whether it be a contribution only to knowledge or to wisdom as well. Unfortunately, even a correct analysis makes little contribution if it is not *seen* to be correct. A fourth-century theologian, Lactantius, attacking the heretical doctrine (as he called it) of the globular form of the earth, asks, "Is it possible that men can be so absurd as to believe that there are crops and trees on the other side of the earth that hang downward and that men have their feet higher than their heads? If you ask them how they defend these monstrosities, how things do not fall away from the earth on that side, they reply that the nature of things is such that heavy bodies tend toward the center like the spokes of a wheel. Now I am really at a loss what to say of those who, when they have once gone wrong, steadily persevere in their folly, and defend one absurd opinion by another." "Up" and "down," "higher" and "lower" must be defined in terms of the earth's center of gravity, or some other such reference point. Not until Newton was this analysis understandable, and not until the space age has it been generally accepted.

In breaking down complex ideas into simple components, analysis may also disclose the complexities, as Russell's analyses have so often done, in what we had taken to be simple. It took until the middle of the second volume of their *Principia Mathematica* for Russell and Whitehead to prove that $1 + 1 = 2$. Often we suppose something to be simple when it is only something we are accustomed to, as we often suppose an idea to have been made intelligible or a phenomenon to have been explained when it has been reduced to the familiar. Unquestionably, one of the functions of philosophy is to dispel the confusions in specific cases between familiarity on the one hand, and clarity, simplicity, or validity on the other.

One of the important contexts of application of this function of philosophy is that provided by myths, symbols, analogies, and the like. These may serve as models, embodying the logical structure of their primary subject matter, or they may provide only suggestive metaphors. Whether a particular comparison can be taken literally or is to be construed as a figure of speech has been a recurrent question in science as well as in theology. For instance, the issue of whether man is a machine depends, in an essential way, on the conception of machine in question. Man is certainly not merely some complicated kind of clockwork, the paradigm of a machine in the eighteenth century, nor only some kind of energy converter, like a nineteenth-century steam engine. Only when the concept of machine is broad enough to include computers and other such devices for processing information can the question be fruitfully pursued today. Similarly, the comparison of the state to an organism, as in Plato's *Republic* or Hobbes' *Leviathan,* shows, in contemporary political and social modelmaking, promise of embodying much more than a figure of speech. Perhaps one of the most basic ways in which a philosophy shapes our thinking is by marking out the boundaries of literal truth amid all-encompassing metaphor. In that case, a difference in philosophy may well make a difference in what we see as myth and what as scientifically established truth.

Philosophy itself has sometimes claimed (or has been charged with claiming) to be capable of arriving at explanations by the sheer power of its abstract ideas, without recourse to direct observation or experiment. What has been produced in this vein is much more easily recognizable as pseudoscience than as some kind of superscience. Hegel, for instance, published a "proof" of why there must be exactly seven planets only a short time before an eighth was discovered (to say nothing of a ninth, and countless planetoids besides). Bergson argued that the eye evolved because the organism willed to see; but such "creative evolution," or at any rate such an application of the idea, could not be formulated as a testable scientific hypothesis.

Throughout its history philosophy has often stood at the frontiers of knowledge. The Greek atomists may not have formulated a scientific atomic theory in the modern sense, but for their time they were far from being only mythmakers. Aristotle founded or distinguished himself in many branches of science. Descartes and Leibniz were mathematicians of the first rank, the former creating analytic geometry (we still speak of "Cartesian coordinates"), and the latter sharing with Newton the creation of the differential calculus. Kant was one of the first to formulate the nebular hypothesis of the origin of the solar system, to propose that it was tidal friction which kept the same side of the moon facing the earth, to explain that trade winds are due to the rotation of the earth, to hypothesize that there are volcanos on the moon, and to lecture on anthropology. Auguste Comte founded sociology. William James was as much a psychologist as a philosopher. The list could be extended. Moreover, analysis is, after all, as important to science as it is to philosophy; often it is impossible to say in which enterprise an analyst is involved. Here examples are provided by the analysis of "consciousness" by William James and the foundations of mechanics by the nineteenth-century philosophical physicist Ernst Mach.

As analysis, therefore, philosophy may be scientific, not only in spirit, but even in substance. To make progress in science it is important to break problems down into simpler parts, the procedure followed by Galileo in practice, and urged by Descartes in principle in his *Discourse on Method*. As philosophy has pursued its analyses, special disciplines have broken off as sciences in their own right. Physics and chemistry were once part of what was called "natural philosophy"; well into the present century, psychology was part of the responsibility of philosophy departments in the United States; from their beginnings political science and economics have been closely bound up with social philosophy; and newer disciplines like mathematical logic and utility theory have an equivocal standing as philosophy or as science.

It is with good reason, from the standpoint of philosophy, that our time has been called "the age of analysis." For the last half-century, in the English-speaking countries, at any rate, philosophy has been largely, often exclusively, engaged in clarification and criticism, analyzing either "ordinary language" or "the language of science." Even when it has occupied itself with law and morals, politics, art, and religion, its work has been the analysis of various ideas (or locutions) in those domains, rather than the promulgation of substantive doctrines or the presentation of broad syntheses. Philosophy has been conceived, not as a body of propositions, but as an activity, the activity of analysis. (It is common nowadays to speak of "doing" philosophy.) One of the early logical positivists declared that he looked forward to the time when there would be no more books on philosophy, but all books would be philosophically written. There are those who would say that his ideal has already been halfway attained.

The practice of analysis has sometimes been associated with a repudiation of any other philosophical aspiration. It is not enough, apparently, for a man to do whatever it is he does; he must also insist that that is the only thing worth doing. The godfather of present-day analysis, David Hume, divided propositions which might embody knowledge into two classes: those which present relations of ideas, as in mathematics, and those which convey matters of fact, as in empirical science. At the very end of his *Enquiry Concerning Human Understanding* he writes, "If we take in our hand any volume; of divinity or school metaphysics, for instance; let us ask, Does it contain any abstract reasoning concerning quantity or number? No. Does it contain any experimental reasoning concerning matter of fact and existence? No. Commit it then to the flames: for it can contain nothing but sophistry and illusion."

The repudiation of any philosophical function but analysis stemmed, I believe, from a perspective in which the only quandaries (or, as we shall see in a moment, the only quandaries to speak of) are puzzles and problems; since problems belong to science, what is left for philosophy are only the puzzles, and the analysis of science itself. In Ludwig Wittgenstein's epoch-making *Tractatus Logico-Philosophicus* (published in 1922), the thesis is put forward that a question can exist only where there is an answer. "We feel that even if all possible scientific questions be answered, the problems of life have still not been touched at all. Of course there is then no question left, and just this is the answer." Thus logic and theology suddenly meet: to the problems of life there are no answers in the back of the book, Sören Kierkegaard once observed. What positivist and existentialist are agreeing to is that the deepest human quandaries are predicaments, not problems in the present narrow sense. When the dying Gertrude Stein asked, "What is the answer?" and Alice B. Toklas did not reply, Stein continued, "In that case, what is the question?" Where no answer can be given, there is nothing to be asked.

All this is only to affirm that predicaments are quite different from problems, but merely to recognize the difference is not necessarily all that is involved in dealing with them. Even if there is nothing to ask, there may yet be something to be said. Wittgenstein's conclusion, "Whereof one cannot speak, thereof one must be silent"—a conclusion shared by mystics in many cultures (§89)—begs just the sort of question whose existence is being denied.

In addition to analysis there is, at the very least, a corresponding task of synthesis. Philosophy has a *synoptic* role, summing up and systematizing the whole corpus of knowledge. By the nineteenth century, specialization had already become so far advanced that the work of the generalist, whatever its shortcomings in matters of detail, was very much welcomed. Philosophers like Georg Hegel, Auguste Comte, and Herbert Spencer had enormous influence as generalists. A century earlier, the French *philosophes* and Encyclopedists attempted to digest the whole of knowledge, an enterprise whose spirit was manifested in our own time by the *International Encyclopedia of Unified Science* published under the aegis of the logical positivists, though here the attempt was not to summarize *new* knowledge but to amplify the thesis of the underlying unity of all science. Positivists like Rudolf Carnap were at one with metaphysicians like Aristotle, Leibniz, Charles Peirce, and Alfred North Whitehead in seeking the most general and abstract conceptual structure within which the whole of knowledge can be expressed.

To succeed in its synoptic role, philosophy must also find room for other domains than knowledge. Human interests and aspirations are expressed, not only in science, but also in politics, art, religion, and other dimensions of culture. It is easy for the philosopher, devoted wholly to the life of the mind, to assume that no other life is possible or worthy of man. For Aristotle, nothing else can occupy God Himself but thinking about thinking. Today we may be digging so far down into foundations that we come to see life only in terms of our own subterranean existence. What we know as philosophical analysis sometimes might better be called "notes from the underground."

The exclusive interest in analysis is at worst a preoccupation with trivia, and even at best, without corresponding synthesis, may achieve only fragmentary and barren perceptions: "Tick, tick, tick what little iambics, while Homer and Whitman roar in the pines." The most influential of the twentieth-century analysts—Russell, Carnap, and Wittgenstein—were men with greatness of spirit; it is to be expected, I suppose, that the epigones would be as inferior in sensibility as in sense. Wittgenstein wrote in the preface to the *Tractatus* that the problems with which the book deals "have in essentials been finally solved," but concluded, "If I am not mistaken in this, it shows how little has been done when these problems have been solved."

That a philosophy aspires to the fullest use of our intellectual capacities is essential to its being identifiable as philosophy at all. It does not follow that philosophy must therefore engage only in analysis and renounce any findings which cannot be put forward as definitive and precise. The so-called "scientific philosophy" of Hans Reichenbach and others ranks, in my judgment, with the very best of the analyses to be found anywhere in philosophy. The question of whether it goes as far as is intellectually acceptable is not settled with anything remotely resembling the definitiveness and precision of its own substantive concerns.

For some time—perhaps from the beginnings of the modern age—science has been the object of quite ambivalent feelings on the part of society. On the one hand, it has been seen as the sole locus of worth, the model to be imitated by every intellectual enterprise, and the great hope of mankind. On the other hand, it has been attacked or, at best, ignored by obscurantists, activists, irrationalists of various sorts as a falsification and dehumanization of experience. I repudiate both these points of view.

Philosophy is not science; neither is it politics, religion, or art. It owes much to all of them and resembles each in one respect or another. But it is nevertheless distinctive and autonomous—as, indeed, are all these enterprises. From time to time, one or another of these concerns has attempted to subdue and even to swallow up the others. I do not see that we must choose from among them which is to dominate all the rest, nor that philosophy must subject itself to any one set of values and standards. Science, politics, religion, and art can each of them, in its own way, lay claim to a certain universality. It seems to me wise to acknowledge or question all these claims equally, at least at the outset.

5. The Philosophic Function

Specialization within philosophy is virtually a contradiction in terms. There are, to be sure, distinguishable areas of interest, such as will be surveyed in the following chapters. But the synoptic role remains; if philosophical specialities were pursued without regard to one another, a supraphilosophy would be needed to unite them, interpreting them in ways which allow for general perspectives. Similarly, philosophy cannot embody its concern only in theoretical formulations. For we would then need another discipline to relate theory to practice, and this new discipline would be recognized as philosophy. Philosophy deals both with the practical import of our theories and the theoretical presuppositions of our practice. Its function is to mediate between the life of the mind and the world of affairs which gives to mind its place and purpose. The task of philosophy is now what it seems to me always to have been—to bring the mind to bear on the great issues and concerns of its time: the pressing problems of the day and the perennial predicaments.

To perform this task, philosophy must stand at the frontiers of knowledge, at the boundaries which separate the different fields of thought, and at the points of contact among the various domains of culture. Philosophy grows only at the edges. In what is called "a philosophy," a world view, or an ideology, action, thought, and feeling are each given what is held to be its proper place and each is provided with a distinctive and more or less general content. It is this task which was performed for their respective cultures by Plato and Kant, Aquinas and Maimonides, Sankara and Chu Hsi. In our time the task has been made more difficult by the explosion of knowledge, the great increase in specialization, and the complexity of modern society. What is significant in our lives has become remote, technical, elusive, and unintelligible. But however multifarious our world, man needs to be at one with himself. More than ever we desperately need principles of integration by which we can achieve a consonance of our beliefs with one another, of what we think with what we feel, and of both thought and feeling with action.

For some centuries, philosophy turned on the conflict between science and religion; more recently, it is the relation between science and politics (both taken in the broadest sense) which shapes philosophy. Copernicus, Newton, Darwin, Marx, Einstein, and Freud have as much bearing on philosophy as on the natural, biological, and human sciences. What they signify is not only the growth of knowledge, but also changes in the import of what we cherish and strive for Kant's work reveals the influence of the man of feeling and action, Rousseau, as much as of the thinker, Newton: perhaps even more, it reveals the impact of the one set of concerns on the other. Kant (in the *Fragments* included in his collected works) speaks for many, perhaps most, philosophers, before and since, when he writes, "I feel a consuming thirst for knowledge and a restless passion to advance in it. There was a time when I thought that this alone could constitute the honor of mankind. This blind prejudice vanished. I should consider myself far more useless than the ordinary working-man if I did not believe that this view [the philosophy derived from Rousseau] could give worth to all others to establish the rights of man." Ours is also a time in which establishing the rights of man is a central concern: the rights of the individual against an oppressive and all-encompassing state, the rights of races to equality, the rights of nations to identity and autonomy, the rights of all men to a life of peace. A philosophy which ignored these concerns might still have intrinsic worth, satisfying intellectual curiosity; but it would surely be, as Kant put it, comparatively useless.

In our time the scientific enterprise and its outcome have often been perceived to be in opposition not only to religious faith and political conviction but to moral commitment as well. The issue has been thought of as rooted in a bifurcation between the domain of fact and the domain of value. In such a perspective the basic function of philosophy is to cope with this bifurcation. That was the lifelong endeavor of John Dewey, as formulated, for instance, in his final reply to his critics: "The problem of restoring integration and cooperation between man's beliefs about the world in which he lives and his beliefs about values and purposes that should direct his conduct is the deepest problem of any philosophy that is not isolated from life."

A philosophy not isolated from life need not have an immediate and direct bearing on the integration of facts and values. The distance between the philosophical abstractions and the concreta of our quandaries may be a measure of the profundity of the philosophy rather than of its isolation. The question is whether there is a path which connects the abstract and the concrete. Spinoza's dictum, "Man's happiness consists in his being able to preserve his own essence," has much the same content as the query, "What does it profit a man to gain the whole world and lose his own soul?" (The example is Matthew Arnold's.) Not every metaphysics of essence has such a straightforward connection with existence, as contemporary existentialists have emphasized.

Here there also arise all the difficulties of philosophical interpretation. It is easy to condemn a philosophy as meaningless when the situation is only that we have not understood it, or to dismiss it as irrelevant when we have only failed to recognize how it bears on our concerns. Dewey observed in his *Reconstruction in Philosophy,* "That which may be pretentiously unreal when it is formulated in metaphysical distinctions becomes intensely significant when connected with the drama of the struggle of social beliefs and ideals." For instance, the problem of universals in the late Scholastic period was usually formulated in some such metaphysical way as this: Are only particulars real (nominalism), or do universals have an antecedent and independent existence (realism)? Or do universals have a reality, but only that given them by the human mind which constructs them out of particulars (conceptualism)? These metaphysical distinctions may have been connected with the drama of the struggle within the Church over the locus of power and authority: whether in the individual communicants, in the papacy, or in the parish priests. (The connection, however, is far from being as straightforward and direct as my simplification suggests; not all Protestant theologians are nominalists.)

So far as their overt and explicit subject matter is concerned, philosophies might be divided into three groups, according to whether they focus on nature, on God, or on man: Aristotle, Plato, and Socrates, respectively; or Descartes, Spinoza, and Kant; or, in our time, Russell, Whitehead, and Dewey. All philosophies must accommodate all three areas of concern; one of these areas—nature, God, or man—is likely to be central and primary, the other two peripheral and derivative. Equivalently, one can look at philosophies in terms of the discipline or domain which provides the point of departure: science or religion, or else politics, education, or other such man-centered fields of interest.

Whatever the proximate content, however, the ultimate subject matter of all philosophies is one and the same: human problems and predicaments. It may be that this declaration points only to my own doctrinal predilections. I believe wholeheartedly with E. E. Cummings (in "One Times One") that

—when skies are hanged and oceans drowned,
the single secret will still be man

We each seek a sense of worth, of being found worthy at least in our own eyes if not in that of others. Thomas Carlyle asks, "What act of legislature was there that thou shouldst be happy?" Happiness is perhaps not to the point; but the pursuit of wisdom surely presupposes that the pursuit is worthwhile, and that such wisdom as a man might attain is worth having. The philosophic function seems to me inseparable from some attempt to specify how a wise man might live.

In terms of the ends of philosophy, if not its means, ethics is the most basic branch of the subject. This is the position made explicit by Friedrich Nietzsche, in his *Beyond Good and Evil,* as a guide to philosophical interpretation: "To understand how the most abstruse metaphysical assertions of a philosopher have been arrived at, it is always well (and wise) to first ask oneself: 'What morality does he aim at?' " It is also the position of a philosopher who is in most respects the polar antithesis of Nietzsche, the ancient Stoic, Epictetus, who writes at the beginning of his *Discourses,* "Whatever subject we are dealing with, our aim is to find how the good man may fitly deal with it and fitly behave towards it."

Yet the intellectual component or aspect of philosophy is not to be forgotten. The aim of philosophy may be to find how the good man may fitly deal with his quandaries, but it is to *find* out, not to take it to be already known or cultivate some passive receptivity (usually religious or political) so that it will be made known to us. The pursuit of wisdom demands not only the moral virtues which Plato emphasized but also the intellectual virtues which Aristotle made explicit. In our time especially, irrationalism has become so rampant that respect for empirical evidence and for reasoned argument is often far outweighed by respect merely for the passion and intensity with which a position is espoused, or the determination and ruthlessness with which it is acted on. I believe that there is no such thing as a philosophical basis for irrationalism in any of its forms (though reason is in no way incompatible with either passion or action). Perhaps the high priests of the cult of unreason are not altogether lacking in either moral or intellectual virtue; but I find it hard to acknowledge them as philosophers.

The philosophic function, then, is to make sense of a way of life. The pursuit of wisdom is essentially a search for meaning, the most fundamental and comprehensive meaning to be discerned in all we are and all we do.

This is not to say that philosophy is confined to making intelligible and acceptable only established patterns—for society, the role of what Marx called "ideology," and for the individual, what Freud called "rationalization." Philosophy also has a prophetic function; many philosophers think that the role of philosophy has been to mediate, as they put it, between a stubborn past and an "insistent future." Not only is philosophy not intrinsically conservative or even limited to reformism; it may also be revolutionary. It does not exclude radical measures but only unreasonable ones—if a tooth is to be pulled, wisdom does not enjoin that we only loosen it a little. Nietzsche said of himself that he philosophized with a hammer. The literal truth behind the metaphor is that he hit hard with ideas; he did not plant bombs.

The point is that philosophy matters. Even a philosopher like Charles Peirce, who held that philosophy has nothing to say about "vitally significant topics" (like moral issues), yet insisted that "every man has to have a metaphysics, and it will influence his life greatly." It is true, however, that often philosophy is only academic, in the sense in which this word is applied to art objects that are mechanical, cold, uninspired, and conforming to conventional norms promulgated and maintained by the socially recognized heads of the profession. The academic is what results when the man himself has no place in his work, and human concerns give way to a preoccupation with what is seen as professional standards. What should be a work of creation becomes a labor without love, governed by occupational anxieties and the unfeeling application of established formulas.

Philosophy is no less subject to such deadening professionalism than other enterprises and may be even more vulnerable to it than most. "The shades nowhere speak without blood," it was once said (by the philosopher F. H. Bradley, in a book of aphorisms written around the turn of the century), "and the ghosts of Metaphysics accept no substitute. They reveal themselves only to that victim whose life they have drained, and to converse with shadows, he himself must become a shade." It is not philosophy itself which is dehumanizing, however, but the folly of pursuing wisdom with one's back turned to his own humanity.

The philosopher faces a dilemma—philosophy itself is caught up in a predicament. On the one hand, it faces the danger of occupying itself with matters of no interest to anyone but other philosophers, topics so involuted or abstract that though they may have intrinsic interest, they lack any, save the most remote, bearing on significant human concerns. On the other hand, philosophy can yield to the demand for what is called "relevance," forfeiting its autonomy and becoming a handmaiden to politics as in the past it was subservient to religion. In short, philosophy is confronted with the dilemma of choosing between impotence and prostitution.

There is another dilemma, less urgent and threatening perhaps, but also important, which arises when the first dilemma is resolved. Suppose the philosopher has gone beyond a preoccupation with puzzles and is prepared to deal with real quandaries. Topical problems are likely to contrast markedly with perennial predicaments, yet there is a temptation to deal with each in ways appropriate only to the other—to dismiss problems as insoluble and to pretend to solutions for predicaments. In the first case, for instance, the philosopher might presume to legislate to the scientist—for example, "Human behavior is intrinsically unpredictable." In the second case, a presumed science is brought forward as a solution to some predicament—for example, a logic of choice or a theory of utility (more accurately, the science may be genuine, as in this instance, but there is a presumption in supposing it to deal with the predicament rather than with certain subsidiary problems). The dilemma is between loose thinking and superficial technicalities—Russell and Whitehead are said to have accused one another of being respectively simpleminded and muddleheaded.

The interplay of problem and predicament puts philosophy into a predicament of its own, one in which art also is caught up, and perhaps religion as well. While all three aspire to a universality of content, they must embody this content in particular forms. The more fundamental our concerns, the more they transcend differences in region, period, and culture. Yet if art, religion, or philosophy abstracts wholly from such differences, it is likely to become void of content altogether. There cannot be any poetry in Esperanto unless there is a community for which it is a living language. Religion degenerates to empty ritual if it stands aside from the moral and social issues of its own time and place. Philosophy, similarly, in its preoccupation with predicaments suffers from a certain slackness and superficiality if it ignores the problems of its culture in science, politics, and so on.

What most stands in the way of recognizing the philosophic function is that we look only at explicit philosophy, formally identified as such. A distinction of enormous importance is to be drawn between *professed philosophy* and the *philosophy lived by*. Carnap, for example, was a professed empiricist, but in habit and temperament he was actually a rationalist; he once identified as the philosopher to whom he felt the closest kinship (excluding contemporaries), not Hume but Leibniz. Reichenbach was a professed probabilist but argued most of his positions with a strength of conviction more often associated with those who maintain the existence of certitudes. Russell devoted his professional life to the dispassionate analysis of logic, mathematics, and the exact sciences; but he was also one of the most passionate advocates in our time of certain unpopular positions on moral and political issues.

I select these examples without the least intention of impugning the intellectual or personal integrity of these men, for all of whom I have the highest admiration and a warmth of personal feeling. Wholly integrated personalities are no rarer among philosophers than among any other groups. But if what is important in a person's life does not appear in his professed philosophy, the philosophy, in turn, is correspondingly unlikely to appear in the important contexts of his life. Thereby philosophy itself becomes unimportant. Epictetus in his *Discourses* seems to be speaking to present-day philosophers: "Is it for this that young men are to leave their countries and their parents, that they may come and hear you expounding petty points of language? Ought they not to return ready to bear with others and work with them, tranquil and free from tumult, furnished with a provision for life's journey, which will enable them to bear what befalls them well and to adorn themselves thereby? And how are you to impart to them what you do not possess yourself?" If the gap between professed and lived philosophy remains great, thought becomes pointless and action thoughtless.

I do not mean by "lived philosophy" what is sometimes called "a philosophy of life." This also may only be professed and not lived by. A person may claim, for instance, that in his philosophy of life a high place is occupied by the ideal of serving others; in fact, "service" may be the name he gives to his efforts to attain wealth or power. Moreover, lived philosophy is not the application in practice of certain principles, for those principles may never have been formulated as such in order to be applied, and a person who lives by them (or for that matter, by their contraries) may not even be aware of their existence. There is, therefore, another distinction to be drawn, between *implicit* and *explicit* philosophy. Implicit philosophy is what is embodied in patterns of action and feeling, whether or not it is also grasped in thought. Professed philosophy is always explicit; lived philosophy may be either. When the lived philosophy is explicit, we sense the integrity and authenticity in a person's life and work, evoking admiration whether or not we share the philosophy.

Spinoza is one of the best examples. Hegel, an idealist, said that to be a philosopher one must first be a Spinozist, while Santayana, a materialist, believed that no modern writer is altogether a philosopher except Spinoza.

Russell called him the most noble and most lovable of the great philosophers. This is chiefly because he lived as he professed a man should live; Socrates is universally admired for the same reason, even by those who repudiate his explicit philosophy.

For the individual, lived philosophies, usually implicit, have been called "paths of life" by Charles Morris, in a book of the same title and in a subsequent empirical study called *Varieties of Human Value.* Morris has identified some eight or ten such paths; in detail, of course, the number that might be discriminated is endless. Each man lives his life in his own way—not, to be sure, in the sense that it is the way he has chosen; for we live, most of us, not as we would, but as we must. Each man's way is different; it is his own just insofar as he is a free and autonomous individual. Indeed, it is in making the path his own that his individuality consists.

For whole societies, the lived philosophies have been called by Ruth Benedict "patterns of culture," and by other anthropologists "culture themes," "ethos" of society, and such like. Edward Sapir has especially emphasized that members of different societies live in different worlds; more recently, Benjamin Lee Whorf reawakened interest in the ways in which such differences of worldview are reflected in differences in basic language structure. Because the lived philosophy is usually implicit, Whitehead has observed that if we wish to understand the philosophy of a culture we should look not to what has been written by its members but to what has *not* been written. What is most fundamental is just what is most likely to remain tacit, either as so deeply presupposed that it does not enter into awareness, or so widely accepted that it goes without saying. It may well find expression, however, in art, mythology, and other such symbolic forms in ways to which Ernst Cassirer and, subsequently, Susanne Langer have directed attention.

As an example, consider the ways in which different societies deal with time, not in their explicit conceptualizations but as embodied in their patterns of action and feeling. For the Greeks time was, in Plato's words, the moving image of eternity, in which alone reality had its locus. Some millennia later, nineteenth-century Europe viewed change and growth, evolution, as a basic reality. Whatever, therefore, the importance of ancient Troy to the Greeks of Plato's era, it was left to others long after to excavate its remains; in Israel today, archaeology belongs even to mass culture. Another example of differences in the implicit philosophies of time is conveyed in this anecdote related by Morris. One of his graduate students who was a Buddhist monk come to study at the University of Chicago, presented him with a projected schedule of philosophical studies. "That is a most thorough and well thought out program," Morris said, "but it would take much too much time to complete it." "But why?" was the unexpected reply, "I have all the time there is!" The belief in rebirth was not a matter of abstract metaphysics only, but was also a component of the lived philosophy.

Because of these differences between lived and professed philosophies and between what is implicit and explicit, we must also recognize a difference between the philosophic function and the profession or professions to which the division of labor in a society assigns that function. At times in the history of European culture the philosophic function has been performed by poets and priests, lawyers and historians; today, psychiatrists, physicists, and political leaders are performing the function—for good or ill—and perhaps even journalists as well. The function is *not* being performed to any significant degree by the professional philosophers; by and large, it is not to them that we look for guidance in our quandaries. The professors of philosophy are professors, after all, and for the most part not philosophers. As I have had occasion to remark elsewhere, the love of wisdom may be quite like other forms of love in this, that the professionals are just the ones who know least about it.

The profession of philosophy seems to suffer a particular disadvantage, noted long ago by Epictetus: "If one hears a man singing badly, one does not say, 'See how badly musicians sing,' but rather, 'This man is no musician.' It is only in regard to philosophy that men behave so: when they see anyone acting contrary to the philosopher's profession, instead of refusing him the name they assume that he is a philosopher, and then finding from the facts that he is misbehaving, they infer that there is no use in being a philosopher."

Yet it may only betray a lack of perspective for us to expect anything else of the profession. Professional philosophy is certainly an anomaly, historically speaking; few philosophers of the past earned their living by philosophy, or even by teaching it or writing about it. Perhaps the profession is even intrinsically an anomaly. A yogi who demonstrated his extraordinary powers for pay, or, for pay, taught how to acquire them, might reasonably be suspected of self-deception or fraud, for the powers are presumably by-products of a state of spiritual growth in which such commercial transactions can scarcely play a part. Beware of the vendor who, at a bargain price, offers a book entitled *How to Become a Millionaire.* Nietzsche once remarked that a married philosopher belongs to comedy; but he was notoriously a misogynist. It may be the professional philosopher who is a comic figure. Aristophanes ridiculed even the very paradigm of the non-professional lover of wisdom—not the Sophists, but Socrates himself. In modern times, Andreyev casts the philosopher quite literally in the role of the clown; in his play *He Who Gets Slapped,* there is little to laugh at, either in the pathos of the clown's life or in the tragedy of a world which can do no other than victimize him.

Those who perform the philosophic function as their own lived philosophy are men for whom philosophy is a calling, a vocation, and not merely an occupation. They are driven, as Socrates by his daemon, to face the problems of men and confront even our predicaments. There may be a kind of pathology here. Although we cannot deal with our quandaries simply by turning away from them—the defense mechanism of denial—we gain nothing by dwelling on them in morbid despair. He who gazes too long into the abyss, Nietzsche warned in his *Zarathustra,* may find that the abyss is gazing back at him. There may be folly, as the Preacher knew, in the very pursuit of wisdom. The search for the meaning of life may only hide the impulse to escape from life.

But one who hears the call runs this risk. What is striking about this situation is that the answer to the call cannot be made in silence (or perhaps we are not aware of the silent response). The pursuit of wisdom is conspicuously bound up with efforts to transmit to others what has been attained—traveler's tales must be as old as travel itself. The first temptation of the Buddha after his enlightenment was to let his attainment die with him; Mara, the god of Death, sent his daughters before the Buddha to this end. But the Enlightened One rose up from under the *bo* tree to set in motion the wheel of the Law and enlighten others. The student of the Torah, said Saadya Gaaon over a millennium later, is not wise for himself only; he must teach what he has learned. In our day Martin Buber pointedly criticized much contemporary philosophy as essentially a monologue. Philosophy is like religion and art, not only in the previously noted aspiration to universality of content but also in the aspiration to being universally understood, accepted, appreciated, lived. "In that day He will be one, and His name one"—that has been the lived philosophy of all who have heard the call.

6. The Folly of Wisdom

True believers are usually quite prepared to do all in their power to hasten the day when He will be one. The faith is spread by fire and by sword; it becomes an orthodoxy; the community of the faithful is thereupon purged of heretics. For the totalitarian countries this description is not far from the literal truth; ideological "correctness" may well be a matter of life and death. Nevertheless, more democratic countries have their own orthodoxies, less forcibly but still quite effectively maintained. The academic Establishment is as entrenched as any other. What is called "education" is often only a process of reshaping the student in the image of the educators.

In philosophy a criterion of validity and truth is very much more difficult to apply, or even to formulate, than in the exact sciences. Judgments of worth, therefore, understandably contain a large subjective component that lends itself to the service of orthodoxy. The acceptability of the philosophical position is mistaken for insight, just as in the arts the merely conventional is characteristically mistaken by the academy for artistic achievement, while what departs from the norm is dismissed as unintelligible and worthless.

The ossification into orthodoxy may point to one of the predicaments confronting the prophetic impulse as it finds expression in institutional life. There is need for priests as well as for prophets, but in philosophy today the voice of prophecy seems to have been stilled, and only the priesthood flourishes. The predicament is that subservience to the priests may serve the spirit better, after all, than whoring after false gods.

In our quandary, however, there is an element not so universal and perennial as the repressiveness of institutional life. The competitiveness and hostility characteristic of so many patterns of our culture is manifested also in the philosophical enterprise. We are divided into schools of thought with no use for one another, coteries and sects marked by uniformities of position and method that exclude any other approaches. This is a state of affairs recognizable almost everywhere in academic life, even in the sciences; perhaps it is no worse in philosophy than elsewhere. Yet it seems to me to be especially alien to the philosophic temper.

Santayana has said in his *Skepticism and Animal Faith,* "The philosophy of the common man is an old wife that gives him no pleasure, yet he cannot live without her, and resents any aspersions that strangers may cast on her character." Professional philosophers seem to be just as jealously protective.

Much contemporary philosophy aspires to scientific standing, hoping for a precision and objectivity which will compel assent. This aspiration subjects philosophy, like science itself, to competitive pressures to achieve priority of publication. In our hurried civilization there seems to be no place for the groves of academe or the garden of Epicurus. Yet surely it is not elitist, reactionary, nor hopelessly old-fashioned to continue to espouse the worth of calm reflection, to nuture the slow growth of ideas, to cultivate habits of deliberation, and to renounce the scholasticism, however entrenched, which substitutes technical forms for substantive content.

The philosophical orthodoxy of our time is a special instance of a more general *monistic* perspective in the lived philosophy of our culture. There is a widespread though implicit acceptance of what I might call *the axiom of linearity:* that all differences can be ordered on a linear scale of value, that is, arranged in order of worth. If two things differ—habits, beliefs, styles, goals, or whatever—one must be better, according to this axiom, and the other worse. No allowance is made for the possibility that the two might just not be comparable, that each might be wholly worthy in its own way, each as acceptable as the other if taken on its own terms.

Monism need not have the form of an *enforced orthodoxy,* however; it may also be embodied in the gentler pattern of *evangelism,* relying on persuasion rather than compulsion to fulfill its mission which, in both cases, is to promulgate and defend the true faith. Even in the absence of evangelism the axiom of linearity may be operative. The policy of *coexistence* takes for granted that the Other (social system, nation, or whatever) is wrong, but recognizes that efforts to right the wrong might well be mutually destructive, or at least not worthwhile for the present. In practice, of course, coexistence is accompanied by a certain amount of evangelism (and enforced orthodoxy on one's own dissidents).

The ideal of *toleration,* while in no way moderating the insistence that "we" are right and "they" are wrong, emphasizes that we can afford to let them be wrong, as the engineer allows a certain tolerance in his specifications—an admissible margin of error. Thereby toleration betrays either indifference to the other or a reaffirmation of implied superiority. What is worse, in toleration there is always the danger that the error of their ways—never doubted to be in error—might become intolerable; in which case, we can no longer let them be wrong, or even let them be. Here, for example, is Thomas Carlyle on tolerance (in his *Heroes and Hero Worship*): "At bottom, after all the talk there is and has been about it, what is tolerance? Tolerance has to tolerate the *un*essential; and to see well what it is. Tolerance has to be noble, measured, just in its very wrath, when it can tolerate no longer. But, on the whole, we are not altogether here to tolerate! We are here to resist, to control and vanquish withal. We do not 'tolerate' falsehoods, thieveries, iniquities, when they fasten on us; we say to them, Thou art false, thou art not tolerable! We are here to extinguish falsehoods and put an end to them, in some wise way!" But surely a wise way presupposes the recognition that no man or group of men can be the sole and absolute judges of falsehood, thievery, and iniquity. The virtue in tolerating falsehoods is that occasionally some of them turn out to be true.

Perhaps the most humane form of monism is *catholicism* in the strict sense of an all-embracing stance. The Other is not denied its right; what is denied is simply that there *is* any other. "In whatever way men anywhere worship," says Krishna in the *Bhagavad-Gita*, "they worship me." Russell tells a story of being jailed as a pacifist in the First World War. The bailiff, filling out documents, asked Russell's religion. "Atheist," he said. "How's that?" was the naïve question. "Atheist!" "How do you spell it?" "A-t-h-e-i-s-t." "Ah, well," came the kind reply, "we all believe in the same God, anyhow." It is this same catholicism which is expressed in the well-intentioned but repugnant argument for equal opportunity, "After all, they're just like us." Here the axiom of linearity is especially obvious, as though to say that if they were *not* just like us, inequality of opportunity might well be justified. The argument thus suggests that freedom from discrimination must be paid for by abandoning whatever it is that makes one man (or woman!) different from another.

Because of a very natural egocentrism, catholicism is the form quite often taken by a monism which supposes itself to be open and accepting. "Let's put religion back into Christmas," says the announcement. "This Christmas, go to the church or the synagogue of your choice!" Also apocryphal, but perhaps closer to the realities, is the anecdote of an American undersecretary who said at the United Nations, "Why can't Israel and her Arab neighbors settle their differences like Christian gentlemen?" To which a Buddhist delegate, overhearing, remarked, "I'm afraid the trouble is that that is just what they're doing!"

In *ecumenism* there is genuine openness, an invitation to an exchange of viewpoints conveyed in the call for "dialogue." In practice there may be little more than reciprocal evangelism. What stands in the way of our truly transcending monism is the almost universal confusion between accepting a different viewpoint and agreeing with it. I accept your viewpoint when I recognize and understand it, acknowledge that it is in fact yours and that you are entitled to it. I agree with your viewpoint only if it is in fact my own as well. As long as agreement and acceptance are confused, my autonomy and integrity will prevent my accepting you, or else my openness to you will demand that I abandon everything that is distinctively my own. I may become an eclectic, taking something from all around me but having nothing of my own to give; a syncretist, who supposes that bits and pieces are unified merely by being put together—the social myth of the mosaic; or I may look for some grand synthesis (for instance, between the philosophies of "the East" and "the West"), in accord with the older myth of the melting pot.

There is a certain openness which derives from intellectual humility, the *fallibilism* which is ever aware that when my views differ from another's *I* just might be wrong. Nor is it necessarily a kind of anxious insecurity at work here, but simply recognition that all perspectives are limited, that every viewpoint is partial and, at best, is correct only as far as it goes. This is the doctrine of the Jain sect of India, from whom we have the fable of the seven blind men and the elephant; they call it *syadvada*—the "maybe so, partly so" theory. It is the doctrine also of pragmatism, which sees life as "confused and superabundant," in the words of William James. He adds, "What the younger generation craves is more of the temperament of life in philosophy, even though it were at some cost of logical rigor and of formal purity." Confronting this superabundant confusion, a man would be a fool to imagine that he has succeeded in attaining a clear apprehension of the whole truth.

A forthright *pluralism* holds, with Nietzsche's Zarathustra, "This is now *my* way; what is yours? As for *the* way, it does not exist." Differences among persons, groups, cultures are real and significant; no one can live by a professed philosophy which does not reflect these differences. A philosophy is not a garment which all men can wear; even when it is made to measure, it must sooner or later bind or hang loose. A multiplicity of viewpoints is not a necessary evil derived from human error and ignorance, human limitations or frailties. It is a conserving of the variety and growth intrinsic to life itself. Here I might borrow another term from Indian thought—*adhikara*, individual circumstances, the level of personal growth and development. The tradition is that Solomon wrote the Song of Songs in his youth, Proverbs in his middle years, and Ecclesiastes in his old age. Pluralism points to the folly of debating which of these truly embodies the wisdom of Solomon.

In short, philosophical orthodoxy is as much a contradiction in terms as is philosophical specialization. There are fashions in philosophy as there are in manners and dress, a circumstance that militates, at the very least, against the critical function of philosophy, its task of standing aside and saying, "However . . ." to all received opinion, and affirming the rights of reason and experience against every claim of established truth. Still, the insistence that philosophy free itself of conformism does not mean that there can be no such thing as style in philosophy, only that there be no fads. On the contrary, there is an endless multiplicity of styles as by right there ought to be. It is not the distinctive bent of thought that is unphilosophical, but the determination to bend all thinking to the same pattern.

The question whether it makes sense to speak of a "Jewish philosophy," say, can be answered in the affirmative (just as there can be Jewish music and Jewish humor), insofar as it makes sense to speak of any distinctively ethnic matters—whether cultural, national, or religious. To say that there are styles of philosophy is to say no more than that there are styles of life. What makes the philosophy of one sort rather than another is not the identification of the philosopher, but his identity, the substance of his thought. Spinoza may have been excommunicated, but the rationalism and liberalism of his thinking have long been a familiar strain of Jewish life.

The idea of a "class science"—"bourgeois genetics" or "Aryan physics" —I find altogether repugnant. There may be a Jewish philosophy, but not Jewish mathematics, chemistry, biology, or economics. To be sure, there are styles of thought in science, too (§28); yet pluralism, though quite applicable on the level of theory, has a much more limited application to questions of fact. Similarly, from the other side one might say that art is not altogether a matter of free play of fancy, but is also subject to certain objective constraints. In this sense, philosophy stands between science and art—less impersonal and disinterested than the one, more logically controlled than the other. "Far be it from me to deride the imagination," Santayana once said, "but after all it is a great advantage for a system of philosophy to be substantially true."

But is it such an advantage? Many men, undoubted philosophers among them, have said no. "In much wisdom is much vexation," in the words of the Preacher, "and he who increases knowledge increases sorrow." The wise man and the fool alike will die, both without remembrance; so what advantage, he asks, has the wise man over the fool? Is not the pursuit of wisdom a striving after wind? At the very least, it has been urged, even if the pursuit is worthwhile, it would be better that it not be too successful. Santayana writes in one of his poems (possibly more revealing than his professed philosophy), "It is not wisdom to be only wise"; we may be so anxious to escape human folly that we forfeit the touch of the divine madness by which we love and create.

In our day the attack on philosophy is part of a more general anti-intellectualism. Activists see in philosophy only the pale cast of thought by which their enterprises lose the name of action. The popular myth of the philosopher as a profound thinker who is at the same time laughably incapable of grasping even simple realities, embodies an ancient ambivalence; when Aristophanes put Socrates up in the clouds, he was undeniably giving the philosopher the advantage of perspective. That the advantage must be taken seriously was argued by Plato: the philosopher's judgment is sounder than ordinary because in the pursuit of wisdom he has experienced and come to know both the better and the worse, and therefore has a basis for his judgment. Commentators have suggested that the Preacher speaks of his former riches and power so that no one can reject his wisdom on the grounds that he knows nothing of the things he disparages. The Hebrew word for wisdom, *chochma,* originally meant skill and craftsmanship; in Scripture it is first applied to the artisan Bezalel; later, to the man skilled in the arts of living, one who is knowledgeable and has good judgment, a man wise in counsel. *Chochma* is nothing if not practical.

A criticism of philosophical pretensions is that philosophical positions apparently cannot be established to the satisfaction even of philosophers themselves. When there are so many different claimants to truth, all become suspect. All the arguments and counterarguments seem to recur over and over again. This is only to say that philosophy deals with predicaments rather than with problems; it does not mean that the attempts to cope with the predicaments are futile. It is in the nature both of predicaments and of the various ways of coping with them to recur again and again. There is no more reason to expect progress in philosophy than in art; puzzles can be disposed of and problems solved, but the essential task of the philosopher, as of the artist, remains to be done over and over. It is only when the aims and methods of philosophy are assimilated to those of science that progress becomes an operative ideal. Lack of progress does not point to the futility of philosophy, but to the futility of viewing science as the sole model for all intellectual endeavor.

What is undeniable is that when the content of philosophical abstractions is couched in concrete terms, it is so often banal. Wisdom seems paradoxically lacking in sophistication; there is something homespun about it; it smells of the cracker barrel and the whittled stick. In American folklore, the village philosopher is as familiar a character as the village idiot, and they are sometimes indistinguishable. It may well be that the most important truths are also the most widely known and the most difficult to put into practice. There may be more reason to find fault with our expectations than with the philosophy that fails to fulfill them. We want something wonderful and astonishing from philosophy, a secret, like the secret name of the demon which will deliver him into our hands. We still betray an archaic belief in the magical powers of the sage. The stereotype of the wise man as a half-naked figure seated at the entrance of his cave may be less a caricature of the philosopher than of our infantile faith in the Old Man of the Mountain.

Many philosophers today recoil from the tasks of philosophy because of their awareness of the infantilism or presumptuousness which the undertaking may reflect. In the claim to more realistic and modest aspirations there is also a danger—that we may thereby be rationalizing our fears of being confronted with what we cannot master or escape. To pretend to wisdom is folly indeed; but to be intimidated from its pursuit lest we learn what fools we remain is cowardice as well. I cannot quite believe that man must choose between being a coward or a fool.

But what is the point to the pursuit of wisdom if when attained it is universally rejected? "In general, indeed, the wise in all ages have always said the same thing," Schopenhauer observes in his *Studies in Pessimism*, "and the fools, who at all times form the immense majority, have in their way too acted alike, and have done just the opposite; and so it will continue.

For, as Voltaire says, we shall leave this world as foolish and wicked as we found it on our arrival." To criticize philosophy as unacceptable because men fail to accept it is clearly to argue in circles. (Schopenhauer himself does not make this mistake.) A more subtle fallacy, what I call the *intellectualist fallacy*—an unreasoning belief in the efficacy of rational argument—is at work here. A proposition may be true and the arguments on its behalf perfectly sound, yet they may fail to induce belief in it; even when assent is secured, corresponding action may not follow. Irrationality is compounded if we then conclude either that the proposition is false or the arguments invalid or the whole enterprise unworthy of a reasonable person. If philosophy has little impact on the world, so much the worse for the state of the world.

There remains to be considered the criticism of philosophy as essentially an acquiescence in things as they are, bad as they may be. Philosophy seems to enjoin the acceptance of all that befalls us, either because, as the Stoics held, to do otherwise is unworthy of a man, or because, as Hegel urged, whatever is, is right. Certainly, what is popularly regarded as a philosophical attitude conveys this spirit of resignation. Many of the aphorisms of folk wisdom are negative in both form and content: you can't have everything; you can't take it with you; you can't win 'em all; you only live once; nobody's perfect; nothing lasts forever. I share the repudiation of quietism. A man who does not at least speak out against the evils around him cannot pretend to a private virtue.

It does not follow that ideas have worth only as weapons. I abhor the absolutism of "Whoever is not with us is against us," and its particularization, "Whatever does not directly contribute to the fight against evil is itself an evil." Romeo has no use for "adversity's sweet milk, philosophy. Hang up philosophy, unless philosophy can make a Juliet!" He may have been no more unreasonable than our politicized contemporaries, only more straightforward in yielding to his passions. Philosophy cannot make a Juliet; it might have made Romeo and Othello love more wisely, rather than too well.

The charge of quietism against philosophy has some substance. It is the business of philosophy to focus attention on predicaments, which are precisely those features of existence that cannot be altered. "Who can make straight that which He has made crooked?" But the charge of quietism must really be laid at the door, not of philosophy itself, but of those unreasoning or confused philosophies which present as predicaments what are only the problems arising from human ignorance, folly, or vice. The effort to deal with these problems is then held to be futile or even impious, as though God created only actualities and not the potentialities in things, and as though our particular uses of things exhaust their potentialities. It is true that the Ethiopian cannot change the color of his skin, but we can certainly renounce our inhuman ways of responding to skin color.

On the other hand, to mistake a predicament for a problem also has vicious consequences. As the efforts to extricate ourselves from the predicament fail, we are either driven to disillusionment and despair, or we resort to magic and violence. Where there are no gods, we worship idols of our own making and, ultimately, make a god of man himself—the dictator, the self-proclaimed prophet, and his church or party. We cannot, by taking thought, add a cubit to a man's stature; it is monstrous to put him on the rack instead. What philosophy aims at is concisely conveyed in the well-known prayer: "O God, give us serenity to accept what cannot be changed, courage to change what should be changed, and wisdom to distinguish the one from the other."

Perhaps the most fundamental presupposition of the philosophical enterprise is the conviction that taking thought is worthwhile—not necessarily because we can thereby fulfill our desires, but also because we can thereby be freed from the burden of those desires which must remain unfulfilled. This is the presupposition of Buddha, of the Stoics, of Spinoza, of Freud. It might be called *the* philosophic axiom: to understand is to transcend. In such transcendence there is indeed an element of acceptance; not a quiescence in evil, but a reaffirmation of meaning and worth in the struggle against evil even though the struggle be endless. This is the affirmation in the recitation of a blessing: not that all is already as we would wish it to be, but that it is yet to be, that it may be, that it should be, that we dedicate ourselves to its becoming. The last word of wisdom is "Amen."

Chapter Two

Semantics

7. Symbol Magic

Man is the animal that talks. To understand what it is to be human is to give centrality to our capacity for speech. There is no possibility of coping with our predicaments without recognizing the resources of symbolism—at the same time that we acknowledge its limitations. Wisdom may enjoin silence, but there is much to be said before the rest is silence; the most silent sage must listen, if only to the voice within.

If the volume of talk were the measure of humanity, there could be no denying that we have risen far above brutishness. But we remain a simian race; much of what we say is only chatter. If to talk we add the written and graphic symbol, the volume is overwhelming. We have books and newspapers; magazines, pamphlets, circulars, and leaflets; brochures, catalogs, and directories; memoranda, letters, postcards; posters, signs, billboards; phonograph records, tapes, electrical transcriptions, telecasts and broadcasts; telegrams, cables, telephone calls, telex messages, ticker tapes, and computer printouts; and even writing in the sky.

Whatever the role of speech in our *predicaments*, many *problems* of our time spring from the volume and stridency of mass communications. The invasion of privacy, the unremitting pressure of advertising and propaganda, and more insidious as well as blunter devices of brainwashing pose urgent problems of freedom and power, ignorance and enlightenment. Epictetus could resist forced compliance: "I will throw you in prison!" "My body, you mean," "I will break your arm." "Yes, but not my will." What could he say if his will was molded? Brainwashing connotes the melodrama of dungeons, drugs, and torture (although melodrama or not, for some men they are very real). On a much larger scale, what matters is the prosaic but equally effective cumulation of subtle and slight but endlessly repeated impacts.

The Book of Proverbs observes that when words are many, sin is not lacking. In a modern idiom, as volume increases the noise begins to drown out the signal. Advertising, for instance, is useful in providing information on what goods and services can be bought, where, and at what price; but there can be no doubt that it is also enormously wasteful. Yet the commercial may be no more problematic than the program. It is in the nature of the mass media to direct their content to the masses; it would be foolish to expect otherwise. It is also foolish, however, to try to persuade ourselves that all is for the best in whatever is good for the most. We are caught up here in a vicious *circle of taste:* the media may have an obligation to give people what they want, but to do so makes it hard for people ever to want anything better.

Whatever the quality of what is presented in news, comment, or entertainment, the content is standard. Standardization increases with improved methods of marketing and distribution on the one hand, and of political controls on the other. At the same time, the difficulties of reaching a significant audience are so great, whether in terms of economic or of political resources, that only a tiny elite enjoys the privilege of access to a large audience.

Worldwide, uniformities in content are accompanied by persistent and even intensified diversifications in form: while there is a large international vocabulary, differences in language are real and are more important than ever. It is doubtful whether merely human translators (rather than computers) can keep pace with the needs for exchange of even purely scientific and technological information.

At the other extreme, the individual finds himself more and more estranged: the stream of communication only flows around him. He is increasingly forced into a passive role in communication. If he is not a member of the ever more common captive audience, he can interrupt the flow; he cannot talk back. Much of what he sees and hears is either empty or else so technical as to be unintelligible. Every day he hears more and understands less. Special vocabularies and idioms proliferate in spite of the omnipresent media. We must always have someone to talk to. Drug users, for instance, may have a distinctive jargon because they use drugs, but they may also use the drugs because they are cut off from meaningful communication with most people around them.

For all that, the importance in human affairs of signs and symbols, language and communication, can be exaggerated. Some problems as well as some failures in coping with predicaments stem from that exaggeration. We suffer from a deep-seated, largely unconscious, and recurrent belief in the *magic of symbols:* the notion that symbols can affect the realities they signify. There is no magic in the simple power of words to evoke a response from their hearers or readers, no irrationality in my expectation that you will open the door at my call. The magic lies in the "Open, Sesame!" which itself opens the door, without any human mediation. The magical belief is that the word reaches *into* things, that what lies at the core of things is a stuff embodied in the word, that each word partakes of *the* Word in which all things have their beginning and their end. When Alice asks what things are called, she is countered with the question of whether they come when they are called, and, if not, what's the good of calling them? That is the quintessence of the belief in the magic of words: every utterance is an invocation.

Even words addressed to people are not necessarily free from magical expectations. Everything hinges on the place we allow to causal agency—including causes we cannot then and there explain. How the words of a psychotherapist alleviate a personality disorder is obscure, as is the working of the words of the exorcist to the schizophrenic who is seen as suffering from demonic possession. The belief in magic is also revealed in our faith in the effectiveness of exhortations, resolves, pledges, solemn vows, and the like.

The magic is overt in a familiar negative form: we insist that some words *not* be used. Laws against obscenity in the English-speaking world were originally directed against profanity and blasphemy, in which the invocation of the Powers is straightforward. Problems not spoken of are thought to have only a shadowy and perhaps temporary existence; if they are referred to euphemistically, they will perhaps be less threatening. If a symbol can invoke reality, suppressing the symbol is keeping the reality in check. When the child is hurt, he cries; I say "Don't cry!" to comfort him, which my expression of concern may indeed do. At the same time, *I* am comforted, for if his cries were to continue they would arouse my anxiety. At bottom, it is magic that I am calling upon: the cry is the symbol of the hurt—by removing the symbol maybe I can destroy the thing.

Belief in the magic of symbols may be rooted in the circumstance that when the infant is learning to talk, the distinctions between self and other, people and things, fantasies and veridical perceptions are blurred. His word is experienced as directly effective, working on things without the mediation of human agency. He reaches people before he has learned to speak, so he feels that he has magically reached out to the things themselves. At the same time, the word may evoke an image or memory which is experienced as a presence magically summoned. The limit of his world is as far as thought can reach, and fantasy can instantly fulfill his every wish. He attains to humanity as his cry becomes an incantation. Forever after, the nature he has transcended exacts a price: his belief in magic must give way, bit by bit, to a painful sense of reality.

From this point of view, the primeval use of words is to get something done. The imperative mood is prior to the indicative mood—psychologically prior, certainly, and perhaps logically prior as well. We talk, in this primary sense, not as disinterested dispensers of information, but seeking to command, cajole, persuade, enjoin. Even when it appears we are merely declaring a truth, that it *is* the truth cannot itself be the point of the declaration, for why should I declare *that* truth, then and there? The truth needs nothing from me; I add nothing to it by my affirmation save as thereby I evoke assent. We talk in order to be believed and seek credence to secure action. This is the *directive use* of words: it is magic matured and sobered, naturalized and humanized. Ritual has become grammar, and incantation a language.

There is an intermediate stage, in which one speaks to produce an effect on the other, but an effect expected to come about whether the other wills it or no—that is to say, magically. The curse, for instance, stands between a magical incantation and a realistic pronouncement of doom. This is what it means to "call someone names," as children pointedly put it. Lucy is most exasperatingly irrational—and human—when she calls out to Charlie Brown, "Sticks and stones may break my bones, but names will never hurt me—you blockhead!" The working of obscenity is much the same: the obscene word and gesture robs the other person of virtue even with nothing more said or done.

The fact is that words do work. A symbol not only stands for a reality; it is itself a reality, produced by its own causes and, in turn, producing its own effects. "Without knowing the force of words it is impossible to know men," Confucius rightly said. Man is not just the talking animal; he is the animal one can talk to. The fundamental *problem of semantics* is that the reality of the symbol by virtue of which it is effective is not its physical shape or sound; yet we cannot surrender to a belief in magic. How *does* talk do its work? What distinguishes meaningful discourse from abracadabra on one side and patterns of pure sound on the other? This question will occupy us in §9; man has always been caught between magic and nonsense.

A distinctive feature of human society is its reliance on symbols. "In this sign you shall conquer!" Constantine's cross and the shield of David, the crescent and the lotus, hammer and sickle, raised fist and open arms—what have these to do with mathematical symbols, engineers' blueprints, explorers' maps, or doctors' prescriptions? The power of the human mind, of knowledge, of the truth—this is what wisdom seeks to take hold; it is wise to acknowledge, first, the power of the word, whatever truth lies within it. The banners of false prophets are also carried high, and men have conquered under the signs of evil. A good symbol is the best argument, Emerson has said in *Poetry and Imagination*—the most effective argument, that is. We should not too hastily admit that good arguments might be ineffective; there must be some sense in which they do the work they should, or else what makes them good?

In the pursuit of wisdom, semantics compels the mind because human folly is so universal and so blatant in our ways with words. "What's in a name?" Anthony asks in Aldous Huxley's *Eyeless in Gaza.* "The answer is, practically everything, if the name's a good one. Freedom's a marvellous name. That's why you're so anxious to make use of it. You think that, if you call imprisonment true freedom, people will be attracted to the prison. And the worst of it is you're quite right." George Orwell developed the same idea in *1984* with his "Newspeak" and "Doublethink." Fiction became fact in my generation, as Americans thought to secure loyalty by oaths, citizenship by singing the national anthem at ball games, patriotism by painting mailboxes red, white, and blue, and religion by introducing the words "under God" into the pledge of allegiance.

It is not surprising that those hostile to the powers that be, disestablishmentarians of all sorts, should resort to a countervailing magic, in which the symbols invoked by the enemy are directly negated. The flag is worn as a patch on the seat of the pants because of the same psychodynamics that in the Black Mass is responsible for reading the words of the sacrament backwards. The flag is *not* "just a piece of cloth, after all," any more than the signature on a contract is just a trickle of ink. The homely use of the flag is not meant as a lesson in semantics (which is almost surely wrong), but as a lesson in politics (which might well be right). Both sides rely on magic. As always, the rebel, in his ambivalence, is bound to what he affects to have abandoned; the proclaimed atheist who spits when he passes the church is as much a believer as if he had made the sign of the cross.

In other types of political symbols and practices, magic may be mixed with a more or less realistic directive use. By making overt a political identification, bumper stickers and lapel buttons might possibly contribute to a social environment in which it is somewhat easier for others to make the same identification, though I believe the magical role of the symbols is the primary one. Demonstrations might apply real political pressures; yet here too the magical element is not altogether lacking. By a demonstration I mean not just any overt application of power short of violence (as in a strike, say, or a boycott), but one intended to make something manifest, to *say* something; it is in the saying that the magic lies, and the references to arousing public opinion may be a rationalization. "Public opinion" is one of the common names of our time for the unseen Power which magic brings into play.

This intense and widespread concern in our culture with saying the right things and not saying the wrong ones makes up what has been well called a *cult of impression*. In this cult the basic article of faith is that symbols do things, for good or for ill, perhaps with an effect greater than can be produced by what they symbolize. In *Sex, Literature and Censorship* D. H. Lawrence once asked of the puritans attacking what they called his obscenity,

Tell me what's wrong
With words or with you,
That the thing is all right,
But the word is taboo!

The answer must be that the word is more dangerous than the thing it stands for; images count for more than realities. The violence on television screens is thought to constitute a significant threat to the well-being of our children, an opinion held by many people who are apparently less concerned about the threat of actual violence in our cities or on far-flung battlefields. British censors some years ago deleted certain "frightening" scenes from Disney's *Snow White and the Seven Dwarfs* at the same time that British children were being given daily exercises in wearing gas masks.

When Henry Higgins said of the French that they don't care what you do if only you pronounce it right, he could just as well have been speaking about all of us.

Symbols of sex and violence might not only *stimulate* corresponding action; they might have the opposite effect, by providing a *catharsis* for such impulses. There is no doubt that under appropriate circumstances symbols may do either; no one really knows which effect will be produced when. Symbols can not only bring us to closer grips with reality but can also lead us away from reality, providing a substitute for and an avenue of escape from it. Not every fantasy is a psychotic delusion; far from being incompatible with mental health, fantasy may even play an essential part in preserving sanity.

The problem of semantics is to explain the effectiveness of symbols. The *semantic predicament* is that their effect is to deny and distort the reality as well as to bring it to us; they may even replace reality. In Garson Kanin's *Born Yesterday,* Paul, who has just met Billie Dawn and shyly expresses an appreciation of her charms, is taken aback by her prompt response, "Are you one of them talkers, or would you like some action?" We are all in his predicament.

These are some of the semantical quandaries. Semantics itself sometimes contributes to the disease for which it pretends to be the cure. Words about words are words after all, and may be uttered with a belief in the magic of words. Not very long ago there was a so-called "General Semantics" movement; its more cautious proponents contributed to an awareness of our misuses of words, but many people saw it as the solution to all our problems, from personal insecurity to world peace. Today many people seem to think that "better communications" is the answer to every human problem. Such notions may stem in part from the intellectualist fallacy (§6); but they have more to do with mistaken ideas about the bearings of words on feeling and action than with their bearings on thoughts.

I call this belief in the magical power of semantics itself *the semantic myth.* It is a myth which has a greater appeal for the more sophisticated—men of letters, psychologists, and even philosophers. Those who worship idols are likely to prefer idols of their own making. Confucius once declared that the great need of society is for a "rectification of names," so that "fathers" will truly be fathers, "rulers" rulers, "subjects" subjects, and so on. What he intended was that we must change our behavior, not the names we apply to what we do. The semantic myth consists in interpreting the rectification of names literally. The injunction to take care of the sense and the sounds will take care of themselves does not go far enough. There are more important matters to care for even than making sense.

8. Semantics and Thought

"Words are wise men's counters," said Thomas Hobbes in *Leviathan;* "they do but reckon with them, but they are the money of fools." To take them as money is to believe in the magic of words; the semantic myth is the belief that it is enough to inscribe on the counters, "Notice: This is not money!" Whether for the wise man or for the fool, words are the tools of thought. There may well be thought without words; whether there can be any thinking without symbols or representations of any kind is more doubtful. The thoughts we share with others—to establish their validity or to make use of what is already established—are those embodied in words. Whoever is interested in thoughts, therefore, and especially in their validity, must also interest himself in the ways of words. The study of language is inescapably propaedeutic to philosophy. The significance of what we say cannot be assessed without an awareness of the resources we have for saying it—the possibilities they present to us, and the price they exact, in diminution or distortion of meaning, for exploiting the possibilities.

From Aristotle to John Locke, therefore, and down to the present day, philosophers have occupied themselves with theories of meaning and symbolism and with guides to interpretation and analysis of language. Because of the central role played by language in human affairs in general, and in human knowledge in particular, the workings of language would in any case be of concern to philosophers. Because symbolism and meaning are so wholly unlike phenomena in the rest of nature, what their existence presupposes and implies is of considerable philosophical import (§13). Moreover, philosophy must appeal to reason in defense of its conclusions, and therefore has a vested interest in words as the tools of reason. A common failing, however, is to allow our concern with the how to displace our care for the what; it is another predicament, one of the most general and pervasive: there can be no content without an appropriate form, whereupon the form itself is mistaken for the significant content. Zen warns: You sweep the house, and never let go of the broom. How do the forms of our words affect the content of our thoughts?

1. There is, first, the *distortion* of meaning: what appears in the conclusion of a communication may be quite different from what entered at the start. The distortion may simply be a matter of "noise," making the signal uncertain and thereby inviting purely projective interpretations. We hear what we would like to hear, or perhaps just what we are most afraid of hearing, but in any case not what has been said. Listening is not merely a native capacity but can also be a cultivated skill whose importance in human relations is rightly receiving increased attention. In reasoning, an important distortion results from the presence of more than one signal: if the word is ambiguous, we may be arguing now in one sense and now in another.

Not all ambiguity is a distortion of meaning; a tool with which we can do more than one thing, even more than one at a time, does not necessarily permit only poor work. If more than one signal is being transmitted, it may be that our purposes are also multiple, and all the better served by multiple meanings. To start with, at any rate, we must acknowledge the possibility of a *functional ambiguity* (§12). What is to be condemned is not ambiguity as such, which can be valuable and which is, in any case, a universal feature of symbols. Distortion of meaning is the result of *equivocation,* the exploitation of ambiguity in an argument which turns on the shift between one sense and another, and which is invalid for just that reason.

In his essay on "Utilitarianism," John Stuart Mill, an influential logician in his day (and a very sound thinker besides), had the misfortune to slip into a classic illustration of equivocation. He is arguing on behalf of an analysis of values in terms of human needs and interests, and proceeds: "The only proof capable of being given that an object is visible, is that people actually see it. The only proof that a sound is audible, is that people hear it; and so of the other sources of our experience. In like manner, I apprehend, the sole evidence it is possible to produce that anything is desirable, is that people do actually desire it." The difference, however, between what *can* be desired and what is *worthy* of being desired is crucial; "visible" means what can be seen, but "desirable" means what is worthy of being desired. There is an equivocation on the two senses of the "-able" ending.

Equivocation need not play on the words used; it may be based on an ambiguous construction (traditionally known as "amphiboly"). This is characteristic of oracles, as in "The Duke yet lives that Henry shall depose," and often of folk humor:

Satan trembles when he sees
The weakest saint upon his knees.

The analysis of such constructions has played a significant part in the development of logic. The arguments, "Half a loaf is better than nothing, and nothing is better than wisdom, so half a loaf is better than wisdom," and, "The Apostles were twelve, Peter was an Apostle, so Peter was twelve" are plainly invalid, although they appear to be valid. The forms of inference they present are indeed valid, but they do not in fact have those forms in the premises acknowledged to be true. The examples are Russell's, I believe, and bear on his important contributions to an understanding of the foundations of mathematics (§20).

In questions of value—political, moral, aesthetic, or whatever—there is a kind of equivocation so frequent and effective as to deserve its own name. Harold D. Lasswell, in various writings on the political process, has called it *normative ambiguity:* the equivocation is between a factual description of certain kinds of actions or their outcomes, and the promulgation of a norm meant to govern such actions. The word "normal" itself, for instance, has an obvious normative ambiguity, since it may have either a purely statistical sense or an unspecified judgmental one. Evidence supporting the sheer description may then be equivocally urged in defense of the value judgment. The question of "normality" is currently the focus of much attention in psychiatry, where the equivocations are by no means always easy to identify and correct.

A very widespread device of equivocation with normative ambiguity is effective because it disarmingly purports to present a definition of the controversial word. The equivocation consists in the fact that the word retains a more or less familiar descriptive sense, while the claimed definition embodies a special normative sense. In this connection, Charles L. Stevenson, who first called attention to the device (especially in his book *Ethics and Language*), speaks of *persuasive definitions.* Words like "art," "religion," "democracy," "justice," and "freedom" are often given persuasive definitions. Under the guise of explaining what a word means, the equivocator hopes to transfer to the things we already know to be meant by the word the attitudes (of approval or disapproval, for instance) we give to what he presents in the so-called "definition." If "religion" is persuasively defined as the worship of "a Supreme Being," polytheistic and nontheistic religions become contradictions in terms, so that "pagans" and "heathens" can be condemned as "irreligious." In the same way, abstract painting can be dismissed as "not really art," or terrorism defended as "national liberation."

2. Meanings are subject to distortion; they can also be *displaced.* A word may have a definite reference but be misused or misinterpreted by wrongfully detaching it from its reference point. Many words whose meanings are, in fact, relational are used as though they had not a relative sense but an absolute one, perhaps because what they relate to is so familiar that it is assumed to be omnipresent, or because it is so subtle as not to enter into our usual conception of the meaning. In themselves, such words are *incomplete;* thought suffers when how they are to be completed is left uncertain and uncontrolled. What a "living wage" is depends on the standard of living, which varies with time and place; the "facts" of a case may vary not only with procedures and criteria of admissibility of evidence but also with presuppositions of relevance—data are always data *for* some hypothesis or other; whether a statement is "clear" or a conclusion "obvious" varies with the reader, for what is clear to one person may be quite obscure to another.

Displacement of meaning may result not from our shifting the reference point but from our adhering to a point that is no longer relevant. The trouble is not that *we* have shifted meanings but that the world has moved and left our meanings behind. "Mother" still denotes the woman who cared for me as a child; but when I am no longer a child she has a different significance for me, and the word, accordingly, might well have a different signification. The example suggests a general label which might apply to this kind of displaced meaning: *fixated* terms, from the psychoanalytic reference to remaining in an earlier stage of development. To take another example, the meaning of the word "communism" is fixated when it is applied to societies like those of Poland, Yugoslavia, and Romania in the sense it had with reference to Stalin's Russia.

Fixation is often a semantic expression of resistance to substantive change—in politics, art, morals, religion, or whatever. Changes in institutions and practices inevitably are accompanied by changes in meanings as well; but to suppose that an insistence on the new meaning gives support to the new patterns of action is only another instance of the belief in the magic of words. Whether meanings belong in one place or another is a matter of indifference, if only we know what place it is, and how to keep them in their places.

There are words which lose their places altogether, or which perhaps never had any. These are the *floating abstractions,* as they have been aptly called, whose relationship to concreta is left almost hopelessly unspecified. "Cosmic harmony," "the general welfare," and "the will of the people," for example, are not easy to interpret in ways which are both specific and generally accepted. Under what conditions such expressions can be said to have any meaning at all, and what the meaning is, if any, are questions which have very much exercised modern philosophy; I shall return to these questions shortly (§11 and §13).

3. Meanings are also subject to a process of *dilution.* Even though what is meant may be univocal and pointed, the content may be so watered down that it provides little food for thought. The signal is weakened, not by noise, but by impeding signals which may interfere with the message even to the point of cancellation. The paradigm is provided by Theodore Roosevelt, who referred to what a writer of his day called "weasel words" in a speech on the issue of the draft, and his proponents' failure to face the issue: "One of our defects as a nation is a tendency to use what have been called weasel words. When a weasel sucks eggs, the meat is sucked out of the egg. If you use a weasel word after another there is nothing left of the other. Now, you can have universal training, or you can have voluntary training, but when you use the word 'voluntary' to qualify the word 'universal' you are using a weasel word; it has sucked all the meaning out the 'universal.' The two words flatly contradict one another." More recent examples might be "democratic centralism," and perhaps "national socialism."

Such dilution of meaning is very possibly more marked in our time than ever before. In fact, public communications today have quite often degenerated into a downright *perversion* of meaning, in which what is intended is just the opposite of the plain sense of the words. Orwell's fictional Ministry of Truth to spread propaganda and Ministry of Peace to conduct war (in *1984*) embody the same sheer negation of meaning illustrated by Huxley in his *Eyeless in Gaza:* "If you want to be free, you've got to be a prisoner. It's the condition of freedom—true freedom. 'True freedom!' Anthony repeated in the parody of a clerical voice. 'I always love that kind of argument. The contrary of a thing isn't the contrary; oh, dear me, no! It's the thing itself, but as it *truly* is. Ask any diehard what conservatism is; he'll tell you it's *true* socialism.' " The example may be old-fashioned; it falls far short of the brutal cynicism of present-day usage in which victims are labeled "criminals" because their resistance triggered the bloodshed, and a people determined to make a last-ditch defense of their lives and homes are condemned as "genocides" or "racists."

4. There are also many instances of *deflection* of meaning: what is being said is blunted by the use of words which do not change the facts but only the light in which the facts are to be seen. Most familiar are *euphemisms* for low-status occupations, bodily functions and the products serving such

needs, and the various painful actualities related to disease and death. Not quite so harmless is the practice of condemning something through the connotations of the words being used to refer to it. In some political quarters, "social science" sounds too much like "socialism" to receive support, unlike "behavioral science"; less troublesome still is the study of "human resources." The scriptural teaching that a good name is rather to be chosen than great riches, and is better than precious ointments, holds true of much more than reputation.

There is a game, often more realistic than cynical, which consists in identifying the *declensions* of the descriptions we apply to ourselves and to others, as for instance: My explanations are lucid, yours are oversimplified, his are childish; I am firm, you are stubborn, he is pigheaded; I am a freedom-fighter, you are a guerrilla, he is a terrorist. As the last example illustrates, there may be real and significant differences to be discriminated. The deflection of meaning makes it hard to recognize the real differences, replacing them by what are only nuances of usage.

Because in everyday discourse meanings are so easily distorted, displaced, diluted, and deflected, philosophers have for a long time been interested in an *ideal language*. In such a language each word would mean only one thing, each thing would be called by only one name, and the way in which our words would be combined would reflect the structure of the facts to which the combination referred. Three centuries ago, Leibniz held out the hope of our one day achieving a "characteristica universalis," a symbolism in which all ideas could be clearly and univocally expressed. In our own day, Russell, after a lifetime devoted to the creation and application of a system of mathematical logic, concluded, "I remain convinced that obstinate addiction to ordinary language in our private thoughts is one of the main obstacles to progress in philosophy. Many current theories," he continued, "would not bear translation into *any* exact language. I suspect that this is one reason for the unpopularity of such languages." The formulation of a language in which all knowledge could be conveyed, and the translation of philosophical questions into such a language, was, after Russell, the lifelong endeavor of Rudolf Carnap, Hans Reichenbach, and a whole generation of philosophers influenced by them.

The greatest of Russell's pupils, Ludwig Wittgenstein, took the position that all philosophy is critique of language, a view already proclaimed by the nineteenth-century philologist Max Müller, who, after translating Kant's *Critique of Pure Reason*, concluded that Kant's achievement was precisely to replace unanswerable questions of metaphysics by problems of language whose solution was well within the powers of the human mind. In the course of Wittgenstein's own development, and especially in the powerful movement he inaugurated (or which was, at any rate, carried forward in his name), the language to be dealt with was not some ideal logical system but just that *ordinary language* Russell had identified as the great obstacle to philosophical progress. The fault is not in the language but in ourselves—that is the prevailing diagnosis. Each word, as Gilbert Ryle puts it, has its own logic; we need only cultivate, perhaps with the help of the philosopher, the sensitivity to such logics which we all already have. The needs of everyday life are very well met by everyday language; properly used and understood, that language is adequate as well for our most profound reflections.

Between ordinary language and the philosopher's ideal stands scientific discourse, or, as it is usually called in this connection, *the language of science*. In a familiar sense of the words, the phrase refers to mathematics; in this context, however, it has a more inclusive reference. It refers to the whole structure of words and symbols by which scientific findings are communicated and proved. Mathematics plays an important part in science, but so does logic and even conventional prose, if it is used with special care and exactness. Many contemporary philosophers, including some of the most distinguished, turn to analysis of the language of science to deal with questions not just of the philosophy of science but also of epistemology, metaphysics, and ethics.

Medieval kabbalists as well as more earthy Renaissance thinkers looked to a special symbolism to facilitate, illuminate, and even replace thought. Raymond Lully, for instance, anticipated by four centuries or so what are popularly called today "thinking machines." But the languages in which modern computers are programmed do not replace thought. Though computers are already of enormous intellectual worth and of even greater potentiality, they are something less than a fulfillment of that ancient dream—just as the transmutation of the elements has at last been performed successfully in ways far more marvelous, but also far less wish-fulfilling, than the fantasies of alchemy.

Moreover, what is called "the" language of science is undeniably an idealization. It does not refer to what scientists in fact say, even in technical journals and treatises, but to what scientists *should* say (in the opinion of philosophers), what they *would* say if only they were philosophically sophisticated and conscientious. There is a danger that the study of language and meaning can become speculative or dogmatic, projecting its conceptions into its subject matter instead of discovering them there. Idealization is a feature of scientific method, but its usefulness ends when we mistake our own constructions for an externally given reality. Noam Chomsky, a leading exponent of what is known as "structural linguistics," holds that the study of language is a branch of theoretical psychology—of sociology, too, it may be—but, at any rate, of an *empirical* discipline, not one which is purely abstract and *a priori*.

Although it is acknowledged to be empirical in principle, semantics as dealt with by philosophers not uncommonly suffers from being insufficiently inductive. We speak too often of "language" and not often enough of "languages." The latter locution is much more demanding, for there we have to be specific and justify our generalizations. There may be certain language universals—features common to all languages—but just which these are can by no means be taken for granted, and just how they are to be formulated is far from clear and unmistakable. A wag has pointed out that there are even languages in which two affirmatives can make a negative—

"Yeah, yeah!" pronounced in the intonations of American Yiddish. Very understandable, but nonetheless objectionable, is the tendency to assume tacitly that all languages must have the basic structure of our own language, or of the language family of which it is a member—as though the creative word of God obeyed the rules of *our* grammar (a metaphor taken literally in Neoplatonist and Gnostic speculation). What we know as the parts of speech do not necessarily embody ultimate categories of existence or of reason. Charles Peirce, whose ideas about symbols and meaning are among the most profound and influential of any philosophical semantics of the past century or so, remarks that Aristotle might have arrived at a very different logic and metaphysics if he had spoken one of the Mexican Indian languages instead of Greek.

Semantics, then, being inductive and empirical, is basically a study of human behavior. If meanings inhabit some Platonic realm of ideas, they are not to that manner born; grammatical forms, too, must be generalizations from usage, not abstractions independent of actual speech and compelling its patterns. Over the last several decades philosophical semantics has fortunately become more and more human in its focus. From an early preoccupation with the structure of language (especially as embodied in mathematical logic and what was called logical syntax), it has moved to questions of meaning and denotation ("semantics" in a narrow sense), then on to considerations of the functions of language, what people do with words and how they do it. (Ironically, the development of linguistics in this century has been in the reverse direction.) The functional and behavioral orientation has been especially characteristic of American pragmatism, and increasingly in recent years of the Oxford school of analysis. This happy convergence of philosophic ideas hopefully reflects more than the common heritage of the English language.

9. Symbols and Meaning

"Colloquial language is a part of the human organism," Wittgenstein once said, "and is not less complicated than it." What we do with words must be not less complicated than anything else we do, for all of our doings can be represented in words. It may be that nature loves simplicity, or, at any rate, that scientists do, but there is such a thing as oversimplification; it would be foolish to frame a simple account of something we know from the outset to be as complicated as anything we can describe.

For all the attention which in the last hundred years has been given to language, the simple notion is still widespread, and not only among laymen, that language is essentially a matter of the transmission (expression and communication) of meanings, that in speech a man has something "in mind" which he "puts into words" so that others may thereby "grasp the meaning" he intended to convey. The promising development of what is known as the theory of information has popularized a more technical phrasing of the same conception: a "message is encoded," then "transmitted through a channel to a receiver" which thereupon "decodes the signal" to restore the original "message."

Both formulations point to important features of the process; yet they leave a great deal to be said. The idioms I have placed in quotation marks are, in the first formulation, obscurely *mentalistic*. What is it to "have something in mind," and what sort of thing is that something? The usual reply, that it is an "idea" or a "meaning," does not leave us more enlightened. In the second, the *mechanistic* formulation, a degree of precision has been attained, but only by restricting the account to the relatively impersonal aspects of language, an account useful only in proportion to the dehumanization of the language process—for instance, in the programming of computers. Who composed the message to be transmitted, why it is sent, and what it signifies to those who receive it—such questions are left unanswered by this account.

The approach which seems to me to be the most useful, not only for philosophy but for any treatment of language which does justice to the human element, is one that is neither mechanistic nor mentalistic but *behavioral*. This sort of account was made influential in recent decades by the philosophical pragmatist and social psychologist, George Herbert Mead, who approached language, he said, not from the standpoint of inner meanings to be expressed but in its larger context of cooperation in the group. Groups of people do things, especially for and with one another; meanings appear within certain of these doings. The frequent reference by Wittgenstein and his followers to what they call "language games" invites attention to this social and behavioral aspect of the matter, though with an unfortunate connotation of lack of serious intent (unless we remember that the British take games very seriously indeed).

In such a behavioral perspective, five characteristics of the language process emerge into prominence.

1. Language is *purposive*. In using language we are doing something and doing it for a reason. In its essentials, what happens is neither accidental nor unintentional. We need not invoke any antecedently given or independently existent entities called "intentions" or "meanings" to give substance to the operative purposes. Language is a species of goal-directed behavior, in the same sense in which the pursuit of goals can be identified and objectively studied in other organisms—and perhaps even in certain inorganic cybernetic systems. What we say does not merely allow others to infer what we think. It is *meant* to tell them; we say it in order that others may do or say certain things in turn. Words are not *symptoms* but, as Mead calls them, *gestures*. Symptoms also mean something, but this is meaning in a derivative sense: A patient's symptoms may "tell" the physician a great deal, but only in that he can make inferences from them, not because the patient "tells" him something. The physician may even be said to "understand" the symptoms, but this differs again from "understanding" what the patient says. Unlike a symptom, a gesture does not merely *indicate* something but *conveys* it.

2. Language is *social*. A symptom simply occurs, it manifests itself; a

gesture is performed—it is made for others to see. Words are *signals* rather than symptoms; they are directed to others—produced so that others will be aware of their existence. Which others need not be specified; one may signal for help without knowing by whom or even whether the signal will be received. The basic transmission is always "to whom it may concern," or, perhaps, "to whom *I* may be of concern." Even when the signal bears an address, so to say, it is essential to its being a signal that it *could* be read by another. The transmission is specific, but not what is transmitted. There is no language without a language community which, in principle, is indefinite in membership. There are secret languages, but a language that is in a strict sense private is a contradiction in terms. There can be no such thing as a cipher except on the basis of a language ("the clear text") which allows for unrestricted access.

3. Language is *personal.* In referring to those for whom gestures are performed, Mead uses the suggestive phrase, "the generalized other," to convey the unrestrictedly social aspect of language. Merely to call out to whoever may hear is not yet to speak. An animal's warning cry or mating call is a signal to the generalized other (or the appropriate community of others), but it is not yet a *symbol.* It is purposive but not deliberate, intentional but not truly intended. In Mead's account a signal becomes a symbol only when the one making the signal responds to it himself as others do—any others. One is using a symbol only when in gesturing he "takes the role of the generalized other." The response need not be an overt action; "implicit behavior" is sometimes spoken of in this connection, or a "readiness to respond."

Such locutions admittedly involve many problems, but these must in any case be faced in psychology, in contrast to the puzzles in which mentalistic idioms are enmeshed. Meanings arise when a signal means the same to the one making it as it might mean to anyone receiving it, the signal being made for that reason. Mead's analysis suggests an explanation for the centrality of speech in language. Vocal gestures leave the hands free for whatever actions are to be coordinated by the signals; what is more, they can be perceived very nearly as others perceive them, in contrast, say, to facial or bodily gestures.

4. Language is *normative.* For signals to be effective in coordinating action they must themselves be coordinated. Behavior can arouse expectations which are fulfilled only if it exhibits a regularity of pattern, socially shared. Language especially must be strictly patterned, for here small differences may make a great deal of difference. In short, language is "rule-governed," in the currently fashionable phrase. The rules need not be explicit and may be unknown and even unrecognizable to most speakers of the language. We may say that their speech *conforms* to the rules, rather than *obeying* the rules—as we obey the rules of mathematics, for instance, or of a foreign language we are struggling to learn. The word "grammar" may refer to the structure of a language, the pattern to which its speakers conform, or it my refer to the system formulated by a grammarian with

the implicit claim that one who obeyed these rules would be conforming to the pattern of the language.

In this sense the rules of grammar as well as those of lexicography display what I called in §8 normative ambiguity: they may be taken as stating how the language *is* spoken or as how it *should* be spoken. In fact, they do both: how an individual should speak is how most members of his language community—or those members who for some reason are selected as standards—do, in fact, speak. "'When *I* use a word,' Humpty Dumpty said, in rather a scornful tone, 'it means just what I choose it to mean—neither more nor less.'" "'The question is,' said Alice, 'whether you *can* make words mean so many different things.'" "'The question is,' said Humpty Dumpty, 'which is to be master—that's all.'" To *that* question there is a definite answer: not *he.* We can, indeed, make words mean just what we choose them to mean—but "we" can, not "I," just as we can establish customs, manners, and traditions, but not as wholly autonomous individuals. Humpty Dumpty, for all his masterfulness, is as capable as anyone of misusing words; he would do so whenever he mistook the norms of usage, and he would certainly mistake them if he thought that the norms embodied nothing more than his own intentions.

5. Language is *contextual.* A particular *use* of a word is to be distinguished from its *usage.* The use is what is done with it by a particular person at a certain time and place; the usage is not particular, but general—it is the norm or rule specifying its proper use. Every use takes place on a definite *occasion;* the usage involves a *context,* a certain kind or class or *occasions.* What occurs on each occasion is an *utterance* of the word expressing some person's *conception.* In conforming to a certain usage for such a context, the utterance is an instance of a corresponding *locution,* conveying a certain *concept.* The word "word" therefore is ambiguous: it may refer to utterances—the sense in which words are counted in a telegram—or to locutions—as with reference to the number of words in a vocabulary. Charles Peirce called a word in the first sense a "token" and in the second sense a "type." Tokens occur as physical objects or processes—marks on paper, sound waves, and the like; C. W. Morris speaks of these as "sign vehicles" (carriers of the meaning, as it were) as distinguished from "signs," the significant types. The same type may be embodied in tokens of quite different kinds. A word may be either spoken or written, for instance, and written in ways which scarcely resemble each other, like block capitals and script. Usually only certain structural features of the vehicle signify; in literature and the arts its perceptual qualities may also be significant (§77).

In general, the channels of communication and expression, even with regard to language in the strict sense, are much broader than dictionaries and grammars make explicit. Intonation, stress, and subtleties of pronunciation can sometimes be crucial—an ironic note of interrogation can be a more effective sign of negation than "not," "no," "never," and all their cognates. Even body movement and gesture may belong to language. Films made of bilingual speakers in New York showed that it was possible to recognize which language the speaker was using even when not a sound was heard—English, Spanish, Italian, and Yiddish have their own gestures just as each has its own vocabulary and syntax.

What makes a vehicle capable of conveying meaning? Peirce distinguishes three grounds of signification.

An *index* signifies by way of a physical bond—a spatio-temporal relation or causal connection—with what it signifies. Examples are the pointing index finger and the smoke that signifies fire. In a certain respect the index embodies the most fundamental kind of signification. Without it, symbols would have no purchase on reality; words and things would slip past one another, each system wholly self-contained (§13).

A second ground of signification is the resemblance of the vehicle to what it signifies; Peirce calls such signs *icons.* The resemblance need not be a matter of direct perceptual similarities but may require subtle interpretation. A map need not look like its territory, and map reading is not always easy; for that matter, even photographs—those made by reconnaissance satellites, for instance—may call for skilled interpretation. Basically, what the icon shares with the thing it signifies is a certain *structure.* Since structures are of central importance in much of modern logic and science, iconic signification has been given a greal deal of attention under a variety of names ("mapping," "representation," "models," and so on) in a number of disciplines (§19).

The third ground of signification is convention. Pierce calls a vehicle with this ground a *symbol* (in a narrow sense, therefor; in the wide sense, Peirce and Morris use the term "sign"). Linguistic convention need not be explicit and formal, as it is when academies coin or fix usage in adapting an ancient language like Hebrew to the vocabulary of modern technology. In using symbols, as in using other signs, we *conform* to rules, but we do not necessarily *obey* rules. What distinguishes symbols from icons and indices is that in the case of symbols the rules are not restricted to any specific material features of the vehicle or of its structure. A symbol could just as well mean something other than what in fact it does mean; an icon, however, can only picture what it resembles, and an index is similarly restricted by its own characteristics as to what it can indicate. That words, generally speaking, are symbols—that is, conventional signs—is not always clearly recognized (see Plato's dialogue *Cratylus,* for instance). In the perspectives of symbol magic (§7), words are often seen instead as indices, connected by a magical force to what they name, or as icons, embodying in their own features of sound or shape the essences they signify.

These three sorts of signs are not mutually exclusive. Though symbols are conventional signs, conventions are not necessarily arbitrary but may be chosen or become established because of certain iconic or indexical features. Onomatopoeic words, for instance, are iconic symbols, as are paintings in which there are marked conventional features of representation or iconography. There are also indexical symbols; for instance, what Reichenbach calls "egocentric terms": "I," "here," "this," and so on. Each of these has a generic meaning which is purely conventional and a specific meaning which is indexical, depending as it does on the time, place, and person speaking. Indexical icons similarly have a composite signification, exemplified by road signs warning of an intersection or sharp curves just ahead and using a representation of the shape of the road, it being understood that what is represented lies a short distance from the sign itself. If the sign also includes words, say "2 mi.," it is an iconic indexical symbol. Another example of this compound form is the familiar representation of a hand, index finger extended, with the word "EXIT" below it.

Whatever its ground of signification, a sign does its work in a context; an essential component of every such context is the person (or persons) using, producing, or interpreting the sign. The relation between the sign and its users, everything concerning the purposes it is serving, its human conditions and consequences, Morris calls the *pragmatical* dimension of the sign (from a root which means action, not something unprincipled or opportunistic). The relation between the sign and what it signifies, everything concerning what it designates, denotes, refers to, stands for, and so on, Morris calls its *semantical* dimension. The relation between the sign and other signs, everything concerning combinations of signs—grammar, form, and so on—he calls the *syntactical* dimension.

For the most part, signs work in all three dimensions; they are used by people in combination with other signs to facilitate their dealings with other people or things. Yet one or another dimension may be of primary importance. Exclamations and interjections are chiefly pragmatical signs: what is plainly more central to their meaning than the things they refer to (like hell and damnation) or what other words they call for (like various personal pronouns) is the feelings they express or evoke—something concerning their users. Similarly, conjunctions and prepositions are chiefly syntactical signs, while most nouns, verbs, and the rest are semantical. This classification can also be applied to nonlinguistic signs. A theatrical gesture is pragmatical, a symbol for a mathematical operation is syntactical, and an architectural blueprint is semantical.

On most occasions of their occurrence, signs are used for whatever it is they signify. Sometimes, however, we produce the sign when it is the sign itself we want to talk about, as when we pronounce a word in asking how it is spelled. In this connection it is usual nowadays to distinguish between the *use* and the *mention* of a sign. Often the mention of a sign is marked by placing it in quotation marks; in that case the composite sign, including the quotation marks, is a name for a part of the sign itself, what appears between the quotation marks. Thus, a post office may have thousands of letters, but "a post office" has exactly eleven. The sudden substitution of a mention for a use is the basis of much children's humor ("What cheese is made backwards?" Answer: "Edam"); not all such humor is childish, as in the White Knight's confusing but careful distinctions between his song, the name of the song, what the name is called, and what the song is called.

Following Rudolf Carnap, a language in which signs are mentioned (not just used) is called a *meta-language,* as distinguished from the language being mentioned, which is called the *object-language* (because it is the object of interest, not because it talks about objects). The term "language" is used here in a rather special sense; not for English or French, say (the "natural languages"), nor for mathematics nor music, nor the language of flowers, but for an explicitly introduced and formally specified logical system. The meta-language consists of three parts, corresponding to the dimensions it is concerned with in the signs it mentions. In a narrow sense, *semantics* deals with the semantical dimension and with the characteristic features of semantical signs; the other two parts of the meta-language are, correspondingly, *pragmatics* and *syntactics*.

The word "grammar" is thus ambiguous, as noted in connection with the difference between conforming to rules and obeying rules. The grammar of the object-language is its structure, its syntactical patterns. The meta-language grammar is a discipline, pursued by grammarians, describing and, perhaps, explaining the grammar of the object-language. The grammarian formulates rules of such a kind that one who obeyed them would be conforming to the grammar of the object-language. (The meta-language has its own grammar, its own structure, describable in some meta-meta-language.)

Characteristic of every *language*, in the strict sense, is what has come to be called a "transformational generative grammar," a structure whereby we may come to an understanding of the meaning of a given pattern of words, from a knowledge of the meanings of separate words, even though the particular sequences may never have been encountered previously. In the absence of such a grammar, the set of symbols constitutes only a *code;* every admissible pattern, and so all the content conveyable by the set, must be listed separately in a *codebook* rather than listed in a *lexicon* which characterizes a language.

A sign, then, signifies in a particular way; it has a particular ground of signification, and does its work, in one or more of the dimensions, in conformity with certain rules. This may be called the *mode* of its signification in contrast to the *use* made of the sign on the various occasions of its production or interpretation. The mode of the sign is its role in the process of signifying, while its use is the role of that process in the larger setting of behavior in which it occurs. Referring to something and expressing something are two different modes of signifying, while the application of the sign to the purposes of science and of art exemplifies two different uses, the didactic and the aesthetic (§10).

All the modes of signification may lend themselves to any of the uses as, for instance, in both art and science the referential mode may be used, say, in representing a certain subject matter and in describing a certain line of conduct; and science may make use both of reference and expression, say, in formulating a certain hypothesis and in challenging its validity. Distinguishing between mode and use is important so as not to prejudice the logical structure of discourse. The view, for example, that science makes no moral judgments does not follow from the relative unimportance in scientific discourse of the expressive mode, nor does the directive use of moral discourse imply that it has no cognitive content.

I have distinguished the use of a sign from its usage, its mention, and its mode; I trust that in the future the context will make clear which is meant. The word "meaning" covers the same range of senses as "use" and more. The meaning of a sign as determined by its mode of signifying is quite different, therefore, from its effects as determined by its use. We may enjoy listening to sad music, and an inflammatory speech may make us shrink from the violence it incites. We understand the music or the speech, then respond to it on the basis of our understanding; the same understanding may lead to different responses in different people or on different occasions.

Understanding, however, is not wholly antecedent to and independent of the response. The situation is more complicated than can be accommodated by simply distinguishing between meaning and effect; we also need some distinction between what is usually called, in a variety of senses, "levels of meaning." Specifically, there is a difference between *knowing* what is said and *grasping* it. By knowing the meaning, I mean something cerebral, reconstructed, detached; we grasp a meaning with the whole of our being, with immediacy and involvement. When we read poetry like Ezra Pound's *Cantos* and T. S. Eliot's *The Waste Land,* referring constantly to the footnotes, we may understand everything, but miss the poetry. Freud found, early in his practice, that it was of no help simply to tell his patients what they had been repressing, even if they understood and believed what he was telling them; they could not grasp what he said until insight came from within. Stephen Leacock has written a delightful essay on Greek drama in which he describes a college Greek society's performance of a comedy of Aristophanes whose program notes refer to a certain bit of dialogue as illustrating Aristophanes' biting Attic wit—and, sure enough, at that moment the professor of Greek could be heard laughing—alone. It is one thing to know a language and quite another to grasp it, as every foreigner can unhappily testify.

Even the cerebral level of understanding is made difficult by the widespread distortion, displacement, dilution, and deflection of meaning, previously discussed (§8). I have been told by a friend who is a linguist that every Arabic word is reputed to have five meanings: (1) its straightforward sense; (2) the opposite of that; (3) a kind of camel; (4) one of the names of Allah; and (5) a variety of sexual intercourse. The situation is not essentially different in any other language. For the most part, we manage as well as we do because of the enormous help provided by the context—the *setting*—the other signs with which a given sign appears—the whole sentence, paragraph, stanza, and even the whole book—the people, the purposes, and so on. On the other hand, what is meant to be said is not necessarily identical with the meaning of what in fact *is* said. Intentions, whether of writer or speaker on the one hand or of reader or hearer on the other, are simply not enough to determine meanings. There are always rules at work to which interpretations must conform.

Peirce localized this generic and normative aspect of interpretation in habit: the meaning of a sign is not a matter of the response made to it on a particular occasion; it involves, rather, a certain habit of responding. Mead would say, and I think rightly, that this is very well as far as it goes, but it does not go far enough. Habits are personal, while meanings are social. We might speak of the habits of a community of interpreters as *conventions* of meaning. Only symptoms, at most, are free of convention; all other signs mean what they do only because a group of people use them to mean just that. Language is a part of culture. Herodotus tells the story of a king who thought to discover which was the most ancient society by having two infants raised together without allowing a word ever to be uttered in their presence; the words they first spoke were then supposed to reveal the primeval language of the most ancient society. But the babblings of infancy become words only because of what the infant hears from other human beings.

It is not only symbols (as distinguished from icons or indices) that are subject to convention. A map has its scale and system of projection, and even pictorial representations are inevitably stylized to some degree. Similar conventions apply to indices, if these are gestures or expressions and not purely symptoms; what is indicated by a smile or a frown, a fist or a forefinger, may seem to us quite simple and "natural," but it is by no means a cross-cultural invariant.

Conventions of meaning are implicit; the formulation of explicit rules to be obeyed, not merely conformed to, is, if I may say so, the exception rather than the rule. Such formulation is the task of our dictionaries and grammars, works of criticism and commentary, and a certain amount of philosophy. Except in the case of artificial signs, formally introduced—like word coinages and mathematical definitions—all such rules are, at best, only suggestions or proposals which more or less meet the case. What matters at bottom are the conventions—how the signs are actually being used. What linguists, critics, and philosophers can do is to explore various *principles of interpretation,* guidelines for the formulation and application of rules—that the meaning of a word depends upon its setting, for instance, is an example of such a principle.

The discipline dealing with principles of interpretation is called *hermeneutics.* It is an ancient discipline, perhaps older than grammar. In many cultures it developed from the task of establishing authoritative and comprehensive interpretations of a sacred text. In the first century of the present era, Hillel made use of three principles of interpretation (*middot*); later, these were increased to seven; by the time of Akiba, a century or so later, seventy different aspects of Scripture were to be construed (according to some traditions, one for each of the languages in which Revelation was expressed). Aristotle's book *On Interpretation,* some three centuries earlier, focused on logic and science rather than on morals and religion. The question remains whether any one set of principles can be made to serve the needs of interpretation of all the varieties of discourse.

10. Expression and Communication

Words are significant because *we* signify something by them; they mean what they do because *we* mean for them to do so. Language is not a self-subsistent system structuring an autonomous domain of meaning; it is a creature of human purposes, and there are doubts whether even mathematics can be understood abstracted from human activity (§20). With regard to language in general, there is no longer any basis for doubt that language conveys meaning only because human beings use language to convey it. We *express* ourselves, or one of our beliefs or attitudes, by means of language. If our *language* is said to express them, this is a derivative locution: what we say expresses something only insofar as *we* are expressing something in saying it.

Just what it is to express something is even more obscure, if possible, than what it is to designate or denote something. The obscurity is made greater by the practice in contemporary semantics of focusing attention on designation, denotation, referring, and other semantic modes, leaving "expression" as a residual category. A wastebasket has its uses in even the best filing system, but the effective retrieval of information is not among them. The concept of "expression" has also been victimized by the popular *dualistic semantics,* which approaches language in terms of presupposed antitheses between cognitions and emotions, beliefs and attitudes, facts and values. In this dualism, expression is seen only as what remains of signification when we have analyzed out cognitive, factual meaning.

The Italian philosopher Benedetto Croce complained about how many different things are called "expression." We can quickly set aside the relation between a symptom and what it indicates—in Croce's examples, the blush of shame, pallor resulting from fear, fever and illness, falling barometer and rain, and even that an unfavorable rate of exchange expresses discredit on the paper money of a state. For these examples the term *indication* is already available, especially where the ground of signification is indexical, as seems to be the case in all these instances.

The term "expression" can be applied to the movement of any action from impulse to consummation through a phase of externalization. It is sometimes useful to distinguish the mere expression of an impulse from what clinicians call "acting out," carrying the impulse through to completion. To mark this difference, terms like "psychic expression" are sometimes used (for instance, by the philosopher R. G. Collingwood) as a label for what I am here calling behavioral expression which has not been *fully* externalized to the stage of acting out.

It is in psychic expression that language and other symbolisms typically play their part. Rage may be behaviorally expressed in swearing (psychic expression) or acted out in a murderous attack; clenching the fists is an intermediate mode of expression. Protestors against America's participation in the Vietnam war sometimes burned their draft cards; in according these actions the protection of free speech, the courts in effect construed them as only expressing opposition to the war and not as acting out that opposition. A single action may do both.

A behavioral expression can be construed merely as an indication: the clenched fist might be seen as indicating anger in just the way that a clenched jaw or glaring eyes indicate it. The fist is expressive only when it is a gesture rather than just a symptom. Expression is a mode of signification; like other modes, it is purposive, social, personal, normative, and contextual (§9). The expressive symbol is produced in order to express what it does; its being lies in its being understood—otherwise it is not expression but merely exposure.

What differentiates expression from purely semantic modes of signification is that its interpreter, whether source or receiver, is essentially involved in its content. All expression is, at bottom, self-expression, not because it is egocentric but because it is so human. To express something is not only to convey it in symbols but to present it as the locus of interests, attitudes, feelings, and whatever else makes it not only signified but significant. Romanticism saw in self-expression the ground of all value in art, politics, religion, and elsewhere. The mistake of romanticism was not in the breadth it assigned to expression but in the narrowness of its conception of the self. I become a self in expressing myself, but I must also *be* a self to have something to express (§46). At best, as Emerson reflected, we but half express ourselves; perhaps that is because we are scarcely ourselves at all in any greater measure.

Indications can be misleading and downright false if construed as assertions. The lie comes into being only with speech. To lie is not to declare what is false in fact but to express a belief, whether true or false, which, in fact, does not belong to the self expressed. Without man, the world is all honesty and truth. When the dog is happy he wags his tail, and when he wags his tail he is happy, but a man can smile and smile and be a villain. Polonius's injunction, "Give thy thoughts no tongue," is as ill considered as most of his moralizations. As more realistic counselors have recognized, the sad truth is that speech was given to man to conceal his thoughts.

We cannot consider expression without being confronted sooner or later with the notion of the inexpressible. The richness and complexity of any self capable of expressing itself makes something elusive of every expression—not vague but evocative, indefinite; what we express is conveyed only in echoes. There is then a question whether we have said anything at all, whether we *can* say what expression reaches for. Here positivism and mysticism unite in their denial that we can say it. What can be expressed depends on the available resources of expression. The infant, says Tennyson in *In Memoriam,* has no language but a cry, but even the grown man, in T. S. Eliot's phrase (in the poem *Portrait of a Lady*), must borrow every changing shape to find expression.

Insofar as expression is effective, its vehicle manifests a certain quality of *expressiveness.* It is this quality which lifts literature above mere language, transfigures a face, and gives eloquence to the hands, transforming into a work of art what is otherwise merely a physical object. Several features of expressiveness are to be noted here (see also §77).

1. Expressive quality is *perceptual,* something directly experienced, not a matter of retrospective attribution. We see or grasp what is expressed, rather than inferring or reconstructing it, but prior analysis may be helpful, or even necessary, for us to be able to see it. What is expressed is fused with

the sensory characters of the vehicle of expression. The resultant quality lies on the surface of what is being perceived, yet at the same time reaches into its depths. The face is not a mere screen on which an expression is projected but the very flesh and blood of the expressive substance. Psychologists sometimes speak of "physiognomic perception" to convey the immediate, holistic apprehension of expressive quality. Contemporary analysis of the process has not gone much beyond Coleridge's characterization of it as the imagination giving "birth to a system of symbols consubstantial with the truths of which they are the conductors."

2. Expressive meaning is *intrinsic*. It is inseparable from the particular signs by which it is expressed. These do not merely convey the meaning, as in a container or a vehicle, but carry it, in John Dewey's metaphor, as a mother does her unborn child. A meaning that can be abstracted from the concreta that signify it might be called a *message*, in contrast to a *content* embodied in its signs. The conclusion of Archibald MacLeish's *Ars Poetica*, that a poem should not mean but be, is an expressive rendering of the principle that poetry does not transmit a message but presents a content. The words of poetry are in some degree opaque; we do not look through them to a meaning which lies beyond but perceive a meaning embedded in their own substance. For that reason, genuine poetry, as T. S. Eliot said in his essay on Dante, can communicate before it is understood. Literature, in Ezra Pound's definition in *ABC of Reading*, is language *charged* with meaning (my italics).

3. What is expressed is *untranslatable*. This follows from the intrinsic character of expressive quality. If what is expressed is a content inseparable from the perceptual qualities of the signs expressing it, no other set of signs, whether from the same language or from a different one, can express that content. By playing on the words *tradurre* and *tradire*, the Italian truism that to translate is to betray conveys a truth in earnest. Expressive meaning is wedded to what specifically expresses it and, betrayal or no, a man cannot lead the same life with another woman, for each relationship is unique and irreplaceable. The Italians go further, with the aphorism that when two say the same, it is not the same; to be sure, for it is two different selves that are finding expression. This is not to deny that an expressed content can be *paraphrased;* we can explicate the content of a metaphor even though no other locution will embody precisely that content. But there is always something missing and something unwanted which intervenes. Reading poetry in translation, said Chaim Nachman Bialik, is like kissing your sweetheart through a handkerchief.

4. Expressed content is *rule bound*. It is not arbitrary or idiosyncratic, nor is it a matter of purely private associations. I can express myself only to those who understand me, and their understanding depends upon shared patterns of action, thought, and feeling. It is upon these patterns, in turn, that interpretation depends. Expressive meaning, like other species of meaning, is social and cultural. Expressiveness may nevertheless have a so-called natural base; the ground of its signification may well lie in the properties of the expressive symbol. That meanings are conventional does

not imply that they are arbitrary. White may be the color of grief rather than of joy; both have their natural ground, since white may be perceived as void of color (the pallor of death), or as bright and radiant (the life-giving sun). Expressive meanings may be contrasted with *associations* precisely because these are likely to be personal and even adventitious, rather than grounded in social perception of intrinsic qualities.

Expression implies *communication;* we express ourselves to others. Not only does an impulse move toward consummation in the act of expression, but a human being reaches out to others of his kind. I express myself not for myself alone but in order to make contact with the other. When Oscar Wilde has Cecily, in *The Importance of Being Earnest,* say of her diary that it is simply a very young girl's record of her own thoughts and impressions, and consequently meant for publication, he is being more than cynical; whatever his intentions, hers are unmistakable.

There is no doubt that communication is purposive; how we classify its purposes depends on how we classify human purposes in general. Some such classification as the following is rather widely accepted. Communication may be *directive,* serving to stimulate and guide action which the communicator takes to be appropriate or otherwise desirable. Here we have instructions, directions, commands, propaganda, and such like. Communication may be *didactic,* serving to induce certain beliefs or to evoke or sustain certain attitudes, values, or perspectives. These are the uses of reports, textbooks, and other carriers of information, as well as of advertising, education, and all the media of shaping opinion. Finally, communication may be *aesthetic,* in the strict sense of serving to provide certain fulfillments or other satisfactions in the experience itself, as is the case not only in the arts but also in such species of communication as profanity, obscenity, humor, and prayer.

These uses are neither exhaustive nor mutually exclusive. In other contexts, classifications cutting across this one will have their own validity. A cognitive element—producing or presupposing knowledge—is a component of all three types of uses discriminated here. I cannot effectively get you to do something without telling you what to do and, perhaps, why; I cannot change your attitude without putting matters in a new light; I cannot provide any significant fulfillments unless what is presented indeed signifies—that is, unless it is relevant to interests and concerns which reach beyond the immediate context.

Why we communicate something is not to be confused with what we are communicating. The "why" we may call the *point* of the communication, as contrasted with its *meaning,* the "what." The two are connected, so that when either one is grasped there is also some hold on the other. I know he wants the window closed because that's what he asked me to do; in learning his language, I surmise that what he said was, "Please close the window," because his actions and the context strongly suggested that that is what he wanted of me. There is no strict implication here, only an inference, and a hazardous one at that. Two utterances with the same meaning may have a different point (one may have been a lie, for instance); and the same point can be made by utterances with a variety of different meanings: instead of asking you to close the window I may shiver and say, "It's cold in here!"

We may understand either the point or the meaning, yet because we have failed to grasp both, misunderstand the communication. Bernard Shaw's "Tragedy of an Elderly Gentleman" in his *Back to Methuselah* is a continuous scene of mutual misunderstandings, in the same language, engendered by different coordination of point and meaning. What lovers say to one another makes its point, but it is not likely to be good poetry because of their indifference to meanings: "Who with love at his command/Dare give truth a welcome hand?" We pedants, on the other hand, are skilled in the apprehension of meanings but often miss the point. "What do you read, my lord?" "Words, words, words"—the point has been lost. Communication can do without meaning, but without a point it is—pointless. Nonsense may serve the purposes of deception and entertainment, and perhaps have a point in religion and philosophy as well; when a communication has been identified as nonsense, we have not solved, but only formulated, the problem of understanding it (§11).

Whatever one's view of expression, there can be no doubt that communication requires not only a self but also some other. The most common cause of breakdown of communication is the denial to the other of any real part in the process. There are compulsive talkers who pour out a stream of words without knowing or caring who is listening. There are also those who apparently listen but without caring about or even hearing what is being said. In many arguments the disputants are unable to state the view they are rejecting. As the White Queen said of Alice, "She's in that state of mind that she wants to deny *something*—only she doesn't know what to deny!" The argument itself is its own point, so that the meaning doesn't matter. Communication, however, is not merely talking *at* someone; it is talking *to* him.

A cannot talk to *B*—at least, he cannot know that he is talking to *B*—unless *B* can also talk to *A*. Communication is *dialogue*, as Martin Buber has emphasized. The breakdown of communication in modern society goes deeper than technology. The problem is not that the mass media transmit signals in only one direction; this situation could be corrected without too much difficulty and some progress is already being made. The problem is that even when a channel of communication is available to me, I must be willing to listen, and I must care whether I am being heard. Buber has rightly criticized modern philosophy as essentially monologue; the same is true of much modern art and a great deal else of what passes for communication. We do not understand one another because the other has no part to play in the process of communication, only providing an occasion for the process. What takes place is neither expression nor communication; it is just words, words, words.

Two-way transmission does not of itself guarantee that there is communication. It is not enough for *A* to talk to *B* and for *B* to talk to *A; A* and *B* must talk *with* one another. Otherwise we have not dialogue but *duologue:* two-way monologues. When one talks, the other is not really listening but only waiting his turn—as in joke-telling sessions, or in symposia and seminars. There is in our society a widespread pattern of *reciprocity* replacing *mutuality:* instead of doing things *with* one another, we alternate doing things *to* one another. There is a certain crude sense of justice at work in the principle of reciprocity, but whatever the justice, there is neither wisdom nor love in allowing you to exploit *me,* in exchange for the so-called privilege of being allowed to exploit *you* in turn.

Communication—social, cultural, and interpersonal—presupposes something shared; as normative, rulebound, and significant, it also produces a sharing. To communicate is to make something common, thereby to create a bond among the communicants. In a word, communication depends upon and sustains *community;* hence the enormous importance attached to the revival or preservation of their own languages in Ireland, Israel, Bengal, Madras, and many other parts of the world. Hence, too, the lack of viability in Esperanto and other universal languages: there cannot be a world language unless and until there is a world community. Artificial languages may suffice for the processing and transmission of information, but they cannot serve as media of expression and communication. Religious communion is above all communication within the community of the faithful (§83).

If communication sustains community, barriers to communication correspondingly weaken community. To be alienated is, fundamentally, to have no one to talk to. Confrontations are both causes and effects of lack of communication. One of the needs finding expression in the widespread "demonstrations" in our time is the need to be heard and talked to. Someone has remarked that the measure of civilization of a society is the number of strangers one can trust. Perhaps the measure of community is the number of strangers one can communicate with. We feel free to talk to strangers only in times of crisis, when the sense of community is intense and widespread. Without communication, we are less than human. A civilization which allows us to be human only in the face of disaster is a civilization headed for disaster.

To communicate with someone is to *understand* him—the person, not just what he says. It is not for lack of knowledge of English, Russian, Chinese, Arabic, or Hebrew that man suffers so much senseless misery and meaningless death. It is for lack of understanding.

To understand someone is to make more of him than an instrument or a channel for the transmission or reception of information; it is to share the self each is expressing in the act of communication. The great desire to be understood is a desire to be accepted. Understanding implies something deeper than forgiveness; it is inseparable from a measure of love. In the process of communicating, both communicants become more than they were. What passes between them is not a message antecedently given but a content which comes to be in the creative act of expression. All genuine communication is a negotiation without preconditions. This is what Buber conceived as the life of dialogue.

That is why what is communicated depends on who is communicating it. The communication is the person; not only what you do but what you are speaks so loud that I cannot hear what you say—unless, in the saying, you are expressing your authentic self. The meaning we convey is given shape and substance by our point in conveying it. A philosophy which depersonalizes meanings and detaches them from human purposes, however subtle its tools and techniques of analysis, is foredoomed to miss the point.

If what we are speaks so loud, communication can sometimes dispense with words altogether. Words can drive men apart as the United Nations often demonstrates. Silence, on the other hand, may bind men together in the most eloquent of expressions. This is especially characteristic of what Abraham Maslow has called "peak experiences." The content of emptiness and silence plays an important part, too, in art and religion, especially in mysticism, and in Taoism and Zen. The haiku runs:

They were silent all three:
The host, the guest,
And the white chrysanthemum.

Our philosophies have been so preoccupied with speech that we have left silence to the poets, perhaps from a dim awareness that our semantics stops short of the most significant communications. Edgar Lee Master's poem *Silence* is worth quoting at length:

I have known the silence of the stars and of the sea,
And the silence of the city when it pauses,
And the silence of a man and a maid,
And the silence for which music alone finds the word,
And the silence of the woods before the winds of spring begin,
And the silence of the sick
When their eyes roam about the room.
And I ask: For the depths
Of what use is language?
. . . .
We are voiceless in the presence of realities—
We cannot speak.
. . . .

There is the silence of a great hatred,
And the silence of a great love,
And the silence of a deep peace of mind,
And the silence of an embittered friendship,
There is the silence of a spiritual crisis,
Through which your soul, exquisitely tortured,
Comes with visions not to be uttered
Into a realm of higher life.
And the silence of the gods who understand each other without speech,
There is the silence of defeat.
There is the silence of those unjustly punished;
And the silence of the dying whose hand

Suddenly grips yours.
There is the silence between father and son,
When the father cannot explain his life,
Even though he be misunderstood for it.

There is the silence that comes between husband and wife.
There is the silence of those who have failed;
And the vast silence that covers
Broken nations and vanquished leaders.
. . . .

And there is the silence of age,
Too full of wisdom for the tongue to utter it
In words intelligible to those who have not lived
The great range of life.

And there is the silence of the dead.

Silence, like other forms of communication—perhaps more than most, because it can embody a so much richer content—can communicate only when there are already bonds of communion to make for the appropriate receptivity. However sweet, unheard melodies remain unheard by the deaf. Sometimes, on the other hand, there is a message to be conveyed, loud and clear. Years ago I visited the Sri Aurobindo Ashram near Pondicherry and was granted an interview with its head, a spiritual leader known as The Mother. Unfortunately, I was accorded the privilege of a silent interview, in the course of which I acquired nothing of what I had come to learn and almost nothing in unanticipated dimensions of experience. There is, after all, something to be said for speech.

The semantics of silence must begin with the recognition that there are two species of silence, only one of which embodies a content, while the other is truly empty. There is the silence of understanding but also the silence of bewilderment; of full knowledge but also of ignorance; of the love which has no need to speak but also of the hatred which has nothing to say. Communication moves from silence to silence; wisdom differs from folly only in replacing one silence by another. T. S. Eliot describes the hollow men of our time as caught in "paralyzed force, gesture without motion"; yet the same imagery was used a century ago by the Master to define the Hassidic fullness of faith: "silent screaming, upright kneeling, motionless dance." In the end, I suppose, if a person does have something to say, he will speak even in his silences.

11. Sense and Nonsense

The failure of communication is not always a matter of shortcomings in the potential communicants. There may also be something wrong in what passes between them. It may be saying too little, even nothing at all; or else it may be saying too much or several different things at once. These two possibilities localize the two problems which, Bertrand Russell said, logic has to deal with in regard to symbolism: (1) the conditions for sense rather than nonsense in combinations of symbols; (2) the conditions for uniqueness of meaning or reference in symbols or combinations of symbols.

How do we distinguish sense from nonsense, signal from noise? Much effort in twentieth-century philosophy has been directed toward the formulation of what Karl Popper called a *criterion of demarcation* between the domains of sense and nonsense, a touchstone by which to recognize the presence and purity of meaning. Since ancient times, philosophy has classified statements into the true and the false, applying respectively to reality and appearance. Occupied through most of its history in carrying out the classification, in promulgating logical or metaphysical principles by which the classification was to be made, philosophy was for a long time indistinguishable from science which, until modern times, was "natural philosophy." It is a characteristic of contemporary philosophy—perhaps the most distinctive characteristic—that the attention of philosophers has shifted from the difference between true and false statements to the difference between both of these, on the one hand, and statements which can be neither true nor false because they say nothing at all or nothing sufficiently definite to be capable of truth, on the other.

For over a century a perspective on meaning has been emerging which puts into focus the relation between meaning and the mind—the essential dependence of meaning on human powers. Three major variants of this point of view have crystallized: *Positivism,* represented by Ludwig Wittgenstein and Rudolf Carnap, emphasizes the dependence of meaning on the possibility of certain sensations or experiences. *Operationism,* espoused by such scientists as the physicist P. W. Bridgman and the psychologist B. F. Skinner, analyzes meanings in terms of the operations necessary to scientific observation. *Pragmatism,* created by Charles Peirce and developed by William James and John Dewey, puts meaning always into some context of purposive behavior.

1. The criterion of demarcation espoused by positivism turns on the conception of *verifiability.* The principle is that only statements capable of being verified have meaning; all others are nonsense. Alice started her adventures as a positivist: as she was falling down the rabbit hole, she "began to get rather sleepy, and went on saying to herself, in a dreamy sort of way, 'Do cats eat bats? Do cats eat bats?' and sometimes 'Do bats eat cats?' for, you see, as she couldn't answer either question, it didn't much matter which way she put it." To the positivist, a question which we cannot answer makes no sense. A statement is meaningful if, and only if, it is verifiable.

Still, there is a difference between the conclusion that we cannot answer a certain question and the conclusion that it *has* no answer. The former marks the limits of knowledge; the latter, the limits of meaning. In philosophy, emphasis on the centrality of experience is, in general, called *empiricism.* The view that *knowledge* arises out of and depends upon experience we may call *epistemic empiricism;* the view that *meaning* arises out of and depends upon experience is *semantic empiricism.* Semantic empiricism implies the epistemic, but not conversely. A statement without any meaning at all is certainly incapable of embodying any knowledge. On the other hand, it might be held—as it was held by Kant, for example—that though knowledge depends on experience, meaning does not; on this view, there are meaningful statements whose truth lies forever beyond our ken.

Positivists are not only epistemic empiricists but also semantic empiricists. What cannot be known even in principle is nothing at all—in such a case no "what" has been meaningfully identified. We cannot answer the question, How high is up? not because some magnitude eludes our capacities of measurement but because no magnitude has been specified to *be* measured. The statement, The Absolute slumbers in eternal repose, a favorite positivist example of metaphysical nonsense, is void of sense because no conceivable experience could indicate to us that, on the contrary, the Absolute enjoys but a fitful sleep. We have just as much reason to make this statement as its opposite; there is no point, therefore, in making either one.

The obvious rejoinder is that at worst we have just as much reason, *so far as experience goes,* for making either statement, but it begs the question to conclude that experience can always extend to the farthest reaches of the mind. Semantic empiricism, however, need not be regarded as a conclusion but rather as a proposal, so that the issue of begging the question need not arise. The positivist criterion was often referred to as "the verifiability *theory* of meaning," but positivists later explained that it is not a theory in the strict sense. It is, rather, a *proposal* or stipulation, a rule for the admissibility of statements into "the language of science." Proposals also call for reasons; the justification offered for this one is that since statements which are not verifiable are not candidates for knowledge, they deserve no further scientific consideration. Whether science exhausts the domain of meaningful discourse is a question still to be faced.

There were a number of other difficulties, met by successive reformulations of the verifiability criterion. For one thing, we cannot speak of verification in absolute terms, as though statements can be definitely established, but only in terms of some *degree of confirmation,* as Carnap called it. A statement is meaningful even though we cannot strictly verify it, provided only that there could be some evidence, however slight, tending to confirm it. Most empiricists would agree with Hans Reichenbach that no empirical statements can be established beyond doubt. Many statements are verifiable only to some degree, and these statements are surely not lacking in meaning for that reason alone.

The verifiability criterion applies simultaneously to a statement and to its negation, for the negation of a meaningful statement is also meaningful, as the negation of nonsense remains nonsense. Falsification (or disconfirmation) serves as well as verification (or confirmation) to establish meaningfulness. When *S* is falsified, the negation of *S* is thereby verified and hence is meaningful; but in that case so is *S*.

Karl Popper urged that in the light of scientific practice the verifiability criterion is better formulated in terms of *falsifiability*. Many scientific laws—perhaps all—can be construed as declaring something to be impossible—that, for instance, there cannot be any perpetual-motion machines (thermodynamics), nothing can travel faster than light (relativity theory), or it is impossible to measure exactly both the position and the momentum of a particle (quantum mechanics). While it is difficult to establish an impossibility, it is quite easy, from a logical point of view, to establish a possibility: we have only to exhibit an actual instance. In the course of scientific inquiry we do not verify hypotheses but falsify their negations. Scientific laws make universal predications, attributing some property or pattern to all cases satisfying certain conditions. But observation, in science and anywhere else, is never of universals, only of particulars. Even one particular serves to falsify a universal. It is the possibility of such falsification which gives meaning to the hypothesis being tested by observation.

The verifiability criterion speaks not of verification but of the *possibility* of verification. For a question to make sense we need not know the answer but only be able, at least in principle, to find the answer. If a hypothesis were not meaningful unless it had in fact been verified (or falsified), we would not be able to design the experiments or plan the observations by which it is to be tested, for we would not be able to say what we want to discover. The criterion of meaning cannot be whether we can imagine a verification, for imagination is altogether too individual and adventitious to serve as an objective basis for meaningful discourse. Not meaningfulness, but only a man's capacity to grasp or entertain meanings depends on his personal powers. Nor will it do to speak of what is conceivable, for insofar as conceivability transcends purely psychological limitations, it coincides with the meaningful and so offers only a circular explanation.

Reichenbach has distinguished three types of possibility of verification, and three corresponding criteria, each specifying its own domain of meaning. *Logical possibility* is freedom from self-contradiction; logical meaning belongs to any statement whose verification is not self-contradictory. *Physical possibility* is consistency with the laws of nature; a statement has physical meaning if natural law would not stand in the way of its verification. The statement that bodies traveling faster than light turn blue has logical but no physical meaning. *Technical possibility* is consistency with actually available resources and procedures of verification; a statement has technical meaning if we can in fact go about verifying it. For instance, statements about life in other galaxies have physical meaning but no technical meaning. The domain of technical meaning changes with our technology; logical and physical meaning, on the other hand, are independent of human affairs, though of course our *knowledge* of logic and science, hence our judgments of what statements have logical or physical meaning, changes with time.

Positivists have usually been careful to emphasize that the verifiability criterion applies only to what they call "cognitive meaning," "scientific meaning," or some such thing. Statements of poetry, for instance, are not verifiable; or if they were construed so as to be verifiable, they would so manifestly be false that their point could hardly lie in their verifiable meaning. In the positivist view, poetry is only without "cognitive meaning"; it is nonsense only in the special sense of the verifiability criterion and is far from being sheer noise. It might be argued, as many positivists *did* argue, that metaphysics is a species of poetry, having its uses, perhaps, but not in science or anywhere in the serious business of life. As the nursery rhyme has it, "A little nonsense now and then is relished by the wisest men"; but men would be fools to take the nonsense seriously. Here positivism seems to me to be more at fault in its conception of metaphysics than of meaning (§36).

Even in science, statements which cannot meet the criterion of verifiability play an important part. This is the case, for instance, with rules and stipulations like the proposed verifiability criterion itself. It makes no sense to ask whether a rule is true; yet its promulgation might be very sensible. The impossibility of empirical verification is even more marked for statements of logic and mathematics (§15 and §20), as Wittgenstein urged. Such statements say nothing at all about the world of experience; no experience could falsify them, and therefore none could verify them either. Yet plainly they are not without meaning, and they undeniably have a great deal to do with cognition even if they are themselves without cognitive meaning. Wittgenstein characterized them as senseless but not nonsensical. If we content ourselves with saying that unverifiable statements are lacking in verifiable meaning, what we mean may be true, but what we are saying seems pointless.

2. For some decades, operationism (or "operationalism") was widely influential, especially in the behavioral sciences. The terms of physics have meaning because they are introduced with specified operations for applying them to experience, and what that meaning is, is determined by the operations. All we need to do in sociology, psychology, and other such disciplines is to avail ourselves of what B. F. Skinner somewhat rashly called "the simple expedient of operational definitions." In the famous formula, intelligence, for instance, becomes what is measured by intelligence tests. The question immediately arises why we call them intelligence tests in the first place. Why select these tests rather than others? And what sense does it make to speak of improving the tests, since what they measure is defined by the tests as they are? Questions of this kind must be faced, however, by every theory of meaning (§13). For operationism there are two specific difficulties.

As a criterion of meaningfulness, operationism faces a serious problem with theoretical terms. These are the terms which do not relate directly to observations, and for whose application, therefore, operations in the usual sense are not specifiable. Such concepts as "chemical bond," "genetic pool," and "social structure" presuppose a whole body of theory and derive their meaning from the theory rather than from any direct observations. Operationists sometimes speak in this connection of *symbolic operations*, those which relate words to other words rather than to experiences. But which symbolic operations mark out the boundaries of sense within the encompassing domain of nonsense? The myth and metaphysics of even the most obscure occultism, like the delusional systems of paranoia, have their own point, however questionable their meaning. The question is, how can operationism exclude systematic nonsense without also rejecting the *systemic meaning* of theoretical terms?

The second difficulty stems from the consideration that operations are taken to be conditions of meaningfulness because they determine meanings. *Whether* a term has a meaning depends on whether there are operations for its application; this is because *what* a terms means is specified by those operations. In the verifiability theory, the corresponding formulation is that "the meaning is the mode of verification." The difficulty is that scientific terms owe their significance largely to the circumstance that a number of *different* operations yield essentially the *same* results. For operationism, instead of converging evidence we have only parallel tracks of meaning. The distance of an astronomical object can be estimated by its brightness, its parallax, its red shift, or by a variety of theoretical considerations (symbolic operations). While it is important to be aware of the different conditions, errors, and uncertainties associated with each of these methods, it is also important to recognize that all of them purport to measure the same magnitude, and it is this magnitude which is meant by the term "distance," however it be measured.

The same difficulty reappears on a more fundamental level. The preceding argument has been that there is a unity of meaning underlying a multiplicity of operations. This conclusion follows from operationist premises themselves. Operationism must posit a unity of operation (and thus of corresponding meaning) underlying the multiplicity of *contexts* in which the operation is performed. It must be possible for the *same* measurements to be made by different people at different times and places. What is it that makes the measurements the same? Presumably, the circumstance that the differences in the contexts are irrelevant. The answer to the question, Irrelevant to what? seems to imply a presupposed meaning. What is thought of as "the" operation being carried out in all these different contexts is no longer something concrete and simple but highly abstract and complex. I do not say that operationism leaves us where we were but that it hardly brings us to the goal of semantic empiricism.

3. The third variant of semantic empiricism is pragmatism. Although the oldest of the three, it had very little influence on philosophy outside the United States until positivism stimulated a renewed interest in the work of Charles Peirce. The focus of pragmatism was not on a criterion of demarcation but on the determination of what is meant by discourse whose meaningfulness was simply not brought into question. Peirce's original formulation of the "pragmatic maxim," as the pragmatist principle of interpretation is called, was contained in an essay written almost a century ago (1878) entitled "How to Make Our Ideas Clear." In one of its many formulations the maxim runs: "Consider what effects, which conceivably might

have practical bearings, we conceive the object of our conception to have. Then our conception of these effects is the whole of our conception of the object."

Although Peirce's language here is mentalistic ("conceivable" and "conception"), his intent is unmistakably behavioral. To understand a term, we suppose ourselves to be in some context or other with a certain set of purposes; for the term to apply in that context entails our acting in such and such ways in order to fulfill those purposes. The meaning of the term is specified by correspondences between contexts and purposes on the one hand and relevant actions on the other hand. To speak of water, for instance, is to say that if we are thirsty we can drink it, if dirty we can wash in it, that it can power our steam engines, supply our irrigation systems, receive our pollution, and cleanse us of sin. Our conception of water is constituted by all such bearings of water on our practice.

It is conceivable that bearings which are in question, not actual bearings, and what is conceivably practical is nothing other than what we call theoretical. The desire to understand, explain, or predict identifies purposes even more relevant to the determination of meaning than the purposes allowing for more immediate gratifications, but in a much more limited set of contexts. In his exposition of the pragmatic maxim, William James unfortunately used the metaphor of the "cash-value" of an idea—an expression which was persistently, and I have sometimes felt willfully, taken in a literal sense, as though pragmatism restricts meanings to what can make money and correspondingly reduces science to technology and morals to expediency. The word "pragmatic" has come to have some such sense as this; this is not the only time in the history of ideas that a word has taken on a meaning very nearly the opposite of what it was originally meant to convey. For the contemporary sense—the one which applies to opportunists, power seekers and money grubbers, unprincipled go-getters of all sorts—for their philosophy, if it can be so called, I prefer the label *vulgar pragmatism*. It has only the most remote connection with the theories of Peirce, James, and Dewey.

As Peirce already saw, the pragmatic maxim yields the same results as the application of the verifiability criterion, the criterion employed by what he called "the experimentalist." Of the experimentalist, Peirce said, "Whatever assertion you may make to him, he will either understand as meaning that, if a given prescription for an experiment ever can be and ever is carried out in fact, an experience of a given description will result, else he will see no sense at all in what you say." The equivalence Peirce makes explicit as follows: "Since obviously nothing that might not result from experiment can have any direct bearing upon conduct, if one can define accurately all the conceivable experimental phenomena which the affirmation or denial of a concept could imply, one will have therein a complete definition of the concept, and there is absolutely nothing more in it." Pragmatism localizes meaning in the action prescribed by our experiences in a given context; positivism, in the experiences predicted by our actions in that context. Both come to the same thing. According to William James, for the pragmatist "the ultimate test" of what a statement means "is indeed the conduct that it dictates or inspires. But it inspires that conduct, because it first foretells some particular turn to our experience which shall call for just that conduct from us."

Some form of semantic empiricism seems to me inescapable. Peirce's arguments, scattered through many writings, are certainly persuasive and to my mind compelling. There is the biological argument that mind, and thereby meaning, evolved out of adaptive behavior and so can be expected to retain some connection, however indirect, with such behavior. There is the psychological argument that a man can be said to believe something only if he is prepared to act in a certain way under appropriate circumstances, and a statement is meaningful only if it is capable of being believed (or disbelieved). There is the sociological argument that meanings are interpersonal and what can be shared in a language community is fundamentally action, not sensation or feeling—if these are thought of as wholly internalized and therefore private. Finally, there is a logical argument, especially distinctive of Peirce's semantics, that meanings are general, applicable in principle to an indefinite set of contexts, and such generality can be localized only in *habits,* patterns of action which allow for corresponding regularities of interpretation. Whether or not these and similar arguments establish semantic empiricism as a criterion of demarcation, they do raise a strong presumption in its favor as a principle of interpretation.

Suppose we know, or can assume, that something makes sense; how is that sense to be specified?

12. Semantic Explanation

"Words are slippery," says Henry Adams, "and thought is viscous." However freely words may flow, thought remains sluggish. At any rate, this is true of *your* thought so far as I can grasp it. I am never quite sure what you are saying. The demand, "Define your terms!" signalizes, if not a breakdown of communication, at least a lack of confidence in the process. The distrust reaches inward as well, especially in the critical thinking essential to science and philosophy. Do I really know what I mean to say, and am I in fact saying it? The Mad Hatter was not so very mad after all in his instruction of Alice on this point.

Even when I succeed in saying what I mean, I may be saying something more as well which I do not intend and of which I may not even be aware. Worse yet, it may seem—to myself as well as to others—that something more is being said than what is actually conveyed by the words. When I say that someone is apathetic because he is "lazy" or "bored," I am only pointing to the apathy all over again, not explaining it by reference to some other condition. Expressions of this kind have what Reichenbach called a *surplus meaning,* a meaning which adds nothing to the verifiable content. If I am not to mislead myself or others, I must strip away this surplus.

Occam's razor enjoins against multiplying entities beyond necessity; in a semantic version we might say, Do not multiply meanings beyond necessity! We need devices which will make it more likely, if never certain, that we say neither more nor less than what we mean.

There are those who cultivate the obscure and even unintelligible, putting upon others the responsibility of finding meaning in what they say and hoping, perhaps, that obscurity will be mistaken for profundity. As Nietzsche says, they muddy the water that it may seem deep. There is a kind of *romantic vagueness* which finds a peculiar charm in the twilight zones of meaning as though imagination can take hold only of what is dimly perceived, or as though understanding is the enemy of insight and appreciation. I am convinced that such a perspective is as alien to art as it is to science or philosophy. When T. S. Eliot has Prufrock exclaim, "It is impossible to say just what I mean!/But as if a magic lantern threw the nerves in patterns on a screen," it is only Prufrock who is inarticulate, not Eliot. Wittgenstein's motto was, "Everything that is known, and that is not mere sound and fury, can be said in three words."

There is such a thing as making meanings too clear and explicit, and words work in many ways, which do not always depend on their precision. The *Brhadaranyaka Upanishad* states that the gods love the obscure, but its own teaching is not therefore obscurantist; the opening line of Lao-tzu's *Tao Te Ching,* "The Tao that can be spoken is not the true Tao," does not reduce Taoism to unspeakable nonsense. A jurist may deliberately seek out vague expressions like "due process" and "reasonable care," just as a diplomat may lean on the language of "secure boundaries" and "just settlements." A certain *intolerance of ambiguity* has come to be recognized as a characteristic trait of the authoritarian personality. In searching for ways to specify meaning, we need not presuppose that we must *always* do what we are capable of doing whenever it truly serves our purposes.

Not all ambiguity makes for equivocation, a fallacious argument which misleads because of a double meaning. On the contrary, ambiguity may be functional, the multiplicity of meaning contributing to the point of the discourse. How the several meanings of ambiguous terms relate to one another and to the point in using those terms provides a basis for distinguishing among several different types of ambiguity.

When the several meanings exclude one another, and the ambiguous term is so used that interpretation in one sense precludes or inhibits interpretations in any other sense, we may speak of *disjunctive ambiguity* ("disjunction" being the name used in logic for the operation which combines two alternatives into a single proposition: *p or q*). The word "depression," for example, exhibits disjunctive ambiguity, with distinct meanings in meteorology, economics, psychiatry, and other contexts.

In the preliminary stages of psychoanalytic dream interpretation, disjunctive ambiguities play a central role. Freud speaks in this connection of "switch-words": "In a line of associations ambiguous words (or, as we may call them, 'switch-words') act like points at a junction. If the points are switched across from the position in which they appear to lie in the dream, then we find ourselves upon another set of rails; and along this second track run the thoughts which we are in search of and which still lie concealed behind the dream." The difference between the manifest and latent content of a dream symbol is disjunctive. The sun, moon, and eleven stars have the latent meaning of Joseph's father, mother, and brothers (as is made manifest in his earlier dream, where the sheaves of grain explicitly belong to his brothers). The dream is not about heavenly bodies and their movements but about his family and his own worldly future.

Oracles, both ancient and modern, so characteristically make use of disjunctive ambiguity that the word "oracular" has come to convey a portentous uncertainty of meaning. The pronouncements of the oracle require interpretation, and since the disjunctive ambiguity covers all possibilities, in retrospect, the oracle is seen to have been prophetic: "Thou shalt go thou shalt return never in battle shalt thou perish!" with the comma after "return" or after "never," as is afterwards seen to be required. Apollo, the deity to whom the most famous of the oracles, that at Delphi, was dedicated, was known as the god of truth, who never spoke falsely; but precision of speech was decidedly not one of his virtues. The philosophers of late antiquity, like Porphyry in the third century, thought it worthwhile to collect and interpret the ancient oracles.

In the seventeenth century a similar enterprise occupied Bernard de Fontanelle, who wrote a widely read history of oracles. His own point, however, made systematic use of disjunctive ambiguity in a technique much favored by the *philosophes* who followed him: to criticize pagan religion in such a way as to expose the weaknesses of Christianity. They spoke of one religion and meant another; what they said, therefore, was disjunctively ambiguous. In our own day, Jean Anouilh wrote a modern version of Sophocles' *Antigone* which, in France under the Nazi occupation, gave a new meaning to Creon's tyranny. Disjunctive ambiguity has been exploited often to evade censorship, whether psychological or political.

In *conjunctive ambiguity* the several meanings are jointly operative ("conjunction" is the name of the operation represented by *p and q*). In disjunctive ambiguity we say one thing to speak of another or, at any rate, intend only one among the two or more things we are saying; in conjunctive ambiguity we mean to say both. If disjunctive ambiguity were eliminated, there would be a gain in clarity without a loss in content, though we might have to pay in other ways for our unmistakable intent. But conjunctive ambiguity makes possible a distinctive content, resulting from the concurrence of the several meanings.

For instance, ambivalent attitudes—combining love and hate, fear and desire—often find expression through conjunctive ambiguities. Freud has called attention to how commonly what he calls "primal words" have an antithetical sense, as does the Latin word *sacer,* which means both sacred and accursed. Conjunctive ambiguity also gives expression to the results of condensation, a process common in dream symbolism in which two or more foci of feeling are combined into a single image—say, a woman who is both mother and sister, or a baby that is also a piglet. Such symbols are like the portmanteau words Humpty Dumpty described in his explication of *Jabberwocky,* where several meanings are packed up in one word, thereby producing unique effects.

Wit of various kinds, especially the kind that exploits puns and double entendres, is largely a matter of conjunctive ambiguity. "How goes it?" asked the blind man of the lame one; "As you see!" was the reply. Among the most significant applications of conjunctive ambiguity is its use for the sake of irony. Irony has been defined variously as "a speech that has the honey of pleasantness in its mouth, and a sting of rebuke in its tail"; "jesting hidden behind gravity"; and "an insult conveyed in the form of a compliment." In all these definitions the double meaning is central: honey and sting, jest and gravity, insult and compliment. Both are essential to the irony. A couplet from "One Times One" by E. E. Cummings provides a memorable illustration:

a politician is an arse upon
which everyone has sat except a man

The play between the literal sense of a word and some figurative meaning it may have is a rich source of irony, as in Alexander Pope's inscription for a dog collar:

I am his Highness' dog at Kew;
Pray tell me, sir, whose dog are you?

In *additive ambiguity* meanings are neither wholly exclusive nor jointly significant. The term has a cluster of meanings whose overlapping range conveys a common center or core of meaning. One country's "friendship" for or "support" of another may signify many different things, ranging from the sending of troops, weapons, or money to formal expressions of sympathy. The ambiguity in the pledge of friendship or support does not call for an interpretation in terms of some one or another of these alternatives nor yet of all of them together, but in terms of the whole range of possibilities, with a content to be made determinate only in specific contexts. The language of the law may use a whole set of near-synonyms for just this reason, to point to the kind of judgments which might be rendered in concrete cases—as in a statute making it illegal to "mar, deface, damage, injure, or destroy" certain property. The psychoanalytic concept of the "overdetermination" of a symptom or symbol similarly turns on additive ambiguity, as is brilliantly amplified in numerous examples in Ernest Jones's essay on symbolism.

Scientific concepts often exhibit additive ambiguity, more or less being included in the concept in various contexts of inquiry. Consider the range around the core of meaning of such concepts as "liquid," "elementary particle," "species," "virus," "inflation," and "culture-pattern." Not uncommonly, a term in everyday use may have disjunctive ambiguity while its scientific meaning may exhibit additive ambiguity, for instance, "cat"; or, conversely, it may be additively ambiguous in its everyday sense and relatively free from ambiguity in scientific usage, for instance, "fruit."

The multiple meanings of a term may be not only co-present but also interacting, evoking, and supporting one another. This is *integrative ambiguity,* characteristic of poetry, iconography, religious symbols and the like. Their interpretation involves the recognition of a complex, shifting, but nevertheless unified pattern of meaning. In disjunctive ambiguity there are several distinct and unconnected semantic fields; in additive ambiguity there is a restructuring of a single field to reveal more or fewer details; in conjunctive ambiguity several fields are connected though remaining distinct; in integrative ambiguity they are fully reconstituted, integrated into one complex meaning.

None of these types of ambiguity should be thought of as subjective, as resulting from inadequate or inaccurate understanding. In a given linguistic community the terms themselves really do have the multiple meanings. When interpretations are in fact subjective, the resultant ambiguity is *projective,* the consequence of projecting meanings onto the term rather than finding them there. In these cases, the term is said to be "hopelessly vague"; but it is a sound principle of hermeneutics not to give up hope until the resources for objectively grounded interpretation have been exhausted. In his novel *Pierre or the Ambiguities,* Herman Melville remarks that "a smile is the chosen vehicle for all ambiguities"—for all projective ambiguities, I would say, but not for those conforming to well-established rules of usage. There are neither dictionaries nor grammars to lay down norms for facial expression—in our culture, that is; the situation is quite different for, say, the Kathak dance of northern India, or the Nō drama of Japan.

I have not been saying that because of their ambiguities, words can mean all things to all men—this is characteristic only of projective ambiguity—but that words can mean more than one thing to most men. An ambiguous meaning can be just as objective as a precise and univocal signification. The literary critic William Empson, in a classic work on types of ambiguity, has extensively documented this position—an achievement all the more impressive because he deals with poetry, where it is too often assumed that meanings are projective.

When we are confronted by ambiguous terms, or find ourselves using them, we ask for or offer explanations of what is meant. These are *semantic explanations,* radically different from explanations of why or how something happens (§34). When we have a semantic explanation we only know what somebody means, but not why he says what he does, and certainly not whether what he says is true. What purports to be a semantic explanation often has quite another point than clarifying a meaning. It may be only a ritualized gesture of obedience to the norms of clarity without in fact conforming to them. Not uncommonly, an introductory chapter or paragraph formulates what profess to be definitions of certain already familiar terms, but these terms are subsequently used in quite other ways than those initially specified. Such *pseudodefinitions* are especially characteristic of enterprises which aspire to more precision of language than is warranted by their achievements of thought.

The simplest type of semantic explanation—simple, that is, provided it is possible to carry it out at all—is *ostension:* pointing to what is meant. The technique encountered by Gulliver in one of his travels, carrying a sack filled with all the things one might want to talk about, is restrictive for even the most hardened empiricist. Of much broader application, though it is still very far from universal, is semantic explanation by way of *description.* The easiest way to explain what is meant by "elephant" or "spiral" is just to describe the thing; indeed, though the description is easy, an exact specification of meaning would call for the skills of a naturalist and a mathematician—or, at any rate, a lexicographer.

A third type of semantic explanation, though of very wide application, is of considerably more limited use than is often supposed; this is *definition:* providing another set of words with the same meaning as the one being defined. Where necessary, we may call it "verbal definition" to distinguish it from other kinds of semantic explanation for which the word "definition" is sometimes loosely used. "Sibling" is defined as "brother or sister"; the word "and" can be defined as follows: "*p and q*" means by definition that it is not the case that *p* is not the case or *q* is not the case. A definition of the second kind, where a word is defined in context, is sometimes called a *definition-in-use.*

Whether a definition succeeds in giving a semantic explanation depends on the intelligibility of the words used in the defining. In his famous dictionary, Samuel Johnson defines a net as a "reticulation of interstices"; this definition is useful only as an example of something or other, but decidedly not as a semantic explanation. A common failing in this connection is to define *A* in terms of *B*, then purport to give a semantic explanation of *B* by defining it in terms of *A*. Such a procedure is appropriately called *circular definition,* as intolerable logically as a circular argument. How to define "obscenity" has been found by the courts to be notoriously difficult; it does not help at all to propose defining "obscenity" as "obscene books, pictures, or films" and then to define "obscene" as "characterized by the presence of obscenity." Nor does it help, in trying to determine the limits of legal responsibility set by insanity, to proceed as does Polonius:

Your noble son is mad.
Mad call I it; for, to define true madness,
What is't but to be nothing else but mad?
But let that go.

In contexts where definitions are to be taken seriously, therefore, as in law or mathematics, definitions occur in a definite order—a *chain of definitions.* (It is a logical order that is in question here, not an order of presentation.) Only terms already defined can be used in later definitions or there will be a circularity. The chain must begin somewhere; such starting points are called *primitive terms*. Though such terms are *undefined*, they are not *indefinable:* we can always define them if we are prepared to choose other terms as our primitives. In the example defining "and," the terms "not" and "or" were undefined; if we are prepared to leave "and" undefined, we can define "or" as follows: "*p or q*" means by definition that it is not the case that *p* is not the case and *q* is not the case. It is best to choose primitive terms which will not call for semantic explanation; when they do, however, something other than verbal definition must be invoked. A semantic explanation for a primitive term is sometimes called a *coordinating definition* or a *rule of designation*.

A particularly useful type of definition gives the appearance of circularity though it is, in fact, perfectly straightforward. It is called *definition by abstraction* and has two parts: to define a property *P* we first state what it is for two things to have the same *P*, then define the property by reference to the whole set of things which are alike in this respect. The appearance of circularity results from the natural assumption that "the same *P*" can only be explained by reference to *P;* the procedure is called definition by abstraction because it dispenses with (abstracts from) a supposed common element. Having-the-same-*P* is a single notion explained by a coordinating definition, not by a verbal definition presupposing that *P* is already understood. The appearance of circularity is avoided from the outset if some other term altogether is used in place of the expression "having-the-same-*P*."

Consider, for example, how the physicist might define the term "weight": (1) Two bodies have the same weight if they balance when placed on the pans of a suitable scale. (2) A weight (say of one gram) consists of the set of all bodies having the same weight as a certain brass cylinder (that a particular body has a weight of one gram means that it belongs to this set). Appearances will be improved without any change in the content of the definition if we use the barbarism "synponderous" to designate the relation, "having the same weight." Reichenbach has proposed a definition by abstraction for meaning itself: Two statements have the same meaning (are semantically equivalent) if they receive the same weight (are confirmed to the same degree) by every possible observation; the meaning of a statement is given by the set of all statements semantically equivalent to it. Russell has also defined number in a similar way (§20).

Verbal definitions provide semantic explanations only if the chain of definitions is linked at last to something other than words. In this way all the verbally defined terms are coordinated to something in experience, whence the linkage is called a "coordinating definition"; equivalently, it is thereby specified what the terms designate, whence the label "rule of designation." The linkage constitutes a vertical specification of meaning, so to speak, as contrasted with the horizontal specification by verbal definition. In this imagery, the vertical dimension is that of the so-called "ladder of abstraction," mounting from the most concrete terms, whose meaning can be explained by ostension, to the remotest abstractions, capable neither of ostension nor description, and to which verbal definitions alone give no empirical content. It is the same as the dimension running from directly observable terms to the highly theoretical ones.

The most general type of semantic explanation I call *indication.* It is a specification of the criteria—either observable or, in turn, linked to observations—by which we can determine whether or not the term whose meaning is being explained applies in a given case. Because of its connection with observation, indication fulfills the requirement of semantic empiricism. Meanings do not reach beyond what can be known, at least in principle. If anyone claims to mean something transcendent, he cannot explain what he means, being limited to offering verbal equivalents which are as unintelligible as his original statement. This is the predicament in which we are placed by floating abstractions (§8); to make sense of them we must provide anchorage, giving indications of the concreta whose observation justifies the use of the corresponding abstractions. Einstein gave meaning to the concept of "electromagnetic field," not in terms of an unobservable luminiferous ether, but in terms of the behavior of matter and radiation in specified space-time regions; Claude Bernard interpreted the abstract concept of a disease in terms of the concreta of certain observable symptoms; and Harold Lasswell explained the meaning of "political power" by reference to who gets what, when, and how.

Generally speaking, indications are indefinitely many. What a term designates—especially a term of some significance—is not usually specifiable in terms of a single property or even of a collection of properties; usually a pattern of properties, a characteristic profile, is involved. The multiplicity of contexts in which the term is to be used inevitably confronts us with a corresponding variety of designated cases. These cases are not usefully regarded as sharing a common property, even a composite one. They bear to one another what has come to be called a "family resemblance." The members of a family need not all have any single trait in common, though any two members of the family share enough traits to be recognizably kin. In this way we may identify a *family of meanings*—quite distinguishable, yet more closely related to one another than are the meanings of wholly distinct terms. Such semantic families contrast with the presupposition of the endeavor traditionally associated with Socrates: to find *the* meaning of "justice," "virtue," and the like. This presupposition, which I am here denying, might be called the *Socratic axiom:* if one and the same term occurs with proper usage in several contexts, some *one* thing must be meant by it.

The possible semantic explanations of related meanings are severely restricted by the resources of verbal definition alone. Either the meanings are wholly distinct, or one is included in the other, or there is some overlapping. With verbal definition we have no way of specifying how close the meanings are to one another, or in what respects. Consider. for instance, the concept of "man" as it appears in physical anthropology, in cultural anthropology, in ecology, and elsewhere. In each of these contexts the concept is differently defined, but there are samenesses, too. Many of the indications are the same, though not all, and different degrees of importance are attached even to the same indications in different contexts. The physical anthropologist may explain what he calls "man" (that is, give indications) in terms of braincase, dentition, and erect posture; the cultural anthropologist by reference to the use of fire, tools, and language; the ecologist in terms of the domestication of plants and animals, the pollution of air and water, and perhaps also—in quite another perspective—the capacity to make fires.

Since contexts are many, it is to be expected that indications might provide a semantic explanation for a term used in certain contexts but leave its meaning unspecified in other contexts. Such conditional semantic explanations are sometimes called *partial definitions* or "reduction sentences." All specifications of meaning other than those provided by purely verbal definitions are, in principle, partial only. A type of partial definition that has been subjected to considerable analysis in modern times, especially by Rudolf Carnap, Carl G. Hempel, Nelson Goodman, and others, is that required by so-called "dispositional terms," which designate a tendency or capacity to respond in certain ways to certain stimuli. To say that a substance is soluble, for instance, is to say that *if* it is placed in a certain solvent, at the appropriate temperature and so on, then it will dissolve. Nothing is said about what will happen if these conditions are not met.

Another important respect in which definitions are often partial derives from the difference between positive and negative indications. Suppose that the presence of a certain property or profile, say a symptom or syndrome, justifies the application of a certain term, say the diagnosis of a certain disease. The absence of that property, however, does not necessarily imply that the term *cannot* be applied; the diagnosis might be correct even though the particular symptom is not observed. By contrast, verbal definitions tell us that a term applies *if and only if* such-and-such is the case. Because such definitions are complete, they may be completely useless.

Semantic explanations by way of indications are partial in another sense. Even if the indications covered all the circumstances in which the question of the applicability of the term might possibly arise, they give to the question an answer always less than certain or indubitable. Each profile is given a weight which, in general, is less than the maximum possible. There are always, at least in principle, borderline cases; in proportion to their frequency we say that the term is *vague*. Some measure of vagueness is an inescapable feature of all terms that have an empirical reference. The triumphant challenge, "But where do you draw the line?" is popularly misconceived as justifying the rejection of terms susceptible of degrees. Usually, however, *there is no line to be drawn*. Discriminations must be made, but it is not to be expected that they can ever be made on a principle so absolute as to apply, beyond dispute, in every case that might possibly arise. Vagueness is objectionable, not in itself, but only when borderline cases become too frequent or too difficult to resolve on the basis of the indications provided. It is then that further indications are called for, with weights closer to the maximal (and minimal) values.

Because of the differing weights of the various profiles, some cases more decidedly warrant the application of a given term than do other cases: there are always good and bad specimens of any class. Verbal definitions presuppose a certain homogeneity; each particular case either does or does not fall under the definition, and all that do are alike in that respect. So far as concerns the term defined, no further discriminations are made. The absence of this homogeneity, and especially the prevalence of poor specimens, I call the *internal vagueness* of the term. It is not so much a question of whether the term applies, as with vagueness in the more familiar sense; it is a question, rather, of whether the boundaries of meaning might not be so redrawn as to give greater centrality to the instances which, though clearly included, are yet only marginally representative of what the term is taken to mean.

A common way of dealing with internal vagueness is to suppose that the term "really means" only what is manifested in the best specimens of the class designated, with the result that the term has very few real applications. Such usage might be called *Platonized,* for Plato held that the ideal of any type most nearly—and clearly—embodies the idea of that type. The Platonized usage is illustrated in what Antony said of Julius Caesar:

His life was gentle, and the elements
So mixed in him that Nature might stand up
And say to all the world, "This was a man!"

and perhaps also in what Hamlet said of his father:

He was a man, take him for all in all,
I shall not look upon his like again.

Whether in the shift from one member of a family of meanings to another, in the movement from vagueness to greater precision, in the reduction of internal vagueness to attain to greater realism, in these and in other ways there is an undeniable growth of meaning. I am not speaking merely of changes in language, of the important but superficial circumstance that a word which at one time might have meant one thing now means another. I am speaking of changes in our conceptions. The growth of knowledge is partly a matter of *epistemic approximation:* coming closer to the truth, or attaining to more of it. This process is accompanied by another, a process of *semantic approximation:* articulating meanings which progressively enhance the effectiveness with which we can make the point we are expressing by that meaning. One process cannot take place without the other. The difference between the present state of knowledge and that of an earlier age is not only that we affirm certain propositions our predecessors denied, and conversely; it is also that we each understand propositions unintelligible to the other. To achieve such understanding it would not be enough for a time traveler to learn another language; he would have to absorb a whole culture.

In short, meanings are open and fluid. Just as atoms, once impenetrable spheres, are now better understood as loci of interactions diffused over indeterminate regions, so also with what were once thought to be semantic atoms. From Descartes and Locke to Russell it was widely assumed that meanings can in principle be made perfectly precise and should in practice be brought to close approximation to that ideal. The principle guiding Wittgenstein's earlier philosophy was: "Everything that can be thought at all can be thought clearly. Everything that can be said can be said clearly." His later thought turned in more fruitful directions than the delineation of an ideal language.

Few, if any, empirical classes exhibit the defining feature of mathematical sets, that with regard to any individual whatever, it is always possible to say whether or not that individual is a member of the set. The more significant a term is, the less likely is it to have a meaning so clearly determinate. It will do its work in many and varied contexts, often in relationship with other terms, also somewhat indeterminate, from which it derives systemic meaning. Meanings can be made superficially precise, especially by way of verbal definition; but the successive redefinition which marks the growth of meaning is precluded by such a *premature closure* of our concepts.

The demand for semantic explanation is, quite properly, persistent. But if it is unremitting and forever unsatisfied, it may reflect more pedantry and scientific pretentiousness than a genuine intellectual virtue. "It is the mark of an educated man," Aristotle wrote at the beginning of his *Nicomachean Ethics,* "to look for precision in each class of things just so far as the nature of the subject admits"—and, I would add, just so far as is admitted by the state of our knowledge and understanding of the subject. Since these always leave something to be desired, meanings, too, can never be explained as well as we would like. Interpretation of any discourse or symbolism which is independently significant (not merely a verbal equivalent for something else) cannot be made on a *codebook principle,* as though somewhere there is a list which gives an indubitable and exact coordination of meaning. Interpretation must proceed, rather, on a *guidebook principle:* much can be said to help us understand, but there is always more to say; our understanding is ultimately to be enriched by our own experience.

13. The Metaphysics of Semantics

The domain of meaning lies between two border regions. On one side lies the field of value which, in the interface with meaning, produces *significance.* On the other side is the domain of what today is called *information,* in a technical sense of that term, not to be confused with such semantic categories as cognitive meaning. In the sense of the recent discipline called the "theory of information," information is not a semantic content at all but a numerical quantity. Roughly speaking, it is the *capacity* for embodying or conveying information, in the more familiar sense, measured in terms of the probability of occurrence of a particular outcome in relation to the ensemble of possible outcomes in that situation. The lower the antecedent probability of a given signal, the greater the information conveyed by its transmission. In the expression "Happy New Year," the "year" tells us little that we would not already surmise from the preceding two words; in the expression "a half-life of one year," the same word conveys a great deal, for, so far as the preceding words are concerned, various other possibilities were just as probable. The details of the measure and the impressive achievements of the resulting theory need not occupy us. So far as the analysis of semantic content is concerned, as Yehoshua bar Hillel and others have emphasized, the theory of information provides a promising approach, but so far it remains little more than a promise.

The attempt to formulate the most general categories and distinctive features of semantic content is as old as philosophic speculation, but progress here has been rather less marked than in other similar areas of philosophic concern. Some such distinction is to be drawn, as that between *substantive* and *auxiliary* terms: the former—like nouns, verbs, and adjectives—embody the semantic content of discourse; the latter—like articles, prepositions, and conjunctions—structure the discourse and help the substantive terms signify what they do. Auxiliary terms often have an undeniable content of their own ("into," "because," "in order that"), while some substantive terms ("fact," "exist," "real") may make only a dubious contribution to what is being said.

Less problematic is the distinction drawn by Charles Peirce between *indexical* and *characterizing signs*. The former identify what things we are talking about, and the latter say something about these things. The difference is not that between subjects and predicates; characterizing signs can play either grammatical role, while indexical signs can appear only as subjects. We may have "Red is a color" as well as "This is red," but not that something "is a this." That there are, however, idioms like "That's that!" illustrates how the study of semantics teaches humility.

Every indexical sign derives ultimately from what Peirce called an index (§9); fundamentally, we can specify what we are talking about only by presenting it to experience. If in the presentation a symbol plays a certain significant part, it can afterward serve in place of the presentation. Such a symbol is called a logically proper name. In the grammatical sense, proper names usually do not name anything on their own but only by way of some descriptive phrase or other by which the name is introduced: " 'Akko' is the Crusader city forty kilometers north of Haifa." A logically proper name need not, and indeed cannot, be introduced by a verbal definition; it itself performs the introduction—by ostension. In semantics complications seem endless: there are indexical signs which look for all the world like proper names, even logically proper names, but which in fact name nothing, like the names in mythology or fiction or the pointing gestures of conjurers.

Language is indifferent to the difference between appearance and reality; there is nothing to prevent us from *calling* an appearance real. This circumstance has baffled philosophers from Plato onward. How is it possible to talk about something which does not exist?—as though when I talk about a thing I am relating to it in a certain way so that it must be there to stand in the relationship. Philosophers have invoked a notion of "subsistence," a shadowy state of being for things which do not really exist, but which, somehow, stand ready to come before the mind when they are summoned. Plato's famous "theory of Ideas" is an attempt to solve this whole nest of problems. There is a domain of certain abstract entities—Ideas or Forms—whose embodiment in things makes these the particular sorts of things that they are, and whose grasp by the mind makes it possible to speak of things and to know what they are.

For all the difficulties and obscurities of this theory, it has not been easy to dispense with it, or something like it. The view that the domain of existence includes at least some abstract entities is called (Platonic) *realism.* The contrary view, that only concrete particulars exist, is called *nominalism.* Whether nominalism is a workable position and can meet the needs of science, logic, and mathematics was examined by Bertrand Russell and more recently by Willard van Quine, with uncertain but tentatively negative conclusions. There are, at any rate, some reasons for wanting to say that certain properties might exist even though no things have those properties, that classes are distinct from their members, so a class may exist with no members at all, and that numbers can exist so large that there are not enough things to be numbered by them.

Being able to talk about something is no more a guarantee of its existence than the expression "It is true that *p*" is a guarantee of the truth of *p*. My talking about unicorns does not commit me to the view that there are such things, else how could I even say, "There are no unicorns!" Language does not of itself bring things into existence; such a belief belongs to magic (§7). In particular, we cannot define things into existence. Two apparent exceptions to this dictum have been given extensive consideration: God, Whose existence, some have maintained, is part of the very concept of a Supreme Being; and mathematical entities (numbers, functions, and the like), for which, it has been held, to be is no more than to be consistent, a virtue to which a definition itself might conceivably certify. I shall say something more of these matters later on (§20, §85).

In the meantime, an apparently simpler yet quite fundamental difficulty demands consideration. When I speak of unicorns and of sea serpents I am speaking of two different things; yet, since neither exists, I am in both cases speaking of nothing at all. How, then, do I differentiate between the meanings of the two sorts of statements? This question was first tackled in a serious way around the turn of the century by the mathematician and logician Gottlieb Frege. He introduced a basic distinction between what he called *Sinn* and *Bedeutung,* or *sense* and *reference.* The former, roughly speaking, is the meaning or concept designated by the term; the latter, the particular existents, if any, subsumed under the concept. These two are sometimes also distinguished as the "connotation" and "denotation," although the former is also commonly used for adventitious or peripheral meanings. With such distinctions in mind, the question when two expressions are synonymous or when one can be replaced by the other is seen to be far from trivial. A typical perplexity (I deliberately do not choose between "puzzle" and "problem" in the sense of §2) is that, though the morning star and the evening star are identical, someone who calls the evening star "Venus" does not therefore believe that Venus sometimes appears in the morning.

Unquestionably the most fundamental concept involving the relation between meaning and existence is that of truth. Of the many senses of that term, the one usually identified as the *semantical concept of truth* can be traced back to Aristotle. To speak the truth, Aristotle concisely remarked, is to say of that which is that it is, and of that which is not that it is not. In the more formidable but essentially equivalent modern locution, a proposition *p* is true if and only if *p;* and this necessary and sufficient condition of truth is taken to define it. Alfred Tarski, one of the founders of present-day formal semantics, then showed how, given the truth conditions for certain simple statements in systems of exactly specifiable structure, it is possible to define the truth of more complex statements. Pilate with his question was not particularly profound, only impatient.

It is easy to make the mistake of supposing that the semantical concept of truth is empty, nothing being added to the content of a proposition by the attribution to it of truth. By the definition, to say that *p* is true is to say neither more nor less than just *p;* why not dispense with the term altogether, save as an honorific, or something of the sort? Yet, as Tarski pointed out, the term is not always eliminable without decided loss of meaning; how else are we to say, for instance, that all the logical consequences of a true proposition are true, or that the first sentence of Plato is true?

The significance of the concept cannot be appreciated before exploring the relations between truth and knowledge (§27). So far as semantics itself is concerned, some preliminary distinctions will be useful. Let us mean by a *proposition* the content of a declarative *sentence* of an appropriate kind—one to which we can attribute truth or falsehood. Then the meaning of such a sentence might be called its *propositional sense,* as distinguished from its *propositional attitude,* embodied in the point of uttering a sentence with that meaning. The same sentence can be used, for instance, to express profound conviction, hesitant acceptance, and suspended disbelief. What is being said in the three cases is partly the same, partly different; the sameness is in the propositional sense, while the difference is in the propositional attitude.

An affirmative sentence signifies an *affirmation;* a negative one, a *negation.* These characterize the propositional sense but not the propositional attitude. In particular, an affirmation is not to be confused with an *assertion.* I can affirm something without expressing my belief in it—for instance, when I am formulating a hypothesis to be tested. The ascription of truth to a statement (the sentence, or the proposition it conveys) implies that the statement is assertable, but that ascription itself is only an affirmation, and neither it nor the statement is thereby being asserted. What justifies an assertion is one of the central questions of the theory of knowledge; semantics is limited to the question of what constitutes an assertion.

The answer to this question is not a matter only of the psychology of belief and its expression; much depends also on the language in which the assertion is to be made. Philosophers are not always less ethnocentric than other mortals; the critic who can see a speck in his neighbor's eye is notoriously ignorant of his own blindness. The language we ourselves speak is easily mistaken for the voice of universal Reason. We can all understand the impression of the American undergraduate that English is a much easier language to learn than German, because in English the words come in the order in which you actually think of them. Philosophers have been affected not only by such *linguistic ethnocentrism* but also by the limitations in received doctrines about language—traditional grammars, for instance—which too often purport to deal with language "as such," rather than with one or another specific language or language family.

Language is intimately bound up with culture, as has been emphasized in our time by such anthropologists as Edward Sapir and Benjamin Lee Whorf. The most obvious, but philosophically also the least interesting, of the ways in which culture is reflected in language is in the lexicon. It surprises no one to learn that the language of the Eskimos has dozens of words for the kinds and configurations of snow, as Arabic does for sand and camels, and as several Asian languages have for rice. Much more interesting, but also more uncertain and even controversial, is the view that which distinctions are embodied in the lexicon affect, to some degree, the ability of the language speakers to make the corresponding perceptual discriminations, as though more colors look different to people with more names of colors in their vocabulary. Certainly, distinctions are not useful if they are not accompanied by corresponding powers of discrimination; whether they enhance those powers is another matter.

The more general form of the thesis has been widely discussed in recent decades: that language suggests, even if it does not compel, certain segmentations and interpretations of experience. An immigrant to Israel, whose native tongue lacked the distinction of gender so characteristic of Hebrew, complained, "Whenever I think of the difference between masculine and feminine, I forget what I was going to say!" In the language of the Wintu Indians, I am told, grammar requires that each sentence contain a prefix indicating the source of knowledge of what is being said—hearsay, direct experience, and one or two other such specifications. Presumably, this should make the Wintu more epistemologically aware, or more resistant to propaganda and promotional techniques. Such an effect is almost impossible to confirm, not only because of the interference of so many other uncontrolled and even unspecified factors in the cultural situation, but also because what analysis after the fact discloses of a certain linguistic form or content simply cannot be assumed to be what was earlier operative on the users of the language. I doubt very much, for instance, whether the norm in English of using masculine nouns and pronouns for the general case ("chairman," "whoever he may be") contributed one whit to the deep-seated prejudice and discrimination against women, or even reflected it.

Now that attention has been focused on this usage, however, changes in the usage might very well play some small part in the liberation of women.

The most far-reaching of the ideas concerning the impact of language on thought and behavior is that the basic categories and principles of philosophy—especially logic and metaphysics—are only formulations of the underlying structural features of the language in which the philosophy is couched. It is not the specific language which is in question but the whole language family—for instance, what Whorf called "Standard Average European" (SAE) contrasted, say, with Hopi, Hebrew, or Chinese.

Max Müller, a nineteenth-century philologist and philosopher, declared with considerable prescience that after Kant philosophy can be nothing else than analysis of language. What Kant identified as the forms of thought are, in fact, the linguistic genera by which thought finds expression. Aristotle introduced his metaphysical categories (substance, quantity, quality, relation, and so on) with the statement, "Expressions which are in no way composite signify. . . ." The word for "metaphysical category" in classical Indian philosophy, especially in the Vaisheshika school, is "padartha" from *pada,* meaning name, term, or word, and *artha,* thought or meaning. That the category of substance basically derives from the subject-predicate form of propositions was argued by Russell in an early book on the philosophy of Leibniz. In a similar vein, Whorf urged that the importance in European philosophy of the distinction between form and matter can be traced to the way in which SAE handles mass nouns, which designate a stuff or material. We cannot speak of these in an undifferentiated way but only as suitably fragmented—that is, formed; thus, we say "a cup of water" or "a piece of wood," not "a water" or "a wood."

Considerations of this kind might also suggest that the preoccupation of Western philosophy with problems of permanence and change reflect the basic contrast in SAE between nouns and adjectives on the one hand and verbs on the other. The trouble is that Heraclitus, who proclaimed that all is flux, and Parmenides, who held that the Real is immovable and unchanging, both spoke (and presumably thought in) Greek. Hebrew has a decided preference for verbs over nouns and adjectives; where English would say, "he was late," Hebrew has "he lated." I scarcely think it follows, however, that the Israeli concern with fixed and secure borders runs counter to the spirit of the language or to some supposedly prevailing metaphysics. Language is important and perhaps indispensable to thought, but it does not determine what we think. Even how we are to go about our thinking is a question which carries us far beyond semantics, to a more austere yet more inviting domain—the field of logic.

Chapter Three

Logic

14. The Uses and Misuses of Reason

Ours is decidedly an age of unreason. It is a time when "reason staggers through the streets with its head to the ground and its legs in the air. Gradually we've got into a state when it's no longer possible to tell the true from the false, the dark from the light, the sun from the moon." Governments whose populations are sunk in the depths of poverty, ignorance, and disease spend vast sums of money and tens of thousands of priceless lives on senseless wars. People feel hatred, fear, or contempt for those who differ from themselves in skin color, sex, or habits of worship; prejudices are expressed in abominable patterns of discrimination. On a planetary scale, we are destroying our only home, eroding its soil, polluting its air and water, while devoting a large part of our resources to accelerating the process. Truly, all this is more than unreason merely; it is madness.

Samuel Beckett, in his *Endgame*—a title of foreboding connotation—puts into the mouth of one of his characters the declaration, "No one that ever lived ever thought so crooked as we." Even this assessment may be crooked thinking, less a realistic appraisal of our failings than a perverse pride in their extent. The quotation with which this chapter begins, on the staggering reason of our time, is from a predecessor of Beckett in the theater of the absurd, and was written at the end of the nineteenth century (Georges Courteline, in *The Commissioner* [*Le Commissaire est bon enfant*], 1899). It may be that we are no more mad than the less agonizingly self-conscious generations which preceded ours. If the good old days are a myth, this seems to be no less true of the old-fashioned idea of progress. There may be no more madness in our time than ever before, but it is hard to lay claim to more sanity, or even to good sense. The faith of a Freud—that the voice of reason speaks soft, but it is insistent, and it will be heard—is not easy to sustain.

Freud also recognizes that he who does not lose his reason under certain provocations has no reason to lose. As American folk humor has it, if you can keep your head when all about you are losing theirs you just don't know what's going on. The world is not only mad but maddening. Victims are condemned as aggressors for refusing to be destroyed; gunmen and hucksters dictate foreign policy; acts of piracy, blackmail, and murder call forth a display of evenhanded, balanced policies; and all the forces of state power are marshaled against so-called hooligans and antisocial elements who want nothing more than to leave the state, for a country and people of their own.

Reason has its limits when we must deal with those who will not listen to reason. The old logic listed among the fallacies the *argumentum ad baculum: the appeal to force* (literally, to the club)—what Humpty Dumpty called a nice, knockdown argument. Such an argument proves nothing, justifying itself only by robbing proof of its point. The Emperor Hadrian who ruthlessly suppressed the last Jewish fight for freedom till modern times, was told by a philosopher, "It is ill arguing with the master of thirty legions." Perhaps our time is even more like the declining days of the Roman Empire, when the philosopher Boethius was imprisoned on false charges and sentenced and executed without trial; his greatest work, written in prison, bore the title *The Consolation of Philosophy*. Everywhere today violence grins obscenely in the face of the most desperate appeals to reason. For those of us still committed to the life of reason it is hard to continue to find consolation. James Russell Lowell, an American lawyer of the last century turned poet, critic, and diplomat, may have been right: the only argument available with an east wind is to put on your overcoat.

It remains important to avoid the intellectualist fallacy, which I have characterized (§6) as an unreasoning belief in the efficacy of reason. Even logic has to be put in its place; the hard thing is to do so without thereby espousing illogic. A lover's quarrel does not call for valid arguments but for understanding, acceptance, and more love. Yet love suffers when intellect and integrity are compromised with a pretense of persuasion.

The intellectualist fallacy involves responding to the meaning of what is being said rather than to the point. But there is no point to illogical thinking, if taking thought is what is called for. Existentialist as well as neoromantic irrationalism supposes itself to be defending the emotional life against the deadening impact of the intellect. "Twice two makes four seems to me simply a piece of insolence," Dostoevski wrote in his *Notes from the Underground*. "Twice two makes four is a pert coxcomb who stands with arms akimbo barring your path and spitting. I admit that twice two makes four is an excellent thing, but if we are to give everything its due, twice two makes five is sometimes a very charming thing too." A. E. Housman takes the same position:

To think that two and two are four,
And never five nor three,

The heart of man has long been sore,
An long 'tis like to be.

Bad arithmetic is not good for the heart, or for anything else. It is not always wise to put two and two together, but if we do add, it is well to get the right answer.

The intellectualist fallacy is not corrected by irrationalism but by the insights embodied in the concept of *rationalization*. To understand human behavior we must distinguish between its *causes* and its *reasons*. The causes of an action are the conditions and forces which bring it about; the reasons for the action are the considerations invoked to justify it. Although there is disagreement among psychologists and philosophers on exactly how the distinction is to be applied in the concrete, that some such distinction must be drawn is beyond dispute. A rationalization is the claim that a stated reason for an action operated as its cause, when in fact other causes were at work. Self-serving policies may be rationalized as "good for the country," or submission to terror rationalized as concern for human life.

It is confusing that a rationalization may indeed be a good reason, one which would justify the action. What makes it a rationalization is not that the reason is a bad one but that the action was not performed for that reason. A hostile criticism may be accompanied by the rationalization that it was made for the victim's good; it may in fact be good for the victim, but this does not falsify the suspicion of hostile intent.

What is wrong with rationalization is that it pretends to a reasonableness which is unassailable, but which is in fact irrelevant, like the accuracy and irrelevance of the intellectualist arithmetic. The mistake is not in the argument but in its application. The insistence that the argument is misapplied does not imply that the argument is mistaken, and certainly not that some mysterious logic of the emotions would provide a better argument.

In contexts where argument is appropriate (and only then) there is a point to distinguishing between *valid* and *fallacious* arguments. There is no point to determining whether an argument is fallacious if it is irrelevant or if the question of validity is irrelevant. A fallacy is a mistaken argument, but it cannot be *mis*taken unless it is *taken* as valid to start with. Like an optical illusion, which is real when recognized for what it is, the fallacy lies in bad judgment rather than in what is being judged. The word "fallacy" comes from a Latin source meaning "deceptive." It is one thing not to be deceived because the force of the argument is not the point—as with didactic poetry; it is another matter not to be deceived because we see through the argument—as with poor propaganda. An argument does not cease to be fallacious by foregoing subtlety.

Ways of classifying fallacies have been almost as numerous as fallacies. It is useful to separate fallacies of proof, of inference, and of argument. In terms of the ground of their deceptiveness, fallacies of argument, which I consider first, may in turn be divided into *substitutes* for argument, *apparent* arguments, and strictly *invalid* arguments.

1. A substitute for argument is fallacious only if it appears in a context in which argument would be appropriate. Substitutes for argument are inverses of the intellectualist fallacy: the latter turns to argument when it is not appropriate, while the former turns to something else when argument *is* called for.

Among substitutes for argument, the *appeal to force* is the most painfully obvious. More widespread, and considerably more deceptive, is the appeal to *self-interest*. Traditionally, this was identified as the argument directed to the money-bag; a more appropriate contemporary designation might be the *argumentum ad oleum*, from the word for oil. The fallacy lies not in pursuing self-interest but in supposing that the interest gives a reason for believing the desired conclusion. The most common occurrence of this fallacy is as a rationalization.

In his *Novum Organum*, the new method to be followed by the burgeoning sciences in the early seventeenth century, Francis Bacon listed some of the "idols and false notions which beset men's minds." The fourth was the *idols of the theatre*, the false notions which come from received systems of thought. The name of the fallacy was chosen because "all the received systems are but so many stage-plays, representing worlds of their own creation after an unreal and scenic fashion." Though the classical ideologies may no longer shape men's minds, ours is still an age of ideology. Party lines and orthodoxies of all sorts in religion, politics, morals, science, and art are still of incalculable importance. Men still look out upon unreal worlds, if not of their own creation, then of those who control the flow of information.

Bacon speaks of the idols of the theatre as deriving from dogmas. A dogma is not just any doctrine in a received system of thought, however orthodox and however tenaciously adhered to. What usefully defines *dogma* is that criticism, doubt, or questioning of the doctrine is prohibited. Behind every dogma is an appeal to force or to lesser but also effective sanctions: if not execution, then excommunication, exile, or incarceration in a mental hospital. Say what you like as firmly and as flatly as you like; you are no dogmatist so long as I can beg leave to differ and you do not exact an intolerable price for that freedom.

There is a great difference between dogmas in the sense just explained and declarations made without being accompanied by a justification. I call these *bare assertions*. There is nothing unreasonable about bare assertion as such; it plays an indispensable part in all discourse. I cannot justify everything I say, for the justification would be a bare assertion or have its own justification, and I must stop somewhere. A dogmatist is one who holds that there are certain assertions we *must* accept or suffer the impact of power. Whether any assertions need no justification—for instance, because they are self-evident—is another matter (§26).

The most common substitute for argument is clothing an assertion in the robes of *authority*. The appeal to authority is not always a substitute for argument; it may be a genuine argument. Everything depends on which authority and on how its force is applied. The dogmatic use of authority is sometimes called an *ipse dixit* ("He himself said . . ."), the expression used in the late medieval period to identify a citation from Aristotle. (By the sixteenth century, the French philosopher Peter Ramus undertook to defend the thesis that every proposition in the writings of Aristotle is false.) In our time, Chairman Mao, like Stalin before him, exercised more authority, and more dogmatically, than was ever imposed in the name of Aristotle.

For the appeal to authority to be a valid argument, it is not enough that the appeal be made undogmatically. The authority must be *competent* to judge the point at issue. Though his knowledge and skills may be well established, the question of competence might still arise, for he might not know enough about the specific matters on which his authority is being appealed to. Academicians tell of an historian who frequented a spirit medium and once, in a learned article, documented some statement about Alexander the Great with the citation, "Personal communication." Few of us enjoy such authoritative support for our opinions.

Expertise in one domain does not necessarily imply good judgment in other domains. Physicists of unquestioned competence in the technical side of weaponry are not to be relied upon when they attempt to forecast outcomes of alternative political policies. Actors and athletes, however incontestable their skills as entertainers, are not thereby fitted to make pronouncements on the issues of the day. Even relevant authorities may have interests or commitments which preclude unbiased judgment. Military observers, journalists, and other intelligence gatherers may lose more to their loyalties than their professional skills can compensate for.

A troublesome type of appeal to authority is that in which the authority is only vaguely identified, if at all. This reliance on *anonymous authority* makes it impossible to assess competence; there is nothing to take hold of. In Soviet rhetoric the phrases, "It is well known that . . ." and "The whole world knows . . ." usually preface a particularly dubious claim. Other substitutes for argument use anonymity to inhibit critical thinking by inducing an uneasy sense of possible exclusion from a select circle: that of "usually reliable sources," "well-informed observers," or even just the "right-thinking" or "intelligent" elite.

2. The fallacies of *apparent* argument are not radically different in kind from those just considered. Here it is acknowledged that there is room for argument, and the attempt is made to advance what appear to be reasoned considerations. But they have only the barest appearance of reason, an ephemeral plausibility which vanishes on second thought, perhaps even on the first.

Among the most transparent of these arguments is the *appeal to ignorance*. Colloquially, it is the "For all you know . . ." argument. The pretense is that a conclusion has been justified by the premise that nothing is known against it. The scholastic logicians countered with the reasonable principle that what is asserted without proof may be denied without proof. If I urge that for all you know *p* is true, you can with equal justice rejoin: Yes, and for all *you* know, it is false.

Scarcely more effective is the appeal to the ignorance of others who might be expected to know. The argument takes this form, "After all, they still don't know . . . the secrets of the human heart" or, "what electricity really is," or even, "what keeps a plane up." If they don't know everything, then they may also not know that *p* is false—so I claim that it is true. Pseudoscience has its supporters who argue in this fashion, appealing to the presumed ignorance of the recognized scientist without realizing that even when the ignorance is real the argument proves nothing.

The appeal to ignorance has a slightly more subtle form in a gratuitous presumption of knowledge which, however, has not been disclosed. The transparent fallacy lies in arguing from the presumption rather than from the knowledge presumed. Typically, it is to authority figures that the hidden knowledge is attributed, while we remain children uninitiated into adult mysteries with no choice but to believe what we are told—and even what we are not told. Our political leaders were justified in taking the action they did, however foolish it may appear, because "they must know something." To be sure, they have access to information we lack, but the argument is only an appeal to ignorance. For all we know, what *they* know justifies the action taken; but for all we know, it does not.

The apparent argument which has the worst reputation is the *ad hominem:* the unreasoning appeal to the emotions. The qualifier "unreasoning" is absolutely essential; that an argument is warmly urged or warmly responded to does not make it one whit more fallacious than a cold or unappealing counterpart. Socrates' repudiation of this fallacy, made in the course of his defense at his trial (as reported in Plato's *Apology*), is itself a most moving defense of reason. Addressing the jury he says:

> It may be that some of you, remembering his own case, will be annoyed that whereas he, in standing his trial upon a less serious charge than this, made pitiful appeals to the jury with floods of tears and had his infant children produced in court to excite the maximum of sympathy and many of his relatives and friends as well. I, on the contrary, intend to do nothing of the sort, and that although I am facing, as it might appear, the utmost danger. It may be that one of you, reflecting on those facts, will be prejudiced against me, and being irritated by his reflections, will give his vote in anger. If one of you is so disposed—I do not expect it, but there is the possibility—I think that I should be quite justified in saying to him, My dear sir, of course I have some relatives. To quote the very words of Homer, even I am not sprung from an oak or from a rock, but from human parents, and consequently I have relatives—yes, and sons too, gentlemen, three of them, one almost grown up and the other two only children—but all the same I am not going to produce them here and beseech you to acquit me.
>
> Why do I not intend to do anything of this kind? Not out of perversity, gentlemen, nor out of contempt for you; whether I am brave or not in the face of death has nothing to do with it. The point is that for my own credit and yours and for the credit of the State as a whole, I do not think that it is right for me to use any of these methods at my age and with my reputation.

After the verdict of the jury was announced, Socrates continued:

> No doubt you think, gentlemen, that I have been condemned for lack of the arguments which I could have used if I had thought it right to leave nothing unsaid or undone to secure my acquittal. But that is very far from the truth. It is not a lack of arguments that has caused my condemnation, but a lack of effrontery and impudence, and the fact that I have refused to address you in the way which would give you most pleasure. You would have liked to hear me weep and wail, doing and saying all sorts of things which I regard as unworthy of myself, but which you are used to hearing from other people. But I did not think then that I ought to stoop to servility because I was in danger, and I do not regret now the way in which I pleaded my case. I would rather die as the result of this defense than live as the result of the other sort.

It is this other sort which is the *ad hominem* argument.

An indirect form of the argument addresses itself not to the adversary, real or hypothetical, but to the audience at large; accordingly, it is called an *appeal to the gallery*. Instead of reasons, it offers ridicule, moral indignation, and the like, presenting opposing views as foolish or wicked. The controversies over the theory of evolution, for example, provide many instances of this kind of argument. "Is man an ape or an angel? I, my lord, I am on the side of the angels. I repudiate with indignation and abhorrence those newfangled theories." Benjamin Disraeli's rhetoric was matched sixty years later (men learn slowly) by William Jennings Bryan, who, on the witness stand at the Scopes trial, was asked whether he did not find that geological evidence contradicted his fundamentalist views and replied that he cared less about the age of rocks than about the Rock of Ages. No less irrational is the more recent opposition to psychoanalysis as obsessed with sex and other such indecencies.

Underlying most apparent arguments of this sort is some personal *prejudice,* whose unreasoning expression Bacon called the *idols of the cave:* "Every one (besides the errors common to human nature in general) has a cave or den of his own, which refracts and discolors the light of nature." A prejudice is literally a prejudgment, asserting what appears to be the conclusion of an argument but what in fact is only a reaffirmation of something taken for granted from the outset (§65).

While the content of a prejudice may be individual, varying from person to person, succumbing to prejudice is hardly a distinctive failing. Such universal shortcomings Bacon called *idols of the tribe:* "The human understanding is like a false mirror, which, receiving rays irregularly, distorts and discolors the nature of things by mingling its own nature with it." We are all in a condition of human bondage, as Spinoza put it: the subjection of our reason to our passions. Hatred and fear becloud the intellect, denying it effective purchase on action. Referring to Othello's jealousy, Desdemona cries,

Alas, the day! I never gave him cause.

to which Emilia rightly rejoins,

But jealous souls will not be answered so;
They are not ever jealous for the cause,
But jealous for they are jealous: 'tis a monster,
Begot upon itself, born on itself.

Cut off from reality, reason gives way to the mindless thrust of impulse. Fantasy finds expression as *wishful thinking.* Our values determine our perception of the facts, rather than the other way around, and feelings dictate belief. The prospect of death is terrifying, so the soul must be immortal. Such apparent arguments are no more rational when directed *against* religious belief. "If there were gods," Nietzsche's Zarathustra proclaims, "how could I endure it to be no god! *Therefore* there are no gods." The emphasis is in the original, but with some irony the passage continues, "It is well that I have drawn the conclusion; now, however, it draws me." This is the essence of the fallacy, to arrive at a conclusion not because we are impelled to it by impersonal reason but because we are drawn to it by our all-too-human desires.

The current interest in astrology must surely be another idol of the tribe. Eight centuries ago Maimonides said of astrology that it is not just a superstition but a disease; he spoke as one of the great physicians of his day as well as a philosopher. There must be powerful forces at work to sustain the belief that fault or fortune lies in the stars. Our time gives no more reason than did the age of Maimonides to despair that we are not masters of our fate. Yet, while a generation ago scarcely anyone in a university would have known his sign of the zodiac, today the rubrics of astrology are a familiar component of the student counterculture. I might even add that, while I take astrology to be nonsense, all of us Gemini feel the same way.

3. Of the fallacies of invalid argument, the most obvious, the *irrelevant* argument, establishes a conclusion which is *beside the point.* Not all instances are as ludicrous as the colloquy between two friends from the town of Tiberius: "What's this I hear, that your wife is sleeping with half the city?" "Since when does Tiberius also call itself a city?"

Law courts provide more serious examples, not always ruled out of order; the classic illustration is that instead of proving that the prisoner is guilty of an atrocious crime, the prosecutor proves that the crime was an atrocious one. In the history of science irrelevant arguments have played a noticeable role, as when a scientific theory is rejected or promulgated on grounds relating to the religion or politics of the scientist—the Nazis with regard to Einstein's relativity, for instance, or Stalin's Russia with regard to Lysenko's genetics. In the latter case, many American intellectuals of the time, eager to establish what they thought of as their objectivity and open-mindedness, engaged in solemn discussions of the merits of Lysenko's biology, while ignoring the crucial point that questions of biology cannot be settled by pronouncements of the Central Committee of the Communist party but only by biologists. Because of the willingness of these intellectuals to condone irrelevant argument, their own arguments were beside the point.

A second class of invalid arguments are those which stem from distortions of meaning, or its displacement, dilution, or deflection—as already discussed in §8. These fallacies constitute what Bacon called the *idols of the market-place:* "The ill and unfit choice of words [which] wonderfully obstructs the understanding."

A particularly insidious type of invalid argument assumes the truth of the conclusion which it purports to establish. The fallacy is called *begging the question.* For centuries mathematicians attempted to prove Euclid's parallel postulate (that only one parallel to a given line can be drawn through a point outside it in the same plane). Many proofs were forthcoming, but they always reached their conclusion by subtly assuming the postulate, or something equivalent, such as the proposition that the interior angles of a triangle must add to 180 degrees, or that figures of different sizes may have the same shape.

A variant of begging the question is *arguing in a circle:* a proposition p is proved on the basis of q, then q in turn is proved on the basis of p. Sometimes there are a number of intermediate steps. That the saint converses with angels is known by his own admission; and, of course, such a holy man would not lie. Not much better are the misguided attempts to establish the truth of Scripture by arguing that it records the occurrence of historical events whose historicity, it turns out, rests only on the Scriptural account. I once heard someone who accepted the orthodox Soviet view that Trotsky played no significant role in the Russian revolution, when confronted with a scholarly history of those events, dismiss its testimony on the ground that the author was obviously a Trotskyite, and so wholly unreliable. Not all circles are vicious; the process of successive approximation has much in common with circular argument, yet makes an important contribution to scientific method (§31).

There is, finally, the *non sequitur,* which means simply that the conclusion does not follow, for whatever reason, from the premises. As a distinctive fallacy (for in virtually all fallacies the conclusion does not follow), it consists in the making of *hidden assumptions,* the unstated additional premises needed to establish the conclusion drawn. Some of the greatest advances in the sciences, even in those where the arguments are most careful and exact, have come from the identification of such fallacies. For instance, from the premise that parallel lines never meet it does *not* follow that the distance between them must therefore always remain the same. Recognition of this point enabled Nikolai Lobachevsky to construct one of the first systems of non-Euclidean geometry, in which there can be an infinite number of lines drawn through the same point all parallel to a given line. His ideas were initially greeted only with ridicule, even by other mathematicians. Even more extraordinary is the *non sequitur* underlying Zeno's argument that Achilles can never catch the tortoise: from the premise that quantities each greater than zero are added together without end. it does *not* follow that the sum increases without limit. The quantity ½ plus ¼ plus ⅛ and so on indefinitely adds up altogether only to 1.

15. The Nature of Logic

The assessment of the uses of reason by way of an analysis of argument suffers from a serious limitation: it puts reason into the context of man's relation with other men rather than the relations of man with nature. Argument is an attempt to persuade or convince, and so presupposes that we already know what we would like others to accept. Here, undoubtedly, is one of the uses of reason, perhaps not the most important and certainly not the only one. In the history of ideas, argument has been the stock-in-trade of dialecticians, lawyers, propagandists, apologists, politicians of all sorts, teachers, and special pleaders—men of whom the Greek Sophists have become the protytype. The present meaning of "sophistry" as fallacious reasoning may reflect Plato's hostility to the Sophists as much as their own practice; the root meaning of the name, after all, is wisdom.

Scientists, too, use argument, as did Plato and Socrates before him, but we must use our reason before argument if we are to have something worth arguing about. The scientist puts his ideas to the test by submitting them to the criticism of the scientific community; the ultimate test, however, is the reaction to his ideas, not of his colleagues but of nature. Galileo marked the transition from scholastic argument with other men to scientific inquiry into nature when he declared, "I value the discovery of a single even insignificant truth more highly than all the argumentation on the highest questions which fails to reach a truth."

It is reasonable to learn what we can from other men, but reason also demands that from time to time we break out of the circle of received opinion. The life of the mind, like all other life, is inseparable from continued growth. An idea is viable only if it can adapt itself to the ever-changing experience which flows in upon us. Conservative thinking is a contradiction in terms; what remains unchanging is only the delusional system of madness.

If reason is the guide by which we find our way in a changing world, logic, as the quintessence of reason, deals with the most general conditions which must be met for the mind to retain a firm grip on reality. This is the gist of John Stuart Mill's definition of logic as treating of "the operations of the human understanding in the pursuit of truth." Mill's own logic, although it endeavors to give full weight to experience, is still too close to the prescientific and extrascientific tradition to do justice to the uses of reason in the interpretation of empirical data and in its mathematical processing. Charles Peirce's ideas show considerable advance in both these respects. His conception of logic is essentially the same as Mill's: logic is the theory of "the conditions which determine reasonings to be secure," where security is to be understood in terms of continued responsiveness to the challenge of new evidence.

For Peirce the ultimate subject matter of logic is *inquiry* and its methods—science, most especially, but also the work of the inquiring mind in any area, even the practical in its narrow sense. In the present century John Dewey developed this viewpoint systematically: his treatise on logic bears the subtitle *The Theory of Inquiry.* Dewey criticized a widely used logic textbook called *An Introduction to Logic and Scientific Method* for using the word "and" in the title, as though logic were something other than scientific method, conjoined to it only because reason finds a use in both.

There is, however, a radical duality in the meaning of the term "logic." It can refer either to the *study* of successful methods of inquiry or to the system of norms making for success. The former is sometimes called "logical theory" or "philosophical logic," the latter "normative logic" or simply "logic." For the two senses Peirce used the scholastic labels *logica docens* and *logica utens:* the logic that is taught as distinguished from the logic that is used. Peirce was much influenced by the Scholastic logicians, especially by Duns Scotus, a penetrating analyst of the late thirteenth century; Scotus was known as "the Subtle Doctor," but because of what a later time unjustly came to regard as his hairsplitting, his name gives us the word "dunce."

I draw very nearly the same distinction, between *reconstructed logic* and *logic-in-use.* The difference corresponds to the difference between professed and lived philosophies (§5). The logic-in-use consists of the norms operative in rational inquiry; the qualifier "rational" does not mark a circularity but calls attention to the circumstance that thinking is sometimes fallacious and so is not logical in either sense. Reconstructed logic is a formulation of norms which the logician enjoins, and which he purports encompasses what, in fact, characterizes rational inquiry. His reconstruction may do more or less justice to the norms scientists apply in their inquiries. Neither the reconstructed logic nor the logic-in-use is a logical theory in the sense of the preceding paragraph. Both are sets of norms, either explicitly formulated or implicit in scientific practice. It is the explication and justification of the norms which is the substance of logical theory. Accordingly, because such a theory is about reconstructed logic in the same way a metalanguage is about another language (§9), it is sometimes called a *metalogic* and its formulations, *metatheorems* (§16).

If the reconstruction is a poor one, a justification for its content may not be forthcoming. This is not necessarily true, however; a reconstructed logic is sometimes a poor reconstruction just because it confines itself to those elements of the logic-in-use for which the metalogic provides clear and simple justifications. Russell has sometimes spoken of the formulation of reasonable hypotheses as no more than making "good guesses," while logic comes into its own only in drawing conclusions from the hypotheses so as to put them to the test. Such a view, as Russell himself later acknowledged, reveals more of the limitations in the reconstructed logic than in the uses of reason in inquiry.

In any case, it is crucially important, in my judgment, to recognize that the validity of the logic-in-use does not depend on the adequacy of the reconstructed logic or its metalogic. As John Locke caustically observed in his *Essay Concerning Human Understanding,* "God has not been so sparing to men to make them barely two-legged creatures, and left it to Aristotle to make them rational." Aristotle may have been the first logician, but he was decidedly not the first to think logically. Though he may have been correct in identifying logical patterns of thought, it does not follow that he was correct in his theory of why those patterns were logical. Newton's calculus was an enormously successful instrument for physicists to apply; the theory of the calculus invoked the obscure notion of infinitesimals ("infinitely small quantities"), a notion subjected to a devastating criticism by his acute contemporary, Bishop Berkeley. This criticism was not adequately met by mathematicians for two hundred years, but the calculus remained useful the whole time.

The conception of logic as dealing with the operations of the mind in the successful conduct of inquiry is often criticized for confusing logic with psychology. In the introduction to his treatise on logic, Kant declares that it is just as inappropriate to bring psychological principles into logic "as to derive the science of morals from life." Psychology, he urges, only tells us how we do think, but not how we ought to think; its principles are only contingent, lacking the necessity of the laws of logic. It is true that how the mind works and how we should use it are two different things. Granted that logic is normative; it begs a fundamental question, however, to assume that the validation of norms has nothing to do with fact. Life *can* teach us something about morals.

If logic shares with psychology the same subject matter, it must deal with it in a different way or to a different end. Logic studies how we think, not to determine actual patterns of thought but to establish which patterns make thinking effective. Medicine has the same subject matter as physiology and biochemistry but views this subject matter from the standpoint of health and disease. That medicine is normative certainly does not imply that we must not bring physiological principles into it but very much the contrary. Just as medicine must invoke a norm of "health," so also does logic presuppose the normative force of consistency and truth. Whence this force derives is one of the basic problems for logical theory and for the theory of knowledge.

Traditionally, the question asked in this connection has been whether the laws of logic are laws of thought, of language, or of being. Does logic depend on the nature of the mind, of meaning, or of things in general? During the past century it has become increasingly clear that the most fruitful answer is that logic imposes itself on thought because of the demands of the language which is essential to thought. (The dependence of logic on the nature of things is now generally held to be restricted *at most* to the logic of inference but not of proof; see §22.)

The central thesis of this position was stated by Wittgenstein: "It is the characteristic mark of logical propositions that one can perceive in the symbol alone that they are true; and this fact contains in itself the whole philosophy of logic." The truths of logic show their truth in their formulation. It is, however, a special and obscure kind of perceiving that is involved here. When a critic of Plato's theory of Ideas objected that he could see the table but not the Idea of the table, Plato is said to have retorted that his critic had eyes with which to see the table, but lacked the mind necessary to see an Idea. Descartes invoked a notion of "clear and distinct ideas" as the ultimate ground for rational belief. His sense of "idea" was quite different from Plato's, but "ideas" are apprehended by that same "mind's eye." Peirce also spoke of logic as resting on the inspection of what he called "diagrams," patterns of logical form or structure, again by a process of observation which is not perceptual in the ordinary sense but which is not purely psychological either.

What are we to do when men differ as to whether it is possible to perceive in the symbol alone that a certain proposition is true? Peirce pointed out that men are as apt to err in their sense of logicality as they are to reason ill. It is hazardous to try to improve reasoning on the basis of fallible powers of perception. One can see a logical proposition without seeing its truth. I may know what it means for a number to be prime (divisible without remainder only by itself and 1) and to be even (divisible by 2); but neither I nor anyone else can yet perceive in the symbol alone whether it is true that every even number greater than 2 can be expressed as the sum of two primes ("the Goldbach conjecture"). Yet this may very well be a logical proposition.

The issue has to do with the ground of the fundamental distinction which modern logic draws between *analytic* and *synthetic* propositions. This distinction can be traced back to the eighteenth century, in David Hume's division of all objects of inquiry into "relations of ideas" and "matters of fact." The first kind include all "intuitively or demonstratively certain" propositions, like those of mathematics; their truth is "discoverable by the mere operation of thought, without dependence on what is anywhere existent in the universe." Matters of fact, on the other hand, are "conceived by the mind with the same facility or distinctness" whether or not they are true. Analytic propositions are relations of ideas in Hume's sense; synthetic propositions are his matters of fact.

The term "analytic" was given wide currency by Kant, though he used it in a narrower sense than today. Kant restricted the term to those propositions "in which the connection of the predicate with the subject is thought through identity." The truth of such a proposition is disclosed by the analysis of the subject, which reveals the predicate as being identical with one of the constituents of the subject. That every *effect* has a cause is analytic, but that every *event* has a cause is synthetic; having a cause is a constituent of being an effect, but not, presumably, of being an event. There is a similar difference between the propositions that every body is spatially extended and that every body is heavy, the first being analytic and the second synthetic.

Kant took it for granted that mathematics is synthetic. The proposition that the sum of 7 and 5 is 12 is not analytic, he said, because "the concept of the sum of 7 and 5 contains nothing but the union of the two numbers into one, and in this no thought is being taken as to what that single number may be which combines both." But a sum is a "union" of a particular sort (different from a product, for instance); it may be that the analysis of this sort of union would after all disclose the number in the predicate as a constituent of the subject. This is just what Whitehead and Russell achieved in their *Principia Mathematica.*

A great deal depends on just what is involved in the process of thinking a connection through identity. I remember being taught in school algebra that true equations are always reducible to 0 = 0, and being puzzled that the most abstruse and presumably important statements could be equivalent to this triviality. I would have been glad to learn that John Locke had anticipated my puzzlement. He distinguished between two sorts of propositions which we can know with certainty, the one "trifling," which are merely verbal, and the other "instructive," in which what is affirmed is "a necessary consequence of the precise complex idea, but not contained in it." Instructive propositions are thus relations of ideas, in Hume's terms, but are not analytic in Kant's sense. The difference between what is trifling and what is instructive is not a psychological matter. It does not depend on the power of insight into ideas but on the objective relations among the ideas grasped—relations like being contained in another idea or being a necessary consequence of it.

The contemporary approach to this whole nest of problems is most closely associated with the name of Rudolf Carnap. If I may put the matter with a looseness quite atypical of Carnap's technical formulations, an analytic statement is one whose truth can be established merely by reference to the rules of the language in which the statement is formulated. Neither empirical observation nor seeing with the mind's eye is called for; one need only be able to recognize symbols and to understand the rules governing their use. In searching criticisms, however, especially connected with the question of what makes two terms synonymous, Willard van Quine and others have shown that much remains obscure in this definition, and that the difference between analytic and synthetic is neither as precise nor as absolute as is presupposed in philosophical "dogmas" (the term is Quine's). We would like to say that the rules should determine only the logical content of our statements, but the rules of the natural languages invoke many distinctions which depend upon empirical discriminations; for instance, between the sexes, between the animate and inanimate, between the human and the nonhuman, and between one social status and another. How are we to formulate the basis of exclusion of such empirical specifications from the rules defining analyticity?

Carnap makes use of a distinction, also drawn by Alfred Tarski, between *logical* and *descriptive* terms. Instead of attempting a definition of these terms, which would run a serious risk of circularity, we simply list the logical terms and declare that all others are descriptive. Terms like "not," "or," and "implies" are logical in content, and it is easy to identify many others like them. But how do we make the identification?

In a word, logical terms are those which determine the *form* of the propositions. This is the cardinal idea Wittgenstein took over from Russell. It is the essence of logical propositions that one can perceive in the symbol alone that they are true because *such propositions are true just by virtue of their form,* not their content. Russell's intellectual humility is characteristic: "I confess that I am unable to give any clear account of what is meant by saying that a proposition is 'true in virtue of its form.' But this phrase, inadequate as it is, points, I think, to the problem which must be solved if an adequate definition of logic is to be found." No generally accepted solution to this problem has been forthcoming.

In this connection Russell made another of his many contributions to modern logic. He called attention to the crucial difference between *logical form* and *grammatical form,* and used this difference to illuminate not only the foundations of logic but also many other philosophical issues. The difference is illustrated in the White King's rejoinder to Alice when she tells him that she saw nobody on the road. "I only wish *I* had such eyes. To be able to see Nobody! And at that distance too! Why, it's as much as I can do to see real people, by this light!" The word "nobody" has the same grammatical form as a proper name, at least so far as concerns being an object of a transitive verb like "see," but it has a radically different logical form. Russell especially applied the distinction to the explication of relational propositions, whose logical form is obscured by the grammar of subject and predicate. In "Russia armed the Arabs against Israel," all three names belong to the logical subject while only "Russia" is the grammatical subject (§19). Russell also applied the distinction between logical and grammatical form in his influential analysis of definite descriptions, phrases like "the present king of France" (§18).

Logic, then, is the domain of formal truth; what cannot be established by logic alone are the propositions whose truth depends on content. What is illogical violates the formal conditions of intelligible discourse and, lacking form, is *a fortiori* void of content. "It used to be said that God could create everything, except what was contrary to the laws of logic." But as Wittgenstein pointed out, "The truth is, we could not *say* of an 'unlogical' world how it would look." The normative force logic exerts on thought derives from the demands of language. That these, in turn, may be grounded in the nature of things is not the prevailing opinion, expressed by Ernest Nagel in an essay called "Logic Without Ontology." In the nineteenth century Georg Hegel, a philosopher of incalculable importance because of his influence on Karl Marx and with considerable influence in his own right, declared, in his *Science of Logic,* "Logic is the thinking of thinking. It is the absolute form of truth, and another name for the very truth itself." Today this inflated rhetoric smacks of another age. How to do justice in more restrained language to the authority of logic is a question that is far from being conclusively settled.

16. A Pudding of Proof

The Stoic philosopher Epictetus was once challenged by a listener, "Prove to me that I should study logic!" Epictetus at once replied, "How will you know whether it is a good proof?" Perhaps there is a simple definition of logic after all: it is the science or doctrine of proof. Logic is the study of the syllogism, in the broad sense which Aristotle gave to it—"a discourse in which, certain things being stated, something other than what is stated follows of necessity from their being so." Instead of "things" stated, we say today that logic deals with *propositions*. If a proposition *q* "follows of necessity" from another proposition *p*, we say that *q* is a *logical consequence* of *p*, or that *p entails q* (the word "implies" is reserved for another sense, though sometimes entailment is called "strict implication"). Logic, then, is the theory of entailment—and of all that this, in turn, entails.

Every proof has its starting point, what is initially stated, called the *premises* of the proof. A *proof* is an orderly sequence of propositions of which every one is either (a) a premise, or (b) a logical consequence of one or more propositions preceding it in the sequence, or (c) a proposition already proved (in which case the premises of the previous proof must also be included among the premises of the proof here in question). The last proposition of a proof is its *conclusion*, which is then said to *follow* from the premises.

Exactly which propositions are logical consequences of a proposition is the central question of logic; the above definition of proof is of no use till this question has been answered. The answer must meet certain conditions if the logic is to serve the uses of reason. The most fundamental requirement is that as we move from step to step we preserve whatever truth was in our possession: logic must not lead us into falsehood, even though it might not save us if we have already sinned.

Keeping in mind that *truth* is a property of propositions, not of proofs, and *validity* a property of proofs, not of isolated propositions, we can formulate the fundamental requirement as follows: *In a valid proof, only true conclusions follow from true premises.* This is *not* to say that only false conclusions follow from false premises. If a conclusion is false, logic should allow us to infer that at least one of the premises must be false, but if the conclusion is true, the premises may be either true or false so far as the logic of proof is concerned. If the premises are true, logic should thereby establish the truth of the conclusion; but if we were in error to start with, it cannot much matter where logic leads us.

To establish a proposition two steps are required: (1) we must show that the proposition follows from certain premises, and (2) we must show that the premises are true. The first is the task of logic; the second, generally speaking, calls for extralogical knowledge. There are, however, certain propositions which are true by virtue of their form alone, analytic propositions (§15). These are *logical truths*. The premises called for to establish their truth are themselves analytic. A proof in which all premises are analytic is called a *demonstration;* if some premises are synthetic the proof is a *derivation* from those premises. The conclusion of a demonstration is called a *theorem*. Sometimes logical truths are not counted among premises, in which case a demonstration can be described as a proof which proceeds without premises. A theorem, in other words, can be proved without appeal to anything outside logic. This is the substance of the explanation I once heard my daughter give when a friend expressed surprise at her daring to take a second course in algebra: "But that's the easiest subject of all—you don't have to know anything; you just figure it out!"

Just as there are logical truths, so also are there logical falsehoods or *contradictions*. The negation of any analytic proposition is a contradiction, a proposition false by its form alone. Conversely, the negation of a contradiction is analytic. This circumstance makes possible a powerful type of proof in which a proposition is established by showing that its negation is false; if the negation is logically false the proposition is logically true, and so is demonstrated. The procedure is called *indirect proof*, or sometimes a proof by *reductio ad absurdum*, since the negation of the proposition to be proved is shown to be an absurdity, that is, a contradiction.

A classic illustration is provided by Euclid's proof that there are an infinite number of prime numbers. Suppose that there were not—the key step in an indirect proof. Then some prime number would be greater than all the others; call it P. Form the product of all the primes up to and including P and add 1 to the result. This number, which is of course greater than P, is not divisible by any of the primes considered, for in each case the division leaves a remainder of 1. The number is therefore either itself a prime, or it is divisible by some prime not in the product. In either case there is a prime number greater than P, which contradicts the assumption.

An enormously influential indirect proof demonstrated the existence of irrational numbers, magnitudes which cannot be expressed as a ratio of whole numbers, and so are "incommensurable." The square root of 2 was proved to be irrational by assuming that it *is* rational, then showing that its expression as a fraction in lowest terms (no factor common to both numerator and denominator) yields the contradictory result that both numerator and denominator are divisible by 2.

A nameless contemporary has offered the following indirect proof that all numbers are interesting. Suppose that not all numbers are interesting; in that case, among all the interesting numbers there would be a largest one. Consider the next higher number: that is the smallest number which is not interesting—and that makes it a very interesting number indeed!

A system of ideas, such as Euclid's geometry or Newton's physics, may be cast in a logical form, that is, with most of its propositions presented as conclusions from a fixed set of premises of the system. These premises are called the *postulates*, and if they are logical truths, *axioms*. (Usage here is by no means uniform, and often these two terms are used synonymously.) All logical systems must proceed from some set of postulates. If they are systems of logic, of mathematics, or of some similar domain of logical truths, their postulates are axiomatic. A notorious exception, subjected to much criticism for that reason, was the so-called "axiom of infinity" (in the usage here, a postulate) of *Principia Mathematica*, that there are an infinite number of things in the world, a proposition which, even if true, does not seem to be a logical truth. Whether any other sort of propositions can be taken as axiomatic—allegedly self-evident propositions, and the like—is a recurrent question (§26).

A logical system requires more than postulates; it also needs a set of *rules.* We must have not only a starting point but also some way of getting to the next step. Legitimizing the movement from premise to conclusion cannot be accomplished by the premises alone without begging the legitimacy at issue. This point was first made explicitly by Lewis Carroll, in a piece of whimsy called "What the Tortoise Said to Achilles." Suppose that from A and B together Z follows. The justification for asserting Z on the basis of A and B depends on the circumstance that if A and B are true, then Z is true. Call this proposition C. If C is added to the premises A and B, the whole situation will be repeated, and so endlessly. The Tortoise says:

"I accept A and B and C and D. Suppose I *still* refuse to accept Z?" "Then Logic would take you by the throat, and *force* you to do it!" Achilles triumphantly replied. "Logic would tell you, 'You can't help yourself. Now that you've accepted A and B and C and D, you *must* accept Z!' So you've no choice, you see."

"Whatever Logic is good enough to tell me is worth *writing down,*" said the Tortoise. "So enter it in your book, please. We will call it (E). If A and B and C and D are true, Z must be true. Until I've granted *that,* of course, I needn't grant Z. So it's quite a necessary step, you see?"

"I see," said Achilles; and there was a touch of sadness in his tone.

That A and B allow us to assert Z is validated by a rule of the system. The rule does not appear as a premise in any proof but is an operative norm determining the course which a valid proof may follow. The rule itself may require justification, but this can only be provided in a *metalogic,* which establishes what the characteristics are of proofs constructed according to the rule. "We have in every respect complete liberty with regard to the forms of language," Carnap has declared in his *Logical Syntax of Language,* but we must be prepared to accept the consequences to which our choices lead. This standpoint he called the *principle of tolerance:* "It is not our business to set up prohibitions, but to arrive at conventions. In logic there are no morals. Everyone is at liberty to build up his own logic, i.e., his own form of language, as he wishes. All that is required of him is that if he wishes to discuss it, he must state his methods clearly, and give syntactical rules instead of philosophical arguments." Philosophical arguments have turned out to be not as expendable in this connection as was once thought, but there is general agreement that within wide limits, at least, we may set up what rules we choose.

In general, these rules must include two types: *formation rules* governing the construction of propositions, and *transformation rules,* or rules of inference, allowing us to assert certain propositions if some others have already been asserted. It is the transformation rules which are loosely called "the laws of logic."

The most fundamental rule of inference is that known traditionally as the *modus ponens:* From the two premises, (1) If p then q, and (2) p, the conclusion q follows. The first is sometimes called the *major premise* and the second the *minor premise.* Closely related to this rule is one called the *principle of the syllogism:* From the two premises, (1) if p then q, and (2) If q then r, the conclusion follows, If p then r. The exposition of a full set of rules for even a simple logical system is a matter of considerable technicality. These rules are justified by certain metatheorems, the most basic of which is that called the *deduction theorem:* If, in accord with the rules a conclusion C follows from premises P, then the proposition, If P then C, is a logical truth. Other metatheorems are that the logical consequences of true propositions are also true and that the logical consequences of logical truths are also logical truths.

17. The Calculus of Propositions

Prophecy is always hazardous, but never more self-defeating than when it sets limits on the future. Immanuel Kant, who was more penetratingly critical of the pretensions of reason than any other philosopher, was nevertheless not only content to rely on traditional logic (he had no choice) but even viewed it as an achievement completed once for all. In the preface to the second edition of his *Critique of Pure Reason* he maintained, "Since Aristotle, logic has not been required to retrace a single step and has not been able to advance a single step, so that to all appearance it may be considered as complete and perfect." But intimations of a new and radically different logic were already to be found a century earlier in the work of the philosopher Leibniz (who also, at about the same time as Newton, independently invented the differential calculus). In the century following Kant, logic made such enormous advances, continuing into the present period, that logic today is as different from Aristotle's as our physics is from his.

What is essential to modern logic is not conveyed by its most common designation, "symbolic logic." Symbols were also used in the tradition, even by Aristotle himself. The old symbols were not much more than abbreviations, conveniences of writing, but not essential to the thought. The nature of modern logic is better expressed in the name "mathematical logic." In spite of its aspirations to exactness and certitude, traditional logic is farther from mathematics than from rhetoric and grammar—together with these two constituting the "trivium," a major division of the liberal arts curriculum in medieval universities. It was less suited to the discovery, development, and proof of new ideas than to the formulation of arguments on behalf of already established truth—that is to say, received opinion. For this reason, in the early seventeenth century Francis Bacon, "the herald of modern science," called for a *novum organum,* a new instrument of thought.

Modern logic provides a better reconstruction of our uses of reason than traditional logic can provide. Aristotle's logic was magnificently suited to the Greek science of his day, as John Dewey appreciatively explicates in a chapter "The Needed Reform of Logic" in his own treatise on the subject. But by the late medieval period, traditional logic presented little more than the trappings of careful thought, without its substance or its form, and grew progressively more remote from and even antagonistic to scientific habits of mind. Russell's assessment is not unjust, I think: "The old logic put thought in fetters, while the new logic gives it wings." One need not subscribe—as I decidedly do not subscribe—to a separation between humanistic and scientific education (both so-called) in order to recognize that as an instrument of reason the language of mathematics is of incomparably more value than Latin and Greek.

The elements of mathematical logic are comprised of four calculi or logical systems: of *propositions, functions, sets,* and *relations.*

Propositions which cannot be broken down into parts independently capable of being true or false are called *atomic,* and otherwise, *molecular.* Molecular propositions may be built up with the help of conjunctions (like "and"), marks of negation (like "not"), and various introductory phrases (like "It is widely believed that"). Among these binding agents are some which have the following fundamental property: the molecule is so constituted that if we know of each of the atoms whether it is true or false—what is called the *truth-value* of the proposition—then we know (or can determine) the truth-value of the molecule. Such ways of constructing molecular propositions are called *truth-functions* or *extensional connectives* (the qualifier is sometimes to be tacitly understood). For instance, if I know whether *p* and *q* are each true, I know whether the molecule *p* and *q* is true—namely, if both the atoms are true, and not otherwise. By contrast, even when I know whether *p* is true, I cannot tell whether, say, most people believe *p,* nor can the inference be made in the converse direction. (I have a friend whose political views I find so outrageous that from the premise that he believes something I am very likely to conclude—with some justification—that it is false.)

If we confine ourselves to binary connectives (those which unite two propositions at a time), surprisingly few are extensional. This is because with two atomic propositions there are four possible combinations of truth-values, and to each of these the connective can assign one of two values, true or false. Each pattern of 4 assignments, one for each possible combination of truth-values of the atoms, defines a different connective. There are exactly 2^4 or 16 patterns, but some of these are trivial (depending on only one of the atoms, for instance), and the rest can be reduced to a few basic ones. These are *conjunction* ("and"), *disjunction* ("or"), *implication,* and *equivalence. Negation,* which operates on only one proposition at a time, is also to be added as one of the fundamental connectives.

Disjunction may or may not allow for both atoms to be true; if it does, it is called *inclusive disjunction;* if it does not, it is called *exclusive.* Inclusive disjunction has been found to be more useful. Disjunction provides a striking example, noted by Reichenbach, of the fact that ambiguous terms can be used to define precise ones. The connective *p dis q* can be defined by the condition that it is true if, and only if, either *p* is true or *q* is true, but not both; this unambiguously defines exclusive disjunction; yet the term "or" used in the definition remains ambiguous. In such a procedure we are no more raising ourselves by our bootstraps than when we use our gross fingers to build a more refined tool.

Implication is used in the propositional calculus in a special sense, to be contrasted with entailment or strict implication (§16); to mark this sense, the extensional connective is called *material implication*. It is entailment which is usually meant when people speak of "logical implication," but usage is uncertain as well as often unclear. (Apropos, only propositions "imply," and only people "infer.") Material implication is so different from the relations understood as "logical implication" that many of its properties have been called paradoxical. The air of paradox results from thwarted expectations which might not have been aroused in the first place if the connective had been given another name. There are real problems, however, in reconstructing the sense of implication in contexts other than those, chiefly mathematical, with which the propositional calculus is concerned.

The definition of material implication is: *p materially implies q* (hereafter I may omit the qualifier) if and only if either *p* is false or *q* is true. The proposition *q* is called the *consequent* and *p* the *antecedent*. Material implication bears the consequence that when *p* implies *q*, the truth of *p* guarantees the truth of *q*. It is for this reason that the connective is called implication, and can be rendered as, *If p then q*. The paradoxes result from the feature that the implication is also said to hold when *p* is false. This feature is incorporated in the definition because it does not much matter what is implied by false propositions— "If what you say is true I'll eat my hat!" The choice made is connected to the point previously noted (§16) that false premises may entail either true or false conclusions; it is only the true premises which must have true consequences. When a material implication is a logical truth (analytic), we may call it *logical implication* in a strict sense (though not in the sense of strict implication). The metatheorem that the antecedent of a logical implication as premise entails the consequent of that implication as a conclusion can be proved. Material implication, in short, suffices for the needs of logic.

The situation is different, however, when we examine if-then propositions in general. It is a paradox of material implication that of any two propositions whatever, one must imply the other, whereas in the ordinary sense they may have nothing to do with one another, let alone guarantee the truth of the other. Moreover, *p* implies either *q* or the negation of *q*, whatever *p* and *q* may state; and *q* is implied either by *p* or by the negation of *p*. When two propositions each imply the other they are said to be (materially) equivalent. The paradox is pinned down, if not dissipated, by the remark that such equivalence means only that they have the same truth-value, but need not have anything else in common.

The uneasiness which material implication arouses can be traced to its basic properties that a false proposition materially implies any other proposition, and a true proposition is materially implied by any other proposition. What might be called the classical modern logic, from Russell through Carnap, was quite prepared to pay the price of such paradoxes in return for the simplicity and power of material implication. The task of defining a nonextensional implication, like that intended, for instance, by the assertion of a causal connection ("If price controls are not imposed, there will be a runaway inflation") has turned out to be formidable, perhaps even insoluble. Notable efforts have been made by Nelson Goodman, Quine, Hempel, and Reichenbach.

All the extensional binary connectives can be reduced to no more than two. For instance, taking as primitive (undefined) negation and disjunction (the primitives of *Principia Mathematica*), we can define the others as follows. Conjunction: *p and q* is defined as *not-(not-p or not-q)*. Implication: *p implies q* is defined as *not-p or q*. Equivalence: *p is equivalent to q* is defined as *p and q, or not-p and not-q*. All the connectives can be reduced to one, the so-called Sheffer stroke-function, "/", which may be read as *not both*. For example, *not-p* is defined as *p/p*, and *p or q* is defined as (*p*/*p*)/(*q*/*q*); the other definitions can then proceed as before.

As for the axioms of the basic logical system, it is to me quite astonishing how few suffice for any but the most scrupulously explicit and meticulous formulations. The following are the axioms of *Principia* for the propositional calculus, with slight emendations to exclude metalanguage rules:

1. (*p* or *p*) implies *p* ("the law of tautology")
2. *q* implies (*p* or *q*) ("the law of addition")
3. (*p* or *q*) implies (*q* or *p*) ("the commutative law")
4. *p* or (*q* or *r*) implies *q* or (*p* or *r*) ("the associative law")
5. (*q* implies *r*) implies that (*p* or *q*) implies (*p* or *r*) ("the law of summation").

These axioms have also been reduced in number, just as were the primitive terms, and various alternative sets of axioms are in common use.

On the basis of the axioms, many interesting theorems can be demonstrated, including all those which played a part in the traditional logic, so far as concerns the relations among propositions. Among others is the *law of double negation:* not-(not-*p*) implies *p*. The principle of the *reductio ad absurdum,* which is that (*p* implies not-*p*) implies not-*p*, corresponds to the metatheorem embodying the method of indirect proof (§16): that a proposition entails its own negation in turn entails that the proposition is false (so that its negation is true). The correspondence is that between a logical implication—that is, a material implication which is a logical truth, or analytic—and a strict implication—that is, an entailment. Several other such correspondences will be noted; they exist for every theorem.

A number of important relations hold between disjunction and conjunction. Two of these, known as *De Morgan's theorems,* after a nineteenth-century pioneer of mathematical logic, are: not-(*p* and *q*) implies (not-*p* or not-*q*); also, not-(*p* or *q*) implies (not-*p* and not-*q*). These laws are often used to define one of these connectives in terms of the other. Two other theorems are the *distributive laws: p* and (*q* or *r*) together imply *p* and *q* or else *p* and *r*. Similarly, *p* or (*q* and *r*) together imply (*p* or *q*) and (*p* or *r*). Many implications, including these, hold in both directions, so that the theorems may be stated as equivalences. The principle pointed to in this remark is that (*p* is equivalent to *q*) implies that *p* implies *q* and moreover *q* implies *p*. (This whole implication also holds in both directions, and so can be replaced by an equivalence.)

Corresponding to the rule of *modus ponens*—that from an implication and its antecedent the consequent follows—is the *principle of inference: p* implies *q*, together with *p*, implies *q*. Two fallacies are especially common here. The fallacy of *affirming the consequent* argues mistakenly: *p* implies *q*, and *q*, therefore *p*. Correspondingly, the fallacy of *denying the antecedent* runs: *p* implies *q*, but not-*p*, therefore not-*q*. In fact, all that can be inferred in each of these cases is that an implication holds. These are the *paradoxes of implication: q* implies that *p* implies *q*, whatever *p* is; and not-*p* implies that *p* implies *q*, whatever *q* is.

Underlying the fallacies of affirming the consequent and denying the antecedent is confusion about the way in which an implication can be reversed. What follows from the fact that *p* implies *q*? Not that *q* implies *p!* When *p* implies *q*, *p* is said to be a *sufficient condition* for *q;* on the other hand, *q* is a *necessary condition* for *p*. This is because, if *q* is not the case, knowing that if *p* were true *q* would also be true, we can conclude that it must be that *p* is not the case either. These relations are summarized in the *law of contraposition:* If *p* implies *q*, then not-*q* implies not-*p*. Lao-tzu makes the characteristically dual pronouncement, "A good man does not argue; he who argues is not a good man." The second part of this statement is the contrapositive of the first part; it may add emphasis, but it adds no new content. A new statement would be: "He who does *not* argue *is* a good man." Conjoined to the other proposition, it would make virtue equivalent to disinterest in logic. Fortunately, the equivalence would in any case be only material.

For the traditional logic, perhaps the most fundamental theorem is the *principle of the syllogism.* This appears in several different forms, of which one is: If *q* implies *r*, then that *p* implies *q* in turn implies that *p* implies *r*. Another form states the *transitivity of implication:* If *p* implies *q*, and *q* implies *r*, then *p* implies *r*. Its significance for implication is illustrated in the argument made by one of Shakespeare's clowns in *All's Well That Ends Well:* "He that comforts my wife is the cherisher of my flesh and blood; he that cherishes my flesh and blood loves my flesh and blood; he that loves my flesh and blood is my friend; ergo, he that kisses my wife is my friend." A full analysis of the argument, however, requires the calculus of functions (§18)—and who knows what else besides!

The traditional logic singled out three propositions as the so-called "laws of thought"; these, though appearing as theorems of modern logic, have no outstanding significance. What corresponds to them in the metalanguage, however, is indeed basic. The first is the *law of identity,* that *p* is equivalent to *p*. Second is the *law of contradiction* (or better, of noncontradiction): not-(*p* and not-*p*). In a logical system, consistency—that is, the absence of contradiction—is, as a famous football coach said about winning, not just the main thing but the only thing. The third "law of thought" is the *law of excluded middle: p* or not-*p*. The corresponding rule underlies the method of indirect proof; there are mathematicians who find this rule unacceptable, although the proposition remains an unassailable theorem. The theorem is also reflected in the construal of propositions as capable of only two possible truth-values: truth and falsehood. There are, however, systems of logic which are perfectly consistent (or as consistent as the usual systems), and which allow three truth-values; there are even some systems with an infinite number of truth-values.

The truth of the law of excluded middle is not a whit lessened or made dubious by either the vagueness of our terms or the indecisiveness of nature. Either it will rain tomorrow or else it will not rain; drizzle has nothing to do with it. We may have difficulty in making up our minds whether to count it as rain; logic tells us only that there are two choices before us, but gives us no assurances whatever that the choice is always easy to make, or even worth making. When, in *Pride and Prejudice,* Elizabeth refuses Mr. Collins's proposal in spite of Mrs. Bennet's insistence, her father declares, "An unhappy alternative is before you, Elizabeth. From this day you must be a stranger to one of your parents. Your mother will never see you again if you do *not* marry Mr. Collins, and I will never see you again if you *do*." The law of excluded middle declares that either she will marry him or she will not; even if they were to live in sin, logic would remain pure and undefiled.

If we are presented with a proposition and asked to decide whether it is a logical truth, we may be fortunate or clever enough to discover a way to prove it (or its negation) as a logical theorem. Suppose we have not succeeded in doing so; can we tell whether or not this is because the proposition is synthetic, and so cannot be established or refuted by logic alone? This is called the *decision problem;* the problem would be solved if there were a *decision procedure* described beforehand, by which, after a certain number of steps—perhaps a large number, but always finite—the question whether or not any given proposition is a logical truth would be answered. For the propositional calculus (though not for all logico-mathematical systems), the problem has been solved. One form of the procedure is called the method of *truth tables.*

Since all the connectives deal within the propositional calculus are extensional, we can display what truth-value a given molecular proposition has for each of the cases—that is, combinations of truth-values—of the atomic propositions. With two atomic propositions there are four cases: both true, the first true and the second false, the second true and the first false, or both false. Using the symbol "1" for true and "0" for false, the following tables are determined by the definitions of the connectives. (The cases are labeled by letters and the propositions by Roman numerals.)

	I	II	III	IV	V	VI	VII	VIII
	p	*q*	not-*p*	not-*q*	*p* or *q*	*p* and *q*	*p* impl *q*	*p* equiv *q*
A	1	1	0	0	1	1	1	1
B	1	0	0	1	1	0	0	0
C	0	1	1	0	1	0	1	0
D	0	0	1	1	0	0	1	1

Columns I and II are the atomic propositions, each row representing one case; for instance, in case C, *p* is false and *q* is true. If there were three atomic propositions there would be eight cases, because, for each of the four cases here, there are two possible cases of the third proposition. In general, for n atomic propositions there are 2^n cases; the situation quickly becomes complicated, therefore, but with no difficulties of principle—like carrying out a long long-division.

Columns III and IV give the negations of the atomic propositions; the negation is true whenever the proposition negated is false, and false when the other is true. Since negation operates on only one proposition at a time, a table defining negation would need only two rows, since there are only two cases to be considered. Here, therefore, there is a duplication; in III, B and D duplicate the other two cases, respectively; and in IV, C and D.

Column V shows that the disjunction is true in all cases but the last; if it were exclusive disjunction it would also be false in case A. When we know that *p* or *q* is true, we know that D is not the case, but we do not know what the case *is*.

Column VI is true only in case A; hence if we know that *p* and *q* is true we also know the truth-values of its constituents, and in particular, that both are true.

Column VII shows that the implication holds in every case except B, when the antecedent is true but the consequent is false. The paradoxes of implication are shown in cases C and D where the implication holds whether *q* is true or false, provided only that *p* is false.

Finally, column VIII shows that equivalence holds whenever the constituents have the same truth-value, in cases A and D, and not otherwise. When we know that *p* is equivalent to *q*, we know that either both are true or both are false, but not which.

None of the propositions in the above table are logical truths so far as this level of specification of their form is concerned. We cannot determine by their form alone whether they are true, nor can we show them to be false on the basis of their form. To determine their truth-values we have to know what the case is. In case B, for instance, *p* is true, and so is the negation of *q* and the disjunction of *p* with *q;* the other molecular propositions are false. But logic cannot tell us whether B *is* the case.

Suppose that we are presented with the proposition formulating the transitivity of implication, that *p* implies *q,* and *q* implies *r,* together imply that *p* implies *r.* How would the decision procedure of truth-tables show that this is indeed a logical truth? The table is as follows:

	IX	X	XI	XII	XIII	XIV	XV	XVI
							p imp. *q*	trans.
	p	*q*	*r*	*p* imp. *q*	*q* imp. *r*	*p* imp. *r*	*q* imp. *r*	of impn.
A	1	1	1	1	1	1	1	1
B	1	1	0	1	0	0	0	1
C	1	0	1	0	1	1	0	1
D	1	0	0	0	1	0	0	1
E	0	1	1	1	1	1	1	1
F	0	1	0	1	0	1	0	1
G	0	0	1	1	1	1	1	1
H	0	0	0	1	1	1	1	1

This time there are eight cases to be considered; wherever the molecule involves only two atomic propositions, four of the cases will be duplicates, respectively, of the other four. For *p* and *r*, for example, case C duplicates A, D duplicates B, G duplicates E, and H duplicates F.

Column XII corresponds to column VII of the first table, with duplications; so also do columns XIII and XIV. In all three columns, just as for column VII, the implication holds in every case where the antecedent is false, as well as in every case where the consequent is true.

Column XV corresponds to column VI: it is a conjunction, with XII taking the place of I and XIII taking the place of II. That is, XV will have a "1" in every case where both XII and XIII have a "1," and a "0" in every other case.

Column XVI is the proposition whose logical status was to be determined. It is an implication, like VII, its antecedent being given in XV and its consequent in XIV. It has a "1," therefore, wherever XV has a "0" or XIV has a "1."

The extraordinary result is that column XVI has a "1" in all eight cases. The test proposition is true no matter what the case is; its truth does not depend upon the truth-value of its atomic constituents but only on the way these are related to one another. In short, it is true by virtue of its form. A proposition true in all possible cases is called a *tautology.* The negation of a tautology is false in all cases, and so constitutes a logical falsehood or *contradiction.* All other propositions, which are true in some cases and false in others, are *synthetic.* To determine their truth-values more than pure logic is needed.

18. The Calculus of Functions

The propositional calculus explores the ways in which molecular propositions relate to one another by virtue of the truth-values of their atomic constituents. There are many other logical truths which are true not because of their molecular form but because of the inner structure of the proposition. The logic of what lies within the atom—nuclear logic, as it were—is called the calculus of propositional functions, or simply, the *functional calculus.*

Symbols may denote either a particular individual of a certain domain, or refer indifferently to any member of the domain. Symbols of the first kind are called *constants,* and the second, *variables;* the domain is the *range* of the variable. When the variable is replaced by a constant in a particular case, the individual so denoted is called a *value* of the variable; the range consists of the possible values which a variable may have. Sometimes a symbol is used to denote a particular individual, but which one is not specified. It therefore has the appearance of a variable, but is in fact a constant; it might be called an *uninterpreted constant.* If the range is men, "everyone" and "somebody" are variables, "Socrates" and "Russell" are constants, and "John Doe" and "Richard Roe" are uninterpreted constants.

The "*p*" and "*q*" used throughout the preceding section are variables whose range consists of all propositions.

As in the case of these symbols, a variable left open for any application consonant with a proper understanding of its range is called a *free* variable. If the interpretations are predetermined in certain ways to be discussed shortly, the variable is said to be *bound*. When a free variable is replaced by a particular value of the variable, the resulting expression is called a *substitution instance* of the original expression. It is a rule of inference, as fundamental as the *modus ponens*, that, given a premise with a free variable, we may state as a conclusion any of its substitution instances; this is called the *rule of substitution*. The logical truths of the propositional calculus hold true for all substitution instances of the postulates and theorems. For instance, "*p* or not-*p*" is a logical truth; by the rule of substitution, we may also assert that either Socrates was unjustly condemned or Socrates was not unjustly condemned. No certification for the proposition about Socrates is needed other than what was called for by the theorem formulated in free variables. In general, formulas containing variables are true for some values of the variable and false for other values.

A formula containing variables which would become a proposition if the variables were replaced by constants is called a *propositional function*. For instance, "x is Greek" is a propositional function, becoming a true proposition when "Socrates" is substituted for the variable, and false when "Russell" is substituted. Another propositional function is: "Socrates has the property f," where values of "f" might include "being Greek," "being ugly," or "having once traveled to the United States and visited the Grand Canyon." The theory of formulas which contain only variables for individuals, and not for properties of individuals, is called the *first-order functional calculus*.

There are two main ways in which the interpretation of a variable may be predetermined: universally or existentially; the symbols or phrases expressing this predetermination are called, respectively, the *universal operator* and the *existential operator*. The free variables affected are said to fall within the *scope* of the operator, and thereby become bound variables. For bound variables substitutions can no longer be made as we choose.

The universal operator gives to the propositional function in its scope an application to every value in the range of the variable. It is expressed in English by words like "all," "every," "each," "any," and so on. "For all x, x is Greek" means the same as "All men are Greek," where the variable is understood to have men as its range. "For all x, x is even or x is odd," where the variable ranges over numbers, means the same as "Every number is either even or odd."

The universal operator applies the propositional function to every one of the values of the variable—that is, to each individually—and not to all together. In traditional terms, it applies *distributively* rather than *collectively*. Confusion as to the difference between these two underlies a pair of simple yet often misleading fallacies. The *fallacy of composition* interprets collectively what applies only distributively; the *fallacy of division* makes a similar mistake in the reverse direction. The first is illustrated in the conception of an all-star team: from the fact that each player individually performs superlatively well, it does not follow that they will do so well together. The second is illustrated in the supposition, to which traveling Americans even these days are exposed, that citizens of a rich country are individually rich.

The existential operator is so called because it affirms that there are values of the variable for which the propositional function becomes a true proposition; but it does not say which these values are. In English, the existential operator is expressed by words like "some" or phrases like "there are," "at least one," and so on. "There is an x, such that x is Greek" means the same as "There are Greeks" (the operator does not distinguish between one and more than one but only between none and one or more). "There is an x, such that x is prime and ends in 7" says that there are prime numbers ending in 7.

What it means for something to exist, and what is common to the existence of people, numbers, or anything else, need not trouble us in this context. The existential operator simply negates what is affirmed by the universal operator. "Some men are immortal" means that not all men die; "There are numbers greater than one trillion" means that not all numbers are less than or equal to one trillion. This relationship can be used to define the existential operator: "There is an x, such that x has the property f" means, by definition, the same as "Not all x's lack f." By the law of double negation (not-not-*p* is logically equivalent to *p*), if one proposition is the negation of another, the second is also the negation of the first. Hence the universal operator negates what is affirmed by the existential operator. "All men are mortal" means "It is not the case that some men are immortal." This relationship can be used to define the universal operator in terms of the existential, instead of the other way around: "For all x, x is f" means, by definition, the same as "It is not the case that some x's lack f."

Whether or not the negation is contained in the scope of the operator is of crucial importance, logically speaking. "Not all x's are f" is by no means the same as "All x's are not-f," since the first says only that some x's are not-f, leaving open the possibility that some x's *are* f, while the second denies this possibility. Colloquially, however, the logical distinction is not preserved, and "All that glitters is not gold" is interpreted as though it read, "Not all that glitters is gold." Spoken language seems particularly casual about negations. "I could care less" is a standard colloquialism with the meaning, "I could *not* care less"—that is, my caring is minimal. When Alice, understandably assuming that "more" implies the existence of some, complained that because she hadn't had any tea yet she couldn't take more, the Hatter pointed out that what she meant was that she couldn't take *less;* but he was mad.

Similar considerations arise when both universal and existential operators play a part in the same proposition. In that case, the order in which they appear makes a crucial difference. "For all x, there is a y such that . . ." is radically different from "There is an x, such that for all y . . ."

The first says, for instance, that every number has a square, which is true; the second, that some number is the square of all numbers, which is absurd. Between "Every man has a father" and "There is a Father of all men," there is, one might say, a world of difference.

An important concept in the calculus of functions is that of *identity*. It is meant here in a sense which applies to any individual thing whatever, not only to human beings (§47). The standard definition goes back to Leibniz, formulated in what he called the principle of *identity of indiscernibles:* two things are identical if it is impossible—not just practically, but logically impossible—to distinguish between them. This formulation won't quite do, because if they are identical they are not two, but one. A better formulation is "x is identical with y" means, by definition, the same as "whatever is true of x is true of y, and conversely." Otherwise put, wherever x appears in a propositional function it may be replaced by y, or vice versa. Such *replacement,* justified by a proposition affirming an identity, is not to be confused with a *substitution,* justified by the affirmation (as postulate, theorem, or premise) of a formula containing an appropriate free variable. There are those who have challenged the principle on the grounds that things might differ in their intrinsic substance even though all their properties were the same. In that case we could not say anything about their distinctive substances, for whatever we might say would ascribe a property to the substance, and the properties are admittedly not distinctive. An indiscernible identity would be simply unspeakable.

Among the most puzzling affirmations of identity are those involving a definite description—a phrase of the form, "the such-and-such." The examples made famous by Russell's analysis of them are "the present king of France" and "the author of *Waverley*." The sorts of puzzles which arise are illustrated by the circumstance that although it is immediately apparent that the author of *Waverley* wrote books, it is by no means apparent that Walter Scott did so; one would simply have to know something about the man—yet Scott is identical with the author of *Waverley*. As to the present king of France, the situation is worse; since there is none, asking whether he is say, bald, seems rather like the chestnut about wife beating; yet one should be able to say *some* things about him—for instance, that he is a royal contemporary. Such puzzles point to serious problems in the foundations of logic, semantics, and mathematics—where we wish to speak unambiguously about, say, *the* roots of an equation, or *the* limit of a function.

Russell's analysis of the definite description was enormously influential, although—like most advances in thought—it raised many questions as well as answering many. In briefest compass, Russell's view was that a definite description is not a substitution instance of self-identity (x is identical with x), for the description has implicit within it an existential claim which might be false. Only if this claim is warranted can we use the description as we would any other symbol naming an individual. The expression "implicit within it" is a loose way of stating that a definite description is an *incomplete symbol,* whose meaning cannot be specified for it in isolation but only in a full context of use.

The classic example is this. The proposition, "The present king of France is bald," means the same as the conjunction of all three of the following propositions:

1. "There exists at present at least one king of France,"
2. "There is no more than one king of France at present (if x is now king of France and so is y, then x and y are identical)," and
3. "He is bald."

The pronoun "He" is a grammatical expediency which is logically dispensable, by using the same variable throughout the scope of that first existential operator. The pronoun usually involves a definite description, presupposing the existence of an antecedent for the pronoun as in Hughes Mearns' "The Psychold":

As I was going up the stair
I met a man who wasn't there.
He wasn't there again today.
I wish, I wish he'd stay away!

Whatever the merits or shortcomings of Russell's analysis in detail, it illustrates the complexities which modern logic is prepared to countenance in the inner structure of propositions. By contrast, traditional logic, for the most part, thought of propositions as simply consisting of a subject (S) and a predicate (P), and then classified propositions by "quality" as being either affirmative or negative, and by "quantity" as being either universal (containing a universal operator) or "particular" (containing either a constant or an existentially bound variable). This classification allows for four fundamental types of proposition, conventionally symbolized by four vowels:

A: Universal affirmative—all S is P.
E: Universal negative—no S is P.
I: Particular affirmative—some S is P.
O: Particular negative—some S is not P.

These were often represented as the four corners of a square, with A and E at the top left and right, and I and O at bottom left and right, respectively. This was called *the square of opposition*. Of continuing importance is the emphasis this representation gave to the different senses in which propositions can be "opposites" of one another—differences obscured in the looseness often found in expositions or criticisms of Marxist dialectic, Chinese metaphysics, and Freudian psychology.

Two propositions are *contradictories* of one another if they cannot both be true nor both be false. If either is false, the other must be true. In the square of opposition, contradictories are diagonally opposite one another: A and O are contradictories of each other and so are E and I. Either all S is P or else some S is not P, and these cannot both be the case; similarly, either no S is P or else some S *is* P, and these cannot both be the case.

Contradictories are often confused with what are only *contraries* of one another: propositions which cannot both be true, though both might very well be false. This relation holds across the top of the square, between A and E. It cannot be true both that all S is P and that no S is P; but both would be false if some S were P and some not. This assumes, as the traditional logic did, that there are some S's to start with; if there were none, whatever we said about them would be true, ultimately because a false proposition implies any proposition. "All unicorns are gentle" has the form, "For all x, if x is a unicorn then x is gentle," which is true if for no other reason than that the antecedent is false for every value of the variable. "No unicorns are gentle" has the form, "It is not the case that there exists an x, such that x is a unicorn and x is gentle." This is also true; since there are no unicorns at all, there are certainly no gentle ones. "No unicorns are gentle" might also be rendered as, "For all x, if x is a unicorn then x is not gentle," which would be true, as above, because of the falsity of the antecedent.

Two propositions are *subcontraries* if they cannot both be false, though both might be true. This relation holds between I and O: either some S is P, or else some S is not P, and perhaps both are the case. As before, this assumes that there *are* some S's of whatever sort. Because of the "existential import" which traditional logic gave to A propositions, it allowed the inference from A to I which modern logic does not countenance. This does not mark a change in the logic-in-use but only in the reconstructed logic, which is simpler and more elegant, even though more paradoxical, in the present form.

The term "contrary" is sometimes used in a wider sense, so as to include subcontrary. This usage makes sense, because the important difference is between both of these on the one hand, and the contradictory on the other. Psychoanalysis, for example is often criticized as being invulnerable to falsificiation—and therefore to verification as well—because of its doctrines of reaction formation, and the like. "If a boy shows love for his mother, that is the Oedipus complex at work; if he shows hate for his mother, that is only an attempt to disguise his love, and so also verifies the hypothesis of an Oedipus complex." But if both p and not-p imply q, q is necessarily true and thus tells us nothing about what is the case. The point is, however, that hate is not the contradictory of love, as not-p is of p, but only the contrary (or subcontrary). It is possible, after all, to relate to someone with neither love nor hate, or indeed both. The psychoanalytic view would be falsified if relations of boys to their mothers were characteristically, or even often, detached and indifferent.

The most important pattern of inference in the traditional logic is the *syllogism*, having two premises and a conclusion which directly follows from them. When the premises are atomic, the syllogism is called "categorical"; the tradition also analyzed "hypothetical" and "disjunctive" syllogisms, in which one of the premises was an implication or a disjunction, respectively. The predicate (P) of the conclusion of a syllogism is called the *major term*, and the premise containing that term is the *major premise;* the subject (S) of the conclusion is the *minor term*, and its premise is the *minor premise.* There must be, in addition, a third term, present in both premises;

it is called the *middle term* (M). Should any of these terms be used equivocally, in two senses, the syllogism is invalid; this failing is called the *fallacy of four terms.*

Since each of the three propositions of the syllogism may be an A, E, I, or O proposition, there are at most 64 (4 × 4 × 4) possible types of premises and conclusions. These are called the *moods* of the syllogism; by no means all of them, however, are valid. The moods are traditionally designated by proper names whose successive vowels indicate the type of the proposition. For instance, a syllogism in "Barbara" consists of two universal affirmative premises, and a universal affirmative conclusion; "Ferio" has as major premise a universal negative, the minor premise is particular affirmative, and the conclusion is particular negative. These are illustrated, respectively, by the classic examples:

All men are mortal; all Greeks are men. Therefore, all Greeks are mortal.

No philosophers are unjust; Socrates is a philosopher. Therefore, Socrates is not unjust.

In each premise, the middle term can appear in one of two places, as either subject or predicate of that premise. There are thus four different patterns of its placing in the premises; these are called the *figures* of the syllogism. In each figure different moods of the syllogism are valid, for reasons to be stated in a moment. Together, the mood and figure of a syllogism uniquely specify its logical form.

The principle traditionally formulated as underlying the validity of the syllogism is the "all and none" principle (the *dictum de omni et nullo*): what is affirmed (or denied) of a whole class may be affirmed (or denied) of any of its members. (It is assumed that the proposition is not meant collectively, or we would have the fallacy of division.) When the whole class is involved, the term designating the class is said to be *distributed.* Plainly, the subject of any universal proposition (S in A or E) is distributed. But so also is the predicate of any negative proposition (P in E or O); when I say that Socrates is not a Sophist I am denying something of *all* Sophists—namely, that any of them is Socrates.

It is a condition of the validity of the syllogism that the middle term must be distributed in at least one of the premises (otherwise it will not serve to link the two). A failing here is called the *fallacy of the undistributed middle.* From the premises, "Some men are not reasonable" and "All logicians are men," the conclusion does not follow that "Some logicians are not reasonable." This may be true, but it does not follow; "men" is an undistributed middle term. It is also a rule that no term may be distributed in the conclusion if it is not distributed in its premise; otherwise we have an *illicit major* or *illicit minor.* From these and other conditions it can be readily established that the conclusion must be negative if—and only if—one of the premises is negative; that no conclusion at all follows from two negative premises; that the conclusion must be particular if a premise is particular; and that no conclusion follows from two particular premises.

Syllogistic logic exhibited considerable subtlety and ingenuity—determining the valid moods for each figure, developing the theory of the hypothetical and disjunctive syllogisms as well as the categorical one, showing how the various valid forms can be reduced to a few basic ones, and working out the properties of chains of inference (the *sorites*). Yet, as a reconstruction, it is far more suited to the contexts of forensics and rhetoric than of science and mathematics. Today it has only historical interest.

19. Sets and Relations

Many of the results of the calculi of propositions and of functions can be formulated in terms of relations among classes or sets of things as determined by the abstract composition of such aggregates. "Sets" is the more recent term; *set theory*, which incorporates the older *calculus of classes*, is nowadays often taken as the basic calculus, and the calculi of propositions and functions are then built up on its basis. I use "set" and "class" as synonyms, unless otherwise stated.

Take as undefined the idea of being a *member* of a class or an *element* of a set. A *set* is defined if, for every individual in the range of the variables being used, there is specified a criterion for the determination of whether or not it is an element of the set. In practice it may be difficult to apply the criterion, even, in some cases, effectively impossible. This corresponds to the difficulty of actually determining the truth-value of a proposition; logic requires only that a proposition be capable in principle of such a determination. A criterion of membership is a necessary condition for the existence of a set; whether it is also a sufficient condition is a vexed question.

The defining criterion is sometimes called the *intension* of the set; its *extension* consists of the elements satisfying the criterion. In the usual treatment, sets are dealt with only extensionally; that is, they are identified by their membership, not by their criterion. This treatment is expressed in the *principle of extensionality:* If x is a member of A whenever it is a member of B, and conversely, then A is identical with B. (The converse is also true.) This may be taken to define the identity of sets.

A set is distinct from its elements. The *unit set* of a particular individual is one which has that individual as its only element. That the set and its element cannot be one and the same was argued by Frege and, subsequently, by Russell. Consider a set A, and let A′ be the unit set of A, that is, having A as its only member; then A′ has only one member, by definition, while A can have any number of members. A and A′ therefore cannot be the same, though one "consists of" nothing more than the other.

Membership is a relation between an individual and a set; as in the case just described, the individual in question may itself be a set. A set which is a member of another set stands in a different relation to it than does a set which is included in that other. One set is *included* in another (A is a *subset* of B) if every element of A is also an element of B. When the converse also holds—that is, when two sets are each subsets of one another—the two are identical. This corresponds to the theorem of the propositional calculus that the conjunction of p implies q with q implies p in turn logically implies that p and q are equivalent. *Principia* gives the illustration of the don who, whenever he looked out of his window, saw a certain undergraduate walking across the quad, and accordingly taxed him with idleness; to which the youth rejoined, "But whenever I cross the quad, I see you staring out the window!" The perfect coincidence entailed may lead us to question at least one of the premises, but the logic is impeccable.

Two special sets are singled out for attention. The *universal set* consists of all the individuals in the range of the variables used. It can be defined, for instance, as the set of all individuals identical with themselves; from the definition of identity (§18) and the theorem that p always implies p (§17) it follows that this criterion admits of no exceptions. If the variables range over the natural numbers, the universal set might be defined as all numbers obtainable by successive additions of 1, together with 0; if they range over people, the universal set is simply "everybody." The universal set is sometimes also called the *universe of discourse,* though this expression often has another meaning, referring to the context relevant to what is being considered.

The *null set* is the set with no elements at all; it is the empty class. I say "the" empty class not "an" empty one, because, by the principle of extensionality, there is only one—classes with the same members (in this case, none at all) are identical. The notion of a null set arouses much the same uneasiness as must have been felt at one time with the introduction of the number zero. This uneasiness may be lessened if we remember that a set is not identical with its elements but only identified by them (consider the unit set once more). In any case, the idea is an enormously useful one in the formal development.

The set of all the things (in the universe of discourse) which are not elements of a given set A is called the *complement* of A. Corresponding to the law of double negation in the propositional calculus is the theorem here that the complement of the complement of set A is simply A all over again. The set consisting of whatever is an element of either A or B is called the *sum* of A and B; elements of both A and B constitute their *product.* These terms mean something altogether different here than they do in arithmetic, but there is a relation nevertheless. When we add apples and pears we get a certain number of fruit—things which are *either* apples *or* pears. When we multiply the number of workers by the number of hours worked we get a certain number of man-hours—units in which *both* men and time are involved.

A convenient system of representation of these ideas is associated with the names of Leonhard Euler, an eighteenth-century mathematician, and John Venn, a nineteenth-century logician; the representations are called *Euler circles* or *Venn diagrams.* A large rectangle represents the universe of discourse, and circles drawn within it, arbitrary sets. The complement of a set is shown by whatever lies outside the circle—the rectangle with the circle cut out. A dot in the circle is an element of the set. One circle inside another represents inclusion. When two-circles overlap, the football-shaped region common to both represents their product, and the 8-shaped figure their sum. Such circles may be used to show what follows from premises about the relations of given sets. They only "show" it, however, and do not prove it, for the circles might have been drawn in ways which tacitly assume relations not given in the premises: two circles may intersect, for example, and their intersection have a noticeable area, yet the sets may have no common elements—the region should be void of identifiable points and the circles should have been drawn separated from one another.

Analogues to many theorems of the propositional calculus are easy to establish. For the law of contraposition we have: If A is included in B, then the complement of B is included in the complement of A. De Morgan's theorems are: The complement of the product of A and B is the sum of their complements; and the complement of the sum is the product of the complements. The distributive laws are not as elegantly formulable in words but are quite as simple: The sum of the product of A and B together with the product of A and C is identical with the product of A together with the sum of B and C; and if the words "sum" and "product" in the above are interchanged throughout, the result is also a theorem. The law of excluded middle is that the sum of a set and its complement is the universal set; and the law of contradiction is that the product of a set and its complement is the null set. Syllogisms are often more easily formulated in terms of the class calculus than the functional calculus. The principles are, for instance: That A is included in B, and B is included in C implies that A is included in C (Barbara); and if A is included in B and x is a member of A, then x is also a member of B (Darii).

One of the most significant advances of modern logic as compared with the traditional discipline is its development of the *logic of relations*, by which such basic mathematical ideas as order, structure, and operation are brought into connection with the rest of logic. Something is lost when relational propositions are parsed as being subject-predicate in form. From the premises that Tom is taller than Dick, and Dick is taller than Harry, it should plainly follow that Tom is taller than Harry, but it is not easy to see how this can be couched in syllogistic form. Another example of a simple inference which does not lend itself easily (if at all) to a syllogistic form is this one, cited by De Morgan, one of the founders of relational logic: Since a horse is an animal, the head of a horse is the head of an animal.

Much of the foundations of the theory of relations corresponds to that of the theory of sets. A (dyadic) relation is defined when it is specified for every couple of elements in the universe of discourse whether or not the relation holds between them, a *couple* being a pair taken in a definite order (x-y is one couple and y-x is another.) The set of couples for which the relation holds is the *extension* of the relation, and relations having the same extension are defined to be identical, however different their intensions, that is, the criteria by which it is determined whether the relation holds.

The extension of a relation consists of couples; the set of individuals which are members of any couple in the extension constitutes the *field* of the relation. Those that appear first in their couples make up the *domain* of the relation, and those that appear second, the *converse domain;* these two may overlap or coincide altogether. For the relation, "husband of," the field consists of married people; the domain, of husbands; and the converse domain, of wives. For the relation, "square of," the field is all numbers, the domain is the squares, and the converse domain is again all the numbers. A set is *closed* under a relation if the set is included in the field of the relation, and every individual which has the relation to a member of the set or to which a member has the relation is itself a member of the set. For instance, an endogamous society is closed under the relation of marriage.

A relation may be such that only one individual can have it to another, although the same individual may have the relation to several others; such a relation is called *one-many.* Thus "square of," the field being positive and negative integers, is one-many; 9, for example, is the square both of +3 and of −3. Similarly, a relation may be *many-one*—a given number has both a positive and a negative square root, while each is the square root of only that number. A *one-one* relation is such that, if any member of its field is specified, another individual is uniquely determined. Finally, *many-many* relations may be multiple in both directions. In various societies, the relation, "husband of," may be defined in one of these four ways, respectively, constituting polygamy, polyandry, monogamy; for the fourth, "communal living" is among the expressions that might be used. A one-many relation allows us to speak of "the R of y"—the one x which has the relation R to y (the father of y); a many-one relation gives us a unique *set* of relata for a given individual (the children of y); and we may form a set of such sets (the families of prisoners).

If a relation is considered in the reverse direction for each couple of its extension, a new relation is defined, called the *converse* of the original—"larger than" is the converse of "smaller than"; "equal to" is its own converse. The converse of a one-many relation is many-one. Forming the converse has some of the properties of negation (but only some!); for instance, the converse of the converse is the original relation again. Converse is itself a relation, the members of its field also being relations. When, as in this case, a relation is taken twice over (the converse of the converse), we may speak of the "square" of the relation; grandparent is the square of parent. Similarly we may have the cube (great-grandparent) and higher *powers* of a relation.

The idea can be generalized to combinations of different relations; the *relative product* of R and S holds between x and z when there is a y such that x has the relation R to y, and y has the relation S to z. Uncle is the relative product of brother and parent. This is not to be confused with the *relational product,* which holds when both of the original relations hold; "older brother" is the relational product of "older than" and "brother of." Similarly, we have a *relational sum* when either holds, as in "greater-than-or-equal to."

The idea of powers of a relation can be generalized in another direction.

If x and y are related by some power of R—and it does not matter which (parent or great-great-grandparent or whatever)—we may speak of the *ancestral relation* associated with R. For instance, if R is successor of (4 is the successor of 3), the ancestral of R is simply "greater than."

A relation may be pictured by an *arrow diagram*, in which individuals are represented by points, and that the relation holds between two individuals is shown by an arrow drawn between the points representing the two individuals, the arrowhead showing the direction in which the couple is to be taken.

It may happen that some of the arrows have two arrowheads—that is, the relation may hold in both directions for that pair of individuals. A relation which holds in both directions, if it holds at all, is called *symmetrical;* if it is never found in both directions, it is *asymmetrical;* and if it holds sometimes only, it is *nonsymmetrical.* Sibling is symmetrical; parent is asymmetrical; brother is nonsymmetrical. A relation which an individual always has to itself is *reflexive,* and as above for *irreflexive* and *nonreflexive.* A relation is *transitive* if, whenever it holds between x and y, and also between y and z, it holds between x and z; if this is never true, it is *intransitive;* and if sometimes, *nontransitive.* "Equal to" is reflexive; "greater than" is irreflexive; and "having a product divisible by 2" is nonreflexive. Ancestor is transitive; parent is intransitive; and half-brother is nontransitive.

Relations which are symmetrical and transitive are an important type called *equivalence relations;* examples are identity, equality, logical equivalence, synonymy, and having the same weight. Sets closed under such a relation are called *equivalence sets* and are often thought of as having a common property (like meaning or weight in the last two examples). Most of what we would like to say about such a property can be said instead by speaking only of the equivalence relation and the equivalence set. That a body has a certain weight, for example, means that it belongs to the same equivalence set as a certain piece of brass, the set being defined with reference to a certain symmetrical and transitive balancing relation.

Relations which are asymmetrical and transitive are *ordering relations.* If such a relation is also connected—that is, holding in one direction or the other between any two members of its field—it is called a *series.* If the relation is not connected, it defines a *partial order;* if it is nonsymmetrical, a *weak order.* Such relations are fundamental in the construction of scales of measurement, as well as in various branches of pure mathematics.

Suppose that two relations, R and S, are of such a kind that a correspondence can be established on a one-to-one basis between the members of their fields, each member of the field of R corresponding to a certain member of the field of S, and conversely. Suppose further that the correspondence is such that whenever R holds between x and y, then S holds between the elements corresponding to x and y. In that case we say that R and S are *isomorphic* to one another. Isomorphism is clearly an equivalence relation, being symmetrical and transitive. A *structure* is the equivalence set of an isomorphism. It is what is pictured in the arrow diagram; if two relations are isomorphic, their arrow diagrams are identical. In a more familiar idiom, the two relations have the same form; only their content is different. Structure is the form of a relation.

All the relations so far considered are dyadic—they relate only two elements at a time. Instead of couples, the extension of a relation may consist of triples, quadruples, or an ordered set of any size. This size defines the *degree* of the relation, dyadic relations having the degree two, triadic relations the degree three, and so on; classes might even be thought of as relations of degree one. Peirce has argued that with triadic relations we can construct all relations of higher degree, but we cannot manage with dyadic relations alone. When x gives y to z, it is not merely that x gives up y and z acquires it; the relation involves all three.

A relation of degree greater than two is often called an *operation*—a *binary* operation if it involves two individuals at a time. The expression x 0 y (the result of performing with x the operation 0 on y) does not constitute a proposition but designates another individual (or several of them). The propositional form would be: x 0 y = z; this can be couched in the standard relational form as: the relation 0 holds for the ordered triple xyz. Among natural numbers, "greater than" is a relation, while sum and product are operations. When the result of operating with x on y is the same as the result of operating with y on x, the operation is said to be *commutative;* this corresponds to the symmetry of a dyadic relation. The operation is *associative* if, when the operation is performed twice successively, it does not matter in which order it is done: x 0 (y 0 z) = (x 0 y) 0 z.

One of the most important developments of modern mathematics is the theory of groups. A set G and an operation 0 are said to constitute a *group* if the following conditions are satisfied:

1. *Closure*—the result of operating with any member of the group on any other is itself a member of the group: if x and y are members of G, so is x 0 y.
2. The operation 0 is *associative.*
3. *Identity* element—there is a particular member I of G which, operating on any member of G, leaves that member unchanged: I 0 x = x.
4. *Inverse*—to every member x of G there corresponds another member x′ operating on which yields the identity element: x 0 x′ = I.

Groups have proven to have extraordinarily broad applications, from crystallography and quantum mechanics to many parts of pure mathematics.

20. Foundations of Mathematics

In the opening paragraph of Russell's *Principles of Mathematics,* he defines pure mathematics as "the class of all propositions of the form '*p* implies *q*,' where *p* and *q* are propositions containing one or more variables, the same in the two propositions, and neither p nor q contains any constants except logical constants." Because mathematics deals only with implications, nothing is asserted in it except that *if* something were the case, something else would also be the case. And because it is formulated in terms of variables, the subjects of even the hypothetical assertions cannot be specified. Hence Russell's witticism that in mathematics we never know what we are talking about, nor whether what we are saying is true.

It has often been supposed that there is some special faculty of mathematical intuition which reaches out into the mathematical domain and guarantees the truth of what it discerns there. Unquestionably the insights of the great mathematicians are often quite astonishing. What is questionable, however, is whether any such faculty provides a secure foundation for the complex systems mathematics erects. It is quite unsatisfactory to accept mathematical truths merely on authority, and the intuitions of ordinary men are grossly inadequate.

The intuitions of most of us would scarcely yield up propositions like the following (all of which are in fact true): a line of infinite length can enclose a finite area; a sequence of decreasing magnitudes, getting as close to zero as you like, can still have an infinite sum; an infinite number of elements can be taken away from a set and leave just as many as there were before. Nor is it only "the paradoxes of the infinite" which defy intuition. Even ordinary arithmetic can be surprising: any integer can be expressed as the sum of not more than four squares; the square of any integer can be expressed as the sum of two squares; and any odd number greater than 1 can be expressed as the difference of two squares. As for geometry, consider propositions like the following: though lines have no breadth, a curve can be defined which fills a given area; another curve can be constructed which intersects itself at every point; and every simple (nonintersecting) closed curve divides the plane into two parts, an inside and an outside. This last (the Jordan theorem) may be obvious to intuition, but how to prove it is far from obvious. Mathematics needs proof as well as insight.

At least since the time of Euclid mathematicians have been interested in the problems of justifying their conclusions. In the twentieth century three main schools of thought about the foundations of mathematics have crystallized. One of these, associated with the name of L. E. J. Brouwer, is called *intuitionism.* Far from supposing that intuition suffices in place of proof, this school is more restrictive in its criteria of acceptable proof than are the others. Its name derives from its emphasis on a basic intuition of succession in a sequence of possible magnitudes; but everything depends on exactly what is subsequently done with this primeval intuition.

The intuitionist views mathematics as a human activity and so acknowledges no significance to mathematical propositions or procedures which transcend what lies, even in principle, within human powers. Its position is "finitist" and "constructivist"—that is, countenancing no proofs which would require an infinite number of steps, and no claims of the existence of a mathematical entity which cannot be constructed by us, at least in principle. In particular, intuitionism does not accept indirect proof—that is, a claim of existence (say, of a number of a certain kind) based on the demonstration that to suppose otherwise is contradictory. Critics have alleged that an intuitionist would be unwilling to say "It is either raining or not raining" till he had looked. Although it seems clear that the reconstruction of mathematics on strict intuitionist principles would seriously impoverish the subject, there is no doubt that the school has significantly enriched our understanding of mathematical existence and truth.

The second school is the *logicist* school, of which Russell is the best-known representative. (I shall speak of the third school, the *formalism* of David Hilbert and others, in the next section.) The logicist grounds mathematics in logic, not only as a way of justifying mathematical procedures but also as an explication of the nature of the entities with which the mathematician deals.

At the turn of the century, Giuseppe Peano provided a remarkably simple set of postulates on the basis of which the familiar arithmetic of the natural numbers could be demonstrated. He used three undefined terms: 0, ′, and N—meant to be interpreted, respectively, as zero, immediate successor, and number; the validity of the demonstrations does not depend on this interpretation or on any other. The postulates are:

1. 0 is an N.
2. If x is an N, so is x′.
3. If x is different from y, x′ is different from y′.
4. There is no x such that 0 = x′.
5. Call a property *hereditary* if, whenever x has it, so does x′; then each N has every hereditary property of 0.

Logicism set out to show how Peano's undefined terms could be defined on the basis of pure logic and his postulates shown to be logical truths.

The essential steps were taken by Frege and Russell, making use of the fundamental idea of a one-one relation. The mathematical concept of the number one is not presupposed here, or there would be a circularity. All that is involved is the logical concept of identity: a relation R is defined to be one-one if, whenever x R z and y R z, x = y; and whenever x R y and x R z, y = z. Two classes are said to be *similar* whenever there is a one-one relation for which one of the classes can serve as domain and the other as converse-domain. In that case, the members of the two classes can be put into correspondence with one another, each to each, with none left out and none left over from either class. The two classes are then said to have the same *cardinality;* colloquially, they are the same size, or, as will be seen in a moment, they have the same number of members.

In an auditorium in which every seat is occupied and no one is standing (or sharing a seat), the class of seats is similar to the class of people making up the audience; there are as many of the one as of the other, the correspondence relation being that which holds between a person and the seat he is occupying. It is crucial that the fact that the two classes have the same cardinality can be determined without first determining what that cardinality is—that is, without counting how many members there are in each class. If we know only that a city has more inhabitants than any inhabitant has hairs on his head, we can immediately conclude that at least two inhabitants have the same number of hairs—there are too many inhabitants to be put into correspondence with hairs. In its general form, this proposition is known to mathematicians as Dirichlet's "pigeonhole principle": if k pigeons occupy k-1 pigeonholes, at least one hole has two or more pigeons in it.

The definition of number which this approach makes possible is startling in its austerity: a number is the class of all classes similar to a given class. The number 2, for example, is the class of all classes similar to any class for which there exist members x and y not identical with each other, and such that if any z is a member of the class, then it is identical either with x or with y. In other words, the number 2 is the class of all pairs, and numbers in general are the equivalence classes of the equivalence relation of similarity (§19). The classic purity of Russell's definition is in striking contrast with the baroque convolutions of Kant's definition of number as "the unity of the synthesis of the manifold of a homogeneous intuition in general," a definition by which Brouwer was strongly influenced.

Once numbers have been constructed, we can *count.* In counting, we establish a correspondence between the members of the class being counted and the numbers (or the numerals by which these are expressed). When the one-one relation used in the counting (for instance, pushing aside the thing being counted while simultaneously calling out a numeral) takes the numbers in a certain preassigned order, it can be proved that the last number used in the correspondence is in fact the number of members in the class. Counting on one's fingers is no less sophisticated, but only more obvious, than relying on other correspondences; but some correspondence there must be.

Apart from the numbers used in counting, there are many other sorts of numbers; where do they come from? By the nineteenth century, so much progress had already been made in constructing the more complex mathematical entities out of the simpler ones that Leopold Kronecker was able to say, "God made the natural numbers; all the rest is the work of man." Integers can be defined in terms of relations among the natural numbers, rationals (fractions) in terms of pairs of integers, real numbers in terms of certain sequences of rationals, and complex numbers (imaginaries) as pairs of real numbers. These successive enlargements of the domain of number serve to make certain operations always possible. Subtraction, for example, cannot always be performed among natural numbers alone—we cannot subtract a larger number from a smaller one. But in the domain of positive and negative integers the difficulty disappears. Similarly, rationals are needed so that divisions will always yield numbers within the domain. With the introduction of complex numbers the domain is complete in the sense that all the basic operations are closed within the domain.

The method of correspondences made possible, around the turn of the century, one of the revolutions in human thought, when Georg Cantor laid the groundwork of the arithmetic of the infinite. As in the case of other thinkers who challenged received opinion and common sense, Cantor was attacked and ridiculed by most professionals and was altogether ignored by laymen. The trouble is that in transfinite arithmetic the whole is not always greater than one of its parts. The set of even numbers, for example, has the same cardinality as the set of all numbers, both even and odd together. To every number there corresponds exactly one even number (its double), and to every even number exactly one member of the whole set of numbers (its half). The one set apparently has twice as many members as the other, but by the method of correspondences it is no more numerous. (A related example—the set of perfect squares and the set of all integers—had already been noted by Galileo; it took a Galileo to make note of it.)

Although such paradoxes abound in transfinite arithmetic, they are only paradoxes, not contradictions. (Inconsistencies were, in fact, identified by Russell and others; however, they affected not transfinite arithmetic as such but logic and mathematics in general.) Numbers, like the number of all integers, which can be put into correspondence with only a part of themselves, are called *reflexive.* All reflexive numbers are infinite.

Cantor used the first letter of the Hebrew alphabet, aleph, as the symbol for his transfinite cardinal number. Its paradoxical arithmetic is that it is made neither smaller nor larger by the subtraction or addition of any finite number; indeed, aleph plus aleph is no larger than aleph, nor is 2 times aleph, nor even aleph times aleph. The question then arises, is there only one infinite number? Do all infinite classes have the same cardinality? A class which has the same cardinality as the set of all natural numbers can, by definition, be counted; accordingly, it is called a *denumerable* or countable set. Are all transfinite sets denumerable? Cantor proved that the answer is no.

It might be supposed that the number of fractions is greater than the number of whole numbers, not only because between any two whole numbers there are an infinite number of fractions but also because between any two fractions there are always other fractions to be found. The series of whole numbers is *discrete:* between any two there is a finite number of others, perhaps none at all; the series of fractions is *dense:* there are always more in between. Yet the set of fractions is only denumerable. The fractions can be counted by first being placed in the following order (ignoring here the complication of fractions not in lowest terms): Arrange them in order of increasing size of the sum of numerator and denominator; and when two fractions have the same sum, place first the one with the smaller numerator. In this order, each fraction has an unambiguously defined place as the first, tenth, or whatever; in short, the set is denumerable.

Cantor proved that the set of real numbers is nondenumerable. He gave the following indirect proof. Suppose the set were denumerable; its members could then all be placed in some definite order—a particular real number first, another particular one second, and so on. Express each number as an unending decimal, and consider the whole sequence as ordered. Contrary to the supposition, it does not contain all the real numbers, for another can be identified which does not appear in the sequence. For instance, consider the number obtained by choosing first some digit *other* than the first digit of the first number; second, any digit other than the second digit of the second number; and so on. This new number differs from each of the numbers in the list, differing in its nth digit from the nth number in the list. Consequently, no such list can be complete, and the set of real numbers is nondenumerable. (Because of the way in which the unlisted number is constructed, the procedure is called Cantor's "diagonal method.")

The set of points in the line, corresponding as these points do to the real numbers, is thus also nondenumerable. As before, there are paradoxical equalities. A short line segment has as many points as a long one (even an infinitely long one). Consider the base of a triangle and any line above it drawn from side to side across the triangle at any angle. Choose any point of the base and draw the line connecting it to the apex of the triangle; this line will intersect the short segment at a definite point, which corresponds to the one chosen in the base. In this way a correspondence can be set up, and the number of points in the short segment is as great as the number in the base. What is more, there are just as many points in the segment as in the square having it as a side, or in the cube, or in the whole space of the galaxy. Here is another infinite number, one greater than aleph. It is called C (for "continuum").

That the number of real numbers is nondenumerable has, among other paradoxical consequences, this one. Since the set of numbers which can be defined in a finite number of words is only denumerable (a finite set of words can be put into just so many combinations), there must be some real numbers—an infinite number of them—which are not definable in a finite number of words. Of course, being a man of few words—that is, a finite number of them—it is impossible for me to give you even a single example of this countless host. There is nothing about a particular number which would make it indefinable in this way so far as this consideration goes. All that has been said here is that whatever choices we make, in a finate system *some* numbers or others must remain undefined.

Cantor also proved that the number of subsets of any set, even an infinite one, is greater than the number of elements in the set. Since in making up a subset we have, for each element, a choice whether to include it or not, the number of subsets of a set having the size n is 2^n, and this is always greater than n. The number of functions of integers (which is the same as the number of their subsets) is thus greater than aleph, and the number of functions of real numbers is greater than C. By using the infinite numbers as exponents we obtain a whole new series of numbers, all transfinite. The smallest, the denumerable set, is now called aleph_0; the next, given by 2 raised to the aleph_0 power, is aleph_1; and so on. The question then arises whether there is a set with a cardinality greater than that of the integers but less than that of the real numbers; that is, is C equal to aleph_1? This is the so-called problem of the continuum, and Cantor's *continuum hypothesis* was that they are indeed equal—that is, that there is no intermediate magnitude. The hypothesis remained unproven for almost a century; in the 1960s, considerable progress was made, but if I am not mistaken the question is still not definitively settled.

The logic of what used to be called the "infinitely small" was worked out some decades before problems of infinity in the large were seriously tackled. These problems had already been posed by the notion of limits involved in seventeenth-century differential and integral calculus; they recurred in the closely related idea of continuity which came to the fore in the succeeding centuries.

A mathematical function of a given variable may be regarded as a relation which associates with each value of the variable, called the *argument* of the function, a certain magnitude, called the *value* of the function for that argument. The function has a certain value as its *limit* when its argument approaches some specified magnitude if, for every degree of approximation, however close, there exists some interval of such a kind that when the argument lies within the interval the value of the function is closer to what was called the limit than the degree of approximation in question. Loosely put, we can come as close as we like to the limiting value. Infinitely small quantities are nowhere involved, only progressively closer approximations.

21. Metalogic

By the turn of the century there had appeared in logic and mathematics a number of bewildering results, unacceptable in themselves yet apparently arrived at by unimpeachable procedures of derivation and demonstration. These results are often loosely called "paradoxes"; I propose to use the term in a more restricted sense. A *paradox* in this narrow sense is a truth which has the air of falsehood, a puzzle which disappears when rightly understood, a seeming which at last reveals the reality of which it is but an appearance. The paradoxes of the infinite (§20) are indeed paradoxes in this sense, appearing as falsehoods only because they are at variance with the truths about the incomparably more familiar finite numbers. An *antinomy* is a genuine falsehood, a logical inconsistency, differing from a flat contradiction in that it is unavoidable within the given framework of logic—not an oversight or fallacy, but a mark of some radical deficiency or failing within reason itself or, at any rate, within the reconstructions of the logic by which reason is guided.

A certain barber shaves all those men of his village who do not shave themselves, and only those; who shaves the barber? If he does not shave himself, then, by the first clause of the description, he does; but if he does shave himself, then, by the second clause, he does not. Here we have only a puzzle, which is readily dismissed with the observation that the paradox proves only that there is no such barber, and there cannot be one; the characterization of his work is self-contradictory. We would be confronted with an antinomy if, for some good and sufficient reason, we were called upon to believe in his existence nevertheless.

Problems arise for the foundations of logic and mathematics because of their quite natural and usually tacit assumption that a set or class exists as soon as a criterion of membership has been specified. Even if the criterion is contradictory, this means only that no element can satisfy it, so that the class defined is simply the null class (§19). But what if the very existence of a class is contradictory, and at that, a class which is known to have *some* members? Just such a class was conceived by Russell. His antinomy is as follows.

Some classes have other classes as members. A number, for instance, is a class of classes similar to a given class; we may consider the class of large classes, or the class of classes all of whose members are kin. Among those classes which have classes as members are some which have themselves as members. The class of numerous classes is itself a numerous class; the class of nonempty classes is itself not empty. Contrariwise, many classes are not members of themselves: the class of unit-classes has more than one member, and so is not itself a unit-class; the class of finite classes is not itself finite. Now, consider the class of all those classes which are not members of themselves; call it Q. Is Q a member of Q? From the supposition that Q *is* a member of Q, it follows that it is not; and from the supposition that it is not a member of Q, it follows that it is. Yet it must be either the one or the other, and not both.

When Russell came to the University of Chicago in the late thirties, my lifelong friend, Irving Copi, today a distinguished logician, was a classmate of mine. Together we greeted Russell with this limerick of joint authorship:

Discouraged from saving the masses,
Defamed for depraving the lasses,
He kicked off his traces,
Came here, of all places,
Where he's teaching this class, of all classes!

What is wrong with the definition of the class which generates the antinomy (and others like it) is not easy to discern and harder to formulate. Most difficult of all is the task of stipulating rules which would safeguard logic from such antinomies without sacrificing any part of the legitimate domain. Russell held that the antinomy resulted from an "illegitimate totality," a kind of vicious circle which arises from supposing that a collection of objects may contain members which can only be defined by means of this collection as a whole. Q was defined by reference to a collection of which it was presumed to be a part. Another instance of an illegitimate totality is provided by a generalization about all generalizations, like this one contained in a letter by Oliver Wendell Holmes: "I dare say that I have worked off my fundamental formula on you that the chief end of man is to frame general propositions and that no general proposition is worth a damn."

What Russell proposed to avoid the antinomies is a rule to preclude the formation of classes of which they themselves might be eligible to be members. This rule, together with its metalogical justifications, is called the *theory of types*. In essence, it introduces a logical hierarchy, resting on whatever the given system takes to be individuals, then mounting successively to classes of individuals, then classes of such classes, then classes of *those* classes, and so on. An entity can belong only to a class of the next higher type. Analogous restrictions hold for properties of individuals, properties of such properties, and so on. The theory involves technical difficulties of its own, and various logicians, notably Ernst Zermelo and Willard van Quine, have worked out alternative devices.

Russell's antinomy and his tactic to avoid it are reminiscent of Groucho Marx's explanation of his refusal to join an exclusive country club: "I wouldn't belong to a club that would have me as a member!" It quickly became apparent that such principled self-denial would not suffice to deal with all the antinomies. Another kind of difficulty seems to call for very different treatment, in spite of a superficial analogy to the preceding problems. Some words have a meaning which makes them applicable to themselves: "noun" is itself a noun, "English" is an English word, and "sesquipedalian" does indeed have many syllables. Call such words "autological." Other words, which we may call "heterological," do not apply to themselves: "adjective," "Chinese," and "monosyllabic," or the heterological injunction, "Eschew obfuscation!" Now consider the word "heterological"; if it applies to itself then it is autological and so does not apply to itself—but if it does not apply to itself, then it does!

Antinomies of this sort are sometimes called the *semantical antinomies* as distinct from the more strictly *logical antinomies* exemplified by the illegitimate totalities. Here, what is essential is that words are being used to say something about words, including those being used in the saying. Other semantical antinomies involve propositions about propositions. Epimenides the Cretan, for instance, declared that all Cretans are liars, as the Psalmist, some time before him, said "in his haste" about all men. A more strict formulation is this: "The sentence immediately following is true. The sentence immediately preceding is false." Call the first sentence in the quotation marks A and the second, B; A says that B is true, and B says that A is false. Now if A is true, then B is, and so A is false; on the other hand, if A is false, then B is not true, but false, in which case A is true. But A must be either true or false, and not both.

The avoidance of the semantical antinomies demands care in the separation of object-language from metalanguage (§9). Alfred Tarski proved that if a language contains enough of its own metalanguage for us to be able to say in the language that some proposition formulated in that very language is false (or true, for that matter) then the language is inconsistent, and antinomies can readily be formulated in it.

How are we to know whether a system of logic or mathematics is consistent? New antinomies might continue to crop up which elude the restrictions of any rules so far formulated. For that matter, what are we to understand by "consistency" in this context? The notion is an extremely broad one. It sometimes means constancy, doing and feeling today as we did yesterday, the quality of a political policy or a love which alters not when it alteration finds. Sometimes it means congruence, not yoking together an ox and an ass, boogie-woogie with Brahms. Consistency may be no more than purposiveness, not undoing with one hand what has been wrought by the other. There is also a sense of consistency in which it is thought to require that if I prefer x to y and y to z then I must prefer x to z.

It may be that all these usages can be reduced to an underlying logical sense, though how the reduction is to be carried out is far from clear.

What I think undeniable is that in some such senses as these consistency might well be foolish and, as Emerson called it, the hobgoblin of little minds. Circumstances do alter cases, and logic itself might demand that I change my mind; incongruence has its own delights and occasional far-reaching surprises; unraveling at night what has been woven during the day may only conceal a more subtle purpose; and preferability may depend so much on context that we are well advised to forego transitivity. To my mind, however, none of this warrants what Hegel called "one of the main lessons of logic," "to see that thought is in its very nature dialectical, and that, as understanding, it must fall into contradiction—the negative of itself."

Here I find the standpoint of Zen Buddhism much more acceptable intellectually than that of the Hegelian dialectic. Rather than seek a so-called higher synthesis of thought with its own negation, Zen, as Daisetz Suzuki puts it, simply contents itself with calling a spade a not-spade. We are not saved from the intellectualist fallacy by disemboweling the intellect. The spirit of Zen is conveyed by this classic Zen stanza:

> *Empty-handed I go, and behold, the spade is in my hands;*
> *I walk on foot and ride on the back of an ox.*
> *When I cross the bridge,*
> *The water stays still and the bridge flows.*

Perhaps these unmoving waters are what my tradition knows as the well of salvation. The life of the spirit does not demand a sacrifice of the intellect, for what is at stake in such a sacrifice is not only science and mathematics but also morals, politics, and every other domain of value. We cannot attain to an unthinking virtue even if we cross the flowing bridge. Reason is no less sacrificed when its name is put in capital letters or when we are told that the opposite of a thing is only its dialectical realization—that freedom is obedience to party dictates, peace is the imposition of an external will by violence and terror, and justice is the interest of a power bloc.

Dialectics apart, what logic understands by consistency is quite straightforward. A system is *consistent* if there is no proposition formulable in the system of which both the negation and the original proposition are provable in the system. There is no p such that both p and not-p are theorems. If neither p nor not-p is provable, the proposition is undecidable. As a postulate, such a proposition is said to be *independent* of the other postulates, not a theorem of the subsystem defined by the other postulates. Its omission would therefore entail the loss of all those theorems for whose proof it must be invoked. On the other hand, if it is not independent, it need not be taken as a postulate but can be proved. The independence of a postulate system is thus one of its desiderata.

Consistency, however, goes far beyond logical elegance or simplicity. There is a compelling reason why contradictions are to be avoided: if a contradiction can be proved in a system, *anything* can be proved in it, and so proofs in that system become worthless. Suppose that we have among our premises both *p* and not-*p*. Given not-*p*, I can infer that *p* implies *q*; from this, together with the other premise, *p*, *q* follows, whatever *q* might be.

If a contradiction has been demonstrated, we need only examine the proof to see whether it is valid; if so, the system has been shown to be contradictory. If no contradiction has so far been demonstrated, it does not follow that none ever can be or will be. How, then, can a system be shown to be consistent? One way is by *interpretation*, exhibiting a model, a configuration of elements and relations truly described by the postulates when these are appropriately interpreted. What is actual is certainly possible, and a contradictory system is a tissue of impossibilities. But for logic and mathematics, the interpretations are perforce in terms of entities whose own status may be brought into question. The consistency proof employed in practice here is usually the method of *translation:* a particular system is shown to correspond to some other system already shown or assumed to be consistent; the correspondence demonstrates that the new system is no less consistent than the old. It was in this way that non-Euclidean geometry was shown to be consistent: a translation was provided whereby to every theorem in Lobachevski's geometry there corresponded one in Euclid's, so that if any theorem and its negation were both provable in Lobachevski's geometry, the corresponding theorem and its negation would both appear in Euclid's geometry, which would thus also be contradictory.

Such a procedure is all very well so far as it goes; but does it go far enough? In this way we can show that one system is as consistent as another; but without being limited to comparisons, is there no rock on which we can build? The program of *formalism,* led by possibly the most distinguished mathematician of the twentieth century, David Hilbert, aspired to this end. Proofs do not depend upon meanings but only upon forms. That a system is consistent means that certain configurations of forms do not appear within it. Let us then make exact and explicit what forms do appear, and into what forms a given form may be transformed. Just so, by analogy, it might be shown that no position in a game of chess can include more than nine queens of the same color, for there is only one queen of each color to start with; in the course of play another queen can appear only by the promotion of a pawn, and each side has only eight of these.

There is no doubt that the symbols themselves do much of the work of logic and mathematics for us. Russell has said that a perfect notation would be a substitute for thought, and Whitehead has seen as the role of mathematics that of sparing us, as much as possible, the painful necessity of occasionally thinking. Systems can undoubtedly be developed in a purely formal manner, and subsequently be given a variety of interpretations. Geometry, for instance, can be formalized, which Hilbert did, and presented as dealing with undetermined elements and relations, specified only so far as they satisfy the formal requirements of the postulates. A typical proposition might be, "If x is a P and y is a P not identical with x, then there is an L such that x and y are both members of L; and if x and y are also both members of L′, then L and L′ are identical." This is the proposition that is more familiar as stating that two points determine a straight line. We need not interpret P and L to make use of the proposition in proofs.

Instead of attempting, as logicism did, to construct the entities with which mathematics deals out of more basic logical ideas, formalism sought to give a complete but formal specification of their structure, since this is all that matters mathematically. To this, Russell retorted, "The method of 'postulating' what we want has many advantages; they are the same as the advantages of theft over honest toil." These advantages were satirized by John Tukey in a paper called "A Contribution to the Mathematical Theory of Big Game Hunting." The Hilbert method is this: "We place a locked cage at a given point of the desert. We then introduce the following logical system. Axiom I. The class of lions in the Sahara Desert is non-void. Axiom II. If there is a lion in the Sahara Desert, there is a lion in the cage. Rule of Procedure. If *p* is a theorem, and '*p* implies *q*' is a theorem, then *q* is a theorem. Theorem 1. There is a lion in the cage." The method of set theory, however, also does not escape: "We observe that the desert is a separable space. It therefore contains an enumerable dense set of points, from which can be extracted a sequence having the lion as limit. We then approach the lion stealthily along this sequence, bearing with us suitable equipment." To this may be added a modern political method: catch a bear in the usual way, then force it to confess that it's a lion.

Perhaps a more telling criticism of formalism is that the formalist approach is quite unable to account for the usefulness of mathematics. Without interpretation, mathematical formulae are no more than counters in a game, one which may be intellectually challenging and esthetically satisfying, but a game nevertheless. "The formalists," Russell once said, "are like a watchmaker who is so absorbed in making his watches look pretty that he has forgotten their purpose of telling the time, and has therefore omitted to insert any works." Whatever one might think of these criticisms, in the course of the development of metalogic a quite serious and perhaps fatal difficulty presented itself: the formalist program simply cannot be brought to completion.

A logical system is *complete* if every logical truth (tautology or analytic proposition) is a theorem of the system. Put otherwise, for a complete system, if a proposition formulable in the terms of the system is not a theorem, adding it to the postulates would make the system inconsistent. The propositional calculus and the first-order functional calculus are both complete. Completeness is not the same as having a decision procedure, an algorithm or mechanical process by which it can be determined in a finite number of steps whether or not a given proposition is a theorem. It is one thing to show that a certain proposition can be proved in a given system, and it is quite another to be able to provide a proof for it. In fact, though the first-order functional calculus is complete, there is no decision procedure for it.

The program of formalism was to provide a complete formal system for mathematics—complete in this technical sense, not in the colloquial sense of exhaustive, which of course is absurd so long as mathematicians continue to make new discoveries. In 1931, Kurt Göedel demonstrated that in every system rich enough to contain arithmetic an undecidable proposition can be formulated—undecidable, that is, unless the system is inconsistent. It can also be shown that if the system *is* consistent, then the proposition in question is true. Of course, its truth is shown outside the system in question. This result is called *Göedel's first theorem.* He also proved—this is his *second theorem*—that the consistency of a system cannot be proved in a language no richer in formal resources than is the system whose consistency is to be proved. Even if we could prove what we like, we could do so only by using a system which contains some true propositions that are unprovable, and whose consistency must remain unproved unless we use still another system of unproven consistency. The goal of absolute assurance recedes to a new horizon with every step we take toward it.

Kant may have misjudged the progress which the logic of his day was yet to make, but today we can say that the elementary parts of logic, at any rate, have been carried as far as the subject allows. The frontiers now lie in fields like modal logic and deontic logic. What is the structure of propositions about necessity, possibility and impossibility, and about what one ought or ought not to do? To my mind, much of the current interest in such questions has lost itself in a preoccupation with puzzles, for the real problems reach far beyond the domain of logic into all we can know and understand of man and nature. Before attempting to deal with such questions, it is plainly wise to look first at the nature of knowledge itself.

Chapter Four

Theory of Knowledge

22. Inductive Logic

Logic can provide two sorts of knowledge: logical and hypothetical. It can demonstrate analytical propositions, using no other assumptions than logical truths, themselves analytic or tautological. This sort of knowledge comes *from* logic. Logic can also derive synthetic propositions, which are true provided the premises from which they were derived are all true. Such hypothetical knowledge is obtained in *accord* with logic, but not from it.

This is why logic sometimes has an air of unreasonableness. A thought process may be in accord with logic, but take its departure from premises so plainly false that the derivation, though valid, seems absurd. Something of this kind is characteristic of the so-called "logic of the insane." A madman, trying to drive a nail into the wall, is holding the head against the wall and pounding on the tip. "Ah!" he exclaims, realizing the cause of his failure, "some fool has put the head of this nail on the wrong end!" "It's you who are the fool," his companion, also mad, replies. "That nail is for the opposite wall."

If we are to maintain contact with reality, we cannot remain enclosed in a pale of unreasonable premises, however valid our derivation from those premises. The reasonableness of a conclusion is the validity of the derivation by which we arrived at the conclusion; but what makes a premise reasonable? This question is a task for *inductive logic*.

There are philosophers who have denied the possibility of an inductive logic—skeptics who repudiate all knowledge, and rationalists who maintain that all knowledge can be derived from logic alone. To both it might be said that knowledge can be worth something even if it is not certain.

Knowledge would, indeed, be worthless if we had no reason to believe the premises on which it rests. Without an inductive logic, we would have to say that the premises must either be accepted because they are analytic or because they are conclusions of previous derivations (as the rationalist claims), or be acknowledged to be quite arbitrary (as the skeptic insists). The question, Why is one set of premises preferred to another? is usually answered, "By their fruits you shall know them." But the inference, "*p* implies *q*; *q*; therefore *p*," is invalid—it is the fallacy of affirming the consequent. Inductive logic is an attempt to find an alternative to this fallacious reasoning.

If premises were unmediated by other knowledge, no reasoning, deductive or inductive, would be called for to establish them (§26). It seems to me undeniable that some knowledge is arrived at inductively. One may know the world, said Lao-tzu, without going out of doors. We make inferences from what we see indoors, from what we remember of the world without, and from what we are told by others about both. We *make* the inferences. In spite of the etymology of the word "data," knowledge is seldom given to us. A more instructive locution is, "I *take* it that such-and-such is the case"; error is a mis-take.

It is possible for us to know something without knowing just how we know it: "Intuition" is knowing without knowing how we know, and reliance on intuition may reflect a logic-in-use which includes among its resources processes of inference that take place beyond the reach of immediate awareness.

To invoke intuition, however, is not thereby to provide a proof. I may rely on my intuition only after it has been shown to be reliable. What brings intuition into disrepute is that it so often claims credit without being willing to establish its credibility. Einstein was characteristically modest, writing in a letter to a colleague, "I cannot provide logical argument for my conviction, but can only call on my little finger as a witness, which cannot claim any authority to be respected outside my own skin."

It used to be said that the difference between induction and deduction is that one infers from the particular to the general, and the other from the general to the particular. But deductions sometimes remain generalizations, and inductions sometimes move from particular to particular. "By a man's finger-nails, by his coat-sleeve, by his boots, by his trouser-knees, by the callosities of his forefinger and thumb, by his expression, by his shirt-cuffs—by each of these things a man's calling is plainly revealed." These examples given by Sherlock Holmes may be somewhat fanciful, but they are not the "ineffable twaddle" Watson at first thought them to be, until Holmes identified the retired sergeant of marines. Contemporary usage differs from Holmes, who speaks here of the "science of deduction," rather than of "induction"; but the difference is only in the name. Generalizations made in the course of the inference may guide us, but need not be central. We may be far more confident that *this* man is a retired sergeant than that *all* men, of a type we are prepared to specify then and there, are retired sergeants.

While the conclusions of deductive inferences follow necessarily from their premises, there are other inferences which are logical even though the conclusions are not entailed (§30). Inductive logic is the logic of uncertain conclusions—uncertain both in themselves and in relation to the premises from which they are inferred. "Life is the art of drawing sufficient conclusions from insufficient premises." Samuel Butler's epigram may be taken to define at least that part of life which is devoted to making inductions.

Suppose we know that a certain crime must have been committed by either A or B. The premise that A or B did it certainly does not entail the conclusion that A did, yet undeniably gives *some* justification for the conclusion. Similarly, the premises that most f's are g and that x is an f do not entail that x is a g but give *some* ground for that conclusion.

Yet there are difficulties. If *p* is true, so is *p* or *q*, whatever *q* might state (this is one of the paradoxes of implication: *p* implies that not-*p* implies *q*). The evidence we have for *p* may show that if *p* is not true then *q* is very likely to be—but a particular *q*, not just any one. We are no longer dealing with a truth-functional operation (§17). Reichenbach calls operations of this kind *connective operations*, but the subtle and complex definitions he has proposed for them have not generally been accepted. As for the other type of inference, suppose that x is also an h, and that few h's are g; is it reasonable to conclude that x *is* a g, because it is an f, or that it is *not* a g, because it is an h? Unlike the contradiction which would vitiate a deductive inference, conflicting evidence is a standard problem for inductive inference.

John Stuart Mill propounded an inductive logic which enjoined us to look for what is common to all the instances of the phenomenon being investigated and for what is distinctive of such instances. These injunctions are applications to inductive inference of the conception of a cause as a necessary and sufficient condition for the occurrence of its effect. Because it is necessary, it will be found in all the instances of the effect, and because it is sufficient, it will be found only in such instances.

This reconstructed logic was not very useful, however. For one thing, it overlooked the difficulties in even recognizing, without guiding hypotheses, what are actually instances of a phenomenon; for instance, it is not easy to diagnose a disease of unknown etiology, because similar symptoms may characterize different diseases. It is even more difficult to isolate and identify the significant factors present in each instance, a difficulty glossed over by the logician's habit of describing instances as "containing the factors ABCDE"; often what turns out to be crucial is some factor hitherto not noticed. Most important of all, traditional inductive logic does not do justice to the circumstance that most of our inquiries are not directed to discovering "causes" but to disclosing stable patterns of change or interaction—as exemplified by the patterns formulated in the equations of chemistry and physics.

The most serious difficulty in providing a rational basis for inductive inference, known as the *problem of induction*, was first put forward by David Hume. The validation of inductive inference rests on some metalogical *principle of induction,* such as "The future resembles the past," "Like causes produce like effects," "Nature is uniform," "What is observed as an invariable succession of events holds true universally," and so on. Such a principle, Hume pointed out, is not analytic and so cannot be established by logic alone; in his terminology, it states not a relation of ideas but a matter of fact. Yet it cannot, without circularity, be established on the basis of experience, for all arguments based on experience presuppose the validity of inductive inference.

There is a type of inference which though called inductive is, in fact, a deduction; that is *induction by complete enumeration,* where the inference is from premises stating that each of a whole set of cases has a certain property to the conclusion that all of them do (there must also be a premise stating that the cases listed are all that there are). This is not the fallacy of composition (§18), mistaking what is true distributively for something true collectively, but only summing up in a single proposition what has already been said in several. It would be fallacious, however, to assume something to be true of a *whole* class only because it is true of *some* of its members. Giving this inference a resounding name, like "inductive generalization," does not make it valid.

The problem of induction is constituted by the circumstance that we seldom have knowledge about *all* the cases to which we mean our conclusion to apply. This is clearly true when we are making predictions on the basis of experience which, at best, reaches only up to the present moment. Wittgenstein endorses Hume: "The events of the future cannot be inferred from those of the present. Superstition is the belief in the causal nexus." The future is not as open to us as is the past—and neither is the past. Knowledge of the past is also inferential; memory is notoriously uncertain. Statements about the past are sometimes called "post-dictions" to emphasize their logical parallelism to statements about the future.

It is easy to be caught up here in circular arguments—arguing, for instance, that all science to date shows how successful inductive inferences are. Even though such inferences have worked in the past, the question is, By what right do we conclude that the future will resemble the past? It might be argued that the past was once a future, and does indeed resemble *its* past; to this, however, there is the rejoinder that what has been pointed out is a characteristic of past futures, while induction is based on the assumption that it will also be characteristic of future futures. Most logicians agree that Mill was guilty of a comparable circularity when he argued that induction is validated by the uniformity of nature to which all scientific generalizations point.

Hume took the position that the inductive inference is a habit; we are conditioned by a succession of concurrences of A with B to expect that when A occurs again it will be accompanied by B. The question is, however, whether it is a good habit, one not leading to thwarted expectations. Russell gives the example of a chicken which has acquired the habit of running up when it is called to be fed, until one day it responds to the call and has its head chopped off. Einstein has said in connection with the search for the laws of nature that God is subtle but He is not malicious. To which I suppose that Russell might retort, "Not so far!"

Many philosophers, from St. Augustine to Charles Peirce, have been struck by the consideration that man is more successful in acquiring knowledge, and acquires it more readily, than can easily be accounted for—without invoking, as Augustine did, the divine light of grace, or, as Peirce did, the natural light of reason. Other philosophers—like Nietzsche, Bergson, and Dewey—are able to give a more plausible explanation, in Darwinian terms. The human mind developed its powers in an evolutionary process which selects those patterns that prove useful for the survival of the organism. Induction does not have to be absolutely safe or else be absolutely without justification. Russell's chicken was, after all, better fed than slower learners among the brood, and though it died sooner, it may well have had more to crow about.

For logical theory, the problem remains. If induction is not valid, then, excluding purely logical truths, we have no knowledge. Hume's question is not how we come to discover so many laws of nature so quickly; Darwin might answer this one. The question is rather, what right we have to believe that there are any laws of nature at all, and that a given proposition is one of them. Kant's profound reply to Hume was that the mind is the lawgiver to nature—the validation of induction is provided by the mind's knowledge of the conditions of its own working. We could not conceive a nature which did not conform to laws.

Knowledge of our minds constitutes what Kant called "transcendental logic." He was speaking, not of one man's mind as distinct from another's, but of the human mind as such. It is often said that Kant set out to save science from the devastating consequences of Hume's skepticism. This formulation misses the point of Kant's argument. The fact is that we do have knowledge. It is not science that needs to be saved from philosophy, but philosophy that needs to be saved from the folly of refusing to acknowledge the existence of what it finds itself unable to explain. The proper question to ask, in Kant's view, is not whether knowledge is possible, but, rather, what follows from its existence. What follows—since our conception of "nature" is of an orderly, intelligible system of events—is that we must think of experience inductively or we cannot think of it at all. The validity of the principle of induction (Kant called it the principle of causality) is a precondition not only of truth but even of meaning.

Kant's argument provides, at most, a justification for conceiving the world in causal terms. It does not provide a justification for the inference, from limited observations, that *this* is the cause of the particular phenomenon being investigated. As Mead points out, "the scientist asks himself not whether the world will be rational and law-abiding but whether *this* observation will be confirmed and whether experiment will pronounce in favor of *this* hypothesis."

I do not know of any alternative to a pragmatic justification of induction. As Peirce puts it, the validity of inductive inference consists in the fact that "it pursues a method which, if duly persisted in, must in the very nature of things, lead to a result indefinitely approximating to the truth in the long run." The inductive principle might be formulated as stating that, with regard to every proposition, evidence will not remain indefinitely divided. If this principle is sound, then anyone relying on the evidence gathered so far—the essence of the inductive method—will sooner or later inevitably arrive at the truth. In Reichenbach's illustration, we do not know whether there are any fish in the stream; but it makes sense to fish if our hook and line will catch what fish there are—and none can be expected to jump into our hands.

Sooner or later we will arrive at the truth—if there be any truth. The extraordinary thing is that so often it is sooner than later. In this connection, scientists as well as philosophers speak of *simplicity*. "What is remarkable," Russell has said, "is not the reign of law, but the reign of simple laws. The principle of induction, as practically employed, is the principle that the simplest law which fits the known facts will also fit the facts to be discovered hereafter." "Nature is pleased with simplicity," Newton declares, "and affects not the pomp of superfluous causes." Similarly Einstein: "Our experience hitherto justifies us in believing that nature is the realization of the simplest conceivable mathematical ideas." And a contemporary Nobel laureate, Richard Feynman: "It is possible to know when you are right way ahead of checking all the consequences. You can recognize truth by its beauty and simplicity."

Two sorts of simplicity are often confused, as Reichenbach especially emphasized. They are easily distinguished in the abstract but hard to disentangle in concrete cases. One is *descriptive simplicity,* an attribute of how we describe things. When one formulation is descriptively simpler than another, the two have the same content and differ only in form. For instance, there is a difference only in descriptive simplicity between (1) If *q* is false then *p* is true, and moreover *r* is true, or else *r* is false, and if *p* is also false then *q* is true, and (2) *p* or *q*. The two numbered statements are logically equivalent; the second is descriptively simpler.

Inductive simplicity, on the other hand, is an attribute of what is being described, not of how we are describing it. A system consisting of a few components is simpler than one with more (paradoxically, if there are a great many, then simple relations might manifest themselves again, on a statistical basis). Linear functions are simpler than those involving quadratic or higher powers; integral values are simpler than irrational ones, and so on. It is a matter of inductive simplicity, for example, not of the descriptive simplicity of Newton's formulation, that the gravitational force between two bodies depends only on their masses and distances, and not also, say, on their composition or shape.

That the inductively simpler hypothesis enjoys a logical advantage is a significant consideration. Yet in spite of the praises of simplicity quoted above, Freud is also deserving of attention when he warns that the simplest explanation is not always the right one, and the truth is very often not simple. The scientific explanation of a phenomenon is often much more complicated, both inductively and descriptively, than the popular account. Freud is far from alone in noting that "the mass of mankind require only a single reason to serve as an explanation, they are not grateful to science for its intricacies, and they like to have simple answers given to their questions and to feel that their problems are settled once and for all."

Simplism may be defined as responding to the psychological appeal of a simple explanation. Simplism is especially frequent where human interests are deeply engaged—in medicine and religion, morals and politics. We look for panaceas and magic keys, vulgarizing Freud to a bedroom theory of history and Marx to economic determinism. Scientific idioms may be as vulnerable to simplism as colloquialisms; for instance, there is not much to choose between "Hatred can only be conquered by love" and "No twisted behavior without somewhere a twisted molecule."

To say of a hypothesis that "the situation is more complicated than that" is to say nothing. There is too much truth in it; it applies everywhere, and so is pointless. Perhaps the last word on the matter is Whitehead's: seek simplicity—and distrust it!

23. Fallacies of Inference

Simplism belongs to a broad class of fallacies—the fallacies of inductive inference. These may be compared with the fallacies of argument, like the appeal to the gallery (§14), and the fallacies of proof, like affirming the consequent (§17). The classification of fallacies is, to a considerable degree, an arbitrary one.

Simplism is one of a whole nest of fallacies which constitute *block thinking.* Such thinking corresponds to the tactics of the slugger rather than the boxer, forgoing finesse in favor of the sheer sweep and force of its ideas. It has no patience with subtleties, and no power of fine discriminations. For instance, what is called "pushing an idea to its logical conclusion" often consists in *illogically* extending it to cases and conditions to which it was never meant to apply. The justification of demands for equal employment and educational opportunity does not rest on a claim of equality in *every* capacity. Valid inductive inferences lead to qualified conclusions—something is affirmed to be true under certain conditions, in certain respects, to a certain degree. It is such qualifications that are missing in block thinking.

The mistake consists in overlooking the principle that abstract ideas make sense only with reference to concrete contexts of application; shifts in context or unnoticed features of a fixed context may easily invalidate an inference. Water is, to be sure, a liquid consisting of hydrogen and oxygen; but it may exist as a vapor or crystal as well, and particular waters contain other substances. Often, as with the materials which serve as transistors, it is precisely the "impurities" which are responsible for the characteristic properties. Romania, Poland, Yugoslavia, Russia, and China are all "Communist countries"; yet differences among them are considerable and significant, and subject to sudden as well as secular change. The same is true of the many Arab countries. A "mother" is identifiably the same person throughout her lifetime; yet even without regard to changes in her habits or behavior in the course of her life, there are enormous differences in what she signifies for the child and for the mature offspring. "Fixation"—remaining at an earlier stage of maturation—reveals block thinking, but it would be another fallacy to suppose that such thinking is the cause, rather than the effect, of the psychopathology.

A common type of block thinking in our age of extremism is the *false dilemma,* thinking which limits choices to one extreme or the other. It is black and white thinking with no place for shades of gray, the position that there are no innocent bystanders, and whoever is not with us is against us. But the alternatives offered might not be exclusive, so that we can choose both in some measure; or they might not be exhaustive, so that we are free to choose neither. "Red *or* dead," "peace *or* territories," "freedom *or* security" are among the false dilemmas on which many in our time have been impaled. I do not mean to say that logic has no place for decisive and even extreme action. No induction warrants pulling a tooth or a trigger only halfway. Yet even when we shoot, it need not be in a total war which disregards possibilities for the peace to come, as well as the most elementary human decencies.

Complex systems—like an organism, a personality, or a state—often provide occasion for other sorts of block thinking. One is the *reductive fallacy*—the "nothing but" position—and the other, its counterpart, is the *seductive fallacy* (so called, I think, by Herbert Feigl)—the "mysterious something more" position. Both engage in block thinking about wholes and parts, differing only in whether the existence of special sorts of parts is to be acknowledged—entities like a life-force, a soul, a national destiny. Ernest Nagel and others have distinguished many different senses of "whole" and "part," and talk about whether one is equal to the "sum" of the other is pointless if the distinctions are not carefully observed.

Learning is a painful experience because we learn from mistakes, which are painful, and because in learning we give up something of ourselves, some old way of belief or action. Thinking is unpleasant not because it demands effort and concentration (so does love) but because our thoughts come trailing wisps of anxiety—we might learn something. It is not surprising that alternatives to taking thought are attractive, especially if they present themselves not as thoughtlessness but as conclusions of profound and proven reflections. The fallacy embedded in this pattern may be called *sloganizing.*

"The exception proves the rule," to be sure; but "proves" here has the sense of testing, not of establishing. A rule does not become more acceptable for having been shown *not* to apply; what the exception establishes is that the rule is not universally true. Again, an idea may be "all right in theory though it won't work in practice," if it states a conditional truth whose conditions are not then and there satisfied. But a theory which just isn't workable is *not* all right, except as a game or exercise; it is not what a theory is meant to be: an account of some feature of reality. "The greatest good for the greatest number" may be devoutly to be wished, but it is very rarely usable as a guide to choice. This is because the greater good almost always, in problematic situations, benefits the lesser number. (A function of two arguments seldom has a value which simultaneously maximizes both variables.) Problems of educational philosophy, tax policy, or social welfare are not solved by sloganizing.

Sometimes, in place of slogans, we protect ourselves from learning by encasing thought in a *closed system,* a set of ideas which provides a place beforehand for conflicting evidence, and which is accompanied by interpretations guaranteeing that the conflict is always removed. In extreme cases, the insulation from reality is so complete as to constitute a psychosis, as with the delusional systems of paranoia. In less extreme forms, patterns range from harmless heresies on the barest fringe of lunacy (Bacon wrote the works of Shakespeare) to the deadly monomanias of the rabid anti-Semite or the self-styled national liberationist. Each must judge for himself how much psychopathology is involved in the closed systems which perceive one set of political policies as invariably peace-loving and aiming at the freedom of oppressed peoples, while another set is invariably the expression of a damnable self-interest, aiming at the perpetuation of imperialism and colonialism.

There is a special type of closed system characteristic of our age of symbolism, stemming from the circumstance that symbols can not only bring us into more effective contact with reality but can also insulate us from reality, offering instead a fantasy world. The stereotype of the scholar shut off from life by his books may occasionally have substance; but a great many people are undeniably shut off from the real world by the pictures of it put before us in the mass media. A lie repeated often enough begins to acquire the accents of truth, and it is sure to be believed if it is a big enough lie to contain what Pooh-Bah called "corroborative detail, intended to give artistic verisimilitude to an otherwise bald and unconvincing narrative."

At a time when the world was being flooded with Nazi propaganda, an American magazine published a sensational article disclosing in a most convincingly circumstantial account that the great wealth of the Astor family was based on an ancestor's having discovered and seized the treasure of the pirate Captain Kidd. In the last paragraph of the article it was revealed to be a hoax, intended to make readers more skeptical in the future. Give a dog a bad name and he'll soon be hanged, the proverb runs. Nowadays, when someone is called an aggressor, you may be sure he is about to be attacked.

A *prejudice* is one component of a closed system, resisting both evidence and argument which might lead to significant change in the system. Prejudice is almost as readily found in the scientific academy as in the councils of other bodies with less claim than science to knowledge validated by reason. Galileo's treatment by the Church is better known but no more prejudicial than his treatment by his scientific colleagues. In a letter to Kepler, Galileo supposedly wrote, "Oh, my dear Kepler, how I wish that we could have one hearty laugh together! Here, at Padua, is the principal professor of philosophy whom I have repeatedly and urgently requested to look at the moon and planets through my glass, which he pertinaciously refuses to do. Why are you not here? What shouts of laughter we should have at this glorious folly! And to hear the professor of philosophy at Pisa, laboring before the grand duke with logical arguments, as if with magical incantations, to charm the new planets out of the sky."

Among the factors making for closed systems of thought is the *bandwagon effect,* what the social psychologist Irving Janis has called "groupthink." It is not only the friends of my friend (or his enemies) that I make my own; I am likely also to take over his opinions and attitudes. This is especially likely if he is perceived as a member of a significant group with which I also identify, for then group norms come into play.

The sheer weight of numbers may also make itself felt. Logic cannot countenance the jury system as anything other than a way of reflecting norms of the community; even in unanimity twelve good men and true can easily be mistaken in their conclusions. There are experiments which suggest that simple perception (for instance, which of two lines is seen as longer) may be affected by what others report they perceive. Even if it is not what we see but only what we say we see that is subject to the bandwagon effect, logic must take this factor into account; the communication of evidence is essential to the process of validation in the scientific community.

There is not much cynicism in Hobbes' remark that if national interests were as much involved in the foundations of geometry as they are in matters of politics and economics, men today would be hotly debating whether two points determine a straight line, and perhaps even appealing to force to settle the issue. Not a geometer in the world would risk putting the matter to a vote in the United Nations. In addition to group interests, there are personal interests to consider as well—what Bacon called the "idols of the cave" (§14). Darwin tells us that he kept a special notebook in which to record evidence against his theory, knowing very well that he would have no trouble in afterwards locating the favorable data.

The replacement of well-grounded belief by groundless rumor, though not strictly a problem for the theory of knowledge, is relevant here as illustrating the workings in the inductive process of personal and group interests. Rumors flourish in situations which are both important and indeterminate—unstructured or uncertain. Intense involvement in an ambiguous situation gives full play to wishful (and fearful) thinking.

There is a widespread doctrine in which reason and emotion are conceived as antithetical. Plato is obviously right when he says in the *Timaeus* that "a man who is in great joy or in great pain, in his unseasonable eagerness to attain the one and to avoid the other, is not able to see or to hear anything rightly; but he is mad, and is at the time utterly incapable of any participation in reason." The fact that strong emotion can interfere with reason scarcely provides justification, however, for the dualism which sees feelings as irrational or, at best, nonrational, and reason as unfeeling and disinterested.

The whole history of science shows it to be very different from the impersonal, dispassionate pursuit that this perspective pictures it to be. Feelings have been engaged in the cause of free inquiry as well as on behalf of dogma, and passions have been aroused by the truth as well as by error. Conversely, detachment has often meant no more than a readiness to adhere to received opinion. Many studies of the "independent voter" have shown that, far from being more rational, with thought processes free from the distortions of partisanship, he is very likely to be only more ignorant and uncaring. It is not feeling, as such, which confounds thought but only certain patterns of emotional involvement. A feeling, interest, or attitude which makes for fallacious thinking I call a *bias.* To be free from bias does not require that we abandon concern for everything else that matters.

Well known to the working scientist is the so-called *personal equation,* which is not an equation at all but a factor at work in observation and even in calculation. What we see is affected by our eyesight and by what we most want or fear to see. Percival Lowell saw canals on Mars which other astronomers, who did not share his conviction of intelligent life there, could not make out. Arithmetical errors in tax returns much oftener favor the taxpayer than the government, although there is no question of fraud. Noteworthy in this connection are what Thorstein Veblen called *trained incapacities,* the shortcomings from which we suffer as the price paid for acquired skills. We find it hard to hear the difference between speech sounds not contrastive in our own language, like "l" and "r" in Japanese. For the stage magician, children are the most difficult audience because they have not yet learned what they should look at, so that he cannot readily misdirect their attention.

Bias and prejudice come together in the formation of *stereotypes,* which assign to members of a class attributes grounded more in our own attitudes to the class than in evidence warranting the attribution. Quite familiar in our time are the stereotypes of racial, national, and ethnic identifications, but many other stereotypes also play a part in our thinking. Thinking is impossible without guiding hypotheses; we approach every situation with a whole network of assumptions. The fallacy does not lie in making an assumption, but in treating it as an established conclusion. Stereotyping might be regarded as reliance on unchecked assumptions. A common instance of such reliance stems from confusing a particular formulation of a *problem* with the *problematic situation* to which the formulation is directed. The growth of knowledge sometimes depends less on finding answers to our questions than on finding better questions which do not rest on the unwarranted assumptions we have been making.

Stereotypes assume that all members of a given class have a certain property. In addition to the fallacy involved in treating the assumption as unquestionably true, the fallacy of *hasty generalization* is also likely to be involved. One or two members of the class may show the property, from which we then conclude that all members of the class have it. How long one must wait before a generalization is no longer hasty is a question to which there is no generally appropriate answer; it depends on the homogeneity of the class. Stereotyping characteristically assumes too much homogeneity.

A type of inference which often reveals bias, yet has a valid foundation, is that which draws a conclusion about the truth of a proposition from the premise that the proposition was put forward by a particular person or group. This is called the *genetic fallacy.* To the question, "Can anything good come out of Nazareth?" the reply, "Come and see," was very much to the point.

The truth or falsehood of a proposition can be determined only by empirical test, or by inference from other propositions already tested empirically. It can not be determined by assessments, on whatever basis, of the people who believe or disbelieve it. When it comes to matters of fact, it is not only politics that makes strange bedfellows. Much of the truth that I cherish is acknowledged also by fools and knaves; it would be both foolish and wicked to abandon the truth for that reason. Yet, I have often been moved to reexamine a conviction when I learned of someone who affirmed or disputed it; there are cities not far from Nazareth which I have reason to view as dubious sources of truth. There is nothing unreasonable, after all, in giving credence to a proposition found in the encyclopedia, and viewing with skepticism the contents of a commercial or political handout.

There is a *genetic method* which seeks to understand and explain a phenomenon by looking to its origins and development. This method has proved useful not only in history but also in fields as diverse as astronomy, anatomy, linguistics, and psychiatry. The method can also be applied to knowledge itself. Genetic considerations are fallacious only when we assume that we already know what must be the outcome of that genesis.

There is an advantage to seeing things in historical perspective, as the genetic method requires: it is that we are not so easily tempted to suppose that the present created the past instead of the other way around. Mistaking an effect for a cause is called the fallacy of *false cause.* It often plays a part in closed systems of thought, rationalizing behavior as justified by a situation created by the behavior. The racist denies opportunities, then defends the denial by pointing to failings produced by that denial. A country is attacked for taking up a position made necessary for its defense by a succession of just such attacks. A man complains of a lack of friends, which is largely the result of his incessant complaints. I am not saying that in these examples the behavior is produced by the fallacy—that might itself be an instance of false cause—but that the fallacy is likely to be committed in the course of trying to justify the behavior.

Perhaps the best known of the fallacies of inference is one for which the label "false cause" might be more appropriate than the fallacy it actually names. This is the inference that because A follows B, A was caused by B: *post hoc, ergo propter hoc.* Political administrations are usually blamed or praised for whatever happens during their tenures of office, even if what happens is not the consequence of any distinctive policies or actions of the administration. On the other hand, beliefs in causal connections not yet understood may be prejudicially dismissed as instances of the *post hoc* fallacy: a nineteenth-century textbook of logic used, as an example of this fallacy, the belief by "natives" that an epidemic was caused by the white man's ship which had docked a few days before.

The appeal of the *post hoc* fallacy has been effectively described by the anthropologist James Frazer in his classic *The Golden Bough:*

The practical savage, with his conservative instincts, might well turn a deaf ear to the subtleties of the theoretical doubter, the philosophic radical, who presumed to hint that sunrise and spring might not, after all, be direct consequences of the punctual performance of certain daily or yearly ceremonies, and that the sun might perhaps continue to rise and trees to blossom though the ceremonies were occasionally intermitted, or even discontinued altogether. These sceptical doubts would naturally be repelled by the other with scorn and indignation as airy reveries subversive of the faith and manifestly contradicted by experience. "Can anything be plainer," he might say, "than that I light my twopenny candle on earth and that the sun then kindles his great fire in heaven? I should be glad to know whether, when I have put on my green robe in spring, the trees do not afterwards do the same? These are facts patent to everybody, and on them I take my stand. I am a plain practical man, not one of your theorists and splitters of hairs and choppers on logic. Theories and speculation and all that may be very well in their way, and I have not the least objection to your indulging in them, provided, of course, you do not put them in practice. But give me leave to stick to facts; then I know where I am." The fallacy of this reasoning is obvious to us, because it happens to deal with facts about which we have long made up our minds. But let an argument of precisely the same caliber be applied to matters which are still under debate, and it may be questioned whether a British audience would not applaud it as sound, and esteem the speaker who used it a safe man—not brilliant or showy, perhaps, but thoroughly sensible and hard-headed. If such reasonings could pass muster among ourselves, need we wonder that they long escaped detection by the savage?

To all this I have a simple counter-question: Who, indeed, are the savages?

24. Subjectivist Madness

Years ago I was called upon to provide evidence quickly about a naturalization proceeding which had taken place a long time earlier and far away. I was able to establish contact with the court clerk where the matter had been handled, and he attested to the facts over the long-distance telephone. But bureaucratic practice demanded written materials, though these would be third-hand and easily forged, instead of the direct, inimitable, but oral testimony. The operative criterion seems to have been that expressed in the last chapter of Job: "I had heard of You by the hearing of the ear, but now my eye sees You, wherefore I abhor my words and repent." Job was contrasting a faith grounded in personal experience with one resting only on tradition and hearsay; but sight is not necessarily better than sound as a basis for rational belief. More information is conveyed, in individual instances and in the aggregate, by sight than by any of the other senses; yet touch, which conveys least of all, is the conventional mark of something "real."

The trouble is that for knowledge of truths other than those of pure mathematics and logic we have no alternative, at bottom, than to rely on the evidence of the senses; but the senses are notorious deceivers. The birth of philosophy may owe as much to simple optical illusions as to the awesome and wondrous spectacle of the night sky. How can a straight stick appear bent in water? If we cannot believe what we see there, by what right do we believe anything else to which our eyes testify? Among the most persistent problems of philosophy is that called the *problem of error*. It can be formulated, initially, as a dilemma: either the senses cannot be relied upon, in which case the world is somehow illusory and the claim to knowledge an empty pretension; or else the world really is what our senses reveal it to be, in which case error becomes inexplicable, if not downright impossible.

The unanalyzed notion that the senses put us into direct contact with reality except when they are "interfered with" is called *naive realism.* What constitutes an interference is the crucial question. The senses require subtle and complex instrumentalities and media: we do not see in the dark or hear through a vacuum. By what right do we countenance and even cultivate some of these intermediates and withhold certification from others? The eye contains a lens and a liquid, both common sources of optical error; but do these interfere with vision or, on the contrary, make it possible?

Critical or *representative realism* holds that the senses never do put us in touch with the world as it is but only provide us with representatives of the real world whose credentials must constantly be scrutinized if we are to trust them. Many do prove trustworthy, but they remain only representatives of the world to be known, and not themselves the objects of knowledge; a certified check can be cashed almost anywhere, but it is not to be confused with the things it can buy.

This has been the position taken by many philosophers, from the Greek atomists down to our own day. Whether things are sweet or bitter, hot or cold, colored this way or that is a matter of how we experience them; in truth, said Democritus, there are only atoms and the void. In the thought of Galileo and his successors, an enormously influential and, to my mind, grossly misleading distinction came to the fore between the so-called *primary qualities,* like mass and state of motion, which belong to bodies in themselves, and the *secondary qualities,* like color, which depend on how we see them. John Locke, perhaps the most representative of the representative realists, took the position that we know of things only the effects they produce in us, by virtue of unknowable "powers" inherent in the things themselves. A similar view has persisted down to the present century, espoused by such philosophers as George Santayana. Its basic weakness is the negative outcome already explicit in Democritus: "In truth we know nothing, for truth lies in the depth." Our experience is confined to the surfaces of things, and the knowledge it provides is, therefore, only superficial.

To the view that things only *seem* to be what our knowledge discloses of them, other philosophers objected, with Hamlet: "Seems, madam! Nay, it is; I know not 'seems.'" The senses put us in touch with things themselves, not with surrogates. What naïve realism does not realize is that what we call "things" consist of the very stuff of sense experience; they are not composed of some contrasting physical substance as we unthinkingly suppose them to be. This position is called *new realism,* its best-known exponents being G. E. Moore and Bertrand Russell. Experience provides us with two sorts of materials of knowledge, which Russell calls *hard data* and *soft data.* The difference between them is a matter of their capacity to withstand subsequent critical reflection and the impact of additional data. We interpret the data of experience, and it is in the course of interpretation that errors creep in. The hard data are just what they are. When I first traveled through desert country I was eager for my first glimpse of a mirage and at last saw what I took to be one. "Sorry!" said my friend, "that's not a real mirage; it's a lake." The appearance common to both was a hard datum, but my judgment was softened by inexperience.

In all these philosophies, what is directly known is something in which the knower is intimately involved. In Locke's terminology, what we know are "ideas"; Hume called them "impressions"; throughout the nineteenth century they were commonly labeled "sensations"; the twentieth-century term is *sense-data.* The chief issue dividing the theories in which these locutions are embedded is whether sense-data somehow represent things or rather constitute them.

Sensationalism, as this general standpoint is also known, suffers from several serious shortcomings. For one thing, the doctrine does not do justice to the fact that it is not the senses that know something, but we who know by way of the senses. "It would surely be strange," as Socrates said long ago, in Plato's *Theatetus,* "that there should be a number of senses ensconced inside us, like the warriors in the Trojan horse, and all these things should not converge and meet in some single nature—a mind, or whatever it is to be called—with which we perceive all the objects of perception through the senses as instruments." For Kant, the unification of experience necessary to knowledge can only be provided by this mind; he gave it the forbidding name, "the transcendental unity of apperception." For William James, experience itself provides, if not unity, at least strands of connection. Sensationalism need not be atomistic; relations among things are as directly given as things themselves. The connections of experiences with one another are themselves matters of experience.

Even if not atomistic, sensationalism must meet another objection. Sensationalism holds that the hard data of experience are sensations, which are interpreted as perceptions. The objection is that sensations are not the original elements of experience, but abstractions or inferences from experience, constructions after-the-fact out of experience. Considerable effort and some skill is required to free experience from the *funded meanings* with which the objects of experience are imbued as a result of a lifetime of learning. Only the proofreader sees the shapes of the letters; the rest of us *read* the letters. What we read depends on the shapes, to be sure; the fact remains that it is precisely *not* those shapes which are matters of direct experience. The same is true of the sounds of speech. I remember a family gathering in which several languages were bandied about, there being, in this era of immigrants and refugees, no one language in which we were all at home. Someone asked, "I didn't quite understand you; would you translate that, please?" To which the reply was, "Certainly! What language did I say it in?"

In knowing, we experience things, not sense-data. To hold otherwise is to do violence either to familiar facts or to the norms of ordinary usage.

This line of thinking is characteristic of the contemporary approach to the theory of knowledge, as it often characterized the approach of the Greeks. In the same passage from which I quoted a moment ago, Socrates says, "To use words and phrases in an easygoing way without scrutinizing them too curiously is not, in general, a mark of ill-breeding; on the contrary, there is something low bred in being too precise. But sometimes there is no help for it."

Transitive epistemic verbs, of which "to know" is the prototype, take as their grammatical objects words naming things rather than sense-data. God spoke to Moses face to face, as a man speaks to his friend. The implied contrast between this encounter and the religious experience of ordinary men is intelligible; but how are we to understand the claim that we do not really see our friends face to face but are confronted only with their appearances? I might loosely say I saw my friend when I saw only a photograph or a television image. But this usage is loose precisely in contrast with the strict sense of seeing him in the flesh. If what I see then is but another image, there is no contrast to be drawn, and seeing him, rather than some manifestation of him, has lost its meaning.

Sensationalism of whatever sort, whether associated with critical or new realism, incorporates the defining principle of idealism (in one of the many senses of the word, the epistemological), formulated in what might be labeled the *idealist axiom:* we know ourselves better than, and logically prior to, our knowledge of other people and things. The idealist's position is that whatever my sensations are of, they are *my* sensations. What is sure is only that there must be something about them peculiarly and distinctively mine; all else is unsure, inferential, and, perhaps, altogether unknowable. All that I know must be built on premises embodying the hard data of my own experience. From that experience I must move, if I can, to the world outside me—a world that may be known to others, but if it is, they are knowers forever excluded from rightful access to my own premises. This supposed situation is called the *egocentric predicament.*

Sensations are being viewed as ineluctably private. You cannot know what I am experiencing unless you are not only in my place but we are literally of one mind. In that case you and I are no longer two; we have not thereby escaped the egocentric predicament, but only negated an ego. Widely quoted in this connection is Chuang-tzu's story of the two philosophers watching the goldfish in a pool. "How pleasant," said the first, "is the life of fishes besporting themselves in the limpid water." "But," asked the other, "how can you, not being a fish, know wherein lies the pleasure of fishes?" To which the first rejoined, "And how can you, not being I, know wherein lies the possibility of my knowing?"

The egocentric predicament is not just a matter of our not being able to reach, save by dubious inference, into another's mind; the question is whether we can get outside our own minds at all. I experience certain sensations and am accustomed to supposing, if I think of the matter at all, that I experience them because something outside me is causing them. But if everything outside me ceased to exist, so long as my sensations remained the same I would never know it. How, then, can I prove that there *is* something outside the domain of my sensations? This problem is traditionally called the *problem of the external world,* which much exercised Hume and his modern followers. To argue that something external must be causing my sensations is simply to beg the question, for the whole theory of causation invoked in the argument, as well as the specific causal connections to which it has reference, from the beginning have been and remain still within the compass of my sensations. Of course, my sensations of light and warmth are produced by the fire; but what reasons can I give for the belief that the fire is something more than another complex of sense-data?

The air of unreality in all this attains to its ultimate in the view that in fact nothing external does exist, save in a sense definable by reference to my own sensations: that the problem of the external world is insoluble simply because there is no such world; in short, that only I exist. This view is called *solipsism.* What solipsism means is correct, Wittgenstein held; only what it says is misleading. For the "I" which embraces the whole of existence "does not belong to the world, but it is a limit of the world." It is what Kant called "the transcendental ego"—not the self known to you and me, which is a part of experience, but a featureless, unknowable presupposition of experience.

A theory of knowledge in which the world is first reduced to a shadow play projected on the screen of the mind, then the screen folded up and put away, such a theory, to my mind (if I may still say so), is nothing less than grotesque. I have no doubt that if there were a society of solipsists, each of its members would aspire to be its president and see nothing absurd in the aspiration. As with the supposed task of saving science from philosophical skepticism (§22), I do not see that the external world is problematic in any wholesale fashion. It is not we who are in an egocentric predicament; the predicament is one into which a philosophy falls when it makes nonsense of its own questions. If I did not sometimes know what you are experiencing, it is doubtful that I would ever know what is happening to me; it is virtually certain that I would not be able to *say* what I am experiencing, for the words are not and never have been solely my own. I would never have learned them at all, but for what I shared with others and they with me.

There is a Zen story of one who came to a *roshi* (teacher) and propounded the following problem: A man put a small gosling into a jar and fed it daily, till it grew too large to be taken through the mouth of the jar; how is he to get it out, without killing the goose or breaking the jar? When the visitor had finished his statement the *roshi* called out, "Sir!" "Yes, *roshi!*" came the prompt reply. "There!" said the *roshi,* "it's out!" In Jewish tradition much the same point is conveyed in the narrative of Abraham. God called, "Abraham, Abraham!" and he answered, "Here I am!" As Martin Buber put it, in every dialogue, in every encounter with the other, we reach out beyond the self, and only then give substance to our own experience.

The most subtle and penetrating defense of sensationalism is that of Bishop George Berkeley. He argued that the difference between primary and secondary qualities makes no difference to their dependency on the process of perception. Accordingly, he arrived at the conclusion expressed in his famous formula, to be is to be perceived. To keep things from popping in and out of existence as we turn our backs on them, the Bishop invoked their continuous presentation to the mind of God (presumably in some extrasensory fashion). His philosophy is memorably summed up in a pair of limericks of (to me, at least) unknown authorship:

There once was a man who said, "God
Must think it exceedingly odd
To find that this tree
Continues to be
When there's no one about in the quad."

The answer:

Dear Sir:
Your astonishment's odd.
I *am always about in the quad.*
That's why this tree
Will continue to be
Since perceived by,
Yours faithfully,
God.

Solipsism, even if it allows for the existence of God as well as self, is a philosophical curiosity, not to say an aberration. The subjectivism of which it is the ultimate expression is rampant in the world today. "To believe your own thought, to believe that what is true for you in your private heart is true for all men—that is genius." Thus Emerson, a century ago. If "true for you" means true *about* you, it is indeed a work of genius to plumb the depths of your own being till you have reached the common humanity you share with all men. But if "true for you" means only, *in your opinion,* to suppose what you believe must be believed by all, that is not genius, it is madness, the subjectivist madness which Russell has said is characteristic of modern thought.

The self-reliance Emerson was advocating is also a matter of intellectual integrity. To think for myself is, in a sense, a redundancy; if, instead, I simply takes over *your* thought, I am not thinking at all. " 'Tis with our judgments as our watches," said Alexander Pope; "none go just alike, yet each believes his own." Of course, or there would not be much point in carrying a watch; but one need not be deluded into mistaking if for the Naval Observatory chronometer. There is more bite in the opening lines of Descartes' *Discourse on Method:* "Good sense is of all things in the world the most equally distributed, for everybody thinks himself so abundantly provided with it that even those most difficult to please in all other matters do not commonly desire more of it than they already possess." The extraordinary thing is that Descartes did not mean to be cynical; he held all men to be equal in their capacity for rational thought, differing only in how well they apply their capacities. But to assess the application is itself a matter of judgment. The subjectivist does not concede the weight of any judgment but his own, and *that* he takes to be self-validating.

There is a widespread form of subjectivism in which its connection with sensationalism is particularly apparent. It is the position embodied in what I call the *axiom of direct experience:* that direct experience of a subject matter is both a necessary and a sufficient condition for knowledge of it. As black studies programs, for example, were introduced, it was taken for granted that they must be directed by blacks—not because, for obvious reasons, blacks were much more likely to have cultivated an interest in the subject but because others would find it impossible to grasp "the black experience." Similarly, it was taken for granted that only ghetto dwellers are competent to handle urban studies, only women can speak authoritatively on problems of women's liberation, and so on. Moreover, it was commonly urged that academic qualifications to deal with such matters are of no more than academic importance, in the pejorative sense, and that direct experience more than makes up for deficiencies of book learning.

There may be good reasons, as a matter of social policy, for such selections of candidates; I repudiate not necessarily the policies but their rationalization by a subjectivist theory of knowledge. It might be desirable to have a teen-ager appointed to a municipal board of education—what an educational experience for him, and what a stimulus to the interest of other youths in the work of the board! But it is absurd to pretend that he would bring to the board "the young experience," or a point of view otherwise inaccessible to them. Even a crude poll would probably provide more reliable data than could be brought by a single member representative only in age.

Direct experience may provide a special motivation and an opportunity for learning. But these alone are grossly insufficient for knowledge; good intentions must be guided into effective channels, and opportunities must be properly exploited. We must *learn* to make observations, to reflect on our experience, analyze it, measure, test, experiment, theorize, and much else. All of us, all of our lives, have had direct experience of moving and being moved by the forces of mechanics and gravitation; but it takes more than an apple to make a Newton.

Direct experience is not sufficient for knowledge, unless the word is understood only as a synonym for experience; nor is direct experience even necessary: male physicians can become expert in both the theory and practice of obstetrics, and psychiatrists—joking aside—need not be mad, nor judges criminal. The axiom of direct experience negates the whole of human culture. Culture consists of all that is learned on a basis *other* than direct experience—the repository, in symbols and practices, of all that the group makes available which not only supplements but shapes, informs, and suffuses the experience of every member of the group.

Subjectivism infects more than knowledge; it reaches out into every domain of value. "The mind is its own place, and in itself can make a heaven of hell, a hell of heaven." This is Milton's Satan speaking, the prince of lies and falsehood. Truth does not rest on him or on any mind but on the realities of God's world. In Peter Weiss's *Persecution and Assassination of Jean-Paul Marat,* the Marquis de Sade declares,

The only truths we can point to
are the ever-changing truths of our own experience
I do not know if I am hangman or victim.

. . . .

You swim all huddled up
alone with your ideas about the world
which no longer fit the world outside
And why should you care about the world outside
For me the only reality is imagination
the world inside myself

The scene is very properly laid in a madhouse. It is enough of a reason to care about the world outside in order to know who the hangman is and who the victim, and perhaps to learn so to change the world and our behavior as no longer to have either hangmen or victims. For that we must recognize, first of all, the world of difference between imagination and reality.

The root error of subjectivism lies in this assumption that the movement of knowledge is from the self to the world outside. Because subjectivism remains locked within the self, it concludes that the only reality is the imagination. Instead, knowledge moves from a world in which both self and not-self have a place, although the place is not always clearly delimited, to a wider world less unsettled and obscure. Knowing is not a relation between a subject and an object; the difference between what is subjective and what is objective is localized in what is known.

The words "objective" and "subjective" once had a meaning almost exactly the opposite of their present sense. The "subjective" was what pertains to a subject, as that in which attributes inhere, while the "objective" was something which exists only as an object of our consciousness, not in itself but only as presented to the mind. By the time of Kant, perhaps coinciding with a shift from religious to secular contexts of application, the terms had acquired substantially their contemporary sense. That is objective which is *independent* of its presentation to a knowing mind. The objective is not independent of thought, because of considerations advanced by Kant and the pragmatists; it is independent only in the sense that thinking so does not make it so. In Freudian terms, the reality principle governs precisely the domain which the pleasure principle finds unconquerable. The objective world consists of all that does not heed the human incantation "Let there be!"

The objective is also the *intersubjective:* "Do you see what I see?" is a reasonable test. That experiences are in their nature subjective is a gratuitous assumption. They may well be *private,* in the distinctive sense G. H.

Mead analyzed—individually observed and directly observable only by the individual. But indirect validation is available for what is private, while what is subjective is revealed to everyone to be without valid foundation. It was a startling and instructive experience to be fitted with new glasses without being asked what I saw through the various lenses, but having the oculist examine my eyeball for himself.

The objective, finally, is *regular,* constant, and reliable in its relations with other components of experience. "Although the whole of this life were said to be nothing but a dream," Leibniz wrote, "and the visible world nothing but a phantasm, I should call this dream or phantasm real enough if, using reason well, we were never deceived by it." This is also the position of Kant. To the question, "How can I tell whether I am awake?" a good workable answer is, "If you have any doubt, you're dreaming." Dreams in which we entertain the question are not uncommon, and we may answer it either way. Fundamentally, it must be recognized that no specific content can differentiate the reality from a dream, for whatever we can experience we can also dream we are experiencing. The objective world is marked by its regularity, its intersubjectivity, its independence. How it comes about that these several criteria coincide, I would not dream of trying to explain here.

25. Empiricism

The name "epistemology" for the branch of philosophy dealing with knowledge has been current for only about a hundred years. Because in this period epistemology has been so much occupied with the difficulties in which it has been involved by sensationalism, I propose to restrict the name to sensationalist views, in an admittedly pejorative usage. The literature of sensationalism, it has been remarked, reads like sensational literature. There is "the adventure of the double cross": if the eyeball is pressed, two images are seen, one of which seems to be an image of the reality, while the other, only of an appearance; but if the untouched eye is closed, it is the appearance which is seen as real. How can we interchange appearance and reality with the touch of a finger or the flick of an eye? There is "the case of the speckled hen": although we see that the hen is speckled, we do not see any definite number of speckles. How can we have a sense-datum of speckles without some determinate number of them? There is the difficulty known as "the missing shade of blue": seeing shades adjoining it in hue we can tell what is missing. How can we know the quality of a sense-datum we have never had?

Perception undoubtedly confronts us with many problems; the solution of problems characteristically frees us from many puzzles. I am inclined to the opinion that the above difficulties are not substantive problems but puzzles, traceable to errors of understanding what we know or to the sort of confused questions which with the growth of knowledge are not answered but are no longer asked.

The *theory of knowledge* (and the adjective "epistemic") may be distinguished from "epistemology" in the narrow sense (and the adjective "epistemological"). The theory of knowledge views knowledge in its biological, psychological, and social context. Rather than dealing with questions which are distinguished as "philosophical"—that is, of no possible significance outside the profession—it asks what happens in the natural process called "knowing," differing from the sciences which study that process, if at all, only in the depth and breadth of its concerns. Here, as in so many other fields, philosophy may be the speculative, prescientific stage of what afterwards comes to be dealt with in more controlled and well-grounded inquiry.

Knowing how to do something is fundamentally different from *knowing that* something or other is true. In the former sense, knowledge is a skill, capacity, or ability. When we know that something is true we may be able to do things which otherwise would not have been possible. This ability is a consequence of our knowledge; it is not what the knowing consists in. Sometimes we speak of knowing *how* something happens when we have knowledge *that* the conditions or patterns of its occurrence are such and such. The distinction concerns knowing how to do something, not knowing how it is done, which is a species of knowledge in the other sense. How skills are acquired, how knowledge-that contributes to knowing-how, and conversely, are questions deserving more attention than the theory of knowledge has given them so far.

Knowing-that is also distinguished from another kind of knowing, usually called being *acquainted* with something. This distinction has been especially emphasized by William James and Bertrand Russell, who uses the expressions "knowledge by description" and "knowledge by acquaintance." The former kind of knowledge is indirect, mediated by words or concepts; the latter is direct, involving immediate experience. I may know where you live in the sense of having an address, knowing a location in some suitable coordinate system; or I may know it in the sense of being able to get there, even though I cannot say where it is. The essence of empiricism is the insistence on the fundamental role played by acquaintance in all knowledge of matters of fact.

Not every experience is cognitive; experience is much else besides an occasion for knowing. When I eat sugar I taste its sweetness; thereby I am made acquainted with the taste. The experience is also something enjoyed or suffered, scarcely noticed or quite unexpected, and so on through an endless spectrum of qualities. The significance of the experience need not be rendered by, "I see, this is sweet"; more appropriate, instead, might be just "Mmmm . . ." John Dewey speaks in this connection of the difference between *having* an experience and *knowing* an experience.

Confusion between these two is responsible for much of the appeal of subjectivism. The experience had is private; the having is my own affair—otherwise it is not I who have the experience but someone else. What is known, however, is not private. No one else can suffer my pain; this is tautological, for the pain is his who suffers. But others can know that I am suffering, can be acquainted with just such suffering of their own, and can know that I am suffering a certain sort of pain even without acquaintance with such an experience.

By knowledge we may mean only what is then and there being thought of and believed with good reason, or what *could* be brought to mind, or *would* be believed, under suitable circumstances. "Consider whether knowledge is a thing you can possess in that way," Socrates says in the *Theatetus*, "without having it about you, like a man who has caught some wild birds—pigeons or whatnot—and keeps them in an aviary he has made for them at home. In a sense, of course, we might say he 'has' them all the time inasmuch as he possesses them, mightn't we? But in another sense he 'has' none of them, though he has got control of them, now that he has made them captive in an enclosure of his own; he can take and have hold of them whenever he likes by catching any bird he chooses, and let them go again, and it is open to him to do that as often as he pleases."

The superficial argument that an "unconscious idea" is a contradiction in terms ignores this distinction. It is indeed contradictory to speak of a bird in the hand if the hands are empty; but a bird in the aviary is after all not in the bush, and might be taken hold of. The distinction between knowing-how and knowing-that may also be relevant. A man might be said to know something unconsciously because he acts in a certain way which would be appropriate if he knew that something or other was true. How he comes to act in that way without knowledge which was at one time conscious is another question. The theory of knowledge has hardly begun to take into account either the empirical findings of depth psychology or the conceptual analyses of the theory of information storage and retrieval.

We might say, "I see that two people have already arrived," whether we ourselves met them at the door, saw two coats on the rack, or have just been told they had arrived. *How* we come to know something is quite distinct from *what* is known. It is sensationalism all over again to identify an experience with its content; this is how we get caught up in the subjectivist involutions of knowing only our own knowings.

Matters which are logically distinct may, nevertheless, stand in close relation to one another. Each mode of knowing provides us with distinctive sorts of things known. Objects of direct experience are *concreta*—trees and stones and stars, all the furniture of earth and choir of heaven, as Bishop Berkeley called them. There are other objects which are not and cannot be directly experienced. These are *abstractions,* defined in terms of concrete things though not themselves concrete. Their meanings are so specified that statements about them are verified by observations of concrete things, so that they are "reduced to" concreta (§12). An orbit, a species, a government are all abstractions; we cannot see them, but it would make no sense to say that they are invisible. We observe concreta, and these observations exhaust all that is meant in statements involving the abstracta.

There is a third kind of objects, objects which, Reichenbach warned, are easily confused with abstracta. He called them *illata;* these, like abstractions, are not objects of direct experience, but physical rather than logical reasons make them unobservable. Molecules, genes, and neural circuits are of this kind. If they were more accessible to observation, or if we were creatures of very different and more refined senses, we might call them concreta. There is nothing absurd in imagining radio waves to be as directly experienced as we experience colors.

What is it, at bottom, that we know, when knowledge is recast so as to make explicit on what each bit of knowledge is logically dependent? An answer to this question is said to specify an *epistemic base.* Such a base is not the ground on which the edifice of knowledge is erected; it is the constitution of the structure itself, the raw material of which its substance is compounded. It is an answer not to the question of *how* we come to know but to the question of *what* we know.

Three epistemic bases have played a major part in the theory of knowledge. The *positivist* or *phenomenological base* consists of sense-data. The position was developed at the turn of the century by the physicist Ernst Mach and the biometrician Karl Pearson, then given logical subtlety and polish by Russell and Carnap. The *realistic base* consists of the concrete things of everyday life and commonsense experience; its claims were especially advanced by Charles Peirce and G. E. Moore. The *physical base,* consisting of subatomic particles, electromagnetic fields, and the like, brings nineteenth-century materialism up to date and has been emphatically affirmed but not developed in any detail—as, for instance, in Carnap's thesis of physicalism (§39). Philosophers as different as Whitehead and Reichenbach are alike in the centrality they assign to physics in the analysis of knowledge.

The "principle of tolerance" which Carnap formulated for logic (§16) has its analogue in the theory of knowledge. It is that all three of these epistemic bases—and perhaps others, too—are admissible. The question, "What is human knowledge really about?" presupposes that the "reality" can be identified in some one unequivocal way; but knowledge can be reconstructed in various ways. This is not to say that anything goes but that in different contexts different bases may suit our purpose. To be able to serve as a base at all, each must be capable of accounting for the other bases in its own terms.

The realistic base is the most serviceable in the philosophical theory of knowledge. A psychologist studying the growth of knowledge in infancy, or what happens when congenital blindness is successfully corrected, may find the positivist base the most appropriate. The neurophysiological exploration of the processes of pattern recognition or of the storage and retrieval of perceptual data may turn to the physical base. Even for the purposes of science the realistic base may be fundamental, for it is used to describe the evidence for scientific theories, and to specify the concreta underlying scientific abstractions, Niels Bohr has made this point with regard to the dependence of quantum physics on classical physics. The description of the experimental set-up and of the observed results in quantum physics is given in the terminology of classical physics, including much of the terminology of everyday life—that is, of the realistic base.

There is still another base (perhaps only a subtype of the realistic), the *pragmatic base.* This base takes as fundamental human actions; it analyzes things, sensations, and scientific entities in terms of various phases, components, or outcomes of action. The pragmatic line of analysis was carried furthest by George Herbert Mead; John Dewey also made notable contributions. The general approach was anticipated by Faust: In the beginning was not the Word but the Deed. A substantive contribution was made earlier by Bishop Berkeley's "theory of vision," which sketched an account of our perception of an external world "out there" in terms of experiences of motion and contact with things. In the present century, the same tack was taken by the mathematician Henri Poincare, to provide an epistemic base for geometry.

From ancient times to the present day, geometry has had a profound effect on the theory of knowledge. In his dialogue *Meno,* Plato defends the view that the soul existed before birth by showing that anyone—even a slave boy—can be brought to the recognition of geometrical truths. As the boy did not learn them in this life, he must have learned them in a previous one. The argument fails because not all we know must have been learned. We must distinguish between *learning* and *maturing.* A young bird does not learn how to fly, nor a human infant how to walk. Their early mistakes do not mark the rocky road of learning but only the inadequate performances of immaturity which correct themselves in the course of time.

Almost all the knowledge we acquire by maturing is knowing-how; geometry is the conspicuous instance of knowledge-that, which, it was widely held, need not be learned. The knowledge of arithmetic is less debatably the maturing of innate capacities than a matter of learning. Experience provides the *occasion* for awareness of mathematical truth but constitutes neither its source nor its ground. *Rationalists* hold that all knowledge is *innate,* embodied in the very structure of reason or of the human mind, and requiring experience only to allow what is latent to become manifest. The rationalists include such distinguished philosophers as Plato, Leibniz, Spinoza, and Descartes. Plato had inscribed over the gate to his Academy, "Let no one ignorant of geometry enter here"; Leibniz invented the differential calculus; Spinoza wrote a treatise on ethics with the subtitle, *Demonstrated in the Geometrical Manner;* and Descartes invented analytic geometry. Their mathematical skills and interests shaped their conceptions of knowledge in general.

The slave boy of whom Plato writes could be brought to recognize the properties of geometrical figures, but he certainly could not be brought to discover the shape of a single thing he had not seen or been told of unless he inferred this shape from what he or others had previously seen. Knowledge of matters of fact inescapably depends, directly or indirectly, on experience. This is the standpoint of *empiricism.* John Locke delivered a crushing blow to the theory of innate ideas, from which it never recovered. But the view that the laws of nature, as distinguished from matters of fact, are grounded in the structure of the mind still finds supporters. What appeals to the mind as simple, reasonable, or beautiful has served as a remarkably effective guide to scientific discovery to a degree which cannot be casually dismissed.

At birth, the mind, in Locke's metaphor, is a *tabula rasa,* a blank page on which experience writes. True, Leibniz replied: there is nothing in the mind before experience—save the mind itself. It has its own structure which is no more determined by experience than the photograph on the negative is determined by the developing solution. The Leibizian position is represented in the present century by the astrophysicist Arthur Eddington, in his *Nature of the Physical World:* "We have found a strange footprint on the shores of the unknown. We have devised profound theories, one after another, to account for its origin. At last we have succeeded in reconstructing the creature that made the footprint. And lo! It is our own."

To mediate the claims of rationalism and empiricism, Kant held that the *form* of knowledge is determined by the mind, while experience provides the *content.* Nature can only answer the questions we put to her; a great deal depends on how a question is put. Knowledge is the outcome of conceptualization as well as of perception. The Kantian formula is that percepts without concepts are blind, and concepts without percepts are empty. The three positions of brute empiricism, pure rationalism, and the Kantian synthesis are prefigured in Bacon's *Novum Organum:* the brute empiricist, like the ant, only collects and uses what he finds; the pure rationalist, like the spider, makes his webs out of his own substance; the true scientist, like the bee, gathers his material from the flowers of the field but digests and transforms it by a power of his own.

It was taken for granted that both the content and the validation of knowledge depend on the origins of knowledge; philosophies differ only in their views of what the origins are. Empiricism localizes the role of experience in knowledge at the point of its entry into the mind. Pragmatism relates knowledge to experience prospectively rather than retrospectively. What is significant are not the experiences in which knowledge originates but rather the experiences to which the supposed knowledge leads in the course of its verification. It is as though pragmatism liberalized an immigration policy: those who come to our shores will be admitted not because they can point to acceptable origins but because they give promise of a productive future.

Kant characterized his standpoint in the theory of knowledge as a kind of Copernican revolution. Copernicus accounted for the apparent motions of the heavenly bodies partly by their own real motions but partly also by the effect of the motion of the earth from which we observe them. In the same way, Kant proposed to account for appearances in general partly by the properties of the objects of knowledge but partly also by the effect of the structure of the mind by which we attain to knowledge. The mind by itself provides knowledge of synthetic propositions (§15); that is, propositions which do not merely amplify identities but which, in their predicates. add to our conceptions.

The propositions of mathematics, in particular, are of this kind. The rationalists were right in their view that reason alone can be a source of knowledge, but this knowledge is limited to the forms in which the mind must conceptualize whatever it seeks to know. The empiricists were also right in insiting that knowledge of the properties of things, and of patterns of events, necessarily depends on experience. All we know independently of experience is that things do have properties, and events do fall into patterns. Because we know this regardless of what happens, these propositions are not only true but are necessarily true.

Russell tells us that the work which ultimately became his contribution to *Principia Mathematica* at first presented itself to him "as a parenthesis in the refutation of Kant." He wished to establish that the truths of mathematics, though known independently of experience, are only analytic—identities, in Kant's conception—and so they say nothing at all about the world of experience, not even about the forms to which that world must conform. The point at issue, perhaps the most basic issue in the theory of knowledge of the last two centuries, is whether there are any "synthetic *a priori*" propositions.

A proposition which is known independently of experience is said to be known *a priori*, and otherwise, *a posteriori*. That 1 + 1 = 2 is *a priori*. True, a gallon of alcohol combined with a gallon of water makes less than two gallons of liquid (the two interact), and this can be known only by experience. But arithmetic says only that if we put a gallon of each into a container, we will have put two gallons there; this remains true regardless of what experience shows to be the outcome. Knowledge independent of a particular experience is *relatively a priori;* if it is independent of all experience it is *absolutely a priori*. In both cases it is logical independence, not psychological (causal) independence, which is in question. Before going to the moon we know something of what we will find there, but such knowledge is *a posteriori*, and only relatively *a priori*.

A proposition is *pure a priori* if none of its components refers to the contents of experience, and otherwise *mixed*. A statement about the sum of two numbers is pure; if it is about the sum of two quantities of apples it is mixed. The propositions whose status is at issue are the pure, absolute *a priori*.

There is no doubt that analytic propositions are known *a priori;* we do not need experience to tell us that siblings have the same father, since they have, indeed, the same parents. It is only through experience that we learn the meaning of the word, but until we have learned its meaning we are not yet entertaining a proposition. That analytic statements, though *a priori*, may tell us nothing, like Locke's "trifling" propositions (§15), is clear from this passage in Act II of *Antony and Cleopatra*, in which Antony describes a crocodile to Lepidus:

> LEP. What manner o' thing is your crocodile?
>
> ANT. It is shap'd sir, like itself, and it is as broad as it hath breadth; it is just so high as it is, and moves with its own organs: it lives by that which nourisheth it, and the elements once out of it, it transmigrates.
>
> LEP. What color is it of?
>
> ANT. Of its own color too.
>
> LEP. 'Tis a strange serpent.
>
> ANT. 'Tis so, and the tears of it are wet.
>
> CAESAR. Will this description satisfy him?
>
> ANT. With the health that Pompey gives him, else he is a very epicure.

The question is whether all *a priori* knowledge is analytic. An affirmative answer is characteristic of most empiricisms of the past century. "No part of our experience is also *a priori,*" said Wittgenstein. "Everything we see could also be otherwise. Everything we can describe at all could also be otherwise." Mathematics is *a priori,* but it is also analytic. "In life it is never a mathematical proposition which we need, but we use mathematical propositions only in order to infer from propositions which do not belong to mathematics to others which equally do not belong to mathematics."

Unfortunately, in many discussions of the issue, "analytic" is defined in such a way as to make it virtually indistinguishable from *"a priori"* (for instance, "what can be established by reference only to the rules of language"). In that case, a *synthetic a priori* would be a contradiction in terms. For the issue to be faced, "analytic" must be defined in terms of the content of the proposition, leaving *"a priori"* to be defined in terms of how we come to know that content. Contemporary discussions have focused on the difficulties of defining "analytic"; the meaning of *"a priori"* has not invited corresponding attention.

Pragmatists—notably Charles Peirce and C. I. Lewis—have emphasized the contextual and functional character of the distinction between *"a priori"* and *"a posteriori,"* an emphasis found also in the work of Quine. When an experience runs counter to a previous belief we may abandon the belief, but we may also cling to it, giving way elsewhere. We may discredit the experience or else reinterpret it—that is, abandon other beliefs involved in the negative impact of the experience. What is at work here is a *pragmatic a priori.* There is a danger of shutting ourselves off from experience altogether in this way and so reducing our thought to a closed system (§23). Yet there is no doubt that the logic-in-use in science often incorporates this pragmatic pattern of thinking.

Whether a proposition is *a priori* now becomes a matter of degree: how impervious is it to modification as a result of experience? Say that measurements are made of the masses involved in an experiment in chemistry or physics; if, whenever the masses differ at the beginning and end of the experiment, we postulate the existence of some unobserved particle with the appropriate mass, the law of conservation of mass is *functioning* as an *a priori* proposition. Yet it may have been formulated and accepted initially on an *a posteriori* basis. Laws of this kind are sometimes distinguished as *principles.*

The decision whether a given proposition is to be interpreted as *a priori* or as *a posteriori* in a specific context is both difficult and inconclusive. The uncertainties are sometimes transferred to the question whether a given sentence should be interpreted as affirming one proposition or another. There is no doubt that what appears to be the dictates of experience may subsequently be revealed as merely the outcome of human decision. "Criticism," said Santayana, "surprises the soul in the arms of convention." The Zen artist commissioned to paint a bamboo grove rendered it in red, to the dismay of his patron, who expected it to be—naturally—in black.

The last word must go to the empiricist. Realism, objectivity, sanity itself all require awareness of the thrust of brute fact. However important the contributions of the mind to knowledge, we live in a world with a mind of its own made known to us in experience. The most compelling argument for empiricism is that stated by Bolingbroke in *Richard II:*

O! who can hold a fire in his hand
By thinking on the frosty Caucasus?
Or cloy the hungry edge of appetite
By bare imagination of a feast?
Or wallow naked in December snow
By thinking on fantastic summer's heat?

26. The Quest for Certainty

Plato, his mind on mathematics, held that nothing was worthy of the name of knowledge unless it was not merely true but universally and necessarily true. A belief about a particular or only contingent matter of fact he called an "opinion," invidiously distinguished from true knowledge. The subject matter of opinion is grasped by the senses rather than by reason; confirmation makes it at best only probable, it being supported by only fragmentary evidence. Knowing is the commerce of the mind with Ideas; to know something is to grasp the Idea.

Aristotle, fundamentally a biologist, was far more interested than Plato in concrete particulars. Accordingly, he gave induction from sensory experience a far more fundamental role in knowing than Plato could assign to it. For Plato the senses only jog the mind into a recollection of the Ideas it has known all along; the diagrams of the geometer do not prove anything about the abstract mathematical figures but only help us understand a truth that must be seen by the mind's eye. Aristotle, however, recognized that the scientist cannot do without careful and patient observation. Yet he, too, felt that the purpose of observation, guided and interpreted by reason, was to yield "first principles," ultimate and unshakable foundations for knowledge.

This point of view persisted into modern times, in the formulation of the mathematical foundations of physics by Galileo, Kepler, and Newton. In the seventeenth century, the conception was given a turn which has plagued thought ever since. *Universality* and *necessity* pertain to propositions. *Certainty,* however, pertains not to propositions but to our knowledge of them. For the past three or four centuries philosophy has exhibited an anxious self-consciousness about claims to knowledge, especially knowledge of good and evil, of social ideals, of spiritual attainment, of artistic achievement; skepticism has eaten into the claims of science as well. Descartes is properly identified as the father of modern philosophy, not because of his rejection of medieval authority but because of his explicit formulation of *the quest for certainty.*

In his *Discourse on Method* Descartes laid down as the first precept, "never to accept a thing as true until I know it as such without a single doubt." This precept was satisfied, he supposed, by the acceptance of his own existence, which was proved by the mere existence of his doubts, in accord with the formula *cogito, ergo sum*—I think, therefore I am. Whether this characteristically subjectivist foundation for knowledge is indeed indubitable does not concern us here; others have employed the same logic to reach different conclusions. It is the way of thinking that is relevant to the quest for certainty, not the particular certitude put forward. The pattern may be called the *logic of the unimpeachable premise.* What follows from a certainty is itself assured; conversely, we cannot know anything at all unless we know something for sure. Here is revealed the close connection between the quest for certainty and dogmatic skepticism. For on this logic, unless an unimpeachable premise can be produced, we must resign ourselves to complete ignorance.

The demand would be met if only there were *self-evident* propositions with a more than tautological content. The premise sought for is a truth with

> ... *such a face and such a mien*
> *As to be lov'd needs only to be seen.*
> —John Dryden, *The Hind and the Panther*

More accurately, since the philosopher is rather more sober than the poet, even a sober poet like Dryden, what is wanted is a truth which to be known—whether loved or otherwise—needs only to be understood. Its truth must be apparent on its very face; if credentials are called for, it is they that serve as premises, which might be impeached in turn.

The trouble is that, like love, self-evidence cannot be forced; over and over a proposition is seen and not accepted by others, though to us it is clearly self-evident. Misunderstanding *is* frequent, but not so frequent as each man's strength of conviction projects. I find it so hard to imagine that anyone alse would not arrive at my inescapably logical conclusions that when I am confronted with someone who disagrees with me I am sure he is misunderstanding me.

Self-evidence rests on a certain measure of self-righteousness; since the immediacy of the claim to truth precludes argument, the self-evident proposition easily becomes a dogma. The history of science is strewn with the shattered remains of what were once taken to be self-evident truths. Even mathematics does not escape the common fate of the sciences: it is not self-evidently true that the whole is greater than any of its parts, or that there can be only one parallel to a line through a given point.

More widespread than the claims of self-evidence, weaker and, for that reason, more acceptable, are the claims of *common sense.* As a quality of realistic good judgment, common sense may well be quite uncommon; as a body of generally received opinion, it is just what is widely shared. The premises common sense provides, while they may not be unshakable, are seldom shaken. What would be the point of challenging their truth? Every "truth" of common sense is seen as such either because it is a "well-known fact" or because "it stands to reason." This is because fact and reason are conceived in just such a way as will accord with the deliverances of common sense. To conceive them otherwise, a man would have to be either a fool or a philosopher; no one would admit to being a fool, and only a fool would lay claim to being a philosopher.

It is easy to be cynical about common sense in general. It is harder to identify falsehoods or confusions in common sense, and harder still to replace these by alternatives better supported by logic and experience. Common sense does, after all, have its reasons; people do not adhere to unclear or mistaken ideas only to provide a living for scientists and philosophers. Knowledge is the functional outcome of intelligent and purposive behavior; this broad pragmatic perspective on knowledge must somehow be incorporated in any acceptable theory of knowledge. The claims of common sense command considerably more respect than is due them if they are seen only as appeals to anonymous authority.

Even when common sense is revealed to be clearly mistaken, the revelation usually also discloses an element of good sense in it. There is a germ of truth in every falsehood which manages to survive reflection on accumulated experience. Of those who thought at all about the shape of the earth, for example, very few, even in the Middle Ages, supposed that the earth was flat. Those who did believe it to be flat were not totally mistaken: the earth *is* flat—on a sufficiently small scale and to a sufficiently crude approximation (the center of a football field is about one-thousandth of an inch higher than it would be on a plane). If we are to believe that the earth is spherical, the sphere must have a substantial radius; on the surface of a sphere with a small radius it does indeed stand to reason that observations of curvature would conflict with well-known facts. The *critical commonsensism* of Charles Peirce holds that common sense is philosophically sound, provided it is taken as the starting point and not as the conclusion of inquiry. Whatever objections might be raised against Peirce's theory of knowledge, it is neither thoughtless nor dogmatic.

Scientific advances have disclosed a world progressively more remote from the simple, concrete, pictorial thinking of common sense. From Copernicus and Galileo to Maxwell and Rutherford, the commonsense physical world was replaced by a fantastic domain of spheres of matter almost unimaginably great and small, caused to move in endless patterns through fields of energy deployed in space and time. With Einstein and Planck the very fabric of commonsense space, time, and causality was so unraveled that imagination was taxed beyond its breaking point. What else can we expect when thought addresses itself to events of altogether different magnitudes than those of commonsense experience?

This is not to say that science has "refuted" common sense. Science has not opened the door to any metaphysics which chooses to ignore the claims of common sense. Such a metaphysics would have failed to recognize the basic obligation acknowledged and fulfilled by science: that what lays claim to account for reality must first of all account for appearances. It was on such a basis that G. E. Moore, in the early years of the century, freed modern philosophy from the pretentious wooliness of the prevailing absolute-idealist metaphysics. It is absurd, he argued, for the metaphysician to declare that time is unreal but admit that he wrote the second chapter of his treatise *before* he wrote the third, and that he finished it only *after* taking much thought. In this same vein the Stoics had castigated the academic moralists who advocate modesty and humility but who do not fail to sign their names to their writings on the subject.

If common sense plays a part in a person's lived philosophy, honesty and consistency demand that it find a place in his professed philosophy (§5). Not every philosopher can say with Santayana, "I stand in philosophy exactly where I stand in daily life; I should not be honest otherwise. I accept the same miscellaneous witnesses, bow to the same obvious facts, make conjectures no less instinctively, and admit the same encircling ignorance."

The fact of his encircling ignorance is the only claim to knowledge Socrates made: "I know only that I know nothing." Lao-tzu, too, professed ignorance, as an ideal if not as an accepted fact: "To know that you do not know is best. To pretend to know when you do not know is a disease." Confucius was characteristically more realistic: "When you know a thing, to hold that you know it, and when you do not know a thing, to allow that you do not know it—this is knowledge." Common to all three sages is the repudiation of the conventional claims to unimpeachable knowledge—whether in the form of common sense, of received opinion, or of metaphysical truth.

Not all doubt expresses the healthy skepticism which is the part of wisdom as well as of the scientific temper of the mind. There is a wholesale skepticism associated with the quest for certainty. Often such skepticism is a reaction-formation to the intensity of the quest—a protesting-too-much which points to the reality of the opposite. Sometimes the skepticism is a device by which it is hoped to attain to certainty at last, a self-denial in the present endured for the sake of the future fulfillment which will be its reward. This is what Descartes called his *methodological doubt*, a determination to discover unimpeachable premises on which to erect the edifice of knowledge. The point to such wholesale but provisional skepticism is made explicit by Bacon: If we begin with doubts, we will end in certainties.

But *will* we end in certainties? The negative answer is called *fallibilism*, the view that for men there is no certitude anywhere, and that even if there were, they could not be certain they had attained to it. Skepticism is not merely a temporary expedient to be abandoned when we have succeeded in our quest for certainty. Even when we hold the grail in our hands, we do well to ask, "What if it is but a common cup after all?"

In defending the claims of common sense, G. E. Moore also maintained that we are, in fact, certain of many of the simple truths of commonsense experience, and that to argue that we *might* be mistaken because our beliefs are about matters of fact which *could* be otherwise is to beg the question. If we really know something to be true, we cannot be mistaken, and the facts truly could not be otherwise. On a noteworthy occasion Moore was presenting this position in a lecture at the University of Michigan, giving a series of examples of matters he was perfectly sure of: "This is a hand that I am holding up; there are other people in this room besides myself; the sunlight is streaming in through the windows"; and so on. Unfortunately, the lecture was being delivered in an interior auditorium which had no windows at all for the sunlight to stream through, a circumstance which escaped Moore's notice because he was reading from a prepared manuscript.

Descartes himself, for all his methodological doubt, once maintained the view that light travels instantaneously (its very rapid but finite velocity was not widely accepted till the next century), and defended it as an unimpeachable truth: "To my mind, it is so certain that if, by some impossibility, it were found guilty of being erroneous, I should be ready to acknowledge to you immediately that I know nothing in philosophy." The only acknowledgment called for is that, like all other men, he is fallible. On the other hand, there is no need for the almost cynical skepticism of Descartes' countryman Montaigne, that men are most apt to believe what they least understand *(Essays)*, or of the more poetic lament in *Measure for Measure*, "Man, proud man, most ignorant of what he's most assured."

Empirical knowledge rests ultimately on processes of perception and memory which involve us in error from time to time. A metaphysics which holds that perception, present or remembered, never provides knowledge of reality but only of unreal appearances is untenable; but this does not warrant the contrary view that perception and memory, if sufficiently vivid and clear, are never mistaken. Common sense itself adheres to fallibilism: things seem to be as we experience them and remember them to be; but from time to time—though not always—we are wrong. The psychology of perception and the psychodynamics of memory can point to the occasions when the mistakes are likely to occur. Nietzsche anticipated Freud with his confession, "'I did that,' says my memory; 'I couldn't have done that,' says my pride! Eventually my memory yields." Folklore also tells of a fallibilist hero with regard to perception. Riding with a companion, he passes a flock of newly sheared sheep. "Well, I see the sheep have already been sheared," said the other; "Yup," was the reply, "on this side anyways!"

As this example illustrates, fallibility stems from the circumstance that knowledge is inferential, and we may always be mistaken in our inferences. The inference that sheep sheared on one side have also been sheared on the other is fairly safe; so is the inference implied in Thoreau's remark about finding a trout in the milk. But inductive inferences are not certain even though they may be safe enough. There is no logical contradiction in affirming the premise and yet denying the conclusion of an inductive inference, as is the case with every valid deductive inference. Only if there were knowledge free of any inferential element whatever could there be certainty. But an experience which does not point outside itself is no more than a having; it is not a knowing. Even to name the "this" I am experiencing, unless the name is a purely conventional label (like a serial number), is to conceptualize—to generalize beyond "this" to an indefinite set of other possible experiences. And these just might not be what they were expected to be.

Fallibilism rests on the ever-present possibility that we might make a mistake. This possibility is grounded not only in our ways of knowing but also in the attributes of what is known. There is a logical as well as an epistemic basis for repudiating the quest for certainty. *Probabilism* is the view that knowledge is always of a probability. This is the objective ground for fallibilism. "It is a mistake," Freud once wrote, "to believe that a science consists in nothing but conclusively proved propositions, and it is unjust to demand that it should. It is a demand only made by those who feel a craving for authority in some form. The capacity to be content with approximations to certainty and the ability to carry on constructive work despite the lack of final confirmation are actually a mark of the scientific habit of mind." The distinction between mere opinion and true knowledge remains, not as invidiously drawn by Plato in terms of certainty but as a matter of the weight of the available evidence. As Milton declared in defense of the importance of the free exchange of ideas, opinion in good men is but "knowledge in the making."

Among modern philosophers of science Reichenbach is noteworthy as a probabilist. Russell once teased him with, "I see that an eclipse of the moon has been predicted for tonight; what do you think?" "Yes," Reichenbach seriously replied, "it is quite probable." A little later they stepped outside and viewed the eclipse. "What do you say now?" Russell asked. "Very much more probable!" was the answer. Archimedes, having discovered the laws of the lever, asked but a place to stand and he could move the earth. So far as knowledge is concerned and an unimpeachable premise on which to take our stand, Reichenbach admonishes that "there is no Archimedean point of absolute certainty left to which to attach our knowledge of the world; all we have is an elastic net of probability connections floating in open space."

How exactly "probability" is to be interpreted in this context is far from a matter of general agreement (§30). For the present, it is enough to recognize that, whatever our degree of confidence in what we know, the proposition known is confirmed only to some degree, not necessarily the same as the degree of our confidence. It has a certain weight or likelihood in the light of the evidence. Fallibilism comes into play with regard to the possibility of our being mistaken in our judgment or estimation of this likelihood; probabilism is the position that the likelihood is always less than that conveyed in the absolute certitude of an unimpeachable premise. The underlings in the employ of Evelyn Waugh's Lord Copper did not dare "Definitely, Lord Copper," but when he was plainly and flatly wrong, the formula was "Up to a point, Lord Copper." Probabilism saved him from confronting his fallibility.

There is a certain margin of error—what the engineer calls "tolerance"—in what is known, so that it has, at best, only a degree of truth. A proposition about all of a class may in fact hold true only of *almost* all of them; there are always exceptions to be taken into account, and if these are taken to falsify the proposition, we never will have knowledge of universals—almost never, that is. A proposition may assign a numerical value to some magnitude, but one which only approximates the true value. A proposition may predicate a certain property which is very nearly how things are, the true property being similar to, but not identical with, the one predicated. A proposition may affirm something which is true under a wide set of conditions, or under the conditions most commonly prevailing, but its truth *is* conditional for all that.

All these elements of uncertainty may also be included under the rubric of probabilism and may contribute as well to the fallibility of our judgment. They give substance to the *syadvada*—the "maybe-so or partly-so" doctrine —of the Jain logic. All truths, Whitehead has said, are half-truths. He calls it the *dogmatic fallacy* to suppose that our ideas can be well enough defined and articulated to fit exactly the complexities of the real world. The search for unimpeachable premises is foredoomed to failure.

In contrast to the skepticism of universal doubt and the dogmatism of the logic of the unimpeachable premise is the pragmatic theory of knowledge of Charles Peirce and his successors. The pursuit of knowledge, said Peirce, can begin in only one place—where we are. Always, where we are is in a state of some knowledge and some ignorance. If nothing at all is taken to be known, even if this attitude be only a methodological doubt, no questions can sensibly be asked. There is no such thing as an uncertainty without *some* givens, no hypothesis for which there are no data whatever. A problem does not arise, Mead emphasized, except over against that which is not problematic. Every area of the problematic, however wide its diameter, is surrounded by what Mead called "the world that is there," the domain of the unproblematic in terms of which problems can be formulated and proposed solutions tested.

Doubt is meaningful only against a background of what is undoubted; in a doubtful situation not everything is doubtful all at once. Puzzles (§2) are the doubts which arise when there is nothing truly doubtful, in contrast to real problems, which have an objective locus. It is not the state of mind which is decisive but the situation in which we find ourselves. Epistemic error lies neither in doubt nor in belief as such, but in skepticism or credulousness which is inappropriate to the objective circumstances. Where skepticism *is* appropriate, it centers on particular features of the situation rather than diffusing itself over the entire situation as an undifferentiated whole.

The failure to realize that doubt is no more self-validating than belief, but must be justified by objective considerations, is one of the root errors of the quest for certainty. There is another—the failure to recognize that such objective considerations are situational, and vary from context to context. There is always something not to be doubted, but there is nothing which is always indubitable. For each problem there must exist unproblematic data, but it is false that there are data unproblematic for all problems. We do not accept conclusions drawn from premises which we have grounds to impeach, but our conclusions do not wait for premises which would be unimpeachable in every imaginable circumstance. Skepticism, Santayana has said, is "the chastity of the intellect, and it is shameful to surrender it too soon or to the first comer." But the unending quest for certainty condemns the philosopher to the sterile life of a perpetual celibate.

27. The Whole Truth

For Descartes and other rationalists, truth is something to be *recognized*—as self-evident, logically necessary, or as otherwise making an irresistible claim on our assent. The trouble is that what is irresistible to one man is not even attractive to another. Descartes himself recognized that no opinion, however absurd and implausible, has not already been maintained by some philosopher or other. What is needed is not recognition but *verification:* evidence or argument proving truth, it being acknowledged that proof is not necessarily conclusive, and that a proposition, in being proven, has not thereby been made unimpeachable.

To say that a proposition is true does not *mean* that it has been verified; but there is no *point* to saying it is true unless it has been verified, or it is expected that it would be verified if it were put to the test. The claim that a proposition *p* is known implies not only that *p* is true but also that we have grounds for believing it, or else the claim is pointless. To the question, "Why do you believe *p?*" the answer, "Because it is true," says too much, or altogether too little. With comparable logic, the notorious bank robber Willie Sutton, on being asked why he robbed banks, replied, "Because that's where the money is."

The point to saying that something is true is that we have or can come to know it. But that is not what we are *saying* in ascribing truth. There is no contradiction in stating that many truths will never be known; the contradiction would come only in giving an example of an unknown truth—or, if not a contradiction, such an utterance would be self-defeating. What we are saying in ascribing truth is not something about *our* relation to the proposition but about the relation of the proposition to the facts. A true proposition is one which corresponds to the facts, represents them, states them as they are. This is the "semantical conception" of truth, or the *correspondence* theory.

What the correspondence consists in and what exactly corresponds to what are very much open questions. Russell and Wittgenstein propounded the view that every fact has a determinate structure, as does every proposition, a true proposition being one which has the same structure as does the fact it states. The correspondence which constitutes truth would be like that between the placement of successive notes higher or lower on a sheet of music and the rising or falling pitch through time of the melody transcribed. But the relative clarity and exactness of this account of the matter is more than matched by the obscurity and vagueness in which it leaves the connection between truth and knowledge.

This connection is central in the *pragmatic* theory of truth. The truth about something may not be limited to what we know about it, but, at best, this is only a matter of some abstract theory; truth as known is all that has any practical significance for us. The truth is what we are justified in believing, what is useful for us to believe. Correspondence is nothing other than this capacity to make itself useful. "To 'agree' in the widest sense with a reality," William James explained, "can only mean to be guided either straight up to it or into its surroundings, or to be put into such working touch with it as to handle either it or something connected with it better than if we disagreed." One experience is a knowing of another, not because it is its representative in some "quasi-miraculous 'epistemological' sense but in the definite practical sense of being its substitute in various operations, sometimes physical and sometimes mental, which lead us to its associates and results." The pragmatic theory of truth, rather than being an alternative to the correspondence theory, undertakes to provide an analysis of the correspondence in terms of what we can do with it.

The identification of truth with usefulness, unless properly qualified, can easily be taken for the most arrant subjectivism, and was so taken by critics of pragmatism. Soviet historians, for example, periodically rewrite history according to what they find politically useful at the time of the writing; but a falsehood remains false however useful it may be to liars and cheats. Pragmatists were accused of rationalizing the pursuit of power and profit and making success a measure of both the true and the good. To this day the word "pragmatist" has a connotation of willingness to sacrifice principle to mere expediency.

While James did characterize the truth as "only the expedient in the way of our thinking," he added the crucial qualification, "in the long run and on the whole, of course." No limited set of interests, contexts and purposes can define usefulness in the required sense. The lie may be useful to the liar but not to his victim, and even the liar must beware of deceiving himself at last. "Who so well as the pragmatist," James asks, "feels the immense pressure of objective control under which our minds perform their functions?" Whatever the shortcomings of his occasional looseness of expression, James made repeated efforts to correct misunderstandings. I sympathize with his rejoinder: "A favorite formula for describing pragmatists is that we are persons who think that by saying whatever you find it pleasant to say and calling it truth, you fulfill every pragmatistic requirement. I leave it to you to judge whether this be not an impudent slander."

What appears to be true can be accepted as true only if it continues to meet the demands of ever wider contexts. This test is central to a third theory of truth, associated with Kant and the post-Kantian idealists. It is the *coherence* theory of truth: a proposition is true if it fits with all the rest of what we already know to be true. Such fitness or coherence is usually analyzed in terms of logical deducibility, or at least consistency, so that this conception of truth is congenial to rationalists, as the correspondence conception is to empiricists. To verify a proposition we turn to the body of established knowledge; if this must be supplemented by additional data, we take care that the new findings are not brought forward at the expense of what has already been confirmed. William James's formulation is as significant for the coherence conception as for the pragmatic: "New truth marries old opinion to new fact so as to ever show a minimum of jolt, a maximum of continuity."

If I may labor his metaphor, divorce is also sometimes called for. Here we have a serious weakness in the coherence conception. Advances in knowledge, especially the significant ones, often mark a rupture between the new ideas and what had always been regarded as old, established truth. In Milton's metaphor, the marriage may never have taken place at all: "Truth never comes into the world but like a bastard, to the ignominy of him that brought her forth." A great deal of attention has been given to the significance for the theory of knowledge of scientific revolutions. If a proposition does not cohere with what has already been acknowledged as true, it may be true nevertheless and our previous acknowledgments mistaken. In the forefront of the fight for acceptance of Darwin's theory of evolution, Thomas Huxley was moved to point out how often new truths begin as heresies and end as superstitions.

The coherence conception of truth faces the inescapable question of the source and validation of the old truths with which the new one is supposed to cohere. Here empiricism and the correspondence theory seem to be indispensable. Somewhere or other I must be able to say, "I know this to be true because of what I am now experiencing—no matter what you or anyone else has to tell me." But to say this I need not be *certain,* nor need I pretend that my conviction owes nothing to what I have brought into the context. I cannot find anything to be true unless to start with it makes sense; here coherence comes into play. And I cannot accept it as true unless I find it to be useful as I move from this context into all the others to which my interests lead me; here the pragmatic theory makes its contribution.

Experience, logical connections, and effectiveness in dealing with the problems which confront us, all three play a part in the process of inquiry from which knowledge issues and by which truth is established. This process is made the basis for the definition of truth proposed by Charles Peirce: "the opinion which is fated to be ultimately agreed to by all who investigate." John Dewey, for whom logic is nothing other than the theory of inquiry, understandably says of this formulation that it is the best definition of truth, from the logical standpoint, known to him. Russell, on the other hand, criticizes the definition for leaving unanswerable the question what investigation aims at, for this would otherwise be described as "discovering the truth." Peirce's definition points to the criterion we employ when we are called upon to specify what we take to be a truth: we turn to the results of actual or anticipated investigation.

Though inquiry is a process which takes place in time, truth is atemporal. At a given time we make a judgment as to what is true, a judgment which may be correct or mistaken, though we cannot ever be sure which it is—judgment becomes progressively sounder as investigation continues. If the judgment made at a certain time is correct, the proposition then judged to be true is not "true at that time" (as though it could be false at some other time), but simply true. Truth is truth to the end of reckoning, not because, as an ideal good, it is eternal but simply because time specifications belong to acts of knowing and not to the propositions known, to the process of inquiry and not to what inquiry progressively discloses. "True at a certain time" is as perniciously misleading an expression as is the expression "true for so-and-so," and for the same reason: they confuse a judgment made at a certain time with what is being judged at that time. My beliefs are different from yours, and what I believe today I did not believe yesterday; but such truth as we have attained to is neither of my time and place nor of yours.

No doubt something of these considerations was intended by Peirce when he spoke of the opinion "fated" to be "ultimately" agreed to—for this ultimate fate cannot be realized at any actual time but recedes into the emerging future. There is another implication here which raises a serious difficulty. How can we be sure that any opinion will ultimately be agreed to? In presupposing this prediction are we not abandoning logic for sociology, and making our conception of truth depend on the vagaries of human behavior?

That in the end truth will conquer must be for Peirce only a tautology, for on his definition, it appears, truth is what conquers in the end. But that truth crushed to earth will rise again is surely not a tautology and may very well be false. A man may be in as just possession of truth as of a city, said Sir Thomas Browne, and yet be forced to surrender. The domain of truth, so far as man has explored it, is the scene of noble conquests but also of shameful or tragically inescapable surrenders. Truth is what *would* be ultimately agreed to *if* investigation were not distorted by power, passion, and the other all-too-human sources of error. The attempt to define truth must fall back upon a conception of logic. Whether such a conception can be developed adequately without somewhere presupposing the concept of truth is another question.

However it has been conceived, truth has been regarded by virtually everyone as among the supreme values for human aspiration. Often, what has been held to be worthy of prizing is only a certain set of truths—more accurately, a certain set of beliefs claimed to exhaust the domain of truth. "Great is truth and mighty above all things," says the Apocrypha; and in the Gospel, "You shall know the truth and the truth shall make you free." The bondage from which man is thereby to be freed is not the bondage of ignorance or error but the bondage of sin. The tree which stood in the Garden was not a tree of knowledge in general but a tree of the knowledge of good and evil.

Ideologues of both politics and religion have often set themselves astride the path of free inquiry, as at best decadent or trivial and at worst as destructive of the faith. "Men seek out the hidden powers of nature, which to know profits not, and wherein men desire nothing but knowledge. As for me," Augustine adds in his *Confessions*, "I care not to know the courses of the stars." The Caliph Omar is said to have justified his burning of the great library at Alexandria with the argument that if what it contained was already comprised in the Koran there would be no loss, and if not it deserved to be destroyed. The burning of books, licensing of publication, censorship, controls of all sorts imposed on the process of inquiry all betray a *lack* of faith, either in the truth of what is being "protected," in its capacity to withstand critical scrutiny, or in its power to reveal its own importance.

Socrates, we are told by Diogenes Laërtius, proclaimed that knowledge is the only good, and ignorance the only evil. This follows from his identification of virtue with knowledge, the plausible view that no one would knowingly choose the worse rather than the better. Knowledge may be identified with a generic good at least in this sense, that few goods drop into our hands of themselves; we must pursue and seize them, and for this we must know how to go about it. Truth is the guide to effective action. Bacon's dictum that knowledge is power is not limited in its application to politics, business, or any other particular endeavor. It is the most general formulation possible of the pragmatic conception of truth as mediating between aspiration and fulfillment.

The value of truth lies even deeper than this mediation. Truth itself may be an aspiration, and knowledge of it sufficient fulfillment. Wherever civilized men have appeared on earth, contemplation of the truth has been recognized as an end in itself, among the noblest of them. In the pursuit of this end, art, science, and religion have been united; perhaps it is this union which best characterizes philosophy. A list of those to whom the pursuit and contemplation of the truth is the highest of human aspirations, in which all that is beautiful and good makes itself manifest, such a list, I say, would include most of the great thinkers of all the world's cultures.

> *Dear friend, theory is all gray,*
> *And green is the golden tree of life.*
> —Faust

These are the words of a devil, not a man, one who has never known the passion for truth, the joy of its discovery, the courage of its defense, the delight in its comprehension. Such a being, in short, has never tasted at all of the fruit of the Tree of Knowledge; that is *his* damnation.

Chapter Five

Philosophy of Science

28. The Myth of Methodology

Science is knowledge par excellence; the theory of knowledge culminates in the philosophy of science. There cannot be any philosophy of science to speak of until there is a significant body of science for it to philosophize about. While many sciences had their beginnings in ancient times, the ancients looked not to empirical science but to mathematics as the ideal form of knowledge. The philosophy of science is therefore the most recent field of philosophy. This circumstance is responsible for a certain injustice in the invidious comparisons often made between "Eastern" and "Western" thought. The philosophy of science and a scientific temper in philosophy are conspicuously lacking in Asia; but they are not very marked in European thought either, before the rise of modern science.

That rise depended upon and, in turn, contributed to the crystallization of the principle of the *autonomy of science*—that only science itself can judge the validity of either its methods or its results. Only validity, truth, verification, and other such logical or epistemic attributes are in question. Whether it is worth allocating certain social resources to a particular investigation, or whether the conduct of the inquiry meets standards of morality, legality, or good taste—these are not questions science can presume to decide for itself. But no agencies outside the scientific enterprise can decide issues of scientific worth, and in such decisions no standards are to be applied which are not certified by science itself.

Scientific autonomy is not compromised by the mere circumstance that scientific research must be paid for, and that whoever pays will expect his money's worth and demand a voice in determining how the money is spent. Autonomy does not imply that scientists are exempt from the obligations of religion, politics, morals, and, indeed, from any duties not of their own definition and choosing. What it does imply is that *scientific* obligations must be autonomously defined and applied. The principle is not violated when questions are raised about social and ethical safeguards to be observed in experimenting on human beings or on radioactive substances. It *is* violated when a church tells a physicist what he must believe about the motions of the planets, or when a political party tells a geneticist what he must believe about the inheritance of acquired characteristics. It is also violated when church or state prohibits the teaching or even the dissemination of a scientific theory on the grounds that such a theory conflicts with a religious or political dogma, or even worse, on the grounds that the theory is the product of minds belonging to people of the wrong race, creed, color, or national identity.

The repudiation of the principle is usually justified by denying that a fundamental distinction can be drawn between questions of a purely scientific nature and those which hinge on political and similar considerations. On this view there is only "class science," or science qualified by other social identifications and aspirations in place of "class." Knowledge and truth thereby become subject to political decision. We must acquire what knowledge we can and use it as best we can to determine what is worth aspiring to and how it can be achieved. To reverse this order and acknowledge as truth only what serves predetermined interests is to deny meaning to rationality and objectivity. Even whether the so-called truth truly serves those interests cannot be rationally and objectively decided on an ideological basis or by the outcome of internal power struggles.

Without minimizing the importance of these issues, I want to call attention as well to the authoritarian control over science sometimes exercised by scientists themselves. The principle of autonomy can be violated when a scientist behaves in an unscientific manner towards his colleagues. Scientists have been persecuted not only by church and state but also by their own fellows. Galileo, who experienced both sorts of pressures, rightly said, "To command the professors of astronomy to confute their own observations is to enjoin an impossibility, for it is to command them not to see what they do see, and not to understand what they do understand, and to find what they do not discover." Just this is what professors sometimes demand of students and colleagues. The astronomer Fred Hoyle has remarked that scientific history is littered with cases of young people who are discouraged from publishing good ideas which subsequently turn out to be correct.

The dilemma in which every academy finds itself is how to provide training without imposing a deadening orthodoxy, which makes for the academic in art and superficiality in science. If science is taught as though the answers are always to be found in the back of the book, the learner will either be incapable of considering more adequate answers—to say nothing of better questions—or else he will abandon science altogether in quest of some book with answers more to his liking.

The history of scientific advances is, to a noteworthy degree, a history of attempts to overcome hostility from within science. This is especially true when the prestige of the profession appears to be threatened by the new conceptions, as illustrated by the cruel fate of Ignaz Semmelweis, who in discovering causes of infection showed that physicians themselves were spreading it. The founder of quantum theory, Max Planck, said that a new scientific truth does not triumph by convincing its opponents and making them see the light, but rather because its opponents eventually die, and a new generation grows up that is familiar with it. Perhaps the new generation is more receptive for the same reason that so many important scientific discoveries are made by youthful investigators; they are less burdened by the weight of their own training and experience. Even in as abstract a domain as philosophy, William James, in his *Pragmatism,* has noted (with an understandable undertone of some bitterness) "the three classic stages of a theory's career. First, a new theory is attacked as absurd; then it is admitted to be true, but obvious and insignificant; finally it is seen to be so important that its adversaries claim that they themselves discovered it."

Science is not only free from the authority of church, state, and the scientific academy; it is also free from the authority of the philosophy of science. What philosophy can attain to is at best a reconstructed logic of science (§15); it cannot dictate the logic-in-use. Philosophers, and scientists of philosophic bent, have contributed to scientific advance by their analyses. That these analyses reflected valid insights could not be prejudged but had to be determined in the course of further inquiry. The logic is as much subject to evaluation and correction by scientific findings as the science is subject to evaluation and correction by logical analysis. A study of the history of science is likely to throw more light on scientific method than can be shed by the philosophy of science. "The history of science," Goethe remarked, "is science itself"; at any rate, inquiry is one of the best guides to an understanding and assessment of the products of that process.

It is sometimes supposed that philosophy can say what constitutes a good (deductive) argument or weighty (inductive) evidence but that it can say nothing about how to arrive at such arguments or evidence. In this view, there is a *logic of proof* but no *logic of discovery*. If a logic of discovery is thought of as providing a mechanical method for making discoveries, like the algorithms for extracting square roots or carrying out long divisions, it may readily be agreed that there is no such thing (though fantasies of such a possibility played a part in the development of symbolic logic and computer technology). Just as the logic of proof, however, is not limited to what *necessarily* follows from the premises but also includes probable inference, a logic of discovery need not guarantee discoveries but only enjoin procedures which would make them more likely. Experience shows that some methods of hunting are more sensible than others. A logic of discovery is an attempt to systematize and distill such experience.

An exaggerated regard for such a logic I call the *myth of methodology:* the notion that if only we used the right methods—in psychology, sociology, or wherever—these disciplines would quickly attain to indisputable scientific achievements. The difference between the logic-in-use and a reconstructed logic, even a reconstructed logic of discovery, remains. The fact is, as Mead pointed out, that all who are familiar with the history of modern science will admit that none of its discoveries have been made because of a technique which logical theory formulated and inculcated. The study of methodology has its uses, but they derive only from what has already shown itself to be useful.

Even so, methodology can be misapplied. The historian of science, Charles Singer, suggested that Bacon overlooked a fifth set of idols (§14), which might be called the *idols of the academy:* their worship involves the fallacy of supposing that a blind though learned rule can take the place of judgment. In the title of one of his papers, a distinguished modern psychologist pointedly asked his colleagues, "When should we use our heads instead of the formula?" As a schoolboy, I learned to scoff at "cookbook chemistry"—performing experiments by carrying out the instructions in the laboratory manual, neither knowing nor caring about their meaning or purpose. Sciences other than chemistry are just as subject to this failing.

Other misapplications of methodology are common. A familiar one is illustrated by the drunkard who was searching for his house key, not at his doorstep where he had dropped it but under the street lamp at the corner, "because it's lighter here." This *drunkard's search* is especially frequent in the behavioral sciences, attention being deflected to areas remote from the real problems because the other areas are so much more accessible or tractable. It is sensible to pursue goals that offer some hope of attainment. The misapplication of method lies less in the choice of goal than in the delusion that we are pursuing the original goal when we have chosen an easier one. An ancient student tactic when confronted with a difficult examination question is to provide an answer, admirable in itself, but to a question that has not been asked.

Closely related to the drunkard's search is a principle I call *the law of the instrument:* give a small boy a hammer and he will find that everything he runs across needs pounding. Over and over problems are formulated not in the terms posed by the problematic situation but according to the distinctive skills and resources of the inquirer. We suit our problems to our methods, rather than the other way around. What else is a man to do, Charles Peirce once asked, but ride his own horse as hard as he can, and leave it to others to hold him back? This is an understandable attitude; yet the horse may only be hurrying back to the stable. Methods make their own demands. While the methods available must be taken into account, this is not all that matters or else improvements of method would seldom be sought for, or if found, seldom adopted.

The shortcomings of the myth of methodology have been dramatically manifested in the part played by chance in scientific discovery—like Roentgen's discovery of X-rays, Fleming's of penicillin, and Freud's of free association. *Serendipity,* a word derived from the hero of a Persian fairy tale with the gift of finding something of value not sought for, is now common usage. Serendipity is not, however, a matter of *pure* chance. Chance favors the mind that is prepared, and such preparation is not accidental. It consists in a mastery of the data and hypotheses and the capacity to appreciate the significance of an unexpected finding.

The importance of preparation is demonstrated by two types of events frequently encountered in the history of science. One is *rediscovery*. For example, Gregor Mendel's achievements in genetics were rediscovered about thirty years later, and the mechanical theory of heat was brought into the focus of scientific attention a half-century after it had originally been formulated. The other mark of the importance of preparation is *synchronicity:* the simultaneous discovery. Newton and Leibniz simultaneously invented the calculus, and Mendel's work was simultaneously rediscovered by no fewer than three independent investigators.

The most widespread misuse of methodology is to confuse general methods of inquiry with particular techniques. The use of established techniques comes to be regarded as the only way to carry out inquiry, and these techniques are considered to be "*the* scientific method." The confusion of methods with techniques is often characteristic of *scientism,* a species of the intellectualist fallacy which finds science to be relevant to all human concerns, and all that is relevant. Scientism often attempts to restrict science to a limited set of preferred techniques. A generation ago these were symbolized by the "brass instruments" employed in these techniques, so that one spoke of "brass-instrument psychology" first in an honorific, and later in a derogatory, sense. Nowadays, a better symbol of scientism is the "computerized" inquiry.

The misconception is that technique itself makes an inquiry scientific. The whole of science, Einstein has said, is nothing more than a refinement of everyday thinking. While "refinement" includes a great deal, there is undeniable continuity between what the scientist does and what is done by every man as he learns by reflecting on his experience. If we try to capture in a single formula all that goes on in the pursuit of scientific knowledge, it is hard to improve on physicist P. W. Bridgman's remark that the scientist has no other method than to do his damnedest.

One feature of scientific inquiry is the *modesty* of its aim. While Galileo's contemporaries were occupied with constructing whole cosmologies, he was content to discover how pendulums swing, or how bodies move down an inclined plane. The method Galileo followed was formulated by Descartes in his *Discourse on Method:* to divide up each difficulty into as many parts as possible, whereby from what is simple and easy, we may rise to what is most complex. This "gradualness" was singled out by the psychologist Ivan Pavlov: "Gradualness. About this most important condition of fruitful scientific work I never can speak without emotion. Gradualness, gradualness and gradualness. From the very beginning of your work, school yourselves to severe gradualness in the accumulation of knowledge."

Galileo's genius showed itself in his willingness to deal with small problems. What he relied upon is the fact that scientific knowledge is *cumulative.* Newton was exhibiting as much intellectual as moral virtue when he declared in a letter to Robert Hooke, "If I have seen further [than you and Descartes], it is by standing upon the shoulders of giants." Because of the cumulative nature of science and the modesty of aim in any particular inquiry, it becomes possible for investigators of moderate ability to make contributions. Bacon said that his new scientific method "leaves but little to the acuteness and strength of wits, but places all wits and understandings nearly on a level." "Individual excellence," as he called it, is not as expendable as he thought. Yet even the insights of genius depend on accumulated findings and ideas.

The cumulation of scientific achievement exhibits two patterns: In *growth by extension,* knowledge occasionally replaces error, but, on the whole, extends what is recognizably the old domain. In the other pattern, *growth by intension,* earlier ideas are deepened and given new meaning. The mathematician Henri Poincaré is referring to these two patterns in his claim that "The advance of science is not comparable to the changes of a city, where old edifices are pitilessly torn down to give place to new, but to the continuous evolution of zoologic types which develop ceaselessly and end by becoming unrecognizable to the common sight, but where an expert eye finds always traces of the prior work of the past centuries" (*The Value of Science*).

Contributions made by different scientists differ not only in amount but also in kind. There are scientists distinguished for their powers of penetrating criticism, and others distinguished for their creative imagination. There is a variety of *cognitive styles;* it is scientism at its worst to identify "scientific method" with only one way of using human resources for the acquisition of knowledge.

Cultures, subcultures, coteries, and schools cultivate their own styles; there are fashions in science as in other social forms. This circumstance does not in itself impugn the objectivity of the scientific enterprise. To aspire to a science free from cultural expression is as pointless as it is futile. What is important is to recognize which demands on the conduct of inquiry are rooted in the problematic situation and which stem from the stringencies of style.

In the latter part of the nineteenth century, British physics, as exemplified by William Thomson, Lord Kelvin, sought for mechanical models as explanatory devices; in France, on the other hand, in the tradition of Pierre Laplace and Adrien Legendre, what was wanted was the abstract mathematical formulation. James Clerk Maxwell, who formulated the fundamental equations of the electromagnetic field, pleaded, in an address to the British Association for the Advancement of Science: "For the sake of persons of different types, scientific truth should be presented in different forms, and should be regarded as equally scientific, whether it appears in the robust form and vivid coloring of a physical illustration, or in the tenuity and paleness of a symbolic expression."

About a half-century later, Werner Heisenberg and Erwin Schrödinger propounded two formulations of quantum theory. Although Schrödinger was able to show a mathematical correspondence between the two, so that they were essentially equivalent, he said of Heisenberg's version, "I was discouraged, if not repelled, by what appeared to me a rather difficult method of transcendental algebra, defying any visualization." For his part, Heisenberg declared, "The more I ponder about the physical part of Schrödinger's theory the more disgusting it appears to me." Differences in cognitive style may be harder to reconcile than differences in cognitive content. Most cases of scientific disagreement involve differences of both sorts; cognitive style is not just a matter of how ideas are presented but of the style of thought. The task is not to adjudicate among styles but to cultivate the individual style in which each one's genius finds its fulfillment.

29. The Experimental Method

Between unchecked speculation and rigidly controlled dogma lies belief based on experience. Speculation may give direction and even substance to inquiry, but it cannot substitute for inquiry. As Newton said, "We are certainly not to relinquish the evidence of experiments for the sake of dreams and vain fictions of our own devising." The Greek atomists and the philosophers of the Indian Vaisheshika school had some notion of fundamental particles, but they did not provide the basis of a scientific atomic theory: we can build nothing on a purely speculative foundation.

Dogma may preclude futile endeavors, but experience may show dogma to be mistaken. After a time, scientists rightly refused to examine any more designs for perpetual-motion machines and methods of squaring the circle; yet the distinguished American astronomer Simon Newcomb published a proof that heavier-than-air flight was impossible—only a short time before the Wright brothers accomplished the impossible. The motto on the crest of the Royal Society was aptly chosen: NULLIUS IN VERBA—"on the words of no man"; that is, on no man's authority.

The sort of experience which constitutes a scientific observation is not merely the unstructured cumulation of the contents of a passive receptivity; the scientist may have to go to great lengths to see what he is interested in seeing. He may embark on a voyage of discovery in the literal as well as the metaphoric sense.

What is of importance for science if often something unusual, not births, psychotic episodes, and the like, sometimes called "nature's experiments." Their scientific value is limited unless we are prepared to take advantage of them for scientific observation when they do come before us. Einstein's theory of relativity could not be subjected to observational testing until the total eclipse of 1919; to measure the bending of starlight as it passes near the surface of the sun elaborate preparations had to be made, many of them involving international collaboration in spite of World War I. Apropos, it was not until World War II that the atom bomb provided experimental verification of the theory.

Preparations are pointless unless techniques are available to do what is needed when the time comes. The history of science is, to a significant degree, the history of scientific instruments. Consider how different science would be without the telescope, the Geiger counter, or the cyclotron; the microscope, electron microscope, and X-ray camera; the electroencephalograph, maze, and projective test. The instruments not only make it possible for scientists to carry out observations but also stimulate and guide inquiry—the law of the instrument (§28) is not always pernicious in its workings.

Scientific observations are systematic. Science, like art, can only exist in "minutely organized particulars," as William Blake put it. The meaning of the data is disclosed as much in its interrelationship with other data as in its relation to theory. Features common to all the data, for instance, may be due to the instrument of observation rather than to an invariant pattern in what is being observed. Errors of observation may be easy to detect by comparisons of data, even though such errors might elude analysis of the process of observation itself.

To have scientific significance, observations must be *interpreted.* Experience cannot be taken at its face value; as the late Norwood Hansen said, there is more in seeing than meets the eye. How to distinguish between appearance and reality in particular cases is the question. Kant characterized the attempt to draw this distinction as "the noblest enterprise of antiquity"; it remains "the noblest enterprise" today.

When observations are reconsidered with the advantage of subsequent interpretation, we are often astonished that it took so long before the observations were made and that it was so hard to understand them. A recurrent feature of the scientific scene is the existence of *invisible data.* Facts are elusive when we have no place to put them. We do not see them if we don't know what to make of them. Freud's observations of hysteria in males as well as of infantile sexuality are cases in point. "Hysteria" is, indeed, so named from the Greek word for the womb, the displacement of which was supposed to cause the symptoms; and "everyone knew" that sexuality began only at puberty—from the Latin word for "adult." It is not the names which made the data invisible, but the invisibility of the data which allowed such misleading usage to become established.

An *experiment* is a planned and controlled observation. It is planned in that it is deliberately undertaken in a certain context which provides a basis for interpreting its results. Both the circumstances of observation and the materials to be observed are controlled so as to maximize the significance of the expected data. The planning may be no more than formulating a question in a poll, and the control no more than selecting the sample to be polled.

Most experiments are more abstract in plan and more concrete in controls than is conveyed by this example. It is the combination of abstractness and concreteness, speculation and manipulation, which is probably most responsible for the rise of modern science. The cultures of ancient Greece, India, and China all attained to considerable subtlety of theoretical abstraction, and all also displayed considerable technological skill and ingenuity. But these two sorts of activities were largely confined to different social strata; it was beneath the dignity of the theoretician to dirty his hands, and above the station of the craftsman to speculate. The ancient philosophers in these societies usually belonged to religious, political, or social elites; in contrast, Copernicus, Kepler, Galileo, Newton, and other founders of modern science were men of lowly social origins. Perhaps the best representative of the skills which shaped modern science is Leonardo: his genius lay in the way he used both his head and his hands.

The first discipline consciously to adopt an experimental method was medicine; it was probably the only discipline in ancient times to experiment systematically to any significant degree. The great modern medical experimenter, Claude Bernard, described observation as "passive experiment" and experiment as "active observation." It is extraordinary that so little activity of this kind for so long satisfied men of powerful intellect but of an almost entirely speculative bent. Not until almost the end of the sixteenth century (if then!) did Galileo drop a one-pound weight and a ten-pound weight from the tower at Pisa in an experimental test of the widely accepted speculation that they would fall at different rates. The first university laboratory was not established until the seventeenth century, at Leyden.

It is not sufficiently appreciated how often the scientist performs experiments not to confirm his ideas "but simply to control them," as Claude Bernard put it. Galileo's experiments, as well as Newton's, were intended for the most part not to make discoveries but to make theoretical conclusions already arrived at more clear and convincing. "Without proper experiments I conclude nothing," Kepler once declared; yet his famous laws, though based on the very careful observations of Tycho Brahe, could hardly be said to have been experimentally verified. In modern times, the ideas of Planck, Einstein, de Broglie, Schrödinger, and many others were developed largely on theoretical grounds, with little experimental support for them at the time they were promulgated. A number of the most significant experiments in the history of science are *thought-experiments,* not actually carried out but only described, and their undoubted results analyzed. Examples are Newton's rotating-bucket experiment and Einstein's experiment of the falling elevator. On the whole, however, there can be no question that without experimental verification, scientific theories are either neglected altogether or viewed with reserve, if not with downright suspicion.

One of the early experimental chemists (and still very much of an alchemist), Paracelsus, compared an experiment to "a weapon which must be used in its particular way—a spear to thrust, a club to strike. Experimenting requires a man who knows when to thrust and when to strike, each according to need and fashion." One of the basic distinctions among experiments is between those experiments intending only clarification and those aiming at proof—*illustrative* and *probative experiments,* respectively. It not uncommonly happens that the degree of effectiveness of an experimental illustration of a hypothesis is mistaken for the weight of the evidence it provides. Rats may be trained so as to dramatically illustrate certain patterns of human relations, but their behavior may prove nothing at all about how such patterns are actually learned by people.

There are *methodological experiments,* to introduce or perfect certain techniques of inquiry. *Pilot studies* are experiments on a small scale, intended to establish certain parameters, like cost or utility, of a later large-scale inquiry. *Heuristic experiments* may be performed to open new lines of investigation or to provide leads for subsequent study. Exploratory studies may be "mere damnable and detestable curiosity," as Darwin said of certain kinds of animal experiments which he contrasted with "real investigation"; yet it cannot be denied that sheer curiosity has sometimes been a powerful and productive motivation. *Fact-finding* experiments may seek only to establish certain data, significant even if not problematic (like the boiling and freezing points of various substances) or important as marking the boundaries of application of already established generalizations. Only relatively few experiments are *nomological*, designed to establish a scientific law or theory, and rarer still are the *crucial experiments* which clearly decide between alternative hypotheses. An experiment may serve several purposes at once, and so may belong to several of these types or to others not distinguished here.

An experiment performed for one reason may subsequently be understood in terms of quite other aims, just as an observation may later be found to have quite another significance. These *secondary interpretations* are often of greater scientific importance than the primary ones. William Prout's finding that atomic weights of elements usually approximate whole numbers (with hydrogen as unit), Henry Cavendish's experimental proof that electrical attraction varies in accord with an inverse-square law, Count von Rumford's observation that friction (the boring of brass cannon) produces heat—these are all examples of data whose significance was made clear only later. That an observation or an experiment allows for continued reinterpretation does not mean that it was a poor one but just the contrary.

Experiments are sometimes performed only in the spirit of scientism, as though the mere fact that an experiment is being done makes an inquiry scientific. The word "experimental" like the word "methodological" is sometimes used as an honorific, to conceal the lack of ideas in the one case, and of substance in the other. Still, it is easy—and absurd—to criticize experiments for no other reason than that they are carried out in special contexts. There would be no point in experimenting if the experimental situation were no different from other situations in which observations might be made. It is similarly absurd to criticize an experiment for no other reason than that it focuses on such limited and narrow observations. Facts are always particular, but their significance may be boundless. "I love fools' experiments," Darwin once said. "I'm always making them."

The fact remains that an experiment is worthless unless we are justified in generalizing beyond the experimental situation. The laboratory is not to be contrasted with "life"; in itself, it is as real and natural a context as any other. Yet the planned controls instituted to make the experiment worthwhile introduce factors which might not have been present were it not for our intended observations. These factors might distort the very data we hoped to obtain. For instance, experiments often involve changes in scale, keeping certain magnitudes small enough to be subject to experimental variation; but what holds true in the small may be grossly misleading as to what happens in the large. Experiments on decision making in risk situations, for example, often involve the use of small sums of money as rewards or as measures of successful action. If these sums were really large, behavior might change radically. The "utility of money," as it is called, is not simply a linear function of the amount: the sum of two dollars does not necessarily have twice the value of one dollar. The small-scale experiment presupposes some knowledge of what happens when the scale is changed.

This knowledge is presupposed only in the experiment in question; there is no reason why it should not itself be made the subject of other experiments. A number of ways present themselves for dealing with experimental error. We may be able to identify the source of error and *insulate* the experimental situation from that source. Knowing that the answers a subject gives in a face-to-face interview may depend on the person he is facing, we may submit the questions in writing, the replies to be made anonymously. We may deliberately introduce other errors to *compensate* for the one whose effect we wish to cancel. A careful weighing on a balance is repeated with the position of the subject and the weights reversed in the pans. We may measure the amount of the error and *discount* its effect by subsequent calculation. This is how resistance of the air or variations in the force of gravity are often taken into account. There is no justification for imposing on experimental results the false dilemma of being absolutely true or absolutely worthless.

30. Statistical Inference

Whatever data we get, even from the most carefully controlled experiment, carries with it an element of uncertainty. It is prudent to allow for a margin of error in all empirical findings. True science, said Claude Bernard, teaches us to doubt. Even if an observation were free of error, we seldom deal with observations singly. Inquiry usually aims at determining a set of facts—not one—and even a single fact is likely to call for repeated observation. The inferences drawn from our data do not always follow by necessity but only with a greater or lesser degree of likelihood. Both for thought and for action there is no alternative to making do with approximations and probabilities. Errors of observation, multiplicity of data, and fallibility of inference—these are the universal features of human knowledge which make statistics relevant to every inquiry deserving to be taken seriously, and to every decision taken after serious thought.

These are features of our knowledge; they do not necessarily mark its boundaries. *Uncertainty* means partial or unmeasured ignorance—in particular, ignorance of the likelihoods that the situation is of one sort rather than another. By contrast, *risk* refers to a well-defined situation which includes several alternatives of specifiable likelihood. To play cards with a stranger is to enter into an uncertain situation; to know the rules of the game, and that the game is being played according to the rules, is to be confronted with a situation of risk. Much effort, in contexts of inquiry as well as of action, is devoted to transforming uncertainties into risks. One of the oldest and most important examples is provided by the principle of insurance, first adopted by shipowners, who individually faced an uncertain ruin but who collectively could deal with a calculable risk. Historically, the gambler as well as the more respectable actuary stimulated the development of the necessary mathematics. Games of chance are paradigms of risk situations. The theory of probability, the mathematical foundation of statistics, arose in the context of gambling games as statistics developed from actuarial problems.

One of the pioneers of the theory of probability, Pierre Laplace, characterized it as "at bottom nothing but common sense reduced to calculus." Neither the content of what claims to be common sense nor how it is to be reduced to mathematical form is unequivocal and beyond dispute. Few fields of mathematics so frequently invite intuition which, afterwards, turns out to have been grossly misled. When it comes to probability, even great mathematicians, men like Pascal, Leibniz, Bernoulli, and d'Alembert, have been guilty of what are retrospectively seen to be errors and even downright blunders. Probability is a domain of illusion in which one must make his way with great caution.

The calculus itself is deceptively simple. To start with, let us say that we will apply probabilities to events (outcomes, alternatives). In some formulations, probabilities are assigned instead to propositions; since these correspond to the events whose occurrence they affirm, whether we speak of events or of propositions as being probable makes no difference to the mathematical treatment. What does matter is that probabilities are assigned to kinds of events, not to specific occurrences: to a coin falling heads, and not to this penny showing heads the next time I throw it. Decisions, on the other hand, are usually concerned with the particular occurrence rather than with the type.

This circumstance, that a mathematical theory dealing with sets of events is applied to individual elements of the sets, constitutes what Reichenbach called the *problem of the single case.* He proposed the solution of treating the decision in the single case as an element of a new set, a set of comparable decisions, and applying the theory to this new set. Whether this is an adequate solution and whether the problem of the single case is properly formulated in this way or is even a genuine problem are matters on which there is no consensus. It is convenient to continue to speak of the probability of an event, meaning a kind of event and not a particular instance of the kind.

Probabilities are relative—that is, they are assigned to events provided only that certain conditions have been fulfilled. When we say that the probability of a tossed coin showing heads is ½, we assume that the coin is of the usual sort (not two-headed, for instance), that it has been tossed and not manipulated, and so on. Under other conditions other probabilities might reasonably be expected. Inferences about probabilities are sometimes mistaken because assumptions about the conditions to which the assigned probabilities were subject were unknowingly replaced by other assumptions. Problems involving probabilities in card games, for example, yield different solutions according to whether or not cards are assumed to be replaced in the deck, which is then to be reshuffled.

In the assignment of probabilities, only numbers between 0 and 1 (inclusive) are used, a decision embodied in what is called the axiom of *normalization.* Negative probabilities and probabilities greater than 1 are meaningless. If an event has a certain probability p, then the nonoccurrence (or negation) of the event is given the probability 1-p; this is called the law of the *complement.* It is sometimes easier to solve a problem by using the complementary probability with the help of the calculus of sets (§19) than to deal with the problem directly. What is the probability that at least one of a certain set of events will occur? We might more easily be able to compute the probability that none of them will occur; then, that at least one will occur is simply the complementary probability, since "at least one" is the negation of "none" ("all," it is to be remembered, is not the contradictory of "none," but its contrary—§18).

Given two mutually exclusive events, the probability that one or the other will occur is the sum of their separate probabilities; this is the law of *disjunction.* If one of the events is the negation of the other, the probability of the disjunction (that one or the other will occur) is 1. This is, therefore, the probability of a tautology. If the events are not exclusive, there is a more general law of disjunction, which states that we must subtract from the sum the probability of the joint occurrence of the events. In the usual deck of cards, the probability of a spade is ¼, and of a nonspade ¾; the probability of a card being either a spade or belonging to one of the other suits is 1. The probability of a card being a picture card is $^3/_{13}$; that of a card being either a spade or a picture is ¼ plus $^3/_{13}$ minus the probability of its being a spade picture, $^3/_{52}$, yielding the answer $^{11}/_{26}$. (In terms of the *a priori* interpretation shortly to be discussed, this answer, the same as $^{22}/_{52}$, might be thought of as counting, among the 52 cards of the deck, the 13 spades plus 12 picture cards, minus the 3 spade pictures already counted with the spades.)

Given two independent events, the probability that both will occur is the product of their separate probabilities; this is the law of *conjunction.* This law can be used to define "independence." An event e is *independent* of another event f if the probability of e given c (the initial conditions assumed to hold) is the same as the probability of e given c and f together. The probability of e, that is to say, is unchanged by the occurrence or nonoccurrence of f. (In its usual sense, independence is thought of as absence of causal connection; here, however, nothing is being said as to why the probability is unchanged. I have not yet considered how the assignment of a probability is to be interpreted.) A more general law of conjunction can be formulated which specifies joint probabilities even when events are not independent, just as the more general law of disjunction does not require exclusiveness of the events. The probability of occurrence of both e and f is the probability of e times the probability of f given e. The probability of both e and the negation of e—that is, the probability of a contradiction—is therefore 0.

The probability that two successive cards will both be spades is ¼ times the probability that the second card is a spade given that the first one was, or $^{12}/_{51}$, for a result of $^{3}/_{51}$ or $^{1}/_{17}$. If, however, the first card is replaced and the deck shuffled before the second card is drawn, the two are independent, and the answer is ¼ times ¼ or $^{1}/_{16}$. In the case of successive throws of a coin and similar games of chance, the events considered are independent of one another (barring effects like the roulette wheel wearing down). That three tosses of a coin will all be heads is simply ½ times ½ times ½, or ⅛ and, in general, that all of n tosses will be heads is $½^n$. The probability of the (n+1)st toss being heads remains just what it was, ½. The mistaken view that a succession of heads makes it more probable that the next toss will be tails is sometimes called the *gambler's fallacy*.

On the basis of these and similar laws, the theory of probability enables us to calculate a great many probabilities, provided certain other probabilities are given as premises. How these initial probabilities are to be obtained and what is meant by them is not specified by the calculus of probability itself. An answer to these questions constitutes an *interpretation* of the calculus. Such interpretations are also sometimes called "theories" of probability; they are not to be confused with the calculus they interpret. Although the various formulations of the calculus are essentially equivalent, a number of different interpretations of probability are current.

One of the oldest is the *a priori* interpretation; because of its relative simplicity, it is the one usually adopted for the exposition of the mathematics. Probability, on this interpretation, is the ratio of the number of cases of the kind whose probability is being specified—the so-called "favorable" cases—to the total number of cases in the set being considered. For instance, the probability of drawing a spade is ¼ because there are a total of 4 suits, and only 1 of these is the favorable case. A coin has only 2 sides, so the probability for each of them is ½.

Suppose we were to argue that the probability of drawing a picture card is ½, because there are 2 cases—a picture card or a number card—and 1 of these is favorable. The *a priori* interpretation requires, however, that the cases counted be equally likely; now, only 12 of the 52 cards are pictures, while 40 are numbers. How are we to establish when alternatives are equally likely? To demand that they be equally "probable" is to be involved in a vicious circle. Picture cards are assigned a probability of 3/13, but only on the assumption that the equally likely cases to be counted are those of the individual cards. What justifies the assumption?

The usual answer given in the *a priori* interpretation is in terms of what Laplace called the *principle of indifference;* sometimes reference is also made to Leibniz's earlier *principle of sufficient reason*. In effect, the principle states that cases are to be judged equally likely if we have no reason to suppose them otherwise. The smaller number of picture cards than number cards constitutes such a reason, as would knowledge of the loading of a pair of dice, and so on. Here it becomes apparent why this interpretation is called "*a priori*." Probabilities are assigned, not on the basis of experience, but on the basis of its absence. To speak in this connection of a *lack* of experience, as I was about to do, might be prejudicial. It would be unjust to object that the *a priori* theory makes of probability a measure of ignorance. In assigning a probability we are claiming knowledge not only of certain counts (the number of various alternatives) but also knowledge of certain symmetries of shape, homogeneities of composition, uniform densities, and the like. The *a priori* interpretation is incomparably the most useful one in a wide class of problems, those propounded by games of chance, as well as many problems in fields like statistical mechanics, genetics, and learning theory.

A second interpretation, the *frequency* theory, goes back to Aristotle and was taken up in modern times by Charles Peirce. The probable, Aristotle, said, is what happens for the most part. Because it derives probabilities from events already experienced, directly or indirectly, the frequency interpretation especially appeals to empiricists. The assignment of a probability is not merely a report of what has already happened; there is an inductive reference to possible future events. Specifically, the frequency theory identifies probability, not with the relative frequency of occurrence (so far) of the event to which the probability is being ascribed but with the *limit* of this frequency as the number of cases increases without limit.

The usual phrase in this connection is "in the long run." Here, the frequency interpretation encounters the familiar difficulties with inductive inference (§22). All actual runs are short as compared with the infinite sequences which stretch into the future, and a given finite initial segment is consistent with any limit whatever in the long run. After a run of, say, ten heads in a row, the number of tails does not need to catch up; ten cases (or any other finite number) have a vanishingly small effect on the ratio that emerges from the infinite number of cases yet to come. But how are we to know now what this ratio will be then?

There is another difficulty. The frequencies obtained depend on the total number of cases being counted as well as on the number of favorable cases. This total number varies with the kind of case selected as a point of reference. Which selection should be made? Consider the probability that a certain individual will die in the coming year. Different frequencies (both now and, presumably, in the long run) result according to whether we count deaths among individuals of his age, or sex, or medical history, among his forebears, or among those displaying the various combinations of these and other relevant traits. Reichenbach takes the position that we are to count the narrowest class for which we have "reliable statistics." The situation may not be altogether satisfactory, but a corresponding problem of choice of reference class faces other interpretations as well; the *a priori* interpretation, for instance, counts only the tosses from a "fair" coin, draws from a "well-shuffled" deck, and so on. The frequency theory is of unquestionable value in problems like those of demography, voting behavior, and stellar distributions.

A third interpretation develops a conception of *personal* probability—the individual's degree of belief or degree of confidence in his belief. In applications of this theory, the personal probability is measured by a willingness to wager at certain odds or by what would be acknowledged, without the actual wager, as a fair bet. This interpretation is sometimes also called "subjective" probability, but this label may be prejudicial, giving the misleading impression that anything goes. Constraints of consistency and other components of rationality are propounded in the theory, so that the resulting calculus does not differ radically, in most respects, from what the other interpretations find acceptable. The theory has the undeniable advantage of applying directly to single cases, which the frequency interpretation cannot do, and of being free from the assumptions of symmetry and the like on which the *a priori* interpretation rests. It is especially useful in the study of decision making, utility theory, and similar fields. But its foundations are more obscure and controversial than is true of the others.

There is also a *logical* interpretation of probability, especially associated with the names of the economist John Maynard Keynes and the philosopher Rudolf Carnap, among others. In this interpretation, the theory of probability is identical with inductive logic in the strict sense; a probability is a measure of the weight or degree of confirmation of an inductive inference. This view calls for the development of a logical system going far beyond the mathematical calculus of probability, and Carnap has provided the foundations of such a system. The objection has been raised, notably by Reichenbach, that at bottom the logical theory of probability is identical with the *a priori* interpretation, resting on assumptions of equal likelihood for equal regions of the logical space, as it were. Here once more, we reach the edges of the domain of consensus.

Whatever interpretation it be given, the calculus of probability finds direct application in science less often than more developed forms of the mathematics of uncertainty and risk, known collectively as *statistical theory.* These applications are of two main types. In one, multiple or uncertain data are mathematically described; in the other, on the basis of such premises probable conclusions are arrived at. The two sorts of applications are called, respectively, *statistical measures* and *statistical inference.*

The virtue demanded of a statistical measure is *reliability*—its degree of invariance as the measure is arrived at by other procedures or with other data. For a statistical inference the virtue sought is *validity*—leading to a conclusion supported by findings other than those comprised in the measures from which the inference is made. Often, both reliability and validity are ascribed to the measure itself, the inferences involved in validity being tacitly contained in the name assigned to the measure. A test of intelligence, for example, is reliable if repetitions of the test or of alternate forms of the test yield substantially the same measure; it is valid insofar as those to whom the test assigns a high or low intelligence behave as the rest of our knowledge and experience would lead us to expect.

A statistical measure, in turn, has two components: a description of the data taken as a whole, the *central tendency*, and a specification of the injustice done thereby to the individual cases, the *dispersion* of the data. The second component of descriptive statistics is obviously pointless without the first and, in less rigorous contexts, is often omitted altogether—sometimes with a highly misleading effect.

Measures of central tendency are loosely called "averages"; since the various measures have different mathematical properties, the general term lends itself to equivocation. The (arithmetic) *mean* is the familiar "average" obtained by taking the sum of the values and dividing by the number of them. The algebraic sum of the deviations from the mean (both positive and negative) is therefore 0. On the other hand, it may well happen that few cases or even none at all are anywhere near the mean value. The mean may be useful in describing several sets of measurements of a certain length, say, but not in describing the income level of a certain society. The *mode* is the most frequent value, but it may be quite rare nevertheless. It is useful in deciding, for example, what sizes to order for sale in a shoe store but not in deciding what flow a traffic system should be designed to serve. The *median* is the point which divides all the values into two equal parts when they are arranged in order of size: there are as many above the median as below it, but how far above or below is not specified. It may be useful for describing the length of stay in a mental hospital but not for describing inflationary price changes.

A principle called "the law of averages" is often misused as a slogan of block thinking (§23) in an attempt to rationalize the gambler's fallacy, as though the law requires more tails to appear in the near future after a run of heads. In fact the law, known to mathematicians as *Bernoulli's theorem,* states that if an event has a certain probability p, then the proportion of such events in n cases will approach p as n increases. As we keep tossing the coin, the proportion of heads will be closer and closer to ½—not because the probability has been changed by the previous results, but precisely because it remains unchanged.

Paradoxically, when the number of tosses increases, the probability gets less and less that the proportion will be exactly ½. As Peirce observed, everything that happens is infinitely improbable. Assuming a modicum of skill, a dart aimed at a target has a high probability of landing somewhere in the neighborhood aimed at; but the probability that it will land precisely at a given point is 0, though it is sure to land at some point or other. The situation is better represented, therefore, by approximate values than by exact ones—the fundamental consideration on which the usefulness of statistics rests. Another formulation of Bernoulli's theorem is the *law of large numbers,* which states that the probability that the mean of a sample will differ from the mean of the whole population being sampled by more than a given amount approaches 0 as the size of the sample increases.

Incidentally, because probabilities are properties of long-run sequences, a probability of 1 cannot be identified with necessity and 0 with impossibility. An event may have an infinite number of exceptions and yet the probability of its occurrence be 1, or it may occur an infinite number of times with a probability of 0. These possibilities are illustrated by a sequence of heads and tails having the structure HTHHTHHHTHHHHT . . . the first tails being preceded by one heads, the second by two, and the nth tails by n heads in a row. Although both heads and tails occur an infinite number of times in this sequence, the probability of heads is 1, and of tails, 0—the values to which the respective successive ratios are readily seen to converge. The fact that such a sequence is hardly to be expected from ordinary tosses of a coin does not alter the mathematics of the case or the meaning of the concepts usually applied in this connection.

Among the measures of dispersion, the simplest is the *range,* the difference between the minimum and maximum values in the set for which the central tendency has been given. A very common measure is the probable error, the median magnitude among the deviations of the values from their mean value; a deviation from the mean is just as likely to be less than the probable error as it is to be greater. The most useful of the measures of dispersion is the *standard deviation:* the square root of the mean of the squares of the deviations from the mean of the values themselves. Squaring deviations gives large errors proportionately more importance, as well as removing the difference between positive and negative deviations. (It can be shown that the probable error is approximately ⅔ of the standard deviation.) The most complete specification of dispersion is given by a *probability distribution,* which assigns a determinate probability to each possible magnitude of the value being considered. In simpler cases this can be approximated by a *frequency distribution,* which specifies how many cases there are of each magnitude (defined to no more than some appropriate degree of precision).

Much interest attaches to the assumptions underlying the type of distribution most commonly considered, the so-called "normal" or "Gaussian" distribution (after the great mathematician who first studied its characteristics). This is the distribution that results from *random* variations in the magnitude of the values in the distribution. The attempt to define exactly what is meant by randomness has turned out to be much more difficult than might be supposed and has led to profound questions of metalogic (§21).

Randomness is not a property of a single element taken in itself. A "random variable" is not one each of whose values is random; in itself, no number is more or less random than any other. The random variable does not have random values but takes on values at random. Moreover, randomness is not a characteristic of a set of values but of a sequence; the same set might be put into another order which would be, indeed, orderly rather than random. What, then, makes a sequence a random one?

One proposal has been formulated as the principle of the *excluded gambling system:* no selection whatever of a subsequence would yield a different probability than in the original sequence. It turns out that this condition cannot be rigorously formulated with consistency, to say nothing of being easily met. Reichenbach has proposed a weaker requirement: that the probability remain unchanged in regularly spaced subsequences (every nth case), and that it be free of aftereffect—that is, that the probability of the favorable case after any specified pattern of antecedents be no different than the original probability. In Reichenbach's sense, a sequence of heads and tails is random if heads are just as common every other time, or every third time, and so on, as in the whole sequence; and if they are just as common after one tail, or after a tail followed by a head, or after three heads, and so on, as in the original sequence.

In practice, random sequences are taken to be those produced by certain procedures, either mathematical—as, for instance, taking the middle digits after five successive multiplications of ten-digit numbers—or physical—as, for instance, taking the last digit of the number of fluctuations, of which there are several thousand per second, in the strength of a given electrical current. It is noteworthy that random sequences are *not* produced by a succession of "random choices" made by the researcher, or by anyone else. We are too likely to stay away from unusual sequences (like ten heads in a row), although these have determinate probabilities in every truly random sequence.

The importance of randomness for scientific method lies in its implications for sampling and, thereby, for all inductive inference. A sample which is not random incorporates a *bias* which invalidates the conclusions drawn from the sample. The paradigmatic case is that given by Bacon in his *Advancement of Learning*. A skeptic as to the efficacy of prayer was shown, in Neptune's temple, a great number of pictures of those who had escaped shipwreck after praying to the god. "Yes," was the reply, "but where are the pictures of those who drowned?"

The notion of a "fair sample" involves us in the *paradox of sampling*. If we know the characteristics of a population, we do not need to sample it; but if we do not know what the population is like, how can we judge whether a sample is fairly representative of it? The resolution of the paradox is that the fairness of the sample does not lie in its unknown or question-begging representativeness but in the characteristics of the procedures by which it was obtained, the so-called *sampling plan*. The plan is a fair one insofar as it yields stable samples free of bias. How these are to be secured often taxes to the utmost the knowledge already available concerning the population in question and others like it.

From a statistical description, or the statistical data themselves, certain conclusions can be drawn. Of particular importance is the conclusion that a correlation exists between two magnitudes, so that a change in the value of one would justify an inference that the value of the second has changed in some corresponding way—increasing and decreasing when the first does (a positive correlation) or doing the reverse (a negative correlation). This is not to say that a causal agency is at work but only that the variations are not a matter of chance (the times shown by two well-regulated clocks, for example, have a high positive correlation without any causal connection). Second-level statistical *tests* are needed to determine what confidence attaches to such a conclusion; they measure the probability that the degree of correlation manifested by a set of data could have resulted from random variation in the magnitudes reported. An explicitly calculated probabilism and fallibilism is not a confession of an epistemic failing but the mark of scientific maturity.

31. Man the Measurer

Measurement is so structuring an empirical system as to allow a coordination between the empirical data and a symbolic system, the *scale* of measurement, so that operations on the symbols yield results which correspond to significant features of the data. Most scales are quantitative, and a qualitative trait is usually contrasted with one that has been measured. The more extreme view, that the qualitative is not merely what has not been measured but what cannot be measured, I call the *mystique of quality*. In this view, measurement always leaves something out, precisely (if the term be permitted) what is most significant and interesting. In order to measure, it is both necessary and sufficient that we impose a structure. The mystique lies in the belief that although what structure can be imposed may reveal something of the form of our subject matter, the content of that form is necessarily left out of account. The subject is thereby distorted, and its significance destroyed; it has been standardized, mechanized, materialized, dehumanized.

The quantitative leaves something out, however, only in the sense that what we measure is but one of the countless traits of a subject that might invite attention. Of those that *have* been measured, the quantitative description tells us more, not less, than the qualitative one. In the expression, "a dozen sweet, red apples," the number does not tell us anything about taste or appearance; but it does not pretend to, and it *does* tell us more about the amount than if we were to speak of "several" or "a handful."

This example also illustrates another confusion, that between knowing something and experiencing it (§25). Knowing that something is sweet is different from tasting the sweetness. The quantitative description is an aid to knowing, not to having the experience; but that does not justify our condemning it as purposeless. As a matter of fact, it might also contribute to having an experience as well as knowing one; a trained musician can enjoy a musical score without hearing it played. The knowing is no less human (to my mind, it is even more distinctively human) than the having. Bergson's distinction between measured time and experienced duration is a real and important one; but it provides no grounds for restricting the intellect and its quantitative bent to a domain of matter contrasted with a domain of memory.

It is of critical importance to recognize that quantification and its associated technology by no means necessitate standardization and depersonalization. These are the consequences—widespread and deeply rooted consequences, to be sure—of our ignorance and ineptness in putting measures to a human use, not of our skill and ingenuity in measurement. Individually tailored garments benefit from careful measurement even more than uniforms do; the arts of design, architecture, city planning, indeed of every aspect of humane society, all have incomparably more to gain than to lose from our capacity to count and to measure.

But *can* we measure everything? The history of science documents the folly of declaring something to be impossible, when the alleged impossibility is not based on the positive ground of a scientific principle but on a purely negative assessment of human capacity. We are, as Marlowe describes us in *Tamburlaine the Great,* the possessors of souls

> *whose faculties can comprehend*
> *the wondrous architecture of the world:*
> *and measure every wandering planet's course.*

If we can measure the world in the large, why not in the small as well? Kant laid down as a fundamental principle of the human understanding that all objects of knowledge are of measurable quantity. Since his time, meanings, values, even reason have all begun to be subjected to quantitative treatment—in the measurement of semantic fields, in utility theory, and in the theory of games.

Qualitative descriptions can also have scientific importance. Kant very rightly also affirmed the principle that all objects exhibit qualitative as well as quantitative differences. In the history of science both quantitative and qualitative considerations played their parts. Differences of density, for instance, were at one time attributed to differences in the number of atoms per unit volume; then atoms were assigned different weights; these weights in turn were reduced to different numbers of protons and neutrons within the atoms; now these constituents are being analyzed in terms of a variety of qualitatively different nuclear particles, which in turn might be explicable on the basis of an undifferentiated field of some sort.

No light is thrown on the progress of science or on knowledge in general by vague declarations like the principle of dialectical materialism that changes in quantity become changes in quality. While it may be useful in one context to distinguish between a difference in degree and a difference in kind, in another context or in the light of different purposes the distinction might be drawn elsewhere, or not at all. Every trait, quantitatively specified or not, can be taken as a quality. A quantity *is* a quality whenever we find it worthwhile to distinguish it from a slightly greater or lesser quantity. The principle in question amounts only to the truism that when differences become great enough, they can always make a difference.

The reverse process—differences in quality becoming quantified—deserves at least as much notice. Chemistry, the science par excellence of qualities, attained to scientific achievements almost in direct proportion to its introduction of quantitative considerations. It is those more than anything else which differentiated the foundations of chemistry laid down by such pioneers as Joseph Priestley, Antoine Lavoisier, and John Dalton from the speculations of the ancient atomists or the medieval alchemists. Very appropriate to the history of the science was the inscription over the laboratory of the great nineteenth-century chemist Justus von Liebig: "God has ordained all things by measure, number and weight." Newton's mechanics triumphed because of the mathematical exactitude of its results; his optics suffered because of shortcomings of measurement. The wave theory of light was dismissed because observations apparently showed that light does not bend around obstacles, as waves do; in fact it does bend, but by an amount too small to be measured then. Galileo suffered from a similar inadequacy in resources of measurement: he proposed that the speed of light be measured by timing its passage between lanterns placed three miles apart. "The delay ought to be easily observable," he said; in fact it amounts to .00003 second for the round-trip.

There is a *mystique of quantity*—an exaggerated regard to the importance of measurement, no matter how and why it is carried out. "In every department of physical science," Kant once remarked, "there is only as much science, properly so-called, as there is mathematics." But that data or hypotheses have numbers in them does not make them scientific, nor does the absence of numbers rob them of scientific significance. In a famous but unfortunate declaration Lord Kelvin proclaimed, "When you can measure what you are speaking about, and express it in numbers, you know something about it; but when you cannot measure it, when you cannot express it in numbers, your knowledge is of a meager and unsatisfactory kind: it may be the beginning of knowledge, but you have scarcely, in your thoughts, advanced to the stage of science."

Kant spoke explicitly of physical science and, no doubt, that was what Kelvin chiefly had in mind. In biology, perhaps the three most basic theories—evolution, the germ theory of disease, and the theory of the cellular constitution of all organisms—are not expressed in numbers; they are not for that reason unscientific. Whatever criticisms might be made of the Marxist conception of the class structure of society, or of the Freudian conception of the unconscious, the absence of numerical expression in these conceptions is hardly the most significant criticism to be made of them.

Apropos, Kelvin regarded Darwin's views as "utterly futile," because the rate of the earth's cooling and the heat still in its interior did not allow it an age of more than 24 million years, far too short a time for evolution to have taken place as Darwin supposed. It was not until the discovery of radioactivity revealed a continuing source of heat that the difficulty was overcome. In retrospect, it is clear that what was "utterly futile" was not Darwin's qualitative theory but the mystique of quantity which relied on measures without a comparable emphasis on the significance of what was being measured and the uncertainties involved in its interpretation.

Quantitative idioms are sometimes employed without any specification of procedures of measurement. "Strength of repression," "intensity of commitment," and "lowering of morale" are examples from psychology. There is no objection to such idioms themselves, only to the tacit assumption that a quantity has been specified when it has only been named. There is a converse failing, the *false precision* of meaningless or irrelevant exactitude. A measurement may be accurate to, say, the nearest tenth of a unit; when two such measurements are multiplied, the product specifies a hundredth of a unit, but this has no empirical content. It is usual to speak here of the number of *significant figures* of a measurement; to use more than this number is false precision. The same failing also occurs when, though the figures are significant, they are pointless. The tenure of office of a political leader can be measured to the day, but this degree of precision may be of little account in a theory of revolution.

The scale with which a measurement is carried out is not a set of symbols but a *system* of symbols. It is a scale only because it is associated with a set of rules for the assignment of the symbols to the empirical materials. These rules determine which operations on the symbols are admissible—that is, which transformations of the symbols yield usefully interpretable results. Differences among scales of measurement are essentially differences among the meaningful operations which can be performed on the resulting measures. Two broad classes of scales are usually recognized: *intensive* scales, which only allow various sorts of ordering, and *extensive* scales, in which arithmetical operations are also meaningful.

Among the intensive scales is the *ordinal scale,* in which some asymmetrical and transitive relation (§19) allows us to order the elements of a set. In the Mohs scale of hardness the ordering relation is the ability of one mineral to produce a scratch on the other. A mineral with a hardness of 1.5 is harder than talc and softer than gypsum, but we cannot say whether its hardness is closer to the one than to the other. In an *ordered metric,* statements of this kind can also be made; intervals between different positions on the scale are themselves ordered.

In an *interval scale* equal intervals are defined, though with an arbitrary origin, as in the familiar scales of temperature. Though these are usually regarded as intensive scales, some arithmetical operations can be carried out—not on the measures themselves but on the intervals between them. We cannot meaningfully say that a temperature of 80 is twice as high as a temperature of 40, but we *can* say that the difference between those temperatures is twice as great as that between temperatures of 70 and 50. Scales for the measurement of utilities are often of this type. A fully extensive scale is the *ratio scale,* where the intervals are equal and a nonarbitrary zero-point is identified. With this scale, all the usual arithmetical operations can be performed, notably addition, and therefore also multiplication and division (whence the name "ratio" scale). Lear seemed to suppose that the number of attendant knights he could bring with him provided a ratio scale for filial affection, saying to Goneril,

Thy fifty yet doth double five and twenty,
And thou art twice her love.

A less dubious example is provided by the measure of amount of heat (number of calories), which contrasts in a precise way with measures of temperature.

Ratio scales may be constructed out of differences on an interval scale, as illustrated above. More commonly, they result from an ordinal scale with which there is also introduced an *additive operation,* a way of combining empirical materials—like placing them end to end, or putting them together on the same pan of a balance—which satisfies certain formal conditions, like being commutative and associative (§19). Two other distinctive conditions are: (1) The principle of the *increment:* if two elements occupy the same place on the ordinal scale, the combination of either (by the additive operation) with any other element yields a result which is higher on the scale than the uncombined element. (2) The principle of *equalities:* if two elements occupying the same place on the ordinal scale are combined, respectively, with two others which are equal to one another in the same sense, the two resulting combinations are also equal. The empirical significance of any measure lies always within the boundaries fixed by the logical structure of the scale with which the measurement was carried out.

From this fundamental constraint on measurement there follow several consequences important for both science and philosophy. One is that it is impossible, in principle, for any measurement to yield the true value of the magnitude being measured. The notion of a "true value" can be given empirical meaning only in terms of the outcome of an unending sequence of measurements, as truth itself can be defined only by reference to continuing inquiry (§27). To improve a method of measurement is, admittedly, to bring its outcomes closer to the true value, but this is a tautology. The empirical meaning of improvement in measurement is the greater reliability and validity of the resulting measures.

A second consequence is that the outcome of any specific sequence of measurements is always only an approximation; measurement is indissolubly involved with statistics. *Successive approximation* may depend, without vicious circularity, on estimates of future outcomes of measurement. On the basis of these estimates we obtain additional data which will improve the new estimates to be made next. The ephemeris is a compilation of astronomical data which is valid to some degree of precision only for specific locations which a navigator determines with the help of the ephemeris.

Third, every measurement produces effects on what is being measured. To measure something is to carry out operations, not only on symbols, but on the empirical materials with which the symbols are being coordinated. In general, measurement produces second-order effects which can be calculated and discounted. Sometimes they are altogether negligible, though in principle they are never wholly absent. When we measure the temperature of a star, what we do cannot possibly have an effect on the star, so distant that it might have ceased to exist long before we performed the measurement. What we are directly measuring is a certain attribute of the radiation we receive from the star, and that is something present to us in the observatory; what we say about the star involves additional inferences. Making an inference about something does not necessarily produce an effect on it; performing a measurement on it does.

It is not this proposition which is a fundamental principle of quantum mechanics. That measurement produces effects is as much a commonplace of classical physics as it is of modern social psychology. The revolutionary insight of quantum mechanics was that the measurement of, say, an electron's position not only changes the electron's motion, but it does so in an indefinite, unpredictable way. This uncertainty is not a corollary of the logic of measurement but a principle of an empirical physical theory, in need of—and triumphantly obtaining—experimental verification.

Finally, although measures involve the use of standards, specified in the definition of the scale, such standards are themselves subject to evaluation and correction. The standard of weight, for example, is a certain object kept in an institute near Paris. The weights used elsewhere may be called *secondary standards,* which must be measured in relation to the defined standard—an indispensable process called the *calibration* of the instruments of measurement. Even the defined standard is only a *relative* or *functional absolute.* It serves as standard for a certain set of contexts, but the measures defined in its terms may suggest the need for replacement of the old standard by a newer, better one.

If the standard meter bar were made of copper, it would always be exactly one meter in length, by definition; but when the weather grew hot in Paris, all things elsewhere would shrink—literally and truly shrink, in the only empirical meaning that can be given to a specification of length, namely, by reference to procedures of measurement. It is to avoid this awkward but logically inescapable consequence that the bar is made instead of a platinum alloy with a markedly lower coefficient of thermal expansion. That this is a better standard of length can only be determined on empirical grounds, not on purely logical ones. Logic can tell us only that a meter is a meter is a meter; but even in Gertrude Stein's Paris some meters are longer than others.

32. Concepts and Laws

Measurement presupposes appropriate conceptualization of its experiential materials. Fixities are needed by which we can find our way in the flow of experience. A concept is the mark of a constancy; it is an *identification,* the permanent possibility of saying "this" many times over with the same denotation. A basic problem in every science is to determine the entities, the units, the elements—in a word, the identities—with which it is to deal. These are captured in the concepts of the discipline.

Brute empiricism imagines that this articulation of its subject matter is thrust upon science, as though we can choose only where to look, but not how to conceptualize what we see. To the contrary, Einstein has urged, scientific concepts are "free creations of the human mind, and are not, however it may seem, uniquely determined by the external world." Modern philosophy of science recognized since John Locke that the essence of things, which ancient and medieval thought took to be embodied in our concepts of the things, are products of our own choices. Without reference to some choice, nothing can be said to be essential. In *Pragmatism* William James put it this way: "What we say about reality depends on the perspective into which we throw it. The that of it is its own; but the what depends on the which; and the which depends on us." The question, "What is this?"

never has a unique answer. The point to the question, and how the multiplicity of our purposes makes for multiple replies, would be better conveyed if the question were couched in the colloquialism, "What's it to me?"

Theories are not only built up out of concepts but are also presupposed by them. We may define concepts as we please, but we are more pleased with one definition than with another because it fits better into an acceptable theoretical structure. Its place in the structure enters into the very substance of the idea. Concepts have *systemic* meaning: their content cannot be fully explicated without involving the whole range of ideas with which they are associated. We do not really understand terms until we know the propositions in which the terms are used.

The converse is also true: we cannot understand propositions without knowing the meanings of the terms in which they are formulated. Some philosophers hold that a science culminates in suitable definitions, while others suppose that science must begin with them. Neither position does justice to the scientific situation. We must have some ideas to get on with, but they are transformed with the growth of the knowledge acquired by their help. The *paradox of conceptualization* is that good concepts are needed for the formulation of good theories, but only good theories make it possible to arrive at good concepts. Such interdependence does not place the scientist in an impossible situation; it calls for successive approximations. Walking does not require that we put only our best foot forward but that we keep our footing as we shift our weight from one foot to the other.

More illuminating than a study of definitions of scientific concepts is a study of the changes in the definitions. It is often thought that the historical development is essentially from vague concepts to precise ones, as though clarity were the supreme virtue of concepts. Clarification *is* a continuing task. The British analytic tradition, from Francis Bacon to Bertrand Russell, can find much support in the history of science for their dicta that "truth will sooner come out from error than from confusion," and, "better clearly wrong than vaguely right." Yet often the removal of vagueness is only a by-product of advances in thought. The continuing importance in biology of the concept of "species" is the paradigmatic case of a key term which remains vague. It might be better to speak of the openness of scientific terms rather than of vagueness, and to recognize that semantic and epistemic approximations go hand in hand (§12).

If a single, general direction can be identified in the development of scientific concepts it is the movement from *artificial* to *natural classes.* In conceptualizing any subject matter our aim must be, as Plato said of the art of dialectic, to carve the animal at the joints. Artificial classes set up divisions to suit our own convenience. They are not therefore arbitrary but serve only limited and superficial purposes—as is true of a filing system, or the arrangement of an inventory in a warehouse. An artificial classification provides a place for everything, but there is no reason other than ease of storage and retrieval that it should be one place rather than another.

In biology, where taxonomic sophistication is especially marked, a distinction is drawn between the *phenotype,* a classification on the basis of overt characteristics, and the *genotype,* dependent on the genetic constitution (someone with brown eyes might nevertheless carry recessive blue-eye genes). The distinction can be generalized; artificial classes tend to be phenotypes, and natural classes, genotypes. An "acid," for example, used to be thought of only as something sour, a conception still reflected in the German name for such a substance—*eine Säure;* the modern conception is in terms of hydrogen-ion concentration. Similarly, the ancient phenotypic classification of heavenly bodies into fixed stars and moving planets (the word means "wanderers") has been replaced by the modern genotypic classification in terms of their luminosity, internal or reflected.

There is no scientific merit in the deprecation of appearances as such; the point is that the more deep-seated traits tell us so much more. Chemical compounds could be classified by color, but no conclusions could be drawn from such premises about their reactions with other compounds. The color of stars, however, *is* significant and is used in classifying them. A wholly artificial classification is one which tells us no more than is specified by the class-definition itself; a wholly natural classification would tell us everything. Every actual taxonomy has something artificial about it; retrospectively, we can recognize its superficial and irrelevant features. The taxonomy of Linnaeus embodied a considerable amount of biological knowledge, as compared with that of Pliny or other ancient naturalists, but it does not tell us as much as a classification based on evolutionary principles. The same is true of Mendeleev's classification of the elements as compared, on the one hand, with the taxonomy of the alchemists and, on the other hand, with the modern periodic table based on nuclear physics.

Corresponding to the distinction between natural and artificial classes is a traditional contrast between *real definitions* and *nominal definitions.* The difference depends on whether the word defined is already in use. A neologism may be defined (nominally) as we choose, even arbitrarily. A term already in use requires a (real) definition which will do justice to its usage. One proposed definition might be evaluated as superior to another. Even though a definition itself has no empirical content (what it affirms is always true, tautologously, by definition), the point of the definition, as distinguished from its meaning, is empirical. An acceptable real definition tells us something—directly, about an established usage, and indirectly, about the more or less natural class which that usage delineates. It is misleading to dismiss as "only an argument about words" substantive disagreements about the location of the joints in the animal we are about to carve.

A definition which incorporates only the artificial elements of a classification can find acceptance only as a nominal definition. There is a story about Diogenes the Cynic that when in Plato's school man was defined as a "featherless biped" (in contrast to Aristotle's proposed real definition of man as "rational animal"), he brought a plucked chicken into the class; whereupon the qualifying phrase, "with broad, flat nails," was added to the definition. Such a definition may put man in his place, but the concept it defines is purely phenotypical.

In sum, scientifically significant concepts embody natural classes; they have more than merely a descriptive use: they appear in scientific laws. What is a scientific law? No answer to this question is accepted everywhere today; there is wide agreement, however, on certain features.

A law is a generalization; it applies to particulars but affirms something about *all* objects or events satisfying certain conditions. The term "generalization" rightly conveys the idea that the universal was arrived at from the particulars. A law must rest on observation, which is always of particulars. Rather than look to its source to explicate the concept of a scientific law, we would do better to look at its functions. A law is a generalization which plays a certain role in inquiry. Several different roles played by generalizations can be discriminated.

A *presupposition* is a tacit belief antecedent to inquiry, stipulating the background and setting for the inquiry. It characterizes "the world that is there," the domain of the unproblematic within which problems are formulated and solutions sought (§26). Some presuppositions occur widely: for instance, that objects of inquiry do not change just because we change our minds about them; that other observations made on the same materials under the same conditions will yield the same results; that the investigator's memory, assisted by notes and records, is by and large reliable. Other presuppositions apply in some contexts and not in others: for instance, that an experiment will yield the same results if performed in January rather than in June (unless it has to do with fields like astronomy, meteorology, or agriculture); that it does not matter if the laboratory is aligned to the north or to the east (unless we are concerned, say, with the earth's magnetic field); that apparatus can just as well rotate counterclockwise as clockwise, or move to the left as well as to the right (unless we are concerned with stereochemistry or parity).

Distinct from presuppositions are *assumptions*. These are not beliefs but only affirmations made for the sake of considering their consequences. Assumptions may be known to be false, yet may be worth making. Typically, it is assumed that certain ideal conditions obtain: that a system is isolated, that there is no friction, that a certain process is taking place in a vacuum, and so on. Or we may assume that certain effects are negligible: that air offers no resistance, that a structure as revealed *in vitro* is the same *in vivo*, that a respondent to a poll knows his own mind and speaks it freely. To say of a proposition that it is only an assumption, or of an admitted assumption that it is false, is not thereby to condemn it; the question is why the assumption is being made and how well it serves its purpose.

A proposition taken to formulate a possible solution to the problem posed for inquiry is a *hypothesis*. Newton's famous statement that he frames no hypotheses was meant in quite another sense, which he explicitly specified as "whatever is not deduced from the phenomena"; these, every empiricist would agree, "whether metaphysical or physical, whether of occult qualities or mechanical, have no place in experimental philosophy." In modern usage, a hypothesis is just what an experiment may be meant to test, and so provides the occasion for the experiment and is chiefly responsible for its design. A possible candidate for serving as hypothesis is called a *conjecture.* When a generalization has served its purpose well and has been sufficiently confirmed by experiment so that it can be presupposed in later inquiries, it is identified as a scientific *law.*

The term "hypothesis" is sometimes used to convey uncertainty. In that sense, there are no laws at all, only hypotheses. Confirmation is always only partial and conditional; we must acknowledge probabilism and fallibilism from the outset. Laws which are so well confirmed and so far-reaching as to be treated virtually as *a priori* are often called *principles* (§25). Near the other extreme, hypotheses which stand in need of more careful formulation or verification, but which nevertheless have a useful part to play in inquiry, are known as *working hypotheses.* More refined distinctions of this kind remain to be drawn and, like these, on a functional and contextual basis.

There are two main schools of thought as to how scientific law, in general, is to be interpreted—a perennial issue in the philosophy of science. The *positivist* view, represented by Russell, Wittgenstein, and Carnap, takes a law to be a "shorthand description" of events, the specification of a pattern whose locus is in thoughts or language rather than in things. The *realist* view, espoused by Plato, Peirce, and Whitehead, localizes the pattern in the world rather than in our knowledge or description. A law is a matter of convenience, but that it *is* convenient is as much a feature of the world as of the workings of our minds. Since Hume, there has been a consensus that on any interpretation a scientific law does not identify any agency enforcing obedience to cosmic legislation; it is impossible in principle for any such compulsion to be observed or inferred.

Kant shared this empiricism, but insisted that although no particular law is necessary, it *is* necessary that the world be lawful. Without the order and pattern embodied in scientific law, not only truth but meaning itself would elude the human mind. The orderliness of our experience reflects the structuring of experience by the conceptualizations which make sense of what our senses provide. It is a tribute to the profundity of Kant's analysis that, like Aristotle's, the philosophy was of continuing relevance to the science that followed it, for decades and even centuries. Twentieth-century philosophy of science is Kantian at least in recognizing, with Einstein, that "knowledge cannot spring from experience alone but only from the comparison of the invention of the intellect with observed fact."

33. Theories and Models

Laws may reinforce one another, sharing verifications and illuminating meanings. They may be unifed by a more comprehensive and profound generalization from which the laws can be deduced and thereby explained. Such a generalization is known as a *theory.* The theory gives order and meaning to the laws as these give order and meaning to the particulars subsumed under them. Kepler's laws, the classic example, provided a very good fit to Tycho Brahe's observations of planetary movements. In themselves, however, the laws were unintelligible and even mysterious. Why should the planets move in ellipses? Why should the line joining a planet to the sun, at one focus of the ellipse, sweep out equal areas in equal times? What lies behind the seeming numerology of Kepler's third law, that the square of a planet's period of revolution is always proportional to the cube of its mean distance from the sun? It was one of the triumphs of Newton's theory of gravitation that it readily answered these questions.

The distinction between laws and theories is not a sharp one. Laws always reach out beyond the data which they are meant to subsume. A generalization which does justice only to the given data, and gives no reason to expect further observations to conform to the generalization, is called an *ad hoc hypothesis,* with a perjorative connotation. Without any theory by which it can be understood, every law is, to a certain extent, *ad hoc.* It fits the facts, but without a theoretical basis the generalization remains as unsure as it is unintelligible. Such a proposition is sometimes called an *empirical generalization* from the narrow sense of "empiric" in the history of medicine.

Since theories give significance to laws, important generalizations have gone unappreciated until later theoretical developments illuminated their importance. Copernicus himself did not realize that the stars were suns; Giordano Bruno, in the next generation, did. The chemist Svante August Arrhenius was barely granted a doctorate with the lowest passing grade for his discovery of ionization; then, less than two decades later, he was awarded the Nobel prize for the same work. Avogadro's law, that equal volumes of all gases at the same temperature and pressure have the same number of molecules, was not generally accepted until a half-century after it was promulgated, when the theoretical significance of the distinction between atoms and molecules had become manifest. In the seventeenth century the mathematician Pierre de Fermat showed that the path of a light ray through various media always minimizes the time taken to traverse the path. In the nineteenth century another mathematician, Sir William Rowan Hamilton, formulated a certain mathematical quantity always minimized by the path of a Newtonian particle. These generalizations had no significance in relation to each other until the development of wave mechanics in our own time.

Theoretical advances do not always strengthen previously accepted laws but may lead to changes in the laws and even to their abandonment. In the same way, the discovery of a law may lead to corrections of earlier data even to the point of discarding some of the data as errors of observation. The appearance of circularity is superficial in both cases. On the other hand, new laws and new theories are not always generalizations or corrections of the old ones. They may have been developed to deal with different problems than those which elicited the older conceptions, and only later were the new ideas seen to be applicable to these older problems as well.

A theory is not a guess at the riddle, an attempt to reconstruct the blueprint by which God created the world. It is an instrument and a resource to be used in ongoing inquiry, freely to be modified or replaced. What J. J. Thomson, the discoverer of the electron, said (in his treatise on the *Corpuscular Theory of Matter*) about theories in his own field holds true generally: "From the point of view of the physicist, a theory of matter is a policy rather than a creed; its object is to connect or coordinate apparently diverse phenomena, and above all to suggest, stimulate, and direct experiment."

Theorizing often makes use of *analogy* and *metaphor.* They have no probative force, serving instead as stimuli to conceptualization and as guides to hypotheses. In the last three centuries, the clock, the organism, and the computer, respectively, provided key metaphors. In the eighteenth century a wide variety of situations, from the solar system to the economic system, were thought of as consisting, like clocks, of a relatively small number of discrete and independent components, interacting by the agency of one or two basic forces, so as to produce a stable and harmonious whole as long as its smooth working was not disturbed by the sudden intrusion of extraneous elements or forces. This gives inquiry a very different perspective from ideas arrived at in analogy to an organism which has parts whose structures can only be understood by reference to their functions in the whole organism, and which is in constant interaction, as a whole, with situations external to it. This is very different, in turn, from the working of a computer.

Analogy also plays a part in building models. I single out four distinctive features of models. (1) A model is *explicit* rather than metaphoric; the ground of comparison is not left to the creative imagination of the interpreter. (2) A model is *systematic,* developing and extending a description far beyond the one or two features which might suffice for drawing an analogy. (3) A model is *abstract,* defining its elements only so far as is demanded by the structure of the model, so that the model may have a number of different concrete interpretations. (4) A model is *hypothetical,* not asserted but only affirmed for the sake of examining its consequences or possible applications; it is not a theory put forward with a claim to explanatory force.

These characteristics make model building an effective technique for producing and testing hypotheses and theories. The drunkard's search (§28) is a particular danger here, however, since it is tempting to omit features from the model which would deprive it of simplicity and elegance. Over a century ago John Stuart Mill, in *System of Logic,* warned against the attempt "to construct a science out of a few of the agencies by which the phenomena are determined, and leave the rest to the routine of practice or the sagacity of conjecture. We either ought not to pretend to scientific forms [like impressively exact mathematical models], or we ought to study all the determining agencies equally and endeavour, so far as it can be done, to include all of them within the pale of the science; else we shall infallibly bestow a disproportionate attention upon those which our theory takes into account, while we misestimate the rest, and probably underrate their importance."

Every model simplifies the situations with which it is to deal; indeed, all theorizing omits something. Conceptualization serves no purpose except as it distinguishes between the relevant and irrelevant, the essential and accidental, the basic and superficial—in short, between what belongs to the reality of its subject matter and what belongs only to its appearance. Although *oversimplification* is always a danger, the question is rather whether the model is too simple to be useful. A model is oversimplified if we do not know the amount or even the direction of the error introduced by the simplification, for in that case, the experimental results cannot be clearly interpreted as either validating or falsifying the assumptions built into the model.

Complementary to the shortcomings resulting from what the model omits are those resulting from features included in the model because they suit the model, not the problematic situation. Misinterpreting the model in terms of such features has been aptly called the fallacy of *map reading.* Colors make maps easier to read and may add to the content by symbolizing different elevations, but the particular colors chosen for the map have nothing to do with the actual colors of the landscape. Atoms are not nearly as much like miniature solar systems as the usual depictions with balls and wires makes them appear. This is one of the considerations which make relativity theory and quantum mechanics so hard to grasp, and which endows them with such philosophic interest.

About quantum mechanics one of its founders, Erwin Schrödinger, has said, "As our mental eye penetrates into smaller and smaller distances and shorter and shorter times, we find nature behaving so entirely differently from what we observe in visible and palpable bodies of our surroundings that *no* model shaped after our large scale experiences can ever be 'true.' A completely satisfactory model *of this type* is not only practically inaccessible, but not even thinkable. Or, to be more precise, we can, of course, think it, but however we think it, it is wrong; not perhaps quite as meaningless as a 'triangular circle,' but much more so than a 'winged lion.'" At a scientific meeting in which Wolfgang Pauli presented certain ideas, Niels Bohr made the response, "We are all agreed that your theory is crazy. The question which divides us is whether it is crazy enough to have a chance of being correct. My own feeling is that it is not crazy enough." Both these great scientists knew very well that it is no particular merit in a model to reflect the preconceived ideas of its potential critics.

It is extraordinary how useful even crude models can be, often in unexpected ways. For some years I had found the theory of evolution hard to accept because I could not believe that there had been enough time for the tremendous number of changes involved in the transformation of a species into another even closely related species; it is hard to appreciate the magnitude of several billion years. Accordingly, I constructed a simple model of a freely interbreeding population, a tiny proportion of which had a certain trait of specified survival value; I wished to compute how many generations it would take for this trait to spread through the population. To my dismay, the result of the numerical values I had selected was that the population quickly died out, a possibility I had not even considered. The very simplicity of the model was useful in focusing attention on the real complexities. (Incidentally, even small advantages in survival value spread with the astonishing rapidity characteristic of exponential functions.)

As in this example, models typically specify certain magnitudes, so that the assumptions embodied in the model can be assessed in terms of their quantitative implications. Astronomers build up the model of a star, choosing values for its mass, size, proportion of helium to hydrogen, and so on, then compare the calculated radiation with what is observed. In a model the uses of mathematics come to a focus—for measurement, for statistical analysis of data, for the formulation of laws and theories, and for the derivation of conclusions from such premises. The importance of mathematics was emphasized from the very beginnings of modern science. Leonardo echoed Plato with his injunction, "He who is not a mathematician must not read me. Study mathematics, and do not build without a foundation." Galileo declared, "Philosophy [we would say "science"] is written in this grand book—I mean the universe—which stands continually open to our gaze, but it cannot be understood unless one first learns to comprehend the language and interpret the characters in which it is written. It is written in the language of mathematics, without which it is humanly impossible to understand a single word of it."

From Galileo's physics to contemporary quantum mechanics there has been an almost unimaginably great advance in our reading of the book of nature; but the language, in its essence, appears to be the same that Galileo knew. P. A. M. Dirac, who, on the basis of purely theoretical considerations predicted the positron, speaks almost in the idiom of Renaissance Neoplatonism: "God is a mathematician of very high order and He used very advanced mathematics in constructing the universe." Like Plato, Dirac sees the aim of "getting beauty in one's equations" as marking out "a sure line of progress." Even though raw empirical data can never have the exactness mathematical elegance demands, it does not follow that approximations are more practical and useful. The square root of 2 raised to the fourth power is exactly equal to 4; but to obtain an answer correct even to four decimal places, we would need to start with an approximation correct to seven places.

For the founders of modern science, as for many of their successors, the beauty of the mathematical system was at least of as much importance as its empirical validity. Copernicus reduced the number of circles needed to describe the motions of the heavenly bodies from 77 to 34; but this ratio hardly begins to measure the aesthetic improvement. Copernicus himself wrote, "We find under this orderly arrangement a wonderful symmetry in the universe, and a definite relation of harmony in the motion and magnitude of the orbs of a kind it is not possible to obtain in any other way." Kepler said of the heliocentric theory, "I contemplate its beauty with incredible and ravishing delight." This delight is well known to other scientists, especially to those whose objects of contemplation are in mathematical forms.

One who delights in mathematics runs the risk of being victimized by the law of the instrument (§28). He may seek out opportunities to use mathematics only because he enjoys the use rather than because the problematic situation makes it useful. There are models whose essential structure is logical rather than mathematical, if mathematics is thought of as necessarily quantitative. The application of the calculus of relations to kinship structures and of the theory of graphs to patterns of interpersonal encounter provides examples. There are theories which are scarcely mathematical at all, as in the examples already given from biology, with regard to cells, germs, and evolution. When mathematics *is* used, it can be very elementary, yet play a part in profound and important researches, as the work of Faraday illustrates. Many working scientists would agree with Richard Feynman's assessment of mathematical rigor of great precision as "not very useful" in empirical science.

The danger is not that the value of mathematics will be overstated, which, in general terms, is very nearly impossible. The danger is that the mathematics will be introduced in the spirit of scientism, as a fashionable mark of scientific status without really entering into the inquiry. It is not enough to "build" a model; we must do something with the model when we've got it. "No calculus without calculation," it has been well said. A structure of definitions and a set of assumptions, however mathematical in form, do not constitute either a theory or a model unless the definitions and assumptions are points of departure for inferences which could not be made otherwise. Euclid started with only ten axioms, then deduced 467 theorems, as well as a considerable number of corollaries. "It is the glory of geometry," Newton said, "that from those few principles it is able to produce so many things." Moreover, the inferences made, even if mathematically valid, must be significant in the given context of inquiry, or they express no more than a belief in the magic of symbols.

Performing operations which, though valid in form, are void of content is a widespread fallacy in measurement, in model building, and wherever mathematics is used. Its paradigm is the "Puzzle of the Missing Dollar": Three men, having paid $10 each for adjoining hotel rooms, are informed that the three rooms constitute a suite, for which the rate is only $25. The difference of $5 is given to the bellhop to return to the guests. He pockets $2, returning only $3, then reasons: "They each paid $10, received a rebate of $3, or $1 each, so that each paid only $9; now 3 times 9 is 27, and $2 I kept, making $29 in all; where is the thirtieth dollar?" The arithmetic is impeccable, but adding $2 to $27 is pointless. If, instead, $2 (the amount kept by the bellhop) is subtracted from $27 (the net amount paid), the answer is $25 (the amount received by the management). What is missing is not the dollar but good sense.

34. Explanation

Many purposes have been assigned to theories: to unify laws, guide experiments, make predictions. Among the most widely accepted functions of theory is to provide *explanations,* but what constitutes a satisfactory explanation is obscure. The psychological impact of an explanation must be distinguished from its logical function. The expressions "to *see* an explanation" and "to *have* an explanation" point to this difference. When Samuel Johnson dismissed a quibbler with the remark, "I have found you an argument; I am not obliged to find you an understanding," he was drawing the same distinction.

We must *have* a scientific explanation before we can *see* it; for its author the two processes may coincide in the moment of insight. Usually, however, explanations are not seen until some time after they have been brought forward. Newton's explanation of the tides by his theory of gravitation, for instance, was not seen by many, even by as great a scientist as Huygens, who wrote to Leibniz, "So far as concerns the cause of the tides given by Mr. Newton, I am far from satisfied, nor do I feel happy about any of his other theories built on the principle of attraction, which to me appears absurd." This is a far cry from the epitaph proposed for Newton by Alexander Pope:

> *Nature and Nature's laws lay hid in night;*
> *God said, Let Newton be! and all was light.*

After the appearance of the theory of relativity, famous for providing explanations most people still find hard to see, a wag added the couplet:

> *The Devil, crying, Ho!*
> *Let Einstein be! restored the* status quo.

It is characteristic of pseudoscience that the explanations it provides are only seen; they are not in fact had. What makes them pseudo is that they do not emerge from, or merge into, the process of inquiry. The path of scientific advance is strewn with discarded explanations. The explanations we see are usually those to which our minds were exposed in our formative years. Insofar as our conceptions have been shaped by what science made available at that time, we also *have* explanations, for what they are worth. The explanations of pseudoscience, being altogether dissociated from inquiry, are altogether worthless.

In the progress of science, an important part is played by findings inexplicable in a given state of knowledge. Such inexplicable facts may provide the key to scientific breakthroughs if pseudoexplanations do not explain the facts away. I call such findings *cryptic data.* A good example is the status of fossils a few centuries ago, seashells found on mountaintops, and the like. Pseudoexplanations—that they were the remains of antediluvian animals or marks of the Flood—at last gave way to the explanations of paleontology and geology. Meteorites provide another example of cryptic data, for which an explanation was had but not seen, when the French Academy, in the eighteenth century, branded the belief that stones fall from the sky "a superstition unworthy of these enlightened times." Cryptic data may remain invisible (§29) if their acknowledgment would impose too severe a strain on the explanations seen at that time. Thus, the "accidental" comes to mean not only what is unimportant, contrasting with the essential, but also what falls outside the framework of purposive or causal explanation, being neither deliberate nor necessary. We do not pay attention to the "accidental" features of things.

Failure to see some of the data, like our failure to see an explanation, depends on our state of mind, our implicit expectations, our mental set. In the sequence 4, 14, 34, 42, 59, the next number—as every New Yorker should know but doesn't—is 125 (they are the streets of express stops on the Independent subway); in the sequence o, t, t, f, f, s, s, e, the next letter—as every speaker of English should know but doesn't—is n (they are the initial letters of the numerals one through nine). We have the explanations but do not see them, however sound they are, if our experience is limited or if we are unable to bring our experience to bear on the explanation.

Considerations of this kind underlie a popular misconception of the nature of explanation as reducing the unfamiliar to the familiar. Michael Scriven has pointed out that phenomena as familiar as rainbows, memory, and the appeal of music were for a long time, or may still remain, unexplained, while matters as unfamiliar as pure elements, ideal gases, and absolute zero enter quite readily into our explanations. Familiarity may stand in the way of genuine explanation, inducing us to see explanations which we do not really have. Russell has wryly remarked that "if all the world consisted of billiard balls, it would be what is called 'intelligible'—i.e., it would never surprise us sufficiently to make us realize that we do not understand it." The formula that to explain something is to reduce it to what is already familiar confuses having an explanation with seeing one. Perhaps it also confuses scientific explanation with semantic explanation (§12)—the elucidation of meanings, which does depend on a reduction to what is already understood.

A more defensible conception is that to have an explanation of a phenomenon is to know under what conditions it occurs, and so to be able to predict its occurrence. This conception, too, faces difficulties; it is possible to predict without being able to explain, and we can explain without being able to predict. Eclipses were predictable long before observers had an adequate explanation of their occurrence; today, pulsars are observed to vary with predictable regularity, but how this is to be explained is still an open question. As for explanation not being sufficient for prediction, a murder might be explained by jealousy or greed, the extinction of a species explained by climatic changes, the explosion of a supernova explained by certain nuclear interactions, but in none of these cases is the power of prediction commensurate with the degree of validity of the explanation. The position that a completely comprehensive explanation would always allow us to predict is not helpful; all explanations fall short of being completely comprehensive.

Two main views of explanation are current among philosophers of science; the two views are not mutually exclusive, and might be regarded as alternative reconstructions of explanations-in-use (§15). The most widespread view is the *deductive model* of explanation, especially associated with logical positivists, notably Carl G. Hempel. In traditional idioms, in this view an explanation identifies the universal in the particular, the general rule governing the special case. More precisely, an explanation of a given event is a generalization (a scientific law) from which, together with specifications of the initial conditions, the event in question can be deduced. Similarly, a law is explained by the greater generalization of a theory, from which together with certain other qualifying premises—stating boundary conditions, for instance—the law can be derived.

The deductive model does not identify having an explanation with the power to predict, for we may not know enough of the initial conditions or of the other laws that are operative. It is useful to distinguish a *forecast* from a *prediction* in the narrow sense, the latter being purely conditional or hypothetical. In the deductive model not every generalization is explanatory, even though the generalization may allow for the desired deductions. That all men are mortal and Socrates is a man allows us to deduce his (eventual) death but scarcely explains it, as it would be explained by reference either to the biochemical properties of hemlock or to the forces making for conformity to social norms. The generalization must be a law; but it might be easier to explicate the concept of a law in terms of explanatory power than to analyze explanation as a statement of the laws which are operative.

The second view of explanation may be called the *pattern model*, associated especially with neo-Kantian philosophy and psychology, like gestalt theory. In this view, an explanation is a pattern within which what is to be explained is shown to fit. This position incorporates the traditional view that to explain is to lay bare the like in the unlike, make manifest the identity in difference, and the one in the many. The explanatory principle relates to the particulars being explained as does a pattern to the elements and relations by which it is constituted. Where the pattern is that of a logical system, the deductive model is subsumable under the pattern model. On the other hand, for something to "fit" into the pattern may be nothing other than for it to be deducible from a description of the pattern and a statement of the particulars with which it must fit in that pattern, so that the pattern model is, in turn, subsumable under the deductive one. Clearly, the usefulness of this second model depends on its invoking patterns that do not especially invite reconstruction in terms of deducibility.

This is especially likely to be true of pattern explanations in the biological and behavioral sciences. In purposive explanation, a pattern of events can be identified in which approximations to a final equilibrium state determine the direction in which the process continues; a particular event is explained by reference to its place in this directed sequence. Where the final state is intended we may speak of *motivational explanation;* if the pattern is purposive but unintended, the explanation is *functional.* The language of motives tends to be used for all purposes, the motives being ascribed to fictitious entities evoked solely in order to have the required intentions. The classic instance is Darwin's "natural selection," as though Nature makes deliberate choices—an ironic locution, because the thrust of Darwin's theories was that the purposiveness of adaptive organs and behavior can be explained in functional terms, without reliance on intentions.

An event conceived as being explicable in a certain way is said to be *interpreted* in a corresponding fashion. The famous red-shift in the light from distant galaxies, for example, is said to be interpreted as the Doppler effect of their recession at high speeds. What differentiates the biological and behavioral sciences from the physical sciences is that for the former purposive interpretations are characteristically presupposed by subsequent explanations even when these are not purposive. The sounds a person emits and the movements he makes are interpreted as having certain meanings in accord with linguistic and other cultural norms; then the psychologist or sociologist can ask for an explanation of the data so interpreted. These new explanations need not follow the same patterns, or even the same model, as those used in interpreting the data. Marking a certain piece of paper or pulling a certain lever is interpreted as casting a vote. This interpretation is purposive, and even motivational. The explanation of the voting behavior may be purely functional, however, as a Marxist might propose, or even not purposive at all, as in operant conditioning theory.

The openness of all knowledge (§26) is nowhere more marked than with regard to explanations. All explanations are, at best, partial: they do not account for every feature of what is to be explained but only those we see as significant. Explanations are conditional and approximate, applying only in certain circumstances and then only up to a point. They are inconclusive and uncertain, confirmed only to some degree, and yielding only probable conclusions. Above all, explanations are never final, not only in the sense that they might be replaced but also in the sense that the explanation itself will call for an explanation in turn. But it can explain even before it has *been* explained: Newton provided excellent explanations even though gravitation was not explained until Einstein's theory of general relativity. The criticism of a theory, "Yes, but it doesn't explain everything," at best only announces that the road of inquiry is still open.

Many different theories and models may each have explanatory force. "We can construct a system of pictures of the appearances in different ways," Ludwig Boltzmann declared at the turn of the century, and the same view was stated by Feynman in our own day: "One of the amazing characteristics of nature is the variety of interpretational schemes which is possible." We can no longer maintain, as did Descartes and many other philosophers, that the truth on any point is one, and only errors are many. There are many ways of stating and applying "the truth," and each may have a part to play in the search for explanations.

The totally inexplicable, like the inexpressible (§10), is so only relative to some context or other. Explanation is limited only by the boundaries of knowledge; these are indefinitely extensible, as is also the domain of what might be explained. At any given moment, the domain is finite; often it is very restricted. Future understanding lies, like Newton's great ocean of truth, all undiscovered before us, while, like children, we play with smooth pebbles and pretty shells on the shore.

It would be childish folly to suppose that from where we stand now we can already discern the boundaries of the distant shore. In 1835 the philosopher and sociologist Auguste Comte pronounced that man will never be able to study the chemical composition of the heavenly bodies and that every notion of the true mean temperature of the stars will necessarily always be concealed from us. Today we know more of the composition and temperature of stellar interiors than we do of the earth under our feet. The poet—in this instance E. E. Cummings—turns out to be the more philosophical thinker:

all ignorance toboggans into know
and trudges up to ignorance again
—"One Times One"

35. Science, Pure and Impure

In the popular mind, science is often identified with the technology which it makes possible. The countervailing distinction between "pure" and "applied" science often invoked by scientists and philosophers involves confusions of its own. Not only has science made technology possible; the reverse is also true. Progress in "pure" science often resulted from applications of technology—for instance, in the construction of new instruments of observation and experiment. The notion of "applied" science implies the preexistence of a "pure" formulation—either wholly abstract or wholly divorced from extrascientific interests—a formulation which is then given a concrete application. Quite often the "application" comes first, the "pure" form is abstracted from it, then the original concrete setting is retrospectively interpreted as an "application."

The history of science amply documents this pattern. Experimental method was first widely and systematically used in the field of medicine. A great deal of chemistry grew out of the attempt to understand and improve industrial processes. The needs of modern armies generated ideas in fields as diverse as statistics, kinematics, and nuclear physics. Agriculture contributed markedly to sciences like genetics, biochemistry, and microbiology. Newton was interested in the motions of the moon in order to improve methods used on ships to determine their location at sea. The attitude not uncommon in the academy of looking down on research which has immediate practical bearings may be a perpetuation of the elitist contempt for gainful employment rather than a defense of scientific integrity.

There *is* an important distinction to be drawn between *basic research* and less fundamental inquiries. Research is basic to the degree that its successful completion opens the way to further inquiries. It raises many new questions as well as providing resources in terms of which old questions can be answered or at least reformulated. Research carried out in a so-called "applied" context is not thereby deprived of scientific value, which may even be greater than the value of the solution of the practical problem. Pasteur was justifiably emphatic: "No, a thousand times no; there does not exist a category of science to which one can give the name applied science. There are science and the application of science, bound together as the fruit to the tree which bears it."

There is no denying that the tree is valued by most people only for its fruit. Basic research struggles for subvention unless it can promise payoffs other than those relating to future inquiry. Such payoffs have in fact been incalculably great. Before man can live well, Aristotle once remarked, he must be able to live. Since his day, the possibilities of living, and living well, have been unimaginably extended by advances in medicine, agriculture, industry, transportation, and communication. In a classic *History of European Morals* William Lecky opines that the inventor of anaesthetics has probably contributed more to human happiness than all the moral philosophers from Socrates to John Stuart Mill. It is an assessment which can only be painfully denied. "Concern for man himself and his fate," Einstein insisted, "must always form the chief interest of all technical endeavors. Never forget this in the midst of your diagrams and equations."

Yet disease, poverty, and hunger remain, and on a vast scale. The population explosion starkly contrasts quantity with an accelerating deterioration in the quality of life, a deterioration which continues not only in spite of but seemingly because of technological advances. Worst of all, these advances are greatest precisely where their impact is most destructive. One of the preserved fragments of thought of the pre-Socratic philosopher Heraclitus puns on the word "bios," from which we get our word "biology," but which also means the archer's bow: "Its name is life but its work is death." Heraclitus could not have foreseen the import of military research, but he must have known man's own destructiveness very well.

It is extraordinary how ancient is the fear of knowledge dissociated from virtue. The declaration that "science without conscience is but the ruin of the soul" is contemporary in content despite its archaic form; it was written by Rabelais early in the sixteenth century. Only a few decades later the legend of Faust, who sold his soul to the Devil for the sake of knowledge and power, found its way into print. The mad scientist is a more recent symbol of the same fear, embodied in such popular images as those of Frankenstein and Dr. Strangelove.

The usual defense against this line of attack on science invokes the notion of the *neutral instrument.* Science itself, the argument runs, produces only means; the ends which these means are used to serve are defined outside of science. Where and how that is done is left obscure by this argument, save that the choice of ends is, in principle, extrascientific if not downright *un*scientific. That the scientist may be implicated in the process of determining ends as well as means, establishing values as well as facts, is readily acknowledged. The idea of *roles* is then thought to preserve the claimed neutrality of the scientific enterprise. The argument is that "as citizen" the scientist shares with other men the concern over the uses and misuses of science, but "as scientist" he must rigorously set his personal values aside.

Whether this purported defense of science can reasonably be maintained depends on the validity of the theory of value it presupposes. If values are a species of fact, the distinction between ends and means can no longer be drawn in an absolute way, and it loses its force in this connection (§54, 55). There is also a dubious philosophy of science implicit in the argument. It is that values, as such, have no part to play in the scientific enterprise, but enter only into the antecedents and consequences of inquiry. Such a position cannot do justice to fundamental features of inquiry. The intellectual virtues are virtues, after all; honesty in reporting the data and dedication to the truth they disclose are essential to the scientific validity of the inquiry, not just to the scientist's personal morality. Moreover, what the scientist judges to be a datum, or which hypothesis he judges to be supported by the data, are matters that depend on his judgment, and in this process values inescapably enter. Decision theory is a powerful tool of statistical analysis which has been applied in recent decades to the decisions made within "pure" scientific inquiry as well as in such "applied" enterprises as quality control; values are equally fundamental in both cases. A scientist who was truly heartless would be, by the same token, quite mindless as well.

It remains true that the outcome of inquiry can be used in very different ways; a knowledge of anatomy is as useful to the assassin as to the surgeon. Only the totally inert is perfectly safe; the knowledge which is power—in principle this comprises all knowledge—can be power for evil as well as for good. This is the core of truth in the defense of neutrality and role-playing. Yet Frankenstein is not the name of the monster but of the man who created him; the name may be misapplied because we would like to shift responsibility for the destructive impulses within ourselves by projecting them onto the scientist as he, in turn, projects them onto the government, the military-industrial complex, and the like. The dilemma is that responsibility is indivisible, while the power to discharge responsibility is elusive or almost hopelessly fragmented.

In his *Theatetus* Plato describes the mind of the philosopher as "measuring earth and heaven and the things which are under and on the earth and above the heaven, but not condescending to anything which is within reach." What is remarkable is that he cites this description with approval. In the same passage he mentions the legend of the philosopher Thales who, while looking up at the stars, fell down a well at his feet. This is a mockery, Plato continues, to which the philosopher must be prepared to be exposed. But the legend may become fact, and we may all of us fall together. The moral to be drawn is not that we should withdraw our gaze from the stars, but that we should also condescend to what is within reach. It may not be true, as Plato's great antagonist, the Sophist Protagoras, declared, that man is the measure of all things. If we are prepared to take man's measure, as well as the measure of earth and heaven, both philosophy and science may yet survive the hatreds that are nourished by ignorance, falsehood, and folly.

Chapter Six

Metaphysics

36. Metaphysics: Pro and Con

Accusations of ignorance, falsehood, and folly have been made of philosophy throughout its history, especially of that branch called *metaphysics*. The meaning of the term has varied widely, attitudes toward metaphysics having depended on what it was conceived to be. It has aroused opposition ranging from skepticism to contempt. The term "metaphysics" was first applied to a work of Aristotle's which he himself called "First Philosophy." For the Western world, the great ages of metaphysics were the seventeenth century—which produced Descartes, Leibniz, and Spinoza—and the nineteenth century—with Hegel and Peirce. In the twentieth century, perhaps only Bergson and Whitehead are already generally acknowledged to be significant metaphysicians. Two Asian metaphysicians of the first rank are the Advaita Vedantin, Sankara, in the ninth century, and the neo-Confucian, Chu Hsi, in the twelfth century.

The most devastating critique of metaphysics is the *positivistic* critique. Only propositions capable of verification, at least in principle, positivists say, make sense (§11). Such propositions constitute the domain of science, or the protoscience of common sense. Transcending science, metaphysics consists of unverifiable and therefore meaningless statements. "Most propositions and questions that have been written about philosophical matters are not false but senseless," Wittgenstein declared in *Tractatus*, adding, "They are of the same kind as the question whether the Good is more or less identical than the Beautiful." Less prejudicial examples might have been whether the Good and the Beautiful are identical with one another, whether everything that happens must have a cause, and whether there is something permanent underlying all change. Such questions are not absurd on the face of it.

The substance of the positivist critique can already be found in Kant and in his predecessor, Hume. Kant conceives of metaphysics as consisting of propositions which, though synthetic—predicating of a subject something not already contained in the very idea of the subject—are yet known *a priori*, independently of experience. Although Kant, unlike contemporary positivists, acknowledges the existence of synthetic *a priori* propositions, he shares in the positivist critique of metaphysics in holding that such propositions tell us nothing about things, only about the structure of our own minds (the positivist would say, "the structure of our own language"). He repudiates a metaphysics which takes on "the proud name of an ontology that presumptuously claims to supply, in systematic doctrinal form, synthetic *a priori* knowledge of things in general."

The failure of this metaphysics, Kant argues, lies in its lack of an experiential basis. Plato, with his realm of Ideas purified of the dross of mere matter and sense, is the paradigm of metaphysicians. "The light dove," Kant writes in a memorable passage in his *Critique of Pure Reason*, "cleaving the air in her free flight, and feeling its resistance, might imagine that its flight would be still easier in empty space. It was thus that Plato left the world of the senses, as setting too narrow limits to the understanding, and ventured out beyond it on the wings of the Ideas, in the empty space of the pure understanding. He did not observe that with all his efforts he made no advance — meeting with no resistance that might, as it were, serve as a support upon which he could take a stand." Hume's critique of metaphysics is on this same basis. Propositions which can be known independently of experience only state relations of ideas and tell us nothing about things. Propositions about matters of fact must rest on experience.

In Hume's *Inquiry* is also to be found the *scientific* critique of metaphysics—that those of its statements which are not void of meaning are worthless as knowledge. "Here lies the justest and most plausible objection against a considerable part of metaphysics, that they are not properly a science, but arise either from the fruitless efforts of human vanity, which would penetrate into subjects utterly inaccessible to the understanding, or from the craft of popular superstitions, which being unable to defend themselves on fair ground, raise these intangling brambles to cover and protect their weakness."

In this criticism, metaphysics is seen as a pseudoscience or, at best, a quasi science—hopelessly speculative. Hegel's arguments as to the number of planets there "must" be illustrates the vulnerability of metaphysics to the first criticism, and the atomism of Democritus to the second. Science itself is unquestionably full of false starts, fixed ideas, and dead ends. There is a notable difference, however, between science and metaphysics in the readiness to subject beliefs to observational test. The entities, qualities, and powers of metaphysics—like Aristotle's entelechies, Descartes' vortices, Leibniz's monads—are not tested and then discarded, but rather bypassed. It is this circumstance which gives bite to Peirce's remark about "the deathly impotency of metaphysical reasoning." For all that, metaphysics has undeniably given impulse and guidance to the scientific enterprise.

Another criticism is the *pragmatic*. Given the pressing circumstances in which we find ourselves, pragmatists say, metaphysical speculation is very much *not* to the point. This criticism has been made by men of such diverse perspectives as Marx, Buddha, and Confucius. For the Marxist the point is not to interpret the world but to change it. Buddha preached that the man caught in a burning house, consumed by the flames of desire, does not discuss the nature of fire, nor does a man pierced by the arrow of longing speculate on its trajectory. As for Confucius, the *Analects* record his refusal to discuss prodigies or the supernatural at all.

Metaphysics is also subject to a *religious* critique, as being too sacred, too precious, or even too dangerous to be studied. The Talmud warns, "Whoever turns his attention to four things—what is above, what is below, what is before, what is behind—such a one were better not to have been born, being one who has not a respect for the honor of his Creator." Again, it enjoins, "Do not seek things too hard for you, do not search out things hidden from you. The things permitted you, think on them; you have no business with the things that are secret." In the Apocrypha, ben Sira combines the religious critique with the pragmatic one: "Do not seek for what is too hard for you, and do not investigate what is beyond your strength. Think of the commands that have been given you, for you have no need of the things that are hidden."

It is hardly to be expected that if something is declared secret, prying eyes will duly turn aside; on the contrary, curiosity may be heightened. It is the glory of the human spirit, not its shame, to persist in thinking forbidden thoughts; even the most totalitarian thought control seems unable to still the inquiring mind. Such prohibitions can make metaphysics an *esoteric* discipline, whose pursuit is limited to a circle of initiates. The Pythagoreans cultivated their philosophy in this spirit, as did the early followers of Wittgenstein. A number of philosophers, notably Leibniz and Maimonides, espoused two sorts of doctrines, one exoteric, for general consumption, and an esoteric doctrine addressed to the few who are unlikely to misunderstand and condemn. The teachings of the Kabbala are said to constitute *chochma nistara*, the hidden wisdom, and those who have acquired it are called *ba'ale ha-sod*, masters of the secret.

Esoteric metaphysics is usually occult. It is important not to confuse the occult with the mysterious. That is *mysterious* at a given time which at that time is not explained; that is *occult* which demands explanation in terms wholly inaccessible to sensory experience. The widespread confusion today between the mysterious and the occult is one of the marks of the irrationalism of our time. Einstein has said of the mysterious that it is the most beautiful thing we can experience, the source of all true art and science. But it is the *source* of these things, in evoking the awe and wonder which stimulate and guide the creative intellect. It is not an excuse for abandoning the critical self-discipline demanded by both art and science and replacing it by the fantasies of uncontrolled imagination.

Systems of occult metaphysics are to be found in all the major cultures, as exemplified by Pythagoreanism, Gnosticism, Kabbalism, Tantrism,

Theosophy, and some versions of Yoga and Taoism. Generally speaking, occult doctrines invoke a domain outside nature as disclosed to reason reflecting on experience. Such a domain cannot be entered by way of the senses but only through symbolism. Occult knowledge does not derive from observation but from interpretation; logic and experiment are replaced by hermeneutics. Argument and evidence give way to a conviction grounded in what is felt to be direct illumination. The masters of the secret are *anshe emuna,* men of faith. These illuminations typically are supposed to result from combining with study of the doctrine exercises of mind and body—abstaining from or taking certain foods or drinks (peyote, soma, and the like); breathing exercises and gymnastic postures, as in Yoga; abstinence from sex and indulgence, as in Tantrism; recitation of magic formulas, or merely of certain sounds (mantras, "aum," and the like); and so through a long catalog of well-intentioned folly.

A central part in occultism is played by symbol magic (§7), exemplified in the Kabbalistic belief in the creative power of letters as numbers. A theory was recently espoused by three physicists named, respectively, Alpher, Bethe, and Gamow; the similarity of these names to the first three letters of the Greek alphabet was inevitably remarked upon. A certain system of bringing order into the array of fundamental particles has been called "the eightfold way," in lighthearted reference to the Buddhist path of salvation. In occult metaphysics such things are taken seriously. The Pythagoreans related numbers to mental and moral qualities. The square, for instance, was seen as embodying fairness and honesty, but the ellipse, incomparably more basic in the actual constitution of things, was not endowed with corresponding significance. Neither experiment nor reasoning played any part in such interpretations, but only directly experienced expressive qualities.

It is the *logico-linguistic* critique of metaphysics which is taken most seriously by contemporary metaphysicians. This critique, too, can be traced to Kant. The human mind, he held, is so constituted that what is not a possible object of experience is mistaken for an object of some extraexperiential encounter; what serves to regulate our ideas is mistaken for something constitutive of them; what should be a *transcendental* metaphysics, stating the necessary conditions for anything to be knowable, is mistakenly replaced by a *transcendent* metaphysics, which purports to state the necessary conditions for anything to exist. The name Plato gave to what he thought was the highest exercise of reason, *dialectic*—the apprehension of the Ideas in which the reality of all things is localized—becomes, in Kant, a name for the critique of transcendental illusion, the self-deception produced by the mistakes just specified. Transcendent metaphysics is impossible; transcendental metaphysics is not only possible but is even necessary to the understanding of all other knowledge.

What Kant thought of as the structure of the mind is thought of nowadays as the structure of the language in which the mind expresses itself. Metaphysics purports to make statements about things when it is only making statements about how we speak of things; its statements consist of what Carnap called "pseudo-object sentences." Instead of "A flower is a substance, but red is a quality of substances," we could more clearly say, "'Flower' is a noun and 'red' is an adjective." The *Tractatus* begins, "The world is the totality of facts, not of things." This might be rendered as "The world is described in sentences, not by names." Metaphysics tells us nothing about existence, but only about how we speak or think of existence. Russell and Wittgenstein espoused the view that what is spoken of as the structure of facts is the logical form of the propositions in which facts are asserted. There is no metaphysics, only science and logic.

This line of argument was followed by Bergson to an unexpected conclusion. All we can *say* is the product of the analytic intellect, but man is capable of more than talk. He can also have direct experience of reality in the intuition of duration—the immediately apprehended flow of time. Metaphysical awareness is just such intuition. Metaphysics can be characterized as "the science which dispenses with symbols." Wittgenstein, too, urged that what is of philosophic significance in our propositions, their form, cannot be said but can only be shown. Such views are modern versions of the classic repudiation by mysticism of discursive metaphysics. In Wittgenstein's doctrine that "whereof one cannot speak, thereof one must be silent," mysticism and logic meet.

Pragmatism shares the scrupulous empiricism of the positivist but insists that knowledge is not limited to science unless the meaning of the term "science" is stretched beyond recognition. We may also seek to know what is presupposed in all our knowings. William James characterized metaphysics (§4) as "nothing but an unusually obstinate effort to think clearly." Thinking is metaphysical not when it is vague and woolly but when it is as precise and straightforward as it can be. Metaphysics lays out the foundations on which all we know is based, making apparent the dependence of our explicit beliefs on their implicit assumptions.

These implicit assumptions are logical. A pragmatist might even define logic as whatever provides the guiding principles for the acquisition of knowledge. "There has hardly been a metaphysician of the first rank," Charles Peirce declared, "who has not made logic his stepping-stone to metaphysics." In this perspective, metaphysics is a functionalist logic looked at substantively. It is the attempt to answer the questions, "What must the world be like for the human mind, constituted as it is, to be able to arrive at knowledge of the world? What part of what we know is intrinsic to the structure of knowledge rather than characteristic of the things known?" These formulations derive from Kant, whose influence on Peirce and pragmatism was incalculable.

Metaphysical questions are sometimes put in terms of a search for "language universals"—features to be found in all languages. This search has not been a fruitful one; languages vary so much that universals seem as much a matter of what is presupposed as of what is disclosed by the data. So far as metaphysics is concerned, the categories of classical modern logic are as serviceable as any. A language able to embody all we know cannot dispense, for example, with relation terms. The world does not consist of wholly separate individuals; characteristics do not belong only to things in isolation. Moreover, some of the relation terms must be triadic; dyads will not suffice. Systems exhibit order as well as relatedness, and order depends on triadic relations, for which "between" may be taken as a paradigm.

The question, what part of what we know is intrinsic to our knowledge rather than to things known, can similarly be formulated in terms of the necessary features of any language suitable for knowledge. Do existential propositions, disjunctions, and negations reflect ignorance, or are they necessary for the expression of all that can be known? When I say, "There is an x which has the property p," if the statement is true, some P-ish x or other makes it true; if I knew which, I could say that *that* x has the property P instead of asserting only that there is one. When I say, "*p* or *q*," if the statement is true, either the truth of *p* or else the truth of *q* (or of both) makes the disjunction true; if I knew what the case was, I could assert that case instead of the disjunction. When I say, "x does not have the property P," if the statement is true it is because x has some other property instead, incompatible with P; if I knew which I could attribute that property to x, instead of denying that x has the property P.

It is not easy to say what language would suffice if we knew everything, for the condition is so contrary to fact. In any case, we might need a more complex metalanguage if only to assert that the language in question suffices. If we could name all individuals, we could assert their properties without needing to say indefinitely that there is an individual with a certain property; but we would have to say that these are all the individuals there are, and "all are" is logically equivalent to "it is not the case that there is one which is not." The advantage is therefore a dubious one. Such issues can as well be said to belong to metaphysics as to semantics or to logic.

This is what Peirce called metaphysics—"the results of the absolute acceptance of logical principles not merely as regulatively valid but as truths of being." We pursue knowledge in certain perspectives because the world to be known is of a certain kind. We cannot be more confident of what we discover than we are of the validity of the perspectives in which the discoveries are made. "No science," Whitehead has said in the same vein, "can be more secure than the unconscious metaphysics which it tacitly presupposes." Peirce thought of his pragmatism as a device for extracting "a precious essence from metaphysics, which will give life to science." The meaning of a proposition lies in its consequences for action; for the most abstract propositions, the actions are correspondingly general—those called for in the conduct of inquiry. The precious essence of metaphysics which gives life to science is illustrated by Virchow's dictum that a disease is not an entity but a complex of symptoms (the example was first analyzed in this connection by the metaphysician Josiah Royce). What Virchow presents as a truth of being regulates the processes by which we attain knowledge.

Though Hume attacked metaphysics because it lacks an empirical basis, there can be an empirical metaphysics (unless the term is *defined* to exclude the possibility). For Artistotle as for Peirce, metaphysics aims at formulating the most general features of reality, the broadest possible truths. Medievals defined metaphysics with the scholastic formula, "the science of being *qua* being," so that, as Roger Bacon put it, it deals with what is common to all things and all sciences, its whole purpose being "to evolve the natures and properties of things." Such strict universality may be so broad as to be meaningless.

Meaningful generalizations of the widest scope can still be looked for. They are not so easy to find as might initially appear. Consider, for instance, the so-called distilled wisdom of the pronouncement, "This too shall pass away." Does this generalization also apply to numbers and other mathematical or logical entities? to the natural constants, like the velocity of light or the strength of the gravitational force? to the patterns described in scientific laws and principles? to atoms and other fundamental particles? to galaxies, or the stellar universe in its entirety?

Answers to such questions belong to or depend upon the various sciences. But the distinction between philosophy and science is a modern one, first clearly drawn by Kant; the word "scientist" was coined only in 1840. Metaphysical questions are so general that they can dispense with the special instruments of observation and well-defined contexts of inquiry characteristic of science. Metaphysics, Peirce said, aims to find out all that can be found out from those universal experiences which confront every man in every waking hour. Asian metaphysics as well as Freudian metapsychology discard even the limitation to the waking hours. It does not necessarily follow from the universality of the experiences that the metaphysical findings based on them will be familiar to everyone. Peirce declared himself sympathetic to a metaphysics and even a theology which would present itself as "a purified instinct," and both James and Bergson acknowledged considerable respect for the "intuitive beliefs of mankind." Metaphysicians like Spinoza and Whitehead, on the other hand, go far beyond what every man would recognize.

However universal the features that metaphysics formulates, the settings in which these universals are experienced are particular; they are conceptualized in correspondingly particular frames of thought. Metaphysics aims at a single mode of thought or discourse into which all others can be cast. Whitehead defines metaphysics (which he calls "speculative philosophy") as "the endeavour to frame a coherent, logical, necessary system of general ideas in terms of which every element of our experience can be interpreted." If the goal is put in terms of the object of thought, rather than of our ideas about it, this definition is not very different from the one formulated by William James: "the quest of the vision of the world's unity."

The unity sought is that which would disclose the commonalities and continuities between fact and value, science and religion, prudence and morality, utility and beauty, and so through a whole range of conflicting dualities. The questions Kant formulated two centuries ago still perplex us: What am I? What should I do? What may I hope? For Kant, these questions depended in turn on the traditional ones: Is there a God? Does man have free will? Is the soul immortal? Metaphysics aims at resolutions of the perplexities. In Whitehead's phrasing, "metaphysical understanding guides imagination and justifies purpose. Apart from metaphysical presupposition there can be no civilization." It is only because metaphysics performs such functions that Peirce could say that "every man of us has a metaphysics, and has to have one; and it will influence his life greatly."

The shortcomings of metaphysics have been formulated with more care than its merits. Metaphysics has been subjected to a positivistic critique as nonsensical, to a scientific critique as superstitious and occult, to a pragmatic critique as verbalistic and pointless, and to a religious critique as presumptuous or heretical. On the positive side, it has been defended as disclosing the presuppositions of our beliefs, exploring the implications of the logic which governs our thinking, formulating the most general features of experience, and presenting the unity of the various domains of value and fact. Much depends on how metaphysics should be conceived, but this itself poses a metaphysical question.

37. Space and Time

Space and time are the loci of reality, at least of particular and concrete existents. Plato's *Timaeus* aptly calls space "the receptacle and nurse of all generation"—that is, becoming. What exists nowhere does not exist at all, except in some special sense; what never has happened and never will happen has no part in the real world. The lover in the farce, discovered in a lady's closet, explains his presence there with the excuse, "Everybody's got to be somewhere!" His metaphysics is undeniably better than his logic. The light that never was on sea or land leaves all in darkness. As for space, we confront the quandary of an emptiness which yet is something after all, a receptacle which has no walls, a void which is by no means nothing, a place without location or boundaries. Is space a concept or a perception, a construction of the mind, an abstraction from experience, or a substance in its own right? All these views have been defended by men of acute intellect. There is scarcely any subject matter in science or philosophy so familiar and yet so little understood.

Although the nature of space is unclear, its properties are known with more exactness and certitude than that of almost any other domain of knowledge. Geometrical proofs are not only clear and convincing but for millennia served as the model of demonstrative knowledge. What is more, although the truths of geometry are apparently *a priori*, they seem to apply to every *experienced* spatial property. While arithmetic leaves experience untrammeled—violations of arithmetic, being contradictory, are sheer impossibilities—geometry imposes real constraints to which reality appears always to conform. Why shouldn't there be more than one parallel to a given line through a given point? This hardly seems as absurd as the supposition that there is more than one sum to a given pair of numbers. If the first case is as impossible as the second, why can't we prove it to be so?

The difficulty was already known to Euclid, who recognized that the proposition asserting there can be only one parallel must be taken as a postulate. A long line of distinguished mathematicians unsuccessfully tried to prove the postulate. Joseph Louis Lagrange once presented such a proof to the Paris Academy of Sciences but halted his presentation with the remark, "I must think this over once more." The trouble with such proofs is usually that they assume the truth of some other propostion equivalent to the parallel postulate—for instance, that the sum of the angles of a triangle is 180°, that the distance between parallel lines remains always constant, or that there are similar triangles. Without the postulate, it can be proved that the angular sum cannot exceed 180°; in one of the non-Euclidean geometries, the Riemannian, the angular sum can be as much as 270°, and there are no parallel lines at all. The pioneers of non-Euclidean geometry distrusted their own findings. Carl Friedrich Gauss did not publish his discoveries for fear of "the Boeotians," as he put it—men of academic narrowmindedness—and because he was distressed that the new geometry involved a constant (of curvature) which he mistakenly thought could be determined *a priori*. Johann Bolyai, among the first to make public a non-Euclidean geometry, in his old age published what he thought was a contradiction in his own system, and therefore a proof of the sole validity of Euclid.

The establishment of non-Euclidean geometries as systems whose consistency is no less than that of the Euclidean is one of the most significant achievements in the history of ideas, not just because of the new turn it gave to the problem of the nature of space but because of its implications for the dependence of *all* knowledge on observation and experience. Ironically, it was mathematics, the paradigm of rationalist knowledge, which put empiricism on a firmer foundation than ever. Geometry is now seen to be a formal system (§21) capable of various interpretations. One of these, the arithmetical interpretation, is Descartes' invention, "analytic geometry." In this interpretation, geometry consists of arithmetical truths, like the existence of common roots for certain sets of linear equations. These truths are known *a priori*, as are any other arithmetical propositions. In other interpretations, the postulates of geometry are propositions of physics, having to do with the paths of light rays, the behavior of rigid bodies, and the like. These propositions can be known only *a posteriori*. Experience gives some reason for preferring non-Euclidean physical geometries.

How can experience provide content to notions like dimensionless points, lines without breadth, and the like? More generally, what features of prescientific experience provide a basis for scientific ideas? One of the few efforts to answer such questions in detail was made by Whitehead with his method of *extensive abstraction*. By this method, the "points" of formal geometry are interpreted as nests of successively enclosed volumes whose boundaries need not be precisely specified so long as appropriate relations of enclosure are satisfied. Such volumes, in contrast to dimensionless points, *are* given in experience; suitably selected and ordered, they fulfill the requirements of the geometrical formalization.

An attempt to sketch the concrete basis for the abstractions of geometry was undertaken by Bishop Berkeley in his *New Theory of Vision.* Its main lines were reaffirmed (independently, I think) almost two centuries later by the mathematician Henri Poincaré. Both the empiricist and the rationalist believed that our ideas of space can be constructed from awareness of bodily movements and contacts. To localize an object means to represent to oneself the movements necessary to reach it; space can be conceived as the ordered array of such localizations. George Herbert Mead formulated a "philosophy of the act" in which our ideas of objects are similarly constructed from experiences of impulses, perceptions, contacts, and consummations. Mead calls a suitably organized set of such experiences a *perspective;* space is then analyzed as an abstraction from objects considered under the widest possible diversity of perspectives. That objects are located in space means that they are capable of being experienced in a certain structure of perspectives.

Such experiential data provide us not with *physical space* but with *psychological space,* both distinct from the *mathematical space* of analytical geometry as well as from the *abstract space* of an uninterpreted, formal geometrical system. Psychological space is not to be confused with our perceptions of physical space in accord with the laws of perspective as described by geometrical optics (which tells us, for instance, that a circular surface, viewed at an angle, appears to be an ellipse). Among the differences between physical space and psychological space is that the former is isotropic, uniform in all directions, while in the latter there are decided differences between up and down, forward and back, and even between left and right. The psychological space behind us closes in on us, and is more viscous, as it were, than the space which stretches before us—corresponding, I suppose, to the difference in the experiences of moving forward and backward. Eero Saarinen's TWA Terminal at Kennedy Airport is an architectural triumph because its soaring concrete vaults so vividly convey the freedom of up-and-down movement which the airplane makes possible.

Many puzzles about the nature of space arise from our assuming that physical, mathematical, and even abstract space must have the familiar properties of psychological space. An important example is provided by the concept of the curvature of a space. We imagine the curvature of a surface by supposing it to be embedded in a three-dimensional space, then seeing the surface as having a variable height in that space. By this method, the curvature of three-dimensional space would require a space of four dimensions for it to be embedded in, and there is no such physical space; the famous "fourth dimension" is *not* a fourth dimension of physical space but of the space-time manifold. The curvature of a surface, however, can be identified *within* the surface, and correspondingly, the curvature of three-dimensional space can be identified without invoking a supposed fourth spatial dimension. On a curved surface of the most familiar sort, π has a smaller value than on a plane, a value which varies with the area of the circle the ratio of whose circumference and diameter is being measured; the sum of the angles of a triangle is more than 180°, and this too varies with its area, and so on. The difference between positive and negative curvature is not a matter of the difference between convex and concave, for this depends only on our point of view; it is a matter, rather, of whether the centers of curvature of the two dimensions of the surface are on the same side—as they are for a sphere, which therefore has positive curvature—or on opposite sides—as they are for a saddle, which therefore has negative curvature.

One of the classic metaphysical issues concerning the nature of space is whether space is subsistent or relational—an object in itself, the Newtonian view, or abstracted from relations among objects, the Leibnizian view. Developments in both mathematics and physics have more and more supported the Leibnizian position. Relational is not to be confused with relative. That space is relational means that physical geometry describes relations among things, not a special kind of thing; that space is relative means that the description depends on the observer. The theory of relativity affirms both propositions. Spatial properties differ when measured by observers in motion relative to one another, the special theory of relativity dealing with uniform motion and the general theory with accelerated motion. Neither theory states that "everything is relative," even everything spatial. What relativity theory looks for are *invariants* which, like all scientifically valid findings, are the same for all observers.

The invariant in question is not a spatial distance but an interval between events, defined in terms of their separation in the three dimensions of space as well as in a fourth dimension or specification—time. Observers in motion relative to one another differ as to how far apart events are in space and how much time elapsed between them, but they will agree on a certain *space-time interval* separating the events. This is a physical fact, observationally and even experimentally verified. The difference between space and time is not invariant, but there is an invariant corresponding difference between "space-like" and "time-like" intervals, according to whether the events are so separated that a signal traveling at no more than the velocity of light might have gone from one to the other.

Another set of metaphysical questions about space concerns its infinite divisibility and extent. Zeno's paradoxes troubled philosophers for millennia; the most famous is that Achilles cannot catch the tortoise because, however fast he runs, it takes him some time to get to where the tortoise was when Achilles started, and in that time the tortoise, however slow his pace, has moved forward some distance. Zeno supposed that his argument showed that the conception of motion is illogical. What in fact it showed is the illogicality of certain assumptions about limits and continuity—in particular, the assumption that an infinite sequence of quantities, each of which is greater than zero, must have an infinite sum.

Kant formulated what he called an antinomy (in the usage of §21 it is a paradox) concerning the extent of space, arguing that we cannot think of space either as having a boundary or as boundless, and so concluding that space is a form provided by the mind rather than something belonging to things in themselves. What his argument showed is that we cannot *imagine* either alternative, though we can *conceive* both. Neither physics nor metaphysics is properly limited by the power of imagination as contrasted with the resources and constraints of logic. Contemporary cosmological models freely postulate both closed and open spaces. A closed space does not have a boundary, for in that case there would also be space beyond the boundary, as Kant rightly urged. It is closed though unbounded, just as the surface of a sphere has no boundaries (within the two-dimensional surface), yet has only a finite area.

The union of space with time in modern physical theory results from the requirement that the theory be capable of observational test. Newton characterized "absolute, true and mathematical time" as being such that "of itself and from its own nature it flows equably without relation to anything external." Actual time measurements, however, always do depend on such a relation. The definition of the simultaneity of events distant from one another so that their joint occurrence cannot be directly observed depends on our being able to send and receive signals from them and then taking into account the time required for the passage of the signal. The velocity of the signal must itself be measured; how that velocity depends on the relative motions of observers measuring it is crucial. The extraordinary findings of observation were, first, that there is a maximum velocity, c, the velocity of light in a vacuum, beyond which no signal can travel and, second, that this velocity is the same for all observers, regardless of their state of relative motion.

This finding is so extraordinary because, on the scale of usual observations, velocities increase arithmetically when one is superimposed on another: a favorable wind of 100 mph gives to a plane traveling with an air speed of 500 mph, a ground speed of 600 mph. But a light signal sent out from a moving body is found to have no more than the velocity c, regardless of the speed and direction of the body's motion. It is now recognized that velocities cannot simply be added except when they are small compared with c, in which case the correction to the formula of simple addition is negligible. Accordingly, a force applied to a rapidly moving body will not accelerate it to the same degree as if the body were moving more slowly. This is equivalent to saying that its mass has increased with its motion; were its velocity to equal c, its mass would be infinite. The famous outcome of this line of considerations is the equation $E = mc^2$.

The velocities in question here are *signal velocities*, possible motions of bodies or light rays, not *phase velocities*, sequences of events not causally related to one another. A searchlight sweeping across the sky from horizon to horizon traces out a semicircle. The time for one sweep is fixed, but the length of the semicircle can be as great as we like; we have but to choose a sufficiently long radius, the beam of light being supposed to continue outward indefinitely. In this way, the terminal point of the beam considered can be conceived to be traveling at any velocity we choose, without limit. Thereby, however, we are not conceiving a signal traveling at that velocity. A signal is a sequence of effects conveying information about their causes. Here we have not a sequence of effects but only the effect of a sequence.

Each radial beam goes on its way; it is only the source of successive beams which is moving from side to side.

According to the interval between two events and the relative motion of observers noting their occurrence, one observer might judge the events to have been simultaneous, another that E_1 occurred before E_2, and a third observer that E_2 preceded E_1. Certain intervals place events in the absolute past and other intervals place events in the absolute future for all observers. In all cases, past and future depend upon the present which is the locus of observations. The past and future I experience depend on *my* observational standpoint. Mead, in a work called *The Philosophy of the Present,* sketched how past and future can be conceived as constructions out of present experiences. This position has important implications for historiography (§68), but it must be carefully formulated. What we say now about the past and the future depends upon what we know now, but we are speaking about other times and not about the present.

That our knowledge of past and future is rooted in the present does not mean that there *is* no past or future. It is one thing to affirm that the present is the locus of all our values; it is quite another to deny reality to past and future. The affirmation is what gives meaning to the present; the denial would shrink the present to a meaningless instant, a moment without depth or dimension. Hillel's question, "If not now, when?" is meant to invite a decision grounded in our past which is to shape our future; it is not meant to deny that we have a past or will have a future. Such denials are familiar components, however, of certain lived philosophies. The infant has no stock of memories on which to draw, and is incapable of postponing gratifications to a future which is for him unimaginable. For the *infant,* only the present is real. Correspondingly, the *reactionary* is imbued with nostalgia, living only in the past, like the Bourbons who were said to have learned nothing and forgotten nothing. For the *utopian,* only the future is real.

Other philosophies of time deny only one of the three temporal domains while affirming the reality (importance, significance) of the other two. The *romantic,* perhaps reacting to the infantilism to which he may still be drawn, denies the present while affirming both past and future—a golden age in the past and glories yet to come, Paradise lost and Paradise regained. The rule enunciated by the White Queen is the epitome of romanticism: jam tomorrow and jam yesterday—but never jam today. The *radical* combines being an activist and a visionary, affirming both present and future but making a complete break with the past. History is felt to be irrelevant to the problems of the present; time begins with the new order, which therefore demands, as did the French Revolution, a new calendar. The *conservative* differs from his kin, the reactionary, in affirming the reality of the present as well as the past; both deny the future. The conservative sees the present as the repository of the meaning and value of the past, but he does not see a corresponding flow into the future. Like the orthodox who resists change without awareness of the changes which produced his orthodoxy, the conservative has a sense of history, but no historical sense.

Only the *realist* acknowledges the significance in human experience of all three—past, present, and future. The *mystic* denies all three, identifying as the locus of meaning and value not time but *eternity*. The relation between time and eternity, and what is meant by the latter, are traditional metaphysical concerns. In his *Timaeus*, Plato speaks of time as "the moving image of eternity," adding obscurely that it moves "according to number, while eternity itself rests in unity." The idea of eternity is central to the thought of the pagan Plotinus as of the Christian Augustine. The eternal cannot be identified with the everlasting. Spinoza said of eternity that it cannot be defined in terms of time, nor can it have any relation to time. Yet it is not sheer timelessness. A logical entailment, for example, is timeless; yet one would not ordinarily say that the syllogism is eternal; on the other hand, numbers and mathematical truths *have* been spoken of as eternal.

Eternity involves an infinity of some kind, but not one of duration—a temporal sequence lacking beginning or end or both. The boundlessness may be one of meaning or value, a measureless significance or worth. In that case eternity might be identified with the present as the limitless locus of meaningful action in pursuit of the good. Wittgenstein echoes this view with his aphorism, "He lives eternally who lives in the present." Yet Spinoza's ideal of viewing the world *sub specie aeternitatis*, in the light of eternity, seems to me also compelling philosophically. *My* present is only mine and that of my contemporaries; but we are the heirs of the ages and bestow a heritage on generations yet to come. The pursuit of wisdom may demand at least this emancipation from slavery to time, as Russell called it, that we see the world not only in our own perspectives but also in those of men dead and as yet unborn.

What is the difference between past, present, and future? The past is often said to be unalterable, in contrast to the future; this is Aristotle's view. The unalterability of the past may be a matter of definition; our knowledge of the past depends on its traces in the present, and these are effects of the past rather than causes capable of affecting the past. If there were closed causal chains—so that an event produced effects which eventually caused that very event, not merely one like it—past and future could not be distinguished from one another, just as any of the knights of the Round Table could be said to be seated either to the left or to the right of any other, if the distance around the table in either direction is ignored. In this view, the properties of time depend on causal relations among events. There is no logical absurdity in supposing that time does not apply to fundamental particles, say, or that in certain processes it moves backward. The nature of physical time, in short, is as subject to empirical determination as is the nature of physical space.

Causal relations alone fail to account for a fundamental feature of time—its irreversibility. Mechanical processes can as easily be conceived proceeding in one time direction as in another: a film of colliding billiard balls could be run backward without detection. Here there is a fixed time *order*, but no univocal time *direction*. What determines this direction has come to be known as the problem of *time's arrow*. The prevailing view, popularized by the philosophical astrophysicist Arthur Eddington, is that the arrow depends on considerations of thermodynamics rather than of mechanics; today, information theory might also be brought into the account. The future is the direction of approach to heat equilibrium, of greater disorder or randomness, of decay of signal into noise. The film of the billiard game can be run in the right order of it depicts a cigarette burning in an ashtray—flakes of ash fall into random patterns; they do not rise to coalesce into a cylindrical form. If at one terminus of the film the balls are to be seen lying in a tight triangle, in perfect numerical order, we recognize that this depicts the beginning of the game, not its end; the balls *might* have arrived at this configuration, but the probability is very low. In this analysis, time's arrow is only probabilistically determined. (The same might be true of causal relations.)

As we experience them, past, present, and future intertwine by way of memory and expectation. James Joyce's *Ulysses,* Marcel Proust's *Remembrance of Things Past,* and Joseph Heller's *Catch 22* all convey the copresence in experience of all three times. Bergson, in his *Creative Evolution,* has emphasized the significance of memory for all living things. "Wherever anything lives," he says, "there is open somewhere a register in which time is being inscribed." This experienced time flow he calls *duration,* in contrast to what he calls the *measured time* of physics. Duration is not just a stretch of time, an interval; it is the experience of the inexorable and irreversible effects of the passage of time. "Real duration is that duration which gnaws on things, and leaves on them the mark of its tooth." There is no doubt of the importance in human affairs of duration in this sense. Behavior is learned and goal-directed so that memory and expectation continuously transform an evanescent past and a shadowy future into an enduring, significant present. This, however, does not make measured time artificial or unreal; it differentiates psychological from physical time.

Psychological and physical time also intertwine in human experience —a theme often explored by Thomas Mann, especially in his *Magic Mountain* and in his hypnotically effective "prelude" to the *Tales of Jacob.* It is not only psychological time that is interwoven with the physical, but *cultural time,* the time which plays a part in the lived philosophy of a culture or subculture (§5). Western man hears always time's winged chariot hurrying near; for the Hindu and Buddhist a succession of lives reach into a boundless future. In some cultures, time consists of a sequence of completed pasts; in others, it is a sequence of fresh beginnings. The Hopi, for instance, put great stress on preparatory actions and ceremonies, as do the Hassidim—the Sabbath lasts only one day, but we can prepare for it all week. Time may fly like an arrow, as it does for societies with cults of modernity and progress; or it may revolve like a wheel, as it does in various traditionalist societies (§40). It may flow continuously or be marked by discontinuities. Fairy tales may end with "and so they lived happily forever after," as early movies signed off with a clinch and fade-out, or stories may go on endlessly, as in Navajo folktales. The New Year may be seen as a diapered infant displacing a graybeard with a scythe, and so as an occasion for turning over a new leaf; or man may be enjoined, as he is in the Talmud, to repent one day before his death. If metaphysics is meaningful at all, we can expect it to be as varied as are the styles of life itself.

38. The Categories

Ontology is the branch of metaphysics dealing with the nature of being, the kinds of entities there are. These kinds—the broadest classes into which all existents can be placed, the ultimate genera of all species of things—are known as *categories.* Space and time, for example, are identified by some metaphysicians, like Aristotle, as two of the categories; qualities and relations are other typical categories. Contemporary linguistic philosophy inclines to the view that most traditional categories are not categories of things but rather projections onto things of the meanings of the form classes of our language (§13 and §36). Ontology undeniably shows the influence of the language of the ontologist. It also undeniably shows the influence of doctrines *about* language—so-called speculative grammar, logical syntax, and the like. The question whether a category has or does not have an extralinguistic content must be decided separately in each case.

The scholastics distinguished certain terms as *transcendentals*—those terms transcending the differences among the categories and being applicable to members of different categories. The traditional instances are "being," "thing," "something," "one," "true," and "good." To these might be added "entity," "existent," "fact," "reality," "actuality," "individual," and "particular." Such terms may be so universal in application as to have little empirical content. Wherever there is an empirical content, it is limited to one category; the application of the term to some other category is, at best, metaphorical or analogical and, at worst, downright nonsensical. The contemporary linguistic philosopher Gilbert Ryle spoke of such usages as *categorial mistakes;* some decades earlier as nonlinguistic a philosopher as Santayana suggested that metaphysics arises from "a confusion of realms of being."

The question what becomes of the soul after death may involve such a confusion. If the soul belongs to the category of "processes," it makes no sense to ask questions about it that presuppose it to be a substance. Aristotle compared the relation between soul and body to the relation between seeing and the eye; it makes no sense to ask where the seeing goes when the eye is closed, as it would to ask what becomes of the filament or glass of a burnt-out light bulb. The soul is not a part of the body, separable or otherwise; it belongs to a different category. What, if anything, survives of a person after death is another question.

A categorial mistake was committed by the first cosmonaut, who said that he did not catch any sight of God as he traveled in space. Only physical objects or fields of physical force can meaningfully be assigned a location in physical space. The denial that God is found in space is not a conclusion from observation, any more than is the denial that the number two is colored blue. To ask for the color of numbers, unless it is meant in some metaphoric sense, is not to raise a profound metaphysical question but to confuse categories. Apropos, the French symbolist poet Arthur Rimbaud devised colors for the vowels: A black, E white, I red, O blue, and U green; synesthesia—seeing sounds as colors—is familiar both to psychology and to aesthetics. The fusion of senses by no means implies that our thoughts no longer make sense.

The categories of the Vaisheshika school of Indian metaphysics may be taken as an example for the interpretation of categories in terms of linguistic structure. The categories are: substance, quality (*guna*), action (*karma*), generality, particularity, inherence, and nonexistence. The following construal of these categories in terms of the calculus of functions (§18) is illustrative only. "Substance" comprises the individual symbols—proper names and the like—which enter into propositions. "Quality" is for the functions predicated of the names as subjects. "Action" might be taken to comprise relations, or at least some of them. "Generality" and "particularity" could be interpreted as the universal and existential operators, respectively. "Inherence" allows for propositions to be formed, marking the union of a predicate with its subject or of a relation with its relata. Finally, nonexistence is the operation of negation on propositions or of the complement on functions. These categories thus identify most of the major structural features of a language which can be used to formulate what we know of the world.

Aristotle's categories coincide with several of those in the Vaisheshika metaphysics—specifically, substance, quality, and action. Notable among the other Aristotelian categories are quantity and relation: in addition, Aristotle includes place and time. The remaining three—position, state, and passion—reflect Aristotle's physics. Rather than conceive of gravitational forces, for example, Aristotle thought of bodies as each having a natural place intrinsic to it, so that it moves up or down as required to return to its place. Aristotle explicitly defined his categories as a classification of what is signified by expressions which are not composite. Kant, the most systematic of philosophers, was critical of Aristotle's unsystematic findings, although he believed Aristotle's aim to be an admirable one: "It was an enterprise worthy of an acute thinker like Aristotle to make search for these fundamental concepts. But as he did so on no principle, he merely picked them up as they came his way." Even in philosophy, one man's principle may be another man's opportunity.

Kant's own categories are derived from the types of judgment of which the mind is capable. They are divided into four groups of three each. The groups are the familiar quantity, quality, and relation, and a fourth group, the modalities, to be considered in the next section. Grouped under relation are the important categories of substance, which I shall examine shortly, and of causality (§41). The relation of Kant's categories to types of judgment is illustrated by his deriving the categories of quantity—totality, plurality, and unity—from the classification of propositions into universal (all S is P), particular (some S is P), and singular (this individual S, say Socrates, is P), respectively. In the same way, the categories of quality—reality, negation, and limitation—are derived, respectively, from affirmative propositions (S is P), negative propositions (it is not the case that S is P), and what he calls "infinite" propositions (S is not-P). Substance is related to the categorical form of proposition (S is P) and causality to the hypothetical form (if A then B).

Kant's fondness for the number three is noteworthy (four follows closely in his scale of preferences). Kant himself recognized this propensity, and in his third (!) *Critique* offers a justification for it—couched in three propositions. The *magic number* favored by a man may be a distinctive feature of his cognitive style. Distinctions are elaborated or reduced as needed until there are exactly as many as the magic number calls for. Explanations are felt to be acceptable only if they invoke the magic number of factors.

Ten and twelve are among the larger of the magic numbers; much more common are four, three, two and one. It is not surprising that Aristotle presented ten categories and Kant twelve. Four is also a very common magic number, finding metaphysical expression not only in Kant's four sets of categories but also in the four categories of Stoic metaphysics (substance, quality, disposition, and relation), in the physics of the four elements (earth, air, fire, and water), the four points of the compass or quarters of earth and heaven, and the four seasons. The last is important in Japanese culture, providing a classification of animals and plants as well as art forms; F. H. Blythe's treatise on the haiku, the classical Japanese poetic form, is in four volumes, one devoted to each of the seasons, one of which must be indicated in every haiku. Mention should also be made of the four humors or temperaments (phlegmatic, choleric, sanguine, and melancholic) of ancient and medieval medicine and psychology.

The number four also plays a significant role in religious categories. There are four letters in the *Shem ha-m'foresh*, the awesome Hebrew name of God, which is therefore known as the "tetragrammaton." The Passover *Seder* (the observance familiar to Christianity as the Last Supper) is shot through with tetrads, beginning with the Four Questions and ending with the Four Cups. Christianity has its Four Gospels, and such symbols as the four horsemen of the Apocalypse. The religions of India give a central place to the number four—in the four *kalpas* or cosmic eras, the four Vedas (scriptures), the four *ashramas* or stages of life (student, citizen, hermit, and sage), the four major castes (farmer, merchant, warrior, and priest or philosopher), very like the four distinguished in Plato's *Republic;* and there is the symbolism of the four-headed god, Brahma. The Jain religion also has four classes of gods and a fourfold division of the community. Buddhism rests on the Four Noble Truths and identifies Four Intoxications, Four Great Efforts, four roads to saintliness, the twice-four or Eightfold Noble Path, and four stages of holiness. To all this might be added the Four Freedoms—freedom of speech and religion, freedom from fear and want—of the contemporary democratic faith.

The magic numbers seven and five are widespread, but by far the most common magic number is three. I acknowledge it to be my own magic number. It is the number underlying compromises and moderation, in accord with the *Goldilocks principle,* better known as the *golden mean:* one bowl of porridge is too hot, one is too cold, and the third is just right. The most influential of the triadic patterns of thinking is that of Hegel and his follower Marx. Hegel added a dimension of time to the Kantian antinomies, replacing abstract logic by concrete history, purporting to provide for every *thesis* and *antithesis* a *synthesis* of the two, which, as a new thesis, generates its own antithesis, and so on in the process of the dialectic. Peirce, remaining closer to Kant's thought, put the problem of the categories back into the context of the mind reaching out for knowledge. He calls the categories he applies to all experience Firstness, Secondness, and Thirdness—qualities, interactions, and meanings or purposes. The properties which the judgments basic to empirical knowledge ascribe to things are qualities (Firstness) given to the percipient (Secondness) by an object (Thirdness). Peirce, one of the most emphatically triadic of all thinkers, assigns primacy to the triad on the grounds that triadic relations are both necessary and sufficient for the construction of all relations, of whatever degree (§19).

The most suggestive of the threefold categories is the triad introduced in the Hindu *Bhagavad-Gita* and elaborated in the metaphysics of the Sankhya school. These three categories (which correspond to Peirce's in reverse of his numerical order) are *sattvas, rajas,* and *tamas.* They comprise a great number of triads important in the history of ideas, including the following: being, becoming and nonbeing, central to Plato's thought; the form, entelechy, and matter of Aristotle's metaphysics; law, action-reaction, and inertia of classical physics, and information, energy, and mass of modern physics; mind, life, and body; consciousness, effort, and ignorance, and the associated pleasure, pain, and indifference of Spinoza's thought; thinking, willing, and feeling, the central themes of Kant's three *Critiques,* and of the psychology of the century following; various typologies of physique and character, like the contemporary ectomorph, mesomorph, and endomorph symbolized in characters like Ivan, Dmitri, and Alyosha Karamazov, or Hamlet, Fortinbras, and Horatio. The Freudian triad of ego, id, and superego might also be taken to exemplify the Sankhya categories.

The *Bhagavad-Gita* introduced these three *gunas*—strands of being—in a context in which three paths to salvation, *yogas,* were distinguished, as they are within corresponding movements in all the major religions. These are the paths of wisdom, of moral action, and of devotion: *jnana-yoga, karma-yoga,* and *bhakti-yoga,* respectively. Triads of many different sorts are singled out for attention in religious literature, in Ecclesiasticus, Proverbs, the Talmud *(Avoda Zara),* the Gospel According to St. John, the *Tao Te Ching,* and the *Analects.* The Egyptians had a tritheism of Osiris, Isis, and Horus, as Tertullian and other Fathers and later Doctors of the Church had their Trinity, and the Hindus their *trimurti* of the gods Brahma, Vishnu, and Siva (who is himself often depicted with three heads). Buddhism has its *triratna,* the Three Jewels, of the *dharma,* or doctrine, the *Sangha,* or the order, and the Buddha, who is himself sometimes known as *Trikaya,* and endowed with three bodies. The Buddhist scriptures, divided into three collections, are known as the Three Baskets, the *Tripitaka,* as the Hebrew

Scriptures, the *Tanach*, consists of the Law (*Torah*), Prophets (*Nevi'im*), and Writings *(K'tuvim)*. The God of Israel is also known as the God of Abraham, Isaac, and Jacob. Vedic Brahmanism, especially, is full of triads, identifying three worlds of heaven, air, and earth, subdivided into three heavens and three earths; there are three classes of gods as well as a tripartite god called Trita, and another, Varuna, with whom several triads are associated; there are three sacrificial deities, and the number three appears over and over again in the arrangements for the sacrifices.

Folklore and mythology also abound in threesomes and triadic categories. The Chinese have their three Auspicious Stars, three Abundances, and three Celestial Palaces. Both the Greek and Roman religions often associate the number three and its multiples with their minor deities, as do Celtic and Teutonic mythologies—in the latter case, especially the number nine (three times three). Folklore and fairy tale provide us with the familiar threesomes of bears, sons, sisters, Fates, witches, and Graces; the nine Muses might also find a place here.

Pairs play a significant role in almost all philosophies. Not every distinction gives rise to a *dualism;* the pair is dualistic only when the difference between them is taken to be irreducible, so that attribution of similar qualities to both would be a categorial mistake. Otherwise, I call the pair only a *dyad*. Meanings of paired terms easily slip back and forth, unfortunately, between dyadic and dualistic usages.

The most noted metaphysical dualism is the *Cartesian* or *psychophysical dualism* of mind and matter, *res cogitans* and *res extensa*. Others are those which contrast matter and form (both Plato and Aristotle), actuality and potentiality (Aristotle), and actual and possible worlds (Leibniz). In physics, Democritus posed the antithesis of atoms and the void, reflecting Parmenides' metaphysical dualism of being and nonbeing. Empedocles emphasized the contrary forces of attraction and repulsion which he called the love and hate which move all things. In early Chinese speculation, great importance attaches to the yin-yang conception, yin designating the passive, negative, feminine feature of things and yang their active, creative, and masculine side. In contemporary physics, a particle-antiparticle symmetry is basic, like that between the electron and positron; there is thus a conception of antimatter consisting of negative antiprotons in the nucleus and positrons in orbit around it.

Perhaps the first of the philosophical dualists in the Western world was the pre-Socratic Anaxagoras, who introduced the epistemological dualism of being and thought, substance and *nous,* matter and the knowing mind. In Indian philosophy a basic distinction is drawn between *prakriti,* the dynamic, ongoing cosmic process, and *purusha,* the silent witness of the cosmic spectacle. This is not the distinction between knower and known, both of which can be subsumed under *prakriti* if only empirical knowledge is in question. It is more like the distinction in Kant's theory of knowledge between the transcendental ego and the phenomenal world. Plato's dualism of the intelligible world of Ideas and the sensible world of matter has had immeasurable importance for epistemology. This dualism is reflected in Kant's contrast between conception and perception, reason and sense. The dualism between the objective and subjective, absolute and relative, truth and falsehood is the most fundamental in modern epistemology.

Dualistic ethical categories have also been of incalculable importance; the first use of the term "dualism," which occurred in the eighteenth century, was in this connection. The difference between good and evil has been central in the philosophies of all peoples in all periods. "I have set before you life and death, blessing and curse; now therefore, choose life!" in the unforgettable words of the Deuteronomist. *Manichean* religious thought identifies two divine powers, in command of the forces of good and of evil respectively. These are exemplified by the *Zoroastrian* deities, Ahura Mazda and Ahriman, by the distinction drawn in Western religious writings between the Children of Light and the Children of Darkness, by warring gods and demons in all the world's mythologies, and by the combination of self-righteous with demonization of the enemy so characteristic of political conflict. Of particular importance for the history of morality as well as of ethics is the Pauline dualism of the spirit and the flesh—known also in the thought of the Pythagoreans, of Plotinus, of Augustine, and of many others—associated with the view that the body is vile, a hindrance to the soul (§61). In modern ethical theory, the most important dualism is the positivistic one of fact and value.

Dualistic categories, finally, play an important part in many theologies (§86). God is both a cosmological and an ethical principle, a locus both of supreme power and of perfection. Within His own nature two sides are often discriminated, most familiarly exemplified by His justice and His mercy. In Kabbalistic thought the names "Yaweh" and "Elohim" are interpreted in terms of these two aspects of divinity; a number of such pairs of aspects known as *syzygies* are identified, one member of each pair being taken to be masculine and one feminine, as in the yin-yang speculations. In all theologies, the most basic dualism is that between God and the world, especially between God and man. Although God is actual, He is not a thing among other things, and although a Person, he is not a man among other men. "Whoever associates the name of Heaven with another object," the Talmud (*Sukkah*) warns, "is rooted out of the world." Whoever confuses God with man must inevitably come to worship only an idol of his own making.

Where one is the magic number, there is no longer a set of categories; there is no point to a classification if everything belongs to the same class. There is a point, nevertheless, in affirming the primacy of some One, usually by contrast to an emphasis on two. A common way of reducing two to one is by denial of the reality or significance of one of the two. This, for example, is how Gottlieb Fichte, an early nineteenth-century German idealist, reduced the dualism of spirit and matter: "Anyone who in any way admits the existence of a material world, though only along with and beside the spiritual—dualism, as they call it—is no philosopher." An atheist reduces the dualism of God and the world simply by denying God. The materialist counterpart of absolute idealism reduces the dualism of spirit and matter by denying the reality of spirit.

A second mode of reduction is by *synthesis:* the two are combined into one or revealed as being one after all. Spinoza declared mind and body to be the same substance seen from different standpoints, within and without, and God and Nature to be but two names for one and the same reality.

A third method of reduction (I cannot rest easy unless there are three) is *interpretation:* the two result from improperly dividing up the one; each of the two in fact contains the other within itself. The thought of John Dewey is to a considerable extent this kind of interpretation of many traditional dualisms—theory and practice, means and ends, facts and values, the individual and society.

However many categories a metaphysics identifies, one of them is likely to be the category of *substance.* It is conceived in several different ways:

1. What is *self-sufficient,* existing of itself rather than because of something else; this is the conception of Descartes and Spinoza. The question may be asked, not how many kinds (categories) there are but how many there are of a given kind; for instance, how many substances there are. A metaphysician who admits only one category may be called *unitarian,* like the materialist and idealist spoken of just above, as distinguished from a *monist,* who affirms the existence of only one substance. The terms are not always used in this distinct way; "dualism" is used ambiguously both for a doctrine affirming two categories and for a doctrine affirming two existents of a given category.

The view that there are many substances is *pluralism,* which is quite compatible with a unitarian or a dualistic metaphysics. Spinoza is a monist, arguing that every existent is in causal connection with every other, so that the only self-sufficient entity is the world as a whole, which thus constitutes a single substance. Descartes is a dualist, holding that the two substances, mind and body, are each self-sufficient; there can be no causal interaction between them. Leibniz is a pluralist, postulating a plurality of *monads* (psychophysical atoms) described as "windowless"—closed to outside influences.

2. Kant, too, is a pluralist, holding that each part of any substance is itself a substance. But he conceives of substance in another way. His conception of substance is that it is the *unchanging,* the permanent substratum of all change. Only in this way, he argues, can we distinguish a change from a substitution of one individual for another. Wherever there is a change, something unchanging—one and the same thing—gives up one of its attributes, which is replaced by another. Substance never changes; only its attributes change. The same point is to be found in the *Bhagavad-Gita:* "Of the non-existent there is no coming to be; of the existent there is no ceasing to be. That by which all this is pervaded is indestructible." The conception of substance as permanent is not to be confused with a law of conservation of matter. Whether it is matter or something else that marks the unchanging is not predetermined by the metaphysical category. Kant's argument

shows, at best, that in all change there is something unchanging but not that there is something permanent beneath all change. We might even identify one and the same individual as having changed, not because there was anything unchanged about that individual but because all the changes took place by continuous gradations.

3. A third conception of substance is that it is the *substratum* in which all attributes inhere, and which enters into propositions only as subject, never as predicate or relation. This is the conception of Aristotle and of Russell. Empiricists insist that substance so conceived must be understood in logical terms and not as a certain kind of thing; such a thing, by definition, would elude all experience. Substance must not be thought of as a featureless something to which attributes belong, as if it were a cabbage into which the cocktail hors d'oeuvres are stuck on toothpicks, but which is itself quite inedible. "We have no idea of substance," Hume said, "distinct from that of a collection of particular qualities, nor have we any other meaning when we either talk or reason concerning it." From the same position, Russell pointed out that "what seems like perception of an object is really perception of certain sensible qualities together with expectations of other sensible qualities."

Yet, an object is not a mere aggregation of qualities, but exhibits a characteristic unity and persistence of these qualities. This, Russell urges, can be analyzed in terms of causal laws, which are unchanging and which unite attributes in the empirically recognized patterns. This *nomothetic unity* (unity by way of law) is much more useful than is a unity of substance in promoting the growth of knowledge. The search for laws and patterns of change has proved to be more fruitful than the search for distinctive substances. The history of science provides a number of examples of the replacement of supposed entities with certain properties by observed processes in identifiable contexts. A supposed caloric fluid gave way to the process of oxidation, the ether to radiation in electromagnetic fields, and protoplasm to coded and catalyzed sequences of chemical reactions. A similar transformation is taking place today in our ideas about personal identity (§47).

39. Existence and Reality

Existence is, for most people, something which can be seen and felt, which offers resistance to the touch—matter. Anything else is acknowledged to exist if it is (a), a condition or attribute of matter, like perceived qualities such as color or hardness; (b), an abstraction erected upon a material base, like potential energy or a planetary orbit; or (c), some special subtle kind of material entity, like gravitation or electricity. Matter itself is still widely thought to be as Newton described it, consisting of "solid, massy, hard, impenetrable, movable particles."

The metaphysics which regards all existence as limited to matter is called *materialism*, sometimes *metaphysical materialism* to distinguish it from the *moral materialism* expressed in the pursuit of pleasure, power, or profit. Metaphysical materialism has often been attacked because of objections to moral materialism, but the metaphysics by no means necessarily implies the morality. Materialism has been widespread in the history of ideas, being espoused by Greek atomists like Democritus, the Hindu school of Carvaka, the Chinese skeptic Wang Ch'ung, the seventeenth-century philosopher Thomas Hobbes, and many thinkers, notably Marx, in the nineteenth century.

In the last hundred years the conception of matter has been radically transformed. What had been thought of as matter was arrived at on the basis of everyday experience. But for the atomic and subatomic scale of quantum theory and nuclear physics very different ideas are called for. Talk about particles which are also waves, about the movement of waves through "empty" space, about a particle as a wave of probability that observation will yield a certain finding—all this reflects the need for models not couched in terms of our ordinary encounters with things. Hume, for example, declared that everything in nature is individual, a view which would be endorsed by materialists; yet electrons and other such entities have no discernible individuality. No empirical meaning can be assigned to a proposition like one affirming that *this* electron was once part of the body of Marilyn Monroe and *that* one of Brigitte Bardot.

Modern materialism is metalinguistic: instead of holding that only matter exists, it asserts that all statements about existents must be based on the statements about attributes and behavior of matter. These statements make up physics; *physicalism* is the view that all science is one, being ultimately reducible to physics. The position was especially defended by Carnap and others of the *unity of science* movement. Many scientists have also taken that position. The atomic physicist Ernest Rutherford, for example, remarked that all science is either physics or stamp collecting. The nineteenth-century founder of theoretical spectroscopy, Gustav Kirchhoff, expressed a view typical of his time: "The highest object at which the natural sciences are constrained to aim is the reduction of all the phenomena of nature to mechanics." To this, rejoined Ernst Mach, ironically one of the forerunners of the logical positivism which in our time provided the philosophical framework for physicalism: "Intelligible as it is that the efforts of thinkers have always been bent upon the 'reduction of all physical processes to the motions of atoms,' it must yet be affirmed that this is a chimerical ideal. In the workshop of the serious inquirer it has discharged scarcely the least function." Earlier in the nineteenth century, the posivitist Auguste Comte described the now familiar pyramid of the sciences, resting on the broad base of physics and moving up through chemistry to biology, reaching its peak in sociology—a discipline which, as coincidence would have it, was founded by Comte himself.

That all the sciences use the same methods, and that all cognitive propositions have their meanings specified on the same basis of observation are generally accepted doctrines (§11 and §28). They affirm the unity of science as a *unity of methods* and a *unity of terms*. Physicalism gives a third sense to the unity of science, the *unity of laws:* that the laws of all the sciences may be derived from the laws of physics. At present, however, and in the foreseeable future, not even all of physical science can be derived from a single set of propositions; only parts of chemistry and fewer parts of biology can be so derived; as for the behavioral sciences, derivations from physics are negligible. The position can only be defended programmatically.

Existence is not limited to actuality: possibilities may also be said to exist. More generally, several *modalities* can be distinguished, corresponding, in Kant's analysis, to the mode of affirmation in a judgment—that something *might* be the case or cannot be the case, that in fact it *is* or is not the case, that it *must* be or need not be the case. These generate the categories of what is possible or impossible, actual or unreal, necessary or contingent. The modalities are taken in a number of senses.

First, there is the *psychological* sense. The necessity which knows no law, which is the mother of invention, and of which men make a virtue, is a psychological need, like hunger. When, in the *Ethics of the Fathers (Pirke Avot),* Simeon ben Azzai enjoins us to deem nothing impossible, and Napoleon declares that the word "impossible" is not French, what the sage and the man of action agree on has to do with human achievements. Along the same lines, "possible" may designate something permitted, or being considered, or falling outside the scope of decisions already made. In short, in the psychological sense the modalities depend on human action or aspiration.

In the *logical* sense, the modalities depend only on logical truths. An exact treatment of the modalities in this sense is provided by *modal logic,* a field pioneered about a half-century ago by the pragmatist C. I. Lewis. That is necessary whose affirmation is an analytic proposition, a tautology, or a logical truth (§15–§17). A proposition is impossible if its negation is necessary; it is contingent if it is neither necessary nor impossible; and it is possible if it is not impossible. The definition of the actual and unreal fall outside the logical modalities unless they are identified with the truth and falsehood, respectively, of a contingency.

On the basis of these definitions, together with postulates formulating properties of the modalities, some of which are far from obvious, many theorems can be derived of the type that if something is necessary, it is not possible that it is not the case, or, that nothing actual is either impossible or necessary. Not all the theorems are obviously true, especially if modalities are compounded; for instance, if something is necessary, is it possible that it not be necessary? can necessity itself be a matter of contingency? The logic requires choices without dictating what choices are to be made.

Once the decisions have been made, however, the logic *can* dictate belief, on pain of abandoning the rationality defined by the logic in question. In the third century, the Church Father Tertullian defended the faith with the formula, "It is certain because it is impossible, and to be believed because it is absurd." This position is itself an absurdity in the strict sense—a contradiction or logical impossibility—for, if something is impossible, it is its *negation* which is certain and so to be believed. Tertullian's position was restated as late as the seventeenth century by the physician and philosopher Sir Thomas Browne, who thought to reconcile science and religion with the declaration, "To believe only possibilities is not faith, but mere philosophy" (§89).

Lewis Carroll, an expert logician, addressed himself to the issue in this dialogue between Alice and the White Queen.

> "Let's consider your age to begin with—how old are you?"
>
> "I'm seven and a half, exactly."
>
> "You needn't say 'exactly,'" the Queen remarked. "I can believe it without that. Now I'll give *you* something to believe. I'm just one hundred and one, five months and a day."
>
> "I can't believe *that!*" said Alice.
>
> "Can't you?" the Queen said in a pitying tone. "Try again: draw a long breath, and shut your eyes."
>
> Alice laughed. "There's no use trying," she said: "one *can't* believe impossible things."
>
> "I daresay you haven't had much practice," said the Queen. "When I was your age, I always did it for half-an-hour a day. Why, sometimes I've believed as many as six impossible things before breakfast."

If the laws of nature are added to those of a system of logic, the resultant modalities have an *empirical* sense. "Possible" then means: consistent with the laws of nature; "necessary," what is required by natural law; "contingent," neither entailed by nor inconsistent with the laws of nature. That the planet Mercury might have a moon—as was recently mistakenly announced—is possible; that the moon would traverse an elliptical orbit, is necessary; that it would be between three and four hundred kilometers in diameter, is contingent; that it would just graze the surface of the planet, without crashing or being shattered, is impossible. If empirical facts as well as laws are also taken as given, we obtain real modalities. Possibility is now to be understood as *potentiality*. There is a real possibility that roses will bloom in my garden—they were planted there. That orchids will grow there is empirically possible—it would not violate any known botanical principle—but it is not really to be expected.

There is, finally, the interpretation of the modalities as *metaphysical*, but their meaning in this sense is obscure. Suppose there were principles constituting what metaphysics called "laws of being *qua* being"—laws applying to all existents, not because they have this or that property but simply because they exist. Then the metaphysical modalities would bear the same relation to these laws (consistent with them, entailed by them, and so on) as the logical modalities have to the laws of logic and the empirical modalities have to natural laws. Causality has been construed—for instance, by Spinoza and Kant—as such a metaphysical principle (§41). For them, "necessary" means causally determined; the other modalities are correspondingly interpreted.

Kant gives as examples of what is impossible, because they violate the sole conditions under which the mind can acquire knowledge of objects, the existence of spirits (immaterial substances), clairvoyance (direct perception, not inferential knowledge, of the future), and telepathy (sharing, without sensory communication, the contents of a mind). I take these to be empirical impossibilities rather than metaphysical ones. It is hazardous for metaphysics to predetermine scientific hypotheses. The contemporary cosmological theory of "the continuous creation of matter" violates the traditional metaphysical principle *ex nihilo nihil fit* (nothing comes out of nothing), and so might be said to be metaphysically impossible; but this theory has been given serious scientific consideration. If it is eventually rejected, as now seems likely, the rejection will be on empirical grounds, not on metaphysical ones.

The modality of actuality is especially perplexing; it raises one of the most troublesome metaphysical questions—the nature of existence. Leibniz, a mathematician and logician of the first rank, presented the idea of *possible worlds,* systems which are consistent but not actual. Two features of a world may each be possible, if considered separately, without being jointly possible or *compossible;* a world may contain an immovable object or an irrestible force, but not both—the existence of either one is incompatible with the existence of the other. The real world, said Leibniz, is distinguished among all possible worlds because it maximizes the compossibles. But the measure of quantity which is presupposed here is quite obscure.

Kant raised a fundamental objection in one of the most penetrating analyses to be found anywhere in philosophy. Existence, he argued, is not an attribute of things: in the mere concept of a thing no mark of its existence is to be found. Thinking of a dollar and thinking of a real dollar cannot be distinguished from one another, as though in the second case we are thinking of something with a property the first thing does not have. If this were so, we could think of that property in the first case as well, but that would not make what we are thinking of real; it would still be only a thought. Actuality cannot be characterized on a purely rationalist basis, as Leibniz supposed; an empiricist element must also be invoked. The real dollar can be seen, touched, spent, and so on; it enters into experience. Whether it does so or not, its description remains the same. Existence is not a property by which the actual world can be distinguished from possible worlds.

When we speak of an individual existing or not—was there really a Robin Hood?—we are asking about the truth of statements containing definite descriptions (§18): Was there someone who lived in Sherwood Forest, dressed in Lincoln green, and robbed the rich and gave to the poor? We are asking whether a certain class has a member. Whether classes themselves exist, as distinct from their members, and in general the existence of abstract entities, is another matter (§13).

It is sometimes assumed that all existence is of the same grade, that there are no degrees of reality. Many metaphysicians repudiate this assumption. The most famous of these repudiations, in Plato's *Republic,* is his myth of the cave, which, slightly condensed, reads:

> Picture men living in a sort of underground cave with a long opening to the light. Conceive them as having their legs and necks chained from childhood, so that they remain in the same spot, able to look forward only. Picture further the light from a fire burning higher up and at a distance behind them and, between the fire and the prisoners, a road along which a low wall has been built. A strange image and strange prisoners, but like us. These men would not have seen anything of themselves or of one another except the shadows cast from the fire on the wall of the cave in front of them, and the same would be true of the objects carried past them. In every way such prisoners would deem reality to be nothing else than the shadows of things. But when one was freed from his chains, at first, because of the dazzling light, he would be unable to discern the objects whose shadows he formerly saw. Yet what he had seen before was all a cheat and a delusion; now, being nearer to reality and turned toward more real things, he could see more truly. At first he would most easily discern the shadows, and after that the likenesses or reflections in water of men and other things, and later, the things themselves.

For Plato, there is a real world of Ideas and a lower order of reality in the objects of sense experience. Even here there are gradations—things are more real than their reflections. There are also gradations of reality among the Ideas, the Idea of the Good being the highest. In theistic philosophies, like those of Aristotle and, following him, Maimonides and Aquinas, God is pure actuality, the *Ens Entium* or *Being of Beings;* the world which He created is also real, but in a lesser degree. Peirce subsumed gradations under a principle of continuity which he called *synechism;* this principle played a significant part in the history of science as the postulate that Nature does not proceed by leaps. The gradations of reality, from the highest to the lowest, make up *the great chain of being* which plays an important part in the metaphysics of Neoplatonism, the Kabbala, Vedanta, and many other systems.

In these metaphysics, the lower grades of reality are *emanations* from the highest. The eleventh-century Jewish theologian ibn-Gabirol (who, in the mid-nineteenth century, was proved to be identical with the Arab philosopher Avicebrón), specified the gradations: God, then simple substances—intellect, soul, and nature—then composite substances. In Indian metaphysics, the grades, starting with the most unreal, are exemplified by: the children of a barren woman, a sea serpent, a rope-seen-as-a-snake, a snake, and finally, Brahman. Mistaking what is relatively unreal for a higher grade of reality is a consequence of what Indian philosophers call *adhyasa,* imaginary attribution, or what we call projection; just as the snake is projected onto the rope, so, the Vedantin argues, the world is projected onto Brahman. God is the magician Who is not deluded by His own spectacle.

Commonly associated with doctrines differentiating grades of being is a metaphysics of *correspondences.* The grades are not independent; their constituents symbolize and are causally connected with one another. The great Kabbalistic treatise, the *Zohar,* says: "Everything in this world is a replica of something in the world above. Whatever is done on earth has been preceded by its prototype in Heaven. From an activity below there is stimulated a corresponding activity on high. Whenever the thing below bestirs itself, there is a simultaneous stimulation of its counterpart above, as the two realms form one interconnected whole." Another correspondence important in the history of ideas, both in Western and Asian cultures, is that between the *macrocosm* and the *microcosm*, a reflection in the small (especially in man himself) of the great world. This notion is to be found in the Neoplatonists, in such Renaissance thinkers as Paracelsus and Pico della Mirandola, and in Leibniz. The *Zohar* says flatly, "There is not a member in the human body but has its counterpart in the world as a whole."

In the metaphysics of graded realities there is frequently a confusion between two ideas, a confusion marked by an ambiguity in the term "appearance." On the one hand, "appearance" designates the manifestation of a reality; when a man puts in an appearance at some occasion, he is there, present, a part of it. On the other hand, "appearance" designates what is contrasted with a reality, a simulation, a copy, something which only looks like the real thing, but which is significantly different from it. Let us call this a *mere appearance*. Not all appearances are mere appearances, and every mere appearance, properly seen and judged, is not mere at all but the appearance of a reality. There are not two grades of reality but two ways in which reality is experienced and understood. Kant is widely misinterpreted as distinguishing between noumenal and phenomenal worlds, of which we can only know the second. His view is not that we know only appearances *rather* than realities but that we know reality as it appears to us. The Vedantist conception of *maya* is also widely misinterpreted as a veil of illusion rather than as our experience of reality.

Instead of several grades of reality into which existents can be classified, there are many perspectives from which they can be experienced and understood. This view is *contextualism;* Mead and Whitehead are among its modern exponents. In the metaphysics of the Jains of ancient India, contextualism is formulated as the basis for their doctrine of *syadvada* (§26), that knowledge is only of half-truths. Knowledge is rooted in experience, and each experience takes place in a limited perspective, as in their fable of the seven blind men and the elephant. Contextualists are divided on the issue of whether there is any absolute perspective or all-inclusive context. For Whitehead and many others, the answer is in the affirmative; the absolute perspective is the perspective of the Absolute. For Mead and other relativists, all perspectives are limited. The Jain speak in this connection of the absolutist fallacy, *nayabhasa*, "naya" designating a perspective or context of knowing. The "new realists" of twentieth-century Anglo-American thought spoke of a similar "fallacy of exclusive particularity."

From a contextualist standpoint, what is unreal in one context is quite real in another; a functional classification of such contexts replaces the hierarchy of ontological categories. Perceived qualities of things, like colors ("secondary qualities"), have been denigrated by many metaphysicians as having some lesser degree of reality than physical properties ("primary qualities"). Value qualities, like those central in art and morality ("tertiary qualities"), have usually been assigned an even lower ontological status. Contextualism implies that all such qualities are real, truly existent in nature, but nature as involved in experiences, apprehended in the perspectives of some context. This position is *objective relativism:* the qualities are objective, relative to the context with reference to which their existence is asserted.

Physical objects and their properties seem to claim a higher degree of reality only because our conception of a physical object results from our assigning perceptual and value qualities to what is revealed in contexts of manipulation—an assignment made because these contexts are significant in the widest range of our experiences and because the properties disclosed in them are most nearly invariant. What is real comes down to what it best suits our purposes to take seriously. Whether a certain choice *will* suit is not of our own choosing; it is a matter of ineluctable fact. This, I suppose, is what is meant by reality, after all.

40. Permanence and Change

Wherever we look we see motion and change; the more we know of the world the more convinced we are that these are pervasive features of things. The aphorisms of Heraclitus are of universal application: "All is flux; nothing endures but change; you cannot step into the same river twice, for fresh waters are forever flowing in upon you." Yet there must be fixities as well, or else our thoughts will have nothing to take hold of. In a dialogue appropriately named after Parmenides, the most noted metaphysician of permanence, Plato argues that "if a man will not admit that every individual thing has its own determinate Idea which is always one and the same, he will have nothing on which his mind can rest, and so he will utterly destroy the power of reasoning."

There are, then two main types of metaphysics—the Heraclitean and the Parmenidean—according to whether or not change is seen as important. Russell, preoccupied with patterns of thought in mathematics and logic, insists that we should not take time seriously; yet Whitehead, also a mathematician, declares, "Nature is a structure of evolving processes. The reality is the process." Most contemporary philosophies are in this sense Heraclitean. Religious philosophies, focused on eternity rather than on things temporal, are usually Parmenidean. Buddhist metaphysics is a conspicuous exception; a basic Buddhist doctrine is the principle of *anitya*—impermanence, universal change, no enduring substantial reality.

Not just any sort of change can serve as a paradigm of the world process. A clock quietly unwinding exhibits a continuous process of change, but it is far from representative of the turbulence so much a part of the world. I once stood at the edge of a volcano in eruption—Kilauea, I think it was. The scene was like one of Gustav Doré's illustrations for Dante's *Inferno*, but of a scale and a palpable reality that made it indescribably awesome—a glowing lake of molten stone, repeatedly bursting in enormous bubbles and cascades, giving off sulfurous vapors and waves of fierce heat, the whole bathed in a weird reddish light. What must the scene be at the surface of a star, with jets of gaseous material more massive than the whole earth streaming out a hundred thousand miles and more, or in its deep interior, with temperatures in the millions of degrees! The galaxies rush away from one another at speeds of thousands of miles a second, reverberations of the Big Bang which many cosmologists today postulate as the beginning of the present structure of the universe. In the microcosm as well, we find waves vibrating with unimaginable frequencies, colliding molecules, and subatomic particles endlessly spinning, revolving, fragmenting, and annihilating one another. The river of Heraclitus does not quietly flow in upon us but engulfs us in rapids, waves, and whirlpools; we live in a tempestuous world.

What is moving we may see as being in motion or as having arrived at a given point. Spinoza distinguishes between *natura naturans,* nature in process, and *natura naturata,* the nature produced in that process. Spinoza's metaphysics, like that of Plato and Kant, attempts to do justice to both product and process, permanence and change. Bergson, a twentieth-century Heraclitean, insists, "Reality is mobility. Not things made [naturata], but things in the making [naturans], not self-maintaining states, but only changing states exist." Most of Bergson's speculations preceded the discovery of the expanding universe and of the incessant mobility of things on the subatomic scale. Such prescience is not uncommon; philosophical insight—like its counterpart, artistic insight—often anticipates scientific discovery.

Heraclitean metaphysics came into its own in the nineteenth century through the influence of Hegel and Darwin. Hegel's dialectical process—thesis generating an antithesis which combines with its opposite to form a new synthesis—was taken up by Marx as a metaphysical basis for his social philosophy. *Dialectical materialism* contrasts with the *mechanistic materialism* of nineteenth-century philosophers of science in emphasizing the significance of change. Though mechanism involves motion, it does not produce any fundamental change; the planets eventually return to their original positions in their orbits. Hegel's dialectic also does not allow for genuine change, for the dialectic is a process of thought; and thinking, as Plato saw, terminates in an Idea which is always one and the same. The idealism of Hegel and his followers yields only a frozen "block universe," as William James called it, as incompatible with pragmatist liberalism as with the Marxist philosophy of revolution.

Darwin's influence on the metaphysics of change is incalculably great. Several centuries earlier, Leibniz had declared that "there is nothing uncultivated, nothing sterile, nothing dead in the universe." But not until Darwinian biology did life and growth become significant metaphysical categories. The following passage from Bergson's *Creative Evolution* is exemplary:

> All organized beings, from the humblest to the highest, from the first origins of life to the time in which we are, and in all places and in all times, do but evidence a single impulsion, the inverse of the movement of matter, and in itself indivisible. All the living hold together, and all yield to the same tremendous push. The animal takes its

> stand on the plant, man bestrides animality, and the whole of humanity, in space and in time, is one immense army galloping beside and before and behind each of us in an overwhelming charge able to beat down every resistance and to clear many obstacles, perhaps even death.

Criticizing this doctrine, near the end of his *History of Western Philosophy,* Russell eloquently expresses the Parmenidean perspective:

> But a cool critic, who feels himself a mere spectator, perhaps an unsympathetic spectator, of the charge in which man is mounted upon animality, may be inclined to think that calm and careful thought is hardly compatible with this form of exercise. When he is told that thought is a mere means of action, the mere impulse to avoid obstacles in the field, he may feel that such a view is becoming in a cavalry officer, but not in a philosopher, whose business, after all, is with thought: he may feel that in the passion and noise of violent motion there is no room for the fainter music of reason, no leisure for the disinterested contemplation in which greatness is sought, not by turbulence, but by the greatness of the universe which is mirrored.

It is unjust to Bergson to charge him with an unthinking activism. What he does say is that the intellect deals with space and matter in ways shaped by the possibilities of action, a view shared by pragmatists and empiricists. Nineteenth-century idealism came to a similar conclusion from very different presuppositions, adopting a *romantic pragmatism.* Gottlieb Fichte, a philosopher of liberal nationalism in the Napoleonic era, saw the world as organized with reference to human tasks and the means for their performance. Nature, he said, is the material of our duty. Matter is a projection of man's will, which hardens into mechanical necessity as his moral impulse slackens. This view is echoed in Peirce's witticism, deriving from his idealist metaphysics, that nature is second habit.

The connection between will and the concept of matter becomes less obscure when we see will as expressed in our strivings, and matter as defining the obstacles to and resources for the fulfillment of our strivings. This view was developed by Friedrich Nietzsche. Our belief in the reality of objects, he pointed out, is derived from our sensations of strength, struggle, and resistance. Thereby we become aware of our own reality as well. "A living thing," he says, "seeks above all to discharge its strength—life itself is will to power; self-preservation is only one of its indirect and most frequent results." Nietzsche's philosophy of the will to power bears only a superficial resemblance to Fascist and Communist rationalizations of their political practice (§70).

Arthur Schopenhauer had earlier formulated a metaphysics of will as "the foundation of all being; it is part and parcel of every creature, and the permanent element in everything. The word 'will,' like a magic spell, discloses to us the inmost being of everything in nature." And of man as well. Man is defined by his values—that is to say, by his desires. Schopenhauer's pessimism is constituted by his conviction that desire cannot master and transform reality; fulfillment can be found only in the denial of will, as Buddhism also urged. Says Omar,

Ah, love! could you and I with Him conspire
To grasp this sorry Scheme of Things entire,
Would not we shatter it to bits—and then
Re-mould it nearer to the Heart's Desire!

This wish-fulfilling fantasy is expressed in art. Art can be seen as a striving of the will, a mastery of materials by which they are transformed in order to impose meaning and value upon them. The aesthetics of romanticism, presented by Friedrich Schelling and Samuel Taylor Coleridge, gives another version of the metaphysics of will. Nature is felt to be a manifestation of a creative urge which is fully self-conscious only in the poetic genius. Nature is a poem whose secret is revealed by art; it is visible spirit, while spirit is invisible nature.

Both the strength and the weakness of these *voluntaristic* philosophies (those which make the will central) are better seen against the background of the more profound and all-embracing metaphysics of Spinoza. One of his basic categories is *conatus,* "the endeavor with which each thing strives to persist in its own being"—inertia in the physical domain, self-preservation in the biological domain, the Freudian libido and the Nietzschean will-to-power in the psychological domain. Spinoza identifies this endeavor as "nothing more than the actual essence of the thing itself." The essence is that by which a thing is known or understood; accordingly, will and intellect, volition and idea are for Spinoza one and the same. In yielding the appetite in the voluntaristic sense, not Spinoza's, the thing may not persist in its being; it may, rather, destroy itself. The appetite grows by what it feeds on, as Shakespeare's Ulysses points out:

Then everything includes itself in power,
Power into will, will into appetite,
And appetite, an universal wolf,
So doubly seconded with will and power,
Must make perforce an universal prey,
And, last, eat up himself.
—*Troilus and Cressida*

Intermediate between the Heraclitean and the Parmenidean metaphysics are those in which the reality of change is acknowledged, but which also discern fixities of pattern underlying change. The easiest way in which this can be done is by a conception of *cosmic eras,* each characterized by certain constancies, while one era gives way to another. Whitehead and a number of scientific cosmologists have seriously considered that in the course of eons the law of nature might change their forms, or that natural constants, like the force of gravity, might change their magnitudes. Eras frequently play a part in philosophies of history set against a metaphysical background. The thirteenth-century Nahmanides made much of the conception of *sh'mitot,* stages in world history, each characterized by the dominion of one or another of the *sefirot,* emanations of the Divine, the stages succeeding one another in regular progression. These speculations considerably influenced the pseudomessianic movements of the seventeenth century.

Another way of combining permanence and change is in the concept of the *return,* a change which reverses a preceding one, canceling its effect. Heraclitus pointed out that the way up and the way down are one; the metaphysics of the return is especially prominent in Asian thought. In the *I Ching* we have, "When the sun has reached its meridian it declines, and when the moon has become full it wanes. In the return we see the mind of heaven and earth." Similarly in the *Tao Te Ching:* "Reversal is the movement of the Tao. All things in the world come from being, and being comes from nonbeing." Chuang-tzu, the philosopher of Taoism, says flatly, "Coalescence is the same as dissolution, creation is the same as destruction." The Sankhya metaphysics describes a process of cosmic involution following an evolution, by which a *kalpa,* a cosmic era, is brought to an end.

A mathematical pastime in which a number of disks of varying size must be transferred from one post to another, by way of a third, without ever being placed on a smaller disk was called by its nineteenth-century popularizer the Tower of Brahmah. In the great temple at Benares, he wrote, are three diamond needles and sixty-four disks of gold, ceaselessly being transferred by the priests. When the task is completed, "tower, temple, and Brahmins alike will crumble into dust, and with a thunderclap the world will vanish," and the game begins anew. In some contemporary cosmologies the return finds a central place in the conception of an oscillating universe; the rate of expansion of the galaxies is slowing down, arriving eventually at zero, when the galaxies will begin to contract, coalescing once more into the Primeval Atom, after which is to come another Big Bang.

Equally familiar as the return is the idea of a cosmic *cycle,* by which things change yet ever remain the same. "When the cold goes the warmth comes," says the *I Ching,* "and when the warmth goes the cold comes." The Preacher writes, "One generation passes away, and another generation comes; and the earth remains forever. The sun rises and the sun goes down, and hurries to the place where he rises." The cycles of days and seasons are symbols of cosmic cycles, reflected in the microcosm by the wheel of fortune determining an individual's fate, and the cycles of savagery and civilization by which the destinies of whole peoples are fixed. Nietzsche made much of what he called "eternal recurrence"; historians like Oswald Spengler and Arnold Toynbee claimed to discern such cycles in all societies. In Clemenceau's sneer at America—that she is the only nation in history to have gone directly from barbarism to decadence without ever having been civilized—there is just enough truth for it to be painful.

In these perspectives, change, though it occurs, is not significant. "That which has been is that which shall be, that which has been done is that which shall be done, and there is nothing new under the sun." In the mid-nineteenth century, a minor writer coined a phrase which has passed into the folk idiom of several languages: *plus ça change, plus c'est la même chose*—the more it changes, the more it remains the same. It was less than ten years later that Darwin published his *Origin of Species.*

What Darwin thrust upon the attention was not only genuine change but change with a direction, whose outcome is functional though unintentional. The will which the voluntarists saw as the foundation of all being is blind—an unpurposed energy of existence; or, if it has a purpose, that purpose is only to maintain and enhance its own energy—like a protest movement with no other aim than to secure amnesty for the protestors. Spinoza declared that nature does nothing for the sake of an end; it could not do so, for nature, being all-inclusive, lacks nothing, and so has nothing to strive for. Many metaphysical systems view nature as purposeless, and account for such purposiveness as undeniably does exist by invoking some guiding agency outside nature. Divine Providence is familiar in Western thought. In Indian metaphysics, *prakriti,* ongoing nature, is guided by *purusa,* the transcendent subject for whom all nature is object; their relation is like that of a blind man carrying a lame man on his shoulders. Nature alone cannot see, and the cosmic Mind alone cannot do; only both together can provide change which embodies purpose.

The view that there are purposes in things apart from those embodying man's own intentions is *teleology* (the purposes themselves are also so called). In some doctrines, the intentions of another Being are invoked, and the reality of purposes is affirmed in spite of our ignorance of His intentions—"all chance, direction, which thou canst not see." The view that there are purposes rooted in nature is *natural teleology.* Aristotle and Dewey expound this metaphysics. It is not irrelevant that the one has a background in biology and the other in behavioral psychology; both are accustomed to looking at things in terms of functions performed and purposes served. In striking contrast to Spinoza, Aristotle declares that nature does nothing without purpose, that is, uselessly (he makes the declaration, of all places, in a book on politics!). Each thing, according to Aristotle, has its own *entelechy*—the energizing form by which its potentialities for growth and development in a certain direction are actualized. It is a kind of abstract and generalized genetic code. The Hebrew notion of *takhlit*—the purpose for which a thing is meant and by which its potential value is realized—combines natural teleology with a belief in Providence: the *takhlit* is in the thing, but the thing has been so endowed by its Creator.

The view which denies that there are purposes in things, whether innately or placed there by a guiding Intelligence, is *mechanism.* The issue of mechanism or teleology was as basic as the issue of permanence or change, with which it was often bound up. The issue frequently was formulated in terms of two sorts of causes distinguished by Aristotle: efficient causes and final causes (he distinguished four causes, but the other two are not relevant). An *efficient cause* is one which produces its effect from behind, as it were, by a push or impulsion, grounded in the antecedent conditions. A *final cause* is localized in a future end or goal by which we are drawn rather than impelled. Mechanism acknowledged the reality only of efficient causes;

the contrasting view was sometimes called *finalism*. A firm exponent of the reality of final causes was Charles Peirce, who preferred the term "agapism," which he coined to designate the causal efficacy of love (the root meaning of *agape* is a kind of love). Whatever the obscurities of his language, Peirce is far from muddle-headed. A succession of acute logicians and mathematicians defended teleology—men like Plato, Leibniz, and Whitehead.

But the issue between mechanism and teleology was falsely conceived; both may be compatible with one another, and with empirical fact. In Schopenhauer's *The World as Will and Idea,* he argues against Spinoza's denial of teleology: "Spinoza says that if a stone which has been projected through the air had consciousness, it would believe that it was moving of its own will. I add to this only that the stone would be right." Consciousness, however, is beside the point. Dewey very usefully distinguishes between ends and ends-in-view; only the latter are present to awareness, but the former are just as purposive. The apple tree in full blossom is the end of the seed, but was not previewed by the seed. What was active was not the future tree but the present structure of the germinating seed; in this sense invoking final causes is misleading. But it would also be misleading to speak only of the structures without regard to the functions which those structures perform in the life of the plant. From the time of Darwin's own work through a variety of modern disciplines like ecology, microbiology, and cybernetics, we are coming to understand more and more of the mechanisms by which teleology comes into play.

The most important teleological doctrine is the theory of evolution; how evolution works has been dealt with partly on a metaphysical basis. Biological explanations focus on random variations (Darwin), on mutations (De Vries), and on the environment (Lamark). A metaphysical explanation was put forward in the early decades of this century by Hans Driesch, in a doctrine known as *vitalism*—that biological phenomena demand unique agencies which Driesch, borrowing Aristotle's term, called *entelechies,* and which Bergson designated as the *élan vital,* the life force. Most biologists view this doctrine as quite useless. A sharply contrasting position had been taken by Ernst Haeckel, an early ardent exponent of Darwinism. Haeckel declared that the theory of evolution assumes that all natural phenomena without exception are subject to the same great law of causation and are ultimately to be reduced to atomic mechanics. The progress of biology showed that Haeckel's position was the more fruitful one. Today, even machines have the capacity not only to pursue goals but also to play a significant and even an indispensable role in determining the goals.

The theory of evolution brought another question to the fore. Does the process produce something genuinely novel, or is everything already prefigured? What is not so prefigured was called an *emergent,* as contrasted with a mechanical *resultant.* A metaphysics of emergent evolution emphasized the unpredictability of the products of evolution. Against this position, Russell urged that emergent properties represent "merely scientific incompleteness which would not exist in the ideal physics." No scientist ever has the ideal physics; it might therefore still be useful to speak of certain properties as unpredictable in a given state of knowledge.

The point of this insistence is to counter a certain kind of finalism which is a mechanism in reverse—the view, called *historicism,* that historical processes move to a predetermined end. This is the position in certain versions of Marxism and in the fascist notion of "the wave of the future." These doctrines were effectively undermined—from a logical viewpoint, if not from a political one—in the critique of historical inevitability by Karl Popper and Isaiah Berlin. Significant directions of historical change can be discerned; each of us can aspire to a share in determining what that direction is to be.

41. Cosmos and Chaos

A world of change can be an orderly world, if changes take place in an orderly fashion. Underlying the issues of permanence and change is this question whether the world is orderly—either because it exhibits some fixed structure, or becaue there is a fixity of pattern underlying changing events. If anything at all might happen, and in any way at all, all would be without form and void, and there would be darkness on the face of the deep. In a word, all would be *chaos.* In fact, there *is* an order in things—some things could not happen, while those that do happen do so in more or less regular and predictable ways. We live, not in a chaos, but in a *cosmos.* Wherever purposes can be discerned there is some measure of orderliness, but underlying both teleology and mechanism is a more fundamental principle of order: *causality.* The world is a cosmos because "There is occasions and causes and why and wherefore in all things."

Things of a particular sort happen only under certain circumstances, and when those circumstances obtain, the things always do happen. A state of affairs A is the cause of another state of affairs B if A is both a *necessary* and a *sufficient* condition of B; necessary means that B cannot occur without A, and sufficient means that B must occur if A does. A particular virus, for instance, is identified as the cause of a certain disease if it is found in all the victims of the disease, and if everyone having the virus shows the symptoms of the disease. Ordinary usage is not precise; we speak of many causes of an event, in which case none of them singly is necessary; and what we call a cause may still not produce its defined effect if the circumstances are not appropriate, so that the so-called cause is not sufficient.

It is usual in such cases to distinguish the *cause* from the *conditions* under which it is effective. The ground of this distinction lies not in things but in our dealings with them. We single out as the cause that feature of the situation which allows for our intervention to produce the effect or to prevent its occurrence; the other features are the conditions. We speak of many causes when each identifies a locus of possible intervention, rather than abstracting as "the" cause what is common to all the causal agencies. This relation to our actions is sometimes very indirect, as when we speak of the cause of a stellar explosion.

The usual explications of causality are in terms of modalities: given the cause, the effect "must" happen, and without the cause, the effect "cannot" happen. But as David Hume urged, we never experience an element of necessity linking cause and effect; we simply observe the one following the other. The modalities (§39) might even be redefined on this basis, as in fact they were by Kant: that is necessary which always happens, the possible is what sometimes happens, and the impossible is what never happens. Although the notion that a cause impels its effect has no empirical application to relations among things themselves, it may derive from our relations to things, especially from the experiences of effort which we have in our interventions, experiences which Nietzsche and others saw as the root of our conception of what is real or objective. In Indian thought the word for causal efficacy is *shakti,* whose root meaning is the capacity of words to mean their objects, as though a cause literally calls forth its effects. There is a core of magical belief in the uncritical notion of cause.

Shakti also has the meaning of sexual power or energy, with the suggestion, therefore, that a cause produces its effect as living things produce their young. Causal idioms with this connotation are common in Western thought as well; Emerson (one of the early Westerners to be directly influenced by Asian thought) once wrote that "cause and effect, means and ends, seed and fruit, cannot be severed, for the effect already blooms in the cause." Putting this idea more abstractly yields a simple formulation of the cause-effect relation, which bypasses both the ground of distinction between cause and conditions and the perplexities of causal efficacy: an effect is the later part of any continuous process, the earlier part being its cause.

But, in practice, the distinction between earlier and later often depends on the distinction between cause and effect, and, in theory, may always depend on it (§37). Hume argued that we never have an empirical basis for asserting a causal relation because we never know that B always follows A but only that so far it has always followed A. Kant replied that our very conception of an objective time order in which B in fact follows A presupposes a causal order in which objects have their places: the idea of a succession cannot be reduced merely to a succession of ideas. To this a Humean might rejoin that the problem remains whether A, rather than C or D, is truly the invariable predecessor and so the cause of B. This is the problem of induction previously discussed (§22).

Another problem concerning the causal connection came to the fore in the age of Newton, especially because of the impressive success of his theory of gravitation. How can causes produce their effects without direct contact between the bodies or with suitable intermediaries? Such causation was called *action at a distance.* Newton said, "Action at a distance through a vacuum, without mediation of anything else by and through which their action and force may be conveyed from one to another, is to me so great an absurdity, that I believe no man who has in philosophical matters a competent faculty of thinking, can ever fall into it." Modern physics speaks of fields—regions for which there is specified at each point what is to be observed when certain conditions are met, like the presence of a body with a given mass or charge. Impulses are thought to be carried through the region by appropriate waves; gravitational attraction is no longer thought to be instantaneous, as it was in Newton's day, but propagated at the velocity of light. The waves are not waves "of" something, serving as a medium of contact; they can as well be regarded as particles traveling through empty space. Physicists speak of "gravitons," postulated as analogous to photons, the particles of zero rest-mass making up a beam of light. Here philosophical questions of interpretation of physical theory become enmeshed in puzzles resulting from the unreasonable demand that theory restrict itself to models drawn from everyday experience.

The view that causality is operative always and everywhere is one of the most widespread metaphysical doctrines. The second of the Four Noble Truths of Buddhism reads: "That being present, this becomes; from the arising of that, this arises. That being absent, this does not become; from the cessation of that, this ceases." With an equally deceptive simplicity, Spinoza asserts: "All things are determined by the necessity of divine nature to exist and act in a certain way." This position is called *determinism*. It affirms not merely that there are causes but that causes are universal—nothing happens without a cause, and it happens just as it is caused to happen. Epicurus emphasized the importance of causes yet held that the atoms, in their primeval motions, can swerve somewhat from determinate paths, so that not all that happens is ordained by its causes. But even "the minutest wiggle of independence," as William James called it, is incompatible with determinism.

At the opposite pole from determinism is the belief that *chance* rules all things—a basic doctrine of the Greco-Roman culture, to be found in Herodotus, Virgil, Ovid, Seneca, Pliny, and many others. In the Judaeo-Christian tradition, chance comes into its own in the conception of an "act of God," applied to phenomena like lightning or disease, which seem to strike by chance. Apparently, people more easily see God's will in chance events than in causal regularities. The history of the warfare between science and theology (the title of a classic study written at the turn of the century by A. D. White) reveals a progressive diminution of the domain of God's will, so conceived (or misconceived), and its replacement by causal explanations. In Mysore I once witnessed a procession appealing to the goddess Kali to revoke the epidemic of smallpox then raging at her will, while I watched in the security of a recent vaccination. The presuppositions of the American Indian rain dance are not essentially different, nor are these presuppositions confined to those called "heathen." They are probably more devoutly believed by the tourist audience than by the present-day performers. The people have not yet ceased to ask a sign of their God.

Sometimes an event is conceptualized as due to chance, not because we are ignorant of its causes but because our knowledge of the causes would be irrelevant. This is involved in the conception of a traffic "accident," which is a matter of chance from the standpoint of the victims and the courts, but not as seen by insurance companies and traffic engineers. (The most famous instance of this pattern of thinking is provided by the actress Helen Hayes, released from her contract because of pregnancy, which was legally declared to be an "act of God.") Methods of prognostication practiced in many cultures rely on chance events—the flight of birds, convolution of entrails, and patterns of tea leaves or of fallen sticks. The apparently chance event is interpreted as a purposive disclosure of an underlying order. Metternich was so wholly politicized that when a diplomat unexpectedly died, Metternich remarked, "I wonder what he meant by that?" The phrase "It is no accident that . . ." is a cliché of Communist rhetoric.

The denial of chance, far from being an affirmation of determinism, may express instead a readiness to see everything as the outcome of intention—often to the point of personifying agencies to whom the appropriate intentions can be ascribed. Freud has remarked that it requires a good deal of intellectual training before we can believe in chance; primitive and uneducated people, and certainly children, can give a reason for everything that happens. It is not this infantile thinking which is expressed in the entry in Voltaire's *Philosophical Dictionary* that chance is "a word void of sense"; here it is a matter of the straightforward determinist view that nothing can exist without a cause. On the other hand, Peirce's doctrine of the objectivity of chance—a doctrine he called *tychism*, from the name of the Greek goddess of fortune—was not meant to derogate the importance of the purposiveness of events. It was meant, rather, to affirm a basis in things for the fallibilism characteristic of our knowledge about things (§26).

After the triumph of Newtonian physics, determinism was widely regarded as virtually proved, and an inescapable presupposition of scientific method. At the beginning of the nineteenth century the doctrine was canonically stated by the mathematician Pierre Laplace: a being who knew the position and momentum (mass, speed, and direction of motion) of every particle in the universe could foretell the entire future course of events in the universe. (Such a being has come to be known as "Laplace's superman.") The fact that we cannot obtain such knowledge, or anything even remotely like it except in severely restricted domains (like the solar system), and then only to more or less crude approximations, was for long regarded as a difficulty only in practice, not in principle. Idealizations are used everywhere in science, and to very good effect. With the development of quantum physics in the present century the situation changed radically.

At the very foundation of quantum mechanics is the principle—known as Heisenberg's *principle of indeterminacy*—that the position and momentum of a particle cannot both be known to an indefinite degree of precision, an increase in the precision of either one being accompanied by a corresponding increase in the uncertainty of the other, according to a quantitatively defined relationship. This is no longer a matter of shortcomings in practice but is as much a matter of principle as, say, the law of conservation of momentum. The law formulating the ineluctable uncertainty invokes a quantity called Planck's constant (named after the founder of quantum theory), a constant of nature as fundamental to quantum mechanics as the gravitational constant is to the Newtonian mechanics. The uncertainty is not a result of human limitations in procedures of measurement; it is intrinsic to the phenomena dealt with. The issue has not been altogether resolved; some uncertainty still remains about the metaphysics of determinism.

Characteristic of quantum theory is its statistical character. By means of statistics we can discern regularity in chance, order in apparent chaos. It is impossible to foretell why one particle rather than another undergoes radioactive decay at a particular instant, but we *can* predict how long it will take for the decay of half the particles in a given mass. We cannot accurately foretell a particular traffic accident or suicide, but we can accurately predict the rates at which these will occur among certain populations under specified conditions. The argument is that just as there are causes and reasons for these events, though we do not know them, so also are there for the subatomic phenomena. "I am, in fact, firmly convinced," Einstein declared, "that the essentially statistical character of contemporary quantum theory is solely to be ascribed to the fact that this theory operates with an incomplete description of physical systems." No one, however, has been able to specify how the description could be made more complete, even in principle.

For Einstein, the notion of statistical laws, though not self-contradictory, is incompatible with his metaphysical faith: "I can, if the worst comes to worst, still realize that God may have created a world in which there are no natural laws—in short, a chaos. That there should be statistical laws with definite solutions, i.e., laws which compel God to throw the dice in each individual case, I find highly disagreeable. I shall never believe that God plays dice with the world." It seems that just such a possibility must be regarded as that most strongly supported by present-day physical theory. In any case, indeterminism is not anarchy, and chance is not chaos. The world appears to be an ordered cosmos, even if not a deterministic one. Whether or not He plays dice with the world, God is in His heaven.

Such locutions are less metaphoric than might appear, as Einstein himself noted: "A conviction, akin to religious feeling, of the rationality or intelligibility of the world lies behind all scientific work of a higher order." From quite different metaphysical premises a similar conclusion was arrived at by Hegel a century and a half ago: "What is rational is real, what is real is rational." This remark, although quoted by Hegel in his *Science of Logic,* appeared first in the preface to his *Philosophy of Law,* ironically enough. "To him who looks upon the world rationally," he repeated in the introduction to his *Philosophy of History,* "the world in its turn presents a rational aspect." This rationality is not just a matter of appearances. Hegel learned from Kant how much the world as we experience it owes to the organizing and interpretative powers of the human mind. Kant went so far as to say that since Newton the comets follow geometric orbits, but in literal truth Newton did not in the least affect the motions of the comets. The laws of nature, after all, are not merely conventional descriptions; they are embodied in real patterns of events (§32).

There is good reason to suppose that these laws are the same always and everywhere. That our position in the universe gives us no distinctive observational standpoint is sometimes called the *cosmological principle;* that this is also true for our position in time as well as in space has been called the *perfect cosmological principle. Cosmology,* incidentally, is that branch of metaphysics which deals with the structure or organization of the universe, as distinguished from *ontology,* which deals with questions of existence or reality. The cosmological unity of the world has been espoused by metaphysicians from Parmenides to Spinoza. The modern emphasis is on an ontological unity as well and, in particular, on the view known as *naturalism,* that all of reality is coextensive, both in its composition and in its behavior, with nature as we experience it (§39). Nothing supernatural need be invoked to help us understand or appreciate the world we know.

The rationality and unity of the world means more than that all events are governed by the same set of laws. What is also being asserted is that the world does not consist of *causal streaks,* each event being nomologically bound to its antecedents and consequences but with no single system uniting them all. If the world does consist of something like Leibniz's windowless monads, their walls must be made of glass: each monad must receive an image of what is transpiring in all the others—a miraculous concordance for which Leibniz could only provide by what he called a *preestablished harmony.* It was to deal with this difficulty that Kant introduced his category of *reciprocity,* in addition to his category of causality, a reciprocity derived from the disjunctive form of judgment as causality was derived from the hypothetical or if-then form. Naturalism is particularly attractive from the standpoint of a belief in the unity of the world, for it can point to the successive unification, in the history of science, of the domains of the celestial and terrestrial, the organic and the inorganic, the human and the animal, the mental and the physical.

A misplaced emphasis on unities for their own sakes, however, was associated at the turn of the century with the metaphysics of emergents, in the form of a doctrine of *holism:* that there is more reality or significance in wholes than in parts; that parts can be understood only by reference to wholes and not the other way around; and that in the important wholes the relations between parts are those characteristic of an organism rather than of a mechanical system. Apart from the fact that in this doctrine many different senses of whole and part were indiscriminately lumped together, there was also a confusion between the *experience* of a quality, unitary or otherwise, and the *analysis* of some composite—an experience of differentiated parts is just as different from their analysis as a unitary experience would be. The mind is as capable of synthesis as it is of analysis; both are needed if we are to make sense of the order of things, as well as of the many things ordered, or those which call upon us to put them in order.

Chapter Seven

Philosophical Anthropology

42. Man and Nature

Central to many philosophies is the question, "What is man?" How does he behave in various situations? What is his nature—if, indeed, he has a determinant nature? How is he different from other creatures? What is essentially human, making man the being he is? The centrality of questions about man is easy to understand, for it is he who asks the questions; preoccupation with oneself is a familiar human trait. There is more occasion to ask why philosophies ignore man than why they focus on him.

From the standpoint of values, man is of primary importance as a starting point, if not as a conclusion. The word *hominocentrism* has been coined as a neutral designation for this initial focus on man as distinct from the pejorative *anthropocentrism*, which takes man to be the most significant fact in the universe and which interprets all else in light of this fact. I do not know of any serious anthropocentric philosophy; hominocentrism, on the other hand, is characteristic of most Asian philosophies, of most European philosophy, and in our own time, of Continental and South American philosophy. Contemporary Anglo-American philosophy does devote some attention to the analysis of questions about human nature, but such questions are not usually assigned to a distinct specialty, such as logic or epistemology.

Man may be the proper study of mankind for reasons other than those concerning values. Philosophies may be hominocentric because philosophy is a human product; quality control of any product demands attention to the process. Man is the instrument of philosophical reflection; it is a basic principle of method to calibrate the instrument so as to become aware of its possibilities and limitations. This is the explanation John Locke gives for his *Essay Concerning Human Understanding:* "I thought that the first step towards satisfying several inquiries the mind of man was very apt to run into was to take a survey of our understandings, examine our own powers, and see to what things they were adopted. Till that was done I suspected we began at the wrong end."

It is not only understanding which invites attention. Understanding is intimately involved with sense and sensibility, perception and emotion; all these shape our experience. We must agree with Hume's declaration in his *Treatise of Human Nature* that "all the sciences have a relation, greater or less, to human nature. The science of man is the only solid foundation for the other sciences." More plainly, the science of man is the only solid foundation for the other disciplines which provide matter for philosophic reflection—ethics and aesthetics, political and social doctrines; our theologies reveal to what degree our gods have been fashioned in the image of man.

Specific questions about the nature of man are dealt with in the sciences of man. The more general questions, necessarily more speculative, elude scientific treatment. The bearings of facts on value, and the methods by which questions about man can be dealt with at all, are recognizably philosophical concerns. In any case, the line of demarcation between philosophy and science is blurred and shifting (§4). The first modern book on physiology was written by Descartes; the first course of lectures on anthropology was given by Kant; sociology was founded by the positivist philosopher Auguste Comte; and psychology was separated from philosophy only in the present century, a thinker like William James being as distinguished a psychologist as a philosopher.

The philosophical discipline dealing with man is known on the European continent as "philosophical anthropology," the designation I have chosen. In Anglo-American philosophy the narrower label is "philosophy of mind," or the more restricted but currently fashionable "theory of action." Expressions like "philosophy of psychology," "meta-psychology," "humanistic psychology," and the self-deprecating "literary psychology" (due, I believe, to Santayana) are also to be met with.

Fundamental to all philosophies of man must be a recognition of his continuity with the rest of nature. In the West, this marks the impact of Darwin. "If man had not been his own classifier," Darwin wrote in his *Descent of Man,* "he would never have thought of founding a separate order for his own reception." For the biologist, man is an animal among others, kin to all of them, and with an undeniable family resemblance to his closer relatives. In cultures other than the European, the intimacy of man with nature made a commonplace of this kinship; an Asian or African Darwin might have had scientific importance, but in philosophy and religion his work would have gone unnoticed. I am not speaking only of the myth and folklore of so-called "primitive" societies, which, in this respect, are more advanced than our own, but also of the sophisticated metaphysical doctrines of the Indian, Chinese, and other cultures. These doctrines, in spite of our stereotypes of their transcendent mysticism, are more naturalistic, so far as concerns man's place in nature, than the Western metaphysics prevailing before the present century.

Darwin's conclusions were unsettling, not because they did not accord with the literal biblical narrative—this had long been recognized to require interpretation—but because they accounted for teleology on a mechanistic basis (§40). The exquisite adaptiveness of organs to one another and of an organism to its environment could no longer be taken as revealing the design of divine Providence (§85).

The theological impact of Darwin was exceeded by a psychological one, a blow of self-esteem. Man's dominion over the beasts of the field was grounded, he felt—as the wielders of power have always felt—on an innate superiority, an unbridgeable difference in lineage, like that claimed by aristocrat over commoner or by a master race over lesser breeds. If man is only an animal, sharing descent with the apes, what becomes of this claim? Since Darwin's day, ethology has documented our behavioral as well as evolutionary kinship with other animals. The history of our times demonstrates that even if our lineage were wholly our own, there is not that much in it to be proud of. "For my part," Darwin wrote, "I would as soon be descended from a baboon as from a savage who delights to torture his enemies, treats his wives like slaves, and is haunted by the grossest superstitions." What could he have said had he witnessed the unspeakable degradations and perversions of the human spirit in our day!

Granted that there is a continuity of man and nature, continuity is not sameness. The point is not to deny differences between man and animal but to assess their significance. Which differences are accidental, trivial, irrelevant to man's estate? Which are characteristic, distinctive, giving man the place that is uniquely his? What is essentially human, defining man's nature and destiny? (This threefold division between accidents, properties, and essence is Aristotle's; its usefulness is more than expository.)

Man is a creature of passions, of insatiable appetites. Scripture tells of four things that cannot say, Enough!—the grave, the parched earth, the barren womb, and the raging fire. Man is surely a fifth—the only animal, it has been said, who eats when he is not hungry, drinks when he is not thirsty, and makes love at all seasons. Man is one of the few animals capable of blushing—the only one, Mark Twain said, who needs to: the only creature with a nasty mind. The "ungrateful biped," Dostoevski called him—and received no thanks for it. Man is clever with his hands, enjoying the incalculable advantages of an erect posture and an opposable thumb. He makes fires and cooks his food; from time to time it is his fellowman whom he puts to the flames—occasionally to take something into his own body, in less savage societies, as they imagine, for the supposed welfare of the other's soul, and among the civilized peoples of our own day, as a final solution to a political problem.

Man is capable of negotiation, of making bargains, a capacity which Adam Smith understandably took to be fundamental. If the negotiation leads to betrayal or the bargain turns out to have been a bad one, man is quite capable of doing the same thing all over again. Man is the only animal that gambles, and if other animals also take risks, man alone apparently gambles just in order to lose. Man is the only animal to regret the past and to worry about the future. Yet he is also the only one to laugh—at his past follies, at his present shortcomings, and at what the future might bring.

What makes the laughter possible is another extraordinary capacity: man can shut himself off from reality, transform it in imagination or replace it altogether in fantasy; in a word, man can pretend. This means that he is also capable of self-deception. He can combine passion and pretense with a firm sense of reality, and play games. The young of many species are playful, but only man carries play into middle age and makes of sport a matter of life and death. The capacity to imagine things as they are not is manifested not only in play but also in art; man is a creative animal, as well as a destructive one. Man can pray; yet as Dostoevski has remarked, it is also true that only man can curse—"that is his privilege, the primary distinction between him and other animals."

In this whole account there is as much conclusion as premise, as much judgment of value as statement of fact by which evaluations can be assessed. However pointed the epigram, philosophy cannot rest on a turn of phrase. Certain distinctive attributes of the human animal must be examined.

In almost universal tradition, man is a creature with a soul. Less debatably, he has a mind. "The situation of man as man," says the contemporary existentialist, Karl Jaspers, (*Man in the Modern Age*) "is a mental situation." Man has the capacity to speak and to use language to transmit what he has learned; man is a teacher (a conception no doubt taught from earliest times). Man can entertain motives as well as act unthinkingly to fulfill his purposes. He can not only adapt means to ends but foresee the adaptation; not only use tools but use them to make other tools. Man has an identity, a sense that he is himself and none other. Man has freedom in some sense, some measure of choice. In his *Notes from the Underground*, Dostoevski characterizes man as "pre-eminently a creative animal, predestined incessantly and eternally to make new roads, wherever they may lead." Finally, in spite of all appearances to the contrary, man is, as Aristotle defined him, a rational animal. It may be, as Kant later insisted and Jaspers reaffirmed in our own day, that man is essentially a creature who poses problems beyond the powers of his reason, which is to say, he is essentially a metaphysician. Such a definition would understandably appeal to a philosopher; but man's humanity cannot be guaranteed by a definition.

The question has been raised whether man can be defined at all. Jean Paul Sartre argues that man is nothing but what he makes of himself. Whatever definition purported to characterize him would impose limits which he would be free to shatter. This is the cardinal tenet of *existentialism:* that man's existence precedes his essence. The fact *that* he is precedes *what* he is. Man is a well of potentiality. His condition is *dasein*, being there, presence, the capacity to respond freely to the fact of his existence. From the premise, I am a man, no conclusion can be drawn that I must be this or that, as it could be drawn from the premise that I am a thing of one kind or another. What differentiates man from a mere thing is that his nature is not given with his existence: man himself decides what his nature is to be.

I do not see that man's freedom makes him indefinable. It is true, as Spinoza said, that all definition is negation: we do not define what a thing is without implying what it is not. But however great man's potentialities may be, they are limited; what lies outside the limits is as significant as what lies within. Whatever man chooses to do, he has a body—he is an animal. The body must be fed and cared for; if it is mortified, even in the name of the spirit, or abused by drugs, even in the name of heightened consciousness, the man has become something less than human. Whatever man chooses to do, he has a mind—he is a rational animal. The mind, too, must be nourished and cared for; the man who chooses to think with his blood, to renounce the intellect for unthinking action, has also made of himself something less than human. My speaking of what is less than human, rather than merely other than human, may point to a presupposed scale of values; but the logic of the situation is not changed if I say instead that the denial of either mind or body is *in*human. Man's essence, like that of any other thing, we are free to define as we choose (§12)—if we are prepared to accept the consequences imposed by reality, consequences which reveal the definition to be useful or pernicious.

The existentialist argument has a point. It is that any definition of man, in providing a concept of human nature, may lend itself to the service of those who resist change. Human nature, becoming by the definition a fixed essence, is invoked to argue the futility of efforts to improve man's lot. The argument is fallacious, since it begs the question whether a particular change lies beyond human potentialities. We would be guilty of a fallacy, in turn, if in order to prevent a conclusion from being improperly drawn we adopted the tactic of denying its premise. I do not believe that human nature makes war inevitable, but this belief does not impel me to the position that no human nature can be specified. On the contrary, it impels me to an even more careful and clear specification of human nature—in this case, as to the place of hostility and aggression in the makeup of man.

At any given moment every man has a determinate character, but his future is always open in some measure. Even in her madness Ophelia can say, "We know what we are, but know not what we may be." Sartre calls these two sides of man's being his *facticity* and his *transcendence*—the purely contingent fact of his existing then and there, as the man he now is, and the potentialities of change, as he chooses to become. Not only the facts but also their potentialities tell us who the man is; more of the man is revealed in his aspirations, the ego-ideal and other goals expressed in his choices.

Freud's conception of man has been widely misunderstood, his position being mistakenly identified with that of the Idealist in the "Walpurgis Night" scene of *Faust:*

> *Ideas can be a tyranny*
> *To give one mental twinges:*

If all my thoughts are really me,
My mind is off its hinges.

Freud's position is that all my thoughts are *not* really me; what comes to mind tells something about me, but what is more significant is what I do with what comes to mind. Santayana argued that "our deliberate character is more truly ourself than is the flux of our involuntary dreams." There is good reason to acknowledge that dreams are not altogether involuntary. But the wishes fulfilled by the dream symbolism are being given only a symbolic fulfillment, because they are inconsistent with other components of the dreamer's personality. Freud did not denigrate human nature by revealing the monstrous immoralities of unconscious desires. On the contrary, he showed man as all the more admirable in that, for all the intensity of these desires, man does not act on them; he does not even allow himself to become fully aware of them. My true self is not only what I already am, and not only what I wish to become, but, most of all, what I choose in fact to become.

43. The Body and Its Mind

Everyone is first of all some*body*. The word "body" has a usage in which it means simply a person. A body is the most immediate and direct associate of every person. Historically, the gulf between man and the rest of nature was seen as so great that the human body was thought to obey its own laws, in contradistinction to the laws governing purely physical objects or even the bodies of animals. Descartes' dualism of mind and body, although later standing in the way of a scientific study of man, in its own time contributed significantly to the sciences of human anatomy and physiology by subsuming the human body under the same category as other bodies. Almost two centuries elapsed before the synthesis in the laboratory of an organic compound bridged the gap between the animals, including man, and inanimate nature.

How a man sees his own body, the complex of his perceptions, ideas, and emotions about his body is his *body image*. It is the body image, rather than the body, which is distinctively human. In the last several decades attention has been drawn to the role of the body image in shaping personality and conduct. This role is most easily recognized in regard to conditions such as obesity, and for occupations such as pilot, dancer, and athlete. It is also important with regard to the image of ourselves which we project to others and to which we ourselves respond. The body image is a central component of what we experience as ourselves. A pervasive theme of folklore and mythology—as in Ovid, but also in such modern writers as Thomas Mann and Franz Kafka—is the transformation of the body, its metamorphosis, as a highly significant event in the life of the person. The body may be a purely external manifestation of personality; it is not a merely superficial one.

Yet the person cannot be identified with the body. My body is mine, but not me; it only belongs to me. However intimate this belonging, it is a relation, and the relata are distinct. How I experience myself is affected to a great degree by what I feel of my body. William James, decades before present-day behaviorism, concluded that "the 'self of selves' when carefully examined is found to consist mainly of the collection of certain peculiar motions in the head or between the head and throat." The idea that a self other than my own is acting in and through my body is not a contradiction in terms. Demonic possession may be an absurd notion, but it is the demon rather than the possession which is the logical absurdity. When what has taken possession is identifiable as also a human personality—as was true of the *dybbuk* of Jewish folklore—the phenomenon is a commonplace of clinical observation.

The body provides a considerable measure of constancy to the self. It is relatively unchanging through many changes of context and conduct; bodily differences in ordinary encounters are likely to be small enough so that there is ample basis for reliable identification. But this is only a likelihood, not a logical necessity. The whole body, not just the eye, is a window to the soul. When Dr. Jekyll gives way to Mr. Hyde, his teeth, hair, and nails grow astonishingly within a few minutes; it is only the tempo of the change which belongs to fantasy. The face that often wears a frown comes at last to have that cast of features. It is said that long-married couples grow to resemble one another; perhaps if their body images are strikingly different they are not as likely to remain long married. It has even been remarked that we can often see a kinship of appearance between people and their pets.

Though the body is not identifiable with the person, neither is it only his local habitation. The child lifts the eyelid of his dozing grandfather with the words, "Are you in there, Grampa?" The question expresses a childish notion: that the person is somewhere inside his skin. Here we have an instance of what Whitehead called the *fallacy of simple location:* the unwarranted assumption that what we know from observations of what is happening in a certain place can be regarded as localized in that place. In this respect a person is like a corporation; the body is only the headquarters—the center, it may be, but of far-flung operations. Just as a corporation may be said to exist wherever it does business, so also may a person's presence be felt in may places. If, to change the metaphor, the body is a light bulb, lit up by a personality, we would be guilty of the fallacy of simple location if we overlooked the fact that the electricity is not just inside the bulb, but flows through the whole circuit.

The body itself is not as separate from other bodies as traditional materialism supposes. The corporation metaphor is useful here also, in allowing for a variety of relationships with other corporations by which the identity of each is significantly affected—through holding companies, interlocking directorates, and the like. The body is a system of biochemical transformations; it is a complex of interacting processes, not a structure of independent substances. In every encounter with other persons we are warmed by one another's heat, we breathe each other's air, and by smell and otherwise we absorb the more subtle bodily exudations. If we are together for any length of time, we are truly members of one body. Biologically speaking, life is an unending effort to maintain organic integrity in the face of a continuing invasion of privacy.

The materialist argument is that the body, isolated or not, is the decisive factor determining all we know as the person. It is the light bulb, after all, together with the generator and the rest of the system, which determines whether and what light will be given off. Mental events, so called, have no explanatory force in themselves, but are themselves to be explained—in physical, that is, biochemical, terms. This position is known as *epiphenomenalism:* the mind is something derivative and dependent, with no efficacy of its own. The nineteenth-century metaphor was the train whistle, which announces the train but which has nothing to do with driving the wheels. Corresponding to every behavior there is a distinctive material substratum; every change in behavior results only from a change in that substratum. Yet, while it is true that a smudge on the Mona Lisa's lips would transform the painting, it might be argued against the epiphenomenalist that he is so preoccupied with the paint that he no longer sees the picture.

As we come to know more about the material substratum we realize how much less we understand than traditional materialists assumed. Cynics have quipped at the expense both of materialists and their critics, "What is mind? It doesn't matter. What is matter? Never mind." Among laymen the most widely accepted view is *dualism:* man consists of two components, each with its own reality and power—the body and the mind. It is usually taken for granted that each of these can act upon the other—the body affecting the mind in giving it a sensation of pain, for example, while the mind affects the body, for example, in willing the legs to move. This position is known as *interactionism.*

How interactions can take place between two such disparate entities has puzzled philosophers as the so-called *mind-body problem.* "Is there any principle in all nature more mysterious," Hume asks, "than the union of soul with body, by which a supposed spiritual substance acquires such an influence over a material one, that the most refined thought is able to actuate the grossest matter?" Descartes localized the interaction in a small organ at the base of the brain, the pineal gland, for which no other function was known. What could possibly happen in that organ to relate body and mind, a physiological process and a feeling, a neural impulse and a thought, remains, when formulated in dualistic terms, as mysterious as Hume held it to be. The frankest acknowledgment of the mystery is in the doctrine of *occasionalism,* put forward by the Cartesian theologian Nicolas Malebranche, that any action by either mind or body is only an occasion for a direct intervention by God to produce the appropriate effect on the other substance.

To bypass the difficulties of interactionism while remaining within a dualistic framework, some philosophers, like Leibniz, proposed a *psychophysical parallelism:* mind and body follow the same course, but without the workings of any causal agency between them. In that case, what accounts for the parallelism? Leibniz could only reply by having recourse to a preestablished harmony—as with two synchronized clocks, which, having been properly set, thereafter keep the same time. This notion is no less mysterious than the interactionism it purports to replace. A more plausible version of parallelism is Spinoza's, that a mind is the awareness of a body. No harmony need be preestablished, for mind and body are the same thing viewed from two standpoints, just as the surface of a sphere is concave or convex according to whether it is seen from the outside or the inside. This view faces difficulties of its own. If body is only mind seen from without, must we not acknowledge that a mind of sorts exists wherever body is present—that is, throughout the material universe? The view that this is indeed the case is called *panpsychism;* it was held by Leibniz, by the Jains of ancient India, by Bergson, and by others. This version of parallelism, too, can scarcely lay claim to greater clarity or plausibility than interactionism.

Such difficulties in conceptualizing the relations between mind and body led many philosophers to abandon dualism. William James and Bertrand Russell independently arrived at a position called *neutral monism:* there is a single stuff which is neither mental nor physical, but which constitutes the one or the other according to whether it is organized and used in one way or in another. This single entity is the stuff of experience, the percepts or sense-data which provide the phenomenological base for knowledge (§25). The felt hardness of the table is mental when it is placed in the context of other feelings, and physical in the context of other experienced qualities; sight is a seeing or something seen; and so on. The position is congenial to empiricism, positivism, and pragmatism. In the end, however, it seems to have had more bearing on how to understand *talk* about the mind than how to understand the mind itself.

Here another aspect of James's philosophy of mind comes to the fore, in a position also developed by John Dewey: the standpoint of *functionalism.* Mind is not a substance at all—neither a substance contrasted with body, nor some neutral stuff. It refers to a certain working of the body. That a clock keeps time does not mean that in addition to springs and cogs there is a subtle temporal entity mysteriously encased within it. The functionalist view may be traced back to Aristotle, who compared the relation of mind to body with the relation of seeing to the eye or of cutting to the axe. (Aristotle did, however, conceive of an intellect or *nous,* contrasted with the mind or *psyche,* as separable from the body.) The distinction in psychiatric medicine between functional and organic disorders—like that between schizophrenic and drug-induced hallucinations, for example—is not, on this view, a fundamental distinction. What we call "organic" disorders are only those which are grosser and more easily identified. In both cases something is not working right; the "something" is what is conventionally recognized as physical, and the "working" is what is conventionally recognized as "mental."

There has been more progress in the last few decades than in several centuries in dealing with the relation of the mind to the body. I refer to developments in information theory, data processing, and related disciplines—developments which, as a distinguished cyberneticist put it, "help pull down the wall between the great world of physics and the ghetto of the mind." The relation of mind to body can be compared to the relation between the storage, processing, and retrieval of information, on the one hand, and of the channels through which the information flows, on the other. The fact that computers are electrical systems and that nerve impulses are also electrical has nothing to do with the point. It is the logic of the situation which is decisive, not its physics or biology.

Only a unitary conception of mind and body is tenable any longer. An American philosopher espousing naturalism (§41) memorably described man as "a tube, one end of which befouls the earth while the other praises the Lord." Pollutions and prayer issue from one source; the difference is in the product, not in the agent producing it, as though one comes from a body and the other from a mind. The mind is no more a distinct agent within the body than the music is a distinct entity inside the violin. In viewing the body as the instrument for the expression of the spiritual life, Yoga and Kabbalah are closer to a scientifically defensible unitary conception of man than many less obscurantist philosophies. Our wonder at the achievements in body control of some Yogis may testify less to the level of the achievement—no more than that of jugglers and acrobats—than to the strength of our dualistic preconceptions.

Such preconceptions are also responsible for the fact that psychosomatic medicine is such a relatively recent specialty, and that it is a distinct specialty. Medicine cannot be anything but psychosomatic. The body works as a *human* body in all its workings, not only in what used to be called "nervous and mental diseases." The hysterical paralysis known as the "glove syndrome" is instructive. In World War I it was noted that battle-weary soldiers sometimes developed a paralysis of the hand, diagnosable as "in the mind," because the region covered by a glove does not correspond to the articulation of the nerves in the arm and hand: damage to the nerves would produce a paralysis of several fingers and the rest of the arm on that side, and never only of everything below the wrist. Medics, however, sometimes suffered from hysterical paralyses which correctly corresponded to the nerve patterns. The knowledge of neuroanatomy which they had acquired apparently is not just stored in the brain. There may be an unexpectedly literal content in the Psalmist's cry, "If I forget thee, O Jerusalem, let my right hand lose its cunning!"

A unitary conception of man may be obtained by a denial of one of the two components—most commonly, the mind. This denial, as a philosophy of psychology, is known as *behaviorism*, or *behavioristic psychology*. Behaviorism was a metaphysical doctrine: it denied the existence of thoughts, images, dreams, and feelings, insisting that psychology confine itself to the data of bodily states and processes. The result was characterized by critics as psychology without the psyche: "First psychology lost its soul, then its mind, then it lost consciousness altogether; and now it is having trouble with its behavior." On the metaphysical side, behaviorism tended to be dogmatic rather than logically analytic; on the scientific side, it was often more programmatic than productive. Many distinguished psychologists subsequently carried out investigations which were behavioristic in content and method although the metaphysical trappings were no longer important. There is some justice in the assessment that what behaviorism contributed to our understanding of man was proof that man, like other animals, is capable of learning if he is suitably rewarded or punished.

Quite distinct from *behavioristic* psychology is *behavioral* psychology, which rests on a methodological base rather than on a metaphysical one. It acknowledges the existence of "mental" phenomena but proposes to specify the meaning of terms designating such phenomena by publicly observable behavior. William James, for all his pragmatism, supposed that introspection is what the psychologist has to rely on "first and foremost and always." Yet, as early as the time of Auguste Comte, who died when James was still a schoolboy, introspection was notorious for fallibility. With the rise of scientific psychology it became increasingly clear that it was far more difficult than had been assumed to introspect in such a way as to yield objectively valid data. In due course, the Cartesian duality of substances—body and mind—was subtly reinstated as a duality of methods—inspection and introspection.

Behavioral psychology relies on the one method, not necessarily to the exclusion of the other, but as the more fundamental one. The insistence that psychology can in principle be made as objective a science as physics is already to be found in Kant. The question is how this is to be done. Objectivity, Kant showed, can be analyzed as intersubjectivity. The trouble with nonbehavioral data is just here. Even trained clinicians called upon to make diagnostic judgments often disagree markedly with one another. True, the diagnostic categories may be ill-defined; the behavioralist holds that the definition can be improved only by appropriate specification in behavioral terms. The combination of psychoanalytic conceptions with behavioral methods is a characteristic and promising development in contemporary psychology. How the mind is to be conceived and studied is a matter to be decided not by metaphysics but by psychology itself.

44. The Human Spirit

Man is more than body and mind, however these are related. On the one side, the body is not brute matter; it is infused with life. On the other side, the mind is too coldly intellectual to encompass human aspiration and feeling. Man is a creature of appetites and emotions, as well as a creature who is able to reason. Moreover, as a personality he seems strangely capable of absenting himself: permanently, in death; temporarily, in sleep and unconsciousness. Even stranger is his apparent capacity to present himself where he is not, in dream images. Furthermore, all his doings belong to some single agent, which cannot be identified either with the body or the mind. For such reasons—apart from more subtle and perhaps unconscious motiviations—man has been conceived in every culture and from earliest times as endowed with a distinctive individualized entity to which he owes his humanity. In a word, he has a *soul.*

The idea of a soul is not found only in primitive, unsophisticated conceptions of man. Everything hinges on just what the soul is thought to be. I am not speaking here of the ghost and shade, doppelgänger and double, *ka* and astral body of myth, folklore, and occult teaching. The concept of soul as a simple, spiritual substance in which the distinctively human attributes inhere is a very different matter, if I may say so; it is a concept found in philosophers such as Plato, Aquinas, Descartes, Leibniz, and Locke. Neither is the belief in a soul necessary to a religious commitment. A fundamental doctrine of Buddhism is *anatta,* the denial of a soul substance. William James, a philosopher with a profound sympathy for religion, nevertheless declared: "My final conclusion is that the soul explains nothing and guarantees nothing!"

The notion of a spiritual substance is far from clear. "Spiritual" can be taken as meaning not-material; and a substance in the relevant sense (§38) is that which has attributes. Whether the soul is immortal I reserve for later discussion (§88). The soul is the bearer of moral responsibility and the protagonist of the religious drama, since it is the agent of all characteristically human action. In this perspective, the Kantian noumenal self and the *purusa* of Sankhya metaphysics also may be seen as conceptions of soul.

For all its immateriality, the soul is called in many languages by a word whose root meaning is associated with the breath: the Sanskrit *atman* (distantly related to the English work "atmosphere"), the Hebrew *neshama,* the Greek *psyche,* and the Latin *anima.* The Hebrew words *nefesh* and *ruach* (types of souls) are also related, as are some of the preceding words, to a root meaning "to blow," as the wind. The word *psyche* also means butterfly, which, like the shadow, is a common symbol of the soul; in Stephen Vincent Benét's story of *The Devil and Daniel Webster,* Scratch says of Webster's soul, "the wingspread would astonish you!"

A common conception is that the soul has three components or aspects, or that there are three distinct souls. In Hebrew thought the *nefesh* is the biological individual, as in the English locution of the number of "souls" lost in a disaster at sea; the *ruach* is the dynamic, emotional side of man, usually translated as spirit, in the sense in which we speak of a man of spirit, or of a spirited horse; the *neshamah* is the specific personality, especially when viewed as the locus of moral or religious attainments or failings—it is the *neshamah* which is pure or defiled. In Plato we have the appetitive soul, the seat of lower emotions; the spirit, locus of noble feelings; and the reason. Aristotle distinguished a nutritive, sensitive, and rational soul. Comparable distinctions are to be found in Saadya Gaon and in other medieval philosophers. The distinction between the faculties of feeling, willing, and knowing—a distinction to be found in the Jain as well as in Augustine and Kant—may reflect the same tripartite soul. I shall refer to the three aspects or entities as the *biological, psychological,* and *spiritual* souls, respectively.

How the biological soul is to be empirically recognized is problematic, to say nothing of how it is to be assessed from a moral or religious standpoint. The problem becomes acute in the context of organ transplants, for example, with the concept of "clincial death" as seen in the perspectives of medicine, law, and morality. Similar problems arise in connection with abortion, contraception, and the issues of the right to die—in cases of severe brain damage, for instance, where a body may survive in a coma while nothing identifiable as the person can be expected to reappear.

What constitutes the psychological soul is also problematic. In folklore, *golem, zombi,* and the walking dead all illustrate the notion of a creature which has a biological soul but not a psychological one, and which is therefore monstrously inhuman in spite of its form. In Karel Capek's play *R. U. R.,* where the word "robot" was first introduced (from a Slavic root meaning "worker"), the mark of a newborn humanity in the robot is his capacity to weep and his willingness to sacrifice himself for another. It is these emotions, not the power of reason, which are conventionally recognized as the manifestation of soul.

Both the psychological soul and the spiritual soul are thought of as distinct from the body, if not separable from the body, which is the locus only of the biological soul. This conception is presented in Plato's dialogue *Phaedo,* where the soul is seen as imprisoned in the body. Epictetus is quoted by the Stoic Emperor Marcus Aurelius as saying, "Man is a little soul carrying around a corpse."

The idea then readily presents itself that the prisoner may be moved to another dungeon or that the soul may carry a new burden. This is the conception of *rebirth,* so widely assumed in Asian thought that it seldom finds explicit formulation. Rebirth is very different from resurrection or a heavenly life after death. Rebirth is an identifiable sameness of the psychological soul in distinct, successive bodies. The belief is therefore subject to empirical test, and would be confirmed by evidence that a person knew certain events, directly accessible only to somebody already dead, without having been told about the events or inferring their occurrence. These alternative explanations, immeasurably more probable, are very difficult to rule out. The common *déjà vu* experience—the uncanny sense of having already seen what is happening—is worthless as evidence, for the knowledge it displays is always hindsight. If it had predictive power, so that when the experience occurred one could write down then and there what will happen next, as we could while watching a movie we had already seen, that would be quite another matter. (It has been suggested that the *déjà vu* experience is due to a slight difference in the time of the nerve impulses transmitting the perceptions to the two hemispheres of the brain, so that the events were indeed already experienced—a tiny fraction of a second earlier.)

The present-day conception of man as a lump of clay given life, mind, and spirit by the soul is a heritage not so much of biblical imagery as of dualistic metaphysics. In this perspective, the soul is a kind of "ghost in the machine," as the contemporary analyst Gilbert Ryle put it. Encased by the physical system making up the body is another kind of stuff responsible for everything about man which is not merely physical. The doctrine of behaviorism, denying the existence in man of anything other than physical objects and processes, has its counterpart in the metaphysical stance of *mentalism,* which affirms the existence of a special mind stuff which accounts for traditional aspects of the soul—feelings, volitions, and thoughts.

Modern formulations of the issues, except in explicitly religious contexts, concern not the soul but consciousness, which William James characterized as "a mere echo, the faint rumor left behind by the disappearing 'soul' upon the air of philosophy." Ironically, the empiricist John Locke was the first to use the abstract noun "consciousness," by which he meant "the perception of what passes in a man's own mind." Empiricism's phenomenalistic approach to the theory of knowledge (§25) brings it close to mentalism, while its positivistic approach to language and meaning inclines it to behaviorism. On the one hand, empiricism must speak of sensations, impressions, and sense-data; on the other hand, it seeks to specify meanings in terms of publicly observable data. This tension in empiricism is rooted in the difference between epistemic and semantic empiricism (§11). An epistemic empiricist grounds knowledge in such data as my sensation of blue here and now. A semantic empiricist dismisses as meaningless, because it is incapable of verification, the question of whether what is in my mind on such an occasion is the same as what is in your mind when you have a sensation which you call seeing "blue."

Pragmatists, and empiricists close to psychological research or clinical practice, incline towards the second standpoint, repudiating mentalism in favor of a behavioral approach, if not a rigidly behavioristic one. They look for characteristic functions rather than for distinctive substances, familiar processes rather than entities consisting of some special stuff. Instead of speaking of a certain entity entering another called "consciousness," we can say that something was done knowingly; instead of attributing a content to the "mind" or "reason," we can say that something was done intelligently; instead of ascribing a state to the "soul," we can say that something was done emotionally or sensitively. There are difficulties in the way of any analysis which comes near to being acceptable. In this perspective such difficulties are seen to be scientific rather than philosophical, much more likely to cluster around genuine problems stemming from ignorance rather than puzzles occasioned by confusions of thought or language.

James and Dewey both had a considerable impact on psychology by their resolutely functionalist approach to mind and consciousness. The vocabulary of mentalism consists largely of abstractions from the concreta of purposive behavior. Thinking is the activity of "resolving entanglements in ongoing behavior, restoring continuity, recovering harmony, utilizing loose impulse, and redirecting habit." Thinking is problem-solving behavior, not an "idea" entering "consciousness" or being entertained by a "mind." The soul is not properly named by a substantive or an adjective; it demands a set of adverbs.

But which adverbs? Granted that we are not to take literally locutions describing an action as produced by a mind; when can we say that the action was performed "mindedly?" The question is not what differentiates intelligent from stupid behavior, or rational behavior from irrational; it is what differentiates any of these from behavior which is unthinking altogether. The line taken by functionalism is that mind is manifested in an action when some percepts serve as substitutes for or directives to others. Equivalently, there is mind when the action exhibits learning.

This approach may provide an acceptable concept of mind; what about consciousness? There is in consciousness a certain turning back upon itself (§47). In the current idiom, consciousness consists in the processing of information *about* information processes within the system. The dials and gauges facing the pilot correspond to the mind of the plane; the pilot's monitoring of these indicators corresponds to its consciousness. When all goes well the pilot withdraws his attention; so, James remarked, "consciousness deserts all processes where it can no longer be of use." From the standpoint of functionalism, consciousness is as purposive as is the mind.

In place of the idioms of information theory, most philosophers and psychologists have used the locutions of semantics. If mind involves the capacity to respond to *signs,* consciousness involves the use of *symbols* (§9). A sign signifies in replacing or leading up to something else; a symbol symbolizes in communicating to others what is being signified. We ourselves can serve as another: only if we do so can we communicate with others. If not, instead of symbolizing something we are only performing gestures which others can take as signs. This is the difference, so far as consciousness is concerned, between an exchange of insults and dogs growling or baring their fangs. The sting of the insult lies in this, that you know what I mean by it, and that I know that you know. George Herbert Mead and C. W. Morris developed this account in some detail; it is prefigured by the remark of Socrates (in the *Sophist*) that what we call thinking is the inward dialogue carried on by the mind with itself.

The empiricism of Locke, Hume, and their followers, because of its phenomenalistic and subjectivistic tendency (§24), found itself in a quandary known as the *problem of other minds.* Your consciousness, conceived mentalistically, is present only to your own mind; how can *I* know that it exists? Nothing better than an argument by analogy presents itself: When I make these sounds and movements I am conscious; I infer that when you make them you must be conscious as well. The trouble is that the argument cannot be validated for even a single instance; its logic therefore is totally unlike the inference of fire from smoke. A strict behaviorist also conceives consciousnesss mentalistically, denying rather than affirming its existence. Consistent with his determination to avoid subjectivism, the behaviorist denies not only your consciousness but his own as well. His treatment of the problem of other minds consists in the response, "What do you mean 'other'?"

Less extreme rejoinders are more acceptable. One is the answer given by a former colleague of mine to the question, "Do you believe in the existence of other minds?" Reflectively, he replied, "Not many!" ("Yost's retort"). The existence of other minds is no more problematic than the existence of my own. I know of both in the same way—through communication. If thinking is a dialogue carried on in the mind, the role of the generalized other, as Mead called it, is part of the process. When you and I communicate, each of us is an other for the other, and only, thereby, for himself. If I had never had anyone to talk to I would never have become able to talk to myself. Subjectivism founders on the most commonplace facts of how language and consciousness are acquired. The so-called problem of other minds is not a problem but a puzzle. The real problem is how to establish communication when the others will not listen, do not care, or cannot understand—how to bridge the gulfs of indifference, prejudice, and hatred. Unless it has implications for the solutions of such problems, "philosophy of mind" remains remote and unreal.

Mentalism faces difficulties because of its assumption that the mind is constituted by a combination of elementary sensory particles. This position is called *associationism.* Something like it is to be found in Aristotle; its most complete formulation was given by James Mill (John Stuart Mill's father). Experience consists of the mind grasping ideas in the broad sense given this term by Locke, a sense which embraces sensations as well as thought; learning consists in appropriately associating these ideas with one another.

Kant's analysis of knowledge showed that the relations among ideas are more intimate, both logically and psychologically, than empiricism recognized (this intimacy he referred to as "the unity of apperception"). Gestalt psychology emphasized the role of pattern and meaning in shaping experience. We not only apprehend parts which we combine into wholes, but also wholes which we analyze into parts. James, too, emphasized our direct experience of relations. Mental life is not an aggregation of discrete elements but a *stream of consciousness.* This position afterwards found expression in the writings of James Joyce, Virginia Woolf, and others.

Another problem of mentalism is the ontological status of the emotions. To say that someone is unfeeling is rightly construed as charging him with being inhuman. Feelings are universal; only what evokes them and how they are expressed is subject to individual and cultural variation. The question is whether an emotion is a self-sufficient entity—causally related to a thought or a bodily state, but existing in its own right.

Emotions, like other mentalistic entities, are viewed by functionalism adverbially, as qualities of action. The emotion is not antecedent to its expression but is the experience of the expression. The usual view, William James urged in his *Principles of Psychology,* is "that the mental perception of some fact excites the mental affection called the emotion, and that this latter state of mind gives rise to the bodily expression. My theory, on the contrary, is that the bodily changes follow directly the perception of the existing fact, and that our feeling of the same changes as they occur is the emotion. We feel sorry because we cry, angry because we strike, afraid because we tremble, not that we cry, strike or tremble because we are sorry, angry or fearful."

This conception does not reverse the causal relation between act and feeling, as though the action produces the feeling instead of the feeling producing the action. The relation is not causal; if we think so, we have fallen back into a mind-body dualism. An emotion is a way of experiencing something, not an isolable content of experience. In some cases, as with a free-floating anxiety, we may not be aware of what we are experiencing but only of the way in which it is present to us, as the melody of distant music might be blocked out though we can still hear its rhythms. Of emotions it may truly be said, "It ain't what you do, it's how you do it!"

45. The Motives of Men

What do men do, and why do they do it? There *is* a "why"—not always, but characteristically. Men engage in purposive behavior; this is what it means to have a mind. If on some alien planet we were to encounter "things" which moved not only when and where we did, as a shadow might, but in ways which anticipated our own course around an obstacle, the conclusion would be irresistible that the "things" are intelligent. "The pursuance of future ends and the choice of means for their attainment," James said, "are the mark and criterion of the presence of mentality." Purpose, meaning, and rationality are all taken by Peirce to be equivalent instances of his category of Thirdness. I once proved that I was more intelligent than a dog by solving the *Umweg* problem: a dog in a U-shaped wire enclosure finds it difficult to get at the food it sees outside the base of the U by moving in the opposite direction, whereas I, needing to go from Philadelphia to Los Angeles, unhesitatingly traveled east to New York where I could catch a nonstop flight to the West Coast.

I enjoyed an advantage, a distinctive privilege of humanity: my end was not literally in view, but it was an end-in-view in a literally more significant sense. My behavior was shaped not by the performance of a function but by the fulfillment of an intention. Both are purposive; only the second is motivational (§34). Both man and beast have minds of their own, in the sense of pursuing ends, and learning which means are most likely to attain those ends. Only man is conscious of his ends, and of why he uses the means he does. In Mead's idioms, it is characteristic of man that the later stages of his acts are controlled by significant symbols which indicate these stages and their bearings on the objects involved in his acts.

If mind and consciousness are analyzed in functionalist terms, which functions are served? To understand what man is, we ask, what is he up to? This question we might answer by asking, in turn, what's in it for him? what is he after? Different answers would be appropriate for different men, especially in different societies. It used to be thought that answers could be given for all men. These supposedly universal purposes were called *instincts.* They presumably belonged to man as man, regardless of his individuality. Instinct was thought of as unlearned response, what man does without being taught. Now, it is recognized that all but the simplest human reflexes are molded by experience—not that man has no instincts, but that for him the very notion of "instinct" cannot be usefully defined.

There are basic needs common to all. The question whether they are rooted in "nature" or "nurture" is now seen to be pointless. It is man's nature to become human only in nurture. Society does not play variations on a biological theme; the theme is an abstraction from concrete melodies which are culturally orchestrated.

Generalizations about the motives of man depend on normative considerations (§57). Motivations frequently identified have to do with sex, anxiety, aggression, achievement, affiliation with others, and so-called "ludic" behavior—perceptual and intellectual activities exemplified by playfulness and creativity.

Humanistic psychology—exemplified by Carl Rogers, Erich Fromm, and Abraham Maslow—distinguishes between the *satisfaction* of needs, the *gratification* from achievement, and the *joy* in creation and love. The sexual drive may be satisfied as a need—the partner is a "sexpot"; it may gratify a sense of achievement—he "makes" her or "makes out" and is, in turn, a "conquest"; or it may find expression in the joy of mutual fulfillment and growth. Food may satisfy bodily hunger; it may provide the gratification known to the fisherman or gardener; or it may be an occasion of the joy of nourishing those we love, a joy expressed in the grace which pronounces the blessing by which we ourselves have been blessed. Each of these levels of fulfillment may comprise something of the others, and each has its own roles to perform in the complex pattern of our purposes.

The *regulatory model* of human behavior is derived from the role in physiology of homeostasis—the maintenance of bodily equilibria, for instance of temperature. Deviations from equilibrium set up countervailing processes until the equilibrium is restored. Ideas of cosmic equilibria play an important part in many religious ethics (§51). The regulatory model is formulated in behavioral psychology in terms such as "tension reduction." As basic needs remain unsatisfied, tensions build up which stimulate and guide behavior to the satisfaction of the needs. In psychoanalysis the "economic standpoint," which uses the idioms of "psychic energy" and its conservation, is a version of the regulatory model.

Plato criticized this conception of human motivation as unworthy of man, accounting only for such ignoble pleasures as scratching where it itches. There is a more fundamental objection: a significant portion of our behavior is devoted to getting the itch. We eat to satisfy our hunger, but we also cultivate appetizers and relishes. Behavior is directed not only to restoring equilibria but also to producing disequilibria which are to be restored. This could be accounted for on the regulatory model by introducing the idea of second-order equilibria: the maintenance of an appropriate amount of first-order disequilibria. Such a hypothesis, however, is unacceptably *ad hoc*.

Another common conception of human motivation, equivalent to the regulatory model, postulates a general *utility* which behavior is presumed to maximize. Utility is not narrowly conceived here as a measure of the efficacy of a means for the attainment of a predetermined end; it comprises the worth of the end as well. At any moment each of us has a system of utilities which define the goals of our purposive behavior. Reason determines which among the alternative courses of action will maximize the utilities attained, and that is the course of action adopted.

It is questionable whether men in fact choose on the basis of rational considerations, even if they have a determinate set of utilities and know what these are. As Dostoevski and other existentialists contended: "How do these wiseacres know that man wants a normal, a virtuous choice? What made them conceive that man must want a rationally advantageous choice? Man everywhere, and at all times, whoever he may be, has preferred to act as he chose and not in the least as his reason and advantage dictated." Men may even act in ways they know to be contrary to their own interests, in pursuit of a masochistic satisfaction. The lady who had been complaining about her children to her fellow passenger, on learning that the other has no children, asks, "No children? So what do you do for aggravation?"

The aggravation may have a utility of its own; this corresponds to the introduction of second-order equilibria in the regulatory model. A course of action in which utilities are occasionally not maximized, and are even minimized, may acquire a special attraction. This is called the "utility of gambling," best illustrated by Russian roulette, where the difference in the utilities of life and death are outweighed by the utility of being in a state of uncertainty. Gambling might also have a negative utility, as for the young man in a story of De Maupassant's who is so afraid he might die in a scheduled duel that he kills himself the night before the event.

This approach easily slips into tautology, telling us nothing about human behavior. Men undeniably act to maximize their utilities if the fact that they pursue a certain goal is taken as revealing that the goal has utility for them. So construed, the principle says no more than that all purposive behavior is purposive. Its emptiness is glossed over by the uncertainties of meaning in the terms usually occurring in its formulation. More common than "utility" are the terms "pleasure" and "happiness," when these are put forward as magnitudes whose maximization is the universal goal of action. If their meanings are given any concrete specification, however, it becomes clear that we do not always choose to obtain pleasure or happiness. When we attain our goal we are pleased or happy because it *was* our goal. What made it our goal depends on the motivations involved, on which the universal principle throws no light. The mistaken idea that this principle explains action I call the *eudaemonian fallacy,* from the term Aristotle used to denote the state of well-being for man.

Hedonism, which singles out pleasure as the end of man, has two forms with radically different content. *Psychological hedonism* declares that men, in fact, seek pleasure; *ethical hedonism,* that they ought to do so (§61). Jeremy Bentham, one of the nineteenth-century precursors of modern utility theory, opens his *Principles of Morals and Legislation* with a declaration of psychological hedonism: "Nature has placed mankind under the governance of two sovereign masters, pain and pleasure." The eudaemonian fallacy is illustrated in the meaning unjustly acquired by the term "epicurean"; Epicurus himself, although a hedonist, was not an epicurean, believing that a life many men would describe as one of austere self-denial was in fact the most pleasurable. Everything hinges on just what gives each man pleasure. As soon as this is specified, the claim to universality is seen to be false; if the concept of pleasure remains general, the principle retains its truth but is emptied of content.

There are difficulties of another sort in the utilitarian or hedonistic conceptions of human motivation. These stem from the consideration urged by Plato, in his *Philebus*, that even in a life devoted to the pursuit of pleasure, reason, memory, knowledge, and true judgment must be given an important place, to calculate what pleasures can be provided by the alternatives before us. The difficulties arising in this connection cannot be sidestepped by assigning a utility to the process of calculation itself. The question is whether the calculation called for by the theory can be carried out.

How is utility to be measured? The ends even of economic action are not all measurable in a single index; even if there were such an index, it cannot be identified with money prices; and even if it could be, the utility of money is not a simple linear function of the amount of money. Utilities are not always transitive: A may be preferred to B, and B to C; yet A might not be preferred to C. There may be values immeasurably great. It may not always be possible to assess the worth of probable utilities, partly because the probabilities may themselves be difficult to estimate (§30), and partly because the utility of gambling may be hard to assess. The mathematical expectation of matching either pennies or hundred-dollar bills is 0 in both cases; there are people who are willing to play such games, and some would be willing to play one game but not the other.

There are additional difficulties, more psychological than mathematical. Calculation refers to the future, but my utilities then may not be what they are now. Even if utilities are presumed to be unchanging, they are affected by the fact that they lie in the future. A miser saves all he can, spends only what he must, while a child does just the reverse; the miser is not for that reason either more mature or more rational, and it is not easy to say which person is truly hedging against inflation. The question must also be faced of how individual utility systems can be combined to make possible defensible social choices—what the economist Kenneth Arrow has called the "aggregation problem." Simple solutions like majority rule do not always yield consistent results.

When to all this is added the element of subjectivism in what a man is satisfied with, whether or not it is truly satisfactory, it is hard to resist Dewey's condemnation of utilitarian theories of motivation as offering no choice except between "a sickly introspection and an intricate calculus of remote, inaccessible and indeterminate results." The utilitarians, such as

Bentham and Mill, were, however, interested not only in psychological questions but also in ethical ones. Utility theory plays an important role in welfare economics where it provides a logic of preferences and their measurement rather than a psychology of motivation or a philosophy of man. It has already made significant contributions, and can be expected to make more contributions, as mathematics continues to illuminate problems of decision making.

46. The Structure of the Self

The central topic of psychology, the human personality, was not treated by the academic discipline until recent years, with the work of Gordon W. Allport and Henry S. Murray. In philosophy, too, the subject received little attention, except for the scattered insights of Schopenhauer, Nietzsche, and a few others. Hume pinpointed the problem: the presumed unity of the self as the recipient of all its experiences. Hume argued that all we ever know are the experiences themselves; we know nothing of a subject who is experiencing them. "For my part, when I enter most intimately into what I call *myself,*" he says in his *Treatise,* "I always stumble on some particular perception or other. I never catch myself at any time without a perception and can never observe anything but the perception. What we call mind is nothing but a heap or bundle of different perceptions united together by certain relations, and supposed, though falsely, to be endowed with a certain simplicity and identity."

The self is *multiple.* Whatever unity it has results from a unification, either by the personality or by those who are conceptualizing it; the unity cannot be presupposed. We must recognize an *epistemic duality:* the difference between the self as known or experienced, and the self knowing or experiencing itself. The terms "me" and "I" are often used to mark this distinction. The self as known or experienced is sometimes called the "proprium"; the knowing subject is then called the "ego."

The epistemic duality can be recognized as a special case of a more general *dynamic duality* between the self as doer and the self that is done by, the active self and the passive one, the agent and what the agent is acting on. When I hate myself, "I" am full of hate, while "myself" is full of guilt, remorse, and humiliation; when I indulge myself, "I" am indulgent while "myself" is pampered. A strict empiricist might hold that in such cases only the passive self is observed, not the active one, only the "me," not the "I." Yet the difference between hatred and remorse is undeniable, as is the fact that they may be jointly experienced. The same is true of what is in the epistemic duality—the experience of looking and the sense of being looked at.

Widely recognized is a *moral duality* within the self: the higher self and the lower, the virtuous inclination and the evil one (*yetzer ha-tov* and *yetzer ha-ra*), the divine element in man's makeup and the bestial. Says Faust:

> *Two souls, alas, dwell in my breast,*
> *each seeks to sever from the other.*
> *The one with robust love's desires*
> *clings to the world with clutching limbs,*
> *the other fiercely rises from the dust*
> *to the high ancestral regions.*

Together with the dynamic duality, the moral duality serves as a defense against guilt and anxiety; we can identify ourselves with the one self or with the other as occasion requires. Facing a fearful prospect, I can dissociate myself from the passive self, as though the disaster will befall, not me, but someone else. Recognizing a shameful action, I can assign it to the lower self as active, while now I identify myself with the passive, innocent side of myself. "When I did that I was beside myself, I was carried away, I wasn't myself that day, I acted against my own better judgment." "Our frailty is the cause, not we; for, such as we are made of, such we be" (Viola in *Twelfth Night*). The same dualities can also be used for self-punitive purposes. Many neurotics have had occasion to complain, "Wherever I go, *I* come along—and spoil everything."

We can also distinguish a *social duality,* the difference between the public and the private self, and declare with Browning that each man "boasts two soul-sides, one to face the world with, one to show a woman when he loves her." Here it might be better to speak of a plurality rather than only a duality, for we show the world many faces, we may love more than one other, and to each we reveal what is his alone. We must not prejudge the nature of personal identity by assuming that the private self is the "real" self, and that what is revealed to others is only an appearance. The private self may be more illusory than the public one; self-deception is a commonplace of everyday life as well as of clinical observation.

The most familiar multiplicty in the self is found in nineteenth-century faculty psychology which, though in scientific disrepute today, is still close to the lay idiom. Kant assigned each sort of action of the psyche to a distinct agent, which came to be known as a faculty. An idea comes into my "mind," "imagination" pictures it attractively, while "reason" tells me that the actuality will fall short of the expectation—a conclusion confirmed by my "memory," which reminds me of past disappointments, so that my "will" falters, and my "conscience" is set at rest. We could say instead that *I* thought, *I* imagined, *I* remembered, and so on.

It is often charged that the other locutions involve us in the fallacy of *reifying* or *hypostatizing,* mistaking abstract entities for concrete things. But the use of a term as a grammatical subject does not commit us to interpreting it as standing for an ontological subject; a substantive does not have to designate a substance. What the fallacy really consists in is the faulty inference that because a noun is an appropriate subject with some verbs it can be used meaningfully with any verbs we choose. We would be reifying "reason" if we inferred that because reason can "tell" us whether a conclusion follows from premises, reason can also "refuse" to tell us something, or "insist" on telling us. But that a word is nonsensical in some uses does not imply that it should never be used.

What is objectionable in faculty psychology is not the mere naming of agents for psychological processes. The question is, first, whether there is a distinctive process to be named, and second, how assigning the name will contribute to knowledge about the process. My "will" is not an agent translating thoughts into actions; if *I* decide and then *I* act nothing is left for my will to do. "We may as properly say," Locke argues, "that the singing faculty sings and the dancing faculty dances as that the will chooses." Knowledge grows only as the distinctive work of the agent is connected with other acts, by the same or by other agents. We know nothing about how we remember if we are told that "memory" does it, but there *is* content in the propositions that memory weakens with age, that it serves self-esteem, and that it depends on reverberating neural circuits.

There is a danger in the faculty idiom that what begins as a distinction may end by being taken as a mark of separation. But there is also a danger in presupposing beneath the multiplicity of unity which, in fact, does not exist. Counterposed to a psychology of reified faculties are the misleading locutions of a presupposed unity. When I am undecided, I have not yet "made up my mind"; if I am inclined in two directions, I am "of two minds" about the matter, as though one mind can take up only one position; and when you and I agree, there has been "a meeting of minds," as a result of which we are "of one mind."

The contemporary version of the multiple self replaces many faculties by many *roles*. In each situation we are expected to behave in certain ways—in our own expectations as well as in the expectations of other people. Something in the situation provides us with a cue, and we then enact a more or less appropriate role. What role is appropriate and how it is to be performed is largely decided for us by others, either by the culture as a whole or by specific persons. The situation is seldom as extreme as in this scene from Friedrich Dürrenmatt's play, *The Physicists:*

INSPECTOR. Newton thinks he is really Einstein.

FRAULEIN DOKTOR. That's what he tells everybody. But in fact he really believes he is Newton.

INSPECTOR. Are you sure?

FRAULEIN DOKTOR. It is I who decide who my patients think they are. I know them far better than they know themselves.

More customary is the situation of the Zen monk who, schooled to accept whatever life brings his way, explained, on being discovered coming from a lady's bedroom, "What could I do? She asked me!" A true Englishman need not be reminded that England expects every man to do his duty; that is part of what it means to him to be English.

Duty is what we *must* do; the role is what is demanded of us, expected of us, imposed upon us. We are cast in a role, cast into it. P. G. Wodehouse in *Carry On, Jeeves,* shows how it is done:

"I'm sorry, but I simply will not break into your beastly house on any consideration whatever."

He gazed at me, astonished and hurt.

"Is this Bertie Wooster speaking?" he said in a low voice.

"Yes, it is!"

"But, Bertie," he said gently, "we agreed that you were at school with me."

"I don't care."

"At school, Bertie. The dear old school."

"I don't care. I will not—"

"Bertie!"

"I will not—"

"Bertie!"

"No!"

"Bertie!"

"Oh, all right," I said.

"There," said young Bingo, patting me on the shoulder, "spoke the true Bertram Wooster!"

True it may be, but far from the whole truth. The self performing in roles which have been assigned rather than freely assumed is the *involuntary self*. It is a significant component of every personality; we live not as we would like to but as we must. If the life is not of our own choosing, how can it be even a part of the self? When roles are too insistently imposed we cry out, "Why can't you let me be myself!" The involuntary self is apparently alien to us.

The language of role theory describes only what a person does, not what he is. The image conjured up is that my innermost self is an actor with a wardrobe of costumes, each equipped with a mask, props, and a sketch of the dialogue and business of a corresponding play. The moment my cue is given—by other actors or by my own sense of the dramatic—I don the costume, adjust the mask, and proceed with my part. But who waits for me in the dressing room, and how do I occupy myself between performances—how do I look unmasked? Zen asks, "What was your original face before you were born?"

The theatrical image is a misleading one, because—as in Max Beerbohm's story of *The Happy Hypocrite*—the face grows to resemble the mask. As we continue to perform in a role, it becomes more and more natural to us; the Master pointed out that the punishment for continually pretending to be a *tzaddik* (saint) is that eventually you really get to be one. Actors do not more often come to be the characters they portray on stage and screen because the roles, in the present sense, which they spend their lives performing are the roles of actors—that is, theatrical celebrities.

In addition to this psychological objection to the role image there is the philosophical objection raised by Hume. We never see the actor, only the roles he is performing; what is the empirical justification for assuming that he exists? He can be eliminated by the same principle of abstraction which dispenses with an underlying substance supposed to serve as a core to which are attached all the attributes of each thing (§38). In place of the multiple self held together by a homunculus—the true self, huddled within and never seen—we may consider a *pluralistic self* in which even the dressing room is part of the set, and not only the actor but also the playwright, producer, and audience are all only performers. How can this pluralistic conception account for the unity of a self with multiple roles? How can it account for the difference between imposed roles and those voluntarily assumed? Who is it who resists or welcomes the role?

The answer is in terms of relations among the roles themselves, just as the unity of the attributes making up a thing derives from their connections with one another. Roles may be mutually supportive or conflicting; each set of roles is *consonant* (or dissonant) to some degree. One component of "the crisis of identity" is the widespread dissonance in contemporary roles. The adolescent is not allowed to vote or drink a glass of beer but is held responsible for his sexual impulses and is liable to military duty; the working woman is expected to be aggressively efficient on the job, but her femininity is culturally defined as passivity and helplessness; the male is to be a ruthless competitor and a hardened and tough protector but also a gentle and tender lover, a caring father and friend. The more dissonant our roles, the more involuntary the self we are experiencing. The *unity* of the self is not that of a transcendent essence distinct from our doings but reflects the support our roles give one another. I am the man I am because I reply to my children's questions with a lecture, and to my students with fatherly advice.

Consonance is only one aspect of the unity of self. We must also account for the *constancy* of the self; I am essentially one and the same man, not only in my various roles but also from day to day. (There is a third component of the unity of the self, the self's sense of its *continuity*, which will be discussed in the next section.) In what does the constancy of the self consist if not in the persistence of an unchanging substance—the real self beneath all its appearances?

Constancy, like the other components of the unity of the self, is not always as great as might be assumed, nor is it antecedently given. People do change; a dissolute Prince Hal can suddenly display the majesty of Henry V and declare to Falstaff,

> *Presume not, that I am the thing I was:*
> *For heaven doth know, so shall the world perceive,*
> *That I have turned away my former self.*

Constancy is often conceptualized as the *character* of the person. Not only does character change; even when constant, character does not exhaust the personality. It serves, rather, as a background for impulsive and unpredictable behavior, which we call spontaneous or capricious. Mead distinguishes between the "me" and the "I" on the basis of the difference between a socially determined constancy and the spontaneity of individual impulse, so that my *in*constant self may be even more truly my innermost self. "Character" as invoked by moralizers—usually with references to backbone, principles, or strength of character—designates the rigid, absolutistic, and authoritarian aspects of personality. That is why Dostoevski and other existentialists hold that man "must and morally ought to be pre-eminently a characterless creature."

Taken literally, such statements would be absurd, and the existentialist's willingness to welcome absurdity is no help. Each man does have a character of sorts after all, and in the existentialist's own scale of values each man should aspire to the affirmation and protection of his own individuality. What makes each man recognizably the individual he is? What allows us to identify him, to see that his actions are indeed his and not that of some other self by which he is possessed?

The answer is that everything a person does is done in a more or less characteristic *style*. (Apropos, the Greek word from which the word "character" derives meant, among other things, a distinctive species of literary style.) Our analysis of style, even in the arts, is as yet quite rudimentary; only recently has it come into vogue with reference to political and administrative behavior. It has, in fact, a virtually unlimited range of application—from a person's gait or handwriting to the subtle patterns of his thoughts and feelings. I do not mean that the same traits are to be found in all his doings—this is a matter of consonance rather than constancy—but that each of the things he does is done each time in more or less the same way. A person need not walk with the same directness or deviousness that characterizes his thinking, but his walk has stable characteristics by which it is recognizable. Constancy combined with the consonance of a person's actions forms the basis of typologies of character.

An ancient classification is that of Galen, court physician to Marcus Aurelius, whose views on medicine and biology exercised a profound influence for over a millennium. His types of character were presumed to correspond to the predominance of one or another of the bodily "humors" postulated by Hippocrates (blood, phlegm, and two sorts of bile), or of glandular secretions, in the contemporary version. Galen's types classify character by way of temperament: sanguine, phlegmatic, choleric, and melancholic—in modern terms, respectively optimistic, apathetic, hostile, and depressive. During the past century, physique has sometimes been combined with temperament as a basis of classification. Carl Jung popularized the types "introvert" and "extrovert," which he further subdivided. In Freud, there are "oral," "anal," and "genital" characters; the so-called "character disorders" received particular attention, classified into the hysterical, narcissistic, obsessive-compulsive, and impulsive (psychopathic personality). Classifications of character are significant only insofar as they are associated with some theory of character; otherwise the name "characterology" by which such classifications are sometimes known is only an honorific. Interest of psychologists has moved from types of character to character traits, and from these to abstract factors, isolable by statistical analysis.

However character is classified, a long tradition, from Aristotle's *Nicomachean Ethics* to Dewey's *Human Nature and Conduct,* traces the roots of character to habit. Not only does a man act as he does because of his character; he has that character because he has habitually acted in a certain way. As Sartre says, man is the sum of his actions. It is not just sheer repetition which forms character. What is important is not the trend of action, definable by mere frequencies, but the tendencies to act in a certain way—the forces which impel a man to one course of action rather than another even though countervailing forces may lead to a different action. A single killing is enough to make a man a murderer, as a single act of treason makes him a traitor. Such actions reveal character, even though the tendencies disclosed are seldom actualized.

A recurrent theme in wisdom literature is that man's character is his fate. Men cannot conceal their character, says Mencius. Lucretius writes that each man flies from himself, but the self he cannot escape clings to him all the more against his will. Emerson gives us the familiar line, "What you are thunders so that I cannot hear what you say." Character shapes action in ways which cannot be eluded by mere resolves or pious declarations. But it is not forever fixed and unchanging. Like the force of habit in which it is rooted, character restricts action but also frees deliberation for significant choices. Who is there to make a choice, if there is any choice? Free or not, who am I?

47. Personal Identity

Every single thing in the world is an individual, with its unique identity; otherwise it could not be identified as single. When two descriptions denote one and the same thing, their denotations are *numerically identical.* The evening star is numerically identical with the morning star; in the same sense, Mark Twain and Samuel Clemens are identical. Numerical identity is known more generally as *logical identity:* the relation between x and y when every property of x is also a property of y, and conversely. In that case, x and y cannot be distinguished, for a distinguishing mark would have to be a property of one and not of the other. The statement that they are nevertheless distinct, even though not distinguishable, would have no empirical meaning. So-called "identical twins" are, of course, distinguishable—one is standing here, for instance, and the other one there. When they move, I may no longer be able to say which is which, although I still recognize them as two. Here another sort of identity is in question: *genidentity* (from "genetic identity").

Genidentity has nothing to do with biology; it refers to continuity of existence. The adult is identical with the infant he once was, although each is very different from the other. The Crab Nebula now revealed in our telescopes is genidentical with the supernova observed by Chinese astronomers in the tenth century. When x is a later state or condition of y, it is genidentical with y; although the two do not coexist, they are genuinely two, numerically distinct, and distinguishable precisely by the properties which have changed in the time interval between them.

Logical individuality is universal: it is the property which each thing has of being logically identical with itself and genidentical with what it was. No individual has this property to any greater or lesser degree than any other. We speak of something or someone as being "highly individual" in the sense of rare or unusual, very nearly unique. There is no reason why such *statistical individuality* should be particularly valued, unless we invoke some absurd generalization of the law of supply and demand. Yet Kierkegaard chose for his own epitaph, "The Individual." The poet also writes in praise of his beloved, "Which can say more than this rich praise, that you alone are you?" The logician might counter, "Which can say less?"

Personal identity makes each of us the person he is rather than merely a logical individual, like any senseless thing; it gives to the experience of each of us a uniqueness, not because the experience is unlike any other but because it is our own. In many of our involvements with others we are only logical individuals, and thus dehumanized—things rather than persons. The crew of a ship used to consist of "hands"; soldiers are "cannon fodder"; in air travel, passengers are lined up and moved from place to place like baggage, and their humanity is not restored by the formalized ministrations of the stewardess. Even when our humanity is acknowledged, we are often *depersonalized,* as personal identity is ignored. The patient or prisoner is a "male Caucasian, age 37 . . ."; we are taxpayers, customers, members of the public—human beings but not persons, unless a bribe is to be paid, a check cashed, or a correction made to a news story.

People are individuated, distinguished from other people, but this is often done without reference to personal identity. The devices which serve for such depersonalized individuation I call *identifications.* Characteristically, they are numbers; because they appear on documents and cards, identifications provide what has aptly been called a "paper identity." The identifications do not convey who I really am but reveal only what I would admit to an enemy: my name, rank, and serial number. They do not prepare for personal relations with me but only make it possible for others to put me in my place. Insurance companies issue policies to compensate for losses sustained if identifications are stolen and misused; there is no insurance against loss or damage to identity.

We may distinguish between nominal and real identifications by analogy to the corresponding types of definitions (§32). Nominal identifications are arbitrary, as names are in our culture, as contrasted with the practice among American Indians, say, of assigning names which have a meaningful relation to the character or biography of the person. In a pointed caricature of life in the future, when all names have been replaced by numbers, a personnel director asks an applicant his name, and on being told, glances at him in surprise: "Did you say '—1557?' That's funny, you don't look Jewish!" A real rather than nominal identification, though literally superficial, is exemplified by fingerprints or, as with Odysseus, by an old scar or the ability to draw a bow—the last coming closer to the identity. A man's dog may know him by his smell or voice; although these also are only identifications, the dog's reawakened love and loyalty belong to the identity.

To know a man's name may allow us to know a great deal about him; it is not yet to know who the man is. Literature is filled with dramatic disclosures of proper identification: Odysseus, Oedipus, Edmund Dantes, Jean Valjean, Birdy Edwards, Lord Percy Blakeney. The correct identification was hard to arrive at because the identifications presented differed so markedly from the character of the man who bore them. Not uncommonly, when a person acquires a new identity he takes on a new name, as Saul became Paul and as Cassius Clay became Muhammad Ali. Whether a person has a certain identification, and how he came by it, are relatively easy to establish; what is it to have a certain personal identity?

Part of the answer to this question is provided by an account of how we acquire an identity. The child takes into himself the roles, styles, attitudes, beliefs, and values of those around him. That we speak of his taking these into his "self" is a grammatical necessity, not a logical one; a self is not presupposed but comes into being in the process. Outside fiction, Mowgli and Casper Hauser could only have had the personality of a wolf, and Tarzan, of an ape. Psychologists call the process *introjection.* In coming to know someone we ask where he is from because so much of the identity is disclosed in its origins; the child is indeed father to the man. That we pray to "our God and the God of our fathers" is the literal truth: He is ours because He was theirs. That we may later come to embrace another religion or lose our childhood faith altogether means that in some measure we will have acquired a new identity; this one also has its origins, to which it owes much.

We become ourselves in the course of incorporating others. In many cultures it is the practice to name a child after a recently deceased relative. There may be a belief in the continuity of the soul, for which the name provides a local habitation; but beneath a myth there is usually a psychodynamic reality; in this case, it is the continuity of identity produced by introjections. When I was a boy, whenever other children heard that my name was "Abraham," they invariably asked, "Abraham Lincoln?"—which for some reason was thought to be funny; it was years before the effective reply occurred to me, "No, but we were named after the same man!" This was true, to be sure; but more directly, I was named after my mother's brother, who died a few days before I was born; my mother learned of his death only when my name was proposed. A generation later a daughter was born to my sister, who learned of our mother's death, in turn, when the infant was named.

Introjections take place not only in childhood but in all our encounters with one another. It is not only parents and teachers who contribute to identity but friends and peer groups and, in some measure, everyone around us. An identity does not come to be, once for all, but is forever in the making.

A forest does not have a precise geographic location. It is an ecological entity, the locus of interactions among plants and animals, and between them and their environment. Its boundaries are fluid, changing with the shifting winds, with fire and drought, with animal migrations, insect plagues, and viral epidemics. Even the tree line on a mountainside varies with changes in climate, just as a self expands in the warmth of acceptance and support. The boundaries are quite permeable; selves literally interpenetrate. The soldier who enters a forest camouflaged as a tree becomes a part of the forest: rain, sun, and shade fall differently because of him; birds alight and insects lay eggs on his "trunk"; vines and creepers may bind him; were he to remain, it would not take long for the forest to make him its own. Incursions into the self need not be thought of in the melodramatic terms of hypnosis, brainwashing, insanity, or a grand passion so all-consuming that the two lovers are one. Every communication marks a region of contact between selves who will never be the same again. Each of us is truly a part of all that he has met.

The self is mistakenly thought to have a certain fixity because of the *principle of self-reference:* each of us stands at the point of origin of the coordinate system by reference to which everything around us is localized. I am always "here," at the fixed point of the turning world, in an eternal present. This epistemic fixity Kant called the "transcendental ego." The psychology of the situation was dealt with by the gestaltist Max Wertheimer, who analyzed how organizational structures are described by members of the organization: each perceives himself in a position of greater centrality than is warranted by his functions in the organization. Self-reference is not selfishness (§58); what each of us is always asking is not "What's in it for me?" but rather "How does it look from here?"

Introjection has been criticized on the grounds that explanations must refer only to immediately antecedent conditions, not to the remote past. This objection is more commonly made by methodologists than by working scientists. Whatever may be true according to the reconstructed logic, the logic-in-use in science often formulates *interval laws:* if something is the case at the time t, something else will be the case at the time t + Δ. Radioactive decay is so described, the usual interval being the "half-life" of the substance. Apropos, in defending the predictability of human actions, Hume gives the example that a bag of gold placed at noon in Piccadilly Circus will disappear after a few hours as surely as if it had been a block of ice.

When there is a nonarbitrary point of origin for the time interval, we speak of *genetic laws.* These describe stages of development, what is to be expected at various intervals after specified early conditions. A child psychologist confronted with a question about a child's behavior will surely want to know first, "How old is the child?" Useful applications of the *genetic method* are not limited to human affairs, as evolutionary biology, geology, and cosmology all exemplify. It is especially important for the understanding of man because, for him, memory and history are so central, as has been emphasized by philosophers as diverse as Aristotle, Hegel, Nietzsche, and Bergson (§68). Culture is the past of a society embedded in its present, as personality is the presence of the individual's past.

Here we face the problem of the *continuity* of the self—the self's perception of its constancy. When I regain consciousness I ask "Where am I?" but not "Who am I?" Whatever else I may be ignorant of, I know who I am. To lose the continuity of the self is to lose one's identity. Memory is crucial here. I perceive myself as continuous with my past self because the past is present to me, in my remembrance of it. I know who I am when I waken because I remember laying me down to sleep. We can forget a good deal without losing the sense of identity. Even in the middle of a sentence I may forget what I was going to say but have no doubt that it was I who was going to say it. When Alice wondered whether she might have been changed into some other child, she checked her identity by testing if she knew all the things she used to know, "but her voice sounded hoarse and strange, and the words did not come the same as they used to do." For my part, it would be quite unlike me if I *did* remember all I tried to recollect.

What underlies the continuity of the self is a transfer of information; its retrieval is another matter. The self that was, bestowed on its successor the patterns which make up its distinctive being—yesterday this day's madness did prepare. In any transfer of information there is always some degradation: distortion and loss. Change of identity may result not only from the loss of information but also from its gain. With a sudden access of significant information a person is never the same again. This is characteristic of religious conversions, of near-misses in accidents or on the battlefield, and of last-minute reprieves from execution (as happened to Dostoevski). I am the same man when I waken in the morning only because I learned so little during the night.

That there is a continuity among memories does not imply that there must be some one self which has all the memories. This is the presupposition expressed in Descartes' starting-point for his philosophy, "I think, therefore I am." What is given is only that there is a thinking, not that there is an agent who thinks, much less that one and the same agent exists for a succession of thoughts. An office may remain unchanging even though the official occupying it may frequently be replaced. The head of the clan is known as "the" Douglas; at his death the new head of the clan assumes that name. "The" Douglas does not die, but all men, even in Scotland, are mortal. For every experience of the self there is an "I" having that experience, the locus of personal identity at that moment in a continuously changing process. It does not follow that there is an "I" which has all the experiences of that person, because of which they are all his. William James put it, "Each thought is born an owner, and dies owned, transmitting whatever it realizes as its Self to its own later proprietor." Each officeholder inherits the problems and achievements of his predecessor and transmits them to his successor; there is continuity of office without a single enduring official.

Illustrated here is the fallacy Whitehead called *misplaced concreteness*, neglecting the abstraction involved in a concept. What remains one and unchanging, providing continuity of self, is of a higher degree of abstraction than the many experiences which succeed each other. The fallacy lies in thinking that the *one* is as concrete as the *many* from which it is constructed. A clan may be Scottish, but it is not some special sort of Scot; an office may be held by a Democrat, but it is not the office, only its occupant, who can cast a ballot. "The king is dead, long live the king!" expresses not a contradiction, but a continuity—the continuity of the monarchy, which can neither live nor die.

Introjection is only one of the two processes by which personal identity is constituted. The other is *investment*, giving of oneself. I am the person that I am because of all I prize, all that matters to me in any degree whatever. In proportion as I lose interest in any of them, the boundaries of my self contract, until, if I care for nothing at all, identity vanishes in a dimensionless point. "In its widest sense," James said, "a man's self is the sum total of all that he can call his." I can call them mine insofar as I make myself theirs; thereby I make my self. This is particularly true when those I call mine are persons. The other that I care for Martin Buber calls "Thou," adding that through the Thou a man becomes an I. The process of defining my identity through another is sometimes called *identification* with that other. Three senses of this term have thus been distinguished: (1) the conceptualization of a presumed constancy in things (§32); (2) an external mark of individuality, contrasting with personal identity, and (3) the process of investing something of the self in an introjected other.

The empiricist, functionalist, pragmatic, pluralistic self I have been discussing comes to be in the two-way process of introjection and identification. I take something or someone into myself, and I give myself to something or someone. The question who performs these actions has no more point than the question who or what does the raining when "it" rains. Agent, action, and outcome are all one. The self is not a black box in which is connected a complex set of inputs and outputs. Instead of a box with inaccessible contents, the self is the locus of those connections. The inputs and outputs themselves are enough to accommodate whatever we can discover of the self.

The "search for an identity" is an attempt to counter the depersonalization and dehumanization to which so many are subjected in our time. Often it is supposed that an identity can be achieved by negation, by emphasizing the difference between "us" and "them." There was a time when many self-styled Americans knew only what it was to be "un-American," and similar *negative identities* (identity by way of what I am not) can be noted today among blacks and whites, Palestinians and Israelis, Catholics and Protestants, Christians and Jews. The Master said, "If I am I only because you are you, and you are you only because I am I, then I am not I and you are not you." The self is constituted by what we give and accept, not by what we reject. My individuality depends more on what I share with others than on what differentiates me from them or what I keep for myself.

The negative identity which consists in rejecting others has its counterpart in the sense of being rejected by them. Man is so constituted that this sense of rejection is then taken into himself, so that the hatred and contempt he displays for others is a self-hatred and self-contempt as well. Psychologists speak of this process as "identification with the aggressor," the outcome of the principle, "If you can't lick 'em, join 'em." The process is self-defeating from the outset.

Because of rejections, role-conflicts, and depersonalizations there are widespread clinical syndromes of identity confusions and crises, whose conditions and consequences have been illuminated by Harry Stack Sullivan and Erik Erikson. The madman may be identified by his idiosyncratic behavior, but such behavior reveals the failure to attain or maintain an identity. The madman suffers from the delusion that he is Napoleon or Jesus just because he is not himself—he is no *one* at all. The situation is not that *he* is confused about his identity; it is his identity which is confused. In less severe pathologies there may be domains of action in which the self can remain far from the edges of its painful uncertainties, and so perform adequately. If I hear voices, so long as *I* hear them and they are speaking to *me,* I may be not mad but inspired.

The difference is between a self torn by conflict and an integrated self, an identity whose component identifications accept one another. This is not a matter of the consonance of our roles, nor of complacency in performing them. I may accept another without agreeing with him, acknowledging his right to his opinion and inviting him to agree to disagree; so also with the personae within the self. In an integrated personality the conversation of the soul with itself is not just talk; what is said is listened to and taken seriously. A self whose personae speak with only one voice is not integrated but regimented, impoverished by what it must allocate to the suppression of dissent. The search for identity may be a search for integration. The question "Who am I?" may mean more pointedly, "*Which* am I?" Which am I to be? What decisions will embody not an authoritarian unanimity but a democratic consensus? The search may also be for acceptance by the other: Who am I in *your* eyes? What am I to you? What can we be to one another?

Personal identity is multiple, fluid, and open. There are many introjections, many investments, each with varying intensities in a changing pattern, loosely held together in memory and expectation, with many components supportive or conflicting in shifting alignments. The metaphysics of man often assumes that every person *is* a self, that he has an absolutely personal identity. It is taken for granted that deep within each psyche is a unique entity, the very core of the self, its quintessential identity. Theories differ chiefly in what they take to be the distinctive attributes of such a self—those which make it a self, and which make it the particular self that it is. But personal identity has many degrees and dimensions; its essential attributes, whatever they are, are partial, relative, and approximate.

Personal identity, far from being antecedently given, is a personal achievement. Diogenes might have had as long a search if he were looking only for a man, honest or no. In the last act of *Peer Gynt,* Peer, on his hands and knees, is picking wild onions, seeing in them a symbol of his life, each layer the role of a self-seeking which remained, layer by layer, unfulfilled; when they are finally peeled away, nothing at all remains. "Nature is witty," he says, "but to hell with brooding!" Perhaps, in the end, the Kabbalists were right: only God can truly say "I."

48. Human Freedom

Each man aspires to the life of his own choosing; but has he a choice? Choice depends on real opportunities which may be restricted or denied by other men (§71). Man's own nature has also been held to deny choice.

One of the most widespread doctrines denying human freedom is *fatalism.* There is a cosmic power—fate—which ordains the course of each man's life, his "destiny." "All things move toward a determined end," says the Koran; this might also be construed as referring to a divine purpose which does not determine the course of individual lives. Marcus Aurelius, in his *Meditations,* was more specific: "Whatever befalls you was preordained for you from eternity." An almost universal component of the fatalist doctrine is the notion that a man's lifespan is foreordained; the Talmud records that a certain epidemic lasted for seven years, but not one man died "before his time." The bullet, says the soldier, will not kill him "if it doesn't have my name on it." Lesser events may also come within the compass of predetermination; fatality is not limited to matters of life and death. The Talmud declares that even the appointment of inspectors of the water supply is ordained.

Whatever is fated will surely come to pass; fate does not make recommendations but decisions which are executed without fail. "No man has ever escaped his destiny," says Homer; the Greek tragedians gave fate dominance even over the gods, whose favor is not enough to exempt man from its decrees. The inevitable fulfillment of fate is a recurrent theme in the *Thousand and One Nights;* O. Henry's *Roads of Destiny* captures the present-day popular belief, which is effectively satirized in Max Beerbohm's story *A. V. Laidler.* Even if a man knew his fate, what he does to avert it is just what brings it about. Recall the tale of the appointment in Samara: A prince, frightened by the menacing gestures of the apparition of Death in the royal garden, mounted his horse and rode off to the distant city of Samara. Confronting the apparition, the king asked, "How dare you frighten my son?" To which the reply was, "I had no intention of frightening him; I merely threw up my arms in surprise at seeing him here, for I know we have an appointment tonight, far away in Samara."

The psychological appeal of fatalism is easy to understand. It not only provides a sense of security but also ministers to the desire to escape from responsibility, better known as the "escape from freedom," after Erich Fromm's book of that title. On the logical side, fatalism is unassailable because it can so easily be interpreted as a tautology, and so as necessarily true. "Things are where things are," says Aeschylus, "and as fate has willed, so shall they be fulfilled"; elsewhere he says more simply: "What is to come, will come." This is true beyond any cavil, but by the same token it tells us nothing about the future.

If fatalism is construed so as to have a content, it is manifestly false. In that case it asserts that what is to come will come no matter what happens in the meantime—an assertion contradicted by all we know of causes and effects. Whether the soldier will be killed depends not only on the bullet but also on whether he exposes himself, whether he is wearing a helmet, and so on; the explanation after the fact that if he was not killed the bullet did not have his name on it explains nothing, but simply repeats that he was not shot. The statement, "It happened because it happened," is a reference to the past of the fatalistic future, "It will happen because it is to happen"—both are equally empty.

A fatalist might rejoin that while causes do produce their distinctive effects, we are fated to set in motion one train of causes rather than another. Had the soldier worn his helmet he would not have been killed, but he was fated not to wear it at that moment. This action in turn has its causes or reasons, and the whole argument is reinstated. Sooner or later fatalism must fall back on a claim of something happening no matter what—this is what it means to ascribe the event to fate rather than the operative causes. It is this claim which is false.

Failure to recognize the "no matter what" element in fatalism is responsible for the mistaken notion that the Asian cultures, especially the Indian, are fatalistic. A basic Hindu doctrine is the law of *karma,* that a man's past actions (in a previous life as well as in this one) determine what befalls him. This is from from saying that all is fated. Quite the contrary; *karma* extends the workings of causality into the moral realm as well as the physical one. A man's present state is the consequence of his past actions; in the same way, his future state will be the consequence of his present actions, not of what has been ordained for him by fate.

Even if a man's future is determined by his present actions, he is still not free, presumably, so long as his present actions are determined by his past. This is *determinism* (§41), the doctrine that all events have causes. Whether we say that causes make no difference, as in fatalism, or that they make all the difference, as in determinism, the result appears to be the same: man is not free. For Aeschylus no one is free save Zeus, as is declared by the spirit of Power incarnate. Only God stands outside the causal order.

The absence of causal determination is called *free will.* This is only one among several possible conceptions of freedom. The question whether man has free will—whether any actions are uncaused—is not the same as the question whether man is free, unless it has already been decided that freedom can only be conceived as free will. Free will is the negation of determinism; freedom presupposes determinism rather than negating it. Philosophers who identify freedom with free will have sometimes argued that quantum mechanics, in upsetting determinism, has provided a foundation for the belief in human freedom. The notion that the uncertainty associated with measurements of the position and momentum of subatomic particles is the basis for the reality of man's control over his destiny is, on the face of it, quite unconvincing. Suppose that man does not have free will, that human actions are causally determined just as are all other macroscopic events. What bearing does this have on human freedom?

If a man pleaded in court that a contract was not valid because he had not entered into it freely, then supported his plea with the argument that causal agencies necessitated his signing, surely his plea would be groundless. If we were to say that because of determinism no man is free to choose his wife, no student his career, no citizen his government, what would become of the differences between arranged and "romantic" marriages, between a society of status and one of contract, between a dictatorship and a democracy? If freedom is equally absent in all these cases, there is something else, call it what you will, which is present in the second member of each pair. The differences are real and undeniable; I see no good reason to depart from ordinary usage here, which is simply to say that sometimes men are free to choose and sometimes not. The existence of causes does not settle which.

Freedom conceived as free will is absolute: man either has free will or he doesn't, and either all men have it or none do. Thereby important issues are glossed over as to the degree of freedom a man might enjoy under certain conditions, the respects in which he is free and those in which he is in bondage, and how his freedom differs from that of other men of different character or differently situated. "Man is free, man is freedom," Sartre proclaims; to this I respond with a paraphrase of the principle enunciated in George Orwell's *Animal Farm* that all animals are equal, but some are more equal than others.

The belief in free will does have a superficial empirical basis, grounded in ignorance rather than in knowledge. "Men are deceived because they think themselves free," Spinoza argues with reference to free will, "and the sole reason for thinking so is that they are conscious of their own actions, and ignorant of the causes by which those actions are determined." Freud later argued that dreams, slips of the tongue, and the syndromes of psychopathology are dismissed as accidental only because their causes are hidden. Understanding human behavior does not rest on the presupposition that no action is freely performed. Freedom does not imply that behavior is not measurable, repeatable, or predictable. It does not even imply that behavior is not controllable; my opponent at the poker table is free to call my bet or not, as he chooses, but what choice he makes will certainly be affected by the size of my bet.

A man is not free when he is acting under compulsion, when he cannot help himself. He has lost his self-possession, if, indeed, it was ever his; a man is under compulsion when there is no whole self to do the possessing. We are all subject to compulsions, less compelling than the psychopath's, less articulate than Socrates' daemon. Every twinge of anxiety and remorse, every seizure of indecision, reveals how far we are from being at one with ourselves, how far from being free. In the grip of any strong emotion, it is not I who act, but the emotion which acts on me. It is because I am passive in suffering or enjoying emotions that they are called "passions." "Among mortals there is no man free," said Euripides; "he is slave to riches or else to fortune." Aristotle quotes this statement to illustrate a certain logical form of argument; it also emphasizes that we are slaves to external circumstance only so far as our hopes and fears determine. The strange god who is not to be worshipped, the Talmud explains, is the god within.

If human bondage is enslavement by passion, it does not follow that human freedom consists in the negation of feeling (§60). The Stoic doctrine that no man is free who is not master of himself is found in all the world's major religions and moral teachings. Where there is a master there is also a slave. I cannot say that I am free when I practice self-control, for who is it then who is being controlled? The question is how to attain freedom without compromising identity.

Freedom, when it is conceived as free will, is antecedent to choice. Instead, freedom is a matter of how the choice is made, and by whom. We are free when choices are made by an integrated self, acting without compulsion, without being divided against itself. The choices must also be rational in some sense, involving both intelligence and knowledge. The truth makes us free. To act thoughtlessly and in ignorance is not in fact to choose anything. To be free I must know what alternatives are open to me, their conditions and consequences. What freedom do I have to choose, in Frank Stockton's tale, between the lady and the tiger, if I do not know what lies behind each door? I have not chosen whichever it is by opening the door—all I have freely chosen is to open that door.

My knowledge must be acted on by an integrated self, or it is not *I* who am free. Confucius said, "At fifteen, I set my heart on learning; at thirty, I was firmly established; at forty, I had no more doubts; at fifty, I knew the will of Heaven; at sixty, I was ready to listen to it; at seventy, I could follow my heart's desire without transgressing what was right." Only when duty and inclination coincide is a man free to do as he likes; only a fully integrated self is without compulsions. Even for a Master Kung this takes a lifetime to achieve.

Nineteenth-century romanticism and today's neoromanticism confuse freedom with acting out each momentary whim. Freedom is as far from caprice as from compulsion. In neither case am I making a decision: in compulsion, because the decision is made for me, and in caprice, because there is no decision, only the resultant of a welter of impulses. A free man is not capricious but deliberate, doing just as he truly and wholeheartedly wants to do. He must therefore be at one with himself and know who that one is. Freud was once asked by someone caught in indecision how to make up his mind. "Toss a coin," was Freud's advise. "What!" a follower exclaimed; "you, the apostle of awareness and rationality, would have him rely on blind chance?" "Not at all!" Freud replied. "After the toss, let him feel whether he is relieved or disappointed with the fall of the coin; that will tell him what he really wants to do."

The conception of freedom as free will, in insulating the self from causes, thereby also detaches it from effects. Freedom implies determinism, rather than being incompatible with it, because to be free is to determine one's own destiny. A free act is not uncaused but is caused in a certain way—it is the outcome of deliberate choice—what Spinoza called determination by reason. A free act is one whose reasons constituted its cause; only the purpose it served impelled us to it. This is the tenor of the Stoic definition of freedom as the recognition of necessity: not to enjoin resignation, but to teach that we are masters of our fate in knowing where we stand in the nexus of causes that make up our natures and the Nature of which we are a part.

Freedom may have been conceived in terms of free will because of a confusion of *autonomy*, which is an essential component of freedom, with causal independence. I am autonomous when I choose for myself without regard to what others in my place might choose. These introjected others help make up my self (§47), but if they exhaust the self there is nothing which I can truly call my own. In Mead's terms, in that case I would be all "me" and no "I." Even when I appear to be making a choice, I would be acting only as the agent of another; the only choice that I myself might have made is to accept him as my principal. "I was only obeying orders" does not absolve the Eichmanns of this world. Totalitarian bureaucracies and armies seek precisely to destroy autonomy; the touchstone of freedom is resistance to this degradation. Autonomy, like virtue, is lost more often to seduction than to rape; bondage is never more firm than when we are bound by silken cords.

In the development of personality, a marked role is played by imitation: the child does as he sees is done by the significant people around him. But as Emerson said, "There is a time in everyman's education when he arrives at the conviction that imitation is suicide." A man cannot give himself to anything if he has no self to give. The Master succeeded his father as head of a congregation which became increasingly uneasy at the young rabbi's deviations from his father's practice. "Your father was such a saint," they complained; "how dare you depart from his ways?" "I depart from my father's ways?" the Master exclaimed. "God forbid! I do exactly as my father did—he did not imitate and I do not imitate!"

We are all realistically dependent on one another; we need one another and are affected by each other. Such realistic dependence is to be distinguished from "infantile dependency," the failure to achieve autonomy. Dependency unquestionably has its pleasures, described in Tom Stoppard's *Rosencrantz & Guildenstern Are Dead:* "It's all done for you, don't worry. Enjoy it. Relax. To be taken in hand and led, like being a child again, even without the innocence, a child—it's like being given a prize, an extra slice of childhood when you least expect it, as a prize for being good, or compensation for never having had one." Who can a man be if not himself, and what can compensate him for being no one at all?

Autonomy can be achieved through dependency, and—the human infant being helpless—only through dependency. In the pursuit of autonomy we rely on the help of a Vedantist *guru,* a Zen *roshi,* a Hassidic *rebbe,* or a secular psychoanalyst. In psychoanalytic theory the dependency on the analyst is known as the "transference" to him of feelings from the patient's experiences of infancy and childhood. The success of the analysis depends on the patient's breaking the transference; he is cured when he learns that there is no one to rely on but himself. This is the culmination of Buddha's teaching in the words he addressed to the weeping disciples around his deathbed: "Be ye lamps unto yourselves!" The six characters of Pirandello who are in search of an author are no different from the rest of us who, in our childishness, imagine that we can have no identities until they are defined for us by the Great Ones of earth or heaven.

The last stage of dependency is rebellion. Autonomy is not as easy to come by as is conveyed in Emerson's slogan that "whoso would be a man must be a non-conformist." Often we rebel against convention, only to conform, with as great a dependency as ever, to the rebellious subculture—a conformity as observable in the basics of politics and life-style as in the superficialities of costume, diet, and the decorative arts. Caliban sings "Freedom!" but the sad truth is that he has only exchanged one master for another.

Rebellion lacks autonomy as much as submission does. In both cases, it is the other who decides; the rebel negates the other's decision, but this is very different from deciding for himself. In both submission and rebellion the self is divided against itself; each part holds the other in subjection. The rebel cannot bring himself to accept his introjected roles, the inputs by which his self was formed, for these are seen by him as external authorities compromising his independence. Rather than fighting for a cause, he is seeking the cause that will fight for him. His defeat is foreordained, since what is gained by the rejecting self can only be lost by the self rejected. Autonomy does not rest on the victory of either party to the conflict but on the achievement of integration without conquest.

In dependency, the roles which are not accepted are those which make up the self by what the self gives itself to. The conformist personality is directed *to* the other so as to take direction *from* the other—from the introjected roles. One part of the self obeys the other part; submission seeks the commanding presence just as rebellion calls on authority to submit. The free man has nothing to do with either command or obedience. He is autonomous because his self comprises all his roles, independent because in his own being there is no other, outside his identity, for him to depend on. All his personae he accepts as truly his.

An autonomous self is what existentialists call "authentic"; so integrated that the public and private selves are at one, so independent that every act reveals the self, not some other for whom the self is only an agent. A free man cannot be deprived of his freedom unless his is destroyed; if he is willing to give it to another, it is no longer his to give. "You are you and I am I," said Mencius; "although you stand by my side with your body naked, how can you defile me?" The talmudic aphorism is that a myrtle remains a myrtle even though it stand among thorns. It is a mad world, but if we, too, behave like madmen, that is of our own doing. "I cook my food in *my* pot"—thus spake Zarathustra; "only when it has been quite cooked do I welcome it as *my* food." In his *Song of Myself* Whitman declares, "I wear my hat as I please, indoors or out." A free man may please to please others; there is a house of worship where a head is to be bared, and another where it must be covered. Whether I must lose myself in order to find myself depends on values more transcendent than freedom.

49. The Rational Animal

A man may be in bondage to his passions, but feeling is not incompatible with freedom. The *Platonist dualism* between reason and emotion is to be found in traditional moral doctrines (§60), as well as in modern ethical theories (§53). The notion is that we can either give ourselves over to feeling or give full play to the intellect; we cannot do both, and what we give to each we must take away from the other. There is an important contrast to be drawn here, but it is not that embodied in the Platonist dualism. The contrast, rather, is between rational and irrational emotions, between feelings rooted in knowledge and understanding of their objects, and feelings rooted in ignorance and confusion. Fear of a cobra is not irrational, as fear of a garden snake is; contrariwise, one who is fearless is not therefore courageous—he may simply not realize the danger.

Reason *is* affected by emotional needs. These needs may stimulate reason—necessity is the mother of invention, after all; they may also interfere with reason. The concealment of such interference is rationalization (§14). The processes (other than transformation of the real situation) by which these needs are attempted to be met are known as "defense mechanisms." These include, in addition to rationalization, denial, the unwillingness to face reality; repression, denial of the realities of the inner life; projection, ascribing to others attributes of our own which we are unwilling to acknowledge; and reaction-formation, acting out impulses contrary to those at work within us.

To defend ourselves from pain and to maintain self-esteem and the respect of others is not irrational. That without defenses we would be defenseless is not a tautology. The defense mechanisms are irrational when they protect us only against the dangers of wars long past, when they demand too large an allocation of our budget, and when they reject or subvert civilian control. It is not our emotional needs which rob us of rationality but the infantilisms in our efforts to satisfy those needs.

Reason might be defined in terms of its effectiveness in satisfying needs. In Bergson's view, "the essential function of our intellect, as the evolution of life has fashioned it, is to be a light for our conduct, to make ready for our action on things." Dewey's philosophy might be summed up in the thesis that the role of intelligence is to act not as the obedient servant of impulse but as its clarifier and liberator. "Rationality is not a force to evoke against impulse and habit. It is the attainment of a working harmony among diverse desires." The Freudian "ego" resolves inner conflicts and subjects desire to the constraints of the "reality principle" rather than the "pleasure principle." Reason is neither the slave of the passions nor their master, but the faculty of organizing and directing their expression and consummation.

The faculty of reason is not intelligence narrowly conceived. Thinking with one's blood is a notion I would dismiss as romanticist nonsense were it not that it has proven to be so vicious. I mean rather to emphasize the difference between insight and learning by trial and error, or the difference between verbal reasoning and the imagistic thinking of poets and painters. Increasing attention has been given to creativity as distinct from intelligence, sharing responsibility for the distinctively human achievement. The metaphysics of man might yet come to agree with Dostoevski that man is preeminently a creative animal.

However broadly "reason" be construed, it cannot be so all-embracing as to wipe out the savagery and folly of mankind. The indictment of Mephistopheles is more damning today than it was when Goethe phrased it: "He calls it reason, and he only uses it to be more bestial than the beasts." Our ingenuity contrives means for the destruction of our fellowmen and, at last, of ourselves; our poverty of thought is nowhere more marked than in our inability to exploit the resources of nature for man's good, and to distribute the good so as to enable us to live in peace; our mindlessness flaunts itself in the perversions of reason by which we justify our devastation of nature and our brutalities to one another.

In spite of everything, I believe still that man is a rational animal. This belief is the most fundamental sense of *rationalism,* the denial of which seems to be a denial of philosophy itself. Man's reason is of his essence, not an accident of his being. It is neither cause nor consequence of his Fall; if he can yet be saved, it will be only by the fullest use of his reason.

Such use depends above all on self-knowledge. This is what philosophers of many times and places have identified as the core of wisdom. "He who knows others is clever but he who know himself is wise," says Lao-tzu. Plato, in the *Philebus,* writes, "It is splendid for the wise man to know everything, but the next best thing is not to be ignorant of himself." Elsewhere, quoting the injunction "Know thyself!" inscribed at the oracle of Delphi, he insists that no man can be wise who does not obey it. With a startling contemporary relevance, Philo Judaeus asks, "Before you have made a thorough investigation into your own tenement, is it not an excess of madness to examine that of the universe? Bring the explorer down from heaven." I doubt whether we would learn more of ourselves by turning away from the great world around us. I agree with Kierkegaard that the thing to understand is myself; but the self reaches out to other men and things, and understanding is all of a piece.

Self-knowledge is not a matter of scale or focus. The problem is that we are not at one with ourselves, and the isolated fragments are either hidden from one another or indifferent to one another's existence. An "unconscious idea" is not a contradiction in terms. There is no commitment here to Freudian theory. William James, too, held that consciousness "may be split into parts which coexist but mutually ignore each other. A part of consciousness may sever its connection with other parts and yet continue to be." Whatever conditions philosophers of mind impose on explanations of the psyche, they must acknowledge the data concerning posthypnotic suggestion, parapraxes (slips made accidentally-on-purpose), processes of creativity, dream contents, symbolisms of myth and ritual, symptoms of psychopathology, and other indications of the unknown self. We can all echo Faust, when he finds himself dissolving in dreams of love: "Unhappy Faust! You are a stranger to yourself."

The situation is worse than this, for strangers might welcome the opportunity to know one another. Not so the stranger within. We hide from ourselves, so skillfully as to conceal that anything has been hidden. The great obstacle in the way of self-knowledge is self-deception. "We deceive no one by such delicate artifices as we do our own selves," said Schopenhauer. But the deceiver is deceived in estimating his success. Mephistopheles does not begrudge the fool's paradise Faust has fashioned for himself:

> *You are welcome to the pleasure*
> *of self-delusion now and then;*
> *you cannot keep it up for very long.*

If he could, so much the worse for him! The Master said: "It is impossible to fool God, and hard to fool other men; to fool oneself is easy, but in that case, a man is nothing but—a fool." Heinz Hartmann defines psychoanalysis as "the systematic study of self-deception and its motivations."

Sartre has argued that at bottom self-deception must be impossible, for "the very essence of the reflexive idea of hiding something from oneself implies the unity of one and the same psychic mechanism." It is honesty with oneself, not self-deception, which is problematic. What is to be explained is not how anyone can deceive himself in *any* respect, but how anyone can know himself in *every* respect. Self-deception is a species of ignorance; it is not ignorance but knowledge which must be accounted for. In the organization which is the self, as in other organizations, members are more surprised to discover that the administration knows something than to find—as they suspected all along—that the administration just doesn't know what's going on.

Every administration needs an intelligence service at least adequate enough to check on the execution of its decisions and on their consequences. Corresponding to the mechanisms of repression and suppression within the self, there must be other mechanisms of *exposure.* Freudian theory distinguishes between the "topographical" and the "dynamic" unconscious—the domain of unawareness and the energies devoted to keeping it hidden. There must also be a *dynamic consciousness:* certain matters are *brought* to consciousness; they do not rise of themselves but are uncovered, forced on the attention. They do not just happen to become known, any more than they just happened to have been hidden. Self-deception is not hiding something from the one who is doing the hiding, or it would be impossible. It is inadequate communication, by accident or by design, among the personae which make up the pluralistic self.

Such a model of the self and of self-awareness allows for an incomparably richer set of possibilities of ignorance and knowledge of the self than is provided by the dichotomy of "conscious" and "unconscious." Adding the intermediate category of "preconscious" falls far short of the degrees and kinds of awareness which we can now recognize. As in every organization, there is a large flow of memoranda, some originating internally, others bringing communications from outside. Every memo is read by someone—by the writer or by the one who opens and distributes incoming mail. No communication is read by everyone, even an announcement that the firm is going out of business or that there has been an across-the-board salary increase—there is always someone who doesn't get the word. Each memo has its own routing list; no one, not even the company librarian, reads every communication. A particular memo may be discarded by some of its recipients, buried in the files by others, made available for ready access by only a few. More important are the differences in how attentively it is read and in the part it plays in subsequent decisions.

The personae which make up the self are in constant communication with one another as well as with the outside world. Even the most heedless of us does more thinking without talking than the reverse; we talk to ourselves in more than words alone. Franz Alexander has suggested that mental health depends on the self-awareness provided by a forum in which each persona can speak his mind and be listened to with respect. Mental illness is characterized by disturbances in this inner communication: one of Freud's formulations of the aim of psychoanalysis is to fill the gaps in memory. Nothing is gained by telling the patient what is hidden in his unconscious; he will not hear what he is told until the fragments of his self are ready to listen. When they are ready, they no longer need to be told.

This is why wisdom cannot be taught: we knew it all from the beginning.

Chapter Eight

Theory of Value

50. The Crisis in Values

In Bernard Shaw's *Major Barbara,* the munitions magnate, Undershaft, is discussing a career for his son Stephen. The young man repudiates, as unsuited to his capacities or interests, a vocation in business, art, philosophy, the army, the church, or the bar. The scene continues:

> UNDERSHAFT. Well, come! Is there anything you know or care for?
>
> STEPHEN. I know the difference between right and wrong.
>
> UNDERSHAFT. You don't say so! What! no capacity for business, no knowledge of law, no sympathy with art, no pretension to philosophy; only a simple knowledge of the secret that has puzzled all the philosophers, baffled all the lawyers, muddled all the men of business, and ruined most of the artists: the secret of right and wrong. Why, man, you're a genius, a master of masters, a god!

Stephen's confidence in his convictions would make him at home anywhere in the world today. Those who believe that there really is a difference between right and wrong are convinced that they know what the difference is, and they know it with such sureness that they are certain they have a moral obligation to impose their standards on everyone. *Absolutism* is often associated with ignorance and insensitivity, if not with thoughtlessness and downright cruelty.

Certitude is characteristic of absolutism: absolutist morality leaves no room for doubt. Even if what morality dictates is less than certain, there can be no doubt for the absolutist about the principles by which the proper course of action is to be determined. These principles are laid down by the person's religion, politics, or whatever, according to his species of absolutism. "It has remained for me to exhibit the true and only genuine and sound basis of morality everywhere and at all times effective. The actual facts of morality are too much on my side for me to fear that my theory can ever be replaced or upset by any other." Schopenhauer's declaration offends conventional modesty but not the convictions which are more widespread today than in his own time. The authority of church and state is more compelling today than nineteenth-century liberals anticipated. We have reentered the Dark Ages, and mistake for enlightenment the pale glow which technology reflects from an earlier age of reason.

The domain of value used to be conceived in probabilistic terms, and our knowledge of it as correspondingly fallible. Ethics, Aristotle held, is concerned with things which are for the most part so, things quite capable of being otherwise. Benjamin Franklin, pressed for absolutes underlying the proposed Constitution, rejoined that nothing's sure but death and taxes. His commitment, though it did not rest on certitudes, was no less than the commitments of today's absolutists. A man may put at stake his life, his fortune, and his sacred honor, without claiming to know anything for sure; but this requires a moral courage rare indeed today.

Absolutism is *doctrinaire:* to every moral question there is but a single right answer. The absolutist cannot countenance dissent, for this acknowledges the presence of a plurality of defensible views. Here Aristotle's contextualism fails him: "One may go wrong in many different ways," he says, "but right only in one." Voltaire, for all his skepticism of conventional doctrine, still declares, in his *Philosophical Dictionary,* that "there is but one morality, as there is but one geometry." Non-Euclidean geometries make his comparison an apt one in a way he never intended: there are spaces quite different from Euclid's, as there is morality in life-styles quite different from the established ones. This is not to say that anything goes—geometries may be internally inconsistent or false to the facts.

Absolutist values are *unconditional;* they do not depend on time, place, and circumstance. Only if they are unconditional can they allow for certitude; however sure we may be of general principles, we cannot claim indubitable knowledge of the particulars to which the principles are to apply. A judge, however learned in the law, must rely on confused and contradictory testimony to establish the facts of the case. Typically, the absolutist has some single standard, an overriding value which is to be pursued or preserved no matter what. The talmudic sage, Hillel, characteristically qualified the rigors of the Law by reference to special circumstances; even truth, he pointed out, is not an absolute, as when a bride is to be complimented on her appearance. The absolutist identifies certain standards as applicable without qualification. The nineteenth-century theoretician of Marxism and anarchism, Mikhail Bakunin, formulated a principle still governing the morality of millions: "To the revolutionist, whatever aids the triumph of the revolution is ethical; all that which hinders it is unethical and criminal."

That a value is unconditional is revealed in its dissociation as an end from the means employed to attain it (§54). The immoralities of terrorism, for example, are held to be justified—except in the eyes of its victims—by its political goals. Absolutism seems to lose its ugliness when seen far away or when it is so close that we are blinded by its rationalizations.

Unconditional value presents itself as nonnegotiable. Compromise is as abhorrent to the absolutist as is dissent; both are seen as betrayals. When we say of virtue that it has been compromised we mean that it has been lost; "casuistry," whose strict sense is the application of general rules to particular cases, has come to mean glossing over with words the abandonment of principle. There is in all devotion to an ideal a disregard of conditions and qualifications. To love only so long as the object of our love remains worthy and the circumstances propitious is not to love at all. That moral aspiration invites an absolutist stance is a predicament of the moral life.

Absolutism denies that the dilemma must be faced, holding that only evil or weak men must struggle with temptation. The absolutist replaces the realities of human frailty with a myth of perfectionism. There is no margin for error; a wrongful act reveals the treachery which must have been at work all along. The dilemma is reduced to the problem of identifying the traitors to the cause as early as possible; this problem, in turn, is often reduced to the task of determining ideological purity. Absolutism contrasts with the self-awareness of the Gospels' "Judge not lest you be judged" and "Let him who is without sin cast the first stone," and the human sympathy of Hillel's injunction not to condemn another until we have stood in his place.

For the absolutist there is no scale of values, only a flat right and wrong. The Stoics are admirable proponents of this stern ethic. Cultivating proper habits of action, they held, approaches the good but does not increase it. The goodness of a man is like the straightness of a stick; there are degrees of crookedness but not of being straight. The literal sense of moral rectitude is fundamental; righteousness is an absolute.

Perfection, even the aspiration to it, is not easy to maintain. Absolutism often turns away from the world, encapsulating itself in a moralistic ghetto where purity can be preserved. This pattern is best known in monasticism. There is a *secular monasticism* as well, common among those who are so disgusted with the immoralities of politics that they turn away from political life, as though their denial of its significance is enough to insulate them from its impact. Others withdraw from the moral issues of our time. Thereby their morality loses in content what it might gain in purity; in their sickly saintliness, they become so good that they are good for nothing.

The weakness of perfectionism is twofold. Since perfection is not of this world, repeated failure saps the energy of moral aspiration which, at last, is abandoned. This is the point of the Preacher's injunction, "Be not righteous overmuch." He was not recommending a soupcon of sin to season tasteless moral life but warning against aspirations so demanding as to be foredoomed to defeat, and thereby inviting defeatism. The second weakness appears when the moralist thinks to forestall defeat by withdrawing from the wicked world. Moral aspiration then becomes an end in itself and, in losing touch with the real issues, loses any bearing on the realities of the inner life. Here is the point of the Buddhist injunction to renounce even the desire for Nirvana. The injunction is not meant to question the desirability of Nirvana but to emphasize the futility of a life with no other content than this desire. No one is so joyless as the man grimly determined to enjoy himself.

Withdrawal is not so characteristic of contemporary absolutism as is the attempt to impose its absolutes on others. Both monastic and authoritarian absolutism suffer from the same sin: spiritual pride. Self-righteousness is expressed in every disagreement on policy. Were I an absolutist and we differed, not only would there be no question in my mind that you are wrong, but I would look upon you as being *morally* wrong: at best as standing in need of reproof, and at worst as having to be removed from the circle of decent men, to the point of ostracism, imprisonment, exile, or execution. The virtue least in evidence in the controversies of our time is humility.

This failing affects not only how controversy is carried on but also what is at issue. Even moral relevance is prejudged by absolutism. Whatever is not positively good in absolutist terms is downright evil, just as whoever is not with us is against us. There is no domain of neutrality; every institution and practice, whatever values it aims at, is subverted to what is taken to be a moral purpose. Every event, from an academic lecture to an athletic competition, is thought to provide occasion for an affirmation of patriotism, a political demonstration, or a religious exercise. Absolutism denies the possibility of partial achievements. Voltaire's epigram that the best is the worst enemy of the better has more point in our day than it had in his. Whoever insists on all or nothing at all will get—nothing.

The contemporary crisis in values is more deep-seated than a conflict among absolutes. The crisis is seen by many as an aspect of a more pervasive crisis of authority. The locus of authority has become elusive and its basis questionable, so that its pronouncements are no longer believed. The credibility gap was as familiar to the Greeks in the age of the Sophists as it is to us. This gap is more than a matter of not trusting officials; it is a matter of no longer being able to believe in anything at all.

Every interpreter of the crisis in values has an explanation of disbelief. For the historian, what is significant is that the major institutions of modern society—church, state, family, school—no longer serve as different means to the same end. There was a time, it is argued, when the rules of law and morals, the themes of art, and the teachings of science all applied one set of principles, those of the divine constitution of the universe; today, chaos is king. The sociologist sees the crisis as a result of the dissolution of the social hierarchy; there is no acknowledged ruling class to enforce a clear-cut schedule of rights and duties. The elites—such as they are—of jet sets and celebrities cannot carry out this function. The psychologist sees modern man as rootless and alienated; one person today and another tomorrow, as he performs in different roles; so mobile in geography and status that standards of value have no chance to take root. Political theorists, East and West, see the consciousness of class and nation struggling with allegiance to other groupings as well as conflicting with an emerging sense of kinship with the whole family of man.

All these explanations have some substance. However the crisis has come about, its symptoms are easily recognized. They are "relativism" and "subjectivism." *Relativism* refers to the diversity of standards and values. Sakini, in *The Teahouse of the August Moon,* is a spokesman for the age:

World filled with delightful variation.
Illustration.
In Okinawa . . . no locks on doors.
In America . . . lock and key big industry.
Conclusion?
Bad manners good business.
In Okinawa . . . wash self in public bath with nude lady quite proper.
Picture of nude lady in private home . . . quite improper.
In America . . . statue of nude lady in park win prize.
But nude lady in flesh in park win penalty. Conclusion?
Pornography question of geography.

In recent decisions, the Supreme Court has given legal standing to this geographical principle; values are relative to the place of the pursuit. It used to be taken for granted that the pagans had no morality, the barbarians no art, the heathens no religion, and the savages no law. Now we say only that *their* ways are different from ours.

This recognition marks a considerable advance, both moral and intellectual. But it has been paid for by a retrogression: the *subjectivist* view that values have no basis outside the minds of those who prize them. All value, like beauty, is only in the eye of the beholder; nothing's either good or bad but thinking makes it so. In Shaw's play, Caesar's slave, Britannus, explains why he is painted all over blue in battle: "Blue is the color worn by all Britons of good standing. In war we stain our bodies blue; so that though our enemies may strip us of our clothes and our lives, they cannot strip us of our respectability." But to his enemies, he may be only ridiculous. Indeed, they may be fighting over moral issues; can such issues be resolved only by fighting? Can I never say, "Win or lose, my cause is just!" Is there no judge but the victor? Does might, after all, make right?

This is the core of the crisis in values. There is nothing to believe if I can believe only in myself, nowhere to go if I can only spin on my own axis. I cannot keep faith if I have none to start with; I have no faith to defend if its substance is only my readiness to defend it. How are we to live with no sense of anything worth living for? Modern man may have no credo, but he is still credulous. We may have seen the end of ideology but surely not of ideals, or else it is the end of man that we are seeing. Objectivity is an admirable ideal, responsible for much of what is most distinctively and nobly human. But if it precludes all values but itself, what ground is there for my sense of worth, what place is there in the domain of values for *me?* If objectivity always demands strict neutrality, who will be on *my* side?

These are the quandaries which give point to the philosophical theory of value. The general theory is *axiology;* each species of value is the subject of its own branch of philosophy—ethics, aesthetics, political philosophy, social philosophy, and the philosophy of religion. Ancient Indian thought distinguished dozens of value domains and corresponding theories; each philosophical tradition has its own classification. The values which guide someone's pursuits constitute his *morals* or *morality*, or abstractly, his *code* or *standards;* analogously for a style of art. The explicit formulation of the goals to be pursued is the moral *doctrine;* in art, this is the content of the manifestos of artists or critics. The analysis and justification of moral codes and doctrines constitutes *ethics;* correspondingly, *aesthetics* deals with the artistic values and with standards of art criticism.

The term "ethics" is sometimes used for the morality or moral code, as when we speak of an individual's high ethics, or his unethical behavior; it is also used for the moral doctrine, as when we speak of the ethics of a profession. It has become common to use "metaethics" in place of the conventional but ambiguous usage, to emphasize that the term refers to a theory *about* standards of behavior rather than formulating such standards. When the word "ethics" is contrasted with "metaethics" it means the same as the word "morals" when this is contrasted with "ethics." The same distinction is sometimes formulated by using "normative ethics" for moral doctrine and "descriptive ethics" or "analytic ethics" for ethical theory, empirical or logical respectively.

Preoccupation with these subtleties of usage can degenerate into scholasticism and pedantry, but the basic distinction is important. The same morality can be defended by different ethical theories, and the same ethics can lead to different moralities. Peace might be an ideal for both a secularist and religionist, and men might kill each other, each in the conviction that he is carrying out the will of God. If we can get concerted action for our ends, it would be folly to insist on the same reasons for the actions; conversely, it would be foolish to suppose that if we appeal to the same reasons we are pursuing the same goals. The ideological and political differences of our time make these considerations especially compelling.

The question arises whether ethics has the significance philosophers, with an understandable professional bias, have attributed to it. A morality may be admirable even if the ethics on which it is based is contemptible, while a philosophically satisfactory ethics might be used in support of a despicable morality. A man might act nobly in the childish hope of a heavenly reward, and be impelled by his conscience to the slaughter of innocents. Although a satisfactory ethical theory might occasionally lead to morally dubious action, if this were generally true the ethics could hardly continue to be judged satisfactory, just as a sound scientific theory might lead to incorrect predictions in special cases, but would be abandoned if it continued to be falsified.

We must not prejudge in what sense an ethical theory "leads to" action. Theory may be invoked retrospectively or play no part either before or after action, appearing only in philosophical reflection about the actions of others. Confucius was concerned with the moral conduct of political affairs in the concrete, but he did not share Plato's interest in the nature of abstract justice. "There can be no question of holding forth on ethics," Camus wrote in his *Myth of Sisyphus*. "I have seen people behave badly with great morality and I note every day that integrity has no need of rules." Yet the acknowledged moral leaders of mankind set great store by such rules.

There is no justification for Charles Peirce's uncharacteristically cynical remark that "nothing makes a man so much of a scoundrel as the prolonged study of ethics"; philosophy is not so demoralizing. On the other hand, there may be an injustice in supposing that the aim of ethics is to contribute to virtue rather than to understanding. That would be the claim of most contemporary proponents of metaethics—that they aim only at clarification.

Philosophy has not always been so limited in its aims. Aristotle says of his treatise on ethics that it "is not for the purpose of mere speculation, as all others are, for the object of our investigation is not the knowing what virtue is but to become good." A little later he adds, "It is not sufficient to know the theory of virtue; we must endeavor to possess and employ it." The Stoics were even more demanding of the role of philosophy, condemning what usually passes by that name as an excuse for turning aside from our moral responsibilities. "Being unable to fulfil the calling of man," says Epictetus, "we adopt that of the philosopher." "Put an end once for all to the *discussion* of what a good man should be," Marcus Aurelius enjoins, "and *be* one." But we cannot well put an end to what we have scarcely begun.

51. Traditional Ethics

The oldest and most widespread ethical theory is that provided by religion. (The word "theory" may connote more explicitness, more systematic self-consciousness about morality than is appropriate.) Questions about the difference between good and bad, right and wrong, and why we should do the one rather than the other are most commonly answered in religious terms. For all the talk about the collapse of religious authority in our time, religion is still the most widely accepted basis for ethics in the non-Communist world and plays a not negligible part even in some Communist countries, like Poland.

All known cultures have attributed to the world an underlying moral order. The religious viewpoint is that this order is not merely a projection onto the cosmos of something within man. If the difference between good and evil is an illusion, it is only a transcendental illusion, discernible only by metaphysical subtleties and relevant only to the higher reaches of metaphysical thought; in plain, everyday terms, the difference is as objective as anything we experience. Many religions hold that, unlike good, evil is of man's making, and has no aboriginal place in the order of things. Yet, once introduced into the world through human frailty, it is only too real; the fight against evil is no play of shadows. In short, as Confucius has it, "there is no place in the highest heavens above nor in the deepest waters below where the moral law does not reign."

Quite often this universal moral order is conceived as a cosmic equilibrium, maintained by forces analogous to those operative in homeostasis (§45). Hebrew, Greek, Chinese, and Hindu thought all incorporate some such idea. Doing wrong means upsetting the equilibrium; thereby, countervailing forces (sometimes seen as "punishments") are brought into play to restore the status quo. The good man is one whose life is in harmony with the natural moral order. Poetic justice—the appropriateness of the punishment to the crime—is a familiar instance of this homeostatic ethics, the achievement of which the "Mikado" rightly characterizes as an "object all sublime." Scripture is full of instances: "His mischief will return on his own head, and his violence crack his own crown" (Psalms); "He who digs a pit will fall into it, whoever sets a trap will himself be caught in it" (Ben Sira); "All who take the sword shall die by the sword" (Matthew); "Because you drowned others they have drowned you, and at last they themselves shall be drowned" (Hillel).

The fundamental difference between religion and magic or superstition is that in religion cosmic powers have been moralized (§86). The forces brought into play by man's actions also have a moral significance. The moral law is as much divinely instituted as is natural law; God governs the world on the basis of moral principles as well as causal ones. In most religious thought the natural and moral orders are not distinguished from one another; only in Western culture, and only in the last few centuries, have we conceived of a domain of fact governed by natural law, in contradistinction to a domain of values governed by moral law. In religious perspectives, the two domains have usually been seen as one: *torah, logos, dharma,* and *tao* all have an ontological as well as an axiological significance. Religion teaches that the true and the good are truly one and that it is good that this is so.

Religious ethics holds, first, that religion points to the *basis of the distinction* between good and evil, or between right and wrong. What makes good things good and right actions right, or evil and wrong respectively, is that God ordained them to be so. Dostoevski's formulation is axiomatic for most religious ethics: if there were no God, everything would be permitted. Corresponding formulations can be found for the nontheistic religions: the ground of moral distinctions is built into the nature of things as well as into human nature; the highest actualities deserving of worship give substance to the moral life.

Critics of religious ethics counter that religion confounds morality with much that has no moral significance—matters of ritual are given the same basis in divine will as are matters of right and wrong. From the religious standpoint, there is no difference between the injunctions inscribed on the two Tablets of the Law, although the one is concerned with matters like the sanctity of the Sabbath and the name of God, and the other with murder, theft, and false witness. It recurrently happens in the history of religion that orthodoxy becomes so preoccupied with ritualistic requirements as to enforce them by immoral means: doctors have had their lives threatened by religionists because their practice of autopsy shows disrespect for the dead. A more fundamental criticism is one which itself rests on religious premises. The argument is that it is not God's command which makes a right action right; rather, being morally perfect, He commands it because it is right. The issue lies outside the field of ethics (§86).

Religious ethics urges, second, that religion is the source of moral *knowledge.* The serpent was indeed subtle in the temptation he held out for eating the forbidden fruit: to know good and evil is to be as the gods. Yet other ethical theories have come to the same conclusions as the religious ones as to which things are good and which evil. Moral knowledge *is* hard to come by, but no more so than the religious knowledge from which it is alleged to be derived. In a number of religions, such as the Jain, Buddhist, and Confucian, the order of priority is reversed—far from religious attainment being a prerequisite to moral knowledge, it is only after a man has achieved a certain degree of moral consciousness that it becomes possible for him to progress to spiritual awareness.

Religious ethics argues, finally, that religion is the source of moral *motivation:* a man does good, or feels that he should, as a fulfillment of the divine element in his nature. The sense of moral obligation is grounded in religious commitment: "Ye shall be holy, for I the Lord your God am holy." Moral decadence is diagnosed in endless sermons as a consequence of the weakening of faith. Questions of motivation, however, are matters of fact, and the facts do not sustain the religionist diagnosis; the evidence is scanty and uncertain. Skepticism of religious doctrine and rejection of religious authority are not necessarily associated with immorality. Men of exemplary morals such as Socrates and Spinoza were accused of "godlessness"; religionists like Aquinas and Maimonides did not escape similar accusations. On the other hand, men of unquestionable religious commitment have been capable of gross immoralities, even without abandoning their religious principles. Pascal, a man of deep religious faith, observed that "men never do evil so completely and cheerfully as when they do it from religious conviction."

Almost as widespread a basis for ethical theory as faith is *conscience;* in the non-Catholic countries of Europe and America it might stand in first place. The workings of conscience are memorably characterized in this dialogue between the two murderers in *King Richard III:*

1 MURD. Where's thy conscience now?

2 MURD. In the Duke of Gloucester's purse.

1 MURD. When he opens his purse to give us our reward, thy conscience flies out.

2 MURD. 'Tis no matter; let it go: there's a few or none will entertain it.

1 MURD. What if it comes to thee again?

2 MURD. I'll not meddle with it; it makes a man a coward; a man cannot steal, but it accuseth him; a man cannot swear, but it checks him; a man cannot lie with his neighbor's wife, but it detects him; 'tis a blushing shamefac'd spirit,

> that mutinies in a man's bosom; it fills a man full of obstacles: it made me once restore a purse of gold that, by chance, I found; it beggars any man that keeps it; it is turned out of towns and cities for a dangerous thing; and every man that means to live well endeavours to trust to himself, and live without it.

The ethics of conscience is a secularized reformulation of religious ethics. The appeal to conscience replaces institutionalized religious authority by the individual's own sense of right and wrong: every man becomes his own priest. The content of religious teaching already lies within him. "The Law which I enjoin upon you this day is not too hard for you nor is it far off," says the Deuteronomist. "It is not in Heaven, that you should say, 'Who will go up to Heaven and bring it to us, that we may hear and obey it?' Nor is it beyond the sea, that you should say, 'Who will cross the sea and bring it to us, that we may hear and obey it?' The Word is very close to you, in your mouth and in your heart." Conscience tells a person when he has done wrong, and when he is about to do it. The Master characterized sin as whatever a man cannot do wholeheartedly.

The Word is very close because something of the divine is in man, and can recognize its own. Although idioms of feeling are commonly used in this connection—we know right and wrong "in our hearts"—ethical theories based on conscience usually connect it with thought rather than with feeling. This is because it is man's mind, not his heart, which distinguishes him from the animals and reveals his divine nature. Reason is the divine element in man, by virtue of which man is fashioned in the image of God. This is the position of Plato, Aristotle, Philo, Maimonides, Spinoza, and Kant.

The most profound and influential theorist of conscience is Kant. In his view, moral laws are given to awareness by reason; conscience is "not a mere faculty but an instinct" by which we judge ourselves in the light of these moral laws. Conscience is not always self-punitive; judgment, after all, sometimes ends in acquittal. With how much mercy justice to onself can be tempered is itself a moral question. The ethics of conscience emphasizes that moral standards, however loose or stringent, must be *internalized.* I recognize the claims of the moral law even though I violate it, or else it does not belong to the domain of morality.

Here is an essential difference between morality and legality: the law of the state is binding on me even though it is laid down by another, but the moral law, in Kant's phrasing, is given to the self by the self—otherwise I am not a moral agent; the possibility of doing either good or evil presupposes freedom (§48). If I act only in obedience to another, my obedience is only as that other's agent. My responsibility for my acts remains, deriving from my prior responsibility for choosing to obey. The issues here transcend the ethics of conscience, and concern moral responsibility (§63).

The conception of conscience as self-punitive is limited in another way. It gives conscience only a retrospective role, a reference to the future only by way of the anxiety evoked by the anticipation of guilt. But conscience can provide prior guidance as well as judgment after the fact. My *ego ideal* —what I admire most in myself, what I aspire to—though distinct from my conscience, plays a significant part in determining moral choices. (The psychoanalytic concept of the superego contains elements of both ideas.) The ethics of conscience thus grounds morality in the principle of acting according to our better natures. The apparent circularity of invoking the notion of a "better" nature is avoided by defining it not as that expressed in moral conduct but as that which expresses the divine in man, the distinctively human, his autonomous, integrated, and rational self.

Whether there is such a component in our human nature universal enough to serve as a basis for ethical theory is not self-evident. Jeremy Bentham, one of the founders of the utilitarian ethics, which bases morality on the consequences of action rather than on its origins (§52), says flatly of conscience that it is "a thing of fictitious existence." Others have objected to the ethics of conscience on the ground that, being psychological in origin, it cannot give to moral judgment the required normative force: mere matter-of-fact cannot provide a ground of obligation. This objection may be an instance, however, of the genetic fallacy (§23). How we acquire a conscience does not determine what we can do with it when we have it. Scientific curiosity may derive from the infant's interest in its own body and the child's preoccupation with the mysteries of sex; such an origin of the scientific impulse would not justify skepticism of scientific findings.

The origins of conscience make it highly *variable* in both content and scrupulousness. Kant's statement that the starry heavens above and the moral law within both filled him with wonder and awe moved Freud to remark that, though the starry heavens are sublime, with regard to conscience God was guilty of an uneven and careless piece of work. Each man feels that he himself has too much conscience while others have too little, and that the little is misdirected. Disraeli said of Gladstone, "he made his conscience not his guide but his accomplice," and Nietzsche, in *Beyond Good and Evil,* observed, "one may so train one's conscience that it kisses one when it bites." The ethics of conscience is at a loss when confronted by differences in moral judgment, unless it can speak of one conscience as being more cultivated or corrupt than another; here there is great danger of a circular argument.

Conscience is notoriously *unreliable.* Let it be admitted, for the sake of the argument, that conscience expresses man's higher nature, as an element of the divine. The question remains how the data of conscience are to be interpreted. The voice of the people may be the voice of God, but it is hard to know what that voice is saying. The analogy can be pursued: several different things are being said at once—conscience may be divided against itself. In the moral life, as in politics, conflicting ideas are the rule, not the exception. Even when a person is of one mind he might be mistaken, just as a majority, however great, can still be wrong. A person's conscience is an expression of his judgment, Thomas Hobbes argued in his treatise on ethical and political theory, *The Leviathan,* "and as the judgment, so also the conscience may be erroneous."

The moral judgment based on conscience usually lacks the saving grace of humility, a sense of fallibility, an openness to correction. The scientific judgment is also capable of error, but scientific method is self-corrective. There is a *tyrannical conscience* no easier to escape than other tyrannies. Such a conscience is unbending, rigid, absolute, rationalizing hatred, destroying the self it pretends to care for, and executing its sentences even more harshly on others. More suffering has been inflicted in obedience to conscience than from the dictates of lust and greed. The moral life demands freedom from compulsion: the sense of moral obligation is not the same as the acceptance of a moral dictatorship, even from within. Whether conscience can be validated by reason, as Kant set out to demonstrate, cannot be decided by the claims of conscience that its demands are quite reasonable.

Ethical theory may focus not on the inner life but on whatever it is external to man which gives content and validity to moral judgment. The appeal to conscience may be seen as a psychological secularization of religious ethics; there is also a metaphysical secularization. Religious ethics identifies God as the external basis for morality; instead, theory may invoke a self-sufficient, objective Good, which can be apprehended by man just as we grasp other features of the external world. The faculty of this apprehension is *moral intuition;* the corresponding ethical theory is *intuitionism.* Though the name of the theory derives from the way in which we arrive at moral judgments, both the meaning of such judgments and their justification is explicated by this theory in terms of what we grasp by moral intuition—the Good—and not in terms of the faculty by which we grasp it.

The Good in the present sense might be regarded as a projection of conscience, but this would beg a fundamental question. Intuitionism would hold, rather, that conscience is the internalization of the claim made by the Good. In Plato's metaphysics, Ideas are the forms in terms of which things can be conceptualized only because the Ideas constitute the objective actuality of the things—they are not merely subjective, psychological entities. Each Idea embodies the ideal of whatever is conceptualized in its terms, the ground of the value implicit in that sort of thing (§39). To grasp an Idea is not only to know something but also to appreciate it, to feel the pull of that ideal. As we apprehend the Idea of the Good we are drawn towards the essence of what is worthwhile. In the romantic rhythms of Robert Burns,

But to see her was to love her,
Love but her, and love forever.

The consonance of this sort of ethical theory with a religious perspective is illustrated by the views of the Karaites, a sect of Judaism which flourished from the eighth to the twelfth centuries, although it has continued to the present time. The Karaites reject talmudic Judaism, with its detailed elaboration of the rules of good conduct. The good in particular cases can be apprehended without the mediation of involuted logical argument or extraneous empirical evidence. Immediate experience itself elicits the impulse to moral action. Moral consciousness provides its own validation in the act of acquiring content. The Good arouses man to do good without any thought of reward either on earth or in Heaven.

The most influential modern formulation of intuitionist ethics is that of G. E. Moore. His intuitionism is so extreme—or so consistent, its advocates would say—as to deny the possibility of even conceptualizing the Good: it must be intuited, or else it eludes us altogether. Plato, rationalist that he was, declared that "whoever cannot define the Good by reason, separating the Idea of the Good from all others, is dreaming and sleeping out his present life." As against this view, Moore held that to suppose we *can* define the Good is only to deceive ourselves; it is Plato who is dreaming. The attempt to define the Good in terms of any set of qualities which do not surreptitiously include the Good under another name is foredoomed to failure; Moore called this attempt the *naturalistic fallacy*. The fallacy, he argued, is apparent from the circumstance that no matter what definition be given, say in terms of ABC . . ., it is always possible to ask whether ABC . . . is really good; if the definition were a genuine one, the question would be nonsensical.

Moore's explanation of the indefinability of the Good is that the Good is a perfectly "simple" quality—not compounded of others. It is therefore not capable of analysis into component parts. A purported definition cannot be in terms of ABC . . . but only in terms of some A or B or C, and whichever it is can only be nothing but the Good all over again. Just as you cannot explain to anyone who does not already know it what yellow is, so you cannot explain what good is. Explanations reveal components and the way in which they are related to one another, but this is impossible in the case of a simple quality. The Good, like other simple qualities, either reveals itself wholly or else it remains hidden from us altogether.

This theory has the merit of emphasizing the *specificity* of what is good. General criteria of goodness cannot be used in the moral life except as applied to particular cases, and how a criterion is to be applied cannot be specified by the criterion. The general doctrine allows us to formulate a rule, but not the relation between the rule and the specific case. Kant calls the application of rules to cases the work of "judgment," which, he argues, is indispensable, for if there were rules for the exercise of judgment, the faculty of judgment would be called for again in the application of those rules. Moral intuition grasps particulars in such a way as to enable us to make moral judgments about them.

Intuitionism also emphasizes the *spontaneity* of moral judgment. What we want in our moral perplexity is to *see* more clearly what we are to do; we cannot calculate our way out. The mathematician Norbert Wiener was once delivering a paper at a scientific congress; the blackboard was covered with equations. "From this," he said, beginning to write another formula, "it obviously follows that. . . ." Then he hesitated, paused, excused himself, and sat down with paper and pencil. After some minutes he rose once more and continued, "Yes, it obviously follows that. . . ." Whatever be true in mathematics, in the moral life a man should be able to rely on his intuition—or, as Freud might say, to trust his own unconscious.

The doctrine of the indefinability of the Good is another matter. True, the moral life recurrently confronts us with dilemmas; but solutions elude us here, not because we are confronted with ultimate simples but because the complexities of our aspirations and of the contexts for their fulfillment do not allow for any simple way out. In any case, definition need not be by way of analysis; the resources of logic have advanced considerably beyond Aristotelian definition via genus and species, and there are other devices than definition for specifying meanings (§12). Modern approaches in ethical theory localize the impossibility of defining what is good elsewhere than in a supposed unique quality accessible only to intuition. The difficulty, according to most contemporary views, is to account for the normative force in an attribution of goodness, if the ground of the attribution is purely factual (§53).

The fundamental weakness of intuitionism is the same as that of religious ethics and the ethics of conscience: differences in moral conviction are frequent and intense, and these traditional theories leave such differences ineluctable. Historically, the true faith has often been spread by force. In our time, conscience and moral intuition are shaped by indoctrination and transformed by brainwashing. Lately, what is euphemistically called "behavior modification" has come into vogue. As technical jargon for teaching and learning by direct experience, it points to the foundation for all moral growth. As designating the manipulation of others until their behavior accords with the norms of the manipulator, it is only a new name for old-fashioned enslavement. Huxley's *Brave New World* describes a society in which infants, destined to spend most of their lives underground, are administered electric shocks when presented with flowers so that they will grow up to feel that flowers are ugly and that it is dangerous and wrong to smell them. Present-day exponents of behavior modification are not so insensitive or depraved; but this judgment, though it is I who make it, calls for a firmer basis than that provided only by my own faith, my own conscience, or my own moral intuition.

52. Moral Motives and Consequences

Traditional ethics focuses on the inner life. Faith and conscience are localized within, and though intuitionism emphasizes an outer Good, central to the theory is the capacity within man of perceiving the Good. The morality of an action is a matter of the moral quality of the inner life. Traditionally, an act is right if it springs from faith or is endorsed by conscience or is guided by a moral intuition. The morality of an act depends on *motive.* The motives of an act may be many and are likely to be obscure, especially to the actor himself. Some of the obscurity, however, is due to unsatisfactory conceptualizations of action.

The impulse from which an act proceeds is the *cause* of the action; the end to which it is directed is the *reason.* The goal of the act is its *aim;* the larger context of which the act is a part is its *purpose.* Conscious purposes are *intentions.* The directly experienced quality of an act seen to have certain causes and reasons is its *intent.* The action of a hunter stalking his prey may be caused by hunger and care for his family; its reason is food gathering, the aim being to kill the animal, the purpose, to feed himself and his family; a subsidiary purpose may be to impress others with his prowess as a hunter, but this is not likely to be part of his intention, except on special occasions, perhaps ceremonial ones; the intent of the act can only be described roughly, in terms of such qualities as skillful, persistent, determined, anticipatory, and merciless. The term "motive" is used in a comprehensive sense for all these grounds of action.

One of the major implications of the ethics in which motive is central is the importance of character (§46). Morality is not a matter of a single act but of a sequence of actions. Moral qualities do not attach to actions at all, except in a derivative sense; it is people who are good or bad. Character, defined by the motives characteristically expressed in action, is the ultimate subject of moral predication. "Nothing in the whole world, or even outside the world," Kant declared, "can possibly be regarded as good without limitation, except a good will."

Morality does not assess actions but takes the measure of the man. "It does not matter how much or how little, if only for the sake of Heaven" (the talmudic expression from which Martin Buber took the title of his fictionalized biography of two of the Hassidic masters). If it is only the motive that counts, an act which does not succeed in its aim may be as meritorious as a successful one; the fact that we make such judgments gives the ethics of motive its plausibility. Kant argues: "Even if it should happen that, owing to special disfavor of fortune, or the niggardly provisions of a step-motherly nature, this [good] will should wholly lack power to accomplish its purpose, then like a jewel it would still shine by its own light, as a thing which has its whole value in itself. Its usefulness, or fruitlessness, can neither add nor take anything away from its value."

The Talmud qualifies this position only to the extent of holding that while a good intention which is unfulfilled because of circumstances beyond control is nevertheless credited as virtuous, an unfulfilled evil intention is not accounted a sin. Such forebearance is more lenient than consistent. The conclusion demanded by logic is that explicit in the Gospels: "You have heard it used to be said, 'You shall not kill, and whoever kills is to be judged'; but I say to you that whoever is angry with his fellow-man is to be judged. . . . It used to be said, 'You shall not commit adultery'; but I say to you that whoever looks on a woman with lust has already committed adultery with her in his heart." The difference between that place and another is surely morally relevant.

Taking either motives or consequences as a basis of moral judgment is a special application of a more general distinction among ethical theories. Two major sets of moral attributes may be identified: those associated with the difference between right and wrong, and those associated with the difference between good and bad. Ethical theories usually take either the one set or the other as fundamental, and the remaining set as derivative. *Teleological ethics* are those for which good and bad are basic; *deontological ethics* are those for which right and wrong are basic. In a teleological ethical theory, good is somehow specified, then right is defined, roughly speaking, as an action whose outcome or aim is good; in a deontological theory, right is first specified, then the good is defined, roughly speaking, as the outcome or aim of right action. The ethics of motive are deontological theories. In these theories, a good motive is one which aims at doing right; a good man is a righteous one.

In deontological ethics, whether or not an act is right does not depend on its consequences. Expected consequences play a part in the determination of moral quality, but it is the expectations rather than the consequences which are significant. The *Bhagavad-Gita* expounds an ideal found in many moral doctrines: *tyaga,* renouncing the fruits of action (as contrasted with *sannyasa,* renouncing action altogether). The righteous man acts as he does, not in order to attain a certain result (even his own righteousness) but because that way of acting is right. His actions remain purposive, but it is not the moral quality of what is aimed at which makes the action right; and the action remains right whether or not the aim is attained.

The key concept underlying this approach to ethics is *duty.* A right action is one that a man performs because it is his duty, and for no other reason. Duty is the "sublime and mighty name," as Kant calls it, invoked, directly or indirectly, in every moral imperative. The Hindu term *dharma* combines the notion of order with that of obligation even more pointedly than does the English word "law." A Hindu clerk taking down off the shelves for the customer's inspection every object of even the most casual interest has no sense of being put upon; the formula, "It's my duty," is taken both to explain his action and to provide justification for it. Duty is accepted on its own recognizance; its claims need only be made to be acknowledged. In the Western world, historically speaking, this is because to act in the name of duty is to do it for the sake of Heaven. Wordsworth calls duty the "stern daughter of the voice of God." "Teach me to do Your will," the Psalmist prays in the same spirit as the Gospels' "Your will be done on earth as it is in Heaven."

Three major arguments have been put forward on behalf of the centrality of duty in ethical theory.

1. The claims of morality are sometimes clear and beyond question. Such claims cannot rest on assessments of consequences, for these are unending and hopelessly complex. If morality did not rest on a sense of duty it could not be as definite and certain as sometimes it undeniably is. The midwives for the Dzhugashvili and Schicklgruber families might have saved millions of lives if they had anticipated the consequences of assisting at the births of Stalin and Hitler; there is no way they could have known those consequences, but they *could* know and do their duty. The path of virtue—so this argument runs—is to do your duty and leave the consequences to God. In Chinese thought, to "know *Ming*" is to recognize that the outcome of our actions depends on circumstances beyond our knowledge and control, and therefore to content ourselves with doing our duty, regardless of whether ultimately we succeed or fail.

2. The claims of morality are universal, applying equally to everyone

who might be in the same circumstances. Now, what we judge to be good or bad varies from person to person, for the judgment depends on what desires are to be satisfied; but the difference between right and wrong is the same with regard to everyone. The fact that I want one thing rather than another can never give moral justification to my doing something which would be immoral if I had other desires. Right and wrong are in no way constituted by my desires but by intrinsic features of my actions; only what is objective can be universal. Therefore the moral man aspires to live not by human passions but by the will of God—"not as I will, but as You will!"

3. Morality is unconditionally binding, in no way dependent upon the ends a person might choose. Outside morality, imperatives are *hypothetical;* they have the form, if you want y, do x! The implication is that doing x will bring about y. The force of the imperative stems from the desire for y; if this condition is not met, no reason is being given for enjoining x. Morality formulates *categorical imperatives,* without any "ifs." "Thou shalt not murder!"—not: provided you want a sense of security, a peaceful society, a contented citizenry, or provided anything else, but unconditionally, simply because murder is morally wrong. Morality may invoke hypotheticals in defining its claims ("If you borrow money, you ought to repay it"), but it is only the applicability of moral principles which is conditional, not their rightness. Morality is not conditional upon desires, or "inclinations," as Kant called them: the law of duty is one "before which all inclinations are dumb."

But moral imperatives have no purchase on action except by way of those "inclinations" which are silenced by the voice of duty. The desire to do right is not self-sufficient either logically or psychologically: it neither tells us what to do nor provides a motivation (as distinct from a reason) for doing it. "I have never yet seen a man whose love of virtue equaled his love of woman," Confucius remarked. If there were such a man, it does not follow that for him the path of virtue would be clear. On the contrary, it oftens happens that the one sort of love disguises itself as the other—desires masquerade as duties. There is a pernicious moral ventriloquism in which self-interest purports to speak in the name of the Lord.

Even where duties are genuine and unmistakable, the task is not simply to make them prevail over contrary inclinations. To resolve the conflict between duty and desire is the moral problem facing adolescence. The moral issues and dilemmas with which the mature man must cope often confront him with conflicting duties. Such conflicts are not illuminated by a theory which insists only that the voice of duty must be obeyed. Discriminations among duties and hierarchies of obligation are often introduced in this connection, but their justification, in turn, is likely to depend upon consequences.

That duties impose obligations is virtually a tautology; what is meant by an obligation is far from obvious, however. Three sorts of obligation can be distinguished, of which only the last is fundamental in deontological ethics. *Social obligation* is an obligation to someone—a person, a group, or a community—incurred because of a commitment or promise. Consideration of such obligations takes us out of ethics into political philosophy by way of such ideas as "the social contract," or into the philosophy of religion by way of the idea of a "covenant." *Physical obligation* refers to the ineluctability of facts and the necessity imposed by natural law. Such obligation is the essence of teleological ethics, being grounded in the relation of means to their ends. *Logical obligation*—the application to action of logical necessity (§39)—is central to the ethics of duty, in Kant's version, at any rate.

Kant's position is that the content of duty is given by reason and that the force of moral obligation derives from the power of reason. Duties follow from the presuppositions of action. The argument has two steps. First is what Kant calls "the fundamental law of the pure practical reason," *the* Categorical Imperative: "Act so that the maxim of your will can always at the same time hold good as a principle of universal legislation." That an act is right implies that it would be right for everyone, similarly placed, to act in that way; if its rightness were not universal it would not be objective. The second step is the recognition of duties as the logical consequences of this universalization. For instance (the examples are Kant's), we cannot consistently believe it right to break a promise, for if promises were universally breakable it would be pointless for us ever to make any promises; we cannot consistently will not to help the distressed, for we desire help when we ourselves are distressed, and this would be denied us if our uncaring will were universalized.

It is not easy to see, however, why every violation of duty must involve an inconsistency. Suicide, for example, is widely held to be morally wrong; true, if it were universalized there would be an end to mankind, but a man for whom life is weary, stale, flat, and unprofitable might consistently rejoin, "What does that matter!" Moreover, when we act contrary to our moral obligations we are likely to do so only in special circumstances; even if the ground of such action were universalized, the circumstances may well be exceptional enough for the universalization not to matter: how often does a man find a million dollars in small, unmarked bills? We seem driven back upon a consideration of the consequences of acting in one way or another. If morality is basically a matter of good intentions, which intentions *are* good seems to depend on their effects.

This is the position taken by Jeremy Bentham: "There is no such thing as any sort of motive that is in itself a bad one. If motives are good or bad, it is only on account of their effects." The paradigm of the ethics of effects is the *utilitarianism* to which Bentham subscribed. Which effects are to be taken into account and on what grounds are they to be assessed as good or bad? The abstract "utility" from which the theory takes its name does not specify the effects. The most common specification is *ethical hedonism:* what is ultimately good is pleasure. (This is to be distinguished from psychological hedonism (§45), the theory that attaining pleasure is the basic human motivation.) "I know not how I can conceive the good," Epicurus declared, "if I withdraw the pleasures."

A basic difficulty with hedonism had already been argued by the Stoics. Pleasure is the companion, not the guide of our course; we do not and should not love virtue because it gives us pleasure; it gives us pleasure because we love it. Epicurus speaks of "pleasures" in the plural: men love many different things. They cannot all be identified with virtue, unless we give "virtue" so universal a scope as to make it meaningless and acknowledge as a man's good whatever he aims at or takes pleasure in. Morality demands that we discriminate higher and lower pleasures as well as those which are virtuous, morally neutral, and downright wicked. The older utilitarianism held that "pushpin [a children's game of the period] is as good as poetry." To this, John Stuart Mill countered with the dictum, "Better Socrates unhappy than a pig satisfied." This would surely be agreed to by everyone whose sense of human dignity has not been blunted by prior commitment to some theory.

Bentham promulgated as "the measure of right and wrong" the famous formula "the greatest good of the greatest number." I have already noted (§45) some of the problems of measuring this presumed magnitude. Setting aside the technical problems faced by contemporary utility theory, we are still left with considerable difficulties. Bentham held that "vice may be defined as a miscalculation of chances," but I find it hard to believe that the chief failing of a vicious man is incompetence in applied probability; nor can I regard such competence as a conspicuous mark of virtue. On being told that a certain man acted only after thinking three times, Confucius remarked, "Twice is quite enough!" No doubt he meant to emphasize the rarity of even that much deliberation. Yet a "calculating" man connotes one given to coldhearted, scheming self-interest. A preoccupation with the possible effects of what we do may rob our doings of spontaneous warmth and impulsive generosity.

There is in the ethics of effects another danger to the moral life, the *utilitarian fallacy:* the mistake of assessing effects with regard to a preselected set of consequences, even though other consequences may also be important. This is the fallacy in the misconceived ideal of "efficiency" in managing a business or training an army. Maximum profits and firepower do not constitute all the good to be attained in these contexts. Decision making may suffer less from unanticipated consequences than from so-called "by-products" of the actions taken—effects which might have been anticipated but which are dismissed from the outset as irrelevant. One of the utilitarians confides that he selected his wife by listing all the eligible women of his acquaintance, arranging their names in order of their desirability, and proposing down the list until he was accepted. The procedure looks efficient, but what about the calculations that must have entered into the preparation of the ordered list, or that may play a part later in a post-audit?

Effects are always many, capable of being assessed in relation to many different values. These are not always commensurable so as to make possible a single maximization—the values at stake in a company's retirement policy, for example, are not limited to those which can find a place in the annual profit-and-loss statement. We can assess a set of diverse values configurationally rather than by way of a presumed conversion followed by a summation; mathematics can deal with vector quantities as well as with scalars. The more fundamental difficulties are not in carrying out the calculations required by utilitariansism but in defining the magnitudes presumed to have been measured.

The following illustration may not be consonant with contemporary moral values, but the point Lecky is making remains valid. "There are few things more pitiable," he wrote in his *History of European Morals*, "than the blunders into which writers have fallen when trying to base the plain virtue of chastity on utilitarian considerations." I have since heard of the apocryphal Balkan decoration, "Order of Chastity, Second Class." Dewey has insisted that the thing actually at stake in any serious deliberation is not a difference of quantity, but what kind of person one is to become, what sort of self is in the making, what kind of world is coming to be. The criticism is not that there are limits to quantification but that so often the measured quantities are beside the point. An ethical theory which, like utilitarianism, defines the good in quantitative terms may succeed in making measurements while the good continues to elude it.

The ethics of effects provides a basis for *prudence* but not for morality. Prudence is a virtue, but not all virtue is prudence. Biblical wisdom literature, exemplified by Ecclesiastes, does not hesitate to ground its injunctions on expected effects. "Cast your bread upon the waters," says the Preacher, "for you shall find it after many days." The Koran has it, "To those who do good, their good shall return again with interest." So everywhere in the world's moral teaching: honesty, like the other virtues, is the best policy. But there are times, from the days of Socrates to those of Solzhenitsyn, when virtue is imprudent. An ethics judging morality only by effects is beset by opportunism. "We cannot divide ourselves between right and expediency," Kant warned; "policy must bow the knee before morality." Today the order of deference is usually the reverse, but perhaps no more than always. That everything is for sale nowadays is conveyed by the historic slip of the tongue by a television announcer at the conclusion of a religious program which ended with the line from Ecclesiastes quoted above; the announcer then proclaimed, "This is the National Breadcasting Company!"

If morality is not a matter only of motives, neither is it a matter only of consequences, especially not of consequences for the pleasure or happiness of the moral agent. "Parents and teachers," said Plato in the *Republic*, "are always telling their sons and their wards that they are to be just; but why? Not for the sake of justice, but for the sake of character and reputation; in the hope of obtaining for him who is reputed to be just some of those advantages accruing to the unjust from the repudiation of justice. They throw in the good opinion of the gods, and will tell you of a shower of benefits which the heavens, as they say, rain upon the pious." Morality, Kant argued, does not deal with how we can make ourselves happy, but with how we can make ourselves *worthy* of happiness.

The same point might be formulated with a more objective reference. The value of the good is inherent; not all goods are good because of the value of something other than themselves, which their pursuit will help bring about. The reward for performing a good deed, according to the *Ethics of the Fathers,* is the opportunity to perform another, and the punishment for committing a sin is the necessity to sin once more. How is the inherent quality of the good to be recognized?

53. The Emotivist Critique

Attempts to specify the basis for moral judgments, or the procedure by which they can be validated, have failed to meet many objections. To the religious basis, it is objected that irreligious men are also moral and that morality is as much a prerequisite to spiritual attainment as derivative from it. Conscience, sometimes insensitive and sometimes tyrannical, is too variable to provide a basis for morality. A supposed moral intuition, though elusive, is subject to manipulation and so is impossible to calibrate. Motives have no moral quality independent of the results of action except for the pure motive of devotion to duty, but duties conflict with one another. Pleasure, happiness and utility are too immeasurable and the effects of action too incalculable to provide a basis for moral judgment.

The history of ideas, in both science and philosophy, has repeatedly shown that a question which remains for long unanswerable is likely to have been improperly formulated. In the positivist view (§11), statements which are in principle impossible to verify are incapable of being either true or false. Such statements, therefore, are not propositions, however much they may resemble propositions in grammatical form. They make no contribution to knowledge, adding nothing to the description or explanation of any fact. This is the position on the nature of moral judgments taken by Wittgenstein in his *Tractatus* (using the term "ethical" in place of "moral"): "There can be no ethical propositions. Ethics cannot be expressed. Ethics are transcendental." "Inexpressible" and "transcendental" refer, in this context, to whatever is neither a tautology of logic and mathematics nor a verifiable synthetic proposition.

What are moral judgements then? Positivism offers a number of answers in terms of *emotive meaning,* which is contrasted with the *cognitive meaning* of verifiable propositions. Moral judgments, according to Alfred Ayer, express the feelings and attitudes of the judger toward the subject of the judgment, rather than predicating an objective attribute; the judgment can be sincere or hypocritical, but not true or false. According to Carnap, "A value statement is nothing else than a command in misleading grammatical form. It is neither true nor false. It does not assert anything and can neither be proved nor disproved." Charles Stevenson, in his influential book, *Ethics and Language,* emphasizes the persuasive function of moral imperatives; what looks like a factual judgment that x is good has a meaning which can be rendered, in a first approximation, "I like x; do so as well!" For Reichenbach, moral judgments express the speakers' volitions and commitments.

Such views, frequently held during the thirties and forties, were met with the indignation and outrage always evoked by departures from tradition in moral doctrine or ethical theory. The emotivist view was widely charges with nihilism, with undermining morality. This reaction is groundless. Emotivism weakens cynicism as well as coercive dogma, since it emphasizes that arguments about moral issues should focus on matters of fact, and that when arguments have carried us as far as they can, we must take a stand for our values. Far from destroying morality, emotivism insists on the obligation we owe to ourselves to express and enjoin our moral standards.

Emotivism is subject to other criticisms, on the basis of alternative analyses of the meaning of moral judgments. The *reflexive meaning* of such judgments—that the judger has certain feelings or attitudes—hardly exhausts their meaning. There is a difference between a *judgment* and an *expression of taste.* This difference is especially marked in art; it is one thing to say that I like a work of art and quite another to ascribe to it beauty or some specific aesthetic quality. The same difference holds between personal morality and moral judgments. The judgments purport to have an objective ground—an intersubjective, impersonal basis.

If the content of judgment is limited to reflexive meaning, how is it possible for me to express a desire for the improvement of my taste? Emotivism may give an acceptable analysis of expressions of taste, but its analysis of moral judgments is unacceptable because that analysis cannot distinguish judgments from expressions. Statements like, "My taste in these matters is uncultivated," or, "My moral judgments about behavior of this sort are often insensitive," are not self-contradictory. If a judgment about values only expresses how I feel, such statements would be incongruous and self-defeating.

A moral imperative is not a bare command, resting only on an implied power to coerce. Though a value judgment does have imperative force, it is a judgment precisely in that it conveys the existence of good grounds for the valuation it expresses; unlike an expression of taste, a judgment purports to be neither thoughtless nor capricious. In the emotivist view, the attitudes expressed in moral judgments relate to the facts of the case since they are caused by our beliefs as to the facts. The content of a value judgment, however, is not that there are *causes* for the valuation but that there are *reasons* for it. So far as causes are concerned,

> *malt does more than Milton can*
> *To justify God's ways to man.*

In his "A Shropshire Lad" Housman continues, "Ale's the stuff to drink for fellows whom it hurts to think"; but moral judgments mean more than such fellows are capable of.

When reasons, not merely causes, are in question, we must distinguish between good and bad reasons, and between relevant and irrelevant ones. It is hardly plausible that these distinctions should be matters of second-level attitudes. The reasons to which moral judgments implicitly refer point to something in the action or situation being judged. That there are such reasons is part of the meaning of moral judgments.

Consider a cry for help, expressed in the exclamation, "Help!" Its reflexive meaning is: I want help. Utterances of this kind also have an *extended meaning*—that the feelings or attitudes they express are fitting or proper in the situation. In this instance, the extended meaning is: I need help—my situation is dangerous and I cannot cope with it alone. The truth of the claim does not depend merely on how I feel, as is the case with reflexive meaning. The utterance has also a *derived meaning*—that the behavior enjoined upon you has desirable consequences for you. In this instance, the derived meaning is that it would be well for you to help me—this is not a trap, for example. Here also, truth is not a matter merely of how I feel. As with the metatheorems of logic (§16), the rule or norm being laid down can be justified by the consequences of conforming to it. The derived meaning of a normative statement is that it has such a justification.

All three components of indirect meaning—reflexive, extended, and derived—can be formulated in correlated propositions. Correlated to the utterance, "Help!" are the propositions, "I want help," "I need help," and "It is in your interest to help me." Although retrospective analysis assigns the correlated propositions to an indirect meaning, they are directly (if implicitly) understood in interpreting the judgment. They are not inferred from it, or in any sense reconstructed. To fail to understand them as contained in the expression is to misinterpret the expression, to miss the point. We would be in the position of the White King, who pretends that his remark, "There's nothing like eating hay when you're faint!" means only that there's nothing *like* it, not that it's a good thing to do.

We can recognize the *normative function* performed by moral judgments without invoking a distinctive emotive meaning to enable them to perform this function. "If ethics were a form of knowledge," Reichenbach argued in *The Rise of Scientific Philosophy*, "it would not be what moral philosophers want it to be; that is, it would not supply moral directives." But the fact that medicine is a form of knowledge does not prevent the rules of hygiene from performing a normative function, nor does it deprive them of imperative force. Quite the contrary; it is our grasp of their extended and derived meanings, and belief in the truth of the correlated propositions, which give them force. The declarative grammatical form moral judgments usually have helps direct attention to this truth claim, while the imperative form may focus on the element of command and its reflexive meaning. The emotivist charge that ethical theory has been misled by sameness of form to treat moral judgments as verifiable propositions might be countered with the charge that emotivism has been misled by sameness of function to treat moral judgments as no more than imperatives. Meaning is different from both form and function.

The issues pertain more to psychology than to semantics. The emotivist view perpetuates the Platonist dualism of reason and emotion, commonly formulated since Stevenson in terms of the difference between "belief" and "attitude." The difference is held to be ultimate and unbridgeable, save by causal interaction (just as in the Cartesian dualism of mind and body). But attitudes and emotions reach out to the world; they are not self-contained, objectless, encapsulated. Attitudes are not merely caused by and conjoined to beliefs but are, in part, constituted by beliefs, rooted in them, existing in them as the color exists in its surface. Hume, the philosopher with the greatest influence on emotivism, held that while reason owes drive and direction to the passions, it repays the debt by adapting environmental stimuli and emotional responses to one another. Such adaptation is not, in turn, only a matter of how we feel about it.

Emotivism ultimately localizes moral disagreements in the presumed situation of two parties sharing all their beliefs but differing in their attitudes. But there are no such situations at all, let alone those characteristic of moral disagreements—if to have an attitude is to hold a certain belief in a particular way. Feeling is a quality of our knowings and doings; when we feel something, we know—or think we know—something, and act accordingly. Moral judgments express how we feel about things, but by the same token they convey what we *think* of them. Moral judgments are right or wrong for the same reasons that other judgments are—the beliefs they express are true or false, respectively.

Feelings *are* more markedly involved in moral judgments than in other propositions. This is due to the subject matter of these judgments and to their implications for action, not to their having only an emotive meaning. In the eighteenth century the existence of a distinctive "moral sentiment" was widely assumed and was supposed to underlie moral judgments—a faculty of feeling rather than the cognitive moral intuition adduced in other periods. As Hume put it, "The final sentence, it is probable, which pronounces characters and actions praiseworthy or blamable depends on some internal sense or feeling which nature has made universal in the whole species." A feeling for our fellowmen is central to morality (§58). Kant's austere ethics of duty was promptly criticized with the observation that on his theory we can only be sure of acting morally in relation to those we hate, for if we are good to those we care for we cannot be certain that we are not motivated by our inclinations rather than only by a sense of duty. Such human-heartedness, as the Chinese call it, is important rather as a component of moral doctrine than as constituting a basis of ethical theory, which is what emotivism maintains.

Feelings abstracted from thought, or emotions abstracted from reason, are wholly unsuited for an ethical basis. Unreasoning appetite, like the Freudian id, has no characteristic object; it is undiscriminating, as contrasted with reason, whose object, as Plato urged, is always the Good. Freud might characterize a man driven by blind appetite as "polymorphous perverse." Feelings dissociated from their objects are rootless, inward turned, subjective in a pejorative sense. The Hebrew greeting for the New Year invokes a "good" new year (*shanah tovah*), not a "happy" one. There are people who are miserable when all is well with them—like Judith Viorst's friend Ida, "the one who suffers the way other people enjoy." Conversely, there is also the so-called "rapture of the deep," in which lack of oxygen produces a subjective and ultimately fatal illusion of well-being.

As a basis for ethics, feelings suffer from another shortcoming: they are ephemeral, of uncertain duration and often unpredictable occurrence. Nietzsche, like other romantics an ardent exponent of the life of feeling, is realist enough to recognize that it is not the strength but the duration of feeling which distinguishes the great man. It certainly distinguishes the good man. In many contexts, morality turns on commitment, not on merely momentary feeling. If we have agreed to meet for dinner, it will not do for you to excuse your absence on the grounds that when the time came you did not feel like joining me; our agreement was not to meet if we felt like it, but to meet. After we meet we can jointly review the decision to dine together; our commitment meant that the decision would not be changed unilaterally.

The moral quality of whatever action we take at any time is not a matter merely of our feelings at that time. "As one swallow or one day does not make a summer," Aristotle remarked, "so one day or a short time does not make a fortunate or a happy man." Herodotus records the reply of the sage Solon to Croesus' question whether that wealthy king were not a happy man: "I have no answer to give till I hear that you have closed your life happily. God often grants men a gleam of happiness, then plunges them into ruin." A feeling, however radiant, is no more than such a gleam.

Moral judgment, in short, cannot be validated by the mere existence of certain feelings, however distinctively or intensely these find expression in the judgment. Everything hinges on such qualities as the depth, range, stability, and sensitivity of the feelings. Above all, the validity of the judgment depends, so far as feeling is concerned, on how well grounded the feeling is in the objective features of the circumstances in which it arises, and on how well integrated the feeling is with ensuing action. Feeling which is rooted in subjectivity and which bears fruit only in momentary impulse may provide data for moral judgment but is unable to establish moral conclusions.

54. The Ethics of Deliberation

The ethical theories so far considered all point to important features of the moral life, to which any acceptable theory must do justice. Morality is a matter of standards which have been internalized, not merely imposed from without; the recognition of moral quality may be as immediate and irresistible as sensory perception; moral action, although it may spring from spontaneous impulse, is guided, and sometimes also impelled, by a sense of obligation; moral choices are the outcome of a responsible concern for the consequences of one choice or another; and the moral life provides occasion for an intense and pervasive emotional involvement. To all these, another feature of what leads to defensible moral judgment may be added: human reason plays a significant part in just determining what is moral. A representative approach which emphasizes the role of intelligence in morals is the ethical theory of John Dewey.

In voluminous writings Dewey has defined moral activity as that "called forth and directed by ideas of value or worth, where the values concerned are so mutually incompatible as to require consideration and selection." Conflict belongs to the essence of the moral life. Like thought in general, reflection on moral matters arises from and is sustained by what is problematic in ongoing conduct. To think about morals is to think about moral issues, or else to mistake for thought the recitation of formulas.

Moral reflection is not occupied with immediate satisfactions. The *myth of the eternal moment* is the notion that everything of meaning and value belongs only to the present. It is the myth implicitly believed by the infant, who is not yet capable of grasping significant time spans; it is often used to rationalize regressive infantile behavior, in relation to sex, drug abuse, and the like; it is a cardinal tenet of neoromanticism, conveyed in the barbarism, of content as well as of form, of "the Now generation." This is not to deny either that the present is the locus of significance (§37), or that there is any such thing as an immediate satisfaction. C. I. Lewis—like Dewey, a pragmatist in both ethics and theory of knowledge—calls any immediately experienced goodness an *intrinsic value,* all others being *extrinsic.* The point is not to deny the existence of intrinsic values but to affirm that morality is occupied with extrinsic values. Moral issues have to do with the worth of what we can reasonably expect to experience. "To say that something is good," Dewey urges, "is to predict what it will do." An extrinsic value is something which can predictably, in suitable contexts, provide intrinsic goodness.

Such predictions relate to what is to be expected on the whole, in the long run. What is being judged is a way of acting, not any specific outcome. Experts in games combining chance and skills speak with contempt of a "results player": one who claims credit for a foolish play which happened to be successful. There is a story by Somerset Maugham about a father worried because his admonitions to his son against liquor, women, and gambling were refuted by a delightful weekend which the young man enjoyed in Monte Carlo, capped by his finding in his possession all the money belonging to the beautiful woman who had been scheming to steal his; the story is called "The Facts of Life," but the father may have been a wise counselor for all that. Sometimes what are thought of as the follies of the law—with regard to the admissibility of certain evidence, for example—seem foolish only when looked at in isolation from the long run and general consequences.

That moral judgments make predictions implies that they deal only with extrinsic values. Their subject matter is restricted in another way: the predictions concern the results of our actions. What we judge are choices, not outcomes considered in abstraction from the processes of which they are the products. Dewey distinguishes between *values* in a narrow sense, as fruits of "intelligently directed activity," and merely adventitious *goods.* Moral reflection aims at identifying not the best abstractly possible state of affairs but the best *choice* open to us. In moral conduct—as Spinoza held on the basis of a similar emphasis on the role of reason—we are active rather than passive, subject neither to outer authority nor to inner compulsion, choosing deliberately rather than yielding to whim or caprice. We *do* good rather than being done by; if there is any passivity here, it is that adverted to by Plato—the response of reason drawn by the vision of the Good.

What seems to be a moral judgment is often only an expression of taste. Rather than predict extrinsic values, such an expression celebrates an intrinsic good. It does not make an *e*valuation but expresses the fact that we value something. To point to this difference, Dewey distinguishes between *appraising* something and *prizing* it. A moral judgment conveys an appraisal; an expression of taste conveys our prizing of its subject. Moral perception and reflection, experiencing intrinsic value and weighing the worth of the probable outcomes of the alternatives before us—this process Dewey calls *deliberation.* A moral judgment formulates the conclusion of deliberation.

Deliberation is possible, we can make appraisals, because values occur always in the context of what Dewey calls the *means-ends continuum.* Alternatives are evaluated, first of all, as means to certain ends, as utilitarianism urged. In contrast to Kant, Dewey holds that moral norms have the logical structure of hypothetical imperatives, not categorical imperatives (§52). If they appear to be categorical, it is only because the ends hypothecated remain tacit, being implicit in the contexts to which the imperative refers, and in those contexts having an unproblematic status (§26). So far as moral judgments do imply or presuppose hypothetical imperatives, they can be validated in the same was as any other judgments about matters of fact. If capital punishment is being proposed as a deterrent to crime, whether or not it is right to execute criminals can be assessed by the facts as to its effectiveness.

On this basis, we can characterize values as *instrumental* or *inherent.* An instrumental value is one valuable as a means to some end; the value of the end is inherent. Both sorts of values are extrinsic; they are actions, situations, or objects of value, not the immediately experienced intrinsic good. Deliberation weighs the instrumentality of our choices. Inherent values are prized rather than appraised; their affirmation as inherent values are expressions of taste, not the subject of moral judgments.

No values are *only* inherent. The distinction separates aspects, qualities, functions of things, not the things themselves. Where there is no instrumentality, apart from the limiting case of serving as the direct stimulus to an experience of intrinsic value, we are confronted with what is indeed only a matter of taste, like the difference between chocolate and vanilla. From the standpoint of inherent value, no question can meaningfully be raised as to which is the better flavor. Yet judgments of value *cán* be made about such things as wine, tea, and works of art, as well as about particular actions and whole life-styles. These judgments hinge on an element of instrumentality.

Because the ends to which value judgments have reference so often remain implicit, it is easy to focus attention on the means. The notion then arises that deliberation occupies itself *only* with means, while ends are either to be taken for granted or to be determined by some other process—for instance, that they are to be given to us by others. A physician, in deciding that something is "good" for his patient, *assumes* certain ends which he identifies as "health." Both doctor and patient may overlook the questions of value, and even the moral issues which may be glossed over in making such assumptions—as occasionally becomes manifest in cases of cardiac conditions, psychoneuroses, and incurable malignancies. Rationalization of this process I have called the *myth of neutralism* (§35). It is the notion that knowledge, skill, and intelligence can be brought to bear only on facts preconceived to be free of value.

As a result of the widespread acceptance of this myth in our time, people in the helping professions—therapists, social workers, lawyers, planners, engineers, economists, and countless others—characteristically make *virtual decisions:* conclusions which have the effect of decisions but which are presented as "mere" hypotheticals, appraisals of means leading to allegedly predetermined ends—whereby such advisers and technicians exercise power without responsibility. What is called for is not the futile and pointless attempt by the adviser to suppress his own values but, on the contrary, greater efforts to articulate them and to include them among the data for deliberation.

How are ends to be assessed? Their value, as ends, has just been declared to be inherent, and so subject only to prizing, not to appraisal. The answer is that what serves as an end does not serve as an end only: it also functions as a means in turn, and so is also an instrumental value to be appraised. There are no *final* ends; each goal, as it is achieved, becomes a point of departure toward new goals. The sequence is cut off not because it reaches a terminus but because our perspectives rightly reach only so far into the future as has a practical bearing on present action. This unending sequence of ends, each serving as means to the next, has aptly been called "the mountain-range effect," in another version of Sisyphus. We cannot cross the mountain range, for whenever we reach a crest we discern new crests rising across the valley. Dewey was once asked, "What happens when you get tired of forever climbing another slope?" His reply was simply, "When you are tired of climbing, you die."

There is no vicious infinite regress here. The enjoyment of a value, the fulfillment of an aspiration, does not depend on reaching some allegedly final goal. Value is present and realizable throughout the process. Ends do have inherent value—they are indeed ends; they are also means to other ends and therefore have instrumental value by which they can be appraised. The judgment that something is of value affirms a matter of fact with reference to another value, but no ultimate value is presupposed by the affirmation. We appraise x as good by assessing it as a means to some y which is prized; to judge that y is good, we assess it in relation to some z, which in turn. . . . The logic of the situation is like that discussed in connection with the quest for certainty (§26), a quest which may also underlie the search for final ends. To know a proposition we must have evidence for it; to know that what is brought forward as evidence is in fact the case, we must have evidence for *that* claim; and so endlessly. Yet, so long as we *do* have evidence of a proposition, that proposition is known; knowledge does not depend upon the existence of any self-evident truths which bring the sequence of verifications to an ultimate closure.

The counterpart of the myth of the eternal moment, which localizes value in the present, is the *myth of the apocalypse,* which localizes value in some final future. The religious version of the myth—the coming of the Messiah at the end of days to usher in an era of blessedness and peace—has been secularized in our time to such final goals as "the triumph of the revolution and the achievement of Communism," or "the liberation of Arab lands and the restoration of the just rights of the Palestinians." The question is always, how are we to live until the apocalyptic moment? How are we to give significance to aspiration whose achievement will inevitably fall short of the ultimate? There is a Yugoslav joke of a speaker who, after a lecture on "Life Under Communism," was asked, "When Communism is finally achieved, will there be money?" "Comrade," he replied, "the left-wing, orthodox Chinese Communists say no, while the right-wing Russian revisionists say yes. But we Yugoslavs, we are the true dialectical Marxists; we say, under Communism, some people will have money, and some will not!" To reject the apocalypse is not to abandon aspiration altogether but to insist on giving it significance in the ongoing present. The child asked to wash his hands argues that they will only get dirty again; and so they will. Maturity demands the realization that we live always only in the meantime.

The means-ends continuum is more than a linear sequence stretching forward into the future. It reaches backward and sideways as well. We evaluate ends not only by the later ends to which they are means but also by the means which they themselves require. These involve other ends, which are thereby implicated in the end being evaluated. To consider only the given end is to be guilty of the utilitarian fallacy (§52), dismissing as by-products effects irrelevant to the measure, although it may be the measure which is to be dismissed. To abstract from something is not to pay attention to it, but it is there and does its work whether or not we take it into account.

Deliberation is cut off not because certain ends are final but because they are thought to be *unconditional.* Every judgment of instrumental value presupposes an end with inherent value; it does not follow that there must exist ends having inherent value with respect to all judgments—unconditional ends. Every end, as an end, is prized. Whatever conditions qualify its value must already have been taken into account in its prizing; it does not follow that this accounting is not subject to appraisal. It is often argued that an end can be evaluated only if we smuggle in other values to serve as reference points. The truth is rather that ends elude evaluation only when we have smuggled *out* all other values. Ends are not projected in isolation. Every judgment of value, as a concrete utterance, is made in a context in which innumerable ends are already at work.

The hoary question whether ends justify means may be seen in fresher perspective. The answer is yes, since means are subject to appraisal according to their effectiveness. The answer is no, in the sense claimed by the maxim that foul is fair in a good cause. That the means are foul implies that among their consequences are some which destroy other ends than the one which they serve, and all the operative ends enter into our deliberations. If only foul means serve a certain cause it is not easy to conclude that it remains a good cause. That no alternative means are possible does not justify the assessment that, after all, the necessary means are not so foul. Though we sometimes do have to choose the lesser evil, the necessity does not make the evil any less.

The outcome of deliberation in specific cases cannot be prejudged by general considerations. What *can* be said in a general way is that a good cause does not transform foul means into fair. The reverse might equally well be true—that the foul means transform a good cause into a bad one. It is not only *other* values that are affected; the intended goal also changes character. Means leave their marks on their ends. Political independence, it has been said, is never served up on a silver platter; it must be fought for. But what has been won in a foul fight retains the taint. If the first page of a country's history has been written in innocent blood, we cannot expect that the second page will record freedom and justice. The counterargument usually heard is that there is no such thing as innocence—no victims, only enemies and martyrs. When moral corruption has reached this stage, it may already be beyond the reach of argument.

Every segment of the means-ends continuum can be seen both as end and as means—an end in relation to its antecedent and a means in relation to its consequents. Correspondingly, it is a locus of both inherent and instrumental value. Every end is in fact a sequence of means, or else it is incapable of functioning as an end. "The moral life of man may be likened to travelling to a distant place," Confucius suggested; "one must start from the nearest stage. It may also be likened to ascending a height: one must begin from the lowest step."

Not all goals can be reached after a determinate number of steps. This distinguishes *objectives* from *ideals*. An objective is a point or region in value-space, while an ideal is a direction in that space. That ideals can never be attained is a matter of simple logic, not a metaphysical shortcoming of the human condition. As ends, ideals allow us to appraise means, as well as other ends in which they are implicated; but they do not define reachable goals. A liberal education is an ideal, associated with such objectives as certain schooling. Social equality is an ideal, while certain job opportunities or rates of pay might be objectives pursued in the light of that ideal. It is folly for a person to proclaim that on a certain day he will have a liberal education, or for a society to promise that with a certain piece of legislation or a certain change in rulers social equality will be realized.

The danger in confusing ideals with objectives is not only that the continued failure to fulfill aspiration may engender cynicism or despair. There is also a danger that unattainability will be used to rationalize the lack of connection between the ends proclaimed and the means practiced. Such purported ideals are *utopias,* in the pejorative sense. What makes them utopian is not the presence of perfection but the absence of practicality. Where not even the first step of the journey can be specified, we can only conclude "you can't get there from here." A utopia is neither a direction nor a region in the value-space; it is a point at infinity. A utopia does not serve as an end, because it is wholly dissociated from possible means. "If it remains a distant end," Dewey has said, "it becomes a mere end, that is, a dream." The last words of *The Old New Land,* a novel by Theodore Herzl, who launched political Zionism, are: "If you will it, it is no dream." Truly to will is already to begin to act.

55. Ethical Naturalism

In my youth, during the Great Depression, a widely played fantasy game began with the question, "What would you do if you had a million dollars?" (There was even a successful movie called *If I Had a Million.*) What made the game unreal was not just the improbability of the assumption but its barrenness; the question how the player was supposed to have come by the money was simply not raised. (Perhaps he should allocate half the amount to his legal defense.) A similar unreality characterized what passed for the moral dilemmas with which we occupied ourselves. You are in a boat with your mother and your sweetheart; if the boat capsizes, which do you save? The implied conflict between duty and desire, or between duties, is real enough; but the concrete data are lacking which alone allow us to solve problems or to cope with dilemmas. How did we come to be in the boat? Why did it capsize? Where are we? These and innumerable other questions must first be answered. The abstract formulation presents us with an impossible quandary, not because it raises profound moral issues but because its abstractness prevents us from coming to grips with the issues. For my part, the quandary could never arise—I do not know how to swim.

Aristotle points out that in discussions of moral action, universal statements are likely to be too vague because actions are always particular. Universal statements may be made just because of such vagueness. A government or a political party may declare its "support" for a certain policy or movement; "support" may mean anything from full-scale military intervention to the mere repetition of declarations of support. Moral quality can be predicated only of specific acts, not of action in general. Moral generalizations *can* be made, but their validation rests on judgments about particulars. In deliberation, both general and particular are taken into account, but the particular provides the dominant considerations. In scientific inquiry, laws and facts, or hypotheses and data, are reciprocally determined, but an underlying empiricism gives priority to facts and data over our conceptual generalizations. Juridical procedures invoke legal principles as well as decisions in particular cases, but it is case law which is ultimately decisive.

This line of thinking in ethical theory may be designated (ethical) *contextualism;* sometimes it is called "situationalism." (Contextualism is also a doctrine in the theory of knowledge and in metaphysics—§39.) A classic expression of contextualism is Aristotle's explanation that the mean, as a moral principle, is not to be interpreted in terms of an abstract universal: "The time when, and the cases in which, and the persons toward whom, and the motive for which, and the manner in which, constitute the mean and the excellence." Similarly, the Preacher says, "A wise man's heart discerns time and judgment; to every thing there is a time." Context determines the meaning of the moral judgment, and thereby its truth. In morality above all, circumstances alter cases. "Virtue itself," says Juliet's Friar Laurence, "turns vice, being misapplied." Contextualism does not provide a rationalization for opportunistic and unprincipled conduct. Rather, it focuses attention on the specifics which alone can define the rational application of principles. The useful category of "the foolish *tzaddik* (saint)" is traditionally explained as meant for one who refrains from rescuing a drowning woman because she is inadequately clothed.

Confucius shares this contextualist realism. "With me," he says, "there is no inflexible 'Thou shalt' or 'Thou shalt not.'" In morality the exception almost does prove the rule; by exhibiting a limit to the applicability of the rule, it may heighten awareness of the rule's validity in general. In legal practice, "equity" serves to redress the injustices which would result from an inflexible application of substantive law. Shylock's demand for his pound of flesh is negated by explicit Judaic tradition: the Talmud (in the tractate *Baba Metzia*) declares that Jerusalem was destroyed because its inhabitants insisted on the fulfillment of the exact law rather than upon equity.

Contextualist flexibility of principle is not to be confused with the fallibilism which applies to moral judgments as it does to any other claims to knowledge (§26). Fallibilism holds that principles must give way in particular cases because the principles might be mistaken; contextualism holds that the meaning of the principles demands specification by particulars. Moral judgments are valid only *relative* to contexts. Flexibility is demanded of moral principles because these contexts cannot be exhaustively specified beforehand. In his *Ethics,* Spinoza points out that music is good to the melancholy, bad to those in mourning, and neither good nor bad to the deaf. Our judgments of the worth of music are not uncertain, but they are relative to circumstances.

The most significant component of the context to which a moral judgment is referred is the person involved. It is common for the one who makes the judgment to overlook this component by tacitly identifying it with himself, taking it for granted that judger and judged are alike. It is as though, being deaf, I do not say that *I* cannot hear and enjoy music but say rather that listening to music is pointless. Even when I am aware of the self-reference implicit in my judgment, I may make my personal interests the standard by which all values are appraised. There is need for the injunction in "The Revolutionist's Handbook" appended to *Man and Superman:* Do *not* do unto others as you would that they should do unto you. Their tastes may not be the same.

Relativism thus implies *pluralism,* the validity of different values, each referred to a different context. This contrasts with the axiom of linearity (§6) that if two valuations differ, one must be right and the other wrong.

Diversity of values does not necessarily imply conflict. Even where there is conflict of values, it need not be resolved only by force. Abjuring force, moreover, does not imply a weakening of the commitment to one's own values; the use of force is itself subject to a contextual judgment.

Pluralism is not a denial of the unique significance, for *me,* of *my* values. A pluralist can proclaim, with Zarathustra, "When you have a virtue, it is your virtue, you have it in common with no one. Speak thus, stammering: it is *my* good which I live, thus does it please me wholly, thus alone will I do the good." What saves such a position from subjectivism is the relativism which recognizes a plurality of values. As Zarathustra also declares, "'This is now *my* way—where is yours?' Thus did I answer those who asked me 'the way.' For *the* way—it does not exist!"

It is the absolutist who is thrown back upon subjectivism, for in his view, he alone has the principles by which moral judgments are validated. As a relativist, I recognize that your judgments, if they refer to a context of which you are a part, must differ from mine, referred to my context, in just the degree to which you and I differ from one another. The advice-giving idiom, "If I were you, I would . . ." is misstated; if I were indeed you, I would be doing just as you are. What is intended is, "If you were *me,* you would do what I am about to convey." The meaning of the qualifier is, "If I were in your situation"; but being other than you, I can never be precisely in your situation.

Contexts can be divided into three types. *Personal contexts* refer value judgments to situations defined by reference to an individual. A judgment made in such a context is not an expression of taste merely because both the judgment and the expression have a personal reference. It is one thing for me to say, "I like this," and quite another for me to say, "This is good for me." The first expresses a prizing or a valuation; the second formulates an appraisal or *e*valuation. Both the prizing and the appraisal are mine, in the sense of being made by me; the appraisal is also *about* me, while an expression of my prizing is not about me or about anyone else, because it makes no judgment about anything.

Standard contexts refer judgments to situations selected as reference points for the purposes at hand. Often the specification of a standard context is vague, as in making judgments about what would be good for the "normal," "healthy," or "average" person. Other common specifications refer to the "community," to various age-groups, or to a certain social or economic status. In aesthetic judgment (§82), the standard context is often the intended audience, or the audience more realistically expected. The distinction between personal and standard contexts can also be applied in the theory of knowledge. Perceptual qualities like visual shape are referred to a personal context when I speak of how something looks to me, and to a standard context when I describe the shape it would have when seen from a point straight above the center of the surface. Colors, similarly, are often referred to the standard context of daylight.

Ideal contexts maximize the values realizable in the situation. Here judgments refer to what would be good in the eyes of the sage or the man of taste and sensibility. Epictetus tells about someone who asked a philosopher whether he should perform in one of Nero's amateur theatricals. On receiving an affirmative reply, he asked again, "Why don't you yourself participate?" To which the philosopher's answer was, "For me the question never arises."

Which contexts are ideal, or approximate it, is not easy to say. There is the danger of arguing in a circle: "This is really good because it is so judged in an ideal context," and, "This is an ideal context because only what is really good is good relative to this context." There is also the danger of identifying as ideal some unique, all-inclusive context which negates relativism—the absolute perspective of metaphysical contextualism (§39). Philosophers as diverse as Heraclitus and Spinoza have held that to God all things are fair and good; only men hold some things to be ugly and wrong. It is only human judgments, however, which concern us, and judgments made only with reference to human contexts.

Repudiation of relativism is often motivated by an aspiration not to an ideal context but to a *universal* context. The absolutist may be less interested in the validity of his judgments than in being secure from adverse criticism because he is so insecure in his own values. Nietzsche, with his emphasis on the self-reliant individual, describes as "the worst of all tastes, the taste for the unconditional." There *are* values which serve as *relative absolutes*—valid for so wide a range of contexts as to invite reappraisal only in the most special circumstances. They are like the functional absolutes which serve as standards of measurement (§31). To use such a standard in making measurements we need not suppose it to have an absolute magnitude—we can measure the standard without circularity and improve the whole system of measures.

Contextualism is radically different from the relativism characteristic of the contemporary crisis in values (§50). *That* relativism is subjective; here we have an *objective relativism.* Values are relative to contexts, and so are as diverse as are people, cultures, and circumstances; but once the context is specified, whether or not something *is* a value relative to that context is objective. One man's meat is another man's poison; yet biochemistry and toxicology remain scientific disciplines. This fact is obscured by the loose usage common in this connection of something being "good for" someone, with the same relativist and subjectivist connotations of the expression "true for" someone (§27). The statement that x is good for a person A may mean three very different things.

1. It may mean that A prizes x, values it. In that case the statement belongs to descriptive ethics—a branch of psychology or sociology. If the statement is made by A himself, then the utterance may instead be an expression of taste, incapable of being true or false, only sincere or hypocritical.

2. The statement may mean that x is to A's interest, a means to his ends. Here A is a constituent of the context of a value judgment, whose formulation is a statement belonging to normative ethics or to moral doctrine. What the statement says depends on A only in the sense that it is

about A; the truth of the statement in no way depends on A. How he feels about x may be relevant to the value x has for him, but his feelings are not decisive; x may be good for A even if A does not prize it (the bitter medicine), or bad for him even if he does (the tasty poison). Suicides are not uncommonly found with their hands on the telephone or in the midst of other futile efforts to save themselves. "The consequences of our actions," say Nietzsche in his *Beyond Good and Evil*, "seize us by the forelock, very indifferent to the fact that we have meanwhile 'reformed.'"

3. A may be judging that x is good with respect to some unspecified context. His judgment does not make it so, even if he himself is a constituent of the context to which the judgment is referred. If the judgment made by A is sound, then that is the only sound judgment which can be made by anyone—true for one, true for all, except in the sense that the one in question knows the truth, sees it, proclaims it, or some such thing.

Ethical objectivity is perfectly compatible with relativism; it does not depend on the knowledge or existence of any absolute context. Neither does it depend on the existence of any transcendent value properties—properties lying altogether outside experience or accessible to experience only by way of some unique faculty such as moral intuition. The argument is often made that because everything in experience is ephemeral, variable, and conditional, values must derive from ideal entities outside experience. We might call this argument the *unnaturalistic fallacy*, the counterpart of the alleged "naturalistic fallacy" (§51) which the appeal to intuition is intended to avoid.

Plato is the most reputable of the secular philosophers guilty of the unnaturalistic fallacy. "The Idea of the Good is ultimate and needs an effort to be seen," he says, "but once seen, compels the conclusion that here is the cause, for all things else, or whatever is beautiful and right." To this, Aristotle's realistic objection seems to be unanswerable: "How will he who has contemplated the Idea of the Good itself be a more skillful physician or a more able general?" Human goods are always concrete and specific. As for the argument that in experience, goods are transient and imperfect, and so derivative from eternal, ideal goods (§3), Aristotle rejoins that something white forever is no whiter than that which lasts but for a day.

In short, values have their local habitation neither in the mind of man nor in the empyrean; they are as much a part of nature as are the other "facts" from which metaphysical commitment has abstracted them. What is at stake here is not metaphysical correctness but the effectiveness of efforts to improve man's lot. I wholeheartedly share the concern with these efforts which was so central to the pragmatism of James and Dewey. "God only knows how many of the sufferings of life," Dewey wrote (in *Essays in Experimental Logic*), "are due to a belief that the natural scene and operations of our life are lacking in ideal import, and to the consequent tendency to flee for the lacking ideal factors to some other world inhabited exclusively by ideals. Such a cut-off, ideal world is impotent for direction and control and change of the natural world."

Russell was as deeply committed as the pragmatists were to improving man's lot and agreed with them in repudiating unnaturalism. Yet human desires and aspirations, as the pragmatists in turn agreed, do not determine truth, and the truth, Russell was convinced, lies with an emotivist theory of value rather than with a naturalist theory. The *ethical dualism* between facts and values, propositions and imperatives, beliefs and attitudes avoids the metaphysics of the unnaturalistic fallacy, while still denying that values have any place in nature.

Naturalistic ethics invokes a distinctive conception of nature. What we identify as facts implicates human purposes—not only those involved in making the identification but also those giving meaning to all our conceptualizations (§32). Purposes, in turn, engender and validate values. Physics abstracts from value properties, for they are properties relative to a set of contexts very limited from a cosmic viewpoint; but physics is not the whole of science. That the guides to action provided by disciplines like psychiatry and economics are either unclear or controversial does not indicate that values lie outside science but only that what we know so far about values belongs to a primitive stage of scientific thought. We would be foolish to abandon the enterprise before it is well begun.

Paradoxically, less scientific cultures than ours have been more thoroughgoingly naturalistic. This is true of the Chinese culture given expression by Confucius and Mencius. "The way of Heaven is evident," said Confucius. "Let me not say that it is high aloft above me. It ascends and descends about our doings," he adds, in imagery reminiscent of the angels on Jacob's ladder, who mounted up to Heaven before coming down to earth, as though they had been here to start with. The question asked by the Deuteronomist, "What great nation is there that has a god so near to it as our God is to us whenever we call upon Him?" seems to be directly answered, in a nontheistic idiom, by these further words of Confucius: "Is virtue indeed so far off? I crave for virtue, and lo! it is at hand."

At any rate, it can be brought near. Moral knowledge, like knowledge of other truths, is fragmentary, but it is not altogether lacking, and our store can be progressively enriched. Society is undergoing widespread and radical change; many cultures are interacting, so that many values are being questioned. Yet the situation does not warrant wholesale skepticism. A foundation for values is lacking only if the condition is laid down that the foundation must be absolute. It is this arbitrary condition which is responsible for the crisis in values; absolutism is itself the disease for which it pretends to be the cure. The logic of the situation is identical with that for knowledge in general (§22). Since Hume, generations of philosophers have been convinced that there is no rational basis for expecting the sun to rise tomorrow; yet men have sensibly planned for the morrow and taken pains to improve their predictions. Judgments of value have no more shaky a foundation than judgments about other matters of fact.

But no less shaky, either! Knowledge is as hard to come by in the domain of values as anywhere else, but values can rest only on knowledge. Whatever virtue may be, it is not identical with innocence. An age-old polarity between city and country identifies wickedness with urban ways and morality with rural habits—a classification which has little in it but age-old prejudice. The word "sophistication" derives from the same root as the word "philosophy." Morality is not the product of naïveté and ignorance, however well intentioned. The tree in the Garden is the tree of *knowledge* of good and evil, after all.

The reason knowledge is so important to morality is that we must know what is to be done if our actions are to have promise, and we must know how to do it if the promise is to bear fruit. Values are not antecedently guaranteed, either in a preexistent realm of the ideal or in a preordained era of fulfillment. If we are to solve any of our problems, or cope with our predicaments, we can rely only on our own efforts. Golda Meir made a characteristically straightforward reply in this vein to the question whether she believed in prayer, instead of evasions like, "Every day I pray for peace," or "Knowing our drivers, I pray every time I enter an automobile!" Israeli naturalism is perhaps better represented by the words attributed to the rabbi of Safed, when that city was faced with imminent capture during the War of Independence. "Not to worry! We will be saved either through natural means or by a miracle. The natural means will be if God delivers us, as He always has; the miracle will be if the army arrives on time!"

Values can be attained only through appropriate action, not by exhortation or by the magic of symbols. Pious pronouncements of the desirability of moral solutions to our problems do not themselves constitute such solutions. The celebration of Brotherhood Week is more an expression of community than a contribution to its attainment, and peace has seldom been secured only by demonstrations and slogans. The basic thrust of ethical naturalism is its insistence, in Dewey's words, that "ideals are continuous with natural events, they but represent their possibilities, and recognized possibilities form methods for a conduct which may realize them in fact." To attain to such a realization, we must know what is in fact true.

56. Ethical Humanism

The truths of morality are truths about man. Job may not have been comforted, but he ought to have been instructed when he was told, "Your wickedness concerns a man such as you are; your righteousness, a human being." Our word "ethics" comes from the Greek for character or habit; the Chinese ideogram for ethics comes from that for man, and the sign for morality from that for the heart. A naturalistic approach to ethics is necessarily a humanistic approach. Ethics deals with human conduct, especially with man's conduct towards his fellowmen. Not only the meaning of moral judgments but also their validity derives from man—his makeup, his aspirations, and his ways of striving to fulfill them.

Human desires are a necessary condition of moral value. This is not the whole of ethical naturalism, however. The existence of a desire is a necessary condition for the existence of a value, but it is not a sufficient condition. Desire can give meaning to a value judgment, but the validity of the judgment depends on all desires that come into play in a broad and long-range perspective. To determine what these desires are and how action will bear upon them is the basic task of moral deliberation.

This task cannot be performed abstractly with anything like the required specificity. One can speak generally only of how human desires shape action and how people are likely to seek to satisfy those desires—in short, *human nature.* This has been the central concept of ethical theory for moral philosophers in every culture. "Human nature is God-given," said Confucius; "to fulfill the law of our human nature is what we call the moral law." So with Spinoza, who defines virtue as "nothing but acting according to the law of our own nature." Similar formulations abound in the writings of Aristotle and Dewey, and of Hindu, Jewish, and Christian thinkers.

Romanticism and existentialism give to the concept of human nature a personal reference. Their version of ethical humanism might be called *romantic individualism.* Morality here is grounded in the specific nature of the individual moralist. Subjectivism is reinstated as a basis for pride and even defiance. "No law can be sacred to me but that of my nature," Emerson wrote in his essay, "Self-Reliance." "The only right is what is after my constitution; the only wrong, what is against it." What if his constitution makes him vicious or foolish? It begs the basic question for a person to maintain that in *his* case these failings are ruled out by definition. *Candida's* James Morell is more consistent (if his vows as a clergyman are excluded) with his confession, "I like a man to be true to himself, even in wickedness." For my part, if a man is wicked, I would rather he were false to his nature.

A fable tells of a scorpion making its way across the countryside, till it came to a river. Approaching a frog, the scorpion said, "I can't swim; please take me on your back across the river!" "Certainly not!" said the frog. "In the middle of the river you'll bite me and I'll drown." "Where would be the logic of that?" the scorpion demanded; "I asked your help only because I can't swim; if you drown, I'll drown too." "True," said the frog; "all right, jump on," and together they started across. In the middle of the river the scorpion bit the frog, and they both began to drown. "Where is logic now?" asked the frog. Came the reply, "I couldn't help it; it's my nature." I recently heard a more topical version; the scorpion's last words are, "Ah, but you forget this is the Middle East!" Beneath the illusion of self-fulfillment may lurk a reality which destroys itself and all around it.

The individual cannot claim to constitute a moral standard. Neither can a statistical aggregation of individuals; the common cold, no matter how common it is, remains pathological. Yet frequency is some guide to the norm. It has happened more than once that a certain fossil was thought to represent a diseased condition of the organism until the discovery of other fossils of the same species, all with the same apparent deformity, led instead to a revision of our ideas. A practice should not be imposed upon a community, Hillel held, no matter how laudable it might be, unless most members of the community could conform to it. Confucius was similarly realistic: "I know now why the moral law is not understood. The noble natures want to live too high, high above their moral ordinary self; and ignoble natures do not live high enough, that is, not up to their moral ordinary self." Recognizing the inadequacy of the merely ordinary as a measure of value, he adds, "There is no one who does not eat and drink, but there are few who really know flavor."

The nineteenth century compensated for its emphasis on the individual by a heightened awareness of the group, especially on a biological basis. *Evolutionary ethics* spoke of the development of higher species as a fundamental goal with reference to which lesser purposes could be assessed. "Improvement of the breed" is still the conventional rationalization for horse racing, which could not be countenanced by our moralistic society if it were frankly acknowledged as an occasion for betting. Nietzsche's exhortations to live for the coming of the "Superman" led by a straightforward political psychology, however perverted the logic, to racist ideologies, genocide, and what is still in some quarters euphemistically called "eugenics." Evolution destroys some species in creating others, and which is morally more fit to survive is irrelevant. External standards of value are tacitly presupposed by evolutionary ethics. Nature, red in tooth and claw, is not enough in itself to define virtue.

Contemporary versions of biologically based ethical theories take life and growth as the basic values; we might call them the philosophies of *salutary ethics.* For Albert Schweitzer it was a lived philosophy as well as professed: "Ethics is the maintaining of life at the highest point of development—my own life and other life—by devoting myself to it in help and love." The spirit of this definition is conveyed by the moving slogan, "War is not healthy for children and other growing things." On the individual level, salutary ethics also finds expression in such categories as the "nourishing" and "noxious" personality. On its metaphysical side, the approach is close to that of Aristotle, whose concept of "entelechy" is the fulfillment of the potentialities inherent in each thing, after its kind. But ethical theory must take into account that man has potentialities for evil just as for good. We do not develop only in accord with our better natures; cancers also grow.

In modern times humanistic ethics relies more on psychology than on biology, especially on psychoanalytic psychology. A certain historical sequence of concepts of human failings is popularly recognized. First the challenge to religion is met by the claim that religion is a necessary basis for morality; then morals are justified by their importance for social order; finally, the norms of society, or proposed improvements on social norms, are defended as essential to the healthy development of personality. What was once identified as sin comes to be regarded as vice, then as crime, and is finally diagnosed as illness.

The contribution of depth psychology to the understanding of human nature is immense. Its contribution to humanistic ethics is correspondingly great, but in what respects is open to question. The dictum of Socrates is that the unexamined life is not worth living; psychoanalysis adds that the unlived life is worth examining. But does the examination disclose a basis for moral action? Freud's triad of id, ego, and superego suggests the ethical theories of Nietzsche, Bentham, and Kant, respectively; all three components of personality must somehow be taken into account. Just how is not fully determined by the needs of a healthy personality. As Erich Fromm, Rollo May, and other humanistic psychologists have urged, psychoneurosis may be a mark of moral failure, but mental health is not necessarily a mark of moral achievement. Therapy may succeed in making moral choice possible; it does not make *im*moral choice *im*possible. Not every villain is a neurotic; if we psychoanalyze a scoundrel, all we can be sure he will become is—a psychoanalyzed scoundrel.

Moral categories cannot be replaced by the categories of illness and health, nor does ethical humanism imply such a replacement. That would indeed constitute the naturalistic fallacy (§51). The human nature invoked as a basis for ethics is a *normative* nature. Distinctive norms *are* called for by ethical theory, but the norms are defined and validated in terms of human aspirations and their fulfillment. Denial of norms is expressed in the superficial aphorism that to understand all is to forgive all; the truth is that sometimes the better we understand an action the less forgivable we see that it is. What wisdom demands is the recognition—found in Spinoza, for example—that it may be as much a part of a man's nature for him to be ungrateful as for a snake to bite the one who warmed it in his bosom; but ingratitude is no less a vice for being part of a man's nature, as the venom is no less poisonous for being characteristic of the species.

Moral responsibility remains an autonomous category (§63). A madman cannot be held morally accountable, and more subtle illnesses than mania may be at work. The legal specification of knowing the difference between right and wrong, and knowing what one is doing, is far from enough to warrant the imputation of moral responsibility, as is also recognized in the legal formula for "acting under an irresistible compulsion." The absence of such compulsions and other marks of psychopathology means only that a person is capable of bearing responsibility, that he is a moral agent, in other words. It certainly does not determine what he can be held responsible for, what his duties are, and why.

This determination can only be made by careful deliberation in particular cases, and cautious generalization from the particulars. Humanism is the view that the basic data for this deliberation concern human satisfactions. Naturalism adds that these satisfactions provide data but not, in themselves, conclusions. Corresponding to the distinction between prizing and appraising, or between valuing and evaluating, is a distinction between what is merely *satisfying* and what is truly *satisfactory*. Things desired are not *ipso facto* desirable, and unrecognized values may be worthy of higher regard than values widely acknowledged—as the history of art amply documents. A satisfaction bears the same relation to a good as an appearance does to a reality (§39). What we see may be distorted or even wholly illusory, and what is real may be unseen, or seen but in part or darkly. Reality is not to be counterposed to appearance but understood as the orderly sequence of appearances under endlessly varying conditions; and just so with goods and satisfactions. Paralleling the positivist formula which characterizes matter as the permanent possibility of sensations is the characterization of a good as a permanent possibility of human satisfactions.

It is important for value theory in general, and more especially for aesthetics, to recognize that even the affirmation of a satisfaction, without the judgment that something is satisfactory, also makes a cognitive claim. There are not only expressions of taste but also *statements of taste.* The expressions are essentially interjections, however elaborate the rhetoric in which they are couched; the statements are as propositional as any other judgment about matters of fact. A statement of taste reports or claims to report an appearance of a value. Whether or not the appearance is of a reality is the subject of a value judgment; both sorts of statements are equally capable of being true or false.

Something may have looked red though it be false that it really was red—the light misled us, it was casting a reflection, it has been painted over, and so on. But we may also be mistaken in supposing only that something *looks* red—the thing we are referring to was secretly replaced by another, what we remember as red is in fact a different color, what we are experiencing is not due to what we think we are looking at but to an electrode in our brain, and so on. In the same way, we may be wrong not only in judging that something is satisfactory but also in supposing that it is satisfying. Regardless of whether we know what is good we may not know what we like—perhaps because we do not know *what* we are liking, or even because what we are mistaking for a positive feeling is an unconscious reaction-formation to an intensely negative one.

Those who subscribe to the axiom of direct experience (§24) presume that I alone can be the judge of what I am feeling, although it is almost as familiar to everyday experience as to clinical observation that often we do not know what we feel. There is substance to the jibe that one psychiatrist greets another with the words "You're feeling fine today! How am I?"

Subjectivism has gone so far in our time as even to deny that there is any objective difference between mental illness and health. It is one thing to criticize the use of vague diagnostic categories, especially their interpretation as designating fixed abstract entities. It is quite another to suppose that the diagnoses express only the personal values of the clinician or the norms of his culture. Such factors admittedly play a part, and can becloud judgment, but there *are* valid objective judgments to be made. Cultures vary in their response to illness; certain illnesses may even be prized and confer social advantages on their victims. The blind man may be venerated as a visionary, and one who is downright mad may be revered as a saint; the madness is nevertheless as objective a fact as the blindness, and as objectively a pathological condition, although the facts may be much harder to establish in the one case than the other.

So far as ethics is concerned, however, these are not the facts to be established; madness may have its insights after all, and many a leader has been driven by neurosis. Illness need not infect the entire personality; the rest may function more effectively than ever. What is to be established is whether the person who preaches to us is a true or a false prophet: the problem for ethics is a moral problem, not a psychiatric one. The problem is seldom so easily solved as in the case of Elijah, who, on Mount Carmel—very near to where I am sitting at this moment—confronted the false prophets of Baal and proposed the test: "You call on the name of your god and I shall call on the name of the Lord; the god who answers by fire, He is God." At any rate, the test is always empirical, as Matthew later expounds, "You will know the false prophets by their fruits; are grapes gathered from thorns, or figs from thistles?" Even for humanistic ethics, it is not the person who validates his morality, but his moral teaching which reveals the person.

The great failing of the reliance on experienced satisfactions is that so often the experience relied on is only retrospective. The approach is empirical but not experimental. It can therefore conserve old values but is unable to encompass the vision of the new. Accepted social norms are taken to be established, not merely in the sense of having been long accepted but in the sense of having been validated. The idiom, "It's simply not done," enjoins a value rather than only reporting a fact about our doings. In all societies mores are moralized, and custom becomes compulsion. Those who conspicuously depart from conventions even of dress are regarded as lost to all decency, as though to say, "If they dress like that, they'll do anything!" What described itself as "the American tribal love-rock musical" was pointedly called *Hair,* a name which would have made as much sense to the Roundheads and Cavaliers of seventeenth-century England as it does to us today. No doubt they had their witticisms then too, corresponding to our sally that so-and-so is getting too old to wear a beard. A few years go, a man could become a rebel as soon as he was old enough not to shave.

In every society, moral practice, if not moral doctrine, makes a cardinal virtue of obedience. Just as hospitals identify as a "good" patient not one whose condition is improving but one who does not make difficulties for the medical and nursing staff, a "good" boy is one who is no trouble to his parents or aging relatives; the categories of a "good student" and "good citizen" may similarly degenerate in meaning. The underlying point of view is that authority has already determined what we are to do and that the determination has been made adequately once for all.

This point of view has also been widely shared by philosophers. Nietzsche's criticism has much justification: "That which philosophers called 'giving a basis to morality' has proved merely a learned form of good faith in prevailing morality, a new means of its expression." The method of Socrates was to bring to awareness the basic Ideas by means of questions designed to disclose to his hearers the content of the Ideas underlying their own familiar experiences. This assumes that the virtue words, like "justice," have a fixed meaning, and that once this meaning is grasped we will have enough understanding to resolve the moral issues confronting us. The objection naturalism raises is that there are no value properties as such, no Ideas of value to provide meanings for our moral vocabulary; what is involved is the function in conduct of events and processes continuous with the rest of nature. An additional objection is that moral quality is as variable as are the contexts in which it is to be attained. There is no point to exhortations to do what is right, as though there is no question what that is. "In fact the most profound lack," as Dewey says, "is not the will to act upon goods already known but the will to know what they are." What everybody knows, especially the knowledge embodied in established usage, verbal or behavioral, is simply not enough.

Negation of accepted values—characteristic of rebellion—is also not enough. Nietzsche's "transvaluation of values," according to which what he calls the Christian "slave morality" is to be replaced by a "master morality," is not a liberation from dogma but the replacement of one dogma by another. "Because of our traditions," Tevye explains, "everyone knows who he is and what God expects him to do." There may be good reason to challenge the claim of tradition that it speaks in the name of God; but tradition is not to be repudiated for no better reason than that it is traditional. Social norms are facts which, for better or worse, must be taken into account in our deliberations. We may find that they are for the worse, but this is not to be presupposed any more than we can prejudge them to be justified. What is to be rejected is not traditional morality but what Dewey calls *customary morality*—morality which is not only a matter of tradition but which is followed only because it is traditional. What is needed instead is *reflective morality*, in which moral judgments are weighed in the light of all we know of past human satisfactions and what we venture to predict about their future.

In the end, ethical theory, like other fields of philosophy, may have a prophetic function as well as an analytic one. It may be that its task is less to save a presupposed morality from skepticism or dogma than to unfold possibilities for moral advance. It is man who is to be saved—from his own inhumanity.

Chapter 9

Normative Ethics

57. The Measure of Man

Man's inhumanities—to himself as well as to other men—pose the major problems and predicaments of moral action. Moral achievement depends on man's potentiality for good, but man is undeniably and perhaps inescapably immoral. Whatever ethical theory we adopt, man and his ways form the chief content of moral judgment; the assessment is usually negative. In some views, it is unqualified condemnation.

Nietzsche characterizes man as the best beast of prey, to which William James adds that he is the only beast that preys systematically on its own species. Wars, massacres, and pogroms; beatings, tortures, and murders on an individual scale; enslavement, oppression, and exploitation on a social scale—a sorry record which makes up a large part of human history. Schopenhauer argues that we know what a savage, horrible beast man is from the magnitude of the task of taming and restraining him which we call civilization. Who could deny that man is still largely untamed and unrestrained? The observation that the missing link between the early hominoids and a truly civilized being is man himself depends more on honesty than on insight.

Especially abhorent from a moral standpoint is man's treatment of those to whom he might especially be expected to have moral obligations. All of us live under the curse of Cain; if we do not murder our brothers, neither do we acknowledge in our conduct that we *are* their keepers. Most wars are between neighbors, often with a common heritage as well as shared regional interests: the bloodiest conflicts are the civil wars; in most murders, the victim and his murderer were acquainted with one another, often intimately, as is also true of the victim of rape and the rapist. The closer man is to his fellows, the greater his inclination to prey upon them. Schopenhauer remarks that in Dante's *Divine Comedy,* the *Inferno* is far better written than the other two parts, which depict purgatory and paradise; no doubt, he urges, this is because Dante had a realistic model on this earth for the *Inferno*—with this difference from Hell, that on earth men are tortured, not by demons, but by other human beings. This is the point of the existentialist Hell presented by Sartre in his play *No Exit.*

What confronts us here is not human folly, great though that may be, but human depravity—shortcomings of character rather than of intelligence. The greater the intellectual resources man has at his disposal, the more dangerous he becomes. The stereotype of modern weaponry as a loaded gun in the hands of a child hardly does justice to the destructive impulses which have always been at work, nor to the magnitude of the destruction these impulses threaten. Here, even history fails us; someone said of the first researchers into nuclear bombs, "Those men are playing with dynamite!"

Ours is not the only culture nor the first generation to recognize and condemn man's pervasive immorality. On the walls of the temple of Apollo at Delphi, along with the injunction, Know Thyself, is also inscribed the proposition that most men are bad. The Koran describes man as "obstinate, stiff-necked, and rebellious." "It may be said of men in general"—thus Machiavelli—"that they are ungrateful and fickle, dissemblers, avoiders of danger, and greedy of gain . . . . You do not know the unfathomable cowardice of humanity, servile in the face of force, pitiless in the face of weakness, implacable before blunders, indulgent before crimes, and patient to the point of martyrdom before all the violence of bold despotism."

This unfathomable cowardice indulgent before crimes has become characteristic of life in our cities. A few years ago in New York a young woman was attacked and murdered in broad daylight and in full view of some hundreds of people; her cries for help went unanswered. Most of the onlookers—subsequent investigation disclosed—took it for granted that help had already been summoned; but it is also true that most of them simply "didn't want to get involved." People are unwilling to testify against apprehended criminals, not only because they fear the vengeance of the criminals' associates but also because of a more basic feeling—or rather, because of a lack of feeling. If modern society faces a moral crisis, fundamentally it is a crisis of *indifference.*

Indifference save where one's own interests are directly involved is displayed also by states and by lesser groupings. Appeals to the "general welfare" or the "public interest" commonly rationalize some private advantage; there is no nation in the world which can rely on world opinion or on an international body to recognize and respond to even the most elementary claims of justice, or to do more than politely "deplore" the most blatant and outrageous violations of human decency. Over a hundred years ago, in the introduction to his *Democracy in America,* Alexis de Tocqueville described the breakdown of political morality in words relevant today: "I cannot recall to my mind a passage in history more worthy of sorrow and of pity," he writes, "than the scenes which are happening under our eyes; it is as if the natural bond which unites the opinions of man to his tastes and his actions to his principles were now broken; the sympathy which has always been acknowledged between the feelings and the ideas of mankind appears to be dissolved, and all the laws of moral analogy to be abolished."

Is this the whole truth about man's propensities? Many philosophers have taken the position that man's intrinsic nature is not evil; it has become so only by the workings of social forces. "There is no man who is not good," Confucius held, "as there is no water which does not flow downwards. You can strike the water and it spashes upwards above your forehead, or you can force it up the hills. But is this the original nature of water and not just due to circumstances? You can make human nature turn to evil in the same way." The followers of Confucius were divided on this issue, a "realistic" wing identified with Hsün-tzu and an "idealistic" one with Mencius. The idealists emphasized the role of poverty and want in driving man to crime and immorality: "If beans and rice were as plentiful as fire and water, such a thing as a bad man would not exist."

In the West, this Marxist view had antecedents in Rousseau and the romantics. The natural man, as romanticism conceived him, was contrasted with the product of civilization, but "civilized" did not connote, as it had for the Greeks, urbanity and refinement. It connoted the overcivilized: what is formalistic, unfeeling, and decadent. The innate goodness of man is corrupted by society: natural man reveals this innate goodness in his simple manners and morals. But the romantic myth of the "noble savage" only masked the savagery. The myth persists in contemporary neoromanticism, so that torture, murders, and massacres carried out by so-called revolutionaries are romanticized as glorious struggles for freedom.

One version of the romanticist conception of the relation between moral man and immoral society (a phrase of the modern Protestant theologian, Reinhold Niebuhr) condems the corrupting effect of technology. "God made man upright," says the Preacher, "but they have sought out many inventions." The same position was taken by the Taoist philosopher, Chuang-tzu, by Mahatma Gandhi, and by many other proponents of resistance to industrialism. It is the belief also expressed in the contemporary faddist preoccupation with handicrafts, organic foods, and the preindustrial decorative arts. An earlier generation blamed what it saw as pervasive immorality on the automobile, just as many moralists today attack television, computers, or nuclear reactors. Not man but the machine is seen as the primary locus of evil.

The argument on behalf of the innate goodness of human nature cannot be casually dismissed. "Can it be said," Confucius asks, "that the mind of any man is without a sense of sympathy and a sense of shame, benevolence and righteousness?" A man seeing a child in the path of an onrushing horse, or one who has fallen into a well—the traditional Chinese illustrations—will unhesitatingly come to the rescue, without thought of reward. If this innate benevolence and righteousness does not always express itself in action, it is only because of the deadening effect of the demands of our daily existence.

"The way in which a man loses his proper goodness of mind," Confucius goes on, "is like the way in which the trees are denuded by axes. Hewn down day after day, can the mind retain its beauty?" There may be more than metaphor in the notion of a moral ecology and moral pollution.

That man is naturally good is a conclusion which need not rest on romanticist premises. Even as uncompromising a realist and rationalist as Voltaire declared in his *Philosophical Dictionary* that man is not born wicked but becomes so "as he becomes sick." What are the germs of this disease? Romanticism says society, especially with reference to the constraints of civilization and the demands of technology. In both Hinduism and Buddhism, man, in his innermost being, is conceived as wholly good; to be born as a human being marks the beginning of the end of the long road to perfection, in life after life. To attain the goal, man need only free himself from the agencies of corruption. In Hindu thought, man is corrupted by *avidya*—metaphysical ignorance; in Buddhism, by *drsta* (from the same root as the English "thirst")—that is, passion or desire. In the realm of appearance man is ignorant and passionate, and therefore evil; but his true being is altogether good.

A similar position was taken by Socrates and developed by Plato. Man would always pursue the Good if there were no interference with his perception of the truth. Those who really know which acts are just and righteous would not be willing to do anything else, as no man knowingly prefers the worse to the better. Such knowledge is ingrained in the soul, which dwelt before birth in the world of Ideas, so that it need only recollect the truth and its intrinsic virtue will shine forth.

How this is to be accomplished remains problematic. Whatever theory may say, in practice virtue cannot be taught as is geometry; even the axioms remain obscure or uncertain, to say nothing of the theorems. Moreover, even if we are confident in our knowledge of what is good, we cannot always bring ourselves to act on what we know. Here the Asians are more realistic than Plato's intellectualism allows: man's innate goodness emerges only after intensive disciplines such as *sadhana, yoga, zazen,* and the like—disciplines which make demands not only on the mind but on the whole personality.

A third set of philosophies regards man as being intrinsically neither good nor evil. Instead, it views human nature as morally neutral, with potentialities for both good and evil. Morality is natural, but only as a potentiality; the proposition that man is a rational animal similarly means only that he is capable of rational behavior. "The virtues," said Aristotle, "are produced in us neither by nature nor contrary to nature, but we, being naturally adapted to receive them, perfect this natural capacity by habit. This is the role of education in the broadest sense: to perfect our natural capacities. Morality is natural to man, but man as educated by society, his impulses guided and transformed by the agencies of social control—family, school, church, state, and the rest. Childhood is innocent only in the sense of naïveté, not as being endowed with a native virtue. That we come to birth trailing clouds of glory, as Wordsworth has it in his Platonic ode, "Intimations of Immortality," is another romantic myth. The unthinking selfishness and cruelty of children is only less calculating and ingenious than that of which their elders are guilty. There is a subtle point in misreading the title of the poem as "Imitations of Immorality."

In his intrinsic nature man is neither moral nor immoral, but *a*moral; the same nature manifests itself in both virtue and vice. The impulses expressed in lust and greed, the Rabbis pointed out, are the same ones which lead a man to raise a family and conduct a business; the passions which set man against man also make society possible. The key to understanding how moral attainment can rest on amoral foundations is the Freudian concept of *sublimation.* Morality is a product of socialization; what is extraordinary is that from time to time it can rise higher than its source. A similar interdependence of traditional attainment and creative advance can be traced also in science and in art (§28 and §78). That human nature includes, in addition to the impulses expressed in moral conduct, an innately destructive bent—like Freud's notion of a so-called "death wish"—is a view which has found little philosophical favor and even less empirical support.

To live outside society, Aristotle said in his politics, man would have to be either a beast or a god. In fact, he is neither; Pascal is not alone in observing that when man mistakes himself for a god he acts like a beast. Such an assessment, like the others discussed in this chapter, weighs man as a moral agent, one who makes and acts on moral judgments. We can also look upon man as an object of moral judgment, whose worth is to be taken. The second assessment is affected by the first: the more praiseworthy man's actions, the more he is to be prized. The two assessments are nevertheless logically distinct—it would be quite consistent to hold that men, on the whole, behave badly, yet embody in themselves the most precious essence in all the world.

This is the traditional religious view of man: that for all his shortcomings, there is in him an element of the divine. The proposition which declares man to have been created in the image of God has been pointed to as the most significant in all of Scripture. The Talmud cites the myth that whenever a man goes forth he is preceded by a company of angels calling out, "Make way for the image of God!" Man was made but a little lower than the angels, and all things have been put under his dominion. Elsewhere, the Talmud declares that wherever you come across the footprint of man, God stands before you. Robinson Crusoe might have done better to have given his man Friday the name "Sabbath," in recognition of his fellowman's essential holiness rather than to mark the accidental day of discovery; but that might have undermined the relation of master and servant so quickly assumed to be natural.

The religious assessment remains in our secularized culture, though the premises on which the assessment once rested are no longer universally assumed. Today disillusionment with humanity may be widespread, but Hamlet's rhapsody on man is as familiar in content as in its mode of expression: "What a piece of work is a man! How noble in reason! how infinite in faculties! in form and moving how express and admirable! in action how like an angel! in apprehension how like a god! the beauty of the world, the paragon of animals." The passage ends, however, with a bitterness shared by every victim of human stupidity, cruelty, and injustice: "And yet to me what is this quintessence of dust? Man delights not me; no, nor woman neither." In the next century, in his *Pensées*, Pascal expresses a frankly ambivalent assessment rather than a disillusionment: "What a chimera is man! What a novelty! What a monster, what a chaos, what a contradiction, what a prodigy! Judge of all things, feeble worm of the earth; depository of truth, a sink of uncertainty and error; the glory and shame of the universe."

The most defensible conclusion is that whatever man's worth, his value is inherent rather than only instrumental (§54). Man is to be cherished for what he is in himself, not for what we can do with him or how we can exploit his capabilities. Morality demands that we see every human being as a person, not simply as cannon fodder, sex object, slave, or taxpayer. This principle Kant formulated as another version of his categorical imperative (§52), the declaration of the fundamental duty on which morality rests: "Act so as to treat humanity, in yourself or any other, as an end always, and never as a means only."

That last word, "only," embodies an important qualification. Morality is not violated by finding instrumental value in man but by failing to find inherent value. It is not immoral to lean on another when I am falling; the immorality is in denying him any life other than as my crutch. Sexual morality, for example, does not imply that the body of another person may not be an instrument of pleasure; but it does imply that the other is a person, and not only an instrumentality, a nameless thing to be exploited.

Inherent values may be compared with one another as greater or less, and in principle quantified. The major religions and moral philosophies agree that man, however, is of measureless worth in the sense that his value is boundless, the locus of all other values. Commentators have remarked that there is a reason man was created by way of a single person, Adam, though the Creator could at once have called millions into existence. It was to teach that whoever destroys or saves even a single human life destroys or saves, as it were, a whole world. In Western tradition, moral teaching begins with Abraham, who transformed infanticide into a symbolic sacrifice whose reality is a dedication to the sacredness of human life. In Jerusalem there is a place where infanticide is supposed to have once been practiced, a place identified as the valley of Gehennom; this name afterwards took on the denotation of Hell. Damnation is the condition of every person who denies the humanity of other people by making them only the means to ends not of their own choosing.

58. Self and Other

Man is damnable—so it has widely been held—because he is so preoccupied with his own well-being as to give no thought to the welfare of others.

Among the issues thought to be central to the moral life, outranking even the supposed conflict between duty and desire, is that formulated in terms of the antithesis of selfishness and unselfishness, egoism and altruism. Man is a selfish creature, a slave to his own desires; duty demands of him that he act unselfishly, to satisfy the desires of others. The view that he is in fact selfish is known as *psychological egoism;* that this is right and proper, that he ought to be selfish, is called *ethical egoism.* If the psychological thesis is correct, the moral issue does not arise: there is no point in enjoining man to do what in any case he cannot help doing. The moral doctrine, while acknowledging an abstract possibility of acting otherwise, is usually defended by the argument that to act unselfishly is somehow perverted, like rejecting pleasure in favor of pain.

In the course of its defense, psychological egoism is sometimes so construed as to become a tautology. Whatever I choose to do I do because it pleases me to do so; therefore, the argument runs, I am, after all, only pleasing myself. Now, of course, my values are mine, in the sense of being valued by me; this truism, however, does not imply the falsehood that all I find valuable is me myself. Every interest of mine is not necessarily an interest in me. When I want to please someone it is *his* pleasure I want, though his getting that pleasure will please me. Satisfying my wants implies my satisfaction, but this says nothing about what I want. In short, the locus of each man's values is tautologically his self, but this self neither constitutes the values nor provides a measure of their worth.

There is no doubt that apparent acts of altruism sometimes are really egoistic. A child may offer his friend the first choice of a divided apple in the expectation that politeness will constrain the other to take the smaller piece; a businessman may contribute to a charity because of the tax deduction and because the advertisement will list him as donor. Yet the child may learn to share, and the benefaction may come to be made anonymously and even survive changes in the tax laws. Indeed, apparently egoistic acts sometimes are really altruistic: a sense of duty does sometimes disclaim the reward which was the apparent motive. Both selfish and unselfish behavior are possible.

Suppose the argument were granted that all human beings are inescapably selfish, because each does what, under the circumstances, he himself pleases to do. Then we can distinguish two sorts of people: those who rarely are pleased to do anything which aims at pleasing others, and those who rather often are pleased to please others. Both sorts of people, on this assumption, are selfish; the difference between them, however, is of considerable social importance, and presumably of moral significance as well. It has been suggested that we might mark the difference by using different words for such people—say, "belfish" and "unbelfish"; then everything which is traditionally expressed in terms of the distinction between selfish and unselfish behavior would be expressible, with no change in content, in terms of being belfish or unbelfish. All that has been accomplished by the thesis of psychological egoism is to universalize the domain of selfish behavior so as to rob the word "selfishness" of meaning; the original distinction might just as well be retained. This combination of tautology and falsehood is a fallacy to be met with in other contexts—for instance, in connection with hedonism (§45) and fatalism (§48).

Egoism is no longer tautological when it is considered dynamically, that is, from the standpoint of the changing dimensions of the self. The self is enlarged in the act of giving itself to another. The situation is not that I love only myself but that those whom I love thereby *become* part of me. The truth in psychological egoism is that insofar as I care about the other, he does not remain wholly other. The voice of my brother's blood cries out to me from the ground because that blood is my own—very well; but the sense of brotherhood is as much an *effect* of hearing that cry as it is its cause. Personal identity is, to a significant degree, the outcome of the investments we make in what once lay outside the self (§47). The injunction to love thy neighbor as thyself does not merely specify a degree, as though to say "as much as you love yourself"; it also specifies the quality of the lover. It is what I feel for my neighbor, how I impinge on all that lies about me, which makes me the person I am.

An understanding of the structure and dynamics of the self undercuts the significance of the supposed antithesis between egoism and altruism. The moral issue, as traditionally formulated, tacitly assumes that the ego is complete in itself, apart from what it takes from and gives to the other. The self-contained ego, seeking to express only what is already embodied within it—this is the central myth of romanticism. It is this ego, lacking all aspiration to anything higher than it can see in itself, which Nietzsche contemptuously dismised as a "refined swindle."

To care only for the self as it is already, is not to nurture it but to improverish it. The more inward turned we are, the less there is within to turn to. The psychoanalyst Jules Masserman reminds us that the nymph who sought Narcissus, and whom he rejected in favor of his own reflected image, was, after all, only his own Echo. Narcissism is a species of psychopathology in which the victim is fixated on an early stage of development, when infantile love has not yet learned to reach outside itself. The maxim of the Mountain King, "Troll, to thyself be—enough!" is a teaching fit only for trolls: inhuman, and making for a twisted and stunted growth. The moral task is not to replace self-love for the other but to achieve a self which identifies with the other. I am indeed my brother's keeper if I am man enough to keep him; to disclaim brotherhood is to be so much the less a man.

John F. Kennedy enjoined the citizen, "Ask not what your country can do for you; ask what you can do for your country." The less we do for our country, the less it is our homeland, the more merely a habitation. The moral dimension of much of the politics of our time is constituted by the struggle of many people to live in a land they can love, give themselves to, and thereby make their own. That every person has a right to a homeland I firmly believe. But that right cannot be defined by a prior presence—there was always someone there before. How far back into the past do such priorities reach? Who are the rightful heirs of Cro-Magnon and Neanderthal? A person can only *make* his home somewhere, as the self is only in the making. The *roshi,* asked the nature of the self, replied, "What would you do with a self if you had one?" The same rejoinder might be made in the political context.

The confusions and distortions in the traditional antithesis of egoism and altruism are especially pernicious in connection with the idea of *self-sacrifice.* Students of human nature from Aristotle to Spinoza and Freud have condemned self-sacrifice as unnatural and unfulfilling. Only a self arrested in its development is capable of rationalizing its own destruction; love can never be served by hatred, even of the self. What one man can give to another is, in the end, himself; if that has been destroyed, there is nothing left to give. The hand of Abraham was stayed from his son; God is served only by life. That the devotees of the god Jagannath fling themselves beneath the wheels of the chariot bearing his image is a traveler's tale; for the worshippers, death makes the temple unclean.

Self-sacrifice is not uncommonly associated with self-pity, for the sacrifice is typically unappreciated; immolation manages to surround itself with what it sees as ingratitude. What is there to be grateful for? Quite often the sacrifice of oneself is a device for the manipulation of others by way of the guilt it induces. Those who make the sacrifice often demand of others the same austerities they practice on themselves: notorious cruelties have been perpetrated by zealots with the excuse that they themselves live by the code they are imposing. In its pathological extreme, self-sacrifice may manifest a sado-masochistic perversion.

There is, to be sure, a genuine self-sacrifice which love sometimes calls for. A self incapable of sacrifice is incapable of love, but love cannot countenance the destruction of the self as a *proof* that it is loving. As an expression of love, the sacrifice must have a meaning transcending the destruction or self-denial: we love and are loved for reasons which lie outside the act of sacrifice. In truth, we cannot sacrifice to idols; for them, we can only destroy.

In the religious ideal of *selflessness* the antithesis of egoism and altruism becomes irrelevant. The unselfish man can say, "What is mine is yours," but for the selfless man neither "mine" nor "yours" has meaning. In selflessness we have transcended the principle of self-reference (§47): we no longer stand at the center of the world but look with detachment even at ourselves. This is what Spinoza called viewing the world *sub specie aeternitatis,* in the light of eternity. The capacity so to view the world has been regarded in many cultures as characteristic of the sage, especially in the Stoic, Buddhist, and Taoist ideals. It is not a matter of adopting an absolute perspective, mistaking oneself for God, but a fluidity of observational standpoints, the ability to look out upon the world through the eyes of any fellow creature, like the actor who can throw himself completely into any role, with no character of his own to interfere. In attaining to selflessness the self is not sacrificed; instead, self-seeking is consummated. "He that finds his life shall lose it, and he that loses his life for My sake shall find it." This is not a crude promise of Paradise for those who die in a holy war but points to the fulfillment in a life of selflessness.

On less than the highest spiritual level—that is, without transcending the self—there is a basic principle governing the relations of self and other for which most moral doctrines have a place. This is the *Golden Rule:* "Do unto others as you would have them do unto you"; the negative formulation ("Do not do unto others what you would not have them do unto you") is sometimes called the *Silver Rule.* Hillel says of the principle, "This is the whole of the Law; the rest is commentary." It is also to be found in Matthew and in Luther; in Zoroastrian, Hindu, Buddhist, Confucian, and Islamic writings; and in many secular philosophers, even those as unmoralistic as Thomas Hobbes.

Morality depends on the capacity to identify with others, if not so as to incorporate them in the self, at least so as to be able to do them justice. Hillel again speaks for a host of other moralists in the injunction not to condemn another man until we have stood in his place. The Golden Rule may also make for condemnation, as we identify ourselves with victims of *in*justice. Defects of identification—its absence or displacement—are widely responsible today for moral failings. Many people who think of their politics as shaped by high moral principles accept terrorism because they identify with the terrorists, not with the victims. There is a tacit assumption that someone with the "right" political views would never be a victim; but what is terrifying is precisely that the victims do not deserve to be victimized.

The Golden Rule is often defended as a counsel of prudence: do as you would be done by because you will be done by as you do. In Confucius there is an explicit formulation of *the principle of reciprocity:* what a man hates to receive on the left, let him not bestow on the right. That a man will receive what he gives is a special application of the doctrine of cosmic equilibrium (§51), the belief in the poetic justice grounded in the nature of things. Such a belief has a certain psychological justification: a loving man is likely to be lovable, and hateful when he hates. How a person acts, however, or how he is perceived as acting, is as much an effect of how he is reacted to by others as a cause of their reaction. As Eliza says, the difference between a lady and a flower girl is not how she behaves but how she is treated. "I shall always be a flower girl to Professor Higgins because he always treats me as a flower girl and always will. But I know that I shall always be a lady to Colonel Pickering because he always treats me as a lady and always will." A habitual liar will himself be lied to; but an honest man is also told lies, and what is worse, he does not recognize them as early or as often as the liar does.

Both justice and prudence support the Golden Rule but not enough to account for its universal appeal. We want others to deal with us kindly even though we are undeserving or powerless to retaliate. The Golden Rule is not enjoined as a matter of self-interest; it may even demand action contrary to self-interest (at least as this is initially defined). The same is true of the injunction to love one's enemy, whether or not it will weaken or win him. The teaching is in the Old Testament as well as in the New. Thus Exodus 23:4–5: "If you meet your enemy's ox or his ass going astray, you shall bring it back to him. If you see the ass of one who hates you lying under its burden, you shall help him to lift it up"; and Proverbs 25:21–22: "If your enemy is hungry give him bread, if he is thirsty give him to drink."

An enemy is one who does me evil; the Golden Rule nevertheless enjoins that I do him good, because that is what I would wish him to do for me. Here is a moral dilemma; when Confucius was asked what he thought of the doctrine of returning good for evil he rejoined, what are we to return for good? To respond alike to both good and evil means to make no moral discrimination between them; yet to return good only for good is to replace morality by utility and moral duty by contractual obligation. This is why the Gospels counter, If you love only those who love you, how are you different from the sinner? Even gratitude is a rare enough virtue; but when gratitude is only a lively sense of favors yet to come, as Ambrose Bierce defines it in his *Devil's Dictionary,* it ceases to be a virtue.

The doctrine of loving your enemy has been carried further. If your enemy strikes you on the right cheek, turn the left to him; if you are compelled to go with him one mile, continue for two; if he takes your coat, give him your shirt as well. To this morality there is an even greater objection than the failure to discriminate between good and evil. It is that by not resisting evil we encourage it. Is it loving the sinner to provide him with more occasion for sinning? In Shaw's *Androcles and the Lion,* the Christian prisoner Ferrovius, a man of obvious brute strength, is tauntingly struck on the face by a Roman dandy. After turning the other cheek Ferrovius says:

> The first man who struck me as you have just struck me was a stronger man than you; he hit me harder than I expected. I was tempted and fell; and it was then that I first tasted bitter shame. I never had a happy moment after that until I had knelt and asked his forgiveness by his bedside in the hospital. . . . God has greatly blessed my efforts at conversion. Shall I tell you a miracle—yes, a miracle—wrought by me in Cappadocia? A young man—just such a one as you, with golden hair like yours—scoffed at and struck me. I sat up all night with the youth wrestling for his soul; and in the morning not only was he a Christian, but his hair was as white as snow.

Shaw is more realistic here than cynical; fear is more readily seen to work miracles than love. Yet this is a matter of argument. The teaching agreed to by Jew, Hindu, and Buddhist as well as by Christian is that we can overcome evil by good and hatred by love. It was the teaching promulgated by men as diverse as Mahatma Gandhi and Martin Luther King; perhaps it is not irrelevant that both, like Jesus himself, were killed. It may be that here, too, as in the replacement of altruism by selflessness, we transcend moral obligation to rise to the demands of religion.

Whatever religion calls for, morality depends on a sense of self, at least sufficiently strong to make us aware how different from ourselves others may be. As was pointed out in connection with pluralism (§55), there is a paradox in the Golden Rule: if I am to treat others as I would be treated, I must treat them differently than I myself want to be treated, for they are different from me, and I want *my* differences to be acknowledged and respected. Love chooses the gift the beloved would prize, not what the giver would wish to receive. Men differ in their tastes and interests, in temperaments and life-styles, in their situations and their stages on life's way, in value scales, philosophies, and aspirations. Ignoring or overriding such differences typifies man's inhumanity to man. Those who claim to be acting for my good are often ignorant of or indifferent to *my* vision of the good.

A sense of the self is important in another way. The injunction to love thy neighbor as thyself is not fulfilled by the person who hates his neighbor and offers the justification that he hates himself as well. Far from condemning what is superficially called "egoism," morality recognizes in self-love the prerequisite to all forms of love. If I cannot be true to myself I will betray all others. From Nietzsche onward this has been a theme of existentialism, reinforced by the depth psychology of the past hundred years. "To love oneself in the right way and to love one's neighbor," said Kierkegaard, "are at bottom one and the same." Karl Jaspers declares, "The other can only thrive when I myself become all that I am capable of being." In Martin Buber we have, "Without being and remaining oneself there is no love." The Hassidic Rabbi Sussya said, "When I am called to account, I will not be asked, 'Why were you not Moses?' I will be asked, 'Why were you not Sussya?'"

The basic role in morality of self-love is not limited to existentialism and romanticism. For Confucius, the "cultivation of the person" is "the root of everything besides." Spinoza declares that "the first and only foundation of virtue, the rule of right living, is seeking one's own true interest." Even the traditional morality of so-called "altruism" recognizes that charity begins at home and that blood is thicker than water. Aristotle unabashedly formulates the Golden Rule as applying to one's friends, not to men in general. At the very least, it is widely recognized that concern about oneself and one's own is not necessarily immoral. Everything depends on the nature and limits of that concern.

One should love oneself in the "right" way and seek his "true" interest. Here moral issues arise again. Which way is the right one? Which of my interests are truly to my interest? Nietzsche attacked the traditional virtues, as, for instance, protecting the weak and helpless, as belonging to what he called a "slave morality," and enjoined instead a "master morality" of pride in one's own strength. But it is the man confident in his strength who is most capable of gentleness. The will to power—in interpersonal relations, if not among states—may motivate chiefly the powerless and reflect anxious self-appraisal rather than secure acceptance of oneself. One need not choose between being master and slave; loving oneself in the right way is a way which impels us to love others also, as our equals in a shared humanity.

Romanticism and existentialism enjoin a morality of *self-realization:* cultivating the self, perfecting it, fulfilling its potentialities. Become what you are! says Zarathustra. Such formulations are broad enough to accommodate most of the world's religions as well as its secular moralities. This generality makes of "self-realization" a question-begging ideal; to guide conduct, the general must be made specific, and which specifications are called for is problematic. Like the salutary ethics (§56) which presupposes a conception of "health," the ethics of self-realization presupposes a conception of growth or self-improvement. What one man pursues as a cultivation of the self another may eschew as its corruption (for instance, the use of "mind-bending" drugs); what one society applauds as the perfection of the self another may condemn as its degradation (for instance, celibacy). The self has potentialities for evil as well as for good; he who cultivates himself may be producing only a poisonous growth.

Moralities fixated on the self ask who is to say what is the right way of self-love, what is truly to one's interest—"who" is to say, rather than on what objective basis to say it. An autonomous self must decide for itself what values to pursue; there is no delegating to another the responsibility for choices each moral agent must make for himself. On what basis is the choice to be made? Romantic individualism holds that the self not only defines values for itself; it defines them in terms of itself. The self measures values; it is also their measure. Here egoism passes into egotism, and self-seeking becomes complacency and conceit. We do not always serve the gods, but we always make divinities of what we serve; those who set out to perfect the self end in self-worship.

Oscar Wilde's blatant egotism may have shocked his Victorian contemporaries, but probably for the wrong reasons—that there is something immoral in thinking well of oneself, or at least something improper in saying so. But this misses the point. Wilde was undoubtedly right that to learn to love oneself is to lay the foundations for a lifelong romance. The real question is whether such a romance, however enduring, has anything more in it than sustained self-deception. Is the object of this love worthy of our devotion? W. H. Auden remarks that Narcissus may well have been a hydrocephalic idiot who, gazing at his reflection in the pool, concluded, "On me it looks good!" The root error of egotism is that it is not sufficiently egoistic: if we make the self the standard of value, we preclude the possibility of truly caring for it since it makes no sense to seek to improve upon perfection. The "libertines of self-love," as Rousseau called them in *Emile,* his treatise on education, are as incapable of love, when all is said and done, as are any other libertines. They are not drawn by Eros in a vision of Beauty and the Good but are driven by the unending frustrations to which in their inward turning they have condemned themselves.

In the end there is no denying the centrality of the self in the moral life because of its autonomy and also because of its role in providing substance to our loving. To love is to give something of ourselves, having made it worthy of acceptance. This centrality of the self may be summed up in the existentialist virtue of *authenticity,* in which the following components may be discriminated:

1. *Responsibility.* The authentic self recognizes and assumes responsibility for its moral choices. Since an act is not truly chosen unless it is responsibly undertaken (as was urged by Spinoza), it can be said that an authentic self lives the life it chooses for itself. Here is the intimate connection between freedom and responsibility, as between autonomy and authenticity. A paradigm of the lack of authenticity is provided by the man who,

imagining he was ready to embark on a new life, yet ashamed to acknowledge his former follies, explained to the Master that he was confessing on behalf of a friend. "Your friend is a fool," the Master said to him; "he could have come to me himself and told me that he was speaking for a friend." Here was not a petty triumph but a stroke which went at once to the heart of the matter. So long as the actions are imputed to another, nothing has changed. Morality can begin only with authenticity, but an authentic person does not need, and cannot accept, absolution from another.

2. *Honesty.* Self-deception is as much an enemy of morality as is spurious self-love; and each of them is impossible without the other. A person can remain locked within the self only under the illusion that it already has everything within it, and perpetuate illusion only if he is indifferent to reality. Maintaining a strict fast on Yom Kippur is notoriously a matter of appearances, for the weaker worshippers surreptitiously refresh themselves. Even if it is real, denial of the flesh does not necessarily nourish the spirit. Whatever be the nature of the good, truth about oneself is indispensable to valid moral judgment.

3. *Self-respect.* Contempt for the self makes moral endeavor futile and pointless. This is the core of correctness in the emphasis on egoism to be found in many moral philosophies, from Hobbes and Spinoza in the seventeenth century to the romantics and existentialists of the nineteenth and twentieth centuries. The prayer listing the sins being confessed is in the form of an alphabetical acrostic, it has been explained, not only to assist the memory—it is easy to forget our shortcomings—but also so that eventually we come to a definite end of the list and leave a basis for self-respect.

What is rightly called a "healthy egoism" is far from megalomania or even from moderate egotism. The relevant difference between egoism and egotism is that between pride and vanity: pride is what an autonomous self finds worthy in itself, while vanity is the spurious self-esteem which insecurity wants to see reflected in the eyes of others. A corresponding distinction may be drawn between humility and modesty, humility autonomously recognizing the limitations of the self, while modesty introjects the low opinion insecurity anticipates from others. Modesty and vanity are counterparts, as pride and humility are linked in a realistic self-awareness. "What is man that you are mindful of him?" asks the Psalmist in his humility; his pride continues "yet you have made him but a little lower than the angels and have crowned him with glory and honor." Only a self capable of both the question and the rejoinder is capable of moral aspiration; but for such a self, moral aspiration has already come to fulfillment.

59. The Human Heart

Man is a social animal; solitary confinement, whatever its setting, is a cruel punishment; we need one another. Widely told is the story of the note found tied to a rock lying just outside the walls of the orphanage and reading, "Whoever finds this, I love you!" We live behind our own stone walls, repeatedly sending out the message but often forgetting to attach the note to the rock. We need others for what they can give to us and for what we have to give to them as well. A man needs someone to talk to; even more, he needs someone to love. It is these needs which make for the internalization of the other. Caring for the other is both condition and consequence of caring for the self. Self and other are intimately bound up (§46 and §58); in embracing the other we fulfill ourselves.

The talmudic sage, Akiba, showed psychological insight as well as moral sensitivity in designating as the most important single verse in Scripture the injunction to love thy neighbor (Leviticus 10:18). The same injunction was promulgated by Thales, and Aristotle remarked that we praise those who love their fellowmen. Confucius, on being asked the meaning of virtue, replied, love of one's fellows; the principles of *chung* and *shu*—conscientiousness to others and altruism—are central in Confucian thought; Mencius sees in benevolence the distinguishing characteristic of man. Compassion is the cardinal virtue in Buddhism; loving care for others is basic to Christianity, is enjoined in the Koran, and in one form or another is to be found in virtually all moral doctrines.

In all of them, moreover, special emphasis is placed on *charity*. "If there be among you a needy man," in the words of Deuteronomy, "you shall not harden your heart, nor shut your hand in his face." "Give and it shall be given unto you," say the Gospels; Paul adds, "Though I speak with the tongues of men and of angels and have not charity, I am become as sounding brass or a tinkling cymbal." In the Talmud, the practice of charity is declared to be equal in importance to the fulfillment of all the other commandments put together: if the poor are invited to share our food, the dining table becomes an altar, and when a poor man stands at our door, God stands at his right hand. Charity is held to be so nearly the whole duty of man that even a beggar who lives on alms is enjoined to bestow alms himself on others more needy than he.

In the extended sense of goodwill, leniency, and tolerance, charity is unexceptionable, but in its narrow sense of gifts of goods and services it faces objections. Easily dismissed is the popular myth of the beggar who possesses secret hoards, a myth which rationalizes the lack of charitableness towards those whose need is beyond suspicion. Beggary, in some cultures, is a profession, adopted not from need but by choice; deformities may be deliberately produced. Charity thus encourages parasitism and the ignoble exploitation of the most noble impulses.

More important is the objection that charity ameliorates inequities, but does nothing to get at their causes. The poor we need not always have with us; guaranteed annual wages, negative income tax, social services, and full employment will accomplish more than the most widespread charitable dispositions. The Community Chest and similar campaigns have little justification, for from a social standpoint they are palliatives which hardly warrant the energies expended in them, and from a psychological standpoint they are too impersonal to have moral significance. Yet, not giving might encourage indifference to human needs and hardheartedness in response to the suffering of others. In India and elsewhere I have many times faced the dilemma of turning away from the outstretched hand of obvious hunger, misery, and disease or else interfering with governmental efforts to provide productive work, health care, and salutary life patterns. Whether charity in these circumstances is sentimental self-indulgence or truly caring is a question which I have never resolved.

Concern for the well-being of others is as nearly universal a component of normative ethics as can be found. Differences among moral doctrines appear when we ask what constitutes a man's well-being. What is thought of as the welfare of the soul is sometimes contrasted with bodily welfare, so that acts such as burning at the stake so-called infidels and heretics are rationalized as charitable, being intended to save the souls of the victims. The moral obligation is to be concerned with the welfare of one's own soul and the bodily welfare of others.

There is also a widely acknowledged obligation to care for something more than physical well-being. There is, for instance, the duty to avoid publicly shaming or humiliating our fellows. The Talmud follows the admirable practice of citing the names only of those authorities whose views it finds acceptable; men whose positions are being repudiated are referred to anonymously with the expression, "There are those who say that. . . ."

The Asian ideal of *ahimsa,* usually translated as nonviolence, is more comprehensive and might be better rendered as noninjury; it includes the avoidance of acts such as insulting or degrading another. In the passage enjoining love for our neighbor, Scripture also urges, "You shall not hate your brother in your heart, but you shall reason with him." The same injunction is to be found in Marcus Aurelius: "Men exist for the sake of one another. Teach them or bear with them." To reason with another rather than coerce him, to teach him rather than to ridicule his ignorance or denounce him for his error—this is truly to respect the other, to care for him as a fellow human being.

There is no gainsaying, however, that it takes two sides to be reasonable. The moral problem becomes acute when the other is seen to be criminal, wicked, or sinful. He who presumes to reason with the tiger is no help to the tiger's prey. Morality may demand that I take vigorous and determined action against another; it does not demand, and indeed prohibits, hostility against him—displaced, disproportionate, and uncontrolled destruction, which rationalizes hatred as some strange love for an ideal. It is in this spirit that Caesar's Rufio kills an assassin in what Cleopatra calls Caesar's way: "without punishment, without revenge, without judgment." The principle at work is the godly doctrine of hating only the sin, but not the sinner.

What is in question is the quality of character as well as of action. Morality is concerned with what we do and also with the spirit in which it is done. An act which is objectively helpful to another may be done so grudgingly or so impersonally as to make its moral status equivocal. Conversely, warmth of personal feeling heightens awareness of the other's needs and guides the search for ways by which they might be fulfilled. A distinction is sometimes drawn between charity and philanthropy; the latter, as an institutionalized pattern, is likely to be impersonal and even dehumanized. Perhaps with large-scale and complex benefactions this is inevitable.

Moral doctrines, therefore, often emphasize the virtue of personal kindness. Among the most basic concepts of classical Chinese thought is *jen*, rendered as humanheartedness, love, and even virtue in the generic sense. The Talmud speaks of *gemilut chasadim,* acts of personal kindness, declaring that the Law begins and ends with such acts, and that they take the place of the rites of sacrifice in the Temple. To deal morally with our fellowman means, above all, to relate to him with the warmth of fellowship. When another disciple tried to find a place for himself in the already crowded carriage, the Master said, "Let us love one another more, and there will be more room!" We may have come to the pass that if we love one another any the less there may soon be room for none of us.

A certain distancing from our fellows, for the sake of privacy, autonomy, or simply freedom of action, may be acceptable and even welcome. The impersonality of everyday greetings lubricates social relations while preserving us from what would otherwise be unremitting claims on our emotional energies. But to be kept always at a distance produces a sense of alienation and loneliness (§63 and §64). Airplane passengers maintain the conventional fiction that it is not another person but a thing sharing the seat; otherwise the whole journey might be committed to an unwanted relationship. Let the plane, however, encounter rough weather or engine trouble, and the atmosphere changes radically. A similar sense of closeness and warmth from strangers is well-known in wartime and in other times of crisis. Some years ago a power failure kept New York City in darkness for many hours; surprisingly, during that time crime, far from flourishing, was as rare as any moralist might desire. Yet, a society in which men are human to one another only in the face of disaster is a society headed for disaster.

A sustained pattern of personal caring constitutes *friendship*. According to many teachings, this is one of the supreme values in life. "Without friends," Aristotle said, "no one would choose to live, even if he had all other goods." Aristotle accordingly devoted two full chapters of his treatise on ethics to the subject of friendship; in modern works one cannot find the subject so much as mentioned in the index. Neglect of this concept may reflect indifference to friendship, in the widespread "marketing orientation" where what is important are not friends but connections. Even in the most moralistic traditions, friends have been valued for their usefulness. "Woe to him who is alone when he falls," said the Preacher. In the folk wisdom of many cultures it is recognized that no barber cuts his own hair and that one hand washes the other. The medieval Neoplatonist, Solomon ibn-Gabirol, compares a man without friends to a left hand without a right. Spinoza says flatly, "To man there is nothing more useful than other men."

A friend, however, is someone who is always there, not just when we need him. I once had a friend, a psychiatrist, who was an ever-present help in time of trouble, but, as it turned out, only then. Eventually I came to recognize his overtures as a barometer of how he saw my mental health or general well-being. He had no friends at all, caring for all his acquaintances with genuine concern, but only as though they were his patients. A friend is an alter ego whose joys we share as well as his sorrows. Because of this sharing, friendship enlarges the range of experience, enriches the significance of all we undergo, and adds to our awareness a dimension of sympathy. Many personal relations demand a certain *reciprocity*, a *quid pro quo:* I scratch your back and you scratch mine. This is the instrumental value in friendship. It has also, however, an inherent value, being prized for its own sake. This is the element of *mutuality:* doing something together which cannot be done alone. The measure of friendship is given by how much is shared, not by how much is exchanged.

Closely allied to friendship, differentiated from it more by intensity than by distinctive quality, is *love.* The philosophical tradition distinguishes several species of love. *Philia* is the love we feel for friends, the sense of affectionate companionship; it is also what we feel for our pets, our hobbies, whatever we give ourselves to in careless (not uncaring) enjoyment. *Agape* is brotherly love, the fellowship of shared devotion to common interests, the love for a comrade-in-arms; it is not irrelevant that a group dedicated to some shared end is called a "brotherhood." *Eros* is love having a sexual component; though self-fulfilling, it is not a reciprocal sexual exploitation but a mutuality of fulfillments, in which sensuality is consummated in awareness of and caring for the other.

In all its species love may be natural, but it is not native—spontaneous, effortless, and owing nothing to experience. We must learn how to love, not merely grow passively to maturity in it. Love attains to an intimate knowledge of its object, but it also depends on such knowledge. I cannot truly care for another if I am ignorant of his needs or of how they might be met. Here may be an existential ground for monogamy: it is hard enough to learn how to love even one person. Yet we have more than one friend and can love all our children. We come to love in the course of continuing encounters and not at first sight, although one glance may be enough to germinate what must perforce grow in its own good time. Love unfolds; it is not antecedently given. The myth of a predestined mate has a kinship with pre-Darwinian notions of special creation; it is hard to realize that the niceties of mutual fit are the product of long processes of adaptation, not the instant outcome of prior design.

This myth is congenial to *romantic love,* because for romanticism there is nothing to be attained: the appearances are all the reality that is wanted. Romantic love is subjectivist; it has no object but love itself. The romantic is in love with love—that is, with his own feelings. Typically, his love is unrequited, so that in place of the mutuality of real loving is the one-sidedness of his own inner life—a readiness for love, as he imagines, perpetuated by the circumstance that it is never called into actuality. The pathos of romanticism, its characteristic melancholy, may reflect its preoccupation with fantasy which is unfulfilling in fact—as conveyed in these lines by John Keats (from "Ode on a Grecian Urn"):

Bold Lover, never, never canst thou kiss,
Though winning near the goal—yet, do not grieve;
She cannot fade, though thou hast not thy bliss,
Forever wilt though love, and she be fair!

Ah, happy, happy boughs! that cannot shed
Your leaves, nor ever bid the Spring adieu;
And, happy melodist, unwearied,
Forever piping songs forever new;
More happy love! more happy, happy love!
Forever warm, and still to be enjoyed,
Forever panting, and forever young;
All breathing human passion far above,
That leaves a heart high-sorrowful and cloyed,
A burning forehead, and a parching tongue.

It is not my intent to deprecate the poetry; there is a profound difference between the romantic, as an aesthetic quality or genre, and romanticism as enunciating a style of life. What is of dubious value is the preference in life, not in art, for unfulfillment—because of the pleasures of anticipation, on the one hand, and the distasteful signs of consummation, on the other. The defense of the life of fantasy—that it enables one to associate with a better class of people—may be witty, but there is little wisdom in it. There is no degradation of taste in the recognition that even a crust of real bread is more nourishing than all the feasts of the imagination. This recognition is especially important because love nourishes not only the lover but the object of his love. A love which forever remains a feeling and is never externalized in action is no more than a potentiality.

The action externalized must be caring, nurturing, supportive, or it does not constitute an act of love. One may reach out to another in overt action in order to exploit him or destroy him; here are the perversions of love. *Promiscuity* is indifferent to the other save as an instrument for the satisfaction of one's own needs; but even these are not met, for the basic need is to care for another. Free love is mistaken for liberation, while in fact it expresses recurrent frustration with its attendant anxiety about one's own capacity to love and to be loved. There is a *smothering* love, which is possessive and manipulating, caring for the other only as an extension or aggrandizement of the self. There is a *killing* love, which finds a pathic fulfillment only in inflicting pain and destruction. The romantic image of *la belle dame sans merci* has come to life in the contemporary pornography of violence, in which a cartridge belt becomes a sexual adornment, whips and boots the tools of tenderness, and the language of love provides the idioms of hatred.

Romanticism, although it speaks freely of loving "forever," is incapable of real time spans of devotion, measured in prosaic years rather than eternities. Love involves a *commitment*, by which both past and future are united in a meaningful present. It is such meaning which makes it more blessed to give than to receive; what is received may enrich the moment, but—unless it is the other face of giving love—it signifies nothing for what is yet to come. There is no purpose in the passivity of successive enjoyments. Love binds the future, thereby freeing the lovers for the continuous achievement of shared meaning. Love reaches into the future because it cherishes what is already there and nurtures a new growth as well. Eros, as Plato saw, is the creative principle; what is miscalled Platonic love would be sterile. Every lover worships at the altar of the god who is not yet; the act of love is meant to give him birth. It is not that we presuppose the perfection of the object of love; we do not love an abstract Idea of the Good but concrete realities with all their imperfections, that something better might yet come to be.

The superficial Platonism in romantic love comes to its final degradation in the contemporary notion of "glamour," which is the projected fantasy of the vision of the Good as the locus of everything desirable. The woman whose image invites such fantasies is appropriately called a "sex goddess." Thereby real men and women are doomed to loveless lives of frustration and failure, unalterable by any magic of advertised brands, but allowing for intermittent vicarious satisfactions before the television or movie screen. Shakespeare's realism is endlessly refreshing: "I grant I never saw a goddess go;/My mistress, when she walks, treads on the ground" (Sonnet 130).

Love is not conditional on perfection but is *accepting* of its object as it is. Paul may be speaking only of agape, but what he says is true of love in all its forms: "Love is patient and kind; love is not jealous or boastful; it is not arrogant or rude. Love does not insist on its own way; it is not irritable or resentful; it does not rejoice at wrong, but rejoices in the right. Love bears all things, hopes all things, endures all things." Love is not dependent on deserts; no one deserves love, not because we are all undeserving but because love does not weigh merit for a measured reward. It is not a payment earned for benefits received or promised. Love can only be freely given; what is sold is necessarily counterfeit. In Elizabeth Barrett Browning's "If thou must love me, let it be for love's sake only" (*Sonnets from the Portuguese*), there is an element of romanticism: a realistic love would, on the contrary, love love for *her* sake. But in the line there is also recognition that love is unreal if it rests on some special virtue in the beloved. What happens when the virtue is lost or lessened? As Shakespeare again reminds us, "Love is not love which alters when it alteration finds" (Sonnet 116).

Here is the substance in the myth that love is blind. The lover's acceptance of the beloved's faults is mistaken for the reaction of one who cannot see the faults. Just so, justice is blind: not that it is unknowing but that it disregards irrelevancies—say, of name and status. For love, all is irrelevant save the one conclusive, ineluctable truth that here is my beloved, my beloved is mine, and I am his.

As the beloved is never found wanting, because never weighed in the balance, so also the love itself is unmeasured. Love is *unlimited.* To Cleopatra's importunity, "If it be love indeed, tell me how much," Antony replies, "There's beggary in the love that can be reckoned." In giving himself, the lover gives all that is his to give, without stint or reservation. Love has in it an element of absolutism, therefore, which has made it suspect in the eyes of reason.

To my mind, it is the locutions of "giving" which are suspect. What is supposedly given in love is not something which has an antecedent existence. If the lover gives himself, he becomes a self in the course of loving; if it is his love he gives, that love is no more preexistent than the walk which he and his beloved take together. There is nothing separable from the lovers themselves to be transferred, as a giving suggests, nor does it go in one direction rather than the other. I do not in fact give love unless it is being accepted, and the acceptance is itself a giving equally essential to love's coming to be. Most of all, the notion that something is given implies that a certain store has been diminished; possessiveness and jealousy thereupon come into their own, and love is perverted or destroyed.

The more we give the more there is to be given, a truth which might be denoted the *paradox of giving.* "The wise man," said Lao-tzu, "does not lay up treasure; the more he gives to others the more he has for his own." Those who love most are most capable of still more love; the mere show of love may be meant to cope with continuing anxiety whether there is a reality beneath the appearance of loving. An insatiable appetite may reveal only the recurrent failure to be satisfied. The truly great lovers love continually but also effortlessly, without either conquest or pursuit. They are not Don Juan and Casanova, but Krishna, Buddha, Hillel, and Jesus.

60. The Life of Feeling

A perennial issue in moral philosophy has to do with the place of feeling in moral conduct. For some—Buddhists, Stoics, and Spinoza, for example—it has no place at all, so far as it is possible to deny feeling. For others, feeling is all in all; life without passion, even were it possible, would be empty and directionless. Still others acknowledge the claims of feeling, provided that these are moderate and duly qualified.

The counsel of moderation meets with the objection that feeling is by its very nature immoderate. "Modified rapture," as Gilbert and Sullivan called it, belongs to comic opera. Plato says about the great multitude of men, "What they desire they desire out of all measure." That certainly seems to be true of the contemporary psychedelic frenzy. Music is played at a volume that is literally deafening; rhythms are insistent and forcefully pounded out; colors are strident, forms and patterns are blatant, lights blink in an alternation of lurid glare and darkness. All this produces not a heightened awareness but its opposite, a kind of sensory narcosis, a waking anesthesia. In moving to ever greater intensity, feeling contains within itself the seeds of its own destruction, coming to an end not by way of fulfillment but out of sheer desperation, like Aesop's frog puffing itself up till it bursts.

Until the moment it destroys itself, feeling is strong enough to overpower all else. In passion, Spinoza emphasized, we are literally passive; we are in the grip of our emotions, and they refuse to let go; we are in bondage to our feelings, enslaved and driven. The passion in the service of Aphrodite, Socrates described as "a raging and savage beast of a master"; indulging the passion makes man himself the beast, and "that sorry outcome is all the return passion makes him for his favors." Circe did not literally transform Odysseus' men into swine; it was enough for her to provide an occasion for their innate swinishness to show itself. Even Odysseus, though retaining a semblance of humanity, spent a year with the goddess of degrading love, forgetting the true goal of his wanderings. No man can resist the enslavement he imposes on himself. The passions get the better of all the sects, said Maimonides, "even the philosophers." For everyman, Karamazov speaks: "Sensual lust is a tempest—worse than a tempest!"

Strength of feeling does not overpower on behalf of some significant end; like the raging beast or tempest it is only destructive. In a famous sermon, Buddha characterized body, mind, and thought as all burning with fire of passions and lusts; the flames destroy whatever they can seize upon. A certain popular entertainer in recent years is a pixieish figure conveying a quality of infantile polymorphism, untrammeled by the norms of adult respectability or even rationality; one of his best-known songs has the childlike refrain, "The ice-caps are melting, the whole world is drowning." When the restraints of reason disappear, we are engulfed. The juxtaposition of these various images of destruction is memorably condensed in "Fire and Ice" by Robert Frost:

Some say the world will end in fire,
Some say in ice.
From what I've tasted of desire
I hold with those who favor fire.
But if it had to perish twice,
I think I know enough of hate
To say that for destruction ice
Is also great
And would suffice.

One thing the life of feeling is claimed to destroy is reason; it is charged that the passions paralyze or pervert reason. Thus Plato: "A man who is in great joy or in great pain, in his unseasonable eagerness to attain the one and to avoid the other, is not able to see or to hear anything rightly; but he is mad, and is at the same time utterly incapable of any participation in reason." For ibn-Gabirol, passion is "the twin sister of blindness"—not the accepting blindess of love but what veils both facts and reason. Spinoza regards passions like avarice, ambition, and lust as "species of madness." Feeling and good sense go their separate ways. Though he is wearing the head of an ass, Bottom is no fool in his remark to Titania, "To say the truth, reason and love keep little company nowadays."

Buddhism sees in the passions the source of all human suffering, the *dukkha* which makes life as ordinarily lived so far from fulfilling. "Desire is the arrow in the side of suffering life; remove the arrow, and the wound will heal. Those who love nothing and hate nothing have no fetters. Cut down the whole forest of desires, not a tree only!" The second of the Four Noble Truths of Buddhism is that the passions are responsible for human misery. The dissonance between pleasure and pain on the one hand and reasoned judgment on the other, a dissonance constituted by a man's hatred of what his judgment pronounces to be noble and good, while he loves and enjoys what he judges vile and wicked—this Plato calls the greatest of all follies. The best that might be said of a life devoted to the fulfillment of desire is that it is without substance or meaning. As Marcus Aurelius sees it, "The things which are much valued in life are empty and trifling. Men are like puppies biting one another, little children quarreling, laughing, and then straightaway crying."

So much for the attack on the life of feeling; its defense begins with a counterattack on the claims of reason. "With the growth of intelligence comes increased capacity for pain," Schopenhauer held; "it is only with the highest degree of intelligence that suffering reaches its extreme point." The cult of unreason in our time owes much to Dostoevski, who disdained the modern rationalization of narcosis as a search for an expanded consciousness: to be too conscious, he declared, is an illness, a real thoroughgoing illness. Moreover, he argued, reason is nothing but reason and satisfies only the rational side of man's nature. The will, which he contrasts with reason, he sees as "a manifestation of the whole life." This does not make a case for the life of feeling, but once reason is out of the way feeling can have full scope. To paraphrase Kant, the aim is to limit reason so as to make room for passion, if not for faith.

Historically, it is the claims of faith which motivated the modern attack on reason. Kant's task was laid out for him several centuries before his time with Luther's declaration that "reason is the greatest enemy faith has": "You must part with reason and not know anything of it and even kill it; else you will not get into the kingdom of heaven." "Reason is a whore." Protestantism shares in the classical condemnation of the passions; yet once reason is dethroned, feeling is no longer to be denied. Even Rousseau, the so-called apostle of sentimentality, recognized that the heart deceives us in a thousand ways. By the time of Kierkegaard the conviction was widespread that "What our age lacks is not reflection but passion. The conclusions of passions are the only reliable ones."

Feeling need not be irrational; it is not to be contrasted with reason, as in Platonic dualism (§49). In his famous myth of reason as the charioteer driving the fiery steeds of passion, Plato specifies two steeds, one noble and the other not. The most principled rationalist must acknowledge degrees of irrationality among emotions; some feelings are more consonant with reason. Plato points out that reason itself can rouse "the might of passion," by "making proclamation of any wrong assailing us from without or being perpetrated by the desires within."

Man's rationality may be distinctive of his humanity, but it does not exhaust his nature. We do not live in motionless thought but engage in action. The link between thought and action, the stimulus and response to both, is feeling. For Spinoza, as for Freud, desire is the essence of man; *conatus* or id manifests itself in all our doings. To eliminate the will altogether, switch off all the emotions, would be a kind of intellectual castration, as Nietzsche called it in his *Genealogy of Morals*. We neither think nor act without the impulsion of feeling, and new feelings are engendered in the process.

For some time the idea was widespread in American life that feeling is not only subjective and immoral but also unmanly. The wooden hero of the Westerns and the callous private eye agree in denial of feeling. Homer's image of Achilles, manly beyond dispute, weeping tears of frustration or grief is too incongruous to be entertained, as patterns of other cultures are so often perceived to be inappropriate. I remember movies about the First World War depicting British fathers briefly shaking hands with their sons about to go off to the front, while in my Slavic-Jewish upbringing I was given far more emotional farewells on my daily departure to school. It is the expression of feeling which is so variable, rather than feeling itself. There is expressiveness in understatement; unexcelled in the world's literature is David's lamentation, "O my son Absalom, my son, my son Absalom! would I had died for thee, O Absalom, my son, my son!" When all is said, "unfeeling" and "inhuman" are nearly synonymous.

Feelings accompany all our doings; it is not necessarily the emotion which is the by-product. What we do may be meant to act out the feeling—not merely express it but bring it to fruition. Hegel, the most thoroughgoing rationalist of modern times, acknowledges in his *Philosophy of History* that nothing great in the world has been accomplished without passion. Without passion the greatness of what has been accomplished could not be recognized. Feeling is the spontaneous response to the apprehension of any value. To deny feeling in the name of morality is as though to enjoin blindness in the name of beauty.

Those who espouse the life of feeling go further than this. Rather than hold that feeling is the response to value, they hold that it is feeling itself which is to be valued. Feeling for *what* does not matter, if only the emotion is sufficiently intense. The thirst for emotional experience is central in romanticism; a *cult of intensity* can be traced from Byron and Shelley to Hemingway and Fitzgerald and many writers of our own day. It is a half-century since Edna St. Vincent Millay wrote "O world, I cannot hold thee close enough . . ./Here such a passion is/As stretcheth me apart" ("God's World"). In substance if not in mode of expression, these lines might still speak to the hippies of our own time.

Similarly, Shelley's invocation to the west wind might serve for the modern neoromantic radical:

If I were a dead leaf thou mightest bear;
If I were a swift cloud to fly with thee;
A wave to pant beneath thy power, and share

The impulse of thy strength, only less free
Than thou . . .

Oh, lift me as a wave, a leaf, a cloud!
I fall upon the thorns of life! I bleed!

A heavy weight of hours has chained and bowed
One too like thee: tameless, and swift, and proud.

. . . Be thou, spirit fierce,
My spirit! Be thou me, impetuous one!

Drive my dead thoughts over the universe
Like withered leaves to quicken a new birth!

—"Ode to the West Wind"

Characteristic is the breathless admiration of and longing for power, the fervent desire for fierce and impetuous action—but to what end? The Fascist formula that a good war justifies the cause has its counterpart in the romanticist principle that an intense feeling justifies what we feel it for. Some such principle today gives terrorism a specious justification.

The most acceptable defense of the life of feeling reaffirms the claims of feeling against the dehumanizing impact of science and technology, as in Charlie Chaplin's *Modern Times,* or René Clair's *A Nous la Liberté.* The analytic intellect is seen as the source of the dehumanizing technology and as weakening and interfering with the expression of human feeling. The following is from E. E. Cummings' collection appropriately named *is 5* (in contrast to "the merely undeniable fact" that 2 times 2 is 4):

since feeling is first
who pays any attention
to the syntax of things
will never wholly kiss you;
wholly to be a fool
while spring is in the world

my blood approves
and kisses are a better fate
than wisdom
lady i swear by all flowers. Don't cry
—the best gesture of my brain is less than
your eyelid's flutter . . .

There is a profound misunderstanding here. If indeed one must choose between kisses and wisdom, it is easy to understand why so few are occupied with the pursuit of wisdom. But love is no folly, the gestures of the brain are at their best when impelled by passion, and attention to the syntax of things deepens our feeling for their wondrous beauty.

Moral dualism (§46) deals with these issues by distinguishing between good and bad feelings, those of our higher and lower selves. Pangs of conscience, the sense of duty, emotional ties to our fellowmen, all we feel in the contemplation of beauty and truth—these are morally acceptable and even admirable. The urgings of passion, greed for possessions, the lust for power—these are damnable faults, or follies at best. Wisdom demands that we bend every effort to rid ourselves of feelings such as these. George Bernard Shaw satirized this moralistic stance by remarking that an Englishman thinks he is being moral when he is only being uncomfortable. Life is not a moral gymnasium in which to build character, and cold showers are not intrinsically virtuous.

Even the lower self is part of the self. Passions enter into the makeup of the creatures that we are; we are not disembodied souls. The Master said, "It is easy enough for angels to be pure; let them descend to earth in human form, and they will know what men endure." Moralism often extols a way of life which rests on a rejection of the claims of life. "Moral principles that exalt themselves by degrading human nature," John Dewey argued, "are in effect committing suicide, or else they involve human nature in unending civil war." Morality must acknowledge the place of feeling and accommodate impulses and actions which generate and are infused with feeling. Otherwise it condemns itself to no more of a role in life than providing pious pronouncements and condemns its adherents to cycles of hypocrisy and remorse.

Feelings must be appraised; after appraisal some are to be rejected. Repudiation of moral dualism does not deny that *any* moral discriminations can be made in the domain of feeling. There is such a thing as developing moral sensibility just as there is cultivating taste and aesthetic sensibility. The question is how moral improvement is to be conceived and actualized. Moral dualism enjoys the advantage of an apparent simplicity. "Is not the noble," Plato asks, "that which subjects the beast to the man, or rather, to the god in man; and the ignoble, that which subjects the man to the beast?" Another common formula is in the *Misrash:* "The wicked are ruled by their heart, the righteous rule their heart." God and beast, head and heart, higher and lower selves—two basic components of man, of which only one is given moral authority.

In such moralities, the capacity for *self-control* is of crucial importance. Thereby a man holds his lower self in check and establishes the sovereignty of his higher self. Buddha said: "'These sons belong to me, this wealth belongs to me'—with such thoughts a fool is tormented. He himself does not belong to himself, how much less his sons and wealth!" Without self-control a man cannot be self-possessed.

To establish sovereignty over the inner domain takes strength of character and courage—virtues prerequisite to wisdom. "He is strong who conquers others," the *Tao Te Ching* acknowledges, "but he who conquers himself is mighty." Aristotle declares, "I count him braver who overcomes his desires than him who conquers his enemies, for the hardest victory is the victory over the self." The same idea appears in the opening lines of *Love's Labor's Lost:*

. . . brave conquerors–for so you are,
That war against your affections,
And the huge army of the world's desires.

Victory over the self is the most difficult of all victories to achieve; it is also, as Plato assesses it, "the first and best." It remains an enduring victory. "Not even a god," Buddha assures us, "could change into defeat the victory of a man who has vanquished himself."

Self-control means different things, however; how the differences are to be formulated in theory and taken into account in practice is far from clear. It is one thing to appraise and redirect impulse; it is quite another to deny its existence or to deal with it by releasing countervailing forces. Repression and conflict hardly define the ideal life. For every victor there is also a vanquished, and what passes for peace may be only a period of preparation for the next war. Better than a conquering self is one so integrated as to have no enemies within. Self-control implies a self which is being controlled; thereby freedom is radically compromised. The games of chess which I play with myself end, except for downright blunders, in draws: the ingenuity of every attack I plan is countered by my faculty for anticipating precisely such an attack. When the Master was petitioned for a touchstone by which to distinguish a true saint from a pretender he advised, "Ask him what to do to keep alien thoughts from obtruding themselves on you while at prayer." The point was in the interpretation: "If he gives you any advice at all he is not a true saint. Such thoughts will always arise; it is our unending task to redirect them to their true destination."

This is the substance of Frued's insistence on the futility of repression and his emphasis on the constructive role of sublimation. Feelings are among the most important data for moral judgment, for they point to facts of the inner life, and facts can be denied only at the cost of making judgment groundless. More fundamental than self-control, therefore, is self-knowledge and self-acceptance. It is *I* who act, rather than being acted upon, Spinoza urged, when what I do is the outcome of the exercise of reason. For me to be active rather than passive—that is, in bondage to passion—does not call for repression but understanding. "In proportion as we know an emotion better is it more within our control, and the less does the mind suffer from it." What is more, "a passion which is evil ceases to be a passion as soon as we form a clear and distinct idea of it." Here philosophy puts itself at the service of both psychology and ethics.

The passion most widely recognized as compelling and evil is that associated with the pursuit of pleasure; the next section looks to the problems in forming a clear and distinct idea of pleasure.

61. Pleasure and Beyond

The doctrine which assigns a central role to pleasure in human life is called *hedonism.* It has two forms; *psychological hedonism* holds that all men are engaged in the pursuit of pleasure, while *ethical hedonism* ("moral" in my usage) holds that pleasure is worthy of the pursuit.

Psychological hedonism, in the usual sense of the word "pleasure," is plainly false. People pursue other things besides pleasure—wealth, power, knowledge, salvation, and mere survival. If it is argued that these all give their pursuers pleasure the doctrine becomes true, but only because it has been so reinterpreted as to become a tautology, declaring that whatever a person pleases to do gives him pleasure, that is, pleases him. If we are told in this interpretation that a certain man is devoted to the pursuit of pleasure, we have learned nothing about him; we can conclude that he is capable of voluntary action, but not that he is likely to choose one action rather than another. If, on the other hand, the characterization is meant to imply that he is a voluptuary, aesthete, or the like, it tells us a great deal—so much that it is false if applied to most men.

Ethical hedonism makes sense only in a restricted interpretation of "pleasure." There is no point in declaring that pleasure is worthy of pursuit if we mean that whatever a man pleases to do is worth doing—unless this is meant as a doctrine of unqualified permissiveness. Critics of hedonism have objected to its permissiveness, but because of *what* it permits, not because it makes no discriminations. Hedonism declares, for example, that pain is *not* worthy of pursuit, although a person may be so thoughtless, unfeeling, or perverted as to accept or even welcome pain.

Pleasure, said Epicurus, the great hedonist of ancient times, is "our first and kindred good," and Bentham, the most notable modern hedonist, declared, "Pleasure is itself a good, nay, the only good." Again, there is a sense in which this position is quite defensible, but at the cost of no longer enjoining a particular way of life. The distinction is sometimes drawn—for instance, by the pragmatist, C. I. Lewis—between the experience of something of value and the value itself, whatever gives us the experience. The former is called *intrinsic value,* the latter *extrinsic value* (§54). For any naturalistic, humanistic theory of value (§55 and §56), intrinsic value is basic; nothing is of value unless it is capable, under suitable circumstances, of providing a certain kind of experience. Values are *experienced* as valuable; if the experience is veridical, our enjoyment of the value discloses its worth. In a word, apprehension of value gives pleasure; something is valuable only if it can give pleasure to the right people at the right time—to those of appropriate sensibility and in an ideal context.

The distinction between intrinsic and extrinsic value is not to be confused with the distinction between inherent and instrumental value—things worthy of being pursued for their own sake and those which are worthy as means to some other end. All worthwhile pursuits provide us with the experience of intrinsic value, but it is not this experience we are pursuing. The commencement orator who enjoins his hearers to go out and do what's right has contributed little moral instruction, but no less than the hedonist who enjoins the pursuit of pleasure in the sense of intrinsic value. What *is* valuable? To assume that whatever gives us the feeling that it is worthy is indeed worthy begs the question.

Pleasure in the sense of the distinctive feeling, not in the all-embracing sense of intrinsic value, has not only failed to secure general acceptance as a good but has been denounced by moralists as downright evil. The Puritans of a century or two ago opposed the "sport" of bearbaiting not because it gave pain to the bear but because it gave pleasure to the spectators. It is one thing to condemn pleasure in itself and another to condemn pleasure which involves the suffering of others. My first spectacle of a bullfight was also the last, because I sat close enough to the ring to hear the matador's sigh of relief, and remembered the chapel just outside where he had prayed for his safety. Although killing an animal for food and inflicting destruction on an enemy in war also provide satisfaction, it is not because of the suffering but in spite of it.

The pursuit of pleasure from whatever source is the chief component of what is sometimes called *moral materialism,* prizing only material possessions and physical well-being. This is logically independent of metaphysical materialism (§39), although critics often attack the latter because of its supposed support for the former. Marxist materialism is commonly denounced in pulpits and the popular press as a moral materialism, while Communists, in turn, denounce the pursuit of pleasure as an expression of bourgeois decadence. The *Carvaka,* metaphysical materialists of ancient India, were attacked as espousing only the morality of "a good digestion and no conscience."

Dulling the moral sensibilities is a major criticism of hedonism. Pleasure, even if not evil in itself, Plato argued, is "the greatest incitement to evil." At the turn of the century, the French novelist Joris Karl Huysmans depicted the life of a complete aesthete in the novel *Against the Grain.* (For instance, his hero constructed an olfactory piano, as it were, to produce symphonies of smell, and set on his Persian carpet a tortoise whose shell had been encrusted with jewels, so that its slow movements across the carpet would enhance the play of color and light.) In a later work, *Down There,* decadence gave way to sadism, portrayed as the fictionalized biography of Gilles de Rais, the original Bluebeard. The doings of the fictional Dracula are also said to have been based on the cruelties practiced for pleasure by a real Transylvanian nobleman. Satanism is not unknown in our time, and to my mind is rightly so called; the cult of the Mansons is a recent example.

Hedonism does not enjoin the monstrous immoralities of sadistic diabolism, but even in its moderate forms it has still been subjected to a number of criticisms—by Plato, for example. Pleasure, he argued, is neither a self-sufficient nor an ultimate good. The value of reason must be acknowledged by the hedonist, at least as providing the necessary knowledge of where and how pleasure can be attained. Though this allows reason only an instrumental value, the inherent value of pleasure is also limited by this consideration. The gourmet is more knowledgeable than the gourmand and for that reason has a more cultivated taste and is capable of greater pleasure. Further, pleasures are not always harmonious with one another. Some other good is needed to mediate conflicts among pleasures. Reason may enhance pleasure by arranging that its various component enjoyments enhance one another; herein lies the artistry underlying aesthetic experience. If pleasure is acknowledged as good, it must also make way for beauty.

Plato and others have criticized pleasure as having value only in contrast to pain. This argument is implausible: the taste of a fine wine is surely pleasurable on other grounds than that it relieves thirst. Although there is undeniably a distinctive pleasure in the sheer relief from pain, it is hard to see why all pleasures should be of this kind. Yet, while pleasure may not be the essence of the good, pain is essentially evil. It does not ennoble the human spirit but degrades it. Suffering may make manifest the nobility of those who endure it; if so, they are noble in spite of their pain, not because of it.

In traditions other than Puritanism, pleasure is not condemned as intrinsically evil. Hinduism, for example, acknowledges three basic objects of pursuit: not only *karma,* or duty, but also *artha,* wealth, and *kama,* pleasure. It recognizes that the last two may be instrumental to the first: pleasure may serve the interests of duty. Jewish tradition showers raisins and almonds on the child undertaking the study of the Torah; these are said to symbolize the delights of the Law, but there is no doubt that they are also meant to strengthen the child's motivation. The Jerusalem Talmud (the more familiar one was composed in Babylonia) makes explicit the religious teaching that the capacity for pleasure and the means to produce it are a gift of God: "Every man must render an account before God of all the good things in life he beheld and did not enjoy." It is a poor guest who disdains the delicacies set before him by his host.

In this and other doctrines defending pleasure, a distinction is usually drawn between "higher" and "lower" pleasures, only the former being morally defensible. The hedonism of Epicurus himself carries this distinction so far as virtually to accept Plato's wholly negative characterization of pleasure. The difference between them is only that while Plato supposes that the logical dependence of the value of pleasure on an opposite deprives pleasure of inherent value, Epicurus is quite prepared to make a negative goal the end of human action. He says, "When we maintain that pleasure is the end, we do not mean the pleasures of profligates and those that consist in sensuality, as is supposed by some who are either ignorant or disagree with us, or do not understand; but freedom from pain in the body and from trouble in the mind." To the true Epicurean, the life of pleasure is simply one without illness or anxiety.

Plato, too, invokes a distinction between pleasures which are morally defensible and those which are not, characterizing the "truest pleasures" as "those which are approved by the lover of wisdom and reason." There is a danger here of a circular argument, since a man's wisdom and reason may come into doubt because of the pleasures he approves. Can acceptable criteria of approval be made explicit?

The search for such criteria extends from utilitarianism to contemporary utility theory, game theory, and decision theory. Jeremy Bentham was one of the first to make a serious attempt at constructing a hedonic scale.

He listed such plausible measures as the following: intensity, duration, fecundity (the degree to which the pleasure being measured is productive of more pleasures), purity (freedom from an admixture of pain), propinquity (like justice, pleasure too long delayed is pleasure denied), and certainty. The interest in a hedonic calculus has in our time been replaced by a concern with the measure of the values, whatever they are, which motivate decisions (say, in economics); an abstract "utility," so called, is far more useful in such analyses than a presumed pleasure.

Particularly troublesome are questions concerning acceptable criteria for decision making even if we assume that we have measured the pleasure or utility being aimed at. The mathematical theory of games, for example, is developed on the basis of a *minmax* principle: choose that strategy which will minimize the maximum loss which might be sustained. Some have argued that a less prudent principle—for instance, maximizing the maximum possible gain—might be preferable. A hedonist might face the question whether to lump his pleasures and disperse his pains, or distribute his pleasures and get the pains over with all at once. A Japanese meal begins with something sweet, unlike the American placing of dessert at the end; is the best always to be saved for the last? Hedonism is not as clearcut and straightforward a doctrine as it sometimes pretends to be.

A major consideration is whether the pleasure has any depth or meaning, whether it signifies anything beyond the experience of the moment. This is one of the distinguishing features of joy in contrast to the satisfaction of a need or desire. Santayana has pointed out that in aesthetic enjoyment—a common paradigm of the "higher" pleasures—the prized feeling is not localized in our senses, but in the external stimulus to the feeling; he proposes as a definition of beauty, "pleasure experienced as a quality of the object." On this basis, Aldous Huxley's fantasy in *Brave New World* of a new artistic medium, "feelies," would be impossible, because it would be too hard to dissociate the quality of what we are touching from the sensation in our own fingers. That something beautiful is said to be "easy on the eyes" is a misleading metaphor. Yet music pleases or offends the ear, and the sense of smell is a type of distal perception which nevertheless has not been thought of as providing one of the "higher" pleasures.

The goal of pleasure is too inward turned, too self-centered to provide meaning to its pursuit. We cannot set out simply to enjoy ourselves without thereby emptying action of any content other than a trivial way of passing time. This underlies the dilemma confronting Faust: "I am too old for mere amusement, and still too young to be without desire. What has the world to offer me?" The answer might be: both work and play, provided the work is not drudgery and the play is not idle, so that both have significance, giving not the passive pleasures of occupying or amusing oneself but the joys of the act of creation. This is the thrust of Nietzsche's critique of the arid ideal of happiness as the goal of human endeavors. "Of what account is my happiness!" Zarathustra exclaims, "I have long ceased to strive any more for happiness, I strive for my work." If this striving could encompass play as well, it would leave little to be desired, even for a hedonist.

The element of desire is at the root of the moralistic condemnation of pleasure. Moralism views desire in the perspectives of Pauline dualism, which distinguishes the *yetzer ha-tov* and the *yetzer ha-ra,* the good and evil claim that Paul's use of the term "flesh" is metaphoric and that he means only to distinguish "higher" and "lower" pleasures. The Judaic tradition which distinguishes the *yetzer ha-tov* and the *yetzer ha-ra,* the good and evil impulses, does not localize them respectively in the soul and the body. Yet the position of Philo of Alexandria, that there are not two things so utterly opposed as knowledge and the pleasures of the flesh, is unquestionably the dominant outlook of Judaeo-Christian thought. Knowledge of the truth and pursuit of the good are traditionally contrasted with devoting oneself to the pleasures of the flesh.

In moralistic teaching, the body has been attacked persistently as the instrument, the seat, the source, and the principle of sin. There are recurrent denunciations of what Paul called "the physical nature with its propensities and cravings." Of those who yield to these cravings, Paul says, "Their end is destruction, their god is the belly, and they glory in their shame." The faithful, on the other hand, await their Saviour, who will transform "the vile body." Meanwhile, we must "bring the body into subjection." A similar doctrine is to be found in Buddhism. The body is "impure, foul, a dressed-up lump, covered with wounds, wasted, full of sickness, a heap of corruption"—in a word, "disgusting."

What is especially condemned in these philosophies is sexual desire. Foremost among the cravings of the flesh, and the most damnable of them, is lust. The poet gives more effective expression to the idea than the philosopher. Here is Shakespeare (Sonnet 129) on lust:

The expense of spirit in a waste of shame
Is lust in action; and till action, lust
Is perjured, murderous, bloody, full of blame,
Savage, extreme, rude, cruel, not to trust;
Enjoyed no sooner but despised straight;
Past reason hunted; and no sooner had,
Past reason hated, as a swallowed bait,
On purpose laid to make the taker mad:
Mad in pursuit, and in possession so;
Had, having, and in quest to have, extreme;
A bliss in proof–and proved, a very woe;
Before, a joy proposed; behind, a dream.
All this the world well knows; yet none knows well
To shun the heaven that leads men to this hell.

Lust is immoral because of the extreme measures it is prepared to take in order to attain its end; the end itself, when attained, is seen not to have been worthwhile; yet the strength of the impulse is virtually irresistible.

For these reasons moralism enjoins self-control. If men cannot contain themselves let them marry, says Paul in a famous passage: "It is better to marry than to burn"—that is, than to be aflame with unfulfilled passion. In Augustine, some three centuries later, the doctrine is explicit that nothing is so much to be shunned as sexual relations. Celibacy became a great virtue. In certain moralities, the term "moral" and "immoral" came to mean specifically what pertains to sexual conduct. Swinburne, the nineteenth-century poet of sensuality, spoke of the "inebriated virtue" of his shocked Victorian contemporaries, and of the "sexless orgies of morality." Nietzsche also recognized the hypocrisy and self-deception of the moralists whose purity only thinly disguises their frustrations. "How nicely," he mocked, "doggish lust can beg for a piece of spirit when it is denied a piece of flesh."

In the puritanical and moralistic attitudes towards sex some critics saw the workings of economic interests and other material concerns. What appeared to be the idealization of women as too pure to have sexual desires, or so virtuous as to rise above sexual pleasure, was in fact—so the criticism ran—a degradation of women as objects for the satisfaction of masculine needs, property valued for just this reason, whose chastity is therefore to be carefully preserved. There is undoubtedly some substance in this charge that the moralistic condemnation of sex sprang from a kind of sexism (§65). There is no doubt, too, that psychological rather than ethical considerations also played a significant part in this condemnation—fears of venereal disease and distaste for the responsibilities of pregnancy. Dissemination of knowledge about contraception, and its availability, as well as heightened awareness of the importance of planned parenthood, have had a growing impact on ideas of sexual morality.

Humanistic ethics in many traditions recognizes sex as the expression and fulfillment of love. Loveless sex is a reaction to the sexless love of the moralists. Platonic love has served as a defense against the guilts and anxieties evoked by explicit sexuality. Conversely, sex can serve as a defense against love. Caring and commitment make considerable demands even on a mature personality. Those who recoil from giving themselves cultivate the illusion of intimacy and mutuality in what is, in fact, a depersonalized and even dehumanized sexual encounter.

The sexuality which provides only the shadow of love without the substance reveals itself by its grimness. There is no joy in it, at most a gratification in achievement and the satisfaction of relieving tension. In place of tenderness there is exploitation of the other, at best a reciprocal exploitation of each by the other, rather than a mutuality of giving. In place of caring there is a withdrawal from the other, a retreat from reality into corridors of fantasy. In place of responsible commitment is a welter of anxiety and guilt, to be countered by determined indifference. Not every sexual relationship, as puritanism seems to assume, makes a mere sex-object of the other. A loving sexuality addresses itself to the whole person, but not as an entity dualistically disjoined from its body.

In some moralities, especially those espoused by religious fanatics, the body is not just denied its due; it is subjected to downright attack. *Mortification of the flesh* is believed to contribute to spiritual attainment and to be a moral achievement in itself. Fasting, silence, immobility, deprivation of sleep, going unwashed, being loaded down with chains, inflicting on oneself periodic beatings, walking about with pebbles or beans in one's shoes—such practices are known in all the major cultures. Simon Stylites on his pillar is spiritual kin to Bodhi-Dharma, the founder of Zen, who remained so long seated in meditation that he lost the use of his legs; *saddhus* in modern India are known to gaze into the sun until they are blinded. The third-century theologian Origen castrated himself, as an act of moralistic zeal (but he was condemned as a heretic). Buddha, in his search for enlightenment, went through a period of self-inflicted pain and suffering; images occasionally depict him as emaciated from starvation. He came to recognize, however, that such mortification is not conducive even to ordinary knowledge; how much less does it lead to wisdom! Even the full possession of all one's faculties is scarcely enough.

Less destructively self-punitive than mortification is the practice of *asceticism*, widely held to be characteristic of the good life. The true art of living, said Plato, is "the art of dying to the senses," learning to turn away from all they present to us, so as to attain a higher vision. But while self-indulgence may be unacceptable, it is not clear that self-denial is correspondingly praiseworthy. The Master said: "A horse works hard, sleeps on the bare ground, eats no meat, drinks only cold water, wears nails in its shoes, and sustains lashes daily—yet it remains a horse." The sense of the original would be better conveyed if the conclusion were "an ass." When Mephistopheles says of himself, "I am the spirit that denies forever," the meaning may be his repudiation of faith, but the point may be his rejection of all that is good in life. The intimate connection in all the world's religions between religious aspiration and the glories of architecture, painting, sculpture, music, and the decorative arts testifies to the recognition that impoverishment of the senses is likely to impoverish the spirit as well.

In many religious philosophies asceticism is to be practiced only by the few who devote themselves entirely to the religious life; but all the faithful are enjoined to turn away from *worldliness*. "Love not the world, nor yet what is in the world," declares the Epistle of John. "All that is in the world—the desire of the flesh and the desire of the eyes and the proud glory of life—does not belong to God." Worldly things have a meretricious worth; the world is the scene of suffering and evil and of lures to sin. Other doctrines, however, hold that, far from being an obstacle on the path to Heaven, the world with all the things in it is itself the path, if we know how to walk upon it.

The impulse to turn one's back upon the world is not limited to religious monasticism; there is a secular monasticism as well, known by the admittedly pejorative term *escapism*. Plato's groves of Academe and the garden of Epicurus are the philosophic prototypes; the ivory tower, in spite of its academic connotation, originally referred to the artist's seclusion from the pressures and distractions of business and politics. The effort to escape from the concerns of all around us is subject to moral condemnation as avoidance of social responsibility. Although its motivation might be moral, that way of life attains at best what Milton called "a fugitive and cloistered virtue, unexercised and unbreathed, that never sallies out and seeks her adversary." In striking contrast is Job's justifiable pride, "Even the cause of him I knew not, I sought out." In a world where the interests of each are so tightly interlocked with the interests of all, it is as hopeless as it is unjust to pursue one's own salvation while all around are damned. The escapist is a parasite, depending on others to maintain inviolate the larger setting within which his refuge can continue to survive.

If it does continue, it offers only a pedestrian existence, as lacking in passion as in heroism, and affording only the palest of joys as the escapist acts out what is in essence only a fantasy. T. S. Eliot's *Fragment of an Agon* is much to the point:

SWEENEY: You see this egg
You see this egg
Well that's life on a crocodile isle.
There's no telephones
There's no gramaphones
There's no motor cars
No two-seaters, no six-seaters,
No Citroën, no Rolls-Royce.
Nothing to eat but the fruit as it grows.
Nothing to see but the palmtrees one way
And the sea the other way,
Nothing to hear but the sound of the surf.
Nothing at all but three things

DORIS: What things?

SWEENEY: Birth, and copulation, and death.
That's all, that's all, that's all, that's all,
Birth, and copulation, and death.

DORIS: I'd be bored. . . .

I don't like eggs; I never liked eggs;
And I don't like life on your crocodile isle.

There are those who do not like life anywhere; the extreme of mortification, asceticism, unworldliness, and escapism is suicide. It is a major social problem in countries as diverse as Sweden and Japan; in the United States it is the greatest single cause of death among young people, excluding only the automobile. The number of suicides in America each year is as great as the number of homicides; since this number includes only the cases officially recorded as suicides, which is a fraction of the total, the actual number is considerably greater. If America is a land of violence, the chilling truth is that the violence is most likely to be directed against the self.

Most moralities, with the conspicuous exception of Stoicism, unequivocally condemn suicide and class incitement to it as murder. Taking one's life, however, describes only an act, not an action; the meaning of the act may differ widely from case to case. It may be an act of despair, like that felt by the victims of incurable and painful diseases or by the ghetto dwellers of the inner city who see their lives as empty and hopeless. It may be an escape from degradation of the spirit, like that faced by the Stoics subjected to the tyranny of the Caesars. It may be seen as a demand of honor, as by the Forty-Seven Ronin of eighteenth-century Japan, who committed hara-kiri after avenging the disgrace of their feudal lord. It may be an act of heroism, the courageous defense of faith or freedom, as by Hannah and her seven sons of the Book of Maccabees, or by the heroes of Masada, and of the Warsaw Ghetto. It may be an act of self-sacrifice, that others may live: "Greater love has no man than this, that a man lay down his life for his friend."

What morality condemns without qualification is self-destruction carried out for no other reason than to encompass the destruction. Self-hatred is as damnable as any other form of hatred. Identifiable acts of suicide are many times fewer than more subtle forms of self-destruction—the lives of the accident-prone, the abusers of alcohol and other drugs, and of those living life-patterns driven by frenzy. A counterpart of the cult of intensity is the modern cult of the anti-hero, with its ideal of failure. In this cult the tragedy of futile heroism has degenerated to the pathos of the midnight cowboys and easy riders, not the defeated but the dropouts, not the fallen but the unsinning who have damned themselves.

There are many types of failure as well as of suicide; there are circumstances in which it is success that is to be morally condemned. Vulgar pragmatism may amount to no more than an unprincipled worship of power. A successful "revolution" or "liberation movement"—both so called—may mark the defeat rather than the triumph of moral aspirations. There is the romantic failure, which values defeat for the gesture it allows: Cyrano, victim of a cowardly assassin, no longer fighting for justice and truth, but still keeping unsullied his white plume. There is the failure of the merely inept, and of the simpleton so innocent as to embody the wisdom of the Fool of God. There is the absurd failure, the comic figure put in such perspective—by Charlie Chaplin, for instance—that his defeats enhance his human greatness. There is the Quixotic failure of the illusory ideel, and the failure of a Daedelus whose high aspirations mistake man for a god. As with suicide, morality can condemn without qualification only the failure sought for no reason save a perverse prizing of defeat itself.

For no reason—but what is the life for which there *is* reason?

62. The Life of Reason

As might be expected, reason celebrates nothing other than the life of reason, in which reason itself is most prized. Reason is precious, it has argued on its own behalf, because it is the faculty most distinctive of the human animal. The tacit assumption that what we have in common with others is less worthy than what differentiates us from them may be questioned. Usually the position has been that reason is precious because it marks the kinship of man with the gods rather than because it sets him apart from the beasts. "Since reason is divine in comparison with man's whole nature," Aristotle has argued, "the life according to reason must be divine in comparison with usual human life." What theism expresses in terms of man's aspirations towards God, nontheistic philosophies formulate in terms of an equivalent distinction between a Supreme Good and a lesser or only apparent good; reason is assigned to the greater or true Good.

The life of reason is one shaped by rational decision; it is the life whose ideal is conveyed in Freud's slogan, "Where id was, there shall ego be!" The ego is what makes rational decisions; reason can provide both form and content to aspiration. Spinoza, who admirably embodied the life of reason, articulates the basic principle: "Things are good only insofar as they assist man to enjoy that life of the mind which is determined by intelligence." The business of intelligence is to apply this principle; the application consists in the fullest use of the powers of the mind. These powers are being used to the full, philosophers have argued, when the mind is occupied with philosophy. God, according to Aristotle, is most divine when engaged in thinking about thinking. He is then most like Aristotle; but Aristotle held that man is then most godlike. The life of contemplation, Aristotle urged, is the noblest because it belongs to the highest part of our natures, it can be continuously pursued without surfeit or distaste, it is the most pleasurable, the most self-sufficient (after the necessities of life have been provided), the most loved for its own sake—in short, the most in accord with wisdom.

In the rabbinic tradition, study as well as prayer is called *avodah*, service; in both we are actualizing what is divine in our natures. The great figures who laid the foundations of the Talmud are pictured as giving expression to their religious devotion by intellectual activity: Hillel almost froze to death lying on the roof of the academy to listen to lectures for which he could not afford tuition; Yochanan ben Zakkai had himself carried out of besieged Jerusalem in a coffin, in order to found a school outside defeated Judea; Shimon bar Yochai with his son hid in a cave for thirteen years, that they might continue the religious studies prohibited by the Romans. "God weeps every day," says the Talmud, "over him who is able to study the Law and does not" (the scholars who compiled the work could not resist adding, "and over him who is unable to study and does"). The life of the mind is extolled even when the mind is not explicitly occupied with religious teaching: one who has a scientific mind and refuses to apply himself is condemned for indifference to the wonders of God.

In this tradition, study is held to be even more important than action because it leads to appropriate action; the reverse is not necessarily true. Whatever the causal relation between thought and action, many ethical theories see in thought the logical basis of moral action. Boethius, in prison on false charges of treason during the last days of Rome, wrote *The Consolation of Philosophy*, defending the thesis that vice is "a sickness of the mind." A millennium later, Pascal pleaded, "Let us endeavour to think well; this is the principle of morality." From Socrates to Jeremy Bentham and John Dewey, philosophers have held that men never knowingly prefer evil; immoral action is the outcome of ignorance, error, or thoughtlessness.

Yet it can hardly be maintained that intelligence, however earnestly cultivated and systematically applied, suffices for the moral life. Scientists and academics in general are not conspicuously more devoted to the pursuit of the Good, or more markedly successful in attaining it, than are persons of more modest intellectuality. Morally speaking, intellectuals are not better than other people—and no worse either, in my opinion. But though the life of the mind may not be sufficient for morality, it is necessary to morality, if not as constituent of the moral life, then as determining its content. "True virtue," Spinoza said, "is life under the direction of reason." That is the life which Socrates described himself as pursuing: "I am and always have been one of those natures who must be guided by reason, whatever the reason may be which upon reflection appears to me to be the best."

To this life-style the objection is that it fails to do justice to the fullness of human nature, and does more than justice to the powers of the mind. Carnap once complained how lonely he had been during the tenure of a certain fellowship. "Perhaps" I said, "people were reluctant to interrupt your work." "Ah," he replied, "but I explicitly invited them to visit me!" Given the premises, they should be capable of deriving the conclusions. But were the required premises really given? Is it reason which is here at fault? Reason in its very nature, Freud insisted, cannot fail to give the emotions the place in life which is rightfully theirs. This is not meant in the spirit of the folk rhyme, "A little nonsense now and then/Is relished by the best of men." Feeling is hardly nonsensical; the life of the mind is not void of feeling but of groundless and insignificant feeling. Santayana's poem declaring "It is not wisdom to be only wise" does not negate his several treatises on the life of reason but condemns the timorous prudence which closes the eyes on the inward vision (§6).

The rightful place which reason gives the emotions is usually formulated in terms of *moderation*. "Nothing in excess" was inscribed in the temple of Apollo at Delphi. Temperance was classically regarded as one of the four cardinal virtues (the others being wisdom, courage, and justice). "We should pursue and practice moderation," said Plato, adding (rather immoderately) "and flee from excess with all the speed of which we are capable." Aristotle declares, "Pleasures should be moderate and few," and also adds the somewhat immoderate amplification, "and not at all opposed to reason." (Perhaps there is no such thing as only a mild opposition to reason, as there cannot be only a slight inconsistency or the merest hint of a pregnancy). In Lao-tzu we find the same counsel of moderation immoderately expressed: "In ruling men and in serving Heaven there is nothing like moderation." The Koran has it: "God wills that you use moderation in all things."

The ideal of moderation is usually specified by contrasting it with excesses of both too much and too little, what is enjoined being the *golden mean*. Buddhism identifies itself as "the Middle Way"—between escaping from life and being a prisoner of life, between an unthinking optimism and a despairing pessimism, between mortification of the flesh and sensual indulgence, between thoughtless dogmatism and unenlightened skepticism. Confucian philosophy expresses what is "just right" in *Chung-yung*, the doctrine of the mean. Plato's *Republic* states unequivocally, "The life that is seated in the mean is the greatest happiness for man." Aristotle echoes,

"The middle course of life is the best"—a statement, it is worth noting today, in his treastise on *Politics;* each virtue is elsewhere located by Aristotle as a mean between two vices. For Judaic thought, the Neoplatonist ibn-Gabirol enjoins, "Abandon both extremes and set about the right mean"; the Aristotelian Maimonides defines good deeds as "such as are equi-balanced between the too much and the too little."

In practice, the point of balance is problematic and can only be contextually determined. In some circumstances moderation may be unwise or impossible: there is no point in extracting a tooth part way; and if one is to shoot, the trigger must be squeezed decisively. Confucianism introduced the concept of *chung-ho,* the "proportional mean"; Aristotle speaks of the "relative mean": one "defined by reason, and as the prudent man would define it." No general formula is possible, for everything depends on the circumstances. What is called for is not an abstract criterion but concrete good judgment. Perhaps, one might add, good taste: a sense of proportion, a feeling for harmony and appropriateness. "Here are two fountains flowing at our side," says Plato; "one, which is pleasure, may be likened to a fountain of honey; the other, which is a sober draught in which no wine mingles, is of water, pure and healthful. Out of these we may seek to make the fairest of all possible mixtures." Recipes for the mixture are not forthcoming, nor are they to be expected.

The outcome of a life of moderation is *tranquility.* "Better is a handful of quietness," says the Preacher, "than both hands full of labor and striving after wind." In the garden of Epicurus the untroubled spirit could live a life of serene leisure, a smoothly flowing existence in a brotherhood of sages. The tranquil gardens of the Zen temples exemplify a similar life-style. Although the Stoics took sharp issue with the Epicureans with regard to the basis of morality, the life Epicurus enjoined was also described attractively by the Stoic Seneca—a life of simple, natural pleasures.

Stoicism and Zen emphasize maintaining one's equilibrium. Daruma, the founder of Zen, is often represented by a roly-poly doll because he lost the use of his legs from having sat so long in meditation and also because the doll is weighted to return upright no matter how it is buffeted about. The corresponding Stoic ideal is *ataraxia,* equanimity regardless of what happens. The Stoic is to play his part no matter what role he has been assigned. This is not a Judaic or Christian resignation to the will of God but a sameness of mind and feeling in all circumstances, an impartiality to all people, things, and situations. Seneca says, "Nothing should cloud the serenity of the sage, or shake his firmness." The Buddhist monk is to eat whatever life puts into his bowl. In the *Bhagavad-Gita* and the Yoga school is to be found a related ideal of *samatva,* but here there is also an element of transcendence—an indifference to anything worldly.

A life which aims only at tranquility is vulnerable to the criticism that it is self-centered, that it lacks moral discrimination, a passion for justice, or even plain human feeling. When something is rotten it is a man's duty to speak up however upsetting the consequences, and not only to speak but to act as truth and justice demand. Seneca urges that the sage should console those who weep but not weep with them, help but not feel pity. But without pity or some other strong feeling, how long will the impulse to help remain? Quite often the shared feeling (sym-pathy) is itself the help. Those who seek only a peaceful life for themselves are not likely to be of much help to those others for whom there is no peace.

Yet there is in the tranquil life of the sage a certain gracefulness, what many philosophers have extolled as *dignity,* another quality of life strikingly lacking in our time. Here is an important link between ethics and art, an aesthetic element in morality. Harmony and proportion are as much features of the good as of the beautiful, Plato and his followers have urged. Confucianism assigned great importance to what it called *li*—ceremonies, forms, rites, customs. By these, feelings are evoked in due degree, proportional to the circumstances, and given expression in channels which harmonize personal feelings with one another and with the color and texture of social life. It is not always easy, for instance, to find expressions of grief which are not destructive either of oneself or of others, or expressions of joy which do not lead to its own undoing. The Confucian sage, like the Stoic, must always be satisfied and composed, and like the Epicurean, lead a life of dignified ease, self-respect without anxious vanity.

Morality need not be grim, and there is no particular merit in crudeness. Austerity may be imposed upon us by scarcities, but we need not make a virtue of necessity. Yet dignified ease does require wealth. Leisure alone may not be sufficient to give a leisurely pace to life, but it is certainly a necessary condition. There is no sense in speaking of moderation, tranquility, and dignity to those whose unremitting efforts are scarcely enough to yield the barest satisfaction of needs and a modicum of security. Diogenes Laertius quotes Socrates as declaring that leisure is the best of all possessions; unfortunately, it is most likely to be enjoyed by those who possess a great deal else. The rejoinder might be made that leisure is not likely to be truly enjoyed by such people—he who possesses little is by so much the less possessed, as Zarathustra and countless exponents of the simple life have insisted. It is a leisurely life, not a life of leisure, which is being held up as the ideal.

A more telling criticism of the aesthetic morality is that in such a life goodness may shrink to nothing more than good taste, as with the aesthetes who first put manners before morals, then come to identify the two. Oscar Wilde's Lord Darlington (in *Lady Windermere's Fan*) expresses this sort of decadence: "Do you know I am afraid that good people do a great deal of harm in this world. Certainly the greatest harm they do is that they make badness of such extraordinary importance. It is absurd to divide people into good and bad. People are either charming or tedious. I take the side of the charming." There is not a great deal of difference between this aestheticism and the neoromantic glorification of kidnappers and murderers, provided their brutalities are committed with what is seen as a certain verve (and provided that the admirer does not himself become a victim).

A more likely consequence of the emphasis on good form is that morality degenerates to the emptiness of sheer formalism. Ceremony loses its symbolic depth and becomes superficial; instead of celebrating values, we merely observe unmeaning rituals. Orthodox Judaism identifies 613 *mitzvot*, commandments comprising both the highest moral injunctions and detailed specifications of temple rites. Confucianism is said to lay down 300 rules of ceremony and 3,000 rules of deportment. Brahmanical Hinduism is governed by comparably numerous regulations. Are such vast normative structures, without taking into account the complexities of civil and criminal law, necessary or even acceptable constituents of the life of reason? It is not surprising that Freud, far from acknowledging as a sage one who lives such a style of life, diagnoses him as suffering from a compulsion neurosis.

At its best, the life of reason is devoted to adventures only of the mind, pursuing in all else moderation, tranquility, and dignity. It finds memorable expression in the prayer recited by Socrates at the end of the *Phaedrus:* "Give me beauty in the inward soul, and may the outer and the inner man be at one. May I reckon the wise to be the wealthy, and may I have as much gold as only the temperate can carry. Anything more? That prayer, I think, is enough for me." This is not a prayer for brotherhood, justice, or peace; yet it bears the unmistakable accents of wisdom so far as it goes. The life it aspires to embodies the qualities of classic Greek art: proportion, harmony, balance, grace, intelligibility.

This style of art, as of life, Nietzsche called the *Apollonian*. There is another style in Greek art, possibly of more aesthetic merit even though lacking in what we have been brought up to regard as "classic purity." Nietzsche calls it the *Dionysian*—it is exaggerated, discordant, tense, vigorous—above all, passionate. The contrast, later applied by Oswald Spengler to whole cultures, is one of the confused strands of meaning in the opposition of "classic" and "romantic." For normative ethics it poses the question whether the life of reason can come to terms with the Dionysian impulse.

What room does reason make for joy? There are philosophers who hold that there is no room for joy in a rational life, and who argue, rather, that our joys are grounded in irrationality and illusion. This is the root pessimism in Schopenhauer, for example (a pessimism, so far as *this* world is concerned, shared by many religious philosophies). "Life is given us not to be enjoyed," he says, "but to be overcome, to be got over." The world he sees as a kind of Hell, where wisdom lies in confining one's efforts to securing a little room not exposed to the fire. Society today, expecially in the developed nations, allocates a significant part of its resources to anodynes, analgesics, anesthetics—if not rooms protected from the flames, unguents to reduce the pain. I cannot believe that these are the ultimate materials of wisdom.

Life is not always painful, Schopenhauer concedes, but when we are not in pain, he says, we suffer even more from boredom. Pain or boredom is the lot, respectively, of the poor and the rich, and of all men on weekdays and Sundays, respectively, in work and at leisure. For Kierkegaard, boredom is the root of all evil—not because the Devil finds work for idle hands but because in boredom life has no point and action no meaning. Man faces the

Void and can only find within himself wherewith to fill the emptiness. My eye was once caught by the title of an article in a psychoanalytic journal, "The Idea of Nothing"; instead of metaphysical insight, what I found was a clinical report of a patient who, whenever he said he was thinking of nothing, was preoccupied with the female genitals. Not even pathology can make of such symbolism the counter to boredom.

For religion as for rationalist philosophy, the problem is how to attain the Dionysian without the demonic, to savor what we call the pagan joy of life without abandoning moral discrimination and aspiration to the ideal. The problem is not how to sin without anxiety or guilt but how to be blessed in truth with the joys of which the Tempter forever lies. "Since humanity came into being, man has enjoyed himself too little," Nietzsche observes; "that alone, my brothers, is our original sin. And when we learn better to enjoy ourselves, then we unlearn best to give pain to others." He calls himself "the last disciple and initiate of the god Dionysus"; perhaps, after him, Zorba. We can find in the teachings of the Preacher as well as of the pagan that there is nothing better for man than that he should rejoice. What is worthy of giving joy and how it is to be obtained is the question.

Here the cult of intensity (§60) unexpectedly finds support from the religionist. "Whatever your hand finds to do," Kohelet advises, "do it with all your might." What you are to do is to give service, *avodah,* by cultivating what is divine in your nature. "Rejoice in God always," Paul enjoins, "and again I say, rejoice." Thereby we shall know the peace that passes understanding, what Hinduism calls *ananda* or bliss. In naturalistic, humanistic terms, what this comes to is a life devoted to love and to work. Each of these has in its turn been condemned as folly. Perhaps here as elsewhere the last word belongs neither to the philosopher nor to the priest but to the poet. "If the fool," says William Blake, "were to persist in his folly, he would be wise."

Chapter Ten

Social Philosophy

63. Responsibility and Alienation

Central to social philosophy is the concept of *responsibility,* as the concept of freedom is central to ethics. Responsibility binds society together—indeed, makes society possible. Socialization is basically assigning responsibilities and defining how they are to be discharged. This is true even for children, who are not yet "responsible individuals." That is what *we* say about them, but there is a child culture, transmitted from children to children without adult mediation. A child comes to be accepted as a member of his peer group as he becomes responsible for a certain pattern of thought, feeling, and action. The carefree days of childhood are largely an adult myth; children are not subject to lesser demands from their society than we are from ours, only different ones. The same can be said of the mythical savage enviably "free from the trammels of civilization"; behavior in so-called primitive societies is subject to more restraints than in our own. Man everywhere, and throughout his lifetime, is a social animal; there is no getting away from responsibility.

Bearing responsibility must be distinguished from having a sense of responsibility, just as being guilty is distinct from having a sense of guilt. A person can act irresponsibly and lack a sense of responsibility. Responsibility is not a matter of how a person feels about his behavior, nor of what he thinks he is doing. He may have been both thoughtless and unfeeling, and for just that reason all the more responsible for what he has done. Another sort of person often feels responsible, even though the responsibility is not, in fact, his.

A sense of responsibility is nevertheless important. It usually marks the difference between the responsibilities *imposed* upon us and those we *as-*

sume. The difference does not hinge on how we got the responsibilities: we usually assume responsibilities which, to start with, were imposed on us. It hinges on whether we ourselves hold ourselves responsible. To assume a responsibility is to choose to discharge it; whatever its source, the responsibility is freely undertaken. Responsibility is not the price demanded by others for our freedom; it is intrinsic to the exercise of freedom. The choice is not truly mine unless I am assuming responsibility for what I am doing (§58).

My assuming it may be only an assumption, in the pejorative sense. An exaggerated sense of responsibility makes unwarranted demands on the overly conscientious. It is not a simple matter to determine anyone's responsibilities, certainly not our own. This is especially true if the determination is being made so as to assign or withhold blame. "It is not easy to define verbally how far and to what extent a man is blamable," Aristotle noted in his *Nichomachean Ethics.* "Such questions belong to particular cases, and their decision belongs to moral perception." Responsibility is contextual, depending on circumstances which cannot be specified exhaustively beforehand. A man who refuses to participate in a war he sees as unjust may be acting on principle; but to demand amnesty afterwards, even though he rejects an equivalent period of nonmilitary service, amounts to a denial of responsibility. The basic law of economics, that there is no such thing as a free lunch, has its counterpart in ethics: there are no moral bargains. Virtue has a price—it is responsibility.

The fact that responsibility is a price to be paid is recognized in acknowledging it as a burden. For this reason, freedom, from which responsibility is inseparable, is felt to be burdensome. The existentialists speak of "dreadful freedom," of man as being "condemned to be free"; we choose, Kierkegaard has it, "in fear and trembling." Caught up in such fear, we pursue the self-defeating course of aspiring to freedom while seeking to evade responsibility. Even when we have the moral courage to assume the responsibilities which are rightfully ours, the world is too amorphous and complex to allow us to define responsibilities clearly and unequivocally.

The most common device for evading responsibility is not to redefine it, but to *project* it onto others. A religious projection speaks of original sin and vicarious atonement: the moral problem was posed by Adam's Fall and was resolved by the death of the Savior. God Himself may serve as the locus of projected responsibility; confronted by a beggar, a Muslim might say "Allah provide!" instead of "No." The Master said, Act as though there is no God—you yourself must help. A variety of psychological projections have long been familiar; not *I* am responsible, but my compulsions, my passions, or simply, my "human nature."

In our time, a sociological projection has become commonplace. Society is responsible for our moral failings—poverty, discrimination, and the ghetto life are the sources of crime and immorality, and, for that matter, so are affluence, privilege, and the emptiness of middle-class aspirations. In whatever social role we act, moral accountability is localized in another, as each institution imposes on others the responsibility for the moral consequences of its workings: the scientist turns to the "citizen," the state to the church, the school to the family, the media to the "public," the government to the "voters." Meanwhile, everyone feeling himself helpless to do *everything* supposes himself thereby freed from the responsibility of doing *anything*. Hence the *Ethics of the Fathers* enjoins, "The work is not yours to finish, but neither are you free to pass it by."

Common to many of these projective evasions is a retrospective conception of responsibility, as though its locus can be fixed by a specification of causes. The assumption is, if I did not cause it to happen, I am not responsible for its happening. The same assumption is involved in the misapprehension of freedom as free will (§48); I am not the cause, and so was not acting freely (responsibly), if what I did was the effect of other causes acting on me. The law, reasonably enough, exempts a person from responsibility only if certain causes were operative, such as criminal coercion or psychopathic compulsion. How to define the class of causes which free a person from responsibility is admittedly not easy. There are cases where the law reasonably assigns responsibility even though there is no question of causal efficacy, or only the most remote causal connection, as in a parent's responsibility for damage caused by his child, or an owner's responsibility for the misdeeds of his dog. That the child or the dog should have been better trained may be true; yet even if they are unteachable, responsibility for them is not thereby discharged.

Responsibility—both assigned and assumed—looks to the future rather than to the past, to effects rather than to causes. To assign responsibility is not to charge prior involvement but to identify a commitment to something yet undone; to assume responsibility is not to confess a completed action but to declare a readiness to undertake action toward an unrealized end.

Two corresponding conceptions of punishment are involved: *retributive* punishment, seeking to restore the moral balance that was upset, and *corrective* punishment, aiming at a more acceptable future. Philosophers, by and large, agree with the corrective view expressed in Plato's *Laws:* "The purpose of the penalty is not to cancel the crime—what is once done can never be made undone—but to bring the criminal and all who witness his punishment to complete renunciation of such criminality in the future, or at least to recovery in great part from the dreadful state."

Punishment thought of as retributive may also be corrective: some would-be criminals are deterred by the prospect of swift and sure retribution. But criminologists and clinicians have also concluded that a person's insistence on retribution—especially when he is insisting on severe punishment—may serve to free him from a sense of guilt for his own evil impulses, and to strengthen their inhibition. If the criminal goes unpunished for what he has done, how am *I* to control my desires to do likewise? Hamlet may have been as much obsessed with his own guilty impulses as with his stepfather's guilty actions. Some such psychodynamics is at work in the irrational and often savage treatment of homosexuals as well as in the absurdities of ordinances governing what is called "lewdness" and "obscenity." Punishment which purports to be corrective may be seen as retributive by those who inflict the punishment—especially capital punishment—as well as by those who receive it. In some cases capital punishment not only does not deter but provides an incentive.

By his death the criminal takes part in a *sacrament of violence.* This may be the symbolic content of terrorist action: blood is spilled so as to compel the gods. That the killing is indiscriminate means that the gods choose their victims. Terrorists have complained that agreements with them have not been honored; they have even complained against the illegality and deceptiveness of having armed guards on planes. Such complaints are by no means absurd; they express the outrage that the sacrificial animal is so ill-bred as to interfere with the ceremony. In the end, the killer himself is to be killed, as the gods are served in return for their help. The crude and bloody ending of the terrorist drama contrasts markedly with the smooth enactment of its early scenes, not because of the terrorists's miscalculations but because his calculations only extended to the moment of killing. "It worries me that I came out of it alive myself," said one of the Molucca terrorists at his trial. The leader of an abortive coup in Iraq a few years ago declared just before his execution, "He who undertakes an adventure of this kind must pay this kind of price." For these disordered minds, paying the price is itself the adventure.

This side of pathology, a major problem of crime and punishment in our time is that constituted by the ethics of *corporate responsibility.* More and more, socially significant action is performed by corporate entities—governments, corporations, and associations. How are such impersonal entities to be held morally responsible? Individual agents of corporate action regularly disclaim personal responsibility; but they are the only *persons* involved. A man put on trial for war crimes claims to have been "carrying out orders"; let us stipulate that he was doing so, not willfully exceeding his orders in committing atrocities. How can this absolve him? On the other hand, how are all of us to be brought to account for conformity to the norms of social action which in every society today are, at best, morally dubious and, at worst, monstrously inhuman?

One response is to dissociate oneself altogether from corporate action. But it is not easy to drop out completely. In any case, to allow others to pay my way hardly saves me from being implicated in the immoralities of *their* life-style. Moreover, in the degree to which I succeed in really freeing myself from a share in the actions of others, I condemn myself to social impotence: I can act effectively only in concert with others. Advertising is a most pernicious influence; however, to succeed in moderating or elevating its influence, we would have to mount a massive advertising campaign to educate and arouse the citizenry. "All these organizations of ours," one Jew complained to another, "are ruining Jewish life. We have religious organizations, philanthropic ones, organizations to combat anti-Semitism, organizations on behalf of Israel, educational organizations, cultural, social. They're strangling us! I'm confident that there are thousands of Jews who feel the same way; I wish we could get together and do something about it!"

Corporate responsibility has been institutionalized since ancient times through the assignment of collective responsibility regardless of the actions of the individuals subsumed under the collectivity. The view which regards a group as a moral agent, and therefore as a bearer of moral responsibility, is *tribalism.* The collectivity is accountable for the actions of any of its members; conversely, each individual is answerable for the failings of any member of the group. Tribalism is familiar as a presuppostion of ethnic prejudice (§65). It is also expressed in the policy of punishing parents for the "social crimes" of their children, or the children for the "crimes" of their parents—for instance, the desire to emigrate, in the Soviet Union, and ideological heresy in China. Tribalism was morally condemned as long ago as the days of Ezekiel: "What do you mean by using this proverb in Israel, 'The fathers have eaten sour grapes, and the children's teeth are set on edge?' You shall not use this proverb any longer, says the Lord. All souls are Mine—the soul of the father, so also the soul of the son. The soul that sins shall die. But if a man be just, and do what is lawful and right, he shall surely live."

Tribalism is socially pernicious: the grossest immoralities are claimed to be justified if they have been committed in the name of a collective entity. Political offenses are often taken to be exempt from moral norms. Martin Buber's principle, that what is wrong for the individual cannot be right for the group, deserves careful consideration. Action on behalf of a group is not necessarily selfless or even unselfish (§58). *Group egotism,* in Buber's terms, means that neither within the group nor in relation to those outside is there genuine respect for the other or a capacity to enter into dialogue with the other, to say nothing of caring for him. Without such care or respect, it is hard to see any basis for exemption from the norms governing actions for the individual. Buber's position is that only those who are capable of truly saying "Thou" to one another can truly say "We" with one another. The love of a country, a people, or a cause can be as consuming and dedicated as any other love; all the more reason why there is no room in it for hatred.

There is a real moral dilemma here. Morality does demand loyalty and devotion to kith and kin. True, "Our country, right or wrong!" is a dangerous doctrine, if unaccompanied by the determination to put her right when she is wrong; but one who cannot say, "With all her faults she is my country still" cannot acknowledge any country as his own. Yet morality makes other demands, not always compatible with the duty to a man's own people. One may arise who proclaims, in the words of Matthew, "I am come to set a man against his father, and the daughter against her mother. A man's enemies shall be those of his own house. He who loves father or mother, son or daughter, more than me is not worthy of me." In contrast, when someone remarked to Confucius, "In my part of the country there is a man so upright that when his father stole a sheep he bore witness against him," Confucius, according to the *Analects,* replied, "Honest men in my part of the country are different—a father screens the misdeeds of his son, and the son the misdeeds of his father. There is uprightness in this." The dilemma is not to be resolved by taking the one stand or the other. Moral conflicts are inevitable within a self sufficiently rich and complex to identify with more than limited interests; there are no preestablished moral harmonies.

Responsibility, whether assumed or assigned, is social through and through. We are responsible always *to* someone or other. If the wicked flee when no man pursues, the righteous answer even when no man calls, for their righteousness is in being answerable, as the flight of the wicked is itself the sin. Responsibility arises and is discharged in a social context. Every responsibility implies an obligation. That responsibility is social means that the obligation must be referred always to a *community of obligation*, within which the responsible man can acquit himself of the duties he has assumed, and on the basis of which he is truly a member of the community. The story in the Book of Numbers of the rebellion of Korach is instructive. He and others of the house of Levi had been singled out for distinctive duties, for which they claimed a corresponding status, rejecting the leadership of Moses. When God threatened to punish Korach, tribalism was repudiated; "Shall one man sin and Your wrath fall on the whole congregation?" Only when the community had separated itself from the rebels were the rebels destroyed. The essence of *civil* disobedience (§73), which is quite compatible with a sense of responsibility, and may even be demanded by such a sense, is that the disobedience preserves community, only redefining the obligations to it.

No community can be so homogeneous or so wholly integrated as to preclude diversities of interests and outlooks. From the moment obligations are recognized, conflicting obligations must also be acknowledged. The sixteenth-century Kabbalist, Moses Cordovero, argued that in every man there is something of his fellowmen, so that whoever sins injures not only himself, but also that part of himself which belongs to another. We belong to various others, and what we owe to one may be what injures another. Moralists are too much occupied with the insistence on doing one's duty and not enough with the dilemmas of conflicting duties. What is widely lacking is not so much a sense of social responsibility as it is a genuine community of obligation, comprehensive enough to embrace all on whom we wish to impose a measure of responsibility.

Responsibility is not only *to* someone; it is also *for* someone. "Social ethics" has been defined in terms of a set of responsibilities in religious teaching and in political doctrine. It is Abraham, and not Noah, with whom God established His covenant; although Noah was righteous in his way, he assumed no responsibility for those about to be destroyed; Abraham, however, sat at the door of his tent to greet the passing stranger. The Master said: "In the cold, one man wraps himself in furs while another lights a fire which casts its warmth on all around; do not be a saint in a fur coat!" The Book of Proverbs is straightforward: "If you say, 'It is none of my business, will not He Who weighs men's hearts call you to account?" Even more explicitly it enjoins, "Speak out for those who cannot speak, for the rights of all the unfortunate." The Talmud later declares that the man whose protest would be of any weight and who does not make the protest when a wrong is about to be committed is himself to be held responsible for that wrong.

To help where one can and to speak out in protest when no other help can be given—this is to be responsibe *to* others and *for* them. But there can be no sense of responsibility where there is no sense of community, no caring for others if we cannot in any way identify with them. This is what it means to be *alienated* from others: they are strangers, they mean nothing to me, I don't give a damn about them. Alienation is the antithesis of responsibility, fragmenting society. Alienation loosens even the inner bonds by which a person attains some measure of wholeness. The alienated person is also a stranger to himself.

The most obvious symptom of alienation is the desperate attempt to escape from oneself, the hell in which the alienated person finds himself. This is the significance of the high incidence of suicide (§61), as the sociologist Emile Durkheim maintained many decades ago, with his concept of "anomie" as the collapse of the collective normative system. It is the significance, too, of the abuse of drugs, not as a source of pleasure but to get away, to go on a "trip." Whether in America, Scandinavia, or the Soviet Union, alcohol is the futile specific against alienation which many prescribe for themselves, so many that in the United States for some time arrests for drunkenness have equaled arrests for all other reasons put together, excluding only those for "disorderly conduct"—an exception not altogether irrelevant. Mental illness, whatever its organic pathology, is also an expression of the flight from an unbearable reality, an alien and hostile world. Psychiatrists are sometimes called "alienists." In the United States as many people are hospitalized for mental illness, to say nothing of the countless sufferers not under institutional care, as for all other diseases put together. If alienation is not pandemic, it is among the most serious of our social ailments.

Alienation is nowhere more important than with regard to members of one's own family. The opening line of *Anna Karenina* reads, "All happy families are alike; every unhappy family is unhappy in its own way." For each family the pursuit of happiness finds distinctive expression, but in modern society family life, by and large, is unhappy indeed. There are now about one-quarter as many divorces each year as there are marriages, and the number is increasing. Many more families have broken up, in a psychological sense if not legally. Prosecutions (not just complaints or even arrests) for criminal offenses against members of the family are three times as numerous as those for drug offenses, which are so much more in public attention.

With this crisis in the family as an institution, the *generation gap* is no longer a simple, universal fact of biology but a social problem. The problem is not constituted by a rate of social change so great that the outlook of the young is radically different from that of the older generation. Between the generations there is always a radical difference in outlook, whatever the rate of social change. The gap poses a problem because of the alienation of the young, expressed by encapsulation (the hippie), by rebellion (the activist), and by apathy (the dropout). The gap need not be a battlefield; it can provide instead a ground for exploration as in *Huckleberry Finn, Ah, Wilderness,* and *Catcher in the Rye.*

Some of the factors creating the problem are easy to identify. On the one hand, the onset of puberty seems now to come earlier; on the other hand, finding a place for oneself in society is more and more delayed. The training expected of the young has increased: a high-school education was once a considerable attainment; now even a college degree is looked on patronizingly. For almost any career, years of experience after training are demanded, while opportunities to acquire experience are denied to the inexperienced—the equivalent in civilian life of *Catch 22*. Social roles, occupational and personal, are continually and rapidly being redefined, so that both training and experience are soon obsolete. At the same time, the range of possible choices, of goals and of preparation for their pursuit (for instance, by travel), is increasing. It is not surprising that the young, like the rest of us, feel condemned to be free.

For all of us, young or old, relations have become more impersonal. "People rush past each other as if they had nothing in common. The disintegration of society into individuals, each guided by his private principles and each pursuing his own aims, has been pushed to its furthest limits." This is a description of life in London, written about a century ago by Friedrich Engels. If there is a difference today it is that now individuals are often organized into groups, each with its private principles and aims, impersonal in relation to outsiders, if not in the relations among members. A generation or so after Engels, the German sociologist Ferdinand Tönnies distinguished between *Gemeinschaft* and *Gesellschaft*, personal relationships and impersonal organizations, friends and connections, a covenant and a contract. The old-time so-called political machine displayed considerable personal involvement of the political boss with his constituents; nowadays the political organization is called a "team" rather than a "machine," but it is more impersonal.

The intimate *community* whose passing is so widely mourned is to some degree a nostalgic myth, but contemporary patterns of personal relations do leave much to be desired. Not only are we separated from one another, but differences among us often evoke hostility. There is no community but only a collectivity, a contrast reminiscent of Schopenhauer's image of men as porcupines huddling together for warmth, till they come close enough to be pricked by one another's quills. We reach out for others, then keep them at arm's length; we give one another no more than an occasion for reciprocal exploitation.

That something more is wanted is recognized by everyone; it is supplied in a spurious way which leaves unchanged the underlying impersonality of our relationships. I call the pattern the *stewardess syndrome:* charm and warmth of manner become forms without content; an apparently personal interest serves only organizational ends. The syndrome is now a staple of advertising: "Visit a friend this week—your Ford dealer"; "The Dodge rebellion wants *you*"; "In a world where everyone is looking out for himself, it's nice to know that someone cares—Hertz Car Rentals." The automobile industry is no worse than any other, and commerce no more falsifies community than do other domains of life with their brotherhood weeks, community chests, cleanup campaigns, Thanksgiving parades, and even Christmas celebrations.

Technology has disenchanted many and intensified alienation. We do not understand what we use daily. The language of scientists and engineers is foreign to us, while they, in turn, must learn still another language in order to communicate with their machines. Technology puts the world into our hands, then shackles us. ("Where did you spend your vacation?" "Majorca." "Majorca! Where is that?" "How should I know? We flew.") We use the machine, but in the process we are used by it. To control it in its larger consequences, we need to know much more than how to push the button, but the requisite knowledge is, for most of us, impossible to come by. Even what is not secret about atomic energy, for instance, must be taken largely on faith; how are we ourselves to assess the dangers which might lie in its development? "If you don't know jewels, know your jeweler," the merchant tells us; the generalization is obvious. We are at the mercy of technicians who are themselves also alienated.

Machines seem to make their own demands—invention is the mother of necessity, someone has said. It is man who makes the demands, for the machines are only means to ends of *our* choosing, but we keep our ends tacit, and articulate only the means needed for them. The moral collapse of the industrialized nations in the face of oil blackmail is not forced upon them by their industries any more than the dagger guides the hand of the assassin. Technology is not an unthinking monster (§35); it is we who are thoughtless or monstrous in our use of it. When Emerson said over a century ago that "things are in the saddle and ride mankind," he was referring to our being driven by our desires for material things. All that seems to have changed in this respect is that the desires are now socially rather than personally defined. Whatever progress we have made in the satisfaction of personal needs, we have also produced a ravaged earth, polluted waters, poisoned air, and the destruction of many species—possibly soon to include our own. These are not consequences of deliberately destructive aims, as in war, but of our technological *development*. In the long run, nuclear reactors may pose a greater threat than nuclear bombs.

Each of us is alienated from a technology which none of us seems to control. In the perspectives of many social philosophers, this condition is basically a consequence of the alienation of the worker from his work. It was Marx who transformed the concept of alienation from its earlier theological content to its modern sociological content. Marx means by it the dissociation of the worker from the instruments and aims of production, with social worth increasingly centering on the system of production itself, which therefore determines human values rather than being determined by them. "As the world of things increases in value," he wrote, "the human world becomes devalued. For labor not only produces commodities; it makes a commodity of the work process itself, as well as of the worker." Since his day we have succeeded in making work shorter, but hardly more meaningful. After the industrial and the cybernetic revolutions, the majority of workers are still occupied with routine operations directed to trivial ends. They are paid more for their work, but there has been no significant increase in the value of their compensation—I am speaking of human worth, not simply of real wages.

More and more, life searches for meaning not in work but in play, while play, in turn, is socially rationalized as allowing us to work better. Those of us who can afford it work hard at playing; we play with our work only in the most pejorative sense of the term "play." Leisure is now a problem not because we do not know how to get it but because we do not know what to do with it when we have it. The problem was already known to Thoreau (*Walden*): "A stereotyped but unconscious despair is concealed even under what are called the games and amusements of mankind."

Concern over lack of social responsibility, the collapse of community, alienation, and the inhuman use of technology is currently coming to a focus in the emerging concept of *quality of life*. But, first of all, how is life, whatever its quality, to be preserved? "Before man can live well," Aristotle has said, "he must be able to live." The principle of the "sanctity of life," virtually a cliché of Western morality, has been made the basis of invidious comparisons with an alleged disregard for life in Asian societies. In practice, our belief in the sanctity of life seems to be expressed only in combating contraception and abortion, prolonging death agonies, putting high prices on burials, and leaving life insurance in the hands of profit-making corporations. It is not conspicuously expressed in the effort to preserve life. In the United States, technologically the most advanced nation in the world, the rate of infant mortality is higher than in a dozen or so other countries; industrial accidents steadily increase; and years of research followed by years of public outcry have still not provided effective social control of carcinogenic agents like tobacco and pollutants.

The quality of life, given that life is preserved, involves more than the production and distribution of goods and services. It concerns the texture of our experience with all we make and use, the style of all our doings, the character of all we undergo. We still aspire to the classic ideals of liberty, equality, and fraternity. New ideals are also emerging: freedom from fear in a world of little hostility, where such conflicts as arise are negotiated and compromised; a life of serenity and dignity, at an unhurried pace, extending and receiving courtesy and considerateness, accepting and being accepted in an awareness of a common humanity, with its failings; a sense of productiveness and creativity, pride of workmanship taking the place of acquisitiveness, and self-respect replacing competitive assessments; and beauty all around, environmentally and in our immediate surroundings. Responsibility for advancing towards a life of this quality lies with all who share in the ideals.

64. Loneliness and Aging

Among the most widespread manifestations of alienation is loneliness. The following story consists of the titles of songs on this theme popular in the last few years:

I am A MAN ALONE, ALL ALONE, ALL BY MYSELF; LET ME BE LONELY, I WALK ALONE on THE LONESOME ROAD, THE LONG LONESOME HIGHWAY; I AM MR. LONELY, THE LONELY ONE—ONE LONELY BOY; ONE IS THE LONELIEST NUMBER. I'M A LONESOME HOBO, I'M A LONESOME FUGITIVE, A LONELY TEENAGER—OH LONESOME ME! WHY SO LONELY? Because I live in EMPTY ROOMS on LONELY STREET in LONELYVILLE—THIS EMPTY PLACE. IT'S A LONESOME OLD TOWN, a TOWN WITHOUT PITY. I'M A STRANGER HERE; I'M A LONELY LITTLE PETUNIA IN AN ONION PATCH. I'm LONELY AGAIN, NOBODY'S BABY AGAIN, DESERTED, ALONE IN THE WORLD, ALL ALONE BY THE TELEPHONE; but all I hear is the SOUNDS OF SILENCE. WHO CAN I TURN TO? I've been ALONE TOO LONG, living through LONELY DAYS, in each week SEVEN LONELY DAYS; SATURDAY NIGHT IS THE LONELIEST NIGHT OF THE WEEK, but I remember EVERY LONELY DAY, all the OLD LONESOME TIMES. So I know A THING CALLED SADNESS, THE BIG HURT. I'm just LONELY; PLEASE DON'T LEAVE ME. I'M SO LONESOME I COULD CRY, but I'm TOO HURT TO CRY. It's CRYING TIME, but NOBODY SEES ME CRY. Yet there are TEARS ON MY PILLOW, INVISIBLE TEARS. I CRIED LIKE A BABY, but BIG GIRLS DON'T CRY, so I WON'T CRY ANY MORE; I'm FRESH OUT OF TEARS. I'm an UNHAPPY GIRL, unhappy as ONLY THE LONELY can be. HELP ME MAKE IT THROUGH THE NIGHT, or I will have my NINETEENTH NERVOUS BREAKDOWN. THINGS HAVE GONE TO PIECES, AIN'T GONNA TRY ANYMORE, except one thing: SELF DESTRUCT. O BURY ME NOT ON THE LONE PRAIRIE!

The sadness, pain, and self-pity in these titles, and even more explicitly in the lyrics, are by no means distinctive of our own day. The themes can be traced back for many decades, and longer. Here is the symbolist poet Arthur Symons writing around the turn of the century:

> *O water, voice of my heart, crying in the sand,*
> *All night long crying with a mournful cry,*
> *As I lie and listen, and cannot understand*
> *The voice of my heart in my side or the voice of the sea,*
> *O water, crying for rest, is it I, is it I?*
> *All night long the water is crying to me.*
>
> —"The Crying Water"

Crying to me, no doubt crying with me, and crying *for* me as well. It is not hard to appreciate the reaction of the self-contained Sherlock Holmes exposed to the "chorus of groans and cries" which filled what he knew as the "agony columns," of the various London journals of his time: "'Every day my heart longs—' Bleat, Watson, unmitigated bleat!" Yet what else is one in pain to do but cry out, if the pain is from being unheard and uncared for?

Loneliness does not consist in being alone. A person can feel lonely when he is among many others, and can be by himself without being lonely. There is one kind of aloneness which, far from being painful, is enjoyed and sought after. It is *privacy,* freedom from unwanted intrusion, control over one's own life space. Privacy, characterized by Justice Louis D. Brandeis as the most comprehensive of rights, the one most valued by civilized men, is increasingly difficult to secure and to maintain. What we say may be secretly taped, and what we do, recorded by unseen cameras; information about our economic affairs and more personal matters is computerizeed and transmitted to others without our knowledge or consent; privacy is increasingly invaded by telephone solicitations and other forms of commercial, political, and even religious importunities; we find ourselves among captive audiences, listening helplessly to announcements or to what someone judges to be soothing music in markets, elevators, mass transports, and public buildings; everywhere we are assaulted by waves of sound pollution. The loneliness being complained of is decidedly not a matter of too much privacy.

There is another form of being alone which is sought for: *seclusion*, aloneness as a condition of creativity. A turning inward can bring us closer to others when we return to them with what we have produced from our inner resources. The artist who shuts himself away is not thereby declaring that his art serves only to express himself (§79); his seclusion may reveal rather that he cares so much for others that only withdrawal can keep his caring from dissipating his creative energies.

Closely related is *constructive loneliness*, discharging a responsibility which cannot be delegated to others without a corresponding diminution of the self. It is for this reason, as Charlie Brown is acutely aware, that the loneliest place on earth is the pitcher's mound. A memorable symbol of constructive loneliness is the image of Abraham Lincoln, wrapped in a shawl, bowed by the weight of the lonely responsibility of preserving the Union. This loneliness, often embodied in depictions of great leaders, is not to be confused with the pretense of greatness in the aloofness of the romantic pose. "On the heights one is always alone," said Nietzsche; but, perhaps, the higher we mount the closer we come to others. The "splendid isolation," which became a political catchword at the end of the last century, has shown itself in our time to be a tawdry self-seeking. Being alone does not necessarily condemn us to loneliness; neither does it necessarily raise us to the heights.

The difference between loneliness, on the one hand, and privacy, seclusion, and constructive loneliness, on the other, is that in loneliness there is a sense of loss of something precious, a painful contrast between the joy we once knew, whether in fact or in fantasy, and the joylessness of our present state. The lonely one has been abandoned, deserted by those who once knew and loved him. The Book of Job has been recognized by many as a supreme expression of loneliness. Job says: "My acquaintances treat me as a stranger, my relatives have failed me, my friends have forgotten me." A modern symbol may be found in T. S. Eliot's "The Love Song of J. Alfred Prufrock."

The lonely one feels that he does not belong; he is a stranger. Loneliness is alienation seen from within, the personal experience of a dissociated society. It might be argued that this is the price which must be paid for the freedom to be who and what we choose. Modern society has been characterized as differing from feudal society chiefly in that social roles are not predetermined by an individual's status at birth but result from contractual agreements, choices freely made. How free such choices actually are has been questioned; but the difference between status and contract is undeniably significant. Proper names commonly derive from occupations—Smith, Baker, Miller, and Cohen—as though what a person does and who he is are co-determined; many other names reveal family descent—Johnson, MacDonald, O'Reilly, and Ben Yehuda—as though a person's origins define his identity. If the family occupation or status no longer fixes a person's social roles, he must expect a loosening of the ties binding him to his fellows, and so know loneliness. This is the condition of the Hindu factory worker cut off from the caste structure of his native village where his family still resides. It is also the condition of the Western student, uprooted from the family and the neighbors of his youth, so that he might learn to be himself, whoever that might be.

The problem goes deeper. Even if our social roles are of our own choosing, we do not live in those roles as we choose. Suppose a person is free to live where he likes and to do the work he likes, within the limits of his capabilities. His relations with others may still be as dehumanized as his interactions with a soulless machine. We are responded to, and respond in turn, on the basis of identifications (§47) which define the social roles to be enacted, not in terms of identities. The set of roles is so circumscribed and each of them so narrowly defined that we remain strangers to one another. No matter how many people I interact with during the day, I remain lonely because *I* had nothing to do with them nor they with *me;* it was only my identifications, my paper identities, that came into play.

A crucial element in the situation is the nature of the self in question. I will not be accepted by others if I am incapable of self-acceptance, and I will not receive human warmth if I do not give it (§58). Clinical data here is unmistakable. "We find man lonely," Carl Rogers has reported, "because of an inability to communicate freely within himself." A person will remain lonely as long as he does not have himself as a friend. There is a societal factor here as well. There are differences among various patterns of social living and among norms governing personal relations; some of these patterns and norms fail to fulfill the needs for human warmth, needs whose frustration is experienced as loneliness. Is loneliness a problem peculiar to our times, or does it point to a predicament with which we must cope whatever the society?

A doctrinaire position can be avoided simply by making a distinction. There is one kind of loneliness which is basically a social problem and another which is essentially a human predicament. The first I call *contingent loneliness.* It is not accidental, a matter of chance, of indeterminate origin, or produced by extrinsic causes; on the contrary, it may be rooted in the nature of the individual, in the conditions in which he finds himself, or in the society which produced those conditions and made him the person he is. The loneliness is contingent because if he were a different sort of person, or his circumstances other than they are, or his society differently ordered, he would not be lonely. Contingent loneliness is likely to be temporary and correctable; like all problems, it has solutions. The traveler is lonely, but journeys end in lovers meeting; the sick child is lonely but recovers from his illness and rejoins his friends; the lonely city dweller or aging bachelor may remain lonely yet need not be were social patterns better adapted to human needs.

There is an *existential loneliness* which cannot be escaped; we can only learn to live with it. It poses a predicament we can only cope with, not a problem to be solved. This loneliness is rooted in our humanity, whatever our individual circumstances or social condition. Constancy, whether in friendship or in love, is compromised by the continuous change which is the fate of all living things; our parents are lost to us as we mature, and our children in turn move off to their own lives; all we were once a part of recedes into a vanishing past; and we are brought inexorably to face our individual mortality alone. If the other were not a part of my very self, or if we were so bound together that he had no life apart from me, loneliness would be only contingent. As things are, there is a loneliness no human being can escape.

Old age suffers from contingent and existential loneliness; aging is both a social problem and a human predicament. In the last two generations, the proportion of the American population over sixty-five has approximately doubled, and similar figures are reported elsewhere. (The proportion of the young is also growing rapidly; they are also the lonely ones.) Old age is discriminated against in our society. Retirements are mechanically imposed at an increasingly early age, as though a man were disqualified for his work by too much experience. At the same time, the crisis in the nuclear family and the virtual collapse of the enlarged family give the aging no place in society save among others similarly homeless. The prevailing individualist ideology has it that our society cherishes the right of each individual to the pursuit of happiness, but we see to it that the pursuit cannot go on indefinitely. The slogan of equal opportunity is counterposed by the unspoken but more dominant theme, "You've had your chance!"

The aging are the victims not only of discrimination but also of contempt. The old-fashioned is by definition out of date; someone who is hopelessly behind the times is an "old fogey." In *Man and Superman*, when Roebuck Ramsden, outraged at the accusation that his moral ideas are backward, declares, "Let me tell you that I was an advanced thinker before you were born," John Tanner replies, "I knew it was a long time ago." This retort was felt to be as effective in George Bernard Shaw's day (himself a paragon of creative longevity) as in our own. A whole genre of humor ridicules the old as being either sexual failures or sex fiends (the "dirty old man" cliché). The hostility hidden in the humor often becomes overt as the old are attacked for what they have or what they keep others from getting. Macbeth, sick at heart, says at last:

I have lived long enough; my way of life
Is fallen into the sear, the yellow leaf:
And that which should accompany old age,
As honor, love, obedience, troops of friends,
I must not look to have; but in their stead,
Curses, not loud, but deep.

As Macbeth reminds us, the curses may be deserved; hostility against old age may have a realistic basis in the disproportionate share of wealth and influence that is theirs and the rigid authoritarianism with which they often use them. The name given to the staunch defenders of things as they are is, after all, the "old guard"; the word "senate" comes from the Latin for elder; and a survey of the owners of property and holders of power would undoubtedly give substance to the semantics. A psychologist might hypothesize that hostility here is rooted in the child's anger at parental discipline and denial, especially the child's exclusion from parental sex. Less conjectural is the idea that the old are hated because they impose an obligation, then make us feel guilty for discharging it so inadequately. It is *their* fault for being a burden on us, as reactionaries have been known to feel about the poor or about other victims of social discrimination.

Such discrimination, hostility, and contempt make very understandable the cantankerousness of old age. How else is one to react to being cast off by life, especially since inner vitality is inadequate to rebellion, and no institutionalized patterns are available for the discharge of continuously aggravated frustrations? The only alternative to querulousness is to turn aggression inward, thereby giving a psychogenic dimension to biological deterioration. Growing old gracefully is the mark of acceptance of aging by self and others.

The rejection of a human being often takes the form of depersonalizing him (§65). The old are depersonalized by the denial of their individuality, which is replaced by stereotypes—"foxy grandpa," "old-timer," "grannie," "auntie." Depersonalization reinforces and is reinforced by imposing a basic passivity on the old: they are allowed very little share in the decisions affecting their own lives, except with regard to trivialities, much as a spoon-fed infant might be allowed to reach for something or other between mouthfuls.

A man who is no longer an autonomous, individual personality certainly cannot feel at home in the world. Here is the fundamental alienation of age, the basis of its loneliness: freedom and identity can be clung to only by a withdrawal into memory and fantasy. Such a withdrawal is movingly portrayed in Edwin Arlington Robinson's "Mr. Flood's Party," describing the celebration of sorts by old Eben Flood, alone on a hillside, looking down on the places he knew and loved and enjoyed with others when he was young:

Alone, as if enduring to the end
A valiant armor of scarred hopes outworn,
He stood there in the middle of the road
Like Roland's ghost winding a silent horn.
Below him, in the town among the trees
Where friends of other days had honored him,
A phantom salutation of the dead
Rang thinly till old Eben's eyes were dim.

... There was not much that was ahead of him,
And there was nothing in the town below–
Where strangers would have shut the many doors
That many friends had opened long ago.

This is the essence of the loneliness of the old: doors are closed that once were opened long ago, and he himself is the stranger.

The problems and predicaments of old age are shared by the young. Both are discriminated against on the basis of age, even in contexts where age is irrelevant; both are depersonalized and stereotyped; both are denied a significant share in the making of decisions about their own lives; both are treated with contempt and often with hostility; both are caught up in a "crisis of identity," their roles in society being uncertain and ill-defined. A child psychologist recently suggested an explanation for the familiar warmth between grandparents and grandchildren: they have a common enemy. Perhaps this also explains the popularity among youth of the outer marks of old age of another time—granny dresses, wire spectacles, beards, and the interior decoration of *l'art nouveau.*

While the young delight in the symbols of age, the old do what they can to deny the reality, and society encourages the effort of concealment. The gray hair which other cultures have seen as a crown of glory we dye or pull out, and other marks of age are blurred by cosmetics or surgery. Plain speaking gives way to euphemism, as the senior citizen is invited to spend his golden years in Leisure Gardens or Paradise Valley. Cosmetology achieves its greatest triumph in the artistry of the mortician, whose substitution of appearances for reality sets the standard to which the living aspire. "Let her paint an inch thick," says Hamlet, musing on the skull, "to this favor she must come." Denial is a well-known defense mechanism but so ineffective that reliance upon it to any considerable degree verges on pathology.

What is there to deny, after all? Somerset Maugham, at a banquet honoring him on the occasion of his ninetieth birthday, responded to the eulogies with, "There are three advantages to being old . . . [long pause] but I forget what they are!" The openness and continued growth of old age is not so much of a rarity as prejudice portrays it to be. The image of Oliver Wendell Holmes in his nineties reading Plato "to improve my mind," as he explained, is uncommon, to be sure; but this aspiration is not common at any age. The old have a perspective which may extend into the future as well as the past. Longfellow was often a sentimentalist, but not, I think, when he wrote

Age is opportunity no less
Than youth itself, though in another dress,
And as the evening twilight fades away
The sky is filled with stars, invisible by day.

I take it that no one would accuse Plato of sentimentality in this exchange in his dialogue *Laws:*

Where the law is overruled or obsolete, I see destruction hanging over the community; where it is sovereign over the authorities and they its humble servants, I discern the presence of salvation and every blessing heaven sends on a society.

Right, sir, right in God's name! You have the long sight of your years.

Why, yes, a man is always most shortsighted in such matters in youth, and most farsighted in age.

Perhaps the old see further and more clearly because they have less to gain from perpetuating illusion, less at stake in self-deception. At his trial, Socrates refused banishment because he knew that his character would not be changed thereby, explaining, "A fine life I should have if I left this country at my age [he was then seventy] and spent the rest of my days trying one city after another and being turned out every time!" After his conviction and death sentence he declared, "The difficulty is not so much to escape death; the real difficulty is to escape from doing wrong, which is far more fleet of foot. I, the slow old man, have been overtaken by the slower of the two, but my accusers, who are clever and quick, have been overtaken by the faster—by wrongdoing." Later, rejecting a plan to effect his escape, he said, "Will no one comment on the fact that an old man of my age, probably with only a short time left to live, should dare to cling so greedily to life, at the price of violating the most stringent laws?" Zen enjoins the policy of acting "as if dead already," when there is no longer anything at stake; age makes the policy more inviting—and no less ennobling.

It is the old who can make a claim, if anyone can, to some expertness in the arts of living. Man does not often learn from experience how to live; it is rarely that he learns how without experience. There may be some irony in Job's declaration, "Wisdom is with the aged, understanding in length of days." Yet in all cultures the wise counselor is old in years as well as in understanding. Robinson Jeffers, in "Promise of Peace," expresses a perception found in virtually all cultures:

The heads of strong old age are beautiful
Beyond all grace of youth. They have strange quiet,
Integrity, health, soundness; to the full
They've dealt with life and been atempered by it.

There is a certain subservience to age amounting to a stifling conservativism, a worship of the past for its own sake. Confucius regarded filial piety as "the root of all virtue, the stem out of which grows all moral teaching," and Plato, in whose ideal state children would be raised communally, enjoined everyone to respect all who are old enough to be their parents. Neither philosopher laid the foundations of an open society. But piety is one thing, and respect is another. The injunction in Scripture to rise up before the grey head and honor the face of the old is amplified in the Talmud with the precept that even an old man who has lost his learning is to be respected: the fragments of the Tablets of the Law which had been broken by Moses were kept in the Ark alongside the new ones. This is, after all, a counsel of prudence: do not dishonor the old, for we shall all be numbered among them—thus Ben Sira. Plato is equally frank: "Seniority is held in highest consideration by all who intend a long and happy life." There is more warmth in the personal values proclaimed by Hardcastle in the opening scene of *She Stoops to Conquer:* "I love everything that's old: old friends, old times, old manners, old books, old wine; and, I believe, Dorothy, you'll own I have been pretty fond of an old wife."

The predicament of aging will remain, but the problems of the aged call for significant changes in social policy. The aged are not to be isolated, confined to the society only of other elders, but are to be integrated into the community. Their right to be heard must be acknowledged as well as their right to share decisions about the future course of their own lives—and deaths. Productive work must be recognized for what it contributes to the worker, not only to the gross national product; there is a place for home industry in even the most technologically advanced societies. Retirements must be gradual and adapted to the capacities of the individual, not legalistically imposed on an all-or-none basis. Continuing education and cultivation of creative potential is a different matter from encouraging what are called "hobbies," as the aged wait for the end in their "vacation villages."

As a single example, the need for manpower in the helping professions, which are grossly understaffed, can be admirably responded to by recruiting the aged, whose natural sympathies and personal situations fit them for the performance of valuable roles in community mental health programs and social services—as foster guardians, older brothers, friends and guides in Outreach programs, and the like. In such interactions it is hard to say who is helping whom; this is the quintessence of human relations at their best.

For a reaffirmation of the meaning life yet holds for the aged, I choose two expressions; the first is from Browning's "Rabbi Ben Ezra":

Grow old along with me!
The best is yet to be,
The last of life, for which the first was made

. . . .

Youth ended, I shall try
My gain or loss thereby;
Be the fire ashes, what survives is gold.

The second is from the end of Tennyson's "Ulysses":

Old age hath yet his honor and his toil.
Death closes all; but something ere the end,
Some work of noble note, may yet be done.

. . . .

'Tis not too late to seek a newer world.
Push off, and sitting well in order smite
The sounding furrows; for my purpose holds

To sail beyond the sunset, and the baths
Of all the western stars, until I die.

. . . .

Though much is taken, much abides; and though
We are not now that strength which in old days
Moved earth and heaven, that which we are, we are
One equal temper of heroic hearts,
Made weak by time and fate, but strong in will
To strive, to seek, to find, and not to yield.

65. Equality

The prejudice and discrimination by which both old and young are victimized are special cases of the general problem of *equality,* on which social philosophy has increasingly focused. No known society is without differentiation among its members, especially if the society has easily identifiable minorities. But not all responses to minorities are prejudicial, nor are all treatment of minorities discriminatory. What constitutes prejudice?

In the literal sense, a *prejudice* is a prejudgment, a conviction reached beforehand, shaped by preconceived ideas. The toddler returning from his first day at school is asked, "Are there any colored children in your class?" "No, just black and white." He does not share the prevailing preconceptions which gave the word "colored" a special meaning. Knowledge always builds on what we already know (§25–§26); we have no alternative but to bring to new experience the ideas we have formed from the old. But in sound judgment we move on from what we know rather than digging in where we are, using new experience to test and improve our previous ideas rather than only as an occasion for reaffirming them. Prejudice is locked into its own patterns of thought, generating premises from conclusions already arrived at.

From a logical standpoint prejudice is a tissue of fallacies characteristic of simplistic block thinking, with its hasty generalizations and closed systems of ideas in which negative evidence is explained away (§23). These patterns of illogic may be summed up as the *fallacy of simple predication:* the individual is not responded to as an individual but as a member of the minority group whose stereotyped attributes are then imputed to the individual. Foregone conclusions classify the individual as a member of *that* group rather than the countless others always possible; however a minority be defined, its members always belong as well to majorities in countless other respects. Preconceptions also operate in forming the stereotypes of the group.

Prejudice may be as much at work in a favorable prejudgment as in an unfavorable one; typically, ambivalent attitudes are involved. A prejudice known from many cultures ascribes unusual sexual attractiveness or prowess to the members of the outgroup—perhaps because the outsiders are exempt from the incest taboos which otherwise inhibit sexual impulses.

Whatever its causes, the attitude is as much a matter of prejudice as if it ascribed negative attributes; ambivalence is expressed in the common imputation to the outgroup of immorality and perversion. That "they" are "clever" is another frequent prejudice with ambivalence: intelligence and skill are implied, but also sharp practice and unscrupulousness. I was once asked to advise the headmistress of a convent school in Kyoto, where my daughter was then enrolled, and agreed gladly, expecting to be consulted on pedagogical or curricular problems; what was wanted instead was the financial advice usually given by "our friend Mr. Goldberg," who was traveling in Europe at the time. It was taken for granted that I, too, being a Jew, would be something of a financial wizard. I regret to say that I happened to advise a step which turned out to be successful and thereby contributed, I am afraid, to the prejudices of an otherwise delightfully innocent lady.

When prejudice is sufficiently widespread it prevents the formation of community or destroys whatever sense of community already exists. Confusions and misconceptions which might be called *fallacies of community* are at work. The *fallacy of comparison* is that all groups have well-defined characteristics whose worth is always comparable with those of other groups; there is always a comparison to be made, one group being better and the other worse (see the axiom of linearity, discussed in §6). If my own group is being compared, the outcome is predictable. The *fallacy of incorporation* assumes that "they" are "after all, just like us," a particularly insidious pattern of thought because it purports to be a repudiation of prejudice, while prejudicially denying differences and also denying that community can accommodate differences. The *fallacy of superiority* does not recognize the right to be average, thinking to overcome prejudice by a compensatory attribution. Here the ambivalent core of prejudice is likely to come into play. As applied to one's own group, this is the pattern of thought underlying *chauvinism:* if it's mine, it must be good, indeed, better than anyone else's. Closely related is the *fallacy of uniqueness*—nothing is valuable unless it is distinctive; hence if "we" have it, "they" don't. This gives rise to an *ego-imperialism,* planting the flag on whatever is worth possessing. It is an inverse of chauvinism, holding that if it's good, it must be mine. Russian claims to various inventions, and the cryptic ancestries assigned to the great by minorities wanting to be identified with them, illustrate the pattern.

As a result of the attitudes sustained by these patterns of thought, community is fragmented. "We" belong, but all others are outsiders—what the Greeks called "barbarians," from a root meaning "to stammer, unable to speak properly." "They" not only are perceived as aliens but ultimately as nonpersons, wholly dehumanized. In the years before the French revolution, ladies of the nobility freely undressed in the presence of servants, much as a woman might unthinkingly do before a pet dog. A century later, Huck Finn, reporting an explosion on a steamboat, was asked if anyone was hurt. "No, ma'am," came the reply; "killed a nigger."

The most deeply rooted and most destructive form of prejudice is *reactive prejudice.* It is the self-contempt and self-hatred the victims of prejudice often come to feel. It may be the result of the mechanism psychologists know as "identifying with the aggressor." It is also the result of the values of the prejudiced majority making their claim on the minority. There are therefore Jewish anti-Semites and racist blacks. Those who suffer from prejudice are often prejudiced themselves, not only as a compensation but as a component of their identification with the envied and emulated majority. The victim may be prejudiced against himself and easily join in the prejudice against other groups. The first act of a new nation which has at last achieved some measure of liberation is to declare its enmity to Israel, as though to show that it has "arrived."

Prejudice in thought and feeling eventually finds overt expression in acts of *discrimination.* What constitutes discrimination is not responding differently to different people. Different responses are appropriate to different stimuli; much learning consists in becoming discriminating in this basic sense. The meaning of discrimination as it bears on social equality is that differential responses are made on the basis of differences which are not *relevant* and, indeed, which may not even exist but are projected by prejudice. The College of Cardinals has more members now than ever before in its history; yet there is not a single Jew among them. Here religion is relevant; the absence of Jews among the top executives of the automobile industry or insurance companies is another matter. It is not always easy to say what is relevant.

Prejudice and discrimination are logically independent; empirically, each strengthens the other. We discriminate against those we view prejudicially; we also become prejudiced against the victims of our discrimination. A teacher recently conducted an experiment in which the blue-eyed children of the class were regularly seated in the back of the room, required to eat at a separate table, not to mix with the others at recess, and so on. Though everyone was fully aware that the discrimination was being artificially imposed, the experience became so painful for the victims that strong parental pressures were brought to bear to stop the experiment. Exclusion from community is a punishment which carries with it a burden of "guilt by dissociation." As the Supreme Court made explicit some decades ago, there cannot be "equal but separate" facilities: inequality is intrinsic to separation.

Many causes of discrimination have been identified. There are political factors; the Hindu castes, for instance, may have resulted from successive waves of invasion. There are economic factors, as in the importation of cheap labor or slaves. Several psychological factors have also been noted: scapegoating—the displacement of hostilities produced by frustrations; the enhancement of an impoverished ego, seeking a content for its negative identity; and insecurity, which imagines that "we" will have nothing to fear if "they" are kept in their place. No simplistic explanation is acceptable; all these factors, and others as well, such as religious ones, are at work.

Probably the largest and oldest identifiable group unable to achieve social equality is women. The theme that women are vicious, dangerous, and destructive is common in the world's folklore and literature, from Jezebel, Xantippe, and Medea to Lady Macbeth and Milady de Winter; they lure men to their destruction or lead them into temptation, like Eve, Helen of Troy, Cleopatra (who "lost Mark Antony the world"), the Lorelei, and Thaïs; they are scheming, willful, and manipulating, like Becky Sharp and Scarlett O'Hara; even when they are weak and foolish, more sinned against than sinning (a phrase first applied to a man victimized by women—King Lear), they are still disastrous, like the Duchess of Malfi or Madame Bovary. The Preacher warns, "I find more bitter than death the woman whose heart is snares and nets." Saint Chrysostom notes that though Satan took so many of his loved ones from Job, he spared Job's wife, for she was doing the devil's work. The ancient Chinese collection of poetry, the *Shih Ching,* includes this ode (as translated by Herbert Giles):

A clever man builds a city,
A clever woman lays one low;
With all her qualifications, that clever woman
Is but an ill-omened bird.
A woman with a long tongue
Is a flight of steps leading to calamity;
For disorder does not come from heaven,
But is brought about by women.
Among those who cannot be trained or taught
Are women and eunuchs.

In the seventeenth century, the dramatist Thomas Otway summed up the prejudice: "destructive, damnable, deceitful woman!"

At best, prejudice presents women as decidedly inferior to men. A woman is only "a lesser man," says Plato in his *Republic,* and Aristotle echoes that woman "may be said to be an inferior man." "I have found one virtuous man among a thousand," the Preacher declares, "but not a single woman among all those." The orthodox Jew daily gives thanks that he was not created a woman—because of the privilege of discharging the religious duties devolving upon man alone; yet the privilege suggests that man is innately more deserving of it. (On the other hand, the *Midrash* explicitly comments that God has given more understanding to woman than to man.) Even a philosopher as concerned about the rights of man (!) as Rousseau denies women aesthetic sensibility: "Women have no love for any art; they have no proper knowledge of any; and they have no genius." Schopenhauer denies that they have any aesthetic attractions: "It is only the man whose intellect is clouded by his sexual impulses who could give the name of the fair sex to that undersized, narrow-shouldered, broad-hipped, and short-legged race." Philosophers are no more free of prejudice than are men who do not profess rationality.

The ambivalent attitudes so often characteristic of prejudice are also expressed here. Women are bad, Nietzsche agrees, but not much worse than men: "Woman was God's *second* mistake." Robert Gordis has pointed out that in the passage quoted earlier, the Preacher found virtue among men to be only one-tenth of one percent more common than among women. Throughout myth and folklore woman is also stereotyped as protective, productive, nurturing, a ministering angel "when pain and anguish wring the brow," as Wordsworth has it. She is the Earth Mother, the source of all strength, as of her son, the giant Antaeus, who was invincible so long as he remained in contact with her; Hercules could overcome him only by lifting him off the ground. Woman is man's indispensable helpmate, a circumstance James Matthew Barrie identified as *What Every Woman Knows;* behind every successful man, so runs the cliché, stands a woman who is man's salvation—as were Ariadne, Medea (what ambivalence there is here!), Solveig. It is woman who is man's inspiration—the Muses, Beatrice, Laura, and Marguerite. All our labor is for her.

With so many prejudices shaping men's attitudes toward women, it is to be expected that discrimination will also be marked, as indeed it has been, from Paul's dictum "Man was not created for the woman, but the woman for the man," to the infamous "Küche, Kirche, Kinder" of the Nazi era. "Sexism" does not consist merely in recognizing women as sexual objects but in restricting them to that role and responding differentially to them on that basis in contexts where the difference is irrelevant. In "sexism" even the sexual role is dehumanized. Don Juan's contrast, "Love is of man's life a thing apart, 'tis woman's whole existence," does a serious injustice to both sexes, denying men meaningful relationships with women and denying women productive work. Even in their sexual role, women are discriminated against in assigning them more the status of symbols than of actualities: their packaged glamour is meant to be looked at but not touched. In other roles the discrimination is more flagrant. In the United States the median income of full-time women workers is two-thirds that of men, often for identical work. (A famous university, defending a legal action against such discrimination, pleaded that it was its male employees who were being *over*paid.)

What is to be done about discrimination? First, we must be ready to acknowledge its existence whenever it does exist. Often it is perpetuated by a conspiracy of silence. Not uncommonly we are prepared to recognize prejudice elsewhere but not to acknowledge that it is at work within ourselves. There is a widespread tactic of *prejudice by projection:* I myself, of course, have no objections at all, but my superiors, or my clients, my colleagues, the public . . ." and so on. Another tactic of denial argues that the response is not discriminatory because it is based on real (and admittedly relevant) differences; the argument is viciously fallacious when it purports to justify discrimination by appealing to the effects produced by the discrimination itself—the *circle of discrimination.* "These people wouldn't know what to do with a college education if it were offered to them," a charge which might be true as a result of continued denial of adequate educational opportunities from the primary grades onward.

Second, we must *deny the relevance* of the bases of discrimination, not deny that differences exist. Discrimination is not overcome but fulfilled if we think to avoid it by abandoning our identity. Some women's liberationists make the mistake of demanding that women be treated like men rather than demanding that society change the way it treats women. On the one hand, the move towards unisex impoverishes both sexes; on the other hand, discrimination is strengthened when it becomes reciprocal and man is treated as an enemy for no other reason than that he is a man. In this state of belligerency between the sexes there are guerrillas and even terrorists, and female chauvinists as well as male. Awareness of a woman's sexual attractiveness is not to be condemned as making her a dehumanized sex object; tenderness towards her does not imply that she is weak; protectiveness does not impute helplessness. There is such a thing as love between men and women after all.

Affirmation of identity, although it implies differentiation from others, does not imply hostility or withdrawal. Prizing one's identity is not sexist, racist, or chauvinistic unless the traits involved in the identification are taken to be innately fixed and invoked in every context whether they are relevant or not. Neither prejudice nor discrimination follows from the recognition that men and women have different habits and preferences, that ethnic groups have different values and characteristic responses, and that nations have different traits and culture patterns. Humanity is all the more enriched by such differences; its life is impoverished when prized differences are replaced by stereotyped and preconceived grounds of hostility and contempt.

Denial of identity leaves an emptiness within when it succeeds, and adds despair to self-contempt when it fails. The most assimilated and the least assimilated European Jewish communities in the first third of this century—the German and the Polish—came to the same dismal end. In India a few decades ago hundreds of thousands of Harijans (the caste of untouchables) converted to Buddhism; other Indians continued to mistreat them as before, with the difference only that when the Indian state was established the converts were no longer eligible for the benefits the new laws were conferring upon members of the lowest castes.

Third, to counter discrimination we must abandon the attempts to deal with it by *symbol magic* (§7): sentimental rhetoric, declarations of principles, and even the intellectualization of "facts and figures." (In the conspiracy of silence mentioned above there is also an element of magic—if we speak no evil, then we will hear no evil and see no evil.) Symbols do have importance when they are used to educate and to stimulate and organize appropriate action. The Master said, "The distance between the mouth and the heart is as great as that between heaven and earth—yet the earth is nourished by rain from heaven."

Fourth, discrimination can be ended only be establishing and maintaining *community*. It is not ended by compensatory discrimination, any more than prejudice is overcome when it is given a favorable content. It did no good to blacks to be seen as having "a great sense of rhythm," to Jews as being "smart," to women as being "intuitive." As to the last, in his autobiography, Henry Adams expressed, almost a century ago, a deeply rooted American myth: "Women have, very commonly, a very positive moral sense; that which they will is right; that which they reject is wrong; and their will, in most cases, ends by settling the moral." This prejudice very probably reinforced the discrimination to which women were subjected: it is not easy to relate as equals to those whom we see as moral authorities and disciplinarians. To provide economic or educational opportunities to members of certain groups on the discriminatory basis that they are members of such groups is likely to impose inequalities on other groups and to legitimize discriminatory practices.

Neither does the tactic of toleration establish and maintain community. To "tolerate" another implies something objectionable as well as a passivity on the part of the tolerant rather than an active involvement with the other on a plane of equality (§6). Here pluralism—the recognition that community does not consist in sameness but in acceptance of difference, the faith that in the house of the Lord there are truly many mansions—is fundamental. Tradition has it that there are seventy ways of interpreting the Law, each nation having its own; only such a pluralistic tradition provides a solid foundation for community.

There is no reason why groups of shared identity should not establish their own communities, provided that there are no ghetto walls, whether their gates are locked from within or without, to preclude the acceptance of differences. To denounce as clannishness the warmth of feeling evoked by shared language, customs, and outlook is not to defend and cherish human values but to undermine them. The person who finds it equally easy to be friendly with everyone is no friend of mine. True, he might deserve veneration as a saint; it is more likely that he is controlling, uncaring, and superficial in his relationships.

Finally, discrimination can be overcome only by *social action*, in contrast to individual resolves and societal pronouncements. The law cannot directly deal with prejudice, for thought and feeling are beyond its reach, and prohibiting the expression of prejudice raises other fundamental issues (§74). The law *can* deal with discrimination, and has been doing so throughout history, for some measure of equality is intrinsic to the very conception of law (§74). The law cannot force a man to love his wife and children, but it *can* compel him to provide for their support. In outlawing discrimination we are also combating prejudice. Over eighteen hundred years ago the martyr Akiba ben Joseph interpreted the Law so as to press the interests of the poor and of labor, to raise the status of women, to secure the rights of aliens, and to limit the prerogatives of priests—all in a spirit of universalism.

Such a religious basis for the ideal of equality—*prophetic universalism*—has played an important part in the history of several cultures. Thus Job: "If I despised the cause of my servant when he contended with me, what shall I do when God rises up? When He remembers, what shall I answer Him: Did not He Who made me also make my fellow man? Did not one God fashion us both?" The brotherhood of man on the basis of the common fatherhood of God has a counterpart in the nontheistic Buddhist religion. "Go into all lands and preach this gospel," said the Buddha. "Tell them that the poor and the lowly, and the rich and the high, are all one, and that all castes unite in this religion as do the rivers in the sea." Such equality is a recurrent theme in *midrashic* lore: God created man from one Adam so that no man could boast of a better ancestry than his fellows; if a messiah claims to be better than any other man he is not truly the Messiah; the voice at Sinai spoke in all languages, truth being revealed equally to everyone; and prayers can be recited by anyone, in any language. The question with which the Talmud begins is, at what time of day is it permissible to recite the morning prayers, after sunset on the preceding evening, after midnight, with the first dawn, when it is broad daylight, or when? Among the various answers discussed, the most memorable is, when there is enough light for a man to recognize his brother; until then we are in such darkness that the time for prayer has not yet come.

An important part, historically, has also been played by a philosophical basis for the ideal of equality: *rationalist universalism,* the doctrine that men are equals as sharing in the faculty of reason. Spinoza echoes the rationalist universalism of Maimonides when he says, "Books which teach and speak of whatever is highest and best are equally sacred, whatever be the tongue in which they are written, or the nation to which they belong." Plato's ideal state institutionalizes inequalities, for he supposes philosophers to be more rational than other men, while Aristotle holds that some men are "by nature" born to be masters and others slaves. The Stoics, however, promulgated equality and internationalism on the basis of man's sharing in universal Reason. "Nature has made us relatives," said Seneca, "when it begat us from the same materials and for the same destinies." "My nature is rational and social," Marcus Aurelius declared; "so far as I am Antoninus, my city and my country is Rome; so far as I am a man, it is the world." Epictetus was forthright: "You are a citizen and a part of the world."

The idea of a fundamental equality of all men passed by way of Stoic philosophical theory and Roman legal practice into the tradition of "natural law," significant contributions being made by Thomas Aquinas in the thirteenth century, Hugo Grotius in the seventeenth century, and John Locke, who, in the eighteenth century, markedly influenced Thomas Jefferson and other founders of the American republic. The Declaration of Independence holds it to be a self-evident truth that all men are created equal, the reference to self-evidence harking back to the philosophical basis of equality, while mention of being created invokes the religious basis as well. There was never any question in either tradition of affirming an equality in regard to the actual capacities of men, but only in regard to their rights—especially in regard to their equality before the law. Kant defines civil equality as "the right of the citizen to recognize no one as a superior among the people in relation to himself"—superior, that is, in the juridical attributes belonging to the citizen as such. Here social and political issues intermingle (§72).

The *cha-shitsu,* the teahouse of the Japanese ceremony shaped by Zen, has a low doorway, through which one is obliged to enter almost on all fours. Zen, though appealing especially to the samurai and noblemen of a stratified aristocracy, nevertheless espoused a certain ideal of equality, for all men are as one when they have reduced their lives to the essentials. The door of the teahouse is so low as to require all who would enter to remove their swords and pass through in the posture of humility. The symbolism is political, moral, religious, and aesthetic. Even so, it proved too fragile to bear the weight of any movement toward social equality.

66. Social Justice

Equality before the law may be purely formal; content must be provided by goods and services which are equally enjoyed or to which there is equal access. "The law, in its majestic equality," Anatole France wrote in *Le Lys Rouge* at the end of the last century, "forbids the rich as well as the poor to sleep under bridges, to beg in the streets, and to steal bread." The most pernicious form of discrimination, felt most painfully and having the most serious consequences, is that which denies equal employment opportunity and equal pay for equal work. *Distributive justice* is the adherence to moral norms of both form and content in the allocation of resources and products. The vague reference here to moral norms seems to me inescapable; no simple quantitative measures can be applied either to the values on any individual's scale or to the comparability of different scales. But though these norms cannot be articulated with any precision in their full generality, they provide ideals and standards for the formation of social policy in specific context.

Injustices of distribution are a shameful feature of modern life everywhere. In the United States, certainly among the most egalitarian of societies, it was estimated in Franklin Roosevelt's time that one-third of the nation was ill-fed, ill-housed, and ill-clothed; in two generations the proportion has shrunk to about one-fifth—but that fraction still represents a damnable social injustice. For every dollar spent by the most prosperous tenth of the nation, the poorest tenth spends less than five cents. The gap between rich and poor is vastly greater in countries like Saudi Arabia; even self-styled socialist countries such as the Soviet Union are characterized by striking differences in living standards, especially when one takes into account privileged access to goods and services, like assigned housing. Bacon said of money that, like manure, it is no good unless it be spread; the good things of life must be widely distributed if they are to fulfill all their potentialities.

Moral norms demand satisfaction of certain minimal needs for everyone. The norms go further. They also demand that what is enjoyed beyond the minimum bear some relationship to deserts; they condemn "unearned increments" in the most general sense. There is also such a thing as an "unearned *de*crement," more familiar as "exploitation," which is thus a moral category. The most widely recognized basis for concluding that a person deserves something is that he has worked for it. The classic doctrine—to be found in John Locke as well as in Karl Marx—is that labor puts the difference of value in everything; wealth is the product of labor.

There is a sense in which pure air and water are of inestimable value, even if, as was true for so long, no labor is required to purify them. Questions here of exact definition may be left to economics and utility theory. Social philosophy emphasizes that the measure of a person's *right* to something (beyond the satisfaction of basic needs) is, in Locke's phrase, "the labor of his hands that he has mixed with it." *Commutative justice* is the allocation to each person of neither more nor less then he deserves to have.

The dictum of the syndicalist Pierre Proudhon, that property is theft, served to focus attention on the abuses of which private property was guilty—and still is, in many respects; but if all property is theft, some thievery is much less reprehensible than the rest, requiring, it may be, years of toil in which the so-called thief gives as much as he gets. What can be said is that ownership itself does not demonstrate that commutative justice has been served. What is owned may have been stolen, acquired by exploitation, inherited, or simply found underfoot; the highest per capita wealth in the world is enjoyed by the residents of Abu Dhabi and Kuwait, but not because they work harder, longer, or more efficiently than anyone else.

A man who meets the standards of commutative justice may have moral satisfaction, but even the most demanding morality here still leaves something to be desired. The Preacher says, "Sweet is the sleep of a working man, whether he eat little or much"—very well, he has earned his rest. But if his children have eaten too little, the workingman knows a certain bitterness as well. Apropos, it has been estimated that even in rich America millions of children go to bed hungry each night; elsewhere, they slowly starve or die of malnutrition. What we earn must support more than just ourselves; there is also a right to be secure that what we earn today will suffice for the morrow.

Social justice is a comprehensive category comprising a certain degree of equality and security, as well as distributive and commutative justice. It contrasts especially with *privilege:* an unjust inequality in the enjoyment of some social good. *Elitism* is the institutionalization of privilege, often rationalized as serving the general welfare rather than the special interests of the elite. Thorstein Veblen, in his *Theory of the Leisure Class,* has drawn attention to patterns of "conspicuous consumption" and "conspicuous waste" as devices by which to display membership in the elite, and so to make a claim for even more privilege. There is a certain *fusion* of the values in any society: however concentrated or diffused any one value might be, all values tend to be allocated to the same people. There is a great overlap among the healthiest group in the society, the richest, the best educated, the most influential, most respected, and most honored. There are ignorant athletes, rich scoundrels, celebrated courtesans, and powerful social outcasts, but these are not representative of the social structure. In a word, societies tend to contain identifiable *classes.*

The term "class," in its present usage, not in the logical sense of §19, is a political symbol; using the term, or suppressing its use, is connected with political identifications and aspirations, or with the movements opposing them. Members of elites are prone to deny that there is any such thing as an "elite" in their society, and ruling classes to deny that there are any classes.

In its broadest sense, a class is any group of people having a distinctive status or function with respect to some societal value; aesthetic value, for example, defines such classes as artists, dealers, critics, connoisseurs, and art lovers. Most important in social thought have been the economic, political, and status classes (or "social" classes in the narrow sense of the term "social"). "Bourgeois," for instance, may refer to shopkeeper, citizen, or socialite. Economic classes have been distinguished and emphasized since ancient times. "Any ordinary city is in fact two cities," Plato wrote in his *Republic,* "one the city of the poor, the other of the rich, each at war with the other." James Madison observed in the *Federalist Papers,* "Those who hold and those who are without property have ever formed distinct interests in society." The idea is to be found in the writings of countless social philosophers before Marx as well as after him.

Because of the fusion of values, social classes, in the wider and more common sense of the term, are likely to include a distinctive status or function with respect to political, economic, and other domains of social life simultaneously. Membership in a social class is rarely ascertainable on the basis of any single specification, nor is the question of membership answerable by a flat yes or no. What constitutes a social class is complicated; even when the complexities are explicitly taken into account with more or less precision, gradations of class composition rather than absolutes are called for. A fixed makeup is not a part of the conception of a class. New members may flow into it as others lose their status—a process described by the political sociologist Vilfredo Pareto as "the circulation of the elites." Plato's utopian social classes, like the Confucian civil service which administered China for many centuries, was to have its members determined by successive examinations. A class whose membership is rigidly fixed is known as a *caste.*

Different classes have different interests, deriving from their different functions in the production, distribution, or consumption of the values by which the class is determined. Theorists of social classes have usually generalized the fiction of economic man ("fiction" because it is seldom sufficiently explicit and precise to be called a theoretical model). Just as the economic man of classic thought was supposed to be a rational, calculating creature, interested only in maximizing his economic advantage, classes were supposed to pursue always only the class interest. What one is interested in and what is *to* his interest must be carefully distinguished (§54–§56). *Class consciousness* has been used, especially by Marxists, to take note of the degree to which the genuine interests of the class are being pursued. If, instead, it refers to the individual's identification with a class—and about ninety percent of Americans identify themselves as belonging to what they call "the middle class"—a distinction is sometimes made between "false" and "true" class consciousness, corresponding to the difference between what one is interested in and what is to his interest, what he finds satisfying and what is truly satisfactory.

What happens to a society if each individual or class pursues its own interest? In the eighteenth century men thought they saw on earth what had been found in the heavens: a self-contained stable system, smoothly operating in accord with immutable laws. A preestablished harmony, ordained by God or Nature, kept all the parts of the system in place, all working together for the common good. Bernard Mandeville expressed the idea in his *Fable of the Bees:* just as the hive flourishes when each bee busies itself with its individual task, so the welfare of society as a whole is secured when each individual pursues his own self-interest. Does society need more shoes? More can be sold, so it will be worthwhile to manufacture more of them, to pay workers enough so that they will want to make shoes rather than something else, and cattlemen enough so that they will raise more cattle for hides. If too many shoes are made, they will go unsold, manufacturing them will become unprofitable, and the least efficient enterprises will go out of business. Society's needs are automatically met if each individual acts so as to get all he can for himself.

The nineteenth century saw nature as an arena of struggle where dialectical oppositions were resolved only to generate new antitheses (§40). The notion of a preestablished harmony was repudiated and replaced by the image of classes in perpetual and intrinsic conflict. "The history of all hitherto existing society is the history of class struggles," the *Communist Manifesto* proclaims. The idea was by no means distinctive of that time and place, nor only of a secular outlook on the world. Millennia earlier, ben Sira had written in the apocryphal *Book of Wisdom,* "What kind of peace can there be between a hyena and a dog, and between rich and poor?" But ideas, like men, do not flourish if they are born before their time; in the nineteenth century, the time for the idea of *class conflict* had come: all life was seen as a struggle for existence, a fierce competition for survival, a clash of opposing forces from which there were to emerge new and advanced social and economic stages, destined to carry on their own struggles.

Any such doctrine is to some degree self-fulfilling; indeed, the doctrine was promulgated by those who saw themselves as the vanguard of the struggle. To some degree, class conflict was—and is—a fact beyond any doubt. I do not see, however, on what basis anyone can deny that class conflict may be only intermittent and even fragmentary. What doctrinaires call "class collaboration" is also a fact of political life, and the position that in its nature collaboration is a betrayal of the class interest begs the fundamental question. Other conflicts—national, religious, racial, cultural—may cut across class lines and, from time to time, play a far more significant part in human history than a class analysis can take into account.

Yet a "classless society" identifies an important deal of social justice, not in the sense of the absence of all functional differentiations but in the sense that such differences are free from rigid stratifications of status and from the fusion of values into a single pattern of distribution. There may still be important differences between factory managers and workers, but workers, too, can share in decisions about production and, in other contexts of social life, they may have primary responsibility or enjoy a greater share of other goods. So conceived, the ideal is far from utopian, and its recognition is by no means limited to countries which embed the ideal in an ideology of conflict. It is the interests of new elites, not the demands of social justice, which are served by the attempts to heighten class consciousness and to intensify class conflict on the paradoxical premise that classes will thereby be destroyed forever.

Nothing said here has been intended to deny that the class structure of society is often a crucially important determinant of events. Nor have I wished to deny the crucial role often played by economic considerations. Moral materialism is the philosophy which localizes the greatest value in the possession and use of material things. The world of the advertiser focuses naturally on such things, for they make up the overwhelming proportion of commodities. It is not surprising that in the image of his world, and in the real world which is expressed in and influenced by that image, all that matters is what can be bought and sold—and this comes close to the essence of moral materialism. The same outlook is no less common and no less influential in countries which profess a socialist ideology, for the understandable reason that in those countries so many material things are still so widely lacking.

Moral materialism is *not* a Marxist doctrine; quite the contrary. It is a gross misreading of Marx to interpret him as ascribing solely or even chiefly economic motives to individual behavior, as though Marx took the fiction of economic man literally. In fact, this view is more likely to be found among defenders of what they call "the profit system." The claim that people are actuated, even in economic matters, solely by a profit motive is another of those equivocal propositions (like fatalism, egoism, and hedonism) which are either true but tautological, or else meaningful but false. The doctrine is tautology if "profit" means *any* gain; it is false if it means the gain distinctively accruing to a middleman, the margin between cost and selling price, or even the wage for one's labor. People are also motivated in economic activity by an identification with the people or organizations for whom they work, by a desire to give service, by self-respect, by creative and productive impulses, by what Veblen called "the instinct of workmanship," by the satisfaction of a job well done, by the desire for the approbation and esteem of their colleagues.

The Marxist doctrine of the primacy of economic factors in human affairs is called *historical materialism.* It does not purport to describe individual, personal behavior but broad societal patterns. The following formulation is from the preface to the *Communist Manifesto:* "The method of production and the organization of social life inevitably arising therefrom constitute in every historical epoch the foundation upon which is built the political and intellectual history of that epoch." Elsewhere Engels explains, "According to the materialist conception of history the determining element in history is *ultimately* production. If somebody twists this into the statement that the economic element is the *only* determining one, he transforms it into a meaningless, abstract and absurd phrase." The acknowledgment of other determining elements in addition to the economic one adds great weight to the doctrine, though weakening its thrust.

The determinants of historical processes interact; it is not always easy or meaningful to decide which is cause and which is effect. While it may be true that a political action is the outcome of a transposed economic interest, it might equally be true in another case that an economic action is the outcome of a transposed political interest. Both the domestic policies and the foreign relations of the Communist countries provide instances in which political history seems plainly to determine rather than be determined by economic arrangements. Max Weber's *The Protestant Ethic and the Spirit of Capitalism* and R. H. Tawney's *Religion and the Rise of Capitalism* marshal impressive considerations on behalf of the thesis that religious and moral doctrines shaped economic institutions and practices, and not only the other way around.

Distinct from historical materialism, though often confused with it (a confusion excusable because of commonly loose usage), is the doctrine of *economic determinism,* which might be described as determinism *in* rather than determination *by* the economic factor. It is the view that economic stages of society are the inevitable outcomes of the preceding economic stages. Each leads to the next by an inner necessity called the logic of the situation: from primitive communism to the rise of private property, feudalism, capitalism, socialism, and, finally, a fully developed communistic society. If historical materialism analyzes the soil, as it were, as resting on and ultimately produced by the underlying bedrock, economic determinism describes the geological processes by which the rock formations come to be. In a metaphor whose use has some historical justification, the system of production takes the place of Fate or Providence in giving shape and meaning to the course of history (§68).

All economic transactions take place in a political setting; there is always power somewhere in the background. Society is a party to every contract, ultimately defining and enforcing the terms. The freedom of contract which marked the end of feudalism was an important advance in social justice; yet the inequalities which persisted robbed the legal form of an effective content. A person is not in fact free to reject an offer to work at a certain wage if his only alternative is to starve. Politics intervened to give substance to the economic right—by providing for collective bargaining, minimum-wage laws, standards of health and safety in working conditions, and the like.

Most important, *property* is socially defined; ownership is fundamentally a relationship among people, not a relationship between people and things. Property rights, as well as the legal persons (including corporations) who enjoy these rights, are legal—which is to say, social—entities. Society defines ownership, and only the readiness of society to exercise power in accord with its definition makes ownership effective. An income tax is a matter of commutative justice because the ability to pay is itself a mark of a benefit received. As with other restrictions to which we have grown accustomed, restrictions on property, essential to the existence of property, are easily overlooked. The conditions operative at a given time in the definition of property are taken as an absolute zero-point and every change in these conditions is then seen as an invasion of "property rights," as though these had an entirely independent antecedent existence. There is far less historical basis for the Leninist view that under socialism the state will "wither away" (this has decidedly not happened) than for the position of democratic socialism, as articulated by Clement Atlee, that it is property rights which are to wither away.

Increasingly subject to appraisal and control are rights concerning *competition.* On the one hand, the conception of a preestablished harmony among diverse economic interests called for a freely competitive system: a monopolist can satisfy his own interests even though the interests of society suffer thereby. It was early recognized that the conditions of free competition are not preestablished but must be legislated or established and maintained by other social forces, such as trade unions. On the other hand, it has also long been clear that unrestricted competition may be wasteful, as in the competition among brands of essentially the same product.

Even worse is the *ethics of competition,* reinforced if not generated by economic practice. In this view, values are not intrinsic but depend on the circumstance that others are unable to attain them. What counts is not to be good but to be better than others; as Lucy demands of Charlie Brown, the born loser, "What's the good if you can't get to be champion?" Competition enters into every domain of life and may be incorporated into the structure of the personality. There is an intimate connection, logical and psychological, between the ethics of competition and the doctrine that might makes right, that success is its own validation, that it does not so much matter what you try to do, provided you succeed in doing it and doing it better than anyone else. Any further talk of social justice then becomes only a cynical exploitation of other people's moral aspirations.

On a more fundamental level, what is at work is an antithesis between individualism and collectivism, as confused as it is familiar. The confusion lies in the failure to distinguish between the individual and the collective good as an end of action, and individual or collective means for the attainment of ends. There is not a single dimension along which the political Left and Right can be ordered but a two-dimensional manifold (at the very least). If the abscissa separates individual and collective ends and the ordinate does the same with regard to means, the four quadrants signify: (1) individualism of both ends and means, as in early capitalist and contemporary feudal societies; (2) individualism of means but toward a collective good, as in the Jeffersonian democracy; (3) collective means toward individual good, the philosophy of democratic socialism; and (4) collective means for a collective good, as in Communist China. The assessment once made by Martin Buber seems to me very much to the point: "Individualism understands only a part of a man, collectivism understands man only as a part; neither advances to the wholeness of man."

The historic irony is how much has been achieved in the aspiration to social justice without acceptance of—indeed, with bitter opposition to—the ideology of collectivism of either ends or means. Among the declared aims in the *Communist Manifesto* a number have been achieved in non-Communist countries—for instance, graduated income tax, an inheritance tax, free public edication, the abolition of child labor, and other measures of social welfare—but there is still a sting in the epigram that while capitalism is the exploitation of man by man, in socialism it's just the other way around. Much can be done, and much remains to be done, by means of *social planning* within a framework of political individualism.

The following are representatives of principles of planning which social justice appears to call for:

1. *Impartiality:* no prior specification is to be made of who in society is to benefit, or who is to suffer—for instance, on behalf of colonial masters, or aginst the Jews.
2. *Individuality:* the ultimate locus of all values is the individual; nothing is of value if it is a value only for the society as a whole and cannot be experienced as valuable by individuals—for instance, military expenditures unrelated, even indirectly, to personal security.
3. *The maximum principle:* the bottom of a value distribution is to be cut off before the top of the distribution is extended, so that those with least have first priority for more—for instance, any acceptable measure of successful policy must give more weight to adequate food, clothing, and shelter than to achievements in the exploration of space.
4. *The distributive principle:* the more people who have a good thing, the better—against the ethics of competition, and any sort of elitism.
5. *Urgency:* the presumption is always in favor of dealing with present needs, so that postponing their satisfaction requires justification—for instance, in giving priority to the production of capital goods over consumer goods.

67. Philosophy of Education

An economy will not necessarily serve the best interests of society without planning, socialization, or various intermediate forms of social control, such as taxation. For any of these, there are needed trained managers, bureaucrats, or other functionaries, who are educated to the required level of performance. The economy itself, based on a more and more sophisticated technology, increasingly needs more and better trained workers. Simply to carry on, if for no other reason, society needs *education*. The philosophy of education is an integral part of any social philosophy.

While the importance of education is constantly reaffirmed in the United States, education ranks surprisingly low in the allocation it receives of the total national resource, especially when compared with how much is allocated to other uses of symbols—for instance, for commerce or entertainment. The United States spends much more for advertising than for schools. Education is not limited to formal schooling; but Americans spend only a fraction in bookstores of what they lose at racetracks; only one American in twenty reads as much as one book a year. Yet, education, especially higher education, is far more widespread among the population of the United States than anywhere else in the world.

In the democracies, education is seen as essential to an informed citizenry capable of self-government and to the democratic goal of individual growth and development. In the Communist countries, education is the essential basis of ideological orthodoxy; it is the handmaiden of politics as in a former day it served religion. In the Third World, education is recognized as indispensable to technological progress. In the developing countries there are pressures to restrict and reduce education to vocational training. In many parts of the world what passes for education is little more than a capacity for passing successive examinations, regardless of whether there has been intellectual growth.

Whatever the social system, education has a fundamental role: the transmission of what has already been learned. Culture is the capacity to learn from what others have undergone, in contradiction to the axiom of direct experience (§24); it is the capacity of the group not to make the same mistake too often. The aim of education is not to ensure that each generation begin where the last left off but to make it possible for the new generation not to have to start again from the beginning. The predicament is that the new generation must make its own start. Inevitably, the parental generation not only nurtures but also controls and even represses. A school that agrees to be *in loco parentis,* imposing what is called "moral discipline," for example, abdicates its educational responsibilities. Affluent societies face the problem of what to do with those who are too young to find their own place in society but too old to stay at home (§63); colleges are often viewed unconsciously as day-care centers for late adolescence.

Education transmits the past and prepares for the future; it is the agency of conservatism and the agency of change. The educator cannot be confined by society to being a curator of a museum of ideas, permitted occasionally to add a few specimens here and there. As knowledge grows, intelligent social policy must change correspondingly; neither can we pretend in the face of every new idea that it is mistaken or that we knew it all along and have been right from the beginning. There are always vested interests in things as they are, and therefore always those who attack education as dangerous. In a sense, the anti-intellectual is right: education *is* dangerous to mentalities such as his. It is the function of education to open the mind to new ideas and to facilitate their absorption into the society.

This is not to say that the school is only an instrumentality of political action. Control of educational practices or content for political ends is the very antithesis of education, especially when that control is exercised from within the educational enterprise itself, as it has been by student radicals, by doctrinaire faculties, and by political administrators. Education promotes change by way of the new ideas it generates, by stimulating and sustaining the inquiring mind in searching out new possibilities, by urging the claims of observational evidence and reasoned argument against preconceived notions however institutionally entrenched. Its function is not to promote change by exploiting its institutional resources for externally defined ends—the resources, for example, of the energy, dedication, and idealism of the young. Not the student strike and other forms of activism but the teach-in represents the role of education with regard to a social problem—contributing to knowledge and understanding of the problem and its possible solutions, rather than merely adding to the already existing social pressures on behalf of a proposed solution. New ideas, in the long run, have far more impact on society than the reenactment, however dramatic, of old ideologies. "Radical" means, literally, pertaining to the root of the matter; research is the most radical activity of all.

In many societies education has served as a means of advancement for deprived minorities. Ironically, in developing countries higher education is sometimes attacked as a luxury. Perhaps this reflects how much it is secretly valued. Perhaps, too, the hostility rationalizes a more pervasive anti-intellectualism shared by conservative and radical alike, the former because the intellectual espouses change, the latter because he insists on thinking independently about how and what change is to be brought about. The artisans in *Henry VI* say of the clerk, "He can write and read and cast accounts . . . . Here's a villain!"

There may be a substance to the charge that education is a luxury, if it is the privilege of an elite, especially if the elite is alienated from the problems faced by others and if membership in the elite bears little relationship to ability. Whatever education has contributed to the rise in social scale of minority groups, the educated themselves everywhere constitute a tiny minority. There is, to my mind, an inescapable moral obligation to use education not just for personal advancement but for a wider social good.

What the aims of education ought to be is among the oldest questions raised by philosophers, in cultures as diverse as those of ancient Greece and China; philosophers have long served as teachers, even if not in formal schooling. Issues in the philosophy of education have occupied philosophers from Aristotle and Confucius to Rousseau and John Dewey. There is a close kinship between philosophy and education, for central to both is the cultivation of the mind. They share, also, if not the love of wisdom, the *love of learning*. To inculcate this love must surely be one of the basic aims of education; no person can truly be said to be educated who does not know the excitement of the adventure of ideas, the joy of making a discovery. Education must aim at freeing us from a slavish mentality which believes what it is told, as well as from a tyrannical one which imposes its beliefs on others without recourse to evidence and argument. Society provides many opportunities to cultivate the strategies of conflict and skills in the use of instruments of violence; only education teaches the uses of reason.

Another aim of education is the transmission of knowledge. This process, far from coextensive with the whole of education, might be called, in a narrow sense, *instruction*. It is directed toward the student's acquisition of data and skills in processing the data—for instance, the traditional three Rs. There are certain minimal needs here which must be acknowledged and satisfied; it is easy, however, to overemphasize them. There is no reason to learn a laborious process of calculation if pocket calculators are freely accessible; the time can better be used to understand mathematics (Russell once said that we bring students to the very portals of the temple of mathematical beauty, then leave them to count the number of stairs). There is no sense in memorizing "facts"; what does make sense is to learn how to use reference books and more advanced technologies of data retrieval. It takes a lifetime to reach the frontiers of knowledge in any direction, however narrow the path. Instruction can give us no more than a tiny foothold; education provides us with maps and other travel aids, with the help of which we can move freely throughout the whole domain and even, perhaps, cross the frontier.

Instruction can be worse than wasteful; it is in continual danger of becoming doctrinaire, of transmitting a fixed body of authoritative "truths." It may purvey only fresh-frozen ideas: simply thaw, add water, and serve. Growth is the very essence of knowledge (§26); the tempo of change in ideas in virtually every field is rapid and accelerating. The visiting alumnus, amused to see on his teacher's desk the same exam he had to take long ago, is properly told, "Yes, but we've changed the answers." In fields where the greatest progress is being made, the questions are changing as well. On the other hand, "method" cannot be taught divorced from any content. But the emptiness of concentration on "methods" is perhaps no more damaging to intellectual growth than the sterility of scholastic content and pedantic instruction. Many "good students" know only what they have been taught, have studied little else, and understand nothing at all.

Instruction has its place, admittedly an important one. But the needs which instruction satisfies mark the beginnings of the educational process, not its end, whether as terminus or as goal. There is little that any of us can *teach* another; we achieve incomparably more if we help the other *learn*. Because in its beginnings education deals with the very young, the process easily becomes infected with the patronizing condescension characteristic of our treatment of children and, subsequently, with a certain subtle disdain of the student. It is not for us to lead the blind but to help the unseeing open their eyes. The young will see well enough for themselves where to go, and their vision will grow with their expanding horizons. In the end, it is our eyes that will be dimmed, and it is we who will have to be led.

A fundamental aim of education is, in a word, to give *perspective:* the ability to see oneself, man, and nature from the standpoint of each of the three. This aim is the basis of the intimate relationship between education and philosophy. Perspective is not guaranteed by "liberal arts" curricula, or a "general" B.A. degree. Too often such education is diffuse and superficial. Perspective can come even from specialized studies if the specialty provides a firm footing from which to scan what is to be found all around, and not an occasion for looking only at what lies beneath our feet. Instead of contrasting specialists and generalists we ought rather to distinguish between the narrow-minded and broad-minded; both sorts of mentalities can be found in special as well as general pursuits. Education breaks through constrictions wherever it encounters them.

Whether we educate or merely instruct, can anything worthwhile really be taught? The question whether virtue is teachable was raised from ancient times. "He who lives as passion directs," Aristotle pointed out, "will not hear argument that dissuades him, nor understand it if he does; how can we persuade one in such a state to change his ways? In general, passion seems to yield not to argument but to force. The character with a kinship to virtue must somehow be there already." Many philosophers have held, with Mencius, that man's character does intrinsically have a kinship with virtue (§57) but that our ingrained morality becomes mislaid, as it were. Hence he states that the great end of learning is nothing else but the search for the lost mind. But where are we to look, and how are we to carry on the search? "Perhaps we are to be content," again as Aristotle said, "if, when all the influences by which we are thought to become good are present, we get some trace of virtue."

To presuppose our antithesis between facts and values (§53) is in effect to abandon the search. There is a certain *factualism* in educational philosophy which condemns every presentation of values as no more than indoctrination. The irony is that every system of schooling does present values; factualism is observed by avoiding the most significant domains of value. We have no hesitation in teaching the cultivation of physical well-being and the appreciation of music, painting, and literature but are downright opposed to teaching the cultivation of the soul and are uneasy about teaching the appreciation of people and of moral achievements. It is not surprising that an education so unnaturally constrained is so crippling and that it produces cynics who, in Wilde's matchless phrase, know the price of everything and the value of nothing. The wonder is that there is so little cynicism and that it passes so soon. It is fortunate that the young learn so much more than we teach.

Whatever we do teach, how are we to do it? Granted that education is not to be indoctrination, nor salesmanship either. The purely *academic* also has unacceptable connotations. The term is used to mean what is pedantic, stilted, and scholastic, a bookish involution for which research is nothing more than re-search. The academic in the pejorative sense stifles imagination, creativity, and spontaneity. It rationalizes vested institutional interests as "maintaining standards," imposing on curricula whatever the holders of academic power happen to be prepared to teach and resisting as "unacademic" whatever new fields of study threaten established statuses. Rigid departmental lines my be defended regardless of whether emerging disciplines call for interdisciplinary studies, joint courses, and combined degrees. Fixed requirements (say, of languages or mathematics) may be rigidly defended, regardless of whether students really need the subjects or are able to use them after the requirements are met—American students, for instance, are made to study too much or else altogether too little of any foreign language.

The academy is the locus only of schooling, not necessarily of education. Continuing education beyond the school years (however advanced or prolonged) is a growing social need, carrying with it the recognition of the important role in education already played by such institutions as libraries, galleries, museums, concert halls, theaters, and public forums, and the enormous potentialities for education, scarcely begun to be actualized, of the mass media.

Among the worst features of academic pedagogy is its judgmental approach in which the student is continually being weighed in the balance. Emphasis is put on grades, whose validity is easily overrated, rather than on pass-fail outcomes or on descriptive assessments and constructive criticism of each individual's work. In any case, grades measure the quality of teaching as much as the achievement of learning. Often exams are treated as obstacles to be overcome rather than as diagnostic and therapeutic devices. There is good ground to regard exams as initiation rites perhaps more cruel than breaking the candidates' teeth. It has been well said that no matter what courts decide about separation of church and state, there will be prayers in our schools as long as we have exams.

The conventional academic approach is also outrageously competitive. Educational opportunity is a scarce resource in all but the most affluent countries and so is understandably allocated to those best able to make use of the opportunity; unfortunately, what is learned may be only how to compete. The dean of a famous law school annually greeted the first-year class with the words: "Gentlemen [women were almost never admitted to start with], look at the man sitting at each side of you; the chances are that next year only one of you three will be here." I doubt whether such a high level of anxiety is optimal for learning; I have no doubt that the hostilities induced compromised the social worth of what was learned. Students learn a great deal from one another, at all ages; peer learning should be encouraged and guided, not inhibited by competitiveness or condemned as dishonest. Group projects and team research in the course of one's education prefigure the forms which learning often takes when it is released from academic constraints.

The "academy" pays too little attention to the individual, especially with regard to differences in interests, capacities, and levels of prior achievement. One or two electives in a curriculum which consists largely of required courses can hardly provide a program suited to each student's unique educational needs and aspirations. The pervasive depersonalization is revealed by the common policy of identifying the writer of an exam by a coded number; because the reader might use irrelevant data, the data available to him are severely restricted, although they could be essential to understanding what the student meant to say, what he has learned, and what is important for him to learn next.

Education must address itself not only to the individual but to the whole personality of the individual. Education is not psychotherapy, but learning cannot be dissociated from the passions which motivate and guide it. Even if instruction could focus exclusively on the subject matter, education cannot. When a student asks a question, to answer the question rather than the student is to respond to a meaning and miss the point (§10). Large enrollments in psychology courses and the widespread student interest in Asian cults result partly from the circumstance that the person is so largely ignored in the educational process. Love of teaching is inseparable from love for students. I cannot help someone learn if I care nothing about him; if I do care for him, it is almost inevitable that I will contribute to his growth.

Claims to "student power" should be responded to in the light of such caring, not as a surrender to coercion. Students deserve a share in academic decision making, first, because the decisions affect their lives and, second, because such sharing can contribute significantly to their education. Students are not the best judges of good teaching, for they may confuse long-run learning with immediate enjoyment; but learning is certainly improved when teaching is being continually assessed. Education is like salesmanship, Dewey has pointed out: no sale is made unless the customer buys. A student never fails a course alone; the failure is shared by those who did not succeed in teaching him.

The call for "student power" cannot be justified by the spurious principle that he who wears the shoe knows where it pinches; knowledge is not a matter of immediate awareness and direct experience (§24). But just as knowledge is not absolute, not all or none, so also with power. A share in the decisions does not imply autonomy or veto power. Extremist formulations reflect the distrust and hostility with which students and the rest of the educational community, or society as a whole, view one another. The myth persists that students are indolent, indifferent to all that is being provided for them. ("How many students have you here?" a college president is asked. "Students? Oh, about five percent!") In fact, a large number of students have part-time and even full-time jobs; the vast majority devote more time to their studies than is common in the society at large to devote to productive work. We have a more just complaint against the careerists in the student body than against those who contribute part of their energies to what they see as the general welfare.

The whole personality of the student enters into the educational process; so does the whole personality of the teacher. Instruction can be carried out effectively by machines and is increasingly being mechanized, automated, and computerized with good results. Education, however, can be carried out only by human beings. The educator inevitably serves as a model for those he is helping to grow, not because of any pretensions on his part but because the aspirations of the learners focus on him as the embodiment of his subject and the life of the mind. Teachers are loved and admired—less deservedly, it may be, but certainly more often, than they are hated and feared. Identification is one of the basic mechanisms by which we learn, provided we are being presented with a person with whom we can identify, not with a depersonalized tool to be used, and by which we ourselves feel used. This is why, incidentally, the dichotomy of teaching and research is ill-conceived: we teach best when we allow others to share in our own learning.

In the role of the teacher as socially defined there is a considerable element of monasticism, for historical reasons, without much functional justification. Low salaries and poor facilities, compared with salaries and working conditions allotted to comparable skills and training in other domains, are not only expressions of disdain for education; they may rather be the contrary, as though to say that teachers are dedicated men and women engaged in holy labors, and that mind and spirit flourish only if the body and matter are disregarded. Faculties, it has been remarked, take the traditional vows: poverty in relation to the alumni, obedience in relation to the administration, chastity in relation to the students. Everyone in the educational community must recurrently remind others that, appearances to the contrary notwithstanding, he is indeed human.

In all these respects, teaching methods are best in the preschool and primary grades and get progressively worse as we mount to the graduate and professional schools. The lowest grades are the least academic, the least judgmental and competitive; they are the most individualized and personalized; enjoy the best, most functional facilities; and all in all show the most inventiveness, creativity, and imagination. It is well that this is so, for the earliest years of teaching are the most important; our teachers of the very young are the least appreciated of all educators.

Perhaps the most fundamental condition that must be met for education to flourish is *academic freedom*. The defense of academic freedom means preserving a forum for the free exchange of ideas. The educational process must provide a place where people can say exactly what they think, whatever the issues of freedom of speech in general (§71). Academic freedom means that there must be free speech on the campus and that the results of academic research can be freely disseminated (though not necessarily the results of research carried out in noneducational institutions). This is not a matter of special privileges for educators; academic freedom must be recognized as a social need in just the degree to which education is acknowledged to have a social function.

Neither does academic freedom imply immunity from the law or exemption from judgment by whatever personal or social values might come into play. Academic and extramural considerations must be carefully distinguished, however, though it may be hard to differentiate between them in a concrete setting. A chemistry professor who is sympathetic to enemies of the state may be an excellent chemist and a good teacher. Academic freedom requires that assessment of his academic competence not be confused with the question of his loyalty, just as a musician's politics is irrelevant to the quality of his music. It is *not* irrelevant, however, to the question of whether we are willing to hear him play; he may use part of the price of the ticket to destroy values more precious to us than listening to his music. The professor of chemistry is no less free—but no more—than the musician, in his political beliefs and personal habits. Academic freedom means that academic activity, not everything a person does, should be subject only to academic appraisal and constraints.

Specifically, it means that tenure must be protected; job insecurity may be as pernicious in its effect on educators as on judges. It means that the educator must be free of censorship, except such as might be imposed on every other member of the society (for instance, with regard to libel or national security). The doctrine of "publish or perish" is less abhorrent than "publish *and* perish," as pressure groups react to ideas they find unacceptable. Academic freedom means that police have no place on a campus except when what is being threatened is the law of the land, not an administrative ruling. It means that educational institutions must be free to formulate for themselves their educational policies, and the procedures by which it is ensured that these policies are carried out. Admittedly, academic freedom is sometimes compromised and even undermined by the academy itself; just so a democracy can be overthrown by enemies from within as well as from without. But there is no more reason in the one case than in the other to surrender freedom from the outset.

Like other forms of freedom, academic freedom carries with it a commensurate responsibility, what Sidney Hook and others have emphasized as *academic responsibility*. It is not to exploit the classroom, from either side of the desk, on behalf of positions on controversial issues irrelevant to the subject matter of the class, or outside the professional competence of the educator. It is not to undermine the willingness to listen to opinions which differ from our own; to weigh the evidence, in whatever direction it falls; to respect valid argument, regardless of who makes it. The objectivity to which education is committed does not mean that neither educators nor students are entitled to any opinion on controversial matters, or only a "balanced" or "neutral" opinion. What it means is that the defense of opinion is to be undertaken in the educational setting only where it is academically relevant, and everywhere only with the fullest use of reason of which the educated mind is capable. In this age of unreason educators have been subjected to pervasive slanders as to loyalty, decency, even simple good sense. Perhaps what is at work is not only anti-intellectualism but also infantile rebelliousness against authority. Those who stone their prophets are more merciful to their teachers; they give them a suspended sentence.

68. Philosophy of History

Education is meant to provide us with perspective; for man, historical perspective is especially important. Man is the only animal with a history he is aware of, and by which his life is shaped. The awareness takes two forms: a *sense of history* is the capacity to recognize the past in the present, to see its bearings on the present; an *historical sense* is the capacity to recognize the future in the present, to see the promise of the present for the future. (The difference is sometimes marked by different usages for the words "historical" and "historic," respectively.) The two forms of awareness of history often interfere with one another: reactionaries have a strong sense of history but no historical sense, while with revolutionaries the converse is true. In our day the historical sense is especially marked; for the first time *futurism* has emerged as a special discipline.

The penalty for ignoring the past is that we are condemned to repeat it, Santayana has remarked. Some years ago a student activist was attempting to take over my class. As I was about to remonstrate with him, he said, "I suppose you're going to talk to me about the Nazis!" That is exactly what I was going to do. I thought then, and still do, that the parallel might have been instructive; but history cannot teach those who refuse to learn. In the introduction to his *Philosophy of History,* Hegel expressed the dismal though plausible view, "What experience and history teach is this—that peoples and governments have never learned anything from history, or acted upon principles deducible from it." The contemporary rationalization of the willful disregard of the past is that the present is so radically different from the past as to make history irrelevant. Without a knowledge of history, even its irrelevance cannot be judged, but it is not easy to argue with prejudice. The present is unique in many ways, but no one can reasonably believe that its every feature is altogether unprecedented. History need not repeat itself to be relevant.

A more rational objection to the study of history is not that the events of the past are without present significance but that what historians write about those events is not worth reading. The arch-conservative Henry Ford expressed over a half-century ago what many present-day radicals maintain, "History is bunk." Quite a few philosophers and even historians agree with them. History is "a fable agreed upon," said Voltaire; "a shallow village tale" are Emerson's words in his essay on history; "a distillation of rumor" it was called by Carlyle, author of the great *History of the French Revolution;* "that huge Mississippi of falsehood" is the characterization by Matthew Arnold. What historians write often does serve, intentionally or otherwise, special interests for which the strict truth is not so sacred as to be inviolable. "Even the law of gravitation," Macaulay acknowledged, "would be brought into dispute were there a pecuniary interest involved"; that political interests may have a great effect on historians is amply illustrated by the periodic Soviet rewriting of history.

To write history with a deep sense of commitment to truth objectively conceived is, admittedly, very hard indeed; I do not see why we should concede beforehand that it is impossible. The philosophy of history occupies itself with the question whether and how it might be done. This belongs to one branch of the philosophy of history, the *methodological:* its task is the logical analysis of the problems of historiography. Methodological philosophy of history is to the writing of history what the philosophy of science is to the practice of scientific method. There is also a *substantive* philosophy of history whose relation to what historians do is more like that of metaphysics to science. It is the attempt to formulate the most general patterns which the historical process is thought to exhibit.

Methodological difficulties multiply rapidly as soon as we move from what is true "in principle" about the writing of history to what in fact historians do. In principle, the description and explanation of what happened in history is no different from what applies to any other sort of happenings; in practice, there are many special problems.

To start with, there is the problem of determining *historical facts.* The materials available to the historian do not constitute his subject matter from the very outset. The *materials,* sometimes called "traces," are remains of certain processes; the *subject matter* is the processes themselves—what actually happened, in the words of Leopold von Ranke, one of the founders a century ago of the modern attempt to put the writing of history on an objective basis. We cannot, as he supposed, "let history speak for itself"; we can let it speak, but there is still the task of determining what it is saying. Did Norsemen really come to America before Columbus, as I was taught in Minnesota? Did John F. Kennedy's assassin have co-conspirators, as some people still believe? Who authored the Dead Sea scrolls? and a certain one of the *Federalist Papers?* A set of comprehensive answers to such questions constitutes an *historical chronicle*—the record of certain historical facts, such as the facts about church history recorded by Eusebius in the fourth century, or the facts about the ownership of pieces of land recorded in the Domesday Book in the eleventh century. In principle, a chronicle is like an ephemeris, an almanac, or an atlas.

In fact, it raises the basic questions concerning the relations between verification and meaning (§11). The evidence on the basis of which something is determined to be historical fact is a trace in the present, but the fact referred to lies in the past. The question is how we move from evidence to meaning, from present to past. As time goes on, we not only uncover new evidence but also new meanings in the evidence we already have; both processes affect what we accept as historical fact. Not only does the past illuminate the present; the present also continually throws new light on the past, enabling us to see a new past (§37). George Orwell's slogan in *1984* which rationalizes the rewriting of history, "Who controls the past controls the future," is not the whole truth; we might add, "Who controls the present, controls the past."

History not only determines what happened; it *reconstructs* it: the facts are presented as effects of certain causes and as causes of certain effects. In such a causal sequence they constitute *historical events* rather than discrete historical facts. The data of history—the historian's primary materials—are certain traces; in moving to his proper subject matter, the historian first determines what facts the traces show, then establishes the connections among the facts so determined. In reconstructing the past the historian is establishing linkages among particulars, for instance, the part played by Trotsky in the Bolshevik Revolution, or by the Munich Pact in the outbreak of World War II. "Did Caesar cross the Rubicon?" is a question of historical fact; an answer to the question, "What difference did it make?" presents it as an historical event. The outcome of such reconstruction is not a chronicle but a *narrative,* a sequence of events bound together in a causal network, like the histories written by Herodotus and Gibbon. The difference between chronicle and narrative is like that between an anamnesis, the background data about a patient, and a case history, a sequence detailing the onset and course of a disease.

An historical narrative connects facts with one another; it does not display facts as governed by general laws. We may have far better reason to assert a particular connection than to proclaim a general law governing connections of that kind; we may know what started a certain war, for instance, without knowing how wars start, as we may know that a man was killed by a certain shot without a knowledge either of ballistics or of pathology. Disciplines dealing with particular cases have sometimes been called "ideographic" in contrast to the "nomothetic" disciplines, which invoke general laws. The distinction must not be drawn too finely nor pressed too far (§32). Historical narrative does not forfeit scientific standing for no better reason than that it particularizes. Geology is a science just as is geophysics, and the *Descent of Man* is as much a scientific treatise as is the *Origin of Species*.

The writing of narrative involves repeated inductive leaps, not merely "reporting what happened." Even if the historical facts have been established, evidence is needed that they are connected in one way rather than another, and that what is identified as a cause of a certain event is not merely among the conditions under which the event occurred.

The attempt may be made to formulate and invoke *historical laws*. A narrative in which events are presented as a sequence of particulars conforming to general laws may be called an *historical analysis*. Examples are the analyses given by Lenin of certain events in French, German, and Russian history. As he himself would say, it is no accident that he so often uses the expression "It is no accident that . . .": Marxist-Leninism is one of the notable efforts to formulate historical laws and apply them in historical analyses. This effort is the basis of what Engels claimed to be "scientific" socialism in contrast to the "utopian" variety. Problems of discovering and applying scientific laws in general (§41) present themselves in historical research as elsewhere.

The question is often raised whether historical laws are possible because of the central role in history played by *chance*. This might be called the "problem of Cleopatra's nose"—"had it been shorter," Pascal said, "the whole face of the world would have been changed." Lenin claims to speak of what is no accident, but it is undeniable that accidents happen and that they may have profound consequences, as unpredictable as the accidents themselves. To this it might be countered, first, that predictability is not a necessary condition for the existence of scientific laws or for our capacity to discover them. Laws may formulate only statistical regularities, or connections which, though virtually without exception in the short range, cumulatively present enough uncertainties to make longer-range predictions impossible. Examples are the gas laws dealing with the average movement of large numbers of molecules, or the laws of fluid dynamics relating to the onset of a hurricane. Second, while outcomes, in their full specificity, may well be accidental, that some event or other of the kind in question would take place might be not at all accidental. The assassin's bullet at Sarajevo could have missed, and the First World War would not have started just when and where it did; yet historical analysis might well support the conclusion that in the situation, war would soon have been triggered in one way or another.

Such considerations evoke objections from the opposite direction: that those who purport to have discovered historical laws promulgate an unacceptable doctrine of *historical inevitability*, as Isaiah Berlin has called it, a kind of social fatalism or apocalyptic determinism. Giovanni Vico, the eighteenth-century Italian philosopher who is sometimes regarded as the first truly modern historian, was certainly among the first in modern times to attempt to formulate historical laws on the basis of empirical research (although Aristotle might be given priority here). Vico wanted to formulate what he characterized as "eternal ideal history, invariably followed by all nations." By the time of Marx, historical inevitability took on a connotation of both physical and moral compulsion, corresponding to the ambiguity in the "necessity" embodied in the natural "law" and in the moral "law." The individual can only delay or ease the birth pangs of the new society which will inevitably come to be; the ultimate victory of the revolution is assured by the laws of history. Fascism, too, saw itself as representing "the wave of the future."

The alleged inevitability of outcomes is by no means a presupposition of every scientific, causal analysis of events. Causal connection does not involve any element of necessity; nothing is added to the report of an event by the purported explanation that it "had to happen," other than the assertion that some causes or other were at work. The determinism which is characteristic of the scientific approach is only methodological or programmatic, not a metaphysical denial of any possibility of averting destiny. It is meant to encourage the search for causes, not to discourage intervention anywhere in the causal sequence. Such intervention would itself be causal and is as acceptable methodologically as is any other cause

A scientific law is predictive only conditionally—*if* the situation is such and such, then. . . . It does not make *forecasts* of the future, for other laws simultaneously govern the many other factors at work in the situation, and the outcome is the result of all of them. Man himself, with his forethought and such resources as are at his disposal, is also one of the factors of the historical situation, sometimes the decisive factor. An historical situation unquestionably sets limits to the possible outcomes; that it leaves us no options at all is only a dogma. Predictions of the inevitability of a stated outcome are self-fulfilling, weakening the will to resist the outcome and inviting support for a sure winner.

What purport to be historical laws sometimes have a specious air of necessity only because they are tautological. "Pendulum" theories of history—"sooner or later there is bound to be a movement in the opposite direction"—are empty unless they contain some specification of how much of a movement is to be expected (there are random fluctuations in every process), and the time interval within which it will occur (nothing lasts forever). A similar criticism can be made of Arnold Toynbee's notion (in *A Study of History*) of the historical process as a succession of responses to challenges, each response "exposing the respondent to a fresh challenge which demands a further response on his part." A society which is insufficiently challenged or for which the challenge is too great does not survive—to be sure, for "survival" means nothing other than continuing to respond, and what makes the challenge "too" great or "too" little is precisely that no response is forthcoming.

The doctrine of historical inevitability may emphasize moral rather than logical necessity, construing what "must" be as what "ought" to be. In this form the doctrine is sometimes called *historicism;* it amounts to the view embodied in Hegel's formula, "Whatever is, is right. " Morton White and others have called it "social Darwinism," survival being taken as evidence of fitness to survive, or even as defining "fitness." In this view, the judgment of history is never mistaken; what should not happen in fact will not happen. The laws of history are seen as belonging to the same system of cosmic harmony which the medieval period found in the feudal order and which the age of the Enlightenment found in the natural laws of physics and economics. These laws, in turn, are promulgations of the divine will, and so are necessarily and intrinsically good.

Karl Popper criticizes historicism as the espousal of a "closed society," blueprinted either in the world of Ideas, as in Plato, or in the dialectic of world Reason, as in Hegel. Those who claim to be establishing the new order proclaimed by history characteristically exercise totalitarian power to prevent dissidents from proclaiming anything different. That historical laws govern the processes of history does not mean that the future is not open but only that real possibilities for the future are no more chaotic than are present actualities and the past conditions by which they were produced.

Some philosophers object to the very notion of historical laws, for such laws are intrinsically temporal in reference, and scientific laws, they maintain, affirm timeless connections between states of affairs which can be abstractly specified. Like the doctrine of historical inevitability, this position too seems to me to be a metaphysical dogma, or else an arbitrary restriction on the definition of "scientific law." There are temporal laws in the physical and biological sciences as well as in the behavioral sciences (§47). There are *interval laws,* stating what happens under certain conditions after a lapse of a specified time, such as hysteresis in metals or the phenomena of forgetting. The are *genetic laws,* governing growth and development, whether of stars or of starfish. There are *pattern laws,* relating phenomena to identifiable stages or a recurrent process, as in the case of rainfall or of economic crises. If historical laws are to be distinguished from those of other behavioral sciences, that they are temporal may be one of their distinctive features, though it is a feature by no means unique to history. The historian can make good use of such laws as other sciences of man can provide him.

Connections among historical events are not only causal; they may also be purposive. *Interpretation* of historical events as shaped by purposes may be distinguished from their reconstruction as an *historical account,* like those given by Thucydides or Macaulay. Some philosophers of history, like Benedetto Croce and R. G. Collingwood, hold that history must be presented only as an historical account, for they see historical events only as expressions of human meaning. That events sometimes can be so interpreted is beyond question. What is questionable is whether the ascription of certain purposes in a given case is warranted: have the purposes been validly inferred or only projected onto the historical situation? Sometimes we have the advantage of comparatively direct knowledge of purposes, as from letters and diaries. In general, indirect and hazardous inferences must be made that are validated by the *coherence* of the interpretation, how it fits with all we already know about human behavior, and the *comprehensiveness* of the interpretation, its capacity to make sense of all the data we have.

A common pattern of inference here is circular but not necessarily vicious. An interpretation made in order to understand what the actors on the historical scene were doing may then be used to explain why they did it. I call this pattern the *circle of interpretation;* its usefulness depends on the diameter of the circle, as it were—how coherent and comprehensive the interpretation is.

More serious difficulties arise when purposes are construed as *motivational* rather than *functional:* motivations relate to deliberate, intended, conscious goals, while functions embody goal-directed behavior without implied anticipation, as in cybernetic and other telic mechanisms. The difference between functions and motivations corresponds to Dewey's distinction between ends and ends-in-view. The difficulties are of two sorts. One is that motives may be ascribed when outcomes are, in fact, unanticipated consequences of decisions made for quite other reasons. Conspiratorial conceptions of history, for instance, imagine that whatever happens was deliberately brought about, thereby projecting onto others the omnipotence typical in paranoid delusions.

The second difficulty is that motives are ascribed to abstract or collective agencies, to social classes, society, the state, "the people," "universal Reason," and "History" itself. Invoking such entities in historical interpretation is sometimes called *historic holism.* There is no objection to holistic concepts in historical analyses if empirical specifications are given for identifying their causal workings; if they are invoked in historical accounts, however, it can be only in functional, not motivational, terms. Even if social classes, for example, act to satisfy class interests (§66), this is no more a matter of literal motivation than in the case of a species developing the kidney "in order to" maintain a stable saline environment for the body cells. Both, however, are meaningful functional interpretations.

Historical accounts characteristically make use of *purposive units;* corresponding to functions and motivations are concepts of *historical periods* (the Renaissance, the Industrial Revolution) and *historical policies* (the "Drang nach Osten" and the Cold War). All concepts presuppose judgments of relevance (§32); such judgments are especially hard to make in connection with purposive concepts, without question-begging simplifications. We can find almost any purpose we choose if we are free to decide which outcomes we will call "side-effects" or "by-products" and which we will identify as the "major consequences." Not everything all together can be taken as purposive; some selection must be made. There cannot be any such thing as "universal history"; neither does history consist only of past politics. What history "really" is about is an inescapable choice of the historian; history does not speak for itself even to announce its identity. Moreover, what sort of interpretation a historian engages in cannot be legislated by methodology; motivational, functional, and causal accounts or analyses are all admissible, even if we cannot then and there reduce any of them to the others.

Historical explanation comprises historical analyses and accounts as contrasted with historical narratives and chronicles. Pattern explanations (§34) have been much more common among philosphers of history than explanations on the deductive model, though the reverse might very well be true among historians themselves. Vico, Hegel, Marx, Spengler, and Toynbee are some of the modern philosophers of history who have sought to explain historical events by assigning them a place in linear, cyclical, spiral, and other such patterns. The basic principle of their pattern explanations is the one enunciated by Vico in his characterization of the "nature" of things as "nothing but the fact of their being born at certain times and in certain manners." Patterns are often so vaguely described that it is impossible to assess the validity of the explanations invoking them, the more so because of the circle of interpretation usually involved. Tests, over and above those already mentioned for validating interpretations, include the *intersubjectivity* of the explanation, to correct for the ideological biases which are so common, and the *stability* of the explanation with continuing historical research, to correct for the effect of selected and misinterpreted data.

The besetting fault of overall historical explanations is their reliance on a *magic key*, some single factor which is taken to be universally explanatory. It is all very well for a science to aim at the widest possible generalization; it is hardly reasonable to suppose that such a generalization can be attained all at once, without induction from intermediate generalizations of more limited scope. There are too many keys for any one of them to retain plausibility: there are climatic and geopolitical keys to history; psychological keys, like the "bedroom" theory of history; institutional keys, economic and other; theological keys; and so on.

Among the most perennially popular is the conception of the *hero* as the key. There is properly no history, only biography," as Emerson has it; every institution is "the lengthened shadow of one man." This is a type of purposive explanation, subject to the hazards of purposive explanation in general. The concept of the hero has been developed by Carlyle and others as a person whose purposes shape history; they do so, however, only because they embody the teleology immanent in pervasive historical forces. The root idea is contained in Hegel's characterization of heroes as people "whose own particular aims involve these large issues which are the will of the World Spirit." The hero, that is, translates an historical function into a personal motivation. Heroic efforts on the part of the historian himself, however, are required to fit all the data of chronicle and narrative into this type of historical account.

Historiography must recognize, finally, that history need not be written only after the model of other scientific discourse. The historian may attempt to *recreate* the events he deals with, in an imaginative evocation which may have as much in common with art as with science. In a classic comparison, Aristotle held poetry to be more philosophical than history because it deals with universals rather than particulars. But history itself might be, as

Macaulay described it, "a compound of poetry and philosophy." Ancient rhetoricians had already characterized history as "philosophy learned from examples"; subsequently, it was religion, then politics, which history was supposed to teach. The historian needs imagination, as all scientists do, because it serves for all as the source of hypotheses, theories, and explanatory insights. Perhaps he needs it more than other scientists do in order to offset the deadening effect of contemplating a past already over and done with; the truth is, we never are done with the past.

As to substantive rather than methodological philosophy of history, little has been achieved which has met with general acceptance. By far the most influential attempts to paint a sweeping picture of what happened in history have been versions of the Judaeo-Christian account of man's Fall and coming Redemption. The constructive force in history was taken to be Providence itself in such standard formulations as Augustine and Bossuet's (bishops both, of the fourth and seventeenth centuries, respectively); the idea was attacked by such historians as Hume and Gibbon; then reinstated, in secular guise, by Hegel and Marx. The root dialectic is the opposition of Good and Evil, the struggle between the forces of light and darkness. Hegel describes history as "the development of Spirit in time"; Marxist materialism does not do away with the Spirit but focuses, as humanism eventually must, on the clay into which the Spirit was breathed.

If I were to recognize any sustained historical development it would be in the growth of knowledge, man's increasing awareness of himself and the world; in the progressive transformation of the world around him, both by creation and by destruction; and in the gradual emergence of a common human culture, increasingly shared by all the members of the family of man.

Whether those are in fact directions of historical development or only temporary movements to be halted and reversed in a coming age of barbarism, I cannot say. Many historians take a dimmer view of human history than is connoted by the rise of science, technology, and a unified world society. To Voltaire, history is "scarcely more than a register of misfortunes"; according to Jefferson, history "only informs us what bad government is"; and for Gibbon, it comprises "little more than the register of the crimes, follies, and misfortunes of mankind." Carlyle quotes Montesquieu, and has been quoted by many others in turn, as saying, "Happy the people whose annals are blank in history books," or as it is sometimes put, "the people whose history is tiresome."

Years ago I was traveling with my family in Europe; we first spent a week or two in England, then went on to France. As we came to the Place de la Concorde in Paris my younger daughter innocently asked, "Daddy, whose head was cut off *here?*" The question was only too appropriate. In Shaw's *Caesar and Cleopatra* Theodotus pleads with Caesar to put out the fire in the library of Alexandria: "What is burning there is the memory of mankind." To which Caesar rejoins, "A shameful memory, let it burn." The more shame if we do destroy the memory; for how, then, can we hope for a less shameful future?

Chapter Eleven

Political Philosophy

69. Power and Authority

Political philosophy no doubt had it origins in bitter reflections on the realities of political life. Tyranny and injustice—the insolence of office and the oppressor's wrong—are surely as old as any person's ability to impose his will on another. Your will cannot coincide with mine unless I am so enslaved that I cannot call my soul my own; when our wills do not coincide and I must do your bidding, I might well ask, silently at least, by what right you decide what I must do. The justification of power poses questions raised by philosophers from earliest times.

That there is a difference between what is and what ought to be is universally recognized and is made the basis of political action. Politically, this difference is great, and the quandaries in which it places people are widespread and perennial. There is a *predicament* of power, underlying the continuing *problems* of decision making.

The oldest justifications of power refer to the will of the gods. I do not command you, but God, speaking through me; I am his vicar. The king is annointed by the priest, and though the king may occasionally take the crown from the priest's hands and place it on his head himself, he keeps the priest by his side as witness to his right. If his exercise of power seems cruel and unjust, the ways of Heaven are inscrutable; even the savage Attila was known as "the scourge of God." In short, the king rules by *divine right.*

How do we know whom the gods have chosen to rule? A justification of power is needed which discriminates between conflicting claims to power; there has seldom been a throne without its pretenders. An ancient expedient is to let the gods themselves disclose their will. As the conflict continues, it will move to its predestined end, and the victor, his victory having been in the hands of the gods, will be shown to have been their choice. He won because he should have won; that he should have won is proved, in turn, by his winning. *De facto* power is thus transformed into power *de jure.* The Declaration of Independence states, "these United Colonies are, and of right ought to be, free and independent"; that they not only *are* but also *ought* to be free is argued by a lengthy series of "facts to be submitted to a candid world." Trial by combat, however, does not call for any argument nor does it allow any; its principle is that *might makes right.* King Arthur's sword in the stone was to belong to whoever could draw it forth; power is rightly his who has the strength to wield it.

This ancient rationalization of power persists and is continually refurbished by "progressive" thinkers and revolutionaries. It was a central component of Stalinism—in practice, if not in its ideology. Stalin, being told during World War II that the pope might strongly disapprove of some step he was proposing to take, countered, "How many divisions does the pope have?" The strategy of confronting others with a *fait accompli* so that what *is* will settle questions of what ought to be, was adopted by the Soviet Union to repress revolution in Hungary and reform in Czechoslovakia. It was also the strategy underlying Lenin's conception of the dictatorship of the proletariat which he once described as "nothing else than power based upon force and limited by nothing—by no law and by absolutely no rule"; this description was echoed by Stalin with the words, "the domination of the proletariat over the bourgeoisie, untrammeled by law and based on violence." Comparable charges of using power as though it were its own justification have been leveled against the United States for the gunboat diplomacy of another age and for the Vietnam war. Terrorist movements provide other examples. "Might makes right" is a living philosophy, though there is sharp disagreement on its habitation.

The doctrine is that might *makes* right, not that the question, what is right, is inadmissible or irrelevant. "Our strong arms be our conscience, swords our law," says Richard III; he is referring to law and conscience as well as to swords. The successful appeal to arms makes virtue triumphant because triumph is construed as the proof of virtue, and it is so construed in order to preserve virtue. When the British ruled India, an attempt was made to stamp out *suttee,* the practice of burning a widow on the funeral pyre of her husband. To a delegation of Hindus who protested this disregard for local customs, the regional administrator replied, "Not at all! We honor your customs, but we have a custom of our own—to hang anyone who burns people alive." What is refreshing, and unlikely, about this story is the presentation of political patterns as established fact without regard to extrinsic justifications.

Thomas Hobbes is among the most incisive exponents of such a political philosophy. The main thing, he said in effect, is to see that things get done in a predictable way, which allows no occasion for argument and no room for violence. Whether one thing is done instead of another is secondary, and even arbitrary, so far as human judgment goes. The position is that of the inveterate gambler who explains why he continues to play in a game known to be dishonest: "Sure, it's a crooked game; but what can I do? It's the only game in town!"

When power is seen as its own justification it easily becomes the supreme value of political life. If power, like beauty, is its own excuse for being, it is most surely worthy of pursuit. The doctrine that might makes right is closely linked, logically and psychologically, with *power politics.* All politics is occupied with getting and exercising power; power politics is distinctive in making of this aim an end in itself. (Similarly, *militarism* does not consist merely in establishing or using an army but in regarding military force and its use as having intrinsic value.) The pursuit of power Hobbes regards as "a general inclination of all mankind, a perpetual and restless desire of power after power, that ceases only in death." Hobbes acknowledges other human aspirations, such as the desire for gain and glory. A purer form of power politics characterizes the revolutionary, as described by Mikhail Bakunin in Article 1 of his *Catechism of the Revolution:* "The revolutionist has no personal interest, no affairs, sentiments, attachments, property, not even a name of his own. Everything in him is absorbed by one exclusive interest, one thought, one passion—the revolution."

Bakunin was an anarchist and criticized Marxist revolutionaries for wanting not to destroy power (an aim for which the anarchist, too, needs power) but to establish themselves in power. The dictatorship of the proletariat is a dictatorship after all, and any dictatorship, he argued, can have only one aim: self-perpetuation. The dictum of the Prussian general Karl von Clausewitz, that war is a continuation of politics by other means, reverses the situation, so far as power politics is concerned. Politics is the continued struggle against rival claimants to power; just as war cannot have any other aim than victory, so politics has no other aim than getting and keeping power. "Seek ye first the kingdom of this earth" is the gospel of power, "and all these things shall be added unto you." A pursuit of power which stops at nothing is thought to be in the very nature of the political animal and of political institutions. This is the position of Heinrich von Treitschke, a nineteenth-century precursor of Nazi ideology: "The State is not an academy of arts. If it neglects its strength in order to promote the idealistic aspirations of man, it repudiates its own nature and perishes." With this doctrine idealistic aspirations are left powerless while power becomes brutalized.

Not all wielders of power adopt such a stance. In all, however, there is an inclination to increase their power and to hold on to what they get. However power has been attained, it comes to be felt as a personal possession: if given up, it is handed on to chosen successors. Nepotism and related practices are known the world over. Fitness to exercise power does not serve, in these perspectives, as a condition for getting power or for keeping it, because there is no external end (the so-called idealistic aspirations) for which power serves as a means and by reference to which fitness can be assessed. Even where such ends are acknowledged, they easily give way to the overriding end of getting and keeping power. The European sociologist Robert Michels, in the early decades of this century, after a study of left-wing political parties, labor unions, and other groups with democratic ideologies, formulated what he called *the iron law of oligarchy,* that power tends always to be concentrated in a few hands, and that it tends to become entrenched. While this may not be an "iron law," it describes a widespread political pattern, discernible even among groups with a contrary ideology. Revolutionaries and dissenters, once they do attain power, have in their turn suppressed any dissent from their rule and even from their policies.

Power has a variety of bases—what accounts for its possession or for the effectiveness with which it is wielded. In the doctrine that might makes right, "might" is interpreted, sooner or later, in terms of brute strength: arms, and the skill and determination necessary to use them—in a word, the capacity for *violence.* Power based on violence may be called *force* (in a narrow sense). It is force which prevails in trial by combat; power politics prizes force above all other forms of power: Force can be applied most swiftly and surely—in the short run. I recently had occasion to visit some border areas; as we approached the zone, the drivers of the two cars in our party carefully placed their Uzis within easy reach. Not to be outdone, I took out my pen, at which one of the men remarked, "If you had time for that, we wouldn't need these."

If we are not frightened, there may be more time than we suppose, and with determination people can make time for alternatives to force. There is a *cult of violence* given to the worship of force which is used far more quickly and far more often than as a last resort. There are violent men who hold that nothing is achieved without violence; in our day such men speak loudly, even in the councils of nations. "All armed prophets succeed," Machiavelli said, "and unarmed prophets come to ruin." A biography of Trotsky is called *The Prophet Armed,* but he came to ruin nevertheless, and so did the cause for which he armed himself. Marx spoke of force as the midwife of every old society pregnant with the new—a bloody metaphor in such a context and one which contrasts strikingly with Socrates' conception of his role as midwife for ideas.

The cult of violence is institutionalized in the symbols and practices of militarism. The worship of force was most blatant in the praises of war common during the Fascist era and the decades preceding it, and is still to be heard in our own time, though the word "war" is replaced by the rhetoric of "revolution," "liberation," and "the fight for freedom." The cult of violence does not rest only on the doctrine that the end justifies the means; force, like other forms of power, is also worshipped as its own justification. The position is not that a war may be fought in a good cause but that the cause itself is justified by a good war. "War has the higher significance," Hegel declared, "that through it the moral health of peoples is preserved." The doctrine is that war provides an occasion for loyalty, sacrifice, and solidarity. But it also provides an occasion for treason to higher loyalties, whether to God or to our fellowmen; for binding human sacrifices to our own altars; for turning against neighbors and our close kin in the family of man.

William James spoke of "a moral equivalent for war," by which supposed instincts of aggression could find other channels of expression. In his more innocent day, and until recently, it was thought that such a possibility was illustrated, both for players and for spectators, by sports. Now the playing field has also become a battlefield, where athletes are murdered or prevented from making an appearance.

Trotsky once said that not believing in force is like not believing in gravitation. That force is used often, and sometimes with effect, is not to be denied. ("Do you believe in baptism?" "Believe in it? Man, I've seen it done!") The issue is whether the fact that force is used is ground for concluding that it ought to be. The reference to gravitation is more to the point than might be immediately apparent, for this is a law of nature, and therefore also—for those who think in such terms—of God. It is the presupposition of trial by combat that the outcome of force testifies to the will of the gods.

This is a presupposition also of the cult of violence, although it may be unconscious. In the worship of force, killing becomes a satanic sacrament of violence by which the gods are compelled to the killer's service as, in archaic religions, the gods were compelled by the shedding of sacrificial blood. There is a link here with a more general belief in *the magic of violence,* as deep-seated in our psyches and in society as a belief in the magic of symbols (§7). When calling out, "Open, sesame!" is not effective, the infantile reaction is to kick the door. Men find it easy to believe that they can achieve anything if they use enough force, in the right place. This belief underlies the reliance on saturation bombing, acts of terrorism, and perhaps also shock therapy. Pascal put his finger on the crucial oversight which nullifies the worship of force: "Force and not opinion is the queen of the world; but it is opinion that uses force."

In its most general sense, power, politically speaking, is the capacity to bend another to our will. *A* has power over *B* if *A* can determine, to some degree, what *B* is to do. In such circumstances, *B* is not making his own decisions, that is, not making them alone; *A* also has a voice in the matter, though it may be soft and disguised. To have power is to participate in the making of decisions. If the effect of the participation is relatively slight and indirect, we usually speak of *influence.* Power in the strict sense is relatively decisive. How much of an effect *A* has on *B*'s decisions is the *weight* of his influence or power over *B; power* may be defined as influence of considerable weight, how much is "considerable" being subject to contextual determination.

A may wield significant power over *B* with respect to some of *B*'s decisions, say, in economic matters, and not with respect to others, for instance, religious practices or personal relations; the controlled areas constitute the *scope* of the power. Power of greater weight is likely to be more limited in scope: a man is subject to some influence with regard to almost everything he does, but only some of his doings are almost entirely imposed from without.

Those over whom *A* has power constitute the *domain* of the power (it is the "converse domain" of the power relation, in the sense of the calculus of relations—§19). Each member of the domain is subject, in principle, to power of different weight and scope—there are always a few free or rebellious spirits; in practice, there is enough homogeneity in a domain so that we can speak of the weight and scope of the power with respect to the domain as a whole.

Usually *A*'s power over *B* depends on the circumstance that *A* is able to impose sanctions on *B*, according to what *B* agrees to do. These sanctions may be rewards or punishments; if they do not matter much to *B*, *A*'s power will be of correspondingly lesser weight. In this respect *B* also has some power over *A*: *B*'s scale of values sets limits to what power *A* can exercise over him. There is a certain power of desperation enjoyed by those who have nothing more to lose. *B* may also be in a position to manipulate *A*'s scale of values so as to influence what sanctions *A* will be willing to impose—an effect Nietzsche identified as "the tyranny of the weak over the strong."

In political contexts, and to some degree in interpersonal relations as well, for *A* to maintain his power over *B* he must keep a firm hold on *B*'s value system; for this reason some type of thought control is associated with all power of sufficient weight (§71). *B* might also escape the effect of *A*'s sanctions if he has alternative ways of attaining his values. In the effort to maintain itself, therefore, power tends towards a totalitarian scope (§72). Power is intrinsically monopolistic; competing powers necessarily weaken each other—the principle underlying political equilibrium maintained by a *balance of power.*

For power to be wielded, sanctions need not actually be imposed; they may remain implicit and be explicitly formulated only by outside observers. What gives the power its weight is the *power base;* how this is seen by the domain is the basis of authority rather than power. The bases of power vary from culture to culture and from time to time within a given society and with the political context. The base may be personal, as is true of "moral force," and the influence of popular heros or respected writers. Considerable influence may be excerised by experts—doctors, scientists, economists. There is a distinctive economic power, identified in American political thought almost a century before Marx: the *Federalist Papers* declare that "power over a man's subsistence amounts to a power over his will." "Political power" in the narrowest sense of the term is power wielded by those skilled in negotiating agreement or organizing support, and by the fixer, the operator, and the "apparatchik." Force is power based on the use of violence, actual or potential. Each of these bases of power may be institutionalized, giving rise to such distinctive elites (wielders of power) as churchmen, the Fourth Estate, plutocrats, technocrats and managerial elites, bureaucrats and mandarins, party bigwigs and war lords.

The centrality of power in political thought characterizes an empirical approach, from Machiavelli to Harold D. Lasswell. In this approach the focus is on the realities of the political process, whatever the images of it which play a part in the process, images which may idealize actualities and distort empirical data. This is not "realpolitik" in the sense of power politics but the realism displayed by any successful politician, however idealistic.

Political science is the attempt to formulate explicitly and in relation to the empirical data the knowledge of political affairs underlying political effectiveness. In its more systematic and abstract formulations it is sometimes called "political theory." This designation is doubly ambiguous, since it is also used in place of "political philosophy," which in turn has two meanings, or two components. These two correspond to ethical theory and moral doctrine (§50): *political philosophy,* in the narrow sense, is the logical analysis of the concepts, laws, and methods of political science; in the broad sense, which I shall call *political doctrine,* it formulates ideals for political institutions, and justifications for practices on behalf of those ideals.

Such ideals and justifications are always forthcoming, even in power politics. A political doctrine rationalizing the quest for power or the manner in which it is wielded is as intrinsic to the political process as is power. Without such a doctrine we have *naked power* (not to be confused with violence). Not all force is naked power, only that relatively rare and always temporary species we know as "brute force," force exercised without any attempt at justification, even the justification that might makes right. "The strongest man is never strong enough to be always master," Rousseau rightly observed, "unless he transform his power into right, and obedience into duty." By such a transformation, power is legitimized; when it is no longer seen as legitimate it will be resisted and overthrown if a competing doctrine can seize power. Every revolution is a rupture of conscience, as Lasswell called it, in which moral principles turn men from one set of loyalties to another. The wielder of power also sees himself in the perspectives of legitimacy and guides his actions by the corresponding political conscience. "The abuse of greatness," in the words of Brutus, "is when it disjoins remorse from power."

The political doctrine consists of beliefs, aspirations, identifications, commitments; it relates to all we feel and will, as well as to what we think. It is expressed, therefore, not only in doctrinal form but also in the political symbols which crystallize political passions: the "credenda" and the "miranda" of political life—things to be believed and evocations of the deep emotions we also know in religious experience. Because of this symbolization there is such an intimate relationship between politics and religion, or so much commonality between them, that the one replaces the other. "There are three powers, three powers alone, able to hold the conscience captive forever," Dostoevski wrote in his tale of the Grand Inquisitor (in *The Brothers Karamazov*); "those forces are miracle, mystery, and authority." Authority is constituted by the perception of power as legitimate; as legitimate, it is the external locus of the sense of moral obligation. This, together with the fear we all feel in the presence of power, bathes authority in the glow of miracle and mystery.

Authority in the political sense is legitimate power, deriving from whatever source is specified as right and proper in the accepted political doctrine. Acceptance of the doctrine transforms the control exercised by naked power to the authority of legitimate power, supreme power becomes sovereignty, and institutionalized rule over others is recognized as a government. The structure of authority within the framework of the institution is *formal power,* distinguished from the *effective power* exercised by other authorities or by those without authority. The king who reigns but does not rule has formal power; effective power may be in the hands of an elected prime minister or of some power behind the throne. Wielders of nonformal but effective power play an important part in every political system. According to the bases of their power the type is illustrated by the patriarch, the Old Man, the king's favorite, the kingmaker, Mr. Big, Number One, the Grey Eminence, the elder statesman, the political boss, Mr. Moneybags, the godfather, and the gangster.

The modern state as the primary locus of formal power rests on a doctrine of sovereignty as formulated, for instance, in the sixteenth century by the French political philosopher Jean Bodin, who adumbrated the replacement of the accumulated feudal and church law by a centralized and secular authority. The detailed structure of formal power is articulated in a constitution, written or unwritten, and a body of statutory law (§74).

Whatever the pattern of formal power, it rests on a political doctrine. Since Marx, such a doctrine has come to be called an "ideology," especially insofar as the formal power it identifies differs significantly from the locus of effective power. More generally, an ideology is any comprehensive political program with its associated doctrinal justification. Ideologies aiming at the replacement of an existing system by another one being proposed are sometimes called "utopias"—as, for instance, by the sociologist Karl Mannheim—the term "ideology" then being reserved for the doctrinal defense of an existing order. A parallel distinction is sometimes drawn—as by the French radical thinker Georges Sorel—between "force" and "violence," the former being employed in defense of the state and the latter against it. Usage in political philosophy is as divided, arbitrary, and confused as is political practice.

70. The Ethics of Power

Power must be legitimized; if it is not its own justification, it must appeal to values and principles generally accepted in its domain. Divine right invoked in this connection was secularized as early as the fourteenth century by Marsiglio of Padua, who formulated a doctrine of the supremacy of secular power without presenting it as an application of divine law. The metaphysical core of the reference to the divine is usually retained in such secularizations. It is not only the will of the gods that power be wielded by those identified as the anointed; the ends to which the exercise of power is directed are also willed by the gods. The power elite constitutes an elect; its members have been elected because, in a word, they are carrying out a *mission.*

In such political doctrines Providence may be replaced by Nature or

History; what is essential is that there be a preordained purpose whose fulfillment is the duty of the wielders of power. The possession and exercise of power is justified by the devotion to duty. In the ideologies of mission, those who hold or pursue power have been given a mandate by destiny; their careers are a vocation—there is no help for it; they must answer the call (§75). A note of self-righteousness is a striking feature of the ideologies of mission: *we* are devoted to a higher good, while others—especially our rivals for power—go whoring after the false gods of self-interest.

In the politics of mission there is a "manifest destiny" to be fulfilled —territorial aggrandizement (the original context of application of this phrase), hegemony, unification, or nationalization. The mission is to be carried out in the name of a holistic entity (§68)—the nation, the state, the people, a race, or a class. The "white man's burden" and black emancipation, pan-Slavism and national liberation, pan-Arabism and world Communism are missions which, in the last hundred years, have been invoked to justify both the struggle for power and its exercise. Those actually wielding power are only the humble instruments of the great Cause they serve. It is not always clear to others what exactly the Cause is and just how it is to be served; the power elite must therefore act as a vanguard, pointing the way, shaping the beliefs and aspirations of the masses. In the relation of power to its domain there is paternalism: care combined with firmness. If there is a dictatorship, it is of (that is to say, *for*) the proletariat; if there is a despotism, it is a benevolent despotism.

Since power is justified by the mission, its justification ceases when the mission is fulfilled. The limited tenure of power is part of the doctrine. The Marxist ideology sees the bourgeois state as an instrument for the suppression of one class by another; in Lenin's phrase, the state is the executive committee of the ruling class. During the transition to socialism, and then to communism, the dictatorship of the proletariat establishes the rule of the formerly suppressed class and leads ultimately to a classless society. There is then no further function for the state, and the state withers away. As Engels put it, government over persons is replaced by the administration of things.

In fact, far from withering away, the states invoking these doctrines have enlarged and intensified their powers. If this growth of state power is acknowledged, it is usually excused by reference to the opposition of other powers. What is at work is the *fallacy of absolute priority:* the notion that what we do in the meantime does not affect our eventual attainment: first I will acquire knowledge, and only then apply it; first I will get rich, then enjoy my wealth; first I will achieve power and make it secure, then use it to attain its proper end. Tomorrow never comes.

Another legitimization of power makes no reference to a special mission but to the maintenance of a social *order* within which alone any meaningful purpose can be pursued. This is the doctrine expounded by Thomas Hobbes in his *Leviathan:* a sovereign is established so as to make society possible. In the "state of nature," as he called it—the fiction or model of man considered apart from political institutions—each man pursues his own welfare. He disregards the welfare of others and is in active conflict with them, as each man seeks to maximize his own power. The state of nature is a war of each against all; life is "solitary, poor, nasty, brutish and short." Where there is no common power to keep men in awe, Hobbes says, all are insecure. The persuasiveness of this analysis can be felt if it is applied to the international scene, where, apart from shifting and unreliable coalitions, something very like Hobbe's state of nature prevails.

Because of their insecurity, men enter into an agreement with one another, a *social contract.* Each undertakes to give up his individual power so that a sovereign can put an end to the state of nature by ruling unchallenged over all. The contract is among men with one another, not between the subjects and their sovereign. The players agree to have an umpire so that they can get on with the game, but the umpire is in no way bound to them. On the contrary, he cannot serve as umpire unless his authority is beyond challenge. The sovereign is absolute, and his power is unlimited. True, there are rules of the game, but the very notion of a rule implies some means of enforcement: "Covenants without swords are but words," Hobbes said. The sovereign power is not subject to external determination, or it would not be sovereign; once established it is not bound by any rules whatsoever. God is supreme over all earthly powers, and only He can call the sovereign to account. If the sovereign violates God's law, men can do nothing but leave him to Heaven; as for injustice as men conceive it, the sovereign cannot be guilty of it. Justice has meaning only in terms of law, and it is the sovereign who lays down the law.

Doctrines of social order have been used to legitimize Fascist power. There is an apt symbolism in the catch-phrase that Mussolini "made the trains run on time": the schedule is an embodiment of a fixed law and order, scrupulously adhered to. Every man is to do his duty unquestioningly. Obedience and loyalty become the cardinal virtues; the alternative is anarchy, which is the worst of all evils.

The social order is too complex to be maintained without delegation of power; such delegation, combined with the perspectives of absolutism, generates bureaucratic hierarchies. Authority flows downward, responsibility upward; power obtains its justification only from above, till the sequence comes to an end with the duce, führer, or generalissimo—the sovereign whose power is beyond challenge. Men are willing to submit to a social contract and give up their individual power, Thrasymachus argues in Plato's analysis of justice, because the pain of suffering injustice is greater than the pleasure of inflicting it. In stratified political structures, the obedience exacted from above is compensated for by what is exacted, in turn, from those lower in the hierarchy. The important thing is that everyone knows his place and knows what is expected of him; in turn, he also knows what he has coming to him. The ideology assures him that he will get it; man's capacity to believe seems limitless.

In sharp contradistinction to this ideology is the doctrine that power can be justified only from below and not from above; as the Declaration of Independence has it: "Governments derive their powers from the consent of the governed." The legitimization of power by reference to *consent* may be traced to Rousseau and Locke. The central point in the social contract, as Rousseau expounds it, is that the power of each individual is given up not to a sovereign conceived as standing outside and above society but to the community as a whole. The people itself is sovereign and perpetually retains sovereignty. In Locke's political philosophy, the social contract holds between the people and the sovereign who is accountable to them for the manner in which he exercises the power they have delegated to him. The state of nature, according to Locke, has been described as a state of good nature; far from being a war of each against all, it is a moral and social condition. The social contract is entered into the better to secure the ends of joint effort. What is needed is a curb, not on the evil propensities of the citizenry but on the abuses to which power is inclined. The people are to hold the government in check, not the other way around.

Power is legitimized by consent when the holders of power *represent* the domain over which it is exercised. Those who represent me are, as it were, my very self; in deciding for me they are exercising no more than my own right of self-determination. That they have my consent is entailed by my choosing them as my representatives. The qualification, "as it were, myself," is crucial: the agent is not identical with his principal. Representation has associated with it a certain *scope of representation:* the areas within which the agent is empowered to act for his principal. Even though John Alden speaks for another in so intimate a matter as a proposal of marriage, he is not expected (except, perhaps, by the lady in question) to do any more than speak. All power by representation is *limited* to what is specified in its scope; residual powers belong to those being represented. A plenipotentiary is empowered to make binding decisions without the need for ratification from his principals; this is not to say that he may make decisions with regard to any matters whatsoever.

Every representative is subject also to a *code of representation,* standards, usually implicit, by which to assess whether he is indeed representing his constituency. He is *responsible* to his constituency, for his representing them is conditional upon their continued consent. Since representation, like other political arrangements, quickly becomes institutionalized, formal power of representation may remain with the representative while effective power lies elsewhere; or else the representative's power may continue to be effective even though he no longer actually represents his constituency. As this comes to be felt widely among the constituency, his power loses legitimacy, and his authority may be rejected altogether, via recall, forced resignation, impeachment, or rebellion. The power enjoyed by government by consent is far from absolute; it is both limited and responsible.

A century after Locke, Edmund Burke, a statesman as well as a political thinker, formulated the *paradox of representation:* the representative must do as *he* thinks best, not as he supposes his constituency might think. He does not represent his constituency as a fair sample represents the population from which it is drawn. He is not to be an average man but a superior one—not in status but in dedication, knowledge, and, above all, in good judgment. He owes his constituency his judgment, for without it they would not have consented to his being their representative; he is to be a leader of his constituency and is not merely to reflect the policies they have arrived at without him. "I *must* follow the people," said Disraeli; "I am their leader!" The paradox of representation could as well be called the paradox of leadership: the leader must turn his back on his followers. A representative may find himself from time to time taking a position far from those he represents. If his position is too far from them, too often, his representation may continue, formally speaking; it certainly does not remain effective.

The doctrine of government by consent imposes conditions on the governed as well as on the government. The consent is to be *freely* given, or it does not confer legitimacy. What a man does at the point of a gun he has chosen to do in preference to being shot; he has not *consented* to do it. Consent must be distinguished from submission, which is not easy to recognize when the force being applied cloaks itself in legitimacy. "I made him an offer he could not refuse" speaks the language of consent in the context of violence. More widespread in our time than criminal coercion are the more subtle forms of manipulating attitude and action; there is a serious problem of *engineered consent* (§48). In this sense, the constituency is also responsible to its representatives: it owes them its free and informed consent.

The powers of the constituency are limited, just as are those of the representatives. Not everything can be freely consented to: a man who is prepared to give up his freedom reveals that it is no longer his to give. Only that power can be legitimized by consent which does not contradict its own premises. This is fundamental to the possibility of democracy defending itself, while remaining democratic (§78). The legitimization of power by freely given consent does not suffice to satisfy all the conditions morality may impose on the exercise of power. Even what *can* be freely consented to may be immoral; in politics, especially, there can be no question that man is capable of sinning. What is more, the people as a whole, sovereign though it is, may be more sunk in iniquity than sinful individuals are. Political crimes may be commited *by* the people as well as in the name of the people; minority rights are recurrently threatened by majority rule. A copy of Rousseau's *Social Contract* was later bound in leather made from the skin of an aristocrat; the same atrocities have been committed in our own day, in the perspectives of very different ideologies. Whatever gods men worship they contrive to give the devil his due.

Why does a people consent to a government at all? In the idioms of the Declaration of Independence, governments are instituted among men to secure certain rights; the question is, which. Even Plato held that the state is not an end in itself but a means to promote the good life and the virtuous conduct of its citizens. In Spinoza we have a formulation which allows each man to pursue the Good as he himself understands it: "The ultimate end of the state is so to free each man from fear that he may live and act with full security and without injury to himself or his neighbor." In Locke and others the triad of "life, liberty, and property" commonly identified the values to be protected by the state. Locke's position was that "The great and chief end of men's uniting into commonwealth, and putting themselves under government, is the preservation of their property." This third member of the triad Jefferson replaced by "the pursuit of happiness." The French Declaration of the Rights of Man, written a few years later, used the phrase "liberty, private property, security, and resistance to oppression." In one formulation or another, rights such as these give content to the code of representation by reference to which government by consent can be judged to enjoy or to forfeit legitimacy.

Legitimacy is one thing; morality is another. Is the state a moral agent subject to moral judgment? Machiavelli held that politics has no relation to morals, a position which gave his name its distinctive meaning. Political science, like all sciences, must be careful not to allow its values to distort the perception of its subject matter. Political science differs from political doctrine precisely in addressing itself to what in fact happens, not to what should happen. The question is whether, in the political process, men are actually guided by moral aspiration.

Plato has Thrasymachus argue that injustice is inherently better for those strong enough to practice it with impunity; the argument goes on to characterize justice as nothing other than the interest of the stronger. On this showing, there is no question of politics submitting to morality, for there is no morality outside politics. What serves political interest is defined to be right and good. This would be only cynicism if it meant that official propaganda and other political symbols give the coloring of morality to whatever is done by the wielders of power. More than this is meant in the doctrines of political absolutism, such as those of Hobbes and Hegel on the basis, respectively, of a materialist and an idealist metaphysics. The sovereign, in their view, truly does define the good. "The State is embodied morality," said Hegel. "It is the ethical spirit which has clarified itself and has taken substantial shape."

This is a hard doctrine to swallow by those victimized by state power; is the state intrinsically incapable of injustice? "I considered all the oppressions which are done under the sun," said the Preacher, millennia ago; "behold the tears of the oppressed, but they had no comforter. And on the side of their oppressors there was power." This is so universal an experience that idealists (in the ethical sense, not the metaphysical) often renounce power altogether, as intrinsically evil. Anarchists and religious radicals alike attack the Establishment, on the principle that might makes wrong—the moralistic counterpart of power politics. But power is needed to destroy power, even to limit it; if the enemies of a power structure succeed in establishing themselves, they become an Establishment in their turn. The sect of Karaites repudiated the burden of rabbinic law not to be found in the Bible, but eventually declared that the practices which had become traditional in their own community were binding.

The price paid for renouncing power is political impotence. That lost causes so often have a moralistic cast is not a consequence of any innate depravity in man but of political naïveté in so many moralists. The cycle of municipal corruption and reform is well known in American politics, reformers characteristically being so distrustful of power that their reforms are never long-lasting or more than superficial. A number of genuine statesmen have declared, "I would rather be right than president"; they were not elected. Conversely, a number of men of principle in high office so carefully insulated their ideals from the powers and responsibilities of office that their principles were compromised or thwarted, and they themselves were disillusioned. (Woodrow Wilson illustrates in addition the difference, so important in politics, between knowledge and the skills of practice: before assuming the presidency he had been a professor of political science.)

Power without morality is in our day exemplified by terrorism. Its inhumanity is the greater for its pretense of moral aspiration. This exchange in Shakespeare's *Julius Caesar* is sadly prophetic:

> BRUTUS. Stoop, Romans, stoop,
> And let us bathe our hands in Caesar's blood
> Up to the elbows, and besmear our swords:
> Then walk we forth, even to the market-place;
> And waving our red weapons o'er our heads,
> Let's all cry, 'Peace, freedom, and liberty!'
>
> CASSIUS. Stoop, then, and wash. How many ages hence,
> Shall this our lofty scene be acted over,
> In states unborn, and accents yet unknown!

Terror is not just any use of force, nor all illegitimate or naked force, nor simply force directed against an established power. The term has a stricter sense, in which it refers to "the propaganda of the deed." *Terror* is the use of violence in order to produce an effect on someone other than the victim of the violence. The one to be affected is the "target" of the terror; the victim is distinct from the target (or from his agents, like soldiers in his armies). There is in addition an "audience," consisting of the terrorist's allies and rivals. By the act of terror the victim is destroyed (or threatened with destruction), the audience is impressed, and the target is terrorized. The expressed "demands" of the terrorist are not to be confused with his aims. The demands provide the occasion and conditions under which the act is performed. The demands are made of the victims or their defenders; the aims relate to the target and the audience.

Terror is sometimes excused as the only recourse available to the powerless. But terrorists in general are far from powerless; they may be well equipped and command considerable resources. Terror may even be resorted to by governments, as in the French Revolution or the Fascist regimes: that you can't make omelets without breaking eggs was said by Robespierre, after attaining power. On the other hand, many movements attacking a superior power have explicitly repudiated terror—the early Marxists in Russia, Gandhi, the French Resistance, and the Haganah.

Whatever political or strategic rationale may be offered for terror is rationalization for quite other motivations. The act of terror may be experienced as establishing an intimacy with the world's great—the victims or those with whom the demands are negotiated. "I loved that man," Robert Kennedy's assassin said afterwards. It may allow the terrorist to discard an unbearable identity and to find a new meaning in his life, symbolized often by a new name. "Happiness is taking part in the struggle where there is no borderline between one's own personal world and the world in general"—this from John F. Kennedy's assassin. Terror may compensate for a blow to the ego, overcoming a sense of helplessness or impoverishment with the feeling of omnipotence which comes with the abandonment of inhibition, especially a deep-seated moral constraint.

Most of all, terror is to be understood in the context of the cult of violence (§69) in which killing is a sacrament. For the terrorist there are no innocent victims, not only because no one is innocent but also because there is no victim, only a sacrifice. That the destruction is indiscriminate means that the gods themselves make the choice. Terrorists have been known to object to the steps taken by authorities or victims to prevent or neutralize the act of terror: no one must interfere with the sacrament, least of all the sacrificial animal. Lasswell has noted that in terror there is often a "symbolic enhancement," the terror being intensified by overt repudiation of accepted moral norms: the Borgias acted when their victims were in church. The greater the horror perpetrated on the victim, the greater the terror of the target, and the more striking the impression on the audience. Pilgrims, participants in displays of sportsmanship, children in schoolbuses or schoolrooms are typical victims; because they are helpless and because they embody moral values. It is not tyrants but statesmen, widely perceived as men of high principle, who are made victims of terrorism (as distinct from assassination in the course of a power struggle). In the Black Mass it is a prayer which is read backwards; only what is holy can be profaned.

Even when power acknowledges the dominion of morality, it is notoriously subject to corruption. "Experience constantly proves," says Montesquieu, "that every man who has power is impelled to abuse it"; that is why Montesquieu urges a system of checks and balances (§72). Things are bad enough when there are restraints on power; when power is absolute, in Lord Acton's memorable phrase, it corrupts absolutely. The trouble is, Kant remarked in his essay "Perpetual Peace," the enjoyment of power corrupts the judgment of reason: whatever a man *can* do he comes to feel he *may* do. Like love, the appetite for power grows by what it feeds on, and, being fed, it supposes that, like love again, the more it has grown, the more it has to bestow, the more it can give joy. The basic corruption of power consists in the self-deception that wielding power is a selflesss devotion to the welfare of others. Not only those who have power but also those over whom power is exercised are subject to corruption, as consent gives way to submission and the sense of legitimacy is replaced by fear. Shelley's rebelliousness makes him aware of the corruption in obedience:

Power, like a desolating pestilence,
Pollutes whate'er it touches; and obedience,

Bane of all genius, virtue, freedom, truth
Makes slaves of men, and, of the human frame,
A mechanized automaton.

—Queen Mab

Morality is sometimes thought to impinge on politics only at the edges, as though corruption were only a matter of violating or evading the law, for private advantage. But laws may be unjust, and a man may be all the more a moral monster for scrupulously enforcing them. Even where the ends for which power is being exercised are disinterested and laudable, the means employed may be corrupt. Plato supposes that the rulers of his ideal state will find a considerable dose of falsehood and deceit necessary—naturally, for the good of their subjects. These things are to be regarded, he adds, as medicines, and so the rulers "may fitly lie for the benefit of the state." Several of the Watergate defendants seem to have been Platonists.

What compromises morality is not that power is used but how it is used and to what end. A state whose ends were truly to promote the virtuous conduct of its citizens could hardly expect to induce such conduct by falsehood and deceit. If the aim of power is only to stay in power, it cannot claim to act for the benefit of the state. Santayana once defined fanaticism as redoubling your effort when you have forgotten your aim. This might also serve as a definition of power politics.

It is easy to condemn authority on the grounds that power is intrinsically tainted; self-righteousness is an inviting stance. "Every actual state is corrupt," Emerson declared; "good men must not obey the laws too well." I do not see that skirting the edges of the law, and occasionally going beyond, contributes to public morality, nor that individual judgment as to which laws are not to be obeyed too well contributes to personal morality. Political morality is not likely to be significantly above the standards prevailing in other dimensions of social life. No politician has ever bribed himself, and men walk the corridors of power with the same gait that brought them there. Power does not so much corrupt men as attract those who are ripe for corruption; dominion over the kingdom of the world was, after all, one of the Temptations in the Wilderness. Although Plato's political doctrine is unacceptably elitist, there is a core of wisdom in his basic thesis which the most ardent democrat can acknowledge: "Unless either philosophers are kings, or those who are now called kings philosophize really and thoroughly, and these two, political power and philosophy, unite in one, and till most of those who now pursue each of these separately are excluded, there will be no end to the miseries of the human race."

71. Liberty and Freedom

To have power over another is to be able to make decisions as to his actions; correspondingly, the greater the power to which a man is subject, the less he can decide for himself. *Liberty* is the measure of the degree to which a man is master of his fate, so far as concerns the power over him which other men wield. The qualification serves to distinguish liberty from freedom (§48), a man's power over himself, his capacity to make his own decisions with integrity and autonomy. In Spinoza's words, a man is free who lives "under the entire guidance of reason"; he enjoys liberty insofar as the reason is his. A man may be free though he is kept prisoner—Socrates is the prime example. Another man may be so sunk in slavishness as to remain in prison even though he is at liberty to leave it—the conditions Spinoza identified as the human bondage to ignorance, fear, and other passions.

Freedom is logically distinct from liberty but causally dependent on it. Freedom is hard to come by and hard to retain without the liberty to hear and read what we please and to say what we think. (This is conventionally called "freedom" of speech, not "liberty"; my own usage will not be strict, if the difference between the absence of internal constraints and external ones is clear from the context.) Freedom also depends on the liberty to associate with like-minded men in pursuit of common goals, on the security of our persons and sustenance which liberates us from fear, and on the quality of treatment without which we sink into subjection to an introjected master.

A free man knows and cherishes both his freedom and his liberty; the slavish mentality is likely not to know its own slavishness and to find liberty a burden, even a threat. It is a tribute to the greatness of the human spirit that the desire for freedom is not wholly suppressed even by the brutal denial of liberties in concentration camps and under dictatorships. Hegel's conception of freedom fails to disentangle it from its perversion as submission to the power of the state; yet there is a genuine idealism in his perspective on the history of the world as "nothing other than the progress of the consciousness of freedom."

The progress of that consciousness has been central to the history of the past few centuries, though with dismal retrogressions as well. The inscription on the base of the Statue of Liberty, from a poem by Emma Lazarus, "Give me your tired, your poor,/Your huddled masses, yearning to breathe free," is an invitation to which millions of immigrants responded, my father among them, for America was seen as the land of liberty, of equality, of opportunity. For many, the American dream has faded; there are those who would agree with the barbed malapropism of Billie Dawn (in Garson Kanin's *Born Yesterday*), "This country and its institutions belong to the people who inhibit it." The vision remains even though men may despair that it is only visionary.

Freedom must be achieved by every person for himself; liberty can be granted by others, as they yield power. By what right was the power theirs to start with? The words with which Rousseau's *Social Contract* begins are: "Man is born free, yet he is everywhere in chains." How this has come about is not only a philosophical question; it is also a political challenge. "I was not born to be forced; I will breathe after my own fashion," Thoreau declared in his *Civil Disobedience*. Must a man disobey in order to preserve his liberty? Is every state an enemy of liberty? Does every system of laws enchain the law-abiding? Plainly, there are significant differences among states and among laws in the degree to which they interfere with liberty and in the justification which can be adduced for such interference as states can rightly be charged with.

By far the most acceptable principle identifying which limitations on liberty are justifiable is that formulated by John Stuart Mill in his essay "On Liberty": "The sole end for which mankind are warranted, individually or collectively, in interfering with the liberty of action of any of their number, is self-protection. The only purpose for which power can be rightfully exercised over any member of a civilized community, against his will, is to prevent harm to others."

There are many problems in the application of this principle. From what dangers is society entitled to protect itself? Laws against sedition are defended on these grounds, but many lovers of liberty find them abhorrent. Are the liberties only of members of "civilized" communities to be respected? Colonialism has long pretended to moral justification on some such basis, but now the argument is generally repudiated. There is universal agreement that psychotics can justifiably be put under restraint; but what is to be said of the tyrannies which incarcerate in mental hospitals anyone who dares speak out against the regime? We are to prevent harm to others, but whether something is harmful—say, the distribution of contraceptives—may be at issue, and what harms one man may be of benefit to another, as in defiance of the Fugitive Slave Law. Similar problems confront any other formulation of a criterion to identify justifiable limitations on liberty; Mill's principle, or one like it, remains basic to the libertarian ideal.

The main thrust of the principle is that we are not entitled to deprive a person of any liberty on the grounds that it is for his own good. Mill says flatly, "His own good is not a sufficient warrant. The conduct from which it is desired to deter him must be calculated to produce evil to someone else." The objection is not merely that if this warrant is accepted as sufficient, the wielders of power will inevitably rationalize whatever they do as being for the victim's own good. The essence of liberty is to be able to act on what we ourselves take to be the good. As Mill states at the outset, "The only freedom [liberty] deserving the name is that of pursuing our own good in our own way." People have a right to make mistakes, provided they also acknowledge responsibility for their mistakes. We are entitled to prevent mistakes which do not harm others only if they are made without free choice (as in the control of drug abuse).

When liberty is not denied, the mistakes that are made are less frequent and less serious, generally speaking, than is feared by those who wish, even for the best of reasons, to deprive others of liberty. Parents immemorially suppose their children not to be ready to lead their own lives, but the decisions which the young make, ready or not, are no worse, by and large, than those which are made for them. If the decisions are not conspicuously better, they have at least this merit, that the young are better for having made them. Politically speaking, at stake is what Jefferson expressed as a faith in the people, a respect for their intrinsic capacity to govern themselves—or, at least, to govern themselves better than they could be governed by others.

Libertarians as diverse as Jefferson, Kant, and Thoreau agree that the best government is that which governs least: the fewer the restrictions a government imposes, the greater the liberty of the people. The rub is that there may be nongovernmental holders of power who interfere far more with liberty. For this reason, an increase in governmental power is not necessarily the road to serfdom (§66). Libertarians have formulated *the principle of the autonomous domain:* governments are to do for the people only what the people cannot do for themselves.

There is a dangerous equivocation here in the meaning of the word "people," which may be meant as the domain of power, the people collectively in contrast to the government, or as the individual members of the domain in contrast to any form of association for collective action. In America, individualism has deep roots in the ethics of the Judaeo-Christian tradition, in the spirit of the frontier, and in the expanding economy which gave scope to the entrepreneur; but most individuals would suffer a severe diminution of liberty if other individuals were not restrained from acting as they choose. Government may well be the most effective instrument for such restraint as well as the most libertarian. "The public be damned!" was not the expletive of a governmental despot, but of a corporation president who was an ardent exponent and exemplar of individualism. Still, it remains true that any increase in power is intrinsically a threat to liberty. The question of how liberty is to be defended must be faced.

First of all, the continuing threat to liberty, the threat which lies in the very nature of power, must be recognized. "The love of power and the love of liberty are in eternal antagonism," Mill observed. Whoever has power wants more—often enough, at any rate, so that what power he has is used as a means to get more rather than to serve its proper end. This is as true of representative power as of power legitimized by any other doctrine—Hitler, for example, attained office via the democratic forms of the Weimar Republic; it is as true of widely shared power as of power wielded by a small elite—the tyranny of a majority may be as destructive of liberty as that of a single despot; it is as true of private power as of power resting on a political base in the narrow sense (§69)—clericalism and plutocracy have, on occasion, done more harm to liberties than the enactments of duly constituted government.

There is a danger, too, which does not stem from the nature of power but from the nature of liberty. Liberty is a capacity, a potentiality, while its denial and the limitations put upon it have actual existence. The sleeping Gulliver was not aware of his bonds until he woke and tried to move. The fact remains, as Montesquieu has it, that "A nation may lose its liberties in a day, and not miss them for a century." Perhaps in our time we would know it sooner if we had not been so brainwashed as never to know it at all.

Just because it is a potentiality, liberty may be actualized only to meet its own destruction. Democracy gives its enemies leave to try to destroy it, provided the effort is made democratically; those who deny liberty also deny the opportunity to oppose its denial. There are Communist parties in the democratic countries, but no democratic parties in the Communist countries. Liberty is in the unhappy position of a country surrounded by enemies sworn to destroy it, repeatedly mounting wars against it: they can try again and again; their target cannot afford to lose once.

Wielders of power characteristically ask their domain to have faith, while they themselves distrust those they rule; the defense of liberty calls for just the opposite. Eternal vigilance has been the watchword of lovers of liberty since ancient times. Vigilance is especially called for because liberty is typically denied and destroyed in the name of high principle, in the name of liberty itself. The Master, being asked in jest whether the Messiah will come as a *hassid* or as a *misnagid* (one who opposes *hassidism*), promptly replied, "As a *misnagid*" explaining: "If he were to come as a *hassid*, the *misnagdim* would not recognize him, but we *hassidim* will recognize him no matter how he is disguised." If he were a false messiah his disguise might be harder to penetrate. The Tempter does not appear before men with cloven hoofs and smelling of brimstone but in an effulgence of virtue—how else can temptation win the souls of the innocent? Only the vigilant can catch a glimpse, from the beginning, of the ugliness of despotism.

Vigilance presupposes caring: we do not pay attention to what does not matter to us. If liberty is of no consequence, the consequence is no liberty. In many parts of the world liberty is abstract and remote from daily life, while poverty is concrete and ever present. Accordingly, whoever deals with the poverty—or even promises to deal with it—is readily granted power, or legitimacy for the power already his. The same is true in regard to the concrete presence of a colonial master or any other overlord; get rid of him, and you may do as you like with our liberties. The foreign devil is felt to be more hellish than the domestic breed.

A tradition of liberty plays an important part in its preservation. The great danger from the side of those subject to power is their apathy about liberty, their ignorance and unconcern about the scope and weight of the power to which they are being subjected. The crisis of indifference (§57) may be more important in politics than in ethics. Liberty must recurrently be fought for, just as evil must perpetually be fought against. The words of Pericles, in his funeral oration for the Athenians who fell in the Peloponnesian War, sound a ringing truth not limited to his time: "Liberty is the sure possession only of those who have the courage to defend it."

Here we encounter the dependence of liberty on freedom. Restraints on action are not so likely to come from without if there is a firm inner determination to resist them, but freedom implies responsibility, and to escape the one we might be willing to abandon the other. Though liberty puts power in our own hands, the power may be so little as to leave us feeling helpless; to overcome this sense of impotence we might gladly give up our liberty to a powerful master with whom we can identify as the extension and expression of our innermost selves.

Rousseau's political philosophy begins with a false premise: a man is not born free—he must achieve freedom, as he must achieve maturity, autonomy, integration, even an identity (§47, §48). "Born free" in the sense of a native right to freedom is another matter, and defines the core of liberty. The interrelation of freedom and liberty—the inner life, and its causes and effects in the outer world—constitutes another of our predicaments. Men cannot be forced to be free, and they cannot be indoctrinated to a love of liberty; these things must come from within.

There is yet another predicament intrinsic to liberty. In many circumstances, liberty must be restricted so that it can flourish. The point is illustrated by the *traffic paradigm:* traffic signals and regulations are denials of our liberty to drive when and where we please; yet without traffic control, our movements might be even more restricted, and would certainly be more hazardous. The danger in the paradigm is that it is so readily construed to justify the appeasement of power—a partial surrender in the hope that complete submission will not be exacted. Such hopes are never fulfilled. Giving up a little of our liberties may save the rest only if what is surrendered and what is saved are connected in *our* actions, not in the actions of the wielders of power. I obey the traffic signals not so that the police will leave me untouched but so that other drivers will. Law is the defender of liberty, not its enemy (§73); the reason for obeying the law is not to stay out of prison but to live at peace with our neighbors.

If any liberties are denied, it is likely that the denial will extend to the right to say what we choose, for this liberty is so important to the preservation of the others. I shall continue to call it freedom of speech, though it is a matter of liberty and more often concerns writing than speaking. I mean *freedom of speech* in the broadest sense, then, encompassing all the media, and comprising exposure as well as expression—viewing, hearing, and reading, as well as speaking and writing.

Lenin's argument against free speech is that made by virtually all who would deny it: a government would not allow opposition to itself by weapons, and ideas are more deadly. The suppressed premise is that a government has the right to defend itself at all costs, regardless of how its exercise of power relates to the ends for which it is instituted. Quite common in our day is another argument, often invoked by activists, that free speech is only talk, and so gets in the way of doing something about our problems. This position was well known in ancient times: Pericles (in Thucydides' account) repudiates it on behalf of the Athenians, who, "instead of looking on discussion as a stumbling-block in the way of action, think it an indispensable preliminary to any wise action at all." For these and other reasons, those who wield power try to discourage the expression of opposition and, if necessary, try to prevent it. Precensorship—like licensing and imprimaturs—is more far-reaching and effective (from the standpoint of the power holders) than imposing sanctions after the unacceptable view has been expressed.

Freedom of speech may be limited substantially even where such limitations are not a matter of explicit policy. Much of what appears in the media is predigested and is so widely syndicated that it is hard to find not only alternative views but even alternative formulations of the same views.

With the passage of time, the channels for the expression of ideas become progressively fewer as the number of independently owned newspapers, magazines, and broadcasting stations steadily declines and they are replaced by giant chains, even by monopolies. Opening new channels is prohibitively expensive (in my student days it was thought that a "revolutionary party" needed only to acquire its own mimeograph machine). To meet the high costs of operation of any of the mass media, subventions are usually needed over and above what consumers are able to pay. Whether such subventions come from government or from advertisers, the effect is the same so far as concerns freedom of speech. The man who pays the piper calls the tune.

The difficulties here are aggravated by the pretense that all is well. Insistence on the right to express a deviant opinion is countered with a cry for "unity," a cry which often serves the cause of regimentation by way of thought control. That we have free speech is somehow taken to be guaranteed by definition: "This is a democracy, isn't it?" Figaro's complaint is not limited to his time and place: "Provided I made no reference in my articles to the authorities or to religion, or to politics, or to morals, or to high officials, or to influential organizations, or to the Opera, or to any theatrical productions, or to anybody of any standing whatsoever, I could freely print anything I liked—subject to the approval of two or three censors!" When a value like free speech begins by losing its meaning, it goes on to lose its worth and ends by losing its existence.

Freedom of speech means nothing if there is no free market of ideas in which they can compete for acceptance. Competition, in turn, is impossible if there are monopolies, trusts, and cartels controlling the market. There must be free access to channels of expression by all who have something to say and by all who wish to hear what is being said.

Free speech does *not* mean that everyone has the right to speak wherever and whenever he pleases. At a political meeting, members of an opposing party do not have a right to the platform on the grounds of free speech. The right they do have is to a meeting place of their own; otherwise, the free speech of each man would be nullified by the alleged right of others to displace him from his platform.

Channels are not necessarily limited to those explicitly identified as such; means of communication may be all the more effective for being subtle and indirect. There is such a thing as *symbolic speech*, in which a gesture like burning a draft card has significance as the expression of a political position rather than as the performance of a political action. Such gestures have been protected by the courts as comprised under freedom of speech.

Speech is not free if it applies only to popular views. "If all mankind minus one were of one opinion, and only one person were of the contrary opinion," Mill declares in his "Essay on Liberty", "mankind would be no more justified in silencing that one person than he, if he had the power, would be justified in silencing mankind." On the other hand, the right to be heard does not carry with it the right to be taken seriously. For every genius who stands on his convictions against the rest of mankind there are a thousand cranks and crackpots; his hearers are not to be blamed for playing the odds. The right to speak our minds must be paid for by the courage to face condemnation and ridicule.

Ridiculous or not, the opinion has the right to be expressed. To be sure, the dissemination of falsehood does harm to society; unless such harm is significant and undeniable, freedom of speech is empty if it is restricted to "harmless" views. The principle commonly invoked here is that formulated by the great libertarian Justice Oliver Wendell Holmes. Only "a clear and present danger" justifies a denial of the right of free speech, as in the case of a man falsely shouting fire in a theater and causing a panic. Another example is the remark made in an airplane or airport, even in jest, that there is a bomb on the plane. Where the danger is debatable or remote—such as undermining national unity or lowering standards of morality—freedom of speech brooks no restrictions. That there may be borderline cases is undeniable; laws against group libel provide a recent illustration. Whether such laws are justifiable limitations on the right of free speech is not easy to say.

It is true that ideas are dangerous; so is liberty of every kind. When men are free to choose they may choose wrongly. But lovers of liberty are committed to living dangerously; to achieve greatly men must dare greatly. Science and technology are also dangerous; by increasing our power over nature they increase our power to befoul and destroy. But to play it safe altogether is also to destroy ourselves, or so to degrade our lives as to rob them of most of what we thought it important to protect.

When it comes to ideas, the situation is worse, for prohibiting the dangerous idea may have the effect of making it more dangerous, focusing attention on it, and, in the eyes of some, making it more attractive. There is likely to be greater danger in the institutions and practices established to control ideas than in what they are controlling. The cure or preventive is deadlier than the disease. Censorship necessarily discards precious ideas together with dangerous ones, for how can discrimination be made when thought is not free? Worst of all, liberty is as much of a piece as is the power which constricts it, so that the denial of one liberty inevitably reaches out cancerously to all the rest.

The attempt is sometimes made to save whatever ideas might be of worth, while suppressing the dangerous ones. Laws governing "obscenity" have in recent years attempted to make an exception for whatever has any "redeeming social importance." How to identify such importance, and how to measure whether it is enough to be redeeming, no one has been able to say. A more fundamental objection is that what is most important of all is to be able to read and write, hear and see what we please. It is so important because it is intrinsic to freedom which, like virtue, has already been lost if we are willing to give it up. Milton speaks for all free men when he declares (in his essay on free speech, the *Areopagitica*), "Give me the liberty to know, to utter, and to argue freely according to conscience, above all liberties." I cannot be myself if it is you who decide what I am to think and say.

It is sometimes argued, especially in Communist countries, that what makes free speech important is to get at the truth. Consequently, a press, though controlled, may be freer than what passes for freedom in an exploiting society, if it is being controlled so as to convey the truth and not the lies which serve the interests of the exploiters. Stated so baldly, the argument reveals its blatant begging of the question, for what is true can only be determined if thought is restricted by the demands of reason and by nothing else, especially not by what has been declared beforehand to be the truth.

Even if what we believe is in fact true, our belief is not on that account a rational one. Who knows what may have caused us to believe as we do? Rationality demands that the cause of our belief be nothing other than our having *reasons* for it. "A man may be a heretic in the truth," Milton says. "If he believes things only because his pastor says so, or the assembly so determines, without knowing other reason, though his belief be true, yet the very truth he holds becomes his heresy." What censorship destroys is not so much what it takes to be falsehood as "that ethereal essence, the breadth of reason itself." Hence, "As good almost kill a man as kill a good book; who kills a man kills a reasonable creature, God's image; but he who destroys a good book kills reason itself."

Control over ideas is murderous from a strictly logical standpoint, in terms of the conditions of inquiry by which alone men can get at the truth. Controls could be justified only if we already had the truth in our possession and already knew it to be true. In that case, there would be no need for inquiry, or indeed for thought altogether, only for obedience. "All silencing of discussion," Mill has argued, "is an assumption of infallibility." Controlled thought, just because it is controlled, is beyond the reach of correction if it should be in error. It therefore presupposes an infallibility which logic cannot accept (§26). Even if the possibility of error is excluded in what is authoritatively proclaimed as true, there is a danger of error in what has not yet been proclaimed. When this danger is invoked to justify censorship, thought is paralyzed. The suffocating fear of heresy robs orthodoxy of the breath of life. I dare not think at all if I dare not think wrongly, and no belief is truly mine if I have come by it all mindless and unknowing.

Politically speaking, freedom of speech is so important because it underlies all other freedoms. In Benjamin Franklin's homely phrase, "Where a man cannot call his tongue his own, he can scarce call anything his own." To be able to speak out is essential in order to get and keep our other liberties, for otherwise we cannot express grievances; without complaint, it is not to be expected that they will be reduced. Censorship does not restrict the liberties only of the writer but of all who are subject to the power of which the censorship is but one application. No man can be wholly free if any man is denied the right to speak out. He may wish to speak of me or of what affects me, and then it is I who have been put under restraint.

Of all liberties, this one is every person's concern; denied to one, it is denied to all. Within itself it is also all of a piece. It cannot be limited unjustly in any measure without being lost altogether, as Jefferson saw. For this reason Holmes and others have emphasized freedom for the despised opinion, the thought we hate: it is tempting to cherish not the liberty but our own beliefs. If we are willing for other ideas to be suppressed, we are no longer secure in the right to express our own.

This right is not bestowed on us by others: neither can it be externally guaranteed. Even more than other forms of power, the power to restrict the public expression of ideas is likely to weigh as heavily as the public will bear. It is quite a general political principle which the *Federalist* applies to this particular case: "The security of the liberty of the press, whatever fine declaration may be inserted in any constitution respecting it, must altogether depend upon public opinion, and on the general spirit of the people and of the government. Here, after all, must we seek for the only solid basis of our rights."

72. Democracy

A state where liberties flourish is commonly called a "democracy." In analyzing the idea of democracy, political philosophy faces special difficulties in that the key terms have such loose, diverse, and ambiguous usages, not because the content of the terms is intrinsically confused or obscure but because the terms figure so largely as political symbols. It is in the political process, as well as in political science, that states are called "democratic" or "despotic," "libertarian" or "totalitarian," "limited" or "dictatorial," "free" or "authoritarian," "commonwealth" or "exploitative," "republican" or "elitist," "egalitarian" or "stratified."

I shall use all these terms, with contents fixed not by definitions but by specifications of meaning (§12), indications by which abstract concepts can be related to concrete observational data. I shall use *democracy* and *despotism* as the most inclusive terms, the two marking opposite ends of a spectrum of continuous gradations or, rather, many spectra, since each of the pairs just listed is meant to identify one of the many dimensions of the complex idea of democracy. The dimensions are empirically interdependent and may have logical interconnections as well. The list is not exhaustive, and the order in which I consider them is not significant.

1. A democracy is a *libertarian* state; the scope of the power being wielded is relatively narrow. Where state control reaches into every phase of life, the regime is *totalitarian.* A libertarian state offers many areas of choice, even though the range of choice in each area may be limited (for instance, by limitations in resources). In a totalitarian state, almost everything that is not a duty is prohibited. In such a state, the cardinal virtue of the citizen (perhaps "subject" would be better) is obedience. Yet the meaning of liberty is that the citizen can decide for himself what to do. There is a rule of law in both sorts of states, and laws are to be obeyed; but laws can protect liberties as well as restrict them. In libertarian states, disobedience and dissent play a significant role (§73). Where there is genuine choice, different people are likely to choose differently; a libertarian state is therefore more or less *pluralistic,* while a totalitarian state is *regimented,* the

opposite of unity being viewed as disunity rather than as diversity. In a libertarian state opinions are often divided; in a totalitarian one, if they are expressed at all they are likely to be nearly unanimous.

2. In democracies, the weight of power is *limited;* in despotic states it is *absolute.* One who wields absolute power is a dictator; a state where power is unchecked is a *dictatorship.* Since it takes power to keep power in check, political theorists speak in this connection of *checks and balances.* Such a system implies a multiple locus of power—not only in the state but also in labor unions, the church, the press, the schools, business, industry, the military, and elsewhere. A dictatorship cannot establish and maintain itself without extending the scope and domain of its power so as to control these potential challenges to its decisions. Hence dictatorships tend to be totalitarian.

Within state power itself a system of checks and balances may be at work, as in democracies. Since Montesquieu, theoreticians speak of the *separation of powers* into legislative, executive, and judicial powers. One of the basic objections to the "un-American activities" committees of the Dies and McCarthy era was that they dictatorially combined these powers—defining the offense, judging guilt, and punishing by way of damaging publicity. A separation of functions is a less misleading characterization than a separation of powers, for political bodies usually perform more than one function. How a policy is administered (the executive function) inevitably helps define what the policy is (the legislative function). The recurrent conflicts and chronic tensions between the president and the Congress in the American system of checks and balances are intrinsic; comparable tensions play a part in the parliamentary system, as in any other nondictatorial pattern of power.

Within each of the power functions further checks and balances can be identified. Judicial decisions are subject to review by other courts or by other bodies sitting in judgment. The executive function is performed by a number of ministries, departments, and agencies, the powers of each being limited by the others. Legislatures often consist of two houses and are subdivided further into committees which keep one another in check. Cutting across all these powers is a party system which, in democratic states, comprises at least two major parties, each of which sets limits to the powers of the others. Dictatorships are characteristically one-party states. This single party functions so differently from its counterpart in multiparty systems that it is misleading to call it by the same name. It has much more in common with a caste, enjoying status as well as power and having a restricted membership. What are called "elections" in a one-party state do not function to arrive at a national consensus but only to ratify—to express submission to—decisions already reached.

3. Democratic states are *free* rather than *authoritarian.* Citizens in fact exercise the liberties they have, autonomously and with integrity. Decisions are made by discussion, for a free choice is one which has been arrived at only after a process of deliberation (§48 and §54), in contrast to imposed alternatives and to alternatives taken only because we have been conditioned to them. Education is therefore as central to democratic states as

indoctrination is to authoritarian states. To distinguish the two processes is not easy. Of major importance is whether there is an unimpeded flow of information, a free exchange of ideas and opinions, and an appeal to reason. Authoritarians usually hold that these are either impossible or that they are contrary to the best interests of the state. Plato justified lying to the people, Lenin wanted the press rigidly controlled, and Confucius held that the people may be made to follow a line of action but cannot be made to understand it.

Enemies of democracy have contemptuously described democratic parliaments as debating societies, with the implication that they are capable only of talk, not action, and that conflicting opinions can only weaken resolve. Democrats have countered that free debate produces reasonable belief as contrasted with prejudice, and that the resulting conviction can be as resolute and energetic as fanaticism. In allowing for continued self-criticism, the democratic process gives policy a flexibility which makes possible continuing change and improvement. Authoritarian states follow a fixed "line," which is only intermittently changed, usually by sudden and often bloody shifts in the power structure.

In a democracy neither institutions nor policies can be established once for all. As John Dewey has it, democracy must be achieved anew in each generation. Freedom can never be handed down to another. In religious symbols the Messiah is born in each generation, but He does not reveal himself if men are not ready for Him; each generation must seek its own Messiah.

Idioms referring to a messiah are more appropriate to an authoritarian ideology than to a democratic one. In authoritarian states the supreme power is the source both of moral teaching and of salvation according to the teaching. In democratic doctrine, there are moral norms whose authority is superior to that of the state, norms by which state action can be judged and which define a higher duty, one which may even enjoin overthrowing the state. Power is legitimized by conscience or by some other moral judgment. Democracy moralizes power, while authoritarian states politicize morality.

Such politicization may be called *statism*—not in reference to the totalitarian scope of state power but to the claim it makes of being the source and ground of all values. Hegel's formulation is explicit: "All the worth which the human being possesses—all spiritual reality—he possesses only through the State." "The highest duty of the individual citizens," he says again, "is to be members of the State. Man must venerate the State as a secular deity." The democratic conception of a free man's relation to the state is the converse: the state possesses worth only through its individual citizens to whom the state owes its highest duty and unqualified veneration.

4. A democracy is a *commonwealth*—a state in which power is exercised for the common weal, the general welfare; despotisms are *exploitative* states, disproportionately benefiting certain segments of society. The difference relates not only to the ends power is meant to serve but also to the quality of the means employed. "Life, liberty, and the pursuit of happiness" may be subscribed to in both sorts of states, and even be sincerely intended as operative ideals, but may be very differently defined by the

means employed for their actualization. Democracy is not to be identified with "free enterprise" (§66), which has been exploitative, as its critics have charged; but neither is democracy to be identified with a "socialism" which operates for the disproportionate benefit of a new class of political functionaries and economic managers, as Marxist humanists have been pointing out. There are no magic formulas for social systems by which the general welfare can be guaranteed.

Experience suggests the advantages of a mixed economy in which there is both a public and a private sector; some state ownership, some cooperative enterprises, and some individually owned enterprises; some centralized planning, some regulation of unplanned economic activity, and some unregulated enterprise left to find its own equilibrium in the market. Every arrangement has its own dangers, for however economic processes are carried on, power is being exercised, and power can always be turned to special advantage. Big business, strong labor unions, entrenched bureaucracies, and owners, managers, and workers providing essential goods or services—all of these have on occasion exploited society for their own interests. Self-seeking is not limited to any segment of society and is about as characteristic of one group as of another.

"If there were a nation of gods," Rousseau remarked, "it would be governed democratically. So perfect a government is unsuited to men." That is the argument commonly used to rationalize an exploitative state: men are selfish and not to be trusted to serve the best interests of society; they must be compelled. A despotism is therefore likely to be a *police state,* to cope with the human impulse to serve one's own interest. Those who wield power, however, are no less selfish, no more to be trusted than anyone else, except in the perspectives of the ideology they themselves promulgate.

An influential formulation of the problem is crystallized in Rousseau's distinction between the *general will* and the *common will.* Roughly speaking (I doubt whether the distinction can be made precise), the common will is the will of the majority, or of the persons and groups making up society, in the aggregate. The general will is what they all would will, if their concern were for the general welfare rather than their own. The question is how the general welfare is to be identified, since each who pursues his own good, as we see his pursuits, sees himself as devoted to the welfare of all: "What's good for General Motors is good for the country." Rousseau provided a point of departure for both democratic and despotic ideologies, according to their answer to the question of who was to be entrusted with determining the general will.

In democratic political patterns, the difference between the common will and the general will is often institutionalized by the device of a bicameral legislature: one body, like the House of Representatives, is presumed to express the common will, each of its members representing the interests of his constituency; the other body, like the Senate, is presumed to occupy itself with the general will, each member having his formal constituency, but serving the nation as a whole as his effective constituency. To what extent these presumptions are warranted is another matter.

5. A democracy is *republican* rather than *elitist:* power is widely shared. Often the sharing is formal but not effective, either because of apathy or because political structures like party conclaves and nominating conventions hinder or discourage participation. In America, even in presidential elections—to say nothing of congressional or local elections—only about two-thirds of those eligible to vote do in fact cast a ballot, and then for a candidate selected by party delegates rather than through a primary election. Power may be exercised through representatives or without intermediaries, constituting *representative* and *direct democracy,* respectively; the representation, in turn, can be either formal or effective. In short, republican institutions are one thing; republican practices may be quite another.

In the abstract, the conception is clear. The intent is to contrast popular government with government by an elite. Jefferson is a dedicated republican: "The mass of men has not been born with saddles on their backs, nor a favored few booted and spurred, ready to ride them." In his day, elites were hereditary—that is, *aristocracies.* Elites may be differently constituted according to the power base which gives effective control. In extreme elitism, power is concentrated in the hands of a few, as in an *oligarchy,* where power is in the hands of two or three effective rulers, like the triumvirates and troikas known since Roman days, or in the hands of a single autocrat, by what is known as the *Führer prinzip.* The *Führer* is a dictator in the sense given above: there are no other holders of power by whom his power is limited.

A variety of practices has been developed to allow a formal sharing of power by the people. (In the degree to which the sharing is purely formal and the actual locus of decision making lies elsewhere, increasing numbers of people may come to feel remote from the centers of power, and a crisis of authority may develop.) Among republican practices are the procedures of initiative and referendum and other devices to ensure the responsiveness of power (the effectiveness of representation)—devices such as full disclosure of decisions taken and of the deliberations leading up to them, and the right of recall. Basic to all republican institutions is *universal suffrage.* Here, too, effective sharing in power may degenerate into a purely formal participation. A Russian voter, the story goes, on coming into the polling place is handed a folded ballot, already marked, and shown where to deposit it. "Can't I even see what is on it?" "Comrade," came the reply, "don't you know that in our State we have the secret ballot?"

Although known since ancient times, republican institutions, even merely formal ones, are on the whole rare. "Nothing appears more surprising to those who consider human affairs with a philosophical eye," said David Hume, a historian as well as a philosopher, "than the easiness with which the many are governed by the few." Those governed by the few in elitist regimes are not only many, but the vast majority; republics, accordingly, are usually characterized by *majority rule.* The justification commonly given for majority rule is that the people know best what is for their own good; this may be doubted. Less doubtful is the consideration that a man is free only insofar as he has the right to define for himself what he takes to be the good, so that only a republican form of government provides freedom for its citizens, and this is more precious than anything else the state might furnish.

In the political theories influenced by Machiavelli and Hobbes, the justification is sometimes advanced that since majority rule only anticipates the outcome of the application of force, the ultimate winners should prudently be allowed from the outset to make the decisions. This presupposes that power is more or less equally distributed, so that counting noses gives a measure of power at the command of each bloc. The assumption is by no means true, even without taking into account the technology of weaponry. We need only remember the hero of the Western saga, setting out to rescue a man about to be lynched: "What can one man alone do out there?" he is asked, to which he makes the immortal reply, "There ain't but one mob, is there?" The general lines of the argument have recently been revived with the speculation, not altogether fantastic, that in the future, wars might not be fought at all, but peace would periodically be renegotiated on the basis of the inevitable outcomes predicted by computers. I have not yet encountered suggestions as to what might be done if the computers of one side yield a different prediction from those of the other side.

Objections to majority rule go back at least as far as that great elitist, Plato. If the Good has an objective reality in the world of Ideas, how is it to be expected that the many, unskilled or untrained, should be capable of grasping it? This is a powerful argument whose force must be acknowledged by every political doctrine which does not rest on a frankly subjectivist theory of value. It is easy to praise the good sense of the majority when the majority happens to agree with us, though such agreement might instead give us ground for questioning our own judgment. When the majority disagrees with us—as it does, at least at first, with all its prophets and teachers—what then? Giordano Bruno, later burned at the stake for his beliefs, spoke for every free spirit and inquiring mind when he declared, "Truth does not change because it is, or is not, believed by a majority of the people." Are not political decisions to be made on the basis of the truth?

The expert pilot, Plato points out, is very different from ordinary sailors wrangling for control of the helm; he is one who has mastered the art and science of navigation. Plato's illustration became reality after the mutiny on the *Bounty*, when Captain Bligh sailed his small boat across thousands of miles to a safe haven; we can be sure that Bligh did not navigate by majority vote of the sailors cast off with him.

Yet Plato also recognizes that the pilot may be uncertain whether he has benefited his passengers, "knowing as he does that those he has landed are in no way better than when they embarked, either in body or in soul." "The ship of state" may be a foolish and dangerous metaphor if the business of the statesman is not to bring the citizens to some predetermined anchorage but to help them become better in body and soul. In that case, while a republic may not make the best decisions, it may still be the form of government which reaches decisions in the best way. Even if Plato were right that most people are incapable of deciding wisely, what government aims at, in Plato's own doctrine, is to bring the people to such wisdom as they are capable of; this can only come about if they govern themselves. We dare not ask if the people are ready for freedom; what could we answer if the same question were asked about us?

It cannot be gainsaid, however, that there may be too much democracy; not every mode of participation in the exercise of power is consonant with the other ends of a democratic state. Majority rule must be limited by minority rights and by the rule of law (§78). Elected officials, even if truly representative of their constituencies, cannot make their representation effective if they are elected for too short a term and so are vulnerable to every vagary of public opinion. Where majority rule is appropriate, it is not always clear how it can be applied. As is true of the voice of conscience, what a majority is saying often needs interpreting, and it may be saying several different things—sometimes incompatible with one another—at once. For that matter, even a dictator does not always know his own mind.

6. Finally, democracies are *egalitarian,* as contrasted with the *stratified* structure characteristic of despotisms. Egalitarianism is the political expression of social equality (§65). Although empirically connected with republicanism, it is logically distinct. The republican principle involves an equality of sorts, as conveyed in the formula "one man, one vote." This relates to the distribution of power, while egalitarianism refers to the power base and to the impact of power on other values. In an egalitarian society power does not depend on social standing, nor does it give such standing. From American history, the model is Andrew Jackson; his exercise of power may have had elements of the dictatorial, but even his enemies could not deny that he met all men on a plane of equality. (This trait made him enemies.)

With Jackson, it was said, "the rabble" came into the White House. Aristocrats, elitists, all those who defend a stratified society have argued that in the mass the people are mediocre, and they pull everyone down to their level. They are lax and undiscriminating, lacking sensitivity, discipline, and restraint. Plato argued that when the masses have power the result, inevitably, is chaos. Unqualified democracy is mobocracy—the rule of the mob—and, ultimately, anarchy—no rule at all. Aristotle does not depart significantly from this assessment. "A democracy," he says, "is a government in the hands of men of low birth, no property, and vulgar employments." The tone is more down-to-earth than Plato's, but the content is as far as Plato's is from egalitarianism.

In practice, the Athenian democracy was more egalitarian (if the slaves, the vast majority of the population, are not taken into account). As Pericles described the regime, "Advancement in public life falls to reputation for capacity, class considerations or social standing not being allowed to interfere with merit; nor does poverty bar the way; if a man is able to serve the state, he is not hindered by the obscurity of his condition." Thereby the state is not only better served; the justification of egalitarianism is a matter of ends as well as of means. The most fundamental principle of democracy, underlying the ideals of freedom and self-government as well as of equality, is, in Mill's words, that the worth of a state in the long run is the worth of the individuals composing it. If the people are as little deserving of respect as aristocrats have argued, the state itself is contemptible—in its attainment, if not in its aspiration. The superiority claimed by the self-styled upper classes is the effect, not the cause or reason, of a stratified society. Spinoza urged that democracy is the most natural of all forms of government, for in it men remain equals as they were in the state of nature—that is, considered apart from differences instituted and maintained by political practice.

The stratified state reaches its culmination in the apotheosis of "the Leader," who is literally deified, like the Caesars, or who is viewed as a savior in a more secular sense, assuming a superhuman burden of responsibility for guiding the state to the fulfillment of its destiny, carrying out the special mission of state power. The Leader becomes the only individual worthy of respect—indeed, the only one worthy of being called an individual; the masses identify with him and imitate him so far as their lesser capacities allow.

Leadership can be conceived functionally rather than structurally: there is need to coordinate social effort and to give it direction, but it begs the fundamental question to assume that the need can be met only by people of distinctive status in a stratified society. Every stratification keeps some from rising to their responsibilities, and demands from others what is not theirs to give. Egalitarianism does not deny differences among people in any respect save in the right to become all they might ever be.

73. The Right of Protest

A tangle of issues basic not only to democratic theory but to political philosophy in general centers around the right of *protest.* Political history for the last four or five centuries might be written as a history of protest movements—from the Protestant Reformation, protesting orthodoxy of belief, down to the latest resistance movement, protesting some regimented action. Protest movements, especially if successful, promulgate their own orthodoxies and institute their own regimentation. Nevertheless, protest can restore awareness of forgotten goals, revitalize sickly values, and adapt old ideals to new conditions. If men live not as they would but as they must, they can at any rate do so in the defiant spirit of the squire's closing words to Death in Bergman's *The Seventh Seal*—"under protest."

The issues hinge on what happens to authority and, thereby, to social order, if the right to reject authority is recognized. It cannot be right to deny legitimate power; if it is the legitimacy which is being denied, others may have an equal right to protest the denial. Social order rests on *law,* and the obligation to abide by law is part of its meaning. Yet there are unjust laws and to protest against these is also an obligation. In the dialectic of authoritarians, obedience to the law is an expression of freedom rather than an obligation. Hegel argues: "Only that which obeys law is free. When the subjective will of man submits to laws, the contradiction between liberty and necessity vanishes." There is a tale of a desert traveler who unknowingly lay down to sleep on a date stone, which germinated by the warmth of his body and grew rapidly during the night; in the morning, finding himself perched high on the treetop, the traveler looked about him, then declared, "I choose to end my travels precisely at this spot, and remain here the rest of my days"—which he did. Freedom may entail the recognition of causal necessity, as was argued by the Stoics and Spinoza; it does not entail, and indeed is not compatible with, submitting to compulsion without protest even if it is authority which compels.

In democratic doctrine political obligation is subject to moral determination, not the other way around. Conscience may demand of a person that he stand against consensus, even if he stands alone. On the other hand, if each person were acknowledged to have the right of a personal veto over legislation, there would be no rule of law at all. A moral intent does not justify violating law or taking the law into one's own hands. The case was recently reported of an embezzler who was found to have wanted nothing for himself, but to have disbursed all he had taken to private philanthropies and other worthy causes; but the firm failed when the losses were discovered, one of the owners committed suicide, and several others were financially ruined. Every rejection of the legal order must be undertaken in fear and trembling, for we may be carrying out not the will of the gods but our own; yet if we fail to protest evil because of the fear that we might be wrong, we are damned as surely as if the failure sprang only from the fear of power. That is the predicament.

There are many forms of protest, each imposing a different set of moral responsibilities. First is *dissent:* the expression of a contrary conviction. Only authoritarian societies have no place for dissent; every characterization of disagreement as disloyalty is a blow to freedom. The possibility of a loyal opposition is essential to every government of free men. Whenever men stand opposed to any decision that has been taken, they must be given the liberty to express their opposition, the right to dissent, or the decision cannot claim legitimacy in a democratic political doctrine. This remains true regardless of the content of the dissent (subject only to some clear and present danger of free speech [§71]). Those who view dissent from democratic decisions as a subversion against which democracy is to be defended are guilty themselves of "defensive subversion." Theirs is the strategy of the general who reported that he had to destroy a certain village "in order to save it." Dissent is the minimal form of protest, the most unequivocally moral and, for society, the most precious form of protest.

Disobedience goes beyond the expression of opinion into action. (An apparent act of disobedience may in fact be serving as an expression of dissent—what has been called "symbolic speech.") One who dissents may nevertheless go along in action even if he is of another mind. In itself this is neither inconsistent nor lacking in integrity: I may strongly disagree with you and say so, yet acknowledge your right to decide and the wisdom of our acting in concert, whatever the decision. In disobedience, the operative principle is "Without me!" The dissenter may think a law unjust and therefore try to change it but abide by the law in the meantime. One who disobeys does not wait for the law to be changed but acts as if it already has been changed as far as he is concerned.

Where each man obeys only the laws of his own choosing there is no rule of law at all. Disobedience is differentiated from anarchy only if it is carried out in a framework of maintenance of the social order. The intent is made explicit in the designation *civil* disobedience. Community is preserved: the law being disobeyed is unjust, but not the whole legal order of which it is a part (the position taken by the revolutionary). Those who have enacted the law, unjust though it is, are men of good will, deserving neither hatred nor contempt. Gandhi, perhaps the greatest practitioner of civil disobedience, explained that to be civil, disobedience must be "sincere, respectful, restrained, never defiant, and it must have no ill-will or hatred behind it." The law is being disobeyed not just in obedience to one's own moral law as in the case of the conscientious objector but as a way of inducing the community to change the law. It is an exercise of what Gandhi made famous as *satyagraha:* moral force.

Such disobedience does not view itself as exempt from paying the penalties of disobedience, or it would be undercutting the very foundation of legal order. On the contrary, acceptance of the penalty adds weight to the moral force being exerted. Only if the law violates not moral standards but the norms of the legal order itself—as in the case of an unconstitutional enactment or of malfeasance of authority—is there ground for repudiating the penalty. Granting amnesty, however, is another matter, for this pardons an offense rather than conceding that no wrong has been committed.

Resistance goes further than disobedience. Here the protester does not obey the law himself, and he also prevents others from obeying it. Dissent may be expressed in a peaceful demonstration against what is felt to be an unjust war; disobedience might consist in the refusal to be inducted into the armed forces; it is an act of resistance to destroy the files of the draft board. The resister is not just preserving his own moral integrity, as in the case of dissent or disobedience; he may also be exercising a moral tyranny, compelling others to his norms of action. Sidney Hook has rightly emphasized the importance for democracy of distinguishing between heresy and conspiracy. Heresy has a right to be heard—it is an expression of dissent. Disobedience also has its rights—the conscientious objector may accept some form of nonviolent service. But resistance is very likely to involve conspiracy which is intolerable to any viable regime, however democratic.

Resistance is also likely to involve a denial of community; it is not "respectful and restrained," in Gandhi's words; it both expresses and evokes ill-will and hatred. There is a species of "passive resistance," so called, to which this characterization does not apply; but "passive resistance" is organized disobedience rather than resistance in the present sense. It is not an attempt to coerce the decision of the community but to dissociate oneself from it and, in concert with others, to exert moral force against it. In resistance, there is a repudiation of the right of the community to have decided as it did and to carry out its decision. There is something self-defeating about resistance, therefore: it wants a law to be changed, but insists on the change in such an unlawful way as to undermine the authority of law, replacing it by the power of whatever group seeks to impose its will. A demonstration in the galleries of a legislative chamber may be an effective expression of dissent; but if it is carried on so as to coerce a certain legislative action it loses its point, for were it to succeed it would only invite those of a contrary opinion to resist the new decision in the same way, and the legislature would no longer have any function.

In a particular regime, dissent may be ineffective and disobedience impossible. In that case, it may be more than a particular decision which is the object of protest; it may be the whole pattern of decision making. The attempt to change this pattern (in ways other than those provided by the pattern itself) constitutes *rebellion*. Resistance moves against a particular exercise of power; rebellion attempts to take power away from those who are wielding it. In the perspectives of claimed legitimacy, rebellion is known instead as *revolution*.

Where there is simply a transfer of power from one set of individuals to another, while both the means by which power is exercised and the ends to which it is directed remain the same, it is usual to speak of a "palace revolution." In a "political revolution" there is a change in the power base, in the ways in which power is acquired; a new sort of elite comes to the fore. If there is also a change in the ends to which power is directed, together with thoroughgoing changes in the ways in which power is exercised, we have a "social revolution." An assassination by which a new king is enthroned illustrates a palace revolution; abolition of the monarchy, or making a pure formality of its power in a democratic state, is a political revolution; replacement of such a state by a fascist or a communist regime is a social revolution. In the concrete, political changes and protest movements may involve elements of all three.

Revolutions, like other forms of protest, are not made by the completely downtrodden. Dissent and disobedience presuppose some degree of free thought, or the deviant belief and action would hardly spring into being; resistance and rebellion are themselves an exercise of power and would be plainly futile from the outset if their perpetrators were wholly powerless. For this reason, acts of resistance are often seen as being carried out by people who are ungrateful for the concessions already made to them, people who are never satisfied. It is their improved position which makes their resistance possible and, in their eyes, quite possibly successful. Revolution requires considerable power, comparable to that which the overthrown had; usually the regime has already lost a great deal of its power before the revolution is mounted, and there has emerged a so-called "counter-elite": wielders of a significant weight of informal power aspiring to legitimacy. It is not the masses but the counter-elite which carries out a revolution.

Political doctrines which legitimize power by mission or by consent imply the right of revolution. If the ruler is not fulfilling the mission for which he was entrusted with power, or is no longer ruling by consent, he has forfeited legitimacy. He is therefore a usurper, a "mere fellow," as Mencius called him; far from having an obligation to obey him, we have a duty to overthrow him. Cromwell is at one with Aquinas in declaring that rebellion to tyrants is obedience to God. This dictum was used by Jefferson as his personal and official seal, for the tree of liberty, Jefferson held, must be watered often with the blood of tyrants.

Yet the stability on which conservatives insist is, after all, one of the needs of society; providing it is one of the important functions of government. In a period of less than thirty years there have been about sixty attempts in the Middle East to overthrow governments, of which about half have been successful; it may have been tyrants whose blood was shed, but the tree of liberty has not conspicuously flourished. Whether revolution is necessary for human welfare, it is certainly not sufficient. There is a place for protest, perhaps even for violent protest; but the background or aim of every protest movement is a structuring of legitimate power—in short, a rule of law.

74. Philosophy of Law

Hegel's argument which equates liberty with obedience to the state, like Rousseau's equating it with submission to the general will, might be valid if the citizen were truly represented by the state, or if his own will were genuinely expressed in what political institutions identified as the general will. In democratic doctrine, only such a state and such political institutions are legitimate. The exercise of authority—the whole system of law—has as its end, in Locke's words, "not to abolish or restrain freedom but to preserve and enlarge it. Law is not so much a limitation as it is the direction of a free and intelligent agent to his proper interest." The traffic signal dictates my movements; earlier (§71) it was argued that as a result of giving up my right to stop or go as I choose, I enjoy a greater freedom of movement, because thereby traffic flows. There is a more fundamental enlargement of my freedom as a result of the signal: I have been freed from dependence on the personal judgment of other drivers as to whether it is safe for them to proceed. This is why I must obey the signal whether or not there is oncoming traffic. *Law* is defined as that use of power which no one is to take into his own hands.

In this conception, law is understandable only in its social setting, in contrast with those schools of jurisprudence—exemplified by John Austin in the nineteenth century and Hans Kelsen in the twentieth—for which law is an autonomous institution, conceptually separable from community processes. Justice Brandeis, deeply responsive to the social background and functions of the law, once went so far as to say that a lawyer who has not studied economics and sociology is "very apt to become a public enemy."

Law does not do its work only in confrontations between the individual and the state, as in criminal law, nor in confrontations among groups and individuals, as in civil law. It also has the function of anticipating and obviating such confrontations before they arise. Law, like the police, is doing its work most effectively when it is not used; the Chinese custom was to pay your physician as long as you were well, and to stop payment during illness, when he was treating you. "In hearing cases," Confucius said of himself, "I am like everyone else. The important thing, however, is to see to it that there are no cases." The concept of *preventive law* is coming to the fore. Law provides more than a rationale for resolving disputes; it also provides procedures for decision making in areas of potential conflict. It may do less of its work by litigation than by mediation, arbitration, negotiation, and other ways of composing differences.

Law prevents conflict by providing a basis for reliable expectations as to how others will react to any contemplated action of our own. For this reason the doctrine of *stare decisis*—being guided by the precedent of decisions made in similar cases—is an important legal principle. Whether a case is sufficiently similar to previous ones in relevant respects is a matter which obviously calls for a certain nicety of judgment. Thereby law can be adapted to changing circumstances. What exactly the law provides is not determinable beforehand with mathematical precision. We can say only that the law is what in fact the courts will enforce—a standpoint known as *legal positivism.* If what the courts will do is too much in doubt, there is no longer a legal order. Hence, jurists have emphasized that it is more important for the law to be certain than for it to be ideal.

The operative ideal is the moral sense of the community as a whole, or of that part of it which is politically effective. A decision of the courts may be in advance of legislative enactment rather than a straightforward application of statutory law. This is especially likely to be true of what are thereafter known as "landmark" decisions. If the decision does not embody what is subsequently crystallized as the sense of the community, the court is likely to be overruled. Reliance on the law as a guide to morality—the view that if what is done is within the law, it is not immoral—is not so much misplaced reliance as it is poorly timed. At any given moment, there are laws destined to be viewed as unjust and areas of conduct morally condemned and on the way to being legally proscribed.

The attitude, in the face of any problem, that "there oughta be a law"—the exaggeration of what can and should be done by legal institutions—is rightly dismissed as *legalism.* In every legal system there are many laws that are no longer enforced, and many laws might well be replaced by other types of social control. The social resource devoted to the legal enforcement of sectarian standards of religiosity and so-called "decency" is grossly disproportionate in light of the vast scale of crime and injustice *not* being dealt with. Without regard to social ideals or libertarian principles, just from the standpoint of sheer effectiveness, it is likely that there are too many laws rather than too few. If nature had as many laws as the state, it has been said, God himself could not rule over it.

That not only unwise but downright unreasonable behavior can manifest itself in the law is surprising only if the law's claim always to have justification is taken at face value. Aristotle characterized the law as "reason unaffected by desire"—in his treatise on politics, which certainly should have led him to a very different conclusion. "The life of the law has not been logic," Justice Holmes wrote in a celebrated passage of his book on the common law; "it has been experience. The felt necessities of the time, the prevalent moral and political theories, institutions of public policy, avowed or unconscious, even the prejudices which judges share with their fellowmen, have had a good deal more to do than the syllogism in determining the rules by which men should be governed." The irrationalities of both governors and governed make themselves felt in legal institutions no less than elsewhere in society. For once, Plato speaks more realistically than Aristotle, although he is occupied with delineating the ideal state: "We are only men, legislating for the sons of men." The sociologist Vilfredo Pareto documented at great length (in his *Mind and Society*) the irrationalities and absurdities of which the law, in many societies, has been guilty.

However irrational at times, the rule of law is essential to the preservation of liberty. Every society imposes controls on the behavior of its members. Everyone belongs to some power domain or other; there are no power vacuums for long. Among the decisions made, some are bound to be felt adversely; it is not to be expected that any social order can generate decisions which will always satisfy everyone. What can be hoped for is that there will always be a possibility of effectively challenging undesirable decisions—a real right of appeal. Where such a right exists, we may speak of *juridical defense* of liberties. Effective challenge does not imply that every appeal succeeds; it implies only that there are norms to be satisfied by the wielders of power as well as by those over whom they are wielding it. Juridical defense does not exempt a criminal from all punishment but only from punishment arbitrarily imposed by a power which cannot be brought to account.

Where juridical defense prevails, we have *a government of laws, not men. Tyranny,* often identified with "despotism" (§72), may be defined as government of men rather than of laws—that is, government by *decree.* Decrees are not always absolute, like the *ukase* of an autocrat, for they may be limited by countervailing powers; decisions are no less tyrannical because several powers share in making them. In a tyranny, neither the ends nor the means of power are subject to determination by procedural norms. The tyrant declares, "*I* am the State"; even more to the point is another dictum of Louis XIV, "It is legal because I wish it." That is the very antithesis of juridical defense. The Talmud remarks that God weeps every day for the community whose leader tyrannizes over it—literally, who exalts himself over it, thereby placing himself above the law; on this account, men shed even more bitter tears.

Every tyranny is also a despotism; democracy, cherishing both freedom and liberty, requires juridical defense. Widespread sharing of power is not enough; the tyranny of an entrenched majority is a familiar spectacle of political life. Democracy attaches importance not only to majority rule but also to *minority rights,* including the rights of each individual against the common will of all the rest. It has been well said that there is no safety in numbers, nor in anything else: majority votes have sometimes resulted in decisions which only effective challenge prevented from undermining the freedom on which majority rule itself depends. Mechanisms like proportional representation give minorities more of a voice than they might otherwise have, but such mechanisms only supplement juridical defense and cannot replace it.

Juridical defense preserves freedom especially by the principle that a person is accountable only for his actions, not for his thoughts. An important case in American constitutional history dates back to the Revolutionary War. Under cover of darkness, a soldier in the American forces gave himself up to the British (as he supposed); it turned out to be another American regiment. Against the subsequent charge of desertion the defense was offered that, though he had intended to desert, in fact he had not done so, and was guilty, at most, of moving without orders from one unit to another in his own army. The defense was upheld. Another principle of juridical defense denies guilt by association unless there has been an actual sharing of a criminal act. A person who habitually consorts with criminals raises certain presumptions about his character which might be relevant to assessing his reliability as a witness or to determining the criminal intent of some unlawful act of his; but by his associations alone he does not stand convicted of any crime. Still another principle of juridical defense is that every person is presumed innocent until he is proven guilty, and he cannot properly be denied any of the rights of the innocent.

Another important component of juridical defense is widely disregarded, increasingly even in democratic states. It is the principle that it is better for the guilty to escape than for the innocent to be punished. On this principle, evidence illegally obtained is inadmissible, even though it establishes a moral certainty of guilt. The method of obtaining it may jeopardize the rights of innocent persons and so must be disallowed. Juridical defense insists on *due process* being followed in any exercise of power. In criminal matters a person is entitled to know with what he is charged, to be able to confront and cross-examine the witnesses against him, to enjoy advice of counsel, and to have a public trial. In civil matters, juridical defense demands corresponding safeguards against arbitrary procedures.

Terms like "due" process and "arbitrary" procedures are, in themselves, quite vague; they can be made specific only contextually, in the framework of the entire legal order and its traditions. Even so, they cannot be made wholly precise. Twilight zones of legality are required by the ambiguities of both act and intention. Power, both governmental and other, would be more tyrannical if the law could not speak of "reasonable" doubt, "community" standards, "proper" care, and so on, provided that their meaning in specific cases is defined by procedures which conform to the norms of due process.

Law limits power on behalf of liberty; it also guides power towards the ideal of justice. Power without justice is tyranny, said Pascal. Not every set of procedural norms is enough to make the exercise of power juridical. An act of tyranny is no less arbitrary for following predictably on personal frustration, as is illustrated by the Queen of Hearts' "Off with his head!" and by the lives of the twelve Caesars. The operative norms must be those of a system of law whose generality of form makes it impartial in the sense of applying equally to all its instances and whose specificity of content embodies the moral sense of the community about a man's deserts in special circumstances.

If justice is to be anything other than the interests of the stronger, it must be specified in terms of a system of law. But it is only specified by law, not defined by it, for the idea of an unjust law is far from a contradiction in terms. Legalism is at its worst when it not only presupposes that there are moral absolutes but presumes to have embodied them in a specific set of laws. Strict adherence to the letter of the law in all cases will almost surely do an injustice in some cases. Whenever power declares, "Let justice be done though the heavens fall!" the heavens do fall.

Equality before the law underlies every other sort of equality, since without it power could be used to institute and perpetuate all other inequalities. Men share only those goods socially produced and distributed which their share of power enables them to secure for themselves. Scripture enjoins: "You shall hear the small and the great alike; you shall not be afraid of any man." Otherwise law is a formality, while effective decisions continue to be made by those who inspire the fear. Very well known in our day are legal processes which move to ends predetermined by political factors wholly extraneous to the legal considerations and even, in some cases, contradictory to them. It is to such factors that justice must be blind. The law is to be impersonal but not inhuman, impartial but not uncaring, indifferent to irrelevancies but not unknowing. These are ideals; realities fall far short of them. While politics makes for injustice in the despotic states, elsewhere economics makes for inequalities before the law: proportionately more poor wrongdoers than rich ones are caught, more of them are punished, more of their punishments are prison terms rather than fines, more are executed rather than imprisoned. All over the world people may still say with Job, "I cry aloud, but there is no justice!"

Even under the best circumstances, and with the most scrupulous intent, justice is notoriously hard to come by. Justice Felix Frankfurter summarized the qualifications required of a judge: he should be compounded of the faculties that are demanded of the historian and the philosopher and the prophet. Any one of the three alone would be a distinguished achievement. All three, moreover, are conspicuously subject to misunderstanding and rejection; yet the functions of preventive law require that justice must not only be done but be seen to be done. A just decision may be widely resisted, and an unjust one may be defended by the entrenched powers of state and society. When there is general agreement both in the courts and among the people as to what is just, injustice is likely to arise because of that very fact: unquestioned ends invite indifference to the means used to secure them. Philo of Alexandria and later commentators remarked that the command "Justice, justice shall you pursue!" repeats the word so as to embrace both means and ends.

The most difficult problem of securing justice is posed by the injustice which power tolerates and even incorporates in legal systems. Montesquieu distinguished two sorts of corruption: "one when the people do not observe the laws; the other when they are corrupted by the laws—an incurable evil, because it is in the very remedy itself." The comparison is apt: what are we to do when it is the physician who spreads the disease? Legal fictions (like treating a corporation as a person) are an important device by which rigid abstractions can be fitted to changing concreta; only a doctrinaire semantics can object to them in general. But there is also such a thing as legalized falsehood—pretended adherence to legal forms while perverting their content, as in the legalistic devices employed to secure tax advantages or to thwart integration of the schools. "If we desire respect for the law," Brandeis has said, "we must first make the law respectable."

Worse yet, centers of authority may value power more than its legitimization, and instead of upholding the law may be guilty of flouting it. Watergate is the most publicized but hardly the most outrageous of modern instances, as both Nazi and Soviet history attest. "If government becomes a lawbreaker," Brandeis also observed, "it breeds contempt for the law." Power must recurrently be brought before the bar of justice; but who has the power to bring it there?

75. The Political Arena

Politics is well said to take place in the arena: conflict is a pervasive fact of political life. In contrast to most physical processes, political differences tend of themselves to move to extremes. There are not just different positions but opposing sides. The opposition between the two is quickly moralized: every political struggle becomes a conflict between good and evil. A process of heroization comes into play with regard to our side, and of demonization with regard to their side; the forces arrayed against us are satanic, while we carry the banners of virtue. The struggle for power is perceived as another battle in the eternal warfare between the Children of Light and the Children of Darkness. If we lose a battle, it can only be because we have been betrayed; there is no margin for error. The human drama plays itself out in either Heaven or Hell; earth, where good is embedded in human frailty, is only a point of departure. Such perspectives are more explicit in the ideologies of despotism, but they are at work in democratic ideologies as well.

In the relations among nations, conflict is more marked and pervasive than it is among lesser groups or among individuals. Here the Hobbesian state of nature, the war of each against all, seems undeniably real. "We are mad," a philosopher has said, "not only individually but nationally. We check manslaughter and isolated murders; but what of war and the crime of slaughtering whole peoples?" I do not know if it is heartening or depressing to learn that these words were written centuries ago, by the Stoic, Seneca (who, incidentally, committed suicide at Nero's command). Have we learned so little?

Hobbes thought that we could rise out of the state of nature only by the establishment of a supreme sovereign; world government, however, seems to be as remote today as it was in Roman times when the Stoics held up the ideal of world citizenship. International organizations have proliferated, but today they chiefly serve the ends of conflict rather than serve to end it. The Law was given us, says the Talmud, for the purpose of establishing harmony among men; one ought to pray for peace even to the last clod of earth thrown on his grave. In our time, is it only the dead who can have peace?

Whether in international relations or on the domestic scene, the omnipresence of unyielding conflict owes much to the hatred evoked and released by the perception of political opposition as satanic; evil is hateful, and the fight against it must be unremitting. The idea of preventive law has been generalized to that of *preventive politics:* the use of power not to prevail in the power conflict but to minimize conflict in both frequency and intensity. What must be learned is the necessity for compromise, even with sin; that is all we *can* compromise with, for virtue is on our side to start with. Politics has been described as the art of the possible, the practical; one of the meanings of "politic" is prudent, shrewd, sagacious. Realism compels the realization that we will never win if only the virtuous are on our side—there are too few of them. Practicality without compromise is possible only in dictatorship, where there is no opposing power to be either accommodated or destroyed.

The idea of compromise seems to contain an element of the morally dubious: when virtue is compromised it is as good as lost. In politics very nearly the opposite is true. If politics is to be practical it must always be prepared to accept the second best. What is best of all is unobtainable; it is the infantile fantasy of fulfillment of every wish, a fantasy which can be sustained only by an associated delusion of omnipotence. If not all power is in my hands, not all that I will is likely to come about. "Political writers," Aristotle said, presumably referring to his teacher, Plato, "although they have excellent ideas, are often impractical. We should consider, not only what form of government is best, but also what is possible." If only men were not the willful, stubborn, foolish creatures that they are! But politics, says Aristotle again, does not make men, but takes them from nature and uses them. "Never hope to realize Plato's Republic," Marcus Aurelius also counsels. "Let it be enough that you have in some slight degree improved the condition of mankind, and do not regard that improvement as a matter of small importance."

Democratic practice institutionalizes compromise, not only in the political form of parliaments but also through the exercise of informal power by pressure groups. Such groups, far from undermining democracy, are essential to its workings. The political order is threatened only when the pressures become monolithic, or when they are so effectively concealed that countervailing power cannot easily come into play. The party system illustrates the centrality of compromise, whether coalitions are formed before elections, as in the American two-party system, or afterwards, as in multiparty, parliamentary systems. Horse-trading, log-rolling, wheeling and dealing are the very life of politics; some give and take is inseparable from any political process where power is not so concentrated as to be irresistible. The politician must be a fixer, or must employ one. In the conduct of international relations a man with these skills is preeminently a diplomat. It is his business to mediate disagreement before conflict intensifies, and to do so in a way which maximizes the image as well as the reality of power. The motto for the whole breed might well be that formulated by John F. Kennedy in his inaugural address: "Let us never negotiate out of fear, but let us never fear to negotiate."

In all times and places, politicians, though they occupy posts of honor, have been widely held in contempt. An eleventh-century Chinese poem (as translated by Arthur Waley) has a modern sting:

Families, when a child is born
Want it to be intelligent.
I, through intelligence,
Having wrecked my whole life,
Only hope the baby will prove
Ignorant and stupid.
Then he will crown a tranquil life
By becoming a Cabinet Minister.

Ignorant and stupid is the best that can be said, in the popular conception. Politics offers only the choice between an honest fool and an able rascal. Either the politician is incompetent and office hungry, or else he is a dishonest scoundrel. An honest politician, says the American cynic, is only one who, when he is bought, stays bought.

In all this there is a kind of scapegoating. The business of the politician is compromise, which is seen as a dirty business, every compromise being felt to be a betrayal. If "practical politics" is a redundancy, so is "dirty politics"—when it means nothing worse than compromise. There is no other way to get and keep power than by selling something of oneself and one's principles, just as it is impossible to get rich if you wrinkle your nose at dirty money. Principles must be compromised; otherwise they are not performing their function of effectively guiding conduct; what is unbending can only be broken.

The politician is also victimized by the impulse to personify social processes. Impersonal forces may actually be at work, like those making for inflation or crop failures. Such outcomes are affected by human decisions, but the effects may be unintended, unanticipated, and beyond control in a given state of knowledge and resources. But the world, especially the world of power, is seen as consisting of benefactors and beneficiaries, villains and victims. The honor and contempt in which the politician is held reflect the ambivalence of the responses to him, according to the impact of power on personal desires.

What is remarkable is how many men there are in political life with high ideals and aspirations. For many, politics is not an occupation but a calling, as Max Weber especially has emphasized. The notion that power is pursued for personal profit, while having some substance, is at best a half-truth; quite often a personal fortune is devoted to political pursuits rather than the other way around. In states adhering to ideologies of mission, political leaders, like the Bolshevik elite, may lead lives of asceticism and self-denial.

Power feeds an appetite, perhaps the most vicious of all, for its satisfaction puts at stake the welfare of so many other people. The ideal political leader should not only not hunger for power but should have a positive distaste for it—an image cultivated in American politics, where every candidate puts on the airs, so far as they suit him, of a reluctant virgin. There is a Southwest Indian tribe which used to select its chieftain by shutting all the eligibles into a lodge, where one by one they gave excuses for refusing the post, till at last one of them had no more to say. The thought of a nominating convention proceeding in this fashion conjures up a tempting vision.

The personalization of politics easily goes so far as to make the personality of a political leader more important than his policies. It is not only in dictatorships that there is a cult of personality. Policies may be obscure and the reasons for them uncertain; who the man is seems much easier to grasp than what he stands for. This is especially true today, when the mass media allow for the widespread and effective projection of an image. There are important functions of leadership—preserving the integrity of the group, maintaining its morale in the face of adversity, formulating policy when choices are to be made, and organizing the shared effort to put policy into effect. Performance of these functions is largely independent of the qualities usually emphasized in the cult of personality. What matters may be, instead, qualities lacking in glamour—such as skills in negotiation and administration and the capacity to make risky decisions. The leader does not need to *give* the group its purpose and direction; his function may be to help the group crystallize and formulate the goals latent in its values. Lao-tzu's view is that a leader is best when people barely know he exists. "When his work is done, his aim fulfilled, they will say, 'We did it ourselves.'"

The problem of formulating group goals is enmeshed with a predicament. Institutions and organizations established to attain certain ends develop other ends not necessarily compatible with the first—the ends, namely, of maintaining and enhancing their own existence. The former are sometimes called the *principled interests* and the latter the *expediency interests;* expediencies have a way of displacing or transforming principles. The church may stifle or pervert religious experience; the school may get in the way of education; the state may endanger or destroy peace and freedom.

The predicament is that organized effort is impossible without organization and that stable social patterns of action are institutionalized by their very continuance.

The difficulties of coping with the predicament are especially severe in political contexts, where power can be allocated not only to the expediencies but also to the concealment of their departure from principle and to the suppression of protest against such departures. Dictatorship is described as "democratic centralism," tyranny as the justice dispensed by "people's courts," and the police state as a defense against "anti-social elements," while the dissidents who protest this doublethink are first rendered powerless, then silenced.

Ventriloquism is a widespread practice in the political arena: expediencies do not speak for themselves but in the name of principle. Power usually claims to be exercised only on behalf of the general welfare, not for the special interests of those wielding power. The general interest, however, is made up largely of special interests. Factionalism in the political arena, like sectarian religion and tribal ethics, is honest in setting itself apart from its rivals, but not in the recognition of the self-seeking which is at the bottom of the separatism. The opposition frequently has no other program than "Let *me* do it instead," and no other principle than "Anything you can do I can do better!"

All this may make for disillusionment. That means only abandoning illusions; but without illusion can we still pursue political ideals? An affirmative answer presupposes that the ideals are realistic, grounded in the potentialities of things as they are, not as our illusions imagine them to be. "Though men be much governed by interest," Hume said, "yet even interest itself, and all human affairs, are entirely governed by opinion." The question is whether the relevant political opinions are rational. Here is where freedom comes to the fore, not only as a political ideal but as a precondition for the effectiveness of all other political ideals. Marcus Aurelius asks the holders of power, "Without a change of opinions what can you make but reluctant slaves and hypocrites?" If opinions are changed by authoritarian control, nothing has been changed after all.

This is why it cannot be said that every people has the government it deserves; indoctrination and terror may make the government acceptable to the people even though they deserve better. Above all, they deserve to be free. The *Federalist* is realistic almost to the point of cynicism as to the role of unreason in the acceptance of government: "In a nation of philosophers a reverence for the laws would be sufficiently inculcated by the voice of an enlightened reason. But a nation of philosophers is as little to be expected as the philosophical race of kings wished for by Plato. And in every other nation, the most rational government will not find it a superfluous advantage to have the prejudices of the community on its side." Plato thought that the people, by and large, were so irrational as to need guardians, like children or the feebleminded; even Jefferson, with his matchless faith in the people, once confessed, "I tremble for my country when I reflect that God is just." Humility teaches the wisdom of praying not for justice but for mercy.

That ideals are at work implies that changes are in the making: the lode star is of use not to tell us where we are but where we are going. As against the reactionary, a principle of growth affirms that no actual attainment is ideal or can remain so. Even Plato (in his dialogue named, appropriately enough, the *Statesman*) acknowledges that no art whatsoever can lay down a rule which will last for all time. The insistent call for law and order may be serving to maintain dehumanizing inequalities and injustices and other conditions far short of the ideal. A political thinker as far from radicalism as de Tocqueville recognizes that "a nation which asks nothing of its government but the maintenance of order is already a slave at heart." But if permanence is not an intrinsic good, neither is change. As against the rebel, a principle of continuity affirms that not every leap is in the direction of the ideal; not every change is an improvement.

In times of desperation the impulse to do something, anything at all, may become overwhelming, and action then rationalizes itself as its own justification. The times are desperate, but they have been so as long as I can remember, and no doubt will continue to be so throughout the foreseeable future. We live in an age of permanent crisis, but so did most ages which have gone before. The body politic suffers less often from genuine ailments than from the anxieties of political hypochondria which, in Emerson's phrase, hears the crack of doom in the sound of every popgun. When danger is felt to be imminent and deadly, it is understandable that we look anxiously to the horizon, to discern the shape of our salvation. Understandable but unreasonable, for our welfare is determined, in politics most of all, by what we ourselves do, not by what is done for us. Machiavelli's faith in people is conveyed in his remark that when men's very lives and fortunes are at stake they are not wholly insane. There is a real question, however, whether we will be sane enough soon enough.

Just as ethical theory has been shaped by the desire to justify a prevailing morality, political philosophy has served as a defense of the political *status quo*. Such motivations play some part in the thought of a conservative like Hegel, who saw in the Prussian state the highest embodiment of universal Reason, as well as of a radical like Rousseau, who admitted, "I feel happy whenever I meditate on governments, always to discover in my researches new reasons for loving that of my own country." Love of what is one's own needs no excuse, but in acknowledging it as our own we are acknowledging also a responsibility for nurturing its unending growth.

Philosophy need not take a stand only on behalf of things as they are (§5); wisdom entails acceptance, but this includes acceptance of potentialities as well as of what has already been actualized. Wisdom implies an awareness of the halting growth by which potentialities come to fruition and of the gap which continues to divide even the best of actualities from the ideal. The wise man, Confucius said, concerns himself with politics, not because he expects his principles to prevail but because it is in accord with his principles to be politically concerned.

Chapter Twelve

Aesthetics

76. The Form of Art

Art has a place among the earliest products of man's skill and inspiration. Cave paintings such as those at Altamira and Lascaux, however they may have been viewed by those who painted them, must be acknowledged as art, and as art of a high order. Very basic needs must have impelled man, in conditions of life so austere, to turn his techniques and imagination to such ends. Undoubtedly his creations were intimately interwoven with all else that mattered to him. Art and life were probably as inseparable in prehistoric times as now. The museum as a repository of art has been known only in the Western world, and then only for the last two centuries or so. The ancients had no word for "art" in the modern sense. Art does not consist of special objects, or of things used only on special occasions. From the beginnings, those who created or responded to art and those who reflected on art were occupied with a quality of experience, not with a presumed essence—"beauty"—localized in special objects produced only to serve as such a locus.

This pervasive quality is least prejudicially identified as the *aesthetic.* In the sense of relating specifically to the arts, modern usage dates back no further than the eighteenth century. Kant used the word to refer to the direct, unmediated aspect of experience. Kant's theory of art emphasizes the mutual coadaptation of perception and understanding in the recognition of purposiveness, which is present throughout the biological domain, as well as in art; his *Critique of Judgment* is as much a philosophy of biology as of art. Hegel's view of the theory as providing "the first rational word on aesthetics" is a tribute to Kant's genius for abstract generalization which created the possibility of liberating the aesthetic quality and *philosophy of art* as dealing with the status and function of works created in order to have such quality; I shall use the terms interchangeably.

The art gallery is no more the sole locus of aesthetic experience than the church is of religious experience or the school is of the work of the intellect. Unless these domains reach out to all that is significant in our lives they lose significance. Art is the prototype and exemplar of any significance, not just artistic. The canons of art are the expression, in specialized forms, of the requisites for depth of experience anywhere, Whitehead has remarked.

Aesthetic theory must be correspondingly broad. "There is no test," said Dewey, "that so surely reveals the one-sidedness of a philosophy as its treatment of art and aesthetic experience." On the one hand, modern philosophy often dismisses aesthetics with a tactic of *mutatis mutandis*, occupying itself with the general theory of value or with ethical theory, and adding that similar considerations apply in aesthetics. On the other hand, explicit focus on aesthetics theory often involves a conception of the aesthetic as wholly separate from other domains of value.

Concern with the quality of the environment reminds us that the aesthetic may emerge in our perceptions of nature, and of the products of man's interactions with nature—in the urban landscape, for instance—even though these products are not explicitly "artistic." Among such interactions are many in which the rudiments of aesthetic quality manifest themselves—parades and processions, pageants, spectacles and tableaux, ceremonies and rituals, celebrations, carnivals, festivities, revels, fiestas, communal dances and feasts, performances, presentations and exhibitions, games, sports, contests, displays of skill, diversions and entertainments, circuses, vaudevilles, mummeries, pantomimes, and shows of all sorts.

Even within the range of the arts, aesthetics must take into account not only major arts, such as painting, music, and literature, but also so-called "minor" arts—architecture, sculpture, theater, and dance—as well as more or less artistic crafts: carpet making, gardening, calligraphy, flower arranging, photography, industrial design, jewelry making and costuming, tapestry designing and the designing of textiles, and fashioning of ceramics. Asian aesthetics, especially in India, recognized over a hundred arts—painters and musicians being grouped with perfumers and cooks, not in derogation but in appreciation of all of them. Many shortcomings of aesthetic theories can be traced to the narrowness of their concern; it is as though we tried to base chemistry only on the properties of metals or organic compounds, important though these substances might be.

Aesthetics can best attain the desired level of generality by turning away from aesthetic objects and situations to the experiences they evoke. Commonalities among aesthetic experiences, in turn, can most easily be identified in terms of the *structure* of such experiences, especially as analyzed by John Dewey.

An aesthetic experience is, first, demarcated from the stream of experience in which it is embedded. It is preceded by a summoning of attention, a fanfare, a hush, a rising curtain, and is followed by applause, a change of place and pace, a resumption of other activity. The devices at work to provide such demarcation of the experience constitute a *frame*. What is within the frame stands out in the intensity of our involvement with it and our detachment, during that involvement, from other concerns—as though we bring our car to a stop, accelerate the engine, and simultaneously put it out of gear (§78).

The course of the experience has *integration:* correspondingly, the things successively experienced have a *unity*. Things are sometimes unified by contiguity—they are related only because they are in the same place, like the items displayed in a drugstore window; they may be causally unified, like the noise, flash, and flying rubble of an explosion; they may be unified by our conditioning, like a sequence of letters in alphabetical order. All such modes of unification are external to the experience. In an aesthetic experience, the unity is an outcome of integration in the experience; things are seen as united because something in our seeing impels us to the unification. The things belong together because of how they successively work upon us. The unity is not imposed from without but results from the structuring of the energies released in the ongoing of the experience.

An aesthetic experience unfolds; it is neither an aimless succession nor a mechanical routine. The former would be felt as boredom, the latter as fatigue; aesthetic experience sustains interest and attention. There are no holes in it, no emptiness, nothing trivial or distracting. Everything is felt to be necessary. This is the thrust of Aristotle's characterization of poetry as a complete whole, representing a single action as a sequence of incidents so closely connected that the transposal or withdrawal of any one of them will disjoin and dislocate the whole. The connections of the parts are also necessary to the whole; they are substantive and dynamic ties, not mechanical junctions. Each part leads into the next. All this is summed up by the famous passage in Aristotle's *Poetics* which defines a whole as "that which has a beginning, a middle, and an end"—a beginning being something which is not itself "necessarily after anything else, and which has naturally something else after it," and correspondingly for the other two. What is "necessary" or "natural" in this context is what the flow of the experience demands.

The integration of aesthetic experience into a dynamic whole underlies the important role in it of *suspense*. This differs from curiosity, Coleridge has pointed out, in that curiosity is a restless desire to arrive at the final solution (whodunit?), while in suspense we are excited by the attractions of the journey itself. Curiosity is a matter of what we know or anticipate, while suspense has to do with an experienced expectation. Suspense is heightened by foreknowledge after curiosity has long been satisfied. A story which would be spoiled if we know how it all turned out has not much to offer even when we do not know. An aesthetic experience is evoked by something to which we can return again and again.

Two implications follow. One is that the aesthetic is continually surprising, but never frustrating: suspense is recurrently heightened, while all is as anticipated. The other implication is that the expectations to be fulfilled are those aroused by the experience, not by the prior knowledge we bring to the experience. For this reason, a plausible impossibility, as Aristotle remarked, is always aesthetically preferable to an unconvincing possibility. What counts is what we feel *should* happen, not what we know is likely to happen in actuality. But not just expectations are fulfilled; the whole experience is fulfilling. It arrives at a certain closure, which is experienced as deeply satisfying.

In the experience we always perceive goals as being attained, but they are only our goals in perceiving. We may be presented with defeats, but it is not we who are defeated; the conflicts presented are enjoyable because they intensify the experience. Aesthetic experience provides continuous consummation, the value of every end to which we are led being incorporated in the steps leading to it, so that means become ends in themselves as the future stages of the experience enhance the present. On the other hand, the value in the means is brought forward to the end, the past reinforcing the present. Every stage of an aesthetic experience, as Dewey has analyzed in some detail, sums up the values which have preceded and evokes the values yet to come.

The *form,* in the aesthetic sense, of any object is the organization of its elements by virtue of which the perception of the object is structured so as to provide an aesthetic experience. Unity in the object corresponds to the integration of the experience; other aspects of form carry the experience forward in its continuous consummation. In Aristotle's analysis of tragedy he identified the plot as the first essential of tragedy, its life and soul; form is a generalization of plot. It is the locus in the experienced object of the succession of happenings which makes the experience aesthetic. Underlying the expectations aroused and fulfilled in the experience are the demands brought forward and satisfied in the object. Form is the outcome of acknowledging and meeting the inner necessities of the work. When Dickens, who published several of his works as serials, narrated the death of Little Nell, he was flooded with objections from sentimental readers. "I couldn't help it," he replied in effect; "she was suffering from a fatal illness."

Form is not a pattern only of abstractions. Such patterns *can* exhibit aesthetic quality, as in mathematics or chess. That Euclid alone has looked on beauty bare, however, is a romanticized Platonism which does not shed much light on geometry or art. Form is virtually always embedded in concrete materials. There are musicians who can enjoy music merely by reading the score, but even for them music is a pattern of sounds, not of wholly abstract relata—how else could they appreciate, for instance, richness of orchestration? In Hermann Hesse's *Magister Ludi* the practitioners of the glass-bead game move freely between abstracta and concreta; but the game belongs to fiction—it is Hesse's concrete presentation of it in words which is the work of art.

Every work of art has *formal values* underlying the fulfillments in our structured experience. (Form is not essential to all aesthetic quality, since the aesthetic experience contains material sources of satisfaction as well as structural; it *is* essential, however, to a work of art.) A formal value is a satisfaction of interest in the work aroused by the work. A Beethoven coda is enjoyed as a coda; hearing it exemplifies perfectly what Aristotle called an end: that which is naturally after something, as its necessary consequent, and with nothing else after it—when Beethoven has done, there is nothing more to be said.

A *style* is *formalist* when formal values are especially marked in it—as with John Dryden, Franz Joseph Haydn, or Piet Mondrian; on the other hand, there are styles which rely rather on expressive and decorative values (§77), form remaining fluid and even inchoate, as with James Joyce, Jackson Pollock, and John Cage.

Quite distinct from the form of a work of art is its *shape:* the physical attributes and their relationships by virtue of which the work has the form it does. Form depends not only on shape but also on what the shapes represent and express; the shape is the purely relational basis of form. The shape of each verse in a sonnet, for instance, is iambic pentameter; what form it has also depends on the meanings of just those words in just that sequence. The shape is suggested by the following patterns of stresses:

When I have fears that I may cease to be
When to the sessions of sweet silent thought

The form of these lines, however, is much better conveyed by

When I have fears that I may cease to be
When to the sessions of sweet silent thought

Many constancies or regularities of shape can be discerned. Such recurrent shapes, when they exhibit conventional simplifications, are *stylizations.* They distinguish the arts of a particular culture, genre, school, artist, or period in the work of the artist. Egyptian wall painting, classical ballet, haiku poetry, Mozart sonatas, and Picasso's blue period are all highly stylized. Marked stylization is often the basis of parody as well as of identification and subsequent interpretation. We must not confuse stylization with another constancy which can serve as a basis of identification, known as a formula. *Formula art* relies on a recognizable shape regardless of whether, in the context of those materials, the shape evokes an aesthetic experience. The formula does not manifest a style but only presents stereotypes. Its regularities mark a recurrence, but not of an aesthetic experience; they allow for recognition, but not for aesthetic perception (§78). Formulas are characteristic of the popular arts—movie westerns, rock group dance tunes, calendar nudes and landscapes.

Form has been singled out by some aesthetic theories as the basic element in art, in terms of which art as such is to be understood. Such theories are *formalist aesthetics.* Formalism as a philosophy of art is not to be confused with an emphasis on formal values as a style of art; formalist art can be appreciated without subscribing to a formalist aesthetics. Such an aesthetic holds that art has no significance except by way of form, so that the material and content of art is aesthetically irrelevant, or at best quite secondary. There is a strong strain of formalism in the aesthetics of both Plato and Aristotle, in the former because of his metaphysics of abstract ideas and in the latter because of his interests in biology and organic unity; both may have been influenced, as aestheticians often are, by the distinctive qualities of the art of their milieu, which was rich in formal values.

The formalist insistence on ruling out of the aesthetic domain what is important in morals, politics, religion, and other "life interests," as formalism calls them, contradicts the actual role of art in all cultures. Modern formalists like Roger Fry and Clive Bell speak of "*significant* form," opening the door to considerations of meaning and content. Formalism makes an important contribution to the philosophy of art in emphasizing the detachment in the aesthetic experience as against didactic uses of art, and in pointing out the blunder of localizing aesthetic quality in what a work depicts.

As a philosophy of art, formalism may be traced to the epoch-making discovery of the Pythagoreans that sounds experienced as harmonies are produced by strings whose lengths are in simple arithmetical proportions. The generalization suggests itself that all perceived beauty and even goodness rest on a similar abstract, mathematical basis. In the Pythagorean spirit theorists have recurrently called attention to "the golden section," which divides a whole in such proportions that the lesser is to the greater as the greater is to the sum of the two, the whole. Although the name is recent, the concept was known to the Greeks and has played a part in painting and architecture from the Parthenon to Le Corbusier. The significance of this or any other formula for the creation or understanding of art is dubious. In giving specificity to formalist aesthetics, however, it stimulated many investigations of form and proportion in the human body and elsewhere, in accord with such definitions of beauty as the Thomist "splendor of form shining on the proportioned parts of matter." The studies in geometrical optics and in related fields by artists like Leonardo and Michelangelo attest to the imaginative use genius can make of mathematical precision.

Theories of form have usually taken their departure from biology rather than from mathematics (in some cases combining the two, as in D'Arcy Thompson's treatise, *On Growth and Form*). Poetry and drama, Aristotle said in his *Poetics,* should have "all the organic unity of a living creature," a view already expressed in Plato's *Phaedrus,* where the point is added that the parts of a discourse, like the body, head, and feet of a living creature, should be "adapted to one another and to the whole." This *organic unity* is contrasted with the uniformity of sheer repetitiveness; the unity of the whole is superimposed on the parts.

That there are differences among the parts is what allows them to be adapted to one another and to the whole. They enter into an order because of such differences, some components dominating over others on the basis of the intrinsic order of sensory qualities as orange is between red and yellow, or one pitch is higher than another, or on the basis of differences in size, scale, frequency, intensity, or centrality. A certain equality in the significance of the parts is also characteristic of form, or else certain phases of the experience would have value only as means to something yet to come rather than always being also ends in themselves. There is in aesthetics an aristocratic principle providing an orderliness in the work of art—some elements are more significant than others; a corresponding democratic principle—that all the elements have a part to play—gives to art a quality of diffuse richness.

Form cannot be static; as generalized plot, it follows a path of unfolding or development. Two sorts of forces mark out this path. *Harmony* is the mutual support which diverse components of a work of art provide, each intensifying the effect produced by the other. Movement on the basis of harmonies gives the work a quality of coherence. Components may be contrapuntal, contrasting yet remaining in balance. Movement on the basis of such balanced contrasts is *rhythm*, sudden interruptions and reinstatements of the rhythm characterizing dramatic development. *Symmetry* is the formal quality of balance between contrastive elements—balance in form, not correspondence of shape. Aestheticians sometimes speak of "dynamic symmetry" to emphasize this point; dynamic symmetry is rhythm caught in action. More detailed analyses of form quickly call for different specifications for different arts.

What are forms *of*? What matter or content does the form have?

77. The Substance of Art

Suppose that form could somehow exist in itself, either as an abstract entity, like a Platonic Idea, or as a psychological conception—a thought in the mind of God or in the mind of the artist. For it to be shared by others it would need material embodiment; few art forms are meant to remain wholly private. Without concreteness, though the form may be eternal in itself or in the mind of God, it would not continue to be accessible to the artist. There are ephemeral art forms, like *ikebana,* whose flowers fade, and Navajo sand paintings, destroyed before sunset on the day of the ceremony in which they figure. By and large, however, art is meant to endure. Matter makes it possible for art to be both public and permanent.

Idealist aestheticians like Plato and like Benedetto Croce in the present century were reluctant to concede to matter anything more than this incidental role. Matter, however, does much more than just preserve and transmit art; it makes form possible to start with. Aesthetic experience is of physical objects and events; even our fantasies derive from what lies outside the mind. Imagination is creative, but the creative impulse defines itself in material forms. Degas remarked to the symbolist poet Stéphane Mallarmé that he himself should have been a poet, for every day he had hundreds of ideas for poems; to which Mallarmé replied, "Poems, my friend, are not made of ideas, but of words." If we do not have the words we do not yet have the idea.

A word is an abstraction (§9) not identical with the marks or sounds embodying it; the words "we do not" occur twice in the preceding sentence, but there are not six words involved, only three. Peirce would say that there are six tokens, two tokens of each of three types; the word "word" may refer either to type or to token. Corresponding distinctions must be made with regard to the material embodiments of the arts. A poem, a symphony, or a play is a type, existing in innumerable tokens (each reading or performance); what range of variation is acceptable for it still to be *that* work of art is a problem with regard to semantic tokens as well. A sufficiently shared deviation in an idiolect makes for a distinctive dialect, and sufficiently different dialects constitute different languages. Problems of the proper interpretation of a work of art and of the limits and requirements of creative interpretation have been overshadowed in much contemporary aesthetics by puzzles as to the ontological identity of the work of art.

The art token, a physical occurrence, is the *art object;* the art type, which delimits a possible range of aesthetic experiences, is the *work of art.* Some works of art can be defined by only one standard object, as in the case of architecture, although there may be wide variation in the perspectives in which the object is experienced. In other arts one object may be standard while other objects allow for nearly identical works of art, as in the case of lithographs and fine reproductions. In still other cases an indefinite multiplicity of objects is more or less specified, each work depending on a supplementary act of creation (apart from the creativity involved in every aesthetic response); here we speak of the "interpretative arts," like music and theater.

The art object has a shape; form belongs to the work of art, since form depends on the interpretation or performance. When the matter, the physical stuff, of an art object is considered in its capability of sustaining form it is a *medium.* Art objects consist of matter or material processes; works of art exist in a medium. The resources of the medium depend not only on the properties of the corresponding matter but also on the skills and inspiration of the artist and the creative imagination of the respondent. Matter remains fundamental, setting the conditions for the emergence of an aesthetic experience.

Abstractly, matter and form are as inseparable as are relations and what they relate; concretely, they may be dissociated in varying degrees. In the degree to which they are dissociated, what we have is not form but a *formula,* as the shape imposed on the matter resists the emergence of an integrated aesthetic experience. On the one hand, the matter is experienced as crude and unformed; on the other hand, the pretense to form is seen as shallow and flimsy. The union of matter and form so dear to critics is, in part, a kind of honesty or genuineness in the use to which the matter is being put, as contrasted with the striving for the cheap effect which can be achieved by deception. Many homes in southern California are equipped with fireplaces of tin, painted to look like marble, and containing gas-burning "logs."

Functionalism as an aesthetic theory ("form follows function") is unacceptably narrow in its conception of the functions art can perform. As a school of architecture and design it made undeniable contributions with its insistence on respecting the demands of the materials being used. Structural members of a building need not be hidden, nor is the perception of the structure to be distorted by fake beams and pillars which support nothing. Functionalism, too, generated its own formulas—streamlining, for instance, makes no sense in the design of objects like typewriters and flatirons, which are not meant to move at high speeds.

The creation of art consists in the transformation of matter—so shaping matter as to bring about the emergence of form. Matter goes its own way and does not yield to our wishes just for the asking. The artist must, first of all, be a craftsman, skilled in bending matter to his will; the root sense of the term "art" is skill or craft. It is in this sense that there is a cumulativeness in art, so that it can be taught. Our achievements in art are not greater than those of ages long before, but our technology has steadily progressed. The artist must master techniques already developed and learn the solutions to problems former artists faced. In our neoromantic perspectives, beginning art students are likely to protest instruction with the plea, "I have it here, inside!" to which the rejoinder must recurrently be made, "You must have it there, on the tip of your brush!"

The achievement of the artist lies not only in mastering old techniques but also in developing new ones, in revealing new possibilities in the materials, and in exploring new materials. The artist's skill allows him to transform matter in accord with human purposes—to attain not an external end, as in other uses of technology, but an end internal to the experience of the matter so transformed. Nietzsche sees in art another expression of what he takes to be a pervasive will to power. A superlative work of art is properly identified as a "masterpiece," something worthy of having been created by a master as contrasted with the work of an apprentice, and even more as the sense of having been created by an artist who has mastered his craft.

The aesthetic response may include appreciation of the artist's skill; in some aesthetic theories, like those of ancient India, such appreciation is given a central place in the response. Skill can claim so much attention as to interfere with the integrated aesthetic experience rather than enhance it. This is likely to happen in the interpretative arts, when what would otherwise be *artistry* degenerates into *virtuosity*—technical perfection displayed without regard to what it contributes to the work of art. Virtuosity may be enjoyed, as we enjoy the performance of a juggler or an acrobat; but such enjoyment is dissociated from the other values in the aesthetic experience.

That the ends of art are internal to the aesthetic experience has been made the basis of an invidious distinction between the fine arts and the crafts, the useful or industrial arts. In Plato, as often in the present day, the distinction is drawn between the liberal arts and the mechanical arts; medieval Europe and the Asian cultures did not mark out a domain of fine arts. There is no reason, other than social prejudice or aesthetic preconception, to suppose that what is useful cannot also be beautiful; on the contrary, adaptiveness to an external end can itself provide aesthetic quality, as the functionalists insisted. Only intermittently, in decadent periods, is a category of fine art separated out, and the prizing of aesthetic quality throughout experience replaced by an aestheticism for which isolated aesthetic experience is the sole locus of meaning and worth. It is one thing to make of every situation an occasion for aesthetic quality; it is quite another to seek in every situation only a rarefied essence called "beauty," which has been emptied of all other values—moral, political, religious, or utilitarian.

Corresponding to the matter of which the art object consists is the *perceptual material* which makes up the work of art, the experienced quality of matter. The columns of the Parthenon, as physical objects, bulge slightly in the center, but they are perceived as straight; if they were straight in physical fact, they would be seen as concave. Abstract formal structures may lack material altogether; a chess game can be played without boards or men, nor are the players necessarily visualizing them. Such indifference to perceptual material is not characteristic of art.

Heard melodies are sweet, but those unheard
Are sweeter; therefore, ye soft pipes, play on;
Not to the sensual ear, but, more endeared,
Pipe to the spirit ditties of no tone.
—"Ode on a Grecian Urn"

These spirit ditties are not music, and not especially dear to Keats, in spite of what he says, if we are to judge by the care he gives to the sounds of his own poetry.

What actually goes on in art with regard to perceptual material is rendered in this haiku:

Plum blossoms! True,
Really to know them, "One's own heart"–
But one's own nose too!

However much flowers are romanticized, without color and scent there would be little to build on. It is the perceptual materials we enjoy first, throughout the domain of the arts. Color is well known to add considerably to the box-office appeal of any movie (I shall say something shortly about its aesthetic relevance). Whatever other values art may have, it provides sensory delight. There are hedonist aesthetic theories which focus on this component of the aesthetic experience (§78); puritancial hostility to the arts has the same basis.

Perceptual material enjoyed without regard to its form is *decorative;* objects which have only decorative value, and no formal value, are *decorations.* Just as in formalist art formal values predominate, in decorative art decorative values are marked—a rich texture of sensory material, as in the work of Berlioz and Matisse, and in the architecture typified by the shrine at Nikko and the temples of Bangkok. There is a corresponding possibility of complex form dissociated from perceptual material; such form is *ornamen-*

tal, as in the gardens where hedges are clipped into geometrical shapes, or Moghul architecture, like the Taj Mahal, where stone flowers are inlaid in marble.

The substance of the arts must be described not only in terms of perceptual material but also in terms of *expressive content.* The nature of expression in general is a topic which belongs to semantics (§10); expression is basic to all contexts in which meaning is involved. Art is almost universally acknowledged to be one such context; only an extreme formalist or aesthete might deny it. Meanings are not only involved in the literary arts; semantic categories are used with reference to other arts as well. Painting may involve important iconographic elements, and we speak of "understanding" music, which is the paradigm of the abstract arts.

Among aestheticians, the more idealist and metaphysical theorists have emphasized a content in art, as distinct from both its form and its perceptual material. The Neoplatonist Plotinus describes beauty as "rather a light which plays over the symmetry of things than the symmetry itself"; Hegel speaks of beauty as "the shining of the Idea through matter"; Coleridge characterizes painting as the "intermediate somewhat between a thought and a thing." Artists themselves often refuse to acknowledge that their art means anything; yet they are likely to insist that their work is not a merely physical structure nor only a representation of one. Whistler called the portrait of his mother "Arrangement in Grey and Black," but the picture presents more than empty forms. This something more is not what is being represented—a lady seated in a chair—but the expressive content of the representation in just those materials having just that form.

Content, like form and material, is one of the components of every work of art. Every work is to some degree expressive, as every work presents some measure of formal and decorative values. *Expressionism* as a school or style is characterized by expressive content of a particular kind—melancholic and even agonized. As a type of aesthetic theory, expressionism may not only focus on expressive content, just as formalist aesthetics focuses on form; it may also emphasize certain functions of art for both the artist and his society (§79). Content is what Braque called the poetical quality in art, all that captures imagination and ignites emotion. When the fifteenth-century Japanese painter Sesshu was a boy, he was tied to a post in the courtyard of the temple where he was serving for some act of disobedience. With his toes he drew in the dust mice so animated that they came to life and, gnawing at the cords which bound him, set him free. In similar stories about other artists, the horses they paint gallop out of the picture. Expression brings the work of art to life.

That all art has expressive quality does not imply that art must mean something in the sense of carrying us to something outside the work of art. Expression is intrinsic to the aesthetic situation. The expressive content is experienced as a quality of the perceptual material then and there presented. Art, though not superficial, is a matter of surfaces; the *aesthetic surface* lies deep. Gestalt psychologists have spoken of a related phenomenon which they call "physiognomic perception," from processes like recognizing the expressions in a face. They give the example of the artificial words "takete" and "maluma"; if we are told that one of them means "sharp" and the other "round" we have no doubt which should be which. Linguists have spoken of such "phonetic symbolism" in actual languages. Here the sounds are perceived as having certain intrinsic attributes which sounds might actually have. Expressive quality is not so restricted, however; perceptual material may be experienced as having the attributes of human action and passion—the foam is "cruel" and the wind "lazy." John Ruskin referred to such perceptions as involving *the pathetic fallacy* (from the root meaning of "pathetic" as pertaining to feeling); there is nothing fallacious about the perception if it is taken for what it is—the recognition of an expressive quality and not the attribution of actual feelings.

Whatever has expressive quality may be called a *symbol,* since such a quality can serve for expression and communication. Unlike other modes of symbolization, the expressive symbol carries us beyond the symbol only to return us to the immediate experience. An expressive symbol is translucent; a certain light shines through and shapes are shadowed forth, but our attention is caught by the surface on which the shadows are cast. When Macbeth says that his bloody hand will "the multitudinous seas incarnadine," the thought of making the oceans red is evoked, but the sound of the words themselves echoes in our minds like waves beating on a distant shore. There is an arresting effect in all expressive quality; when symbols become wholly transparent, because of overfamiliarity or because we exploit their meanings for extrinsic ends, they lose their expressiveness.

Expressiveness is doubly involved in *metaphor.* The metaphor itself—say, "a sea of troubles"—is a set of words with a literal meaning (there are pictorial metaphors as well, whose literal meaning is something represented). The metaphor has a *subject,* what the metaphor applies to (in this case, troubles), and—to follow the usage of I. A. Richards—a *vehicle* (in this case, the sea) which conveys the metaphoric meaning. Embodied in the vehicle is a certain expressive quality, the *tenor* of the metaphor (in this case, the sea as all-encompassing, uncontrollable, irresistible, and so on). The tenor is not something first experienced in responding to the metaphor but is brought to mind from previous experiences of the vehicle. The *point* of the metaphor is that the tenor characterizes the subject (the troubles are all-encompassing, uncontrollable, and the rest). The characteristics of the subject which makes the metaphor appropriate constitute the *ground* of the metaphor, while the characteristics of the vehicle by virtue of which it has the tenor it does is the *basis* of the metaphor. The relation of the basis to the subject distinguishes the kinds of metaphors or figures of speech.

Fundamentally, the ground of every metaphor is a similarity between subject and vehicle, in respect to the tenor expressively embodied in the vehicle. If experience does not present us with such an expressive quality, or with the corresponding characteristic of the apparently very different subject, the metaphor is felt to be inappropriate. For this reason Aristotle speaks of metaphor as a mark of genius, since a good metaphor "implies an intuitive perception of the similarity in dissimilars." This complex interplay of meanings and expressiveness, in addition to the expressive qualities of the words of the metaphor, gives the metaphor, and not only its vehicle, expressive quality.

A literal statement of the metaphorical content is a *paraphrase* of the metaphor. However accurate the paraphrase, it always lacks expressive quality, just because of its literalness. Expressed quality is subtle and fluid, so that metaphoric meanings are characteristically embedded in a network of integrative ambiguity (§8). The point of the metaphor can be more or less plainly stated, but not its expressive content; if the content shrinks to coincide with the point (for instance, by always being used just to make that point), there is no longer any expressiveness, the metaphor is dead, and a new literal meaning has been born. For such reasons no work of art can be translated; since the translation uses other materials than the original it will differ from the original in its own perceived qualities, and so can provide only a more or less adequate paraphrase. (It has been remarked that "furze" and "gorse" are the only pair of words in the English language which are expressively as well as semantically equivalent—which may give comfort to translators of Robert Burns but scarcely to anyone else.)

What is expressed by an expressive symbol is by no means arbitrary, adventitious, or private. Expressive quality is projected onto its embodiment only in the sense of the pathetic fallacy, not in the sense of projective ambiguity (§12). Like all meanings, expressive content is rule-bound (§10).

> HAMLET. Do you see yonder cloud, that's almost in shape of a camel?
> POLONIUS. By the mass, and 'tis like a camel, indeed.
> HAMLET. Methinks, it is like a weasel.
> POLONIUS. It is back'd like a weasel.
> HAMLET. Or, like a whale?
> POLONIUS. Very like a whale.

Polonius is only humoring a madman, as he supposes; artists cannot expect to be so indulged. William Blake's images of the tiger burning bright in the forests of the night and of the meek and mild little lamb depend significantly for their poetic effectiveness on the perceived qualities of those animals and not on any personal associations, whether his or the reader's. Conventional factors may be at work as well as natural properties; there are cultural differences in responses even to shapes and colors, to say nothing of concrete objects and events. Whether natural or conventional, expressive meanings are given in social experience and are not individually imposed.

Several sources of expressive quality can be identified. If the work has referential meaning, as in the literary arts or representational painting, this meaning may contribute to what is expressed (§80). The events narrated in *War and Peace,* like those depicted in Goya's war drawings, effect the expressed content of the respective works. Expressiveness may be based on the sheer physical properties of the matter employed, as something of the timeless majesty of ancient Egyptian sculpture depends on the unaging hardness of the diorite from which the figures are carved. Where expressive quality is conspicuously at variance with the properties of the underlying matter we speak of *frosting,* characteristic of what is aptly called wedding-cake architecture or of papier-mâché monsters. Art is always a matter of surfaces, but there is a crucial difference, aesthetically, between a veneer and a patina: the veneer has been laid on by artifice, while in the patina the matter itself is expressive.

By and large, it is neither external reference nor self-contained matter which is responsible for expressive quality, but the perceptual material of the work of art. If there is a referential meaning, the sound must seem an echo to the sense, as Pope has it. Sound dissociated from sense—as often with Swinburne, to say nothing of the jingles of ad men—makes expression shallow or gives it the effect of being forced. The material may have decorative value, but it is used unaesthetically if it provides no ground for expressive quality. Color may add to our sensory enjoyment of a film; it is used very differently in Laurence Olivier's *Henry V,* when the resplendent costumes of the French nobles at the battle of Agincourt are afterwards displayed splashed with dirt and blood. The pianist and wit, Oscar Levant, once said of Hollywood that underneath all that false tinsel is—real tinsel.

Above all, material is expressive because of the form it sustains. In art, matter is transformed in order to make it expressive. Where form is elaborated without regard to resulting expressive quality, it is a mere refinement, a formality in the pejorative sense. On the other hand, an expressive effect not grounded in form is likely to be mere sensationalism, like Andy Warhol's painting of an electric chair, surrealist eyes being slashed, and the formless brutality of much screen violence. Music, which comes closest of the major arts to being purely formal, is the most expressive of the arts. We do not hear Bach's music as religious because it is so often played in church; it is played there because it is religious music—it is so understood and responded to. In rhythms and melodies, said Aristotle, we have "the most realistic representations" (mimesis) of anger, benevolence, and the like. "Melodies have the power of representing character in themselves. There seems to be a sort of kinship of harmonies and rhythms to our souls." Perhaps this is because they are movements, he says, as actions also are—an idea developed in our own day by Susanne Langer and other aestheticians. Whatever the reason, music, like all the arts, is a structure of expressive meanings. How do such structures come about, and how do we respond to them?

78. Creation and Response

Art is significant because thought went into its making; it speaks to us because the artist had something to say. The artist has not simply indulged a wish-fulfilling fantasy: the primary process, as psychoanalysts call the generative impulse of such fantasies, has been subjected to a secondary elaboration, reworked in the interests of realism and rationality. If the creative vision is to result in art rather than remain a tenuous and evanescent dream, it must be objectified, given substance in a material embodiment. Wordsworth's characterization of poetry (in the preface to *Lyrical Ballads*) applies to all art: it is "the spontaneous overflow of powerful feelings," the product of "emotion recollected in tranquillity." What happens during the state of tranquillity differentiates art from dream and fantasy. That is when the artist is taking thought and exercising his skill, transforming the materials provided by an inner sensibility so that they do not remain private and confused.

This is why the outpourings of madness, in words or in paint, have so little artistic merit. Too disordered to structure aesthetic experience, they are intelligible only as symptoms with clinical significance, not as symbols with an intrinsic meaning presented in the immediacy of expressive quality. The notion that art is the product of neurosis is more widespread among belle-lettrists than among psychiatrists. The creation of art, like all else we do, may serve the needs of the artist's psyche (§79); but the skills which come into play in the creative process are a measure of the health of the psyche, not its illness.

A weaker variant of the notion that art is produced by neurosis traces art instead to an "artistic temperament": overemotional, unstable, self-centered. The modicum of truth in this stereotype is more relevant to sociology than to psychology or aesthetics. The social structure may assign the artist a place only on the fringes of society, where life-styles are by definition unconventional; the resulting freedom from conventional restraints, though these are likely to have been self-indulgent eccentricity. The artist is autonomous, but for just that reason he is not merely rebellious; sensitive, but not irritable; a dreamer, but uncompromisingly realistic in his relations with his materials. Artists live in Bohemia only when Philistia has no place for creativity.

The stereotype of the artistic temperament is sustained by the continuing impact of the Platonist dualism of thought and feeling (§49). The artist is distinguished not so much by his capacity for feeling as by his ability to unite thought and feeling. His skill lies in bringing about such a union, but there is nothing to unite if there has been no thought to start with. The artist's skill is not mindlessly physical; it is intellectual, unless that term is given a prejudicially narrow sense. "One paints," said Michelangelo, "not with one's hand, but with one's brain." The intellectual effort underlying creativity is marked in the work of artists as diverse as Leonardo, Goethe, and Beethoven. The point of departure for art is emotion, but it is a point of departure after all. Science, too, may originate in a passionate interest; for both art and science the question is what critical faculties are brought to bear on our impulses. The artist, like the scientist, confronts problems, has ideas as to how they might be solved, tries out those ideas, testing them in his own experience, and offers them at last for general acceptance.

Intellectual effort is needed not only to produce form but also to endow materials with expressive content. When someone says that he has an idea which he can't put into words, he has not yet thought it through; this is as true for the use of words in poetry as in science. The principle was stated by the spokesman for neoclassicism, the seventeenth-century French critic, Nicolas Boileau-Despréaux, in his *Art of Poetry:*

> *As your idea's clear, or else obscure,*
> *The expression follows, perfect or impure;*
> *What we conceive with ease we can express;*
> *Words to the notion flow with readiness.*

(His poetry is inferior to the doctrine he expounds here.)

Wordsworth's distinction between "imagination" and "fancy" points to another locus of intellectual effort in art. Fancy is capricious, undisciplined, arbitrary, while imagination looks to the objective ground for its metaphors as well as to the demands imposed by what has already been incorporated in the work. Similar considerations apply to ideas to be expressed in sounds or colors, for what is involved is not semantic meaning but expressive content. There is a chess maxim that any idea is better than just "wood pushing." Thoughtlessness produces neither form nor expression, but only formulas and academic art (§83).

In Edgar Lee Masters' poem on silence already quoted (§10), the old soldier relives the battle in which he lost his leg, but to the curious boy who asked how he lost it he can say only, "A bear bit it off."

> *. . . if he could describe it all*
> *He would be an artist.*
> *But if he were an artist there would be deeper wounds*
> *Which he could not describe.*

Every skill has its limits; what lies beyond we call *inspiration*. Artistic creation is very different from routine, unfeeling production, however carefully planned and skillfully executed. Otherwise the result can be seen to be artificial rather than artistic, something contrived, mechanical, calculated. Children's art, though often imaginative, is likely to fail aesthetically because the thought in it is too little developed to be infused with imagination. The child's drawing of a figure is blatantly a conceptual construction, the various parts, joints, and features being represented as childishly conceived, not as they enter into structured and expressive perceptual experience. (It is illuminating to compare the childlike but thought-out creations of, say, Paul Klee or Lewis Carroll with actual childish productions.) In science, too, creativity calls for inspiration to raise it above pedestrian fact gathering and unimaginative "research."

Because inspiration transcends what can be attained by reason, Plato speaks of it as a kind of madness, which "taking hold of a delicate and virgin soul, and there inspiring frenzy, awakens poetry." Without such inspiration, he continues (in the *Phaedrus*) there can be no art: "He who, having no touch of the Muses' madness in his soul, comes to the door and thinks that he will get into the temple by the help of skill—he, I say, and his poetry are not admitted." The lunatic, the lover, and the poet may be of imagination all compact, an imagination which bodies forth the forms of things unknown, as we are both told and shown in *Midsummer Night's Dream;* but the poet does not suffer from hallucinations or delusions. There are two kinds of madness, as Plato rightly pointed out: one produced by human infirmity, the other a divine release of the soul. Aristotle contents himself with attributing to the poet either a special gift for assuming the mood required by poetry, or else a touch of madness: being, in the moment of inspiration, actually beside himself with emotion.

The source of inspiration is experienced as lying outside the self. The artist, like the prophet, is a channel for an outer reality which flows through him. The Muses are emblematic of the external source of inspiration. "Art," Andre Gide once said, "is a collaboration between God and the artist, and the less the artist does the better." Divine creativity evokes the image of Michelangelo's *Creation of Adam:* there is a touch of God's finger, and the clay comes to life. The myth of the blind artist may contain an element of punishment for the hubris of sharing in the creative work of the gods; it also symbolizes the inwardness of the vision on which creativity depends.

The divine madness is the work of the unconscious. That the artist must rely on inspiration as well as skill means that the whole psyche—indeed, the whole person—must throw itself into the creative act. The work of art is born of the tension between untrammeled impulse and what Plato called "the yoke of custom and convention"; creation is the result of the consummatory embrace of wish and reality. Much of the creative process takes place beneath the level of awareness, with regard to both skill and inspiration. The genius builds better than he knows, and not knowing how he did it. There is in all art a certain freshness and spontaneity; what is heavy and labored is also lifeless. This is not to say that art comes into being fully formed, even for a Mozart. A period of gestation is part of every creative process, however spontaneous it appears to be; the seeming effortlessness is a mark only of the complete integration of all the resources the artist is drawing on.

What enters into the creation of a work of art has its counterpart in the aesthetic response, which might be spoken of as re-creation. First of all, a certain approach to the art object is needed, a spirit of contemplation without which the aesthetic experience cannot unfold. The *aesthetic attitude* is a receptivity combined with detachment. Aesthetic interest differs from intellectual and practical interests not in content but in the relation of that content to external concerns. A painter, geologist, and engineer looking out over a valley may be occupied with much the same materials, though their thoughts are directed to different ends. The painter does not care only about textures and colors; El Greco's *View of Toledo* and Sung landscapes are hardly patterns of meaningless shapes. The painter aims at an expressive embodiment of the scene, while the geologist seeks to account for it, and the engineer to make use of it. In taking up the aesthetic attitude, we contemplate the valley and neither explain nor exploit it.

Essential to the aesthetic attitude is the continual shift in *psychic distance,* from the wholly committed to the wholly detached. At one pole is the pragmatic and utilitarian: an erotic subject becomes pornographic, a political content becomes propaganda, a religious quality becomes idol worship. At the other pole is the theoretical and conceptual response to the art object as we calculate its market value, conjecture who produced it, and analyze the basis of its effects. The aesthetic attitude does not lie just betwixt and between; in the middle distance our response would be conveyed by saying of the work of art that it is "interesting." Instead, we are continually being caught up by the work, then brought up short before we exploit it for external ends; on the other side, ideas are continually generated, but idle curiosity recurrently gives way to passionate involvement.

The frame of the work and stylizations within the frame maintain distance, heightening awareness of the difference between art and reality. Were we aware only of the difference, an aesthetic experience would hardly emerge. Art has a life of its own and defines its own reality. The first-century Greek aesthetician Longinus, author of an influential work, *On the Sublime,* stated a widely accepted assessment: "Art is perfect when it seems to be nature, and nature hits the mark when she contains art hidden within her." There is in all art an artful artlessness, the compelling directness of reality.

Kant saw the commonality of art and nature in their manifestation of purpose, the difference being that in art no external end is served, so that the aesthetic is defined by *purposiveness without a purpose.* This may be a necessary condition for art, incorporating the emphasis on the shifts of psychic distance characteristic of the aesthetic attitude; it cannot be a sufficient condition. The point is demonstrated by an ingenious novelty, a small cubical box equipped with a switch; when the switch is pressed, the top of the box opens, a mechanical arm reaches out, turns off the switch, then withdraws into the box, which then closes once more. Contemporary anti-art has produced a number of similar devices—complicated machines which operate to accomplish nothing, and others designed to destroy themselves.

Psychic distance differentiates the aesthetic response from uncritical rapture. The artist's intellectual activity is matched, in kind, not in degree, by an identical component in the subsequent aesthetic experience. We *understand* the work of art, grasping both its form and its expressive content; the work does more than trigger an abstract emotion or evoke a vague mood. Art is meaningless for the philistine because it is unintelligible to him; it may elude the so-called art-lover as well, because it overwhelms him with awareness of his own feelings rather than invite him to contemplate the objectification of feeling.

Art does not, in fact, produce the emotions it expresses; we are not saddened by the sad music but enjoy it. Aristotle speaks of tragedy as arousing pity and fear, but he goes on to say that the incidents arousing them accomplish the *catharsis* of such emotions. Whether art does have a cathartic effect has been debated ever since. What is beyond dispute is that however intense the feelings experienced in the aesthetic situation, there is enough detachment from them so as to keep us from acting on them as we would in other contexts.

We are not always so detached, and it is not easy to say how much involvement is compatible with the aesthetic attitude. The eighth-century Buddhist painter Wu Tao-tzu depicted hell so fearfully that butchers and fishmongers abandoned their occupations so that they would no longer violate the Buddhist injunction against taking life. Children not only shout warnings to the threatened hero but sometimes try to interfere with the course of the dramatic action. They are victims of the *aesthetic illusion* in which the distinction between art and reality is dissolved. A measure of illusion is intrinsic to art.

The aesthetic response is a recreation of the work of art, not a reconstruction of it, as though we were solving a puzzle or deciphering a code. We may initially engage in such reconstructions as we learn to understand a new genre, style, or art form. But the language of art must be sufficiently transparent for us to respond to what is being said and not only to the saying of it, or else we are not experiencing anything aesthetic. It is all very well to admire the artist's skill, but his skill is most effective when we are aware instead of what he directed it to. When Cicero spoke, men acclaimed his oratory, but when Demosthenes spoke, they said, "Come, let us march against Philip of Macedon!" Art persuades us of its reality.

This feature of the aesthetic response, contrasting with psychic distance, is known as *empathy*. The work of art takes hold of the responder, compelling his imagination and engaging his feelings. In his essay on the sublime, Edmund Burke speaks of "that sinking, that melting, that languor which is the characteristic effect of the beautiful." Such feelings are more characteristic of romanticism than of the aesthetic response in general, but some such element of feeling there must be: to say of something that it leaves me cold is to say that I cannot respond to it as a work of art. The aesthetic response is an affective, organic, even a motor response; it is full of tension and excitement, as well as a melting languorousness.

This is especially the outcome of the apprehension of form. "Rhythm and harmony," said Plato, "find their way to the inmost soul, and take strongest hold on it." Studies of physiological changes in members of movie audiences showed that their excitement was greatest when they were viewing not scenes of sex or violence but running horses. "I galloped, Direk galloped, we galloped all three" may only have the sound of folk-ballad doggerel, albeit from as skilled a hand as Browning's; but the rhythm it exploits plays a part in masterpieces of all media.

In literature and the representational arts, empathy is also evoked by the subject matter. There is a close relation between art and fantasy both as to origin and as to subsequent function. Tales of adventure and romance, of loyalty and courage, of struggle and achievement provide vicarious fulfillments. Human frailties and failures are also irresistibly acknowledged as our own. The role of the unconscious in artistic creation provides art with universal themes and archetypes, for in the depths of his being there is little that distinguishes one person from another.

Empathy is not limited to the effect of form or of subject matter: it is evoked by the whole substance of the work of art and by every feature of the aesthetic situation. Several different sorts of *identification* play a part. We identify with other members of the audience, our responses mutually reinforcing one another—telecasts employ the gimmickry of sound tracks of laughter so that the viewer will not feel alone in his response. We identify with the artist, sharing his triumph in the mastery of materials, his pride of workmanship, his joy in the exercise of skill, his humility as a vessel of inspiration. (For such reasons scenes of natural beauty may elicit religious feeling as we reach out for identification with the artist.) We identify with the characters and the situations represented, with the heroes and the victories as well as with the villains and the defeats.

Fundamentally, we make a metaphysical identification, experiencing ourselves as living in the world which the work of art defines by its form and expression. Wu Tao-tzu painted a landscape on a wall of the palace. "Look!" he said to the emperor; "there is a cave at the foot of this mountain." He clapped his hands, the door of the cave opened, and saying, "Permit me to show you the way," the artist passed within; the whole scene then faded and vanished. Unless we too pass within, the world of art remains closed to us.

We ourselves must take the step; the artist can only show us the way. We can enjoy only a work of art of our own recreation. An aesthetic experience is the result of a *creative interpretation* of a work of art, not of a predetermined, mechanical reaction to it. What distinguishes an aesthetic *response* from a *reaction* to art is just this creative aspect: in making a response we are reacting in part to stimuli which we ourselves provide—our own imagination is at work. Just as there are shifts in psychic distance in the response, there are shifts in *psychic level,* from the purly cerebral, controlled, and calculated to the spontaneous, impulsive, and imaginative. These two poles correspond to the artist's skill and inspiration respectively. In making a creative interpretation of the work of art, the responder shares with the artist something of both his skill and his inspiration. "To understand," the modern painter Vasili Kandinski once said, "is to elevate the onlooker to the artist's level"—and to bring him down to the artist's psychic level as well.

The interpretative arts, which require a performing artist, manifest to a marked degree a requirement of all the arts. We are all performing as artists in every aesthetic experience; the quality of the experience depends on the level of our artistry. Every art object is only the score of the music to be heard, the book of the play yet to be produced, a sketch, a blueprint. Baudelaire remarked about the paintings of Corot, "A work of art need not be finished to be complete." It *cannot* be finished, except in the process of creative interpretation. The sense of finish which distinguishes, say, the Dutch masters from the French impressionists, Haydn from Chopin, and Heine from Baudelaire is not what is involved here, as was made explicit by another contemporary painter, Marcel Duchamp: "The creative act is not performed by the artist alone; the spectator brings the work into contact with the external world by deciphering and interpreting its inner qualifications." The same thing was said more simply by Emerson: "The good reader makes the good book."

The question arises whether he may not be reading into the book something not there; the answer is that what characterizes a work of art is integrative ambiguity, not projective ambiguity (§12). If the artist does too little, he invites projection; if he does too much, he discourages a creative interpretation. Movie music may only signalize to the audience what their mood should be while viewing a certain scene; without the funereal harmonies, say, they might suppose that the victim of a murderous attack was not fatally wounded. That each respondent might have his own associations to a work of art is irrelevant to the question of whether responses are creative or projective. Expressive quality is quite different from disembodied and adventitious associations. The *Ride of the Valkyrie* may be associated with a battle, a storm, or lovemaking (program notes aside), but all three responses may testify to the apprehension of the quality of a tempestuous crescendo. An interpretation which did not distinguish between Wagner's Valkyries and Handel's Water Music, say, would be a pure projection.

That the content of a work of art is rich, complex, and embodied in its perceptual materials makes adequate interpretation far from easy, while the fact that expressive quality is immediately given makes it seem deceptively simple. The naive viewer supposes that he has seen at once all there is to see, while informed critics debate endlessly the acceptability of their interpretations. Expressive clarity is as hard to achieve as the referential, and perhaps harder to learn to grasp. The aesthetic response can appropriately make use of a guidebook, but not of a code book: there is no dictionary of expressive content, except what is tacitly built up through the cumulation of sensitive and informed awareness of the culture, style, school, artist, and the work. Iconology is another matter, for there can indeed be a dictionary of referential or representational symbols—saints are depicted with characteristic accoutrements, and the position of the Buddha's fingers, hands, or feet indicate events or functions of his ministry. But such iconographs guide the apprehension of expressive content; they do not predetermine what is there to be apprehended.

Clear-cut misinterpretations are occasionally unmistakable. Virgil was regarded for some time as having been a crypto-Christian, so that his *Aeneid* was misread in terms of a supposed covert Christian teaching. This is why Dante chose the figure of Virgil to be his guide through the *Inferno;* in turn, readers ignorant of this tradition would be misreading Dante, just as they would if they knew none of the characters and events of Dante's times which enter into his work.

Biography is a useful guide to proper interpretation, but only a guide, for what matters to the aesthetic response is not what the artist meant to say but what, in fact, he did say—what he succeeded in embodying in the work. Other guides to interpretation are provided by the referential elements, by the natural expressiveness of the perceptual materials, by the conventions governing in that period and style, by the coherence of the interpretation (how well it fits other parts of the work, or other closely related works), and by its comprehensiveness (how much it does justice to).

The problems here have much in common with those of historical interpretation (§68), with the added complications of an interplay with judgments of aesthetic value (§83).

Creative interpretation presupposes that it really is the work which is being responded to, not some secondary or superficial image of it. Essential to an aesthetic response to an art object is a process of *aesthetic perception,* contrasted with a mere *recognition* of the object. Aesthetic perception involves attention, a sensory exploitation of everything available to the senses, an active looking at the object rather than a passive receptivity. Aesthetic perception makes subtle sensory discriminations far beyond the slight cues which suffice for recognition. It is faithful to what is actually being presented, not to what we antecedently presume to be the perceptual content—grass does not always look green nor the sky blue, certainly not in paintings. Ancient Chinese artists speak for all their successors in complaining that people look at pictures not with their eyes but with their ears; the complaint may refer as much to the effect of reputation as of perceptual hearsay.

As in science, so also in art, fidelity to the data of experience is fundamental. In art the reward for that fidelity is more immediate and more easily recognizable; it is the pleasure which the work of art can provide if it is responded to with sensitivity and awareness. Pleasure is a necessary mark of the occurrence of an aesthetic experience; if it is not pleasurable it is not an aesthetic experience. (Those who regard pleasure as evil or suspect (§61) condemn or distrust art.) Pleasure does not show that the experience is aesthetic; there is no distinctively aesthetic pleasure except by reference to the characteristics of what produces it. In an aesthetic experience we are taking pleasure in form, in perceptual materials, in expressive content, and in the unfolding of our own creativity. Any other sources of satisfaction are extra-aesthetic, though they may supplement as well as threaten the aesthetic satisfactions.

Aesthetic pleasure has a characteristic structure. It is a summation of cumulating satisfactions, successively more fulfilling; there are riches everywhere, something to be enjoyed wherever we turn. The progressive intensification of pleasure does not go so far as satiation, or even worse, transformation into pain, the likely outcomes outside an aesthetic context. Attention is restructured and shifted before that happens.

Most important, aesthetic pleasure stands in a special relationship to all else that matters to us. The pleasure derives significantly from interests and concerns outside the aesthetic situation; what is left of art if it is emptied of all that relates to love, death, religious fulfillments, and the whole host of our lesser concerns? Yet the pleasure is intrinsic to the aesthetic situation or else the art is only being exploited for other ends. In the course of the aesthetic experience we become aware not of our own pleasure but of something to be prized. Santayana proposed that beauty be defined as "pleasure regarded as the quality of a thing, pleasure objectified." Perhaps we should go further: in the aesthetic experience it is the work of art which enjoys being seen, heard, or read.

79. Functions of Art

Art gives pleasure, but few would regard this as its primary function, the ground of its significance. One of the most popular positions is that the chief function of art is to provide the artist—and derivatively, his audience—with a channel for self-expression. This is a modern view, no doubt connected with the modern ideology of individualism. Art was characterized by Oscar Wilde as "the most intense mode of individualism that the world has known," and many of his contemporaries would have agreed with him. In the most general sense (§10), all expression is of the self, or of something within the self, some thought or feeling. In the view I am now considering, art is seen as preeminently a device for expressing one's most deeply felt concerns. "Whatever of mine has become known," Goethe wrote in his *Poetry and Truth,* "represents only the fragments of a great confession." Art is *self-expression.*

Certainly the artist is intimately involved with his work; unless he gives of himself unstintingly in the act of creation, the result will not have any life of its own. In the course of creation the artist serves as his own first critic; the work he creates must satisfy him first of all, and so it reflects his tastes and standards. The history of art provides innumerable instances of works destroyed or suppressed by their creators, dissatisfied with the outcome. The style is the man, at least in the sense that each artist, if he has attained a style at all, has one peculiar to himself, on pain of being purely imitative (§83). Flaubert pointed out that "style, all by itself, is an absolute way of looking at things." When we also take into account referential and representational subject matters, the role of art as self-expression is unmistakable. The artist's religious commitments and ambivalent feelings about his native city are more explicit but no more significant for James Joyce and Dublin than for Dante and the city of Florence; scenes of the artist's childhood are vividly portrayed by Mark Twain and Marc Chagall; nationalist loyalties are marked in the music of Elgar, Chopin, and Grieg.

In the aesthetics of romanticism, self-expression provides the only metaphysically acceptable locus of aesthetic value. Johann Gottlieb Fichte's philosophy of art typifies the view that beauty exists not in the world but in the beautiful soul, and that art is the manifestation of that spiritual beauty. Hegel, too, held that only the soul and what pertains to it is beautiful. Many aesthetic theories, like those of Plato, Plotinus, and Asian aestheticians, connect art with the life of the spirit. Romanticism is distinctive in assigning the spirit a subjective locus. Art is not conceived as a ladder to the empyrean, in the imagery of Plato's *Symposium,* but as a disclosure of what is already present here below. Even as religious a philosopher of art as Tolstoy maintained that whatever the artist depicts, we seek and see only the artist's soul. What we appreciate in art is only the artist's sensitivity, his depth of feeling.

Just as aesthetic theory suffers from preoccupation with one or another dimension of the work of art, so also is it distorted by focusing attention on a period or style. Until modern times and in most cultures art was produced anonymously, often in cooperative efforts; under these circumstances it would not occur to anyone to think of art as essentially a means of self-expression. What we know as personal art—art identified with an individual, not just by signature but also by content—emerged in the Renaissance. The image of the lonely artist turning to his work for fulfillment has few actualizations before Rembrandt. In the Asian cultures artists throughout the centuries have been integrated in their societies as professionals practicing the skills of a traditional craft, not as individuals driven to give expression to their unique personalities.

Psychology corroborates what sociology discloses. The self is complex and many-sided (§46); at best we must say not that the style is the man but the *men*. All artists show in some measure—what is so striking, say, in Picasso—developments and even radical changes in style. It is not easy to maintain that there are correspondingly basic changes in the self supposedly being expressed. Keats went so far as to say that the poet has no identity of his own, but is "continually informing and filling some other body"; every artist is to some degree an actor, identifying himself with the roles being defined in the work he is creating. This may be one of his reasons for creating it. Poetry, said T. S. Eliot, "is not the expression of personality, but an escape from personality." If there is a self expressed in art, it is a self expanded and transformed by the creation of the work of art.

Eliot has drawn attention to the circumstance that what is important to the poet may be quite unimportant to him as a person, and something which matters a great deal to the human being may be insignificant to the artist. Inferences about the artist's personality based on characteristics of his work are highly unreliable. The music of both Mozart and Mendelssohn is gay and lighthearted, but the one man lived a much sadder life than the other; moral tales bordering on sentimentality were written by both Wilde and Tolstoy, but the men were very different from one another in morals; most of Dostoevski's novels contain a character suffering from epilepsy, as Dostoevski did, but most of Steinbeck's novels contain a character who is feebleminded—shall we not recoil from the inference? Great art is more likely to embody a universal content than an idiosyncratic one; we all have in us something of Hamlet and Macbeth, Puck and Falstaff; but what do we know of the man Shakespeare?

There is a verbalistic device, of a type we have already encountered several times, by which the conception of art as self-expression can be made to accommodate all these considerations. It is to reinterpret the thesis so that it becomes true though tautological, while it relies for significance on an equivocal meaning which is almost certainly false. The reinterpretation is achieved by introducing a distinction between the *empirical personality* and the *aesthetic personality* of the artist. The former is the real man, the whole man, while the latter is the abstract entity constructed from what is to be found in the work of art. It is undeniable that every work of art expresses the aesthetic personality of the artist, for this is true by definition. The question is what relation the aesthetic personality has to the empirical one, and to this question no simple answer is acceptable.

We may draw a corresponding distinction between the *motive* for a work of art and the *purpose* in it. The motive belongs to the artist, as the person he is, in his situation; the purpose is a goal in the work of art—a theme as to content, a motif as to form, a genre as to materials. Self-expression can hardly be recognized as a universal or even as the most common aesthetic motive. Fra Angelico and Fra Filippo Lippi both painted religious pictures; the former did so as a mode of worship, but the latter was hardly concerned about the greater glory of God. Samuel Johnson hurriedly wrote *Rasselas* to pay his mother's funeral costs; its theme of the vanity of man's search for happiness is reminiscent of Voltaire's *Candide*, written in the same year but hardly from the same motive. At an early stage in Braque's career, he painted a number of pictures with very wide but short frames, because he was bound by contract to turn over to a certain dealer all his paintings of more usual dimensions; other artists followed suit because they were exploiting given formulas. Purposes and motives are as varying in their relations as are aesthetic and empirical personalities. Many novels, to give a final illustration, have been written with the purpose of exposing the decadence of a certain society; the motive may have been personal, as for Proust; reformist, as for Dickens; or religious, as for Dostoevski.

There are certain genres, like lyric poetry, in which the purpose *is* self-expression; but there is narrative poetry too. Mahler's last symphony is generally recognized to be autobiographical, but his symphonic mentors, Beethoven and Bruckner, were far less subjective. Artists do not, in general, impose their own needs onto the work but submit to the demands made on them by the work. Shakespeare and Moliére wrote their plays as they did to meet the requirements of the theater companies with which they were associated; they are not for that reason unprincipled hacks. What the work calls for is largely grounded in the requirements of form and expressiveness, not in projections of the artist's personal urgencies. Ibsen wrote by having constructed a small model of his set, with appropriately placed dolls; then, he said, he watched and listened, and simply recorded what was happening. This is no more just introspection than is a mathematician's exploration of the consequences of his postulates.

Reaching out to what lies beyond the self is intrinsic to the act of creation. Even when what impels us, both motive and purpose, is rooted in our own basic needs, art is always directed outward. The oldest and, psychologically speaking, perhaps the most fundamental of the arts is dance. In every culture the dance is associated with the needs for food, safety, and sex; it is not the dancer's hunger which is expressed, however, but the hunting of the animal or the growth of the crops; not his individual lust but the social rituals of courtship and fertility; not his personal hatred or courage but the triumphs of the coming battle.

Art needs its materials, even if it be only the artist's body; the Creator Himself worked on clay. The outcome of the creative act is likely to owe more to the material than to the artist's idiosyncrasies. Thereby, it is dependent also on the state of the art, on technologies far removed from personal considerations. Bach's music owes much to the physics of the well-tempered clavichord, as Leonardo's painting does to geometrical optics, and Fellini's films to the resources of the camera.

The theory of art as self-expression founders on the ineluctable fact that a work of art is not a private, insubstantial vision but something conveyed in public material, formed and expressive. The art object is not a constellation of symptoms, a repository of data on which inferences are to be based; it is the locus of a structured and meaningful experience. What matters to that experience is neither the artist's motive for creating nor the purpose of the creation; it is the *intent* of the work—the expressive form and content embodied in it. Whatever the artist meant to say, knowingly or unknowingly, all that is aesthetically relevant is what in fact he *did* say. For art, it is not sincerity that matters but the *ring* of sincerity. Philosophy of art, like the aesthetic experience, must begin and end with the work of art itself.

More plausible than romanticist aesthetics are the philosophies of art which conceive of art as *social expression*. The artist is not revealing his own soul; he is, rather, the spokesman for his age. Artists, like Hamlet's players, are "the abstracts, and brief chronicles, of the time." What Hamlet says later in the scene about the theater is applied by many aestheticians to all the arts—their end "both at the first, and now, was, and is, to hold, as it were, the mirror up to nature; to show virtue her own feature, scorn her own image, and the very age and body of the time, his form and pressure." The artist is sensitive to his milieu and skilled in embodying its qualities in his materials.

Whitehead, in his essay on *Symbolism*, gives as an example the contrast between Whitman's continental reference to "the wide unconscious scenery of my land" and Shakespeare's insular line, "this little world, this precious stone set in the silver sea." The social history of England can be traced without difficulty in English literature: the fourteenth-century social types in Chaucer; the Elizabethan middle class in Shakespeare and Ben Jonson; the vigorous bourgeoisie of the eighteenth century in Fielding and Smollett; the Victorian strata in Thackeray and Dickens; and the decadent aristocracy in Evelyn Waugh and P. G. Wodehouse. Painting is also a rich repository of social history: the worldliness of the Renaissance in Titian; the self-confidence of the rising Dutch republic in Frans Hals; the torments of the Counter-Reformation in El Greco; the social ferment of the thirties in the Mexican muralists; and into our postindustrial age, with innumerable examples.

The objections to the theory of art as social expression are essentially the same as the objections to the theory of self-expression. Just as we can identify an aesthetic personality which differs from the empirical personality, an *aesthetic society* is sometimes all that can be said to be expressed. A good deal of folk art, for example, is nowadays deliberately created by sophisticated artists to have just that expressive quality—not only by popular singers but also by serious writers like Carl Sandburg and Stephen Vincent Benét. Art not only reflects its culture but is one of the defining components of the culture, and apart from the dogmas of historical materialism (§66), is one of the factors shaping it. Cubist painting, atonal music, the theater of the absurd, and other such styles do not merely express modernity; they constitute it.

Society is far from homogeneous; it contains many subcultures. We would have to say that each work of art expresses its own society, just as each finds its own audience. In this way the notion of an aesthetic society generates a tautology, just as with the aesthetic personality. That every work expresses its own subculture is true by definition. Empirically, different strands must be acknowledged. Robert Frost and E. E. Cummings, with all their enormous differences of style, were both New England poets of the early decades of the twentieth century. New Hampshire is not Massachusetts, but it is possible to distinguish counties too, towns within them, and so tautologously down to the individuality of each work or art. The distinguished art historian, Bernard Berenson, has concluded: "Protest against the theory of the milieu is no longer necessary. The classical instance is Perugino, the most Arcadian of artists, but living in the most turbulent and sanguinary town in Italy and himself an assassin. Art more ecstatic than in early fifteenth-century Siena the Western world has never seen. Yet Siena at that time was notoriously sensual, ribald, and factious."

Social expression is limited as much as self-expression is by the constraints imposed by materials, by techniques, by the state of the art and its traditions, and by the requirements of the work. The significance of art owes more to its expression of a common humanity than of a particular historical situation. *Don Quixote* marks the end of the age of chivalry, but the predicaments of man's aspirations, which make up its substance, are not limited to feudalism. Capitalist institutions are the background for Jane Austen and Dostoevski, but it is universal human relations their artistry captures. Art may provide evidence for the interpretations of the sociologist and historian, but in doing so it is not functioning aesthetically; how well it performs one function has no direct bearing on its performance in the other. If we are to have museums, it might be well to insist on a sharper separation than is usual between art and archaeology. Age alone does not guarantee beauty, and a magnificent work of art has more than once turned out to have been created, even with willful deception, centuries later than had been supposed.

A popular conception of the function of art, one which combines elements of the aesthetics of self-expression and of social expression, is that art serves as a means of *communication*. The best-known exponent of this philosophy of art is Tolstoy, who, in his *What Is Art*, defines art as follows: "Art is a human activity consisting in this, that one man consciously, by means of certain external signs, hands on to others feeling he has lived through, and that other people are infected by these feelings, and also experience them." Art does involve a sharing of feeling—with the artist, and with others who are responding appreciatively. But this is neither sufficient nor necessary for the experience to be aesthetic. Feelings are also shared as a result of advertising and political speeches; the huckster and demagogue consciously, by means of certain signs, hand on to others feelings they have lived through. On the other hand, the artist may embody contents he has *not* lived through and may have no conscious desire to hand something over to others; Wilde's position that "a true artist takes no notice whatever of the public" is a typical overstatement, but it cannot be casually denied.

The aesthetics of communication is likely, as in Tolstoy's case, to adopt the stance of a didactic moralism. The claim is that art communicates certain ennobling feelings; what fails to do so, or communicates a content of another kind, is rejected as lacking in aesthetic value. Tolstoy's own artistic assessments, just because of their consistency, reveal the weakness of his position. He speaks disparagingly of Baudelaire, Ibsen, Liszt, Wagner, and Brahms; includes among "the highest art flowing from love of God and man" Dickens' *Christmas Carol* and Stowe's *Uncle Tom's Cabin;* regards Shakespeare's works as "detestable"; identifies as "the most universal and therefore[!] the most excellent artist of modern times"—Molière; and consigns his own work to "the category of bad art" except for one or two of his moral short stories. Aestheticians, like artists, need not be good critics; but an aesthetics is surely untenable if its principles do not allow for even a moderate consonance with what experience discloses of aesthetic worth.

The root error in the philosophy of art as communication is that communication implies something communicated—a *message* conceived as existing antecedently to and independently of the work of art which communicates the message. But the content of art is not separable from the work; it is fused with the perceived qualities of just those materials having just that form. Art does not mean anything in the sense of transmitting a signal; in *this* sense even the most magnificent music is all noise. The sense in which art does communicate, Dewey pointed out, is that it makes something common. The experience is shared as well as the values both *of* the experience and embodied *in* the experience. This is a consequence of the successful performance of the aesthetic function; it does not define the function itself.

In this political age, when the arrangement of soccer matches is a matter of foreign policy and hair-styles raise presumptions of revolutionary intent—it is not surprising that art, too, is seen in terms of its political significance. The aesthetics of communication has been redefined by Marxist and other philosophies of art in political terms. Art created with political motive or having a marked political effect may be called *directive art* (avoiding the prejudicial label, "propaganda art"). The jibe that the directive artist has sold his birthright for a pot of message scores a hit, unquestionably; it is not to be lightly dismissed. Picasso was expressing artistic as well as political convictions when he said that painting is not made to decorate apartments but is "an instrument of war." It has certainly been a powerful weapon in the hands of Goya, Daumier, and Siqueiros, as literature has been for Dickens, Zola, Ibsen, and Solzhenitsyn.

The effectiveness of directive art, however, may well be extra-aesthetic if not downright anti-aesthetic. The rigid traditionalist, Boileau-Despréaux, wrote,

I like an author who reforms the age,
And keeps the right decorum of the stage

The question is how the artist can do both simultaneously. Psychic distance does not strengthen the reformist impulse; on the other hand, close involvement with the work can make for catharsis, providing a substitute for action rather than a stimulus to it. If action does follow from the response to a work of art, the action is likely to relate to referential or associational subjects, not to expressed content. Music, for instance, being abstract, is usually directive only if it is martial, or by way of a program, as in the words of a song or a libretto. *Finlandia,* the *1812 Overture,* and *Pomp and Circumstance* are, I suppose, political; for aesthetics what is important is that their nationalism is expressed, not externally associated with the music, as in the case of most anthems. But such aesthetic value as those compositions have surely does not depend on their political significance.

80. Art as Truth

Since Horace's *Art Poetica,* the functions of art have been described as being to instruct or to entertain, to provide profit or pleasure. Functions like expressing the self or society, communicating, or directing our emotional responses may sometimes and to some degree be performed by the arts; but these functions are not essentially aesthetic. However, art is always and everywhere something to be enjoyed. The view that art serves as an escape from harsh realities, an idle song for an empty hour, is known as *the doctrine of the inn,* formulated by Epictetus in a comparison of art with philosophy: an inn is pleasant for a night, but not a place to spend one's life. In small doses art is an embellishment to life, but man has more earnest purposes to fulfill.

Art does have something in common with *play.* It is an exercise of skills dissociated from any external end, practiced for the satisfactions then and there provided, while the illusion is cultivated that we are engaged with realities. There is in art the same outpouring of excess energies which we find in play, the joyous creativity which the Hindus know as *lila:* the playfulness which engenders the universe, as symbolized in the dance of Siva. This is very different from escaping life; it is, rather, throwing ourselves more wholeheartedly into life by not taking it so seriously. Art heightens our sensibilities rather than deadening them—the effect produced by the anodynes provided in the mass media. Art so conceived, though prized, is being denied any great importance; worse yet, this philosophy leaves every other domain of life somber and joyless. John Dewey, for all his instrumentalism, had a more vivid sense of inherent value than many of his critics: "If art is the beauty parlor of civilization, neither is secure."

One of the perennial issues in the philosophy of art centers on whether art has any deep significance. In his *Symposium,* Plato argues that the sense of beauty prefigures our awareness of the divine, that art provides a ladder on which we may mount from material existence to ideal reality. If, on the lower rungs of this ladder, art is no more than illusion, it serves even so to carry us upward to the contemplation of things as they are. This is the philosophy in Picasso's dictum that art is the lie which makes us realize the truth. Because of art we see the truth more clearly, appreciate its depth and subtlety, commit ourselves to its pursuit and service. Poetry, Wordsworth said, in his preface to *Lyrical Ballads,* is "the breath and finer spirit of all knowledge; it is the impassioned expression in the countenance of all science."

In the Platonist tradition running through Neoplatonism, romanticism, and contemporary neoromantic currents of thought, art is considered as more than a doorway to the truth through which we may pass to recognize and embrace her. Art is itself a source of truth, improving on what is yielded by more prosaic modes of apprehension. For Plato, what is seen by the mind's eye is closer to reality than the objects of sense, as geometrical figures are only suggested by the mathematician's drawings, not truly presented in them. Art supplies what is lacking in the world of sense—ideals, things as they should be, which is how things really are if the truth were known. "The poet grows in effect another nature," Philip Sidney wrote in his *Apology for Poetry,* "making things either better than nature brings forth, or quite new forms." In our own day, Eugene Ionesco takes a similar position: "I have always thought that the truth of fiction is more profound, more charged with meaning, than everyday reality. Realism falls short of reality. It shrinks it, attenuates it, falsifies it; it does not take into account our basic truths and our fundamental obsessions: love, death, astonishment. It presents man in a reduced and estranged perspective."

From the time of the Greeks, knowledge in the fullest sense (as contrasted with what they called "mere opinion") was held to be always of universals. For this reason Aristotle accounted poetry as more philosophical—"scientific," we might say today—than history, because history deals only with particular people and events while poetry presents the type, and the *kind* of thing that would happen to such characters. Samuel Johnson delcares, "the business of a poet is to examine, not the individual, but the species; to remark general properties and large appearances." The truths of science are ephemeral, changing with shifting viewpoints and experiences, and with the matters of fact which it takes into account, while the truth in art is eternal and universally acknowledged.

The late medieval conflict between faith and reason was compromised by some philosophers with a doctrine of "two truths" by which there was a disengagement of forces between science and religion. As science began to come into its own, it was subjected to a new attack from another direction; art now claimed knowledge which eludes empirical cognition. Vico, in a work called the *New Science,* held: "Poetic truth is a metaphysical truth. If physical truth is not in conformity with it, then physical truth must be reputed false." Eventually, the Platonist tradition came full circle: not mathematics but poetry is the queen of the sciences. Shelley's *Defense of*

Poetry maintains that poetry is "at once the center and circumference of all knowledge; it is that which comprehends all science, and that to which all science must be referred. It is at the same time the root and blossom of all other systems of thought." A philosophical basis for such a position was offered by the post-Kantian idealist Friedrich Schelling: Art is "the highest means of knowledge" because it is "the uniting of the subjective with the objective, of nature with reason, of the unconscious with the conscious."

Plato himself had an ambivalent attitude towards art. Though an appreciation of physical beauty may bring us closer to an apprehension of the world of Ideas, in itself art is a tissue of illusion. It presents us with "imitations thrice removed," for concrete objects are "imitations," crude embodiments of the abstract Ideas, which in turn, imitate the Idea of the Good, while art presents only imitations of the objects. Some say that Plato had wanted to be a sculptor and never quite resolved an internal conflict. Whatever his personal motives, his position makes art both divine and foolish. The poet is compared to the priest and prophet, but it is a dubious honor. None of them owes his eminence to knowledge; if they do utter truths, it is by divine inspiration and not to be credited to their own effort. The artist's truth is, in any case, partial and impure. Aristotle is more straightforward: poets are men who have learned the art of "telling lies skillfully."

There is certainly *some* sense in which art is the domain of illusion; to fail to distinguish art from reality is certainly to be deceived. There are undeniably fewer things in heaven and earth than are dreamed of in our art: gargoyles, angels, mythical monsters of all sorts, the divinities of Hindu sculpture and the demons of Hieronymus Bosch; the fantasies of *A Midsummer Night's Dream* and *Through the Looking-Glass;* the perspectives of impressionism, cubism, and surrealism; the subjectivisms bordering on delusion of black comedy and the theater of the absurd. Science is objective, impersonal, public; art—it is argued—is subjective, personal, private, occupied not with fact but with feeling, presenting not realities but a vision of an unreal world, but one closer to the heart's desire.

Contemporary analytic philosophy has elaborated this position in compelling detail, with its dualistic semantics and emotive theory of value (§53). The elaboration has been largely negative, however, fully articulating the nature of scientific truth and characterizing art only as being all that science is not. Truth is conveyed in propositions, cognitive in content and in function. Art, on the other hand, if it involves meanings at all, is a matter of emotive meaning. Its function is not to explain anything but to evoke or express feeling. It gives pleasure, but we need not be so intellectualist as to suppose that the only pleasure worthy of man is the joy of grasping a truth. If it is truth we want, we must turn to science; poetry is only a halfway house; it fills in, as Hobbes put it, till science takes over. Boileau-Despréaux was mistaken in supposing that the philosophy of Descartes (the scientific philosophy of his day) had "cut the throat of poetry." What it did was destroy the poet's pretensions. We need not follow Plato in expelling poets from our ideal republic—provided they keep their place.

Whatever be said about the functions of art, we cannot do justice to its content if we speak only of emotive meaning. We must give some account of the part played in art, if it is not wholly abstract, by its referential dimension; art often tells a story or represents something. Everything represented or referred to in art is its *subject matter* for which there may or may not be a real *subject* as a point of departure. Questions about the truth in art require clarification of the aesthetics of subject matter.

A work of art is *abstract* in the degree to which the subject matter departs from the subject not by way of distortion but along the referential dimension, away from subject matter. Sometimes the word "abstract" is used to mean what has *no* subject matter; "nonobjective" is a less equivocal term with this meaning. Virtually all art, if it has subject matter, is to some degree abstract: words can tell only part of the story, painted representations are in fact two-dimensional, sculptures are likely to lack the color and texture of what they represent. Abstract art is not distinctively modern but is found in ancient and even neolithic works; geometrical abstractions are characteristic of primitive art the world over.

The opposite of "abstract" is *realistic*, the subject matter more or less closely resembling its subject. Zeuxis, a Greek painter of about the fourth century B.C., made a fortune with his realistic painting. In a contest, he is said to have painted a bunch of grapes so realistically that birds flew down to peck at them, whereupon he asked his opponent, Parrhasius, to draw the curtain hanging over *his* painting, only to discover that the curtain had been painted on. Apelles painted a horse so realistically that live horses, seeing it, neighed; Philip IV is said to have mistaken a Velasquez portrait for a man. A number of nineteenth-century American painters were accomplished illusionists, producing *trompe l'oeil* art ("deceiving the eye"). By way of precisionists like Stuart Davis it moved into contemporary pop art. The extreme of realism, using subjects themselves as a subject matter, was attained in surrealist assemblages, functionalist constructions, and junk art (a label, not an appraisal).

Value is often attached to the quality of realism, an appraisal hard to understand since the invention of the camera, save, perhaps, as an appreciation of virtuosity (§77). This ground of valuation of art is the *photographic fallacy*. There is nothing wrong with such appraisals of, say, a police "artist's" sketch of a wanted criminal. A painter, however, who is asked, "What's it supposed to be?" would do well to reply, "A painting—something to look at," rather than, as expected, to identify a subject. The photographic fallacy is allied to the blunder of attaching too much importance to titles, as though the most serious failure of a work is not to present realistically the subject designated in the title; we might call it *titular criticism*. Constantin Brancusi's abstraction in polished bronze, called "Bird in Space," was denied the status of art object and was declared dutiable as imported metal, the customs official explaining: "He claims that this represents a bird. If you met such a bird out shooting, would you fire?" But if you met such a statue, would you look? Surrealist and other modern painters should have put an end forever to titular criticism; the following titles are all works by well-known artists:

Accommodations of Desire (Salvador Dali)
Bride Stripped Bare by Her Bachelors, Even (Marcel Duchamp)
Broadway Boogie-Woogie (Piet Mondrian)
Dance, Monster, to My Soft Song (Paul Klee)
Disasters of Mysticism (Sebastian Matta)
Human Lunar Spectral (Hans Arp)
King and Queen Traversed by Swift Nudes (Duchamp)
Mama, Come Quick, Papa Is Wounded (Yves Tanguy)
Nostalgia of the Infinite (Giorgio De Chirico)
Objects Arranged According to the Law of Chance or Navels (Arp)
Person Throwing a Stone at a Bird (Joan Miró)
Slowly toward the North (Tanguy)
Soft Construction with Boiled Beans: Premonition of Civil War (Dali)
Treacher (Or Perfidy) of Images (René Magritte)
Triumph of Wit over Misfortune (Klee)
Two Children Are Threatened by a Nightingale (Max Ernst)
Virtual Virtue (Jean Dubuffet)

There is a species of art where realism is unquestionably important—scientific illustration. Audubon's birds are certainly not without aesthetic quality, owing in part to the meticulousness of their details. There is a crucial difference between Howard Pyle's realistic illustrations for the tales of Robin Hood and King Arthur and John Tenniel's illustrations for the books of Lewis Carroll. In the former, it is the subject matter which captures our attention, while in the latter case the illustration interests us. The one may evoke emotion, while the other is itself the object of emotion. The former is *evocative illustration*, as contrasted with expressive illustration; it is characteristic of popular art: erotic, nostalgic, sentimentally religious, or patriotic.

Whatever the degree of its realism, art is not merely evocative illustration. Formalists rendered a service to the appreciation of art in emphasizing the unimportance of subject matter. Roger Fry pointed to the artistry of Rembrandt's painting of a carcass in a butcher shop, and to the triviality of the fruit and crockery on a kitchen table which Cezanne was able to take as subjects for superb works of art. Painting can be altogether nonobjective, just as a composer is not limited to program music. Aristotle remarked that "the most beautiful colors laid on without order will not give one the same pleasure as a simple black-and-white sketch of a portrait." Unless "without order" means formless, this is plainly untrue, as every abstract expressionist would insist. There may be a distinctive pleasure in identifying subjects—Aristotle was a thoroughgoing intellectualist. There are works which are visual riddles, like the hidden figures in Tchelitchew's painting or the impossible architectural structures of M. S. Escher. But this is a matter of recognition, not of aesthetic perception (§78).

What enters into the aesthetic experience is neither subject nor subject matter, but the *substance* of the work of art, the formed and expressive subject matter, the embodiment of the work. To a studio visitor who complained that she had never seen a sunset like the one the artist was painting, he replied, "No, madam, but don't you wish you had!" It is not a question of art improving on nature, in the sense of the Platonists, but rather of the difference between aesthetic experience and apprehension of objects, either directly or by way of a representation.

Subject matter is not altogether irrelevant aesthetically—a view suggested by some of the formulations of formalist aesthetics. Subject matter is relevant not in itself but by way of its contribution to form and expression. A painting of the Crucifixion is very likely to have a different expressive content from a painting of the butcher shop or a wholly nonobjective painting, and its being hung upside-down would do violence to more than its form. Integration of subject matter with expressive content is not easy to achieve; deliberate incongruities between them can produce an effect of irony, of the comic, the tragic, or the absurd—an effect quite different from that of the evocative illustrations of the surrealist formulas, such as fur-lined teacups and flatirons studded with nails.

The classic doctrine of *mimesis* is easily misunderstood, especially if loosely translated as "imitation." Aristotle says of man that he is the most imitative creature in the world because he expresses things rather than because he apes them. Music is identified as the *most* mimetic of the arts, in spite of its abstractness. Realistic art is a particular species of mimesis, the reproductive. That all art is mimetic does not mean that representation is of its essence. Aristotle states a view which comes dangerously near to the photographic fallacy, that the pleasure we take in a representation is not far removed from the same feeling about the realities represented—the principle defining evocative illustration.

In this perspective, nature comes to be seen as not only providing the subject for art but also as constituting the standard of artistic excellence. "Depart not from nature," Albrecht Dürer enjoins, "neither imagine of thyself to invent aught better, for art stands firmly fixed in nature." What art adds is such a way of putting things as will make the beauty of nature more readily apparent to the human eye and the laws and purposes of nature more readily grasped by the human mind. In Pope's incomparable phrasing,

True wit is Nature to advantage dressed,
What oft was thought, but ne'er so well expressed.

. . . .

First follow Nature, and your judgment frame
By her just standard, which is still the same:
Unerring Nature! still divinely bright,
One clear, unchanged, and universal light,
Life, force, and beauty must to all impart,
At once the source, and end, and test of art.

—*Essay on Criticism*

Neoclassicist aesthetics found a basis for art criticism in the acknowledged masterpieces of antiquity ("classics") whose achievement was held to be that they disclosed nature to us. The principles promulgated by the academy, though derived from what is to be found in the classics, are justified by nature herself. To turn to Pope again:

> *Those rules of old, discovered, not devised,*
> *Are Nature still, but Nature methodised.*

A later age became aware that nature imitates art, not only because of the impact of art on culture patterns but also for a more fundamental reason. We see the world in perspectives which are more vividly articulated in art. The concept of nature cannot comprise what lies outside experience, and experiences takes as much from art as it gives. Not just the museum wall but the whole world is transformed by the artistic vision.

We can now return to the question of artistic truth. A number of different types of "truth" can be distinguished, according to their mode of signification and their aesthetic function.

Factual truth is truth in a straightforward sense about any matters of fact referred to or depicted in a work of art—whether Cortez and not Balboa discovered the Pacific (from a peak in Darien), as Keats apparently supposed, or whether Lincoln had a wart on the left or right side of his face. Factual truth is plainly of no aesthetic importance, unless the falsehood is so gross as to interfere with the psychic distance necessary to an aesthetic response. Facts are often glossed over in art, not to idealize the subject but because the gloss is aesthetically more important than the facts. Art reveals illusion to be a part of reality, deepening our awareness of the shortcomings of what we know as truth. This is the role of the masks in the plays of Euripides and O'Neill, of the relativized narratives in Pirandello's *Right You Are* and Kurasawa's *Rashomon,* and of the varied perspectives in impressionism and cubism.

Modal truth is truth so far as concerns laws rather than matters of fact. It is being "true to" the type depicted, showing people, things, and events as they would be in reality, if they were of the kind in question. Factual truth characterizes *realistic* art; modal truth, *naturalistic* art. Aristotle takes the difference between modal and factual truth to be the ground of the distinction between poetry and history: the poet's function is to describe a kind of thing that might happen, not the thing that has happened. Factual truth is unimportant, if modal truth is sufficiently present to engage our attention and evoke our empathy. It is a lesser error in an artist, Aristotle says, not to know that a hind has no horns than to produce an unrecognizable picture of one. Art helps us recognize reality; it is true to the world art discloses to a deepened perception rather than the world as we already know it to be. Even though the picture is overdrawn, the exaggeration heightens awareness of reality. This is the artistry of Molière, Dickens, Daumier, and Gogol.

Art also defines its own kinds to be true to—there is the art of the *fantastic,* as well as naturalistic art. Here a *formal truth* is at work in the sense of aesthetic coherence rather than in the strict sense of logical consistency. The language of logic is useful here because logic is so far beyond aesthetics in the subtlety and complexity of its analysis of formal structures. The artist sets down certain postulates, then derives their necessary consequences. Perhaps it is logically as well as psychologically relevant that the greatest writer of fantasy, Lewis Carroll, was by profession a mathematician. The analogy must not be pressed. What art presents is not a logical system but a formal unity. The fantasy world makes sense in its own way, partly because of its modal truth as, say, in *Gulliver's Travels,* and in Karel Capek's *The War with the Newts,* and partly because contemplation of the fantasy world provides an integrated aesthetic experience.

In *contained truth* a subject is presented in a subject matter having an appropriate expressive quality. Both factual and modal truth may be compromised or sacrificed, as in the multiarmed figures of Hindu deities or the horns on Michelangelo's *Moses* (derived from a mistranslation of the Hebrew word "keren," which means a beam or ray of light as well as a horn, but revealing an incomparable aesthetic sensibility). These falsifications enhance certain qualities of the images, far from making the subjects absurd or grotesque, and thereby contribute to their contained truth.

Religious opposition to imagery in the Iconoclastic Controversy of the eighth and ninth centuries was resolved in the Second Council of Nicaea on the principle that the honor which is paid to the image passes to that which the image represents. For this it is necessary that the image show what it represents in such a way as to reveal how worthy of being honored it truly is. The Maitreya Buddha of Koryuji, the Avalokitesvara of Ajanta, and the paintings of the Sistine Chapel are imbued with unmistakable religious feeling. Whether they are taken to exemplify contained truth clearly depends on the apprehension of the relevant expressive qualitites, as well as on the convictions according to which the qualities are or are not appropriate. What is controversial here is not art but religion; in other instances of a putative contained truth what is at issue is a question of politics or morals.

Finally, there is an *embodied truth* of a work of art, the appropriateness of its expressive content to the whole of our experience rather than to a particular subject. We judge a work of art to embody truth insofar as the world of the work fits our world, has become our world. No referential or representational subject matter is needed; music can embody truth as effectively as literature and painting. Beethoven, as much as Shakespeare and Rembrandt, can evoke the conviction, "Yes, that's how it is in human life!" Aristotle is struck by the circumstance that objects, painful to see in themselves, may nevertheless be represented in art we enjoy. His explanation of our delight in seeing the picture is that we are at the same time learning, "gathering the meaning of things." Art does allow us to gather a meaning, but not of the subjects depicted. The subjects, if they exist at all, are not of central importance. Who would wish to endure the events of a Greek tragedy, walk the agonized gardens of El Greco, or confront the monsters and corpses of *Guernica?* Art is fulfilling because of its form and expression; that the fulfillment is significant beyond the joy of the moment is what is conveyed by ascribing to art embodied truth.

Confusion of this truth with factual and modal truth, or with a contained truth about a subject, poses puzzles for aesthetics because of the role in art of distortion, exaggeration, fantasy, and other types of falsification corresponding to the various sorts of truth. One solution to the difficulty was proposed in Coleridge's formula, "the willing suspension of disbelief." This may do for a response with empathy and identification; but in maintaining psychic distance it is belief which is suspended. Are we to say that in aesthetic experience we alternate belief and disbelief? Does it help to say that we both believe and disbelieve? More to the point is what we are supposed to be believing or disbelieving. Sidney apologized for poetry with the argument that the poet never lies because he never affirms anything. Why then should he be taken seriously? If art offers only what is to be enjoyed then and there, no question of its truth can arise; but in that case it has no meaning as well. What is the significance of art?

81. The Meaning of Art

There are artists, aestheticians, and critics who hold that art has no significance, that it has nothing to do with life outside the aesthetic context. This was the position taken by the school of *l'art pour l'art*. The slogan of art for art's sake rightly emphasized the inherent value of art, as against its exploitation by politics, religion, and moralistic sentimentality. But that something has inherent value does not imply that it cannot have instrumental value as well. Ironically, art was just at that time becoming enormously valuable as a commodity, although it had for long been created on behalf of the church, the nobility, the state, and the plutocracy. It would be unjust to derogate a work of art simply because it has commercial value; everything depends on whose taste determines the price. What is true is that this is an *extra*-aesthetic value. Can nonartistic interests be intrinsic to the aesthetic situation?

The question would not even arise were it not for critical prejudice and aesthetic dogma. Form and content are intrinsic to the work of art, but they may be *derived* from without. The female nude has been prominent in painting and sculpture from the prehistoric Venus of Willendorf to Willem De Kooning; it would be foolish to pretend that this fact has nothing to do with human interest in the body. No doubt the female figure lends itself to beauties of form, but I have no doubt that if the human animal gave birth in litters we would find in six or eight breasts as much beauty as we now see in two. It is interesting to speculate on what nonobjective forms would be cultivated if man were constructed, like spiders and crabs, with radial symmetry rather than bilateral, or if our perceptual apparatus had evolved in a condition of weightlessness.

That art may have bearings on morality is not to be denied *a priori;* there is an obvious point of connection by way of subject matter. Aristotle held that to acquire the habit of being pleased or pained at representations goes a long way towards acquiring the same dispositions towards the originals. But there is a great difference, aesthetically, between the expressive substance of William Hogarth's works, such as *A Rake's Progress,* and the merely evocative sentimentality of Jean-Baptiste Greuze's *The Father's Curse* and other moralistic scenes. Plato thought that form itself had implications for morality—for instance, that simplicity in music is, as he put it, "the parent of temperance in the soul." From the time of the Greeks to the Victorian moralists aestheticians took the position that art—via its subject matter, its form, or its sensory materials—could serve the interests of morality by displaying vice as repugnant and revealing the charms of virtue: a generalization of the classic theme of the contrast between sacred and profane love. "The poet not only shows the way," wrote Philip Sidney in his *Apology for Poetry,* "but gives so sweet a prospect to the way as will entice any man to enter into it. The poet is food for the tenderest stomach, the right popular philosopher."

This argument cuts both ways. If art can entice man to virtue, it can also seduce him into vice. Art, especially the theater, was attacked by the Church Fathers Lactantius and Tertullian, by St. Jerome, St. Augustine, St. Francis, and by countless moralists in the clergy and the laity. Apart from objections to the subject matter, there is the moralistic condemnation of the sensory pleasure which art provides. Plato formulates a more basic moralistic objection to art, that it evokes emotion, which he views as a threat to the good life: "Poetry feeds and waters the passions instead of drying them up; she lets them rule, although they ought to be controlled, if mankind are ever to increase in happiness and virtue."

Art has recurrently been subject to censorship: first in regard to blasphemy, then obscenity, and, most widely today, in regard to disloyalty or "antisocial" features. Abstract arts like music are as much subject to controls as are the representational arts; in Russia, nonobjective painting is highly suspect. The counterclaim of the artist to poetic license and artistic freedom is sometimes based on the groundless presumption that art is exempt from moral or political appraisal. But censorship can be condemned on both moral and political grounds (§71).

The bearing of art on morality is more subtle than both moralists and aesthetes recognize. Art serves morality in a more general fashion than by way of a doctrinaire content like "socialist realism." It illuminates character and the human situation, widens the range of our sympathies and identifications, intensifies the sense of human worth, and can do all this by way of its expressive substance, without a referential or representational subject matter. Shelley's argument (in his *Defense of Poetry*) may be dubious psychology, but it is aesthetically sound: "A man to be greatly good must imagine intensely and comprehensively. The great instrument of moral good is the imagination; and poetry administers to the effect by acting upon the cause." There is something revolutionary in all art: every act of creation is an exercise of freedom, as is also every act of creative interpretation. The service art renders to society, Whitehead remarked, is its adventurousness —and, I might add, its continuous exemplification of the rewards which can be reaped by the spirit of adventure.

Philosophers have noted a commonality between art and morality on a more fundamental level. Art is in itself the prototype of what is most precious and most praiseworthy, and not because it leads to some extrinsic end. It is the exemplar of what makes life worth living and what man can point to in justification of human existence. It serves as such an exemplar because the form of art is the form of all value. Listening to music is an activity, Aristotle observed, which has all the qualities that something intrinsically good possesses, and the same might be said of other aesthetic experiences. Plato spells out the reason: the principle of goodness can be reduced to the law of beauty, "for measure and proportion always pass into beauty and excellence," a position echoed in our day by Whitehead's dictum that the principles of morality express the same requisites as do the canons of art.

This is not a shallow aestheticism. Not every work of art manifests generic value equally, any more than every gesture of kindness or generosity reveals the nature of the good equally. There is a quality of *greatness* in art which is called for in this connection. It is found in art which embodies the deepest and most abiding of human interests, which comprehends the entire spectrum of thought and feeling, which opens perspectives on the sweep of nature as on our innermost being, which, in short, sees life steadily and sees it whole. The eighteenth century was much occupied with what it called "the sublime" in art, which gives us a sense of our finitude, our human frailty; that this genre is of no particular interest to contemporary aestheticians may reflect the banal, petty, and self-centered preoccupations of our politics and religion more than a lack of greatness in our art. The quality of greatness is not the same as aesthetic worth. The minor arts, and minor works of art in the major media, may nevertheless exhibit aesthetic value in a superlative degree. A Chopin waltz, a De Maupassant short story, a Toulouse-Lautrec poster may not be great art, but each is excellent after its kind.

The moral significance of art, by way of its form and its content, is illuminated by a consideration of the nature of tragedy as an aesthetic genre.

Underlying all that tragedy presents is a collapse of values, the destruction of something precious. The theme is in Ophelia's line, "O, what a noble mind is here o'erthrown!" or in Antony's, "O, what a fall was there, my countrymen!" There is a sense of waste, of irremediable loss: insanity and violent death, as in *Hamlet* and *Lear;* moral collapse, as in *Macbeth, Othello,* or *Père Goriot;* lost ideals, as in *Don Quixote* and *The Wild Duck;* injustice, as in much of Euripides; lost faith, as in *The Brothers Karamazov*. Tragedy is rightly described by the schoolboy's phrase, a story with a sad ending. It confronts us with the finality of death—as in the closing scene of *Hamlet*—or with utter ruin, as at the end of *Peer Gynt*. Throughout is the bitterness of temporality, even more ineluctable than mortality: the irreversibility of time, as in *Lear;* the right moment lost forever, as in *Romeo and Juliet;* the niggardliness of time which is too little to allow either healing or forgetfulness, as in *Macbeth*. Prometheus speaks also for other tragedies than his: "Painful are these things to relate, painful is silence, and all is wretchedness."

The movement of the tragic events, as in all drama, stems from oppositions—man against fate (Oedipus), against society (Antigone), against other individuals (Lear), against himself (Hamlet). Our interest, however, is not in the struggle and its outcome, an interest which is characteristic, rather, of melodrama. Instead, our response is to the logic of events which lies in character: the tragic oppositions are among the conflicting motives within the self. It is the progressive revelation of character by way of this conflict which makes Medea, Hamlet, and Peer Gynt so memorable. Tragedy requires a tragic hero, else we have only pathos, as in *Death of a Salesman.* There must be a greatness of soul, a capacity for suffering, a strength of will, as in Aeschylus' *Prometheus,* and the *Seven against Thebes.* It is Aristotle's conception that tragic events are the consequence of a *tragic flaw* in a character otherwise noble and great—of which Macbeth and Othello are later examples—a flaw essential not to serve a narrowly moralistic sense of justice but by contrast to bring out the heroic qualities and by oppositions to intensify them.

In general, it is specific values which collapse, not value as such. An underlying moral order is presupposed: fate, God, or the gods. What happens is not a matter of poetic justice but of poetic injustice. The language of large and universal accents is used to describe intensely personal wrongs, as to Job, Agamemnon, or Othello. Human helplessness to avert the divine decree is what is painful: in the words of Euripides' Andromache, "God has undone me, and I cannot lift one hand, one hand, to save my child from death"; Gloucester says in *Lear,* "As flies to wanton boys are we to the gods, they kill us for their sport." In short, tragedy confronts us compellingly with what Nietzsche called "the terrible and questionable character of things."

Some give tragedy a moralistic interpretation, construing the tragic events as the consequence of wrongdoing. There may be a moral satisfaction in the tragic outcome, but not the petty confirmation of moral bigotry: our sympathies for the victims remain engaged. We do not gloat over Hedda Gabler, Anna Karenina, and Madame Bovary in the spirit that they got what was coming to them. The blinded Oedipus says, "Apollo was he that brought these my woes to pass, sore woes; but the hand that struck the eyes was none save mine." If Oedipus is thought to be unconsciously guilty, there are certainly other tragic victims whose fate is undeserved like Lear or Juliet, and others whose punishment, even if deserved, is out of all proportion to the wrong, as with Hamlet.

Philosophers have seen in the nature of tragedy a validation of their own doctrines. In tragedy, Hegel argued, what is evil from the standpoint of the individual is morally justified by the larger cause which is being served. Antigone's family loyalty is upheld by the punishment of Creon, but her sacrifice is necessary to uphold the more basic value of the sovereignty of the state. Tragedy also presents sufferings of the innocent, such as Cordelia, without furthering any higher cause. Schopenhauer sees in tragedy what his own philosophy espouses: a negation of the will, a calm resignation in the face of evil. Recognition of necessity, of inevitability, may make for resignation, as it did for the Stoics and for the tragic heroes of Sophocles. But there are others who remain defiant and protesting, as is often true in Aeschylus; his *Prometheus* ends with the cry, "Behold what wrongs I endure!"

Tragedy *is* a triumph rather than a defeat, but not of larger causes, stoic detachment, or anything else focused on the outcome of the story. The fulfillment, as always in art, is a matter of the expressive content, of the form which has that content. Suffering is objectified in being given form and expression, so vivid in *Lear* and *The Trojan Women;* the tragic hero objectifies not only our own ego ideals but the selves we know ourselves to be.

Tragedy does not provide the gratification of achieving our ideal, but the thwarting of aspiration is here beside the point. This is because the opposite of the tragic is not the successful or the victorious; it is the sordid, the trivial, the meaningless. The great periods of tragedy—Periclean Athens and Elizabethan London—were not times when life was seen as dark and defeated but when it was exalted with possibilities. The fulfillment of tragedy is its capacity to impose meaning—form, expression, closure—even on what most inflexibly stands opposed to human desires. Near the seacoast at Haifa is preserved as a monument a small boat which was used to land refugees illegally before the establishment of the state; the boat is called *Af Al Pi Chen*—"The Nevertheless." Israelis are also fond of another expression, *b'chol zot:* even so, in spite of that. . . . Such idioms express a sense of the tragic in life combined with a sense of its meaning and worth—a combination characteristic of the aesthetic experience of tragedy.

At the end of the *Symposium* Socrates remarks that the genius of comedy and tragedy is the same. We find in comedy as in tragedy the same reaffirmation of values which seem otherwise to be in question.

To start with, we can easily see an element of playfulness in comedy, which as a theatrical genre has its origins in the Dionysian revel. Comedy, like all art, is childlike in its dissociation from external concerns, in its carelessness, its mock seriousness in its pretenses. The pirates of Penzance demand special treatment due them as orphans; the protagonist of William Saroyan's *The Time of Your Life* unashamedly plays with toys.

As might be expected of forms connected with the worship of Dionysus there is in comedy an intermission from the sober demands of daily life. We are released from the self with its inhibitions—for instance, in a Rabelaisian defiance of the proprieties of cleanliness and continence. On the stage, comedy suspends for a time control of sexual impulses, from Aristophanes' *Lysistrata* to Kenneth Tynan's *Oh! Calcutta!* It allows for an uninhibited release of aggressive impulses as well: the clown beats everyone within reach with a symbolic, possibly phallic, club, and the jester is allowed a more savage though more sublimated attack. Gilbert and Sullivan's Mikado lingers over the image of punishing wrongdoers by boiling them in oil or melted lead, with something of the near-sadistic cruelties in Grimm's fairy tales and Charles Addams's cartoons.

There is a release not only from the self but from an oppressive external reality as well. Logic, especially as construed by Victorian presumptions of good sense, is defied by all the characters in Wonderland and behind the looking-glass, which appropriately enough reverses everything; in Peer Gynt's madhouse the madmen are reckoned as normal and the so-called sane are thought to rave. Comedy makes the conventional, not the deviant, ridiculous, as in Richard Brinsley Sheridan and Neil Simon. For once we can feel superior to the demanding, imposing, even frightening world around us. Hobbes thought that the comic gives one a sense of "sudden glory"—of ego-enhancement, we would say. A pervasive theme of comedy explodes the pretensions of pomposity of all sorts, on Penguin Island or among the opera-loving dowagers of the world of Groucho Marx.

In comedy the element of form is crucial, from "timing," as the theatrical jargon has it, to details of dramatic structure. Comedy exaggerates familiar shapes and patterns; Cyrano's nose has a long history and many counterparts. The comic artist inflates in order to deflate, as in Don Quixote, and in Mark Twain's device of putting the knights of King Arthur's court on bicycles. The rigidity of human responses is a rich source of comic effects; Henri Bergson, for metaphysical reasons, took the lapse of the organic into the mechanical as the essence of the comic. Sheer repetitiveness intensifies the comic if it does not of itself produce the quality. Arthur Schnitzler's *Reigen* ("Merry-Go-Round") presents a succession of love scenes—all the same for all their differences—in which A makes love to B, then B to C, C to D, till Z makes love once more to A. In Jean Giradoux' *Amphitryon 38*, dealing with the loves of Jupiter, the herald refuses to sound his trumpet until he knows the substance of the announcement to follow, for though his trumpet plays but one note, he must first mentally prepare an appropriate composition ending with that note; the end, he explains, is always the same—but the approach, ah, the approach!

An important technique of the comic is contrast—Falstaff followed by a diminutive page, Don Quixote accompanied by the earthy Sancho Panza; one of Chaplin's films begins with the little tramp discovered asleep in the arms of a statue just unveiled as a civic monument. Reversal of role and status is a similar technique, exploited at length in James Barrie's *The Admirable Crichton*, in Samuel Butler's *Erewhon* (the title itself is spelled backwards), and in innumerable other social satires. Many of the epigrams of Oscar Wilde and George Bernard Shaw depend on simple inversions: the difference between a caprice and a lifelong passion is that the caprice last longer; a hotel provides one with a refuge from homelife.

These contrasts and reversals are instances of a more general comic device: the surprise which does not, as in melodrama, heighten tension or bring it to closure but which leads us on only to let us down. This is what Immanuel Kant formulates as the essence of the comic: the sudden transformation of a strained expectation to—nothing. In William Kopit's *O Dad, Poor Dad,* Rosalie is wrestling with Jonathan on the bed in a seductive rape, when the closet door suddenly opens, depositing his father's corpse next to them, at which she says to Jonathan, "Stop looking at him and look at me!" Comedy offers unthinking pleasure in a world of horror.

Eugene Ionesco once confided to an interviewer that the three biggest influences on his work were Groucho, Chico, and Harpo Marx. Thereby he cut down to size the whole fabric of conventionalism which he and the Marx brothers alike were tearing to shreds. It is the world of respectability which is nonsensical. The practice of the modern theater of the absurd is not far removed from the theory of George Meredith a century ago that the comic spirit is the warning voice of common sense and sanity in a mad world.

Comedy, in the form of satire, is unexcelled as a medium of social criticism: Aristophanes scored off both Socrates and the Athenians in *The Clouds;* in *Candide* Voltaire disposed of Leibniz's easy optimism; Jonathan Swift ridiculed theological disputes with his Big-Endians and Little Endians; Heinrich Heine spoke for generations of citizens when he said of a politician of his day that the man was insane but enjoyed moments of lucidity when he was merely stupid. In Bergson's view, laughter is always the echo of a group; the comic is a defense of social unity, an enforcement of group norms, as is illustrated by what Ben Jonson and Jean Baptiste Molière did to misers and hypocrites, George Meredith to egoists, and Charles Dickens and William Makepeace Thackeray to the whole vanity fair.

Comedy is not always hostile, however, although Freudian and other theorists take it to be so. There is in the comic a component of sympathy—in dealing with Falstaff's cowardice and sensuality, or with Cyrano's beautiful soul in an ugly body. In all the world's art there are few scenes more evocative and more expressive of sympathy than Charlie Chaplin's lonely dinner party in *The Gold Rush* or Don Quixote's journey homeward, caged as a madman. Comedy, rather than attack the other, may enlarge the self, bringing awareness of other components of the self than those we readily acknowledge, and of other possibilities yet to be realized in the self—traits, patterns of action, and values we have not yet countenanced.

Laughter is the mark of our capacity for self-detachment, differentiating man from the angels, who have nothing to laugh at, and from the animals, who are incapable of seeing their own absurdity. Man is the only creature which can take a joke; the only creature which sees all creation as comic, and himself as the cream of the jest. A noble philosophic tradition holds that man is never so ridiculous as when he is taking himself seriously, and never so well worth taking seriously as when he is laughing at himself. The wise fool is a familiar figure; correspondingly, every philosopher is something of a clown (§5). Comedy transforms every failure into a success, which is the more successful the more gross the failure. To the comic spirit, the more absurd the self and the world, the more readily acceptable they become; the more trivial things are, the more significance they convey. In Leonard Andreyev's *He Who Gets Slapped* the philosopher literally becomes a clown; it is from his blows that he learns wisdom at last. Comedy brings an awareness of human failings without which we do not have a sense of being human at all. Surely one of the greatest comedies is *Don Quixote:* in this world only a madman can act like a hero, and to live with sanity takes all the heroism we can muster.

What both tragedy and comedy achieve, what is achieved by great art of all genres, is *aesthetic redemption.* The trivial in life becomes a source of delight in color and texture, the pathetic is elevated to high tragedy, the ridiculous is transformed into the richly comic. Matthew Arnold described literature as a criticism of life; so is all art, in the sense of criticism as heightening appreciation through fuller awareness. The tyranny of time is softened by the aesthetic awareness of time as an ageny of creativity, not as a merely passive and deadly receptacle—the theme explored by Marcel Proust and Thomas Mann. The past is redeemed in the eternal present of art, not only on the stage—*Life with Father* (C. S. Day), *I Remember Mama* (John Van Druten), *Our Town* (Thornton Wilder)—but also in painting, as in Marc Chagall's fantasies of his childhood, and in music, as in Sergei Prokofiev's *Classical Symphony*, or the ghostly echoes of the past in Gustav Mahler's *First Symphony*. The future presents itself, in one of the most universal themes of art, as the locus of man's endless quest: the *Odyssey* (Homer), *Parsifal* (Richard Wagner), *Pilgrim's Progress* (John Bunyan), *Moby Dick* (Herman Melville), *The Long Voyage Home* (Eugene O'Neill), *The Castle* (Franz Kafka), *The Old Man and the Sea* (Ernest Hemingway), and countless other works, in many cultures and media.

The enterprise of art, philosophers have noted, is itself a part of the quest, using these as steps. We begin with the beauties of earth, said Plato, and mount upwards to the contemplation of absolute beauty. This absolute beauty has in it something of the divine. In all societies art and religion are intimately related; art is intertwined with myth, ritual, and cultic practice. The aesthetic emotion is akin to, perhaps identical with, that which is felt when we become aware of the divine, so that the creation and response to art is a *sadhana*, a *yoga*, a link uniting man with the gods. The religious dimension is fundamental in the analysis of the aesthetic experience by the Neoplatonists, Goethe, Blake, Schopenhauer, Schiller, and many other aestheticians. The material thing becomes beautiful, said Plotinus, by sharing in the thought which flows from the One. In a typical romanticist formula Schelling characterizes beauty as "the perception of the infinite in the finite."

If the formula were taken as definition, I do not know whether it or its converse would be primary: whatever produces a sense of the divine is beautiful, or whatever is beautiful produces a sense of the divine. In either case, there is no question of art's tempering the painfulness of objective reality with the comforts of subjective illusion. Art reveals the human significance of a world which, without art, would be felt to transcend the merely human. Art does not make a heaven of earth but shows that it is the earth which is heavenly. Art does not invite us to lose ourselves in some private Eden but to find ourselves in a Paradise regained. Plato's highest assessment of the artist may be the key to the meaning of art at its greatest and best: The poets, he says, are our fathers, as it were, and conductors in wisdom. But how are we to know when art is at its best?

82. Aesthetic Judgment

Apart from its vagueness, the term "beauty" suffers from a radical ambiguity: it can be a synonym for aesthetic worth, or it can refer to a distinctive quality whose aesthetic merit is logically open to question. The term "ugly" can mean lacking in aesthetic worth, and it can also refer to a distinctive quality which may or may not have aesthetic merit. The first usage in each case can be called *judgmental,* and the second *descriptive.* It is a tautology that all art embodies beauty in the judgmental sense, but artists have recurrently repudiated the quest for beauty in the descriptive sense. What is repudiated is better conveyed by a term like "prettiness"—symmetry of shape not form, and a certain sweet softness of the aesthetic surface, as is illustrated by the painting of Fragonard, the music of Henryk Wieniawski, the poetry of Dante Gabriel Rossetti, and, on a higher level of merit, by the works of Raphael. There is in such art a quality of the picturesque and graceful, something glossy and enticing, melodic and harmonious.

That art, as such, aspires to this quality is a dogma of criticism, imposing the restrictions of a style on the whole domain of aesthetics. Throughout its history art has struggled to free itself from this *dogma of beauty.* The modern movement in art can profitably be viewed in this perspective, as can the various fringe movements of anti-art or non-art; the descendants of Dada and earlier rebellions. Francis Bacon, in an essay on beauty, remarked that even the most excellent beauty has some strangeness in the proportion, so that to get a perfect model—a really pretty one, I might say—the artist must combine features from several sources. But the "strangeness in the proportion" might be just what is called for aesthetically.

Even a quality of the grotesque has been cultivated in cathedral ornamentation, in Renaissance sculpture, in the paintings of Bosch, and to a degree in some of Goya, Shakespeare, Dostoevski, Kafka, Beckett, and Ionesco. The grotesque, Dürenmatt has said, is "only a way of expressing in a tangible manner, of making us perceive physically the paradoxical, the form of the unformed, the face of a world without face." If art is the fulfillment of a wish, the wish is not that the world present always a pretty face, only that it not look upon us with vacant eyes.

Art satisfies a quest for meaning, as defined by the values of the culture of which the art is a part or which it is bringing into being. Because the artist is revitalizing old values or enlarging the domain of value, his work may at first be unintelligible. John Ruskin saw no more in James Whistler than cockney impudence flinging a pot of paint in the public's face. Two types of artistic achievement can be distinguished: *conservative,* which sums up a tradition, bringing it to perfection, and *revolutionary,* which opens new possibilities, establishing new traditions. It is the difference between Mozart and Beethoven, Velasquez and Goya, Thomas Mann and James Joyce. Ours is so much an age of revolution that new developments in the arts no longer depend on the acclaim of an *avant-garde:* movements like pop art and op art now win almost immediate mass circulation.

Revolutionary art is not to be confused with the *unconventional* schools or styles which attack established values and categories of meaning—schools such as surrealism, atonal music, and the theater of the absurd. These are undeniably rebellious; whether they are revolutionary, marking out paths for future development, remains to be seen. The distinction is all the harder to draw, as it is in politics, because of the professional radicals—artists, dealers, critics and snobs—who have much at stake in the unconventional. On the other hand, conservative art is not to be confused with the merely *academic,* art which fails to attain aesthetic quality because of its reliance on formulas of form, matter, and content. There are now academic surrealists, just as there are formulas for the absurd. Great artists are seldom academic, but they are often conservative, especially with regard to the work of other artists. Many of the contemporaries of Courbet and Manet were hostile to their work; Signac had contempt for Matisse's *Joi de Vivre;* Matisse was very critical of Picasso's *Demoiselles D'Avignon* and Braque's cubism; the Cubists attacked Duchamp's *Nude Descending a Staircase.*

The assessment of aesthetic worth is bedeviled by a confusion of the judgmental senses of beauty and ugliness with their descriptive senses. Descriptively, beauty might be defined in Santayana's terms as "the expected modified by pleasure." The important word is "expected"; what we call ugly is an incongruity with what we have been led to expect. When the baby which Alice was holding turned into a pig, she reflected that it would have made a dreadfully ugly child, though it was rather a handsome pig. The question is what it is *supposed* to look like: the expectation is both anticipatory and normative. An unfulfilled expectation can heighten suspense and amplify discriminations beyond the superficial and obvious; it can thereby contribute significantly to the unfolding of an aesthetic experience. Distortions can be highly expressive by breaking through our patterns of recognition of things which look as they are supposed to look, so that *we* can look at them with aesthetic perceptiveness. Van Gogh wrote in one of his letters, "It is my fervent desire to know how one can achieve such deviations from reality, such inaccuracies and such transfigurations."

Because art is viewed with expectations grounded in the art tradition, revolutionary art is likely to look ugly, until new sets of expectations have developed. Something is beautiful, said Plotinus, when it is true to its own being; ugliness is in "going over to another order." What is the true being of what we are judging? Which order does it really belong to? Dirt has been defined as misplaced matter; ugliness, in the descriptive sense, is misplaced beauty. Religious philosophers like John Scotus Erigena have a simple formula for ugliness so conceived: it is apprehending something out of relation to the will of God. This is reminiscent of the definition of sentimentality offered by the scholar of haiku, R. H. Blythe: loving something more than God does. Art often discloses the beauty in what is conventionally ugly by putting it in its proper place, true to its own being—as in the poetry of Issa and of Robert Burns, and the paintings of Dürer and Rembrandt.

What we are accustomed to acknowledge as beauty, in the judgmental sense, constitutes our *taste.* That there are great differences in taste does not imply a subjective relativism of aesthetic judgment (§50); the possibility is not thereby excluded of distinguishing between good and bad taste, and of acknowledging an objective relativism of style and culture. Hiroshige consummately renders the beauties of rain, a subject almost absent in Western painting; but only European art has shadows. The Renaissance, it has been pointed out, did not discover classic sculpture but only that it was beautiful; it was some centuries later that mountain scenery came to be appreciated. An object can be recognized to have aesthetic status even though it is not being responded to with aesthetic perception or in the aesthetic attitude. Objects designed to be so recognized, without sustaining an aesthetic experience, are known as *kitsch;* they carry the label of Art, with a capital "A," satisfying either a wholly uncultivated or a quite decadent taste.

With the rise of the ideal of social equality, philosophers like the French encyclopedists held that art has merit if it pleases "the average cultured and right-minded man." In Tolstoy's aesthetics a century or so later, even the highest art is capable of being understood by "simple, unperverted, peasant laborers." "Good art," Tolstoy maintained, "always pleases everyone. The majority have always understood what we also recognize as being the very best art." If this is taken as an allegation of fact, not as a tacit criterion of the best art, it is simply false. Understanding and acceptance of art varies markedly with styles and periods, especially with whether the art is conservative or revolutionary. Above all, it varies with the general level of taste; it is as absurd to hold that a majority always has good taste as to hold that what most people believe is always true.

Mark Twain remarked that the public is the only critic whose opinion is worth anything. If this is meant to affirm the primacy of aesthetic experience over the presumptions of so-called authoritative judgment it is unexceptionable. It is certainly to be rejected if it implies that public taste is beyond improvement. The policy of pleasing the public cannot claim justification by reference to public taste, for this can be elevated only if it is offered what initially does not please it. The attempt at such justification is the *circle of taste* (§7). We can break out of the circle only if we assume responsibility for an independent aesthetic judgment.

A statement that a work of art is beautiful, in the judgmental sense, may be only an *expression of taste* if its point is to convey a liking; it is an *aesthetic judgment* if it implies that the taste expressed is good taste—that is, that the work being judged is worthy of being liked. The view that no such distinction can be drawn, that the claim to worthiness is only a restatement of our liking, constitutes *subjectivism.* Like emotivism in ethical theory (§53), subjectivism in aesthetics derives from Hume, who held that beauty lies not in the object but in the beholder, being felt rather than perceived, so that criticism, like morals, is not properly an object of the understanding but of "taste and sentiment."

Subjectivism is not meant to lessen our enjoyment of the value or to weaken our commitment to it—Hume says of literature that it has been the ruling passion of his life. The issue is whether the passion must serve as its own justification, whether there is any sense in saying, in some cases, that it is unfounded or misguided. I once participated in a symposium on modern art whose chairman introduced the subject by reading a news story of a hoax in which a donkey's tail was dipped in a bucket of paint; the donkey was then backed up against a canvas, and swishing its tail, it produced something which was then offered as a work of modern art. My comment was that thousands of Philistines were once slain with the jawbone of an ass; their descendants were apparently now seeking revenge with the other end of the animal. Who is truly the victim of such a hoax?

A person *can* seek to improve his taste, that is, to make it more in keeping with the judgments he accepts, an aim which would be logically impossible if his judgment conveyed nothing other than his taste. Charles Morris had a number of persons rank a set of paintings according to the individual's taste and according to his judgment of aesthetic merit. Not only were the instructions meaningful; the two rankings for each person were closer for just those persons who might be expected to have a more cultivated taste, the ones who were more knowledgeable and more experienced in the arts. Experimental aesthetics, although it would be absurd to expect it to settle questions of aesthetic judgment, can contribute more to the domain of aesthetics than is recognized by the obscurantist mystique of the qualitative which is characteristic of contemporary neoromanticism.

Contextualism and objective relativism are as basic to aesthetic theory as to ethics or the general theory of value (§55). People differ not only in their tastes but also in their capacities for experiences. Some genetic differences can unmistakably be identified; a certain proportion of the population can taste the bitterness of PTC (pentathiocarbamide), while for the others it is tasteless. There are also marked differences in experiences in a variety of settings: how a painting is hung and illuminated will affect the observer's experience of it. The distinctions between personal, standard, and ideal contexts introduced in connection with ethical naturalism (§55) are also important for aesthetics. Reference to an ideal context marks out a *sphere of aesthetic worth* within the *sphere of aesthetic relevance* which personal and standard contexts provide. In calling something a work of art we may be implying a certain level of worth, or classifying it among those things certain people respond to aesthetically, leaving open the level of taste in the response. There is much room here for C. L. Stevenson's "persuasive definitions" (§8) in which judgments of aesthetic worth masquerade as descriptive statements about what a painting or poem "really is."

In practice, ideal contexts are specified in three different ways. One is by reference to aesthetic theory; the influential German philosopher of the Age of Enlightenment and man of letters, Gotthold Lessing, considered Aristotle's *Poetics* "as infallible as the *Elements* of Euclid," a view approximated by many aestheticians before and since Lessing. A second specification of ideal contexts is by reference to the practice of critics; Plato looked to judgments of value made by the wise, whose judgment is better than that of ordinary men, he argued, because they are acquainted with both the good and the bad, and so are in the best position to judge of the difference between them. A third specification is in terms of the cumulative effect of aesthetic experience and cultural tradition; that is really great, Longinus urged, which bears a repeated examination. There are serious difficulties with each of these specifications. The issues can be brought to a focus by considering the functions of art criticism and how it can best perform them.

If criticism consists largely of expressions of taste, it is indeed, as T. S. Eliot remarked, as inevitable as breathing. Our likes and dislikes demand articulation even more pressingly than our beliefs. Another modern poet and critic, William Empson, drew his metaphor from an equally basic physiological need; critics, he said, like dogs, are of two sorts—"those who merely relieve themselves against the flower of beauty, and those, less continent, who afterwards scratch it up." The question is whether the scratching serves to reveal something or only to cover it.

Dogmatic criticism takes as premises of its aesthetic judgments definitions or basic principles of art in general or of the genre in question. It is criticism rooted in aesthetic theory, in a metaphysics or a social philosophy, in cultural tradition, or in the rules promulgated by the coterie of critics and successful artists making up the academy. Pope speaks for them all with his lines,

> *Learn hence for ancient rules a just esteem;*
> *To copy Nature is to copy them.*

The weaknesses of dogmatic criticism are those of its philosophical sources, magnified by the legalism and scholasticism inevitable in the attempt at a rigorous application in specific cases of vague and uncertain general principles. Questions are easily begged as to which genres are immediately relevant, which requirements are essential to the genre and which are merely groundless tradition. It is these weaknesses which Hamlet satirizes when he says that the actors are the best in the world, "either for tragedy, comedy, history, pastoral, pastoral-comical, historical-pastoral, tragical-historical, tragical-comical-historical-pastoral, scene indivisible, or poem unlimited."

Scientific criticism purports to substitute judgments of fact for judgments of value, a tactic which Santayana takes as a sign of "a pedantic and borrowed criticism." The scientific critic takes refuge in the technicalities of the medium and its treatment, or of the psychology and sociology of the creation of the work and of the response to it. What is to be found in the work is not construed as constituting its aesthetic worth (the strategy of dogmatic criticism) but as providing evidence of such worth. Basically, the work is being judged by its effects. Why some effects are better than others, however, is not dealt with; in practice, scientific criticism reduces to some version of dogmatic criticism.

Impressionistic criticism is the *fin de siècle* equivalent in aesthetics of contemporary emotivism. Criticism is meant only to express the critic's personal response. "The good critic," said Anatole France, "is he who relates the adventures of his soul among masterpieces." If the critic were quite frank he ought to say, for instance, "Gentlemen, I am going to talk about myself on the subject of Shakespeare." Oscar Wilde was no more than usually presumptuous in characterizing criticism as "the only civilized form of autobiography." The question is whether it really is among masterpieces that the critic has had his adventures, and why we should care about his autobiography when it is the work of art we are interested in. Impressionistic criticism lacks both purpose and justification.

Certain norms of critical practice are called for if criticism is to have any purpose or justification—*procedural standards*, applying to criticism, as distinguished from the *substantive standards* meant to apply to the work of art being criticized. A valid aesthetic judgment is one sustained by continued criticism conforming to the procedural standards, just as a scientific judgment is validated by being sustained by a continuous process of scientific inquiry, and not by the conformity of its content to a given truth.

Among such procedural standards is a *principle of experience* which gives primacy to the qualities the work reveals in experience of it, as contrasted with qualities ascribed to it *a priori* by prejudice, snobbishness, academic blindness, personal favoritism or enmity. The *principle of inclusion* emphasizes the importance of considering the entire work of art, as against hasty or one-sided condemnations or enthusiasms. It is a lack of critical integrity to plead that one need not eat the whole egg to know it is rotten; Homer may nod, but there is not much to be said for the critic who falls asleep with him, then writes a review. A *principle of interpretation* insists that criticism is not to confine itself to surfaces, or only to such depth as traditional interpretations easily allow for; the work is to be understood, and understood in its own terms, not projectively. A *principle of individuality* demands that each work of art be judged on its merits, not in terms of a genre which it is presumed to typify nor by reference to a "touchstone" which is taken as a fixed standard of comparison.

A number of similar procedural standards can be formulated. What they all point to is a conception of the function of criticism as basically *catalytic* rather than *judicial*. The business of the critic is to heighten appreciation, in the strict sense which goes beyond a blind prizing to an awareness of what is being prized. The function of criticism is not to rhapsodize or denounce, and certainly not to provide a scale of merits and demerits. Carlyle described the critic as an interpreter, standing between the inspired and the uninspired. This may do an injustice to both artist and audience, for the skill of the artist is to give expression to his inspiration, and the audience must, in turn, contribute its creative imagination. A more homely statement of the critic's business is to call him a *shadchan*—a marriage broker—helping artist and audience to find one another and thereby themselves. Maybe the two accounts are, at bottom, the same; for like inspiration, marriages are made in heaven, and the critic is also an inspired artist.

Chapter Thirteen

Philosophy of Religion

83. Religious Institutions

Religion in the Western world is usually conceived in terms of belief in a Supreme Being directing and controlling human life. So central to religion is such a belief thought to be that "atheism" is virtually synonymous with irreligion. Belief in God *is* central to the major Western religions: Judaism, Christianity, and Islam. But doctrine is only one of a number of cardinal elements in religion, and in a philosophical perspective the Western religions cannot be taken as the only ones deserving of the name. The religion of the Jain and the schools of Mimamsa and Sankhya in orthodox Hinduism are explicitly atheistic. Vedanta acknowledges the gods but assigns them a status somewhere between a useful fiction and an image of a reality. Buddhism and Confucianism, in their more philosophic formulations if not in the popular mind, are nontheistic, not denying gods but assigning them only a peripheral role in human affairs. Philosophy of religion comprises more than a consideration of the existence and nature of God.

Among the religions in which the belief in God is central there is still such a wide range of conceptions of deity that it is hard to identify a core of meaning. Russell's bailiff (§6) would have been more typical if he had taken the position that whoever did not believe in *his* God did not believe in any God at all. "Men who can form no idea of God," Spinoza remarked, "unblushingly accuse philosphers of atheism"—as happened to him, to Socrates, to men identified with orthodoxy, men such as Maimonides, Aquinas, and Sankara, as well as to men of unconventional faith, such as Savonarola and Russell.

Similar considerations apply to points of doctrine other than belief in God. There is no savior, for instance, in Judaism or Hinduism. Buddhism, though it centers on the perfections of an individual, regards him as a teacher rather than a savior and focuses on what he taught rather than on the significance of his life and death, as is true also of those who revere Confucius and, with some qualifications, Mohammed. Belief in immortality, in the sense of survival of personality in something other than an earthly life, is not to be found in any of the Asian religions. A hereditary priestly caste is important in Hinduism (Brahmans), vestigial in Judiasm (*Kohanim*), established instead by ordination in Catholicism, and replaced by a lay leadership in a number of Protestant and Buddhist denominations. Hinduism and Buddhism have no Sabbath—in marked contrast to the long religious weekends in Israel, Friday being sacred to the Muslims, Saturday to the Jews, and Sunday to the Christians. Monasteries are important to Buddhists and Catholics, exist in a related form as Hindu *asrams,* but are unknown to Jews and Protestants. Even within the framework of a single religion, there are often significant differences in religious belief and practice.

Not only the terms designating religious concepts but the names of the religions themselves conceal changes of content which may go well beyond differences in shades of meaning. The position of "Judaism," say, on any religious issue, cannot be unequivocally stated. Which Judaism—Orthodox, Conservative, or Reform? If only the Orthodox is granted the name, which orthodoxy? The Patriarchs were Jews before Sinai; the Hebrews practiced Judaism before the Talmud, a Judaism preserved, with considerable variation, by Karaites and Samaritans; for a long time, there were Christian Jews; rabbinic Judaism was transformed in certain respects by Hassidism (so much so that orthodox Jews were once prohibited from intermarrying with Hassidim, who as a body had been declared to be heretics). Judaism is the religion of men of such diverse belief and practice as Abraham, Moses, David, Philo, Maimonides, the Baal Shem Tov, and the Chief Rabbi of Israel—or rather, the two Rabbis, one Sephardi and one Ashkenazi.

Throughout history, new meanings have recurrently been put into old symbols, while forces of conservatism have retained distinctions without differences. For the philosophy of religion, what must be avoided is *semantic rigidity,* the notion that the concepts being analyzed or used in the analysis have a clearly specifiable and fixed meaning, changed or replaced only as a device of special pleading. Freud thought that philosophers who "try to preserve the God of religion by substituting for Him an impersonal, shadowy, abstract principle" should be admonished, "Thou shalt not take the name of the Lord thy God in vain!" As to "shadowy," I cannot say; but the God or Nature of Spinoza and the Brahman of Sankara are impersonal and abstract principles, as are corresponding conceptions in other religions; it is debatable who is to be admonished. The difference between philosophical and religious conceptions of deity is important (§85), but which concepts are "properly" religious is not to be prejudged by personal commitments seeking semantic justification.

Prejudice is more prevalent in the philosophy of religion than in any other branch of philosophy, among apologists for religion as well as among its opponents. An attitude of acceptance of religious ideas, even if we do not share the ideas, today is more likely to be a mark of indifference to the subject than of an open mind. Modern prejudices against religion as such contrast with previous prejudices against all but the one true faith. Prejudices today, as in the past, are rooted in parochialism, and ignorance in all but the most superficial respects of even the one or two religions familiar to us. Religious education often ends with childhood, so that we come to identify religion with childish beliefs; a man who has heard no poetry but nursery rhymes, no stories but fairy tales, and who has read nothing for himself can hardly be expected to take literature seriously. There are, besides, ideological commitments—political, psychological, ethical, and metaphysical. Nietzsche once declared, "Whatever a theologian regards as true must be false: there you have almost a criterion of truth"; I should prefer to say, almost a criterion of prejudice. Emerson may have been right: "If in our philosophy we meet no gods, it is because we harbor none."

It would be a prejudice on the part of the religionist to regard all opposition to religion as basically the same—in content, if not in causes and motivations. There are several different kinds of opposition.

Skepticism is the refusal to accept traditional teaching just because it is traditional, or on the basis of some other authority. The skeptic does not necessarily reject the teaching but insists on subjecting it to rational examination. Skepticism is expressed in Nietzsche's barb, "It is a curious thing that God learned Greek when He wished to turn author—and that He did not learn it better." From the middle of the eighteenth century, the so-called "higher criticism" was directed not only to textual analysis but also to substantive questions about the religious tradition, with outcomes which served the interests of religion as well as the interests of its opponents.

Agnosticism is the refusal to take a position on the basic religious issues on the grounds that no position, pro or con, can establish its claims. "The mystery of the beginning of all things is insoluble by us," Darwin said, "and I for one must be content to remain an agnostic. The whole subject of God is beyond the scope of man's intellect." *Anticlericalism* is opposition not necessarily to religion but to the church and the clergy, especially to their power in secular affairs. The prophet often set himself against the priest who, as Hosea put it, feeds on the sins of the people, while the priest himself has forgotten the law of God.

In seeking to improve religion or to restore it to its purpose, *reformism* is opposed to vested interests. "Superstitution, idolatry, and hypocrisy have ample wages," said Luther, "but truth goes a-begging." Where the truth lies is another matter; *heresy* is the pejorative term used by the orthodox for a claim to truth they find unacceptable. Thomas Huxley's aphorism that new truths begin as heresies and end as superstitions has as much application to the history of religion as of science (§27). *Atheism* is the repudiation of belief in God, or at least in the conception of deity held by those applying the label; it is often confused with *irreligion*, perhaps from ignorance of the nontheistic religions rather than from a doctrinal refutation of their possibility. The most extreme form of opposition to religion is, like other extremes of attitude, close to its opposite; *diabolism* is the worship of Satan rather than God, religion stood on its head.

No useful purpose would be served by attempting to formulate a definition of "religion" broad enough to comprise all actual religions yet narrow enough to distinguish religion from related domains such as magic, superstitution, ideology, and philosophy. Instead, the meaning of the term can be specified by reference to four components of most religions; each component itself stands in need of specification. A religion may be viewed as a *church*, a *cult*, a *creed*, and a *faith*.

For every religion there is a community of the faithful. There is no religion without worshippers any more than there is a state without citizens. Religion is actualized, again like a state, not in isolated individuals but in a society. "Communion" and "community" come from the same root; *religio* means to bind together. Whether or not religion unites man with God (perhaps the root sense of "yoga," cognate with the English word "yoke"), it unites men with one another: "synagogue" means, literally, to bring together. The Talmud has it that if two men enter a synagogue together to pray, and when one of them has finished he leaves without his friend, his prayer is not accepted. The village skeptic, asked why he is so often to be found in the synagogue, explains, "My friend Chayim goes to the synagogue to talk with God; I go to talk with my friend Chayim." The fact is that they both go.

Where there is community there is a bond which unites people at a given moment and also unites the shared past with the present and the present with a shared future. If we worship a God, it is the God of our fathers. Each generation worships in its own way: commentators explain that the expression reads, "God of Abraham, God of Isaac, God of Jacob," and not simply "God of Abraham, Isaac, and Jacob" because each of the three made God his own; but there is continuity nevertheless. There is also loyalty. Moses, pleading with God on behalf of the people, at last declares, "If You will forgive their sin—very well; if not, blot my name out of Your book." No doubt the reference is to the Book of Life, that is, take my life instead of theirs; to which God replies, "Whoever has sinned against Me, his name will I blot out of My book." Yet there is also in the words of Moses something of the spirit, "If You abandon my people, my place remains with them."

Community implies a certain structuring of authority; for the community of the faithful this structure constitutes the *Church*. Church authority is as variable in its distribution and exercise as is political authority. The weight and scope of its power may be slight or considerable; it may demand unquestioning obedience or allow for considerable dissent; it may grant autonomy to local groupings (congregationalism) or centralize power in an Establishment (the original locus of this term). It may recognize the right of other churches to exist or hold with the Church Father Origen that "Outside the Church no one is saved," and with Calvin that "Beyond the bosom of the Church no remission of sins is to be hoped for, nor any salvation."

Characteristically, the authority of the church is associated with a body of authoritative *scriptures*. Hinduism distinguishes between orthodox and heterodox systems of thought—*astika* and *nastika*–not on the basis of doctrinal content but in terms of whether they accept the authority of the Vedas. There is a position that one must believe in God because this is enjoined by scripture, rather than that one must accept scripture because it has been revealed by God. For the community of the faithful, as distinguished from their founders or prophets, what comes first is the book; the source is inferential. There are churches for which writings are quite secondary—for instance, Zen. In all churches the written law is supplemented—to the point of being overlaid or even transformed—by an oral law, with all the power of tradition conjoined to the claim to authority. Sophocles' Antigone could be speaking for virtually any church when she refers to "the immutable unwritten laws of God. They were not born today nor yesterday; they die not; and none knows whence they sprang."

Like other forms of power, church authority has its ultimate locus in individuals, those who are exercising the power. Every church has a *priesthood,* not necessarily intermediates between man and God but distinctive functionaries of the church. Their duty may be to provide authoritative interpretations of scripture and of the oral law; to perform the rituals of the cult; to transmit the teaching; to strengthen faith; to serve as pastors of the community of the faithful, disseminating the consolations and celebrating the joys of the religion. In many religions, personal relationships develop between faithful followers (disciples, *hassidim*) and those perceived as being able to lead them: the *guru, roshi,* and *rebbe.* There may also be a class, overlapping with such leaders, of communicants perceived as having gone very far along the Way—an *arhat, saint, bodhisattva,* and *tsaddik;* or even having attained to the goal—a *jivanmukti* or *buddha.* There are, besides, many who, without distinctive functions to perform for others, are recognized as having seriously embarked on the Way: the monk, *swami, saddhu,* and *nazir.*

Whether in a theocratic or a secular society, religion is everywhere institutionalized, a matter of cultural forms and social organization. The only alternative to organized religion is a disorganized one, or a personal philosophy rather than a religion. Anticlericalism and reformism do not mean to transcend institutional life but to change an institution or replace one institution by another. Such changes and replacements are features of the history of all religions and may mark the emergence of one religion from another. The Hebrew religion gave way to Judaism when the Temple was replaced by the synagogue, the priest by a rabbi, and sacrifices by prayer; Christianity emerged from Judaism, as distinct from being a Jewish sect, when there were comparable institutional changes; Buddhism emerged from Brahmanic Hinduism; and Protestant Christianity, in some of its denominations, at any rate, might well be regarded as a quite different religion than that of, say, the Greek Orthodox Church.

The attack on prevailing religious institutions by such devout religionists as Luther and Kierkegaard is the result of a universal feature of institutional life: institutions have their own interests which may diverge from, and even conflict with, the interests which the institution supposedly serves (§75). No church remains forever free of decadence and corruption—

simony, the selling of church offices or other religious rights and privileges; elitism, a self-centered priesthood indifferent to the needs of the religious community; degradation of religious values in pride of power and self-indulgence with unearned riches; and perversion of religious principle, such as burning heretics in presumed conformity with the prohibition against shedding blood, or mounting a holy war against a persecuted people so as to safeguard "holy places."

"Christendom," said Kierkegaard, "has done away with Christianity." No church is exempt from the tensions between principles and expediencies. Religious as well as political polemics usually compare "our" high ideals with the betrayal of principle in "their" institutional practice. On a visit to a Hindu temple I, as a non-Hindu, was not permitted to approach the altar, and watched with some chagrin as a cow freely wandered up to eat the flowers placed there. On recounting the incident some time later to a Zen abbott, I was told that Zen has no such concern about outer forms and observances—"and now," he added, "if you will remove your shoes, we can enter the Meditation Hall."

It is the church, particularly in the Western world, which has made religion so divisive a force, with its *jehads* and crusades, pogroms and sectarian persecutions: the Thirty Years' War between Protestant and Catholic in Germany and the present bloodshed in Ireland; wars for centuries between Christian and Muslim; extermination of heretics and infidels; and always and everywhere death to the Jews. In its three and a half centuries, the Inquisition put to death, in proportion to the populations involved, about ten times as many human beings as America, throughout its whole history, has executed for murder. "We have just enough religion to make us hate, but not enough to make us love, one another," wrote Jonathan Swift, himself a churchman (Dean of St. Patrick's Cathedral in Dublin). Nietzsche, in the next century, was even more biting: "Not their love of humanity, but the impotence of their love, prevents the Christians of today burning us." Both Christian and Jew were burned shortly thereafter, by men who were making a religion of power. Where religion and power combine, prospects are grim.

Throughout history, governments of every political complexion have been guilty of adding incalculably to the burden of human misery; yet there are few anarchists. Most men suppose that what is called for is not the abolition of government but its reform or transformation. In this respect, the church is less fortunate than the state; or rather, it is religion, not the church, which is victimized by this discriminatory logic.

84. Ritual and Symbol

Associated with every religion is a *cult,* a complex of rituals and symbols. Special places are set aside, like tombs and churches; special days, like the Sabbath and festivals—that is, holy days; special objects are employed—chalices, candles, bells, incense, robes; certain foods are taboo and others mandatory; various gestures are given religious significance—genuflection, the sign of the cross, sitting in the lotus position. There are differences among religions in the richness and complexity of ritual and in the importance attached to it, differences embodied in the contrast between "High Church" and "Low Church" denominations. No church is so "low" as to dispense with symbolism altogether. Just as the religious community is always institutionalized, religious practices are always ritualized and come to be performed in fixed and formal ways. Rituals usually appear prior to the doctrines by which they are explained and justified, and they usually survive changes in doctrine as well as in the church. The "statutes and ordinances" of which scripture speaks (*hukkim* and *mishpatim*) are sometimes interpreted as referring respectively to purely ritualistic precepts and to social and moral precepts—"Remember the Sabbath," for instance, as contrasted with "Thou shalt not steal." The former precepts, together with the oral tradition in which they are detailed, define the cult.

While the demands religion makes on conduct are susceptible, in principle, to rational explanation, its requirements as to ritual can only be explicated. The meaning of the symbols can be specified, but the symbols can be explained only in the sense of tracing a historical or doctrinal derivation of the meaning. The benediction over bread and salt at the beginning of a sacramental meal unites in one symbolic complex nature, man, and God. What purpose is served by such a symbolic union? In many philosophies of religion, practice of the cult is meant to develop the disposition for communing with God (the position of Judah Halevi, for instance), or attaining whatever other goals are specified in the religious doctrine (as in Vedanta, or Hinayana Buddhism). Maimonides holds that ritual serves moral and even intellectual perfection.

How it does so is a question which seems to invite rationalization. Philo of Alexandria explains the Judaic prohibition against eating pork by the consideration that the meat, being so delectable, is a symbol of the sensual life which man is to renounce; Maimonides, on the other hand, as a physician, explains the prohibition on hygienic grounds. In other words, such food is either too good for the Jews or else unfit for human consumption. There is a conjecture that food taboos are connected with totemism, in which the totemic animal is symbolic of the ancestors of the clan and so may not be eaten by members of the clan. Yet sacramental bread and wine may be explicitly identified as body and blood and be enjoined rather than prohibited.

Apart from religious doctrine or doctrinaire anthropology, there are certain general functions of ritual. For one thing, the symbol provides a concrete embodiment of an abstract idea, making the idea vivid and easily grasped. This is true, for instance, of birth rituals—christening, circumcision, the Sioux Reception of the Child, baptism, redemption of the firstborn, and the like—with their content of dedication to a certain community and its principles. For another thing, ritual brings the meanings and values of both past and future into the immediately given present, thereby providing continuity and significance to the stream of experience. Here we have the rites of passage—Bar Mitzvah, confirmation—and the celebration of festivals connected with historical events. In the third place, a practice of the cult may serve to socialize action, endowing it with group sanction. Wedding ceremonies include symbolic enactments of the union in the eyes of man as well as of God. Finally, ritual provides a channel for the expression of strong feelings which would otherwise remain inchoate or incoherent. This is especially likely to be true of grief and the rituals of burial and mourning. In short, the cult is intimately involved in whatever motives and purposes are served by religion.

A certain perversion of ritual from the standpoint of its religious functions has been known in all religions. *Ritualism* relates to ritual as chauvinism does to patriotism, or as in art a "formula" relates to artistic form (§77). In ritualism, the symbol is dissociated from content; the symbolic act is carried out in a mechanical, unfeeling way, robbing it of significance. The performance may be perfunctory or overly scrupulous. Ritualism may well justify the Freudian view of religious practices as expressing the compulsions of an obsessional neurosis.

On the religious side, ritualism is a preoccupation with cult at the expense of faith. Insistence on prayers at public functions or in schools, a reference to God in oaths of allegiance or on coinage, enactment of cult into civil law—all this has in it more of ritualism than of religion. A *roshi* declared, "There is one word which I don't like to hear, and that is 'Buddha.' When you say 'Buddha,' wash out your mouth." Seminary students refer contemptuously to one who is overly free with religious language as a "Christer." There is such a thing, after all, as taking the Name in vain. The Master said, "The distance between the mouth and the heart is as great as that between earth and Heaven"—then he added, "yet the earth is nourished by rain from Heaven."

Rituals may be performed for reasons far removed from religion. Adherence to the cult may be a matter of respectability or social status; it may have political motivations. Aristotle advises a ruler to appear to be particularly earnest in the service of the gods, so that the people will be less afraid they will suffer injustice at his hands, and will believe that the gods are on his side—provided his religion is not thought to be foolish. Pareto has documented the possibility of believing in the efficacy of certain rites of a religion without believing in the religion; here ritual becomes *magic*, and response to religious symbols no more than superstition. Examples familiar in every society are such practices as rain ceremonies; medals or images to ensure safety at sea or on the roads; protective amulets worn by soldiers; exorcisms to cure mental illness and processions to prevent or restrict epidemics—an endless catalogue of the follies to which we are driven by our anxieties and our sense of helplessness.

In general, rites are to be performed for no other reason than that they have been commanded or that they are traditional, that they define "what is done." This emphasis on carrying them out for their own sake helps free the religious impulse from magic but threatens it with ritualism. Religious doctrine may recognize that the ritual has only a symbolic content, yet insist that it be performed with the same scrupulousness which would be devoted to a substantive action. Among the reasons offered for purely informal details of the observance is that they provide "a fence for the Law," as the area around a high-voltage installation, though not itself dangerous, is fenced off to ensure that the actual installation will not be touched. If the Law requires that something be done by morning, the rite may specify that it be performed before midnight even though no special significance attaches to that hour except in subsequent rationalization. The priest may instruct the faithful that the rites make "the word of prophecy more sure," serving as "a lamp shining in a dark place until the day dawns and the morning star arises in your hearts."

The lamp shining in a dark place may produce a willingness to dispense with daylight altogether: the rite is transformed from a means to an end in itself. Often associated with ritualism is religious *formalism,* which adds to an exaggerated regard for ritual an insistence on the unchanging preservation of its symbolic forms. The demand that prayers be recited on any and every occasion illustrates ritualism; the insistence that the prayers must be be in a certain language and that only a specific wording is allowable illustrates formalism. Formalism is conservative and even reactionary; reformists may nevertheless be highly ritualistic. In all the world's major religions, rapidly changing social patterns and conditions of life are posing challenges to religious forms, while new rituals are constantly in the making. The danger of formalism lies in the fact that forms are so well-defined. They may therefore foster the illusion that religious demands have been met when only forms have been satisfied, as justice and equity give way to legalism. This is how the letter kills while the spirit gives life.

The cult may acquire a self-contained importance, so that the religious life is imagined to be one devoted exclusively to ritualistic practices. Monasticism is an institutional form of what the Hindus know as *sannyasa:* withdrawal from any activity other than what is prescribed in the cult. It is religion withdrawn to a circumscribed sphere, the locus of religious life being removed to a holy place, on a holy day—what Buber described as some "sacred upper story" to the house in which we live or, in Franz Rosenzweig's phrasing, "a safe and quite corner." Often, "eternal truths" are not even contemporary, as religion turns aside from the problems and predicaments of life outside the cult. The Talmud declares that one hour of fulfillment of the Law in this world is better than the whole life of the world to come.

Asceticism may be enjoined by religion as the consequence of a dualism between everyday life and the religious life defined by the cult. The injunction to turn aside from worldliness (§60) is too much honored, if one can judge by the poverty and filth so often characteristic of cities and men identified as "holy." If "worldliness" means luxury and indulgence it might be condemned by religion and morality alike, but not if it means the satisfaction of any need other than the compulsion to fulfill ritualistic requirements. The Master was both religious and realistic in his recognition that spiritual ends may be served by fasting, but also by eating. Apparent self-denial may be gratifying spiritual pride or indulging the illusion that something of substantive significance has been achieved, when only forms have been observed. The Master also said: Better only to pretend to fast, and to fool others, than really to fast, and fool oneself.

From a social point of view, a pernicious consequence of withdrawal is *parasitism.* Shimon bar Yochai observed that punctilious observance of the Law is possible only for a man who lives on manna or from the labor of other men. Religion, like the lust it condemns, is too often an expense of spirit in a waste of shame. It is often the countries with the lowest per capita income which allocate the largest part of their resource to the support of a church and cult. In such circumstances it is not surprising that a religious life may be viewed as an occupation rather than as a calling. In various religions, those most distinguished for their spiritual attainments do not earn a living by their attainments ("making a spade of the Torah"). Even monastic institutions often regard the labor of earning one's bread as the fulfillment of a religious duty: to work is to pray. In Hebrew, the same word (*avodah*) is used for both work and religious performance, a duality of meaning also conveyed by the English word "service."

Prayer is the central element in every cult, in the broad sense of any ritualistic use of language. Narrower definitions point to various types or uses of prayer:

1. Prayer may be *magical,* the recitation of the words being supposed to bring about the desired results. The words need not even be recited; there are prayer-wheels on which the words are inscribed, merit accruing to the worshipper who turns the wheel or who constructed the device by which the wheel is made to turn by wind or water. If not magical, prayer may still be thought to be effective by way of the words themselves rather than their meaning, as is shown by the frequent use for prayer of dead languages, or living languages not understood by the worshippers—Latin, Greek, Hebrew, Aramaic, Sanskrit, Pali, and others. In such cases, the prayers are likely to be recited from an inner compulsion as an unthinking routine or as a matter of formalistic observance.

2. Prayer may be *petition,* asking the Powers for preferential treatment. The petition may be on behalf of oneself (all the examples in what follows are from the book of Psalms, unless otherwise indicated): "My God, my God, why have you forsaken me?" "I am brought very low. Deliver me from my enemies; they are too strong for me." It may be on behalf of loved ones, or of the community of the faithful: "Blessed be he who comes in the name of God." "By the rivers of Babylon we sat down and cried when we remembered Zion. They who had taken us prisoner pressed us, 'Sing one of the songs of Zion!' How shall we sing God's song in a land that is not our own?" The petition may be for all who are in need: "Let the mountains bear peace to the people!" "God frees the prisoners; He opens the eyes of the blind; He raises up those who have been brought low; He protects the aliens; He defends the orphan and the widow."

Morality and religion may unite in condemning prayers of petition which ask for something worthless, trivial, or childish. A prince who had run away from home was, after long travels, overtaken by a messenger who informed him that he had inherited the throne. "In that case," said the prince, "I want a new pair of sandals." The injunction of Seneca is to the same point: "Live among men as if God saw you, speak with God as if men heard you." It is shameful to ask only for ourselves, and to ask anyone for what is not worth having. Such petitions may nevertheless enjoy a place in the cult. An Indian friend, contrasting what he saw as Asian spirituality and Western materialism, pointed out that in his country merchants began their working day with prayers; it did not occur to him that the prayers were to Laxmi, the goddess of wealth.

Instead of examining the significance of prayer, philosophy of religion too often is caught up in the issue of whether prayer is effective, an issue construed—by tacit and unwarranted assumption—as the question of whether petitions are granted. "Whatever you desire when you pray," say the Gospels, "believe that you receive them, and you shall receive them." Huckleberry Finn put the principle to the test: "Miss Watson she took me in the closet and prayed, but nothing come of it. She told me to pray every day, and whatever I asked for I would get it. But it warn't so. I tried it. Once I got a fishline, but no hooks. It warn't any good to me without hooks. I tried for the hooks three or four times, but somehow I couldn't make it work." For him, apparently, prayer itself was in a way fishing for something, though he stopped short of the realization that your true fisherman enjoys going fishing even when he doesn't catch anything.

A more fundamental criticism of prayer of petition than the charges that it is immoral or uncertain is that it is illogical in its implication that God has infinite resources but suffers from an inadequate intelligence service. "Your Father knows what you need, before you ask Him," Matthew reminds us. That the petition has not been granted need not mean that the prayer has gone unanswered:

> *We, ignorant of ourselves,*
> *Beg often our own harms, which the wise powers*
> *Deny us for our good; so find we profit,*
> *By losing of our prayers.*

Antony and Cleopatra unexpectedly points a religious moral.

3. Many deeply religious philosophers, such as Spinoza, would agree with Kant that the wish to talk to God is absurd, and the uses of prayer are therefore only subjective. Prayer does not for that reason stand condemned in Kant's eyes: "People may say of Pietism [his own religious background] what they will. Those in whom it was sincere were worthy of honor. They possessed the highest thing that man can have—the quiet, the content, the inner peace, which no suffering can disturb." Prayer may be *psychological,* heightening resolve and sustaining hope and trust. Unlike autosuggestion and self-hypnosis, it gives expression to a commitment already made—to that faith without which prayer is empty—and which is strengthened by being expressed in the shared patterns of the cult.

Thus we have prayers of resolve: "If I forget you, O Jerusalem, let my right hand forget her cunning!" The Talmud records the heartwarming fantasy that God Himself prays; it is a prayer of resolve: "May My mercy prevail over My justice, that I may deal with My children in kindness." There are prayers of hope: "Though my father and my mother have forsaken me, God will gather me to Him." There are prayers of trust: "God is my shepherd; I shall not want." "Though a whole army should be camped against me, my heart shall not fear; though war should come, even then I will be confident. Wait for God; be strong and take courage."

4. The word "prayer" comes from a root meaning to beg or entreat; the root of the Hebrew word, *hitpalel,* means judging oneself. Prayer may be a matter of self-appraisal, examination of one's conscience, confession of fault; we may refer generically to prayers of *humility.* "God looked down from heaven on mankind, to see if there were any men of understanding who sought Him. Every one of them is corrupt; they conspire together. There is none that does good, no, not one." "Man's days are as grass; he flourishes as a flower of the field—the wind passes over it and it is gone, and its place knows it no more." "When I behold Your heavens, the work of Your hands, the moon and the stars which You have set in their courses, what is man, that You are mindful of him, the son of Adam, that You visit him?"

5. Humility combined with appreciative awareness of undeserved good leads to the prayers of *gratitude:* "How can I repay God all His bountiful dealings toward me?" "I will give thanks to You, for I am fearfully and wonderfully made, and wonderful are all Your works." The Midrash on the Book of Psalms remarks that in the world to come all prayers will disappear except prayers of thanksgiving, and these will last forever.

6. There are prayers of *praise:* "The heavens declare the glory of God, the firmament shows His handiwork." The last verse of the Book of Psalms is: "Let all that breathes praise God—Hallelu-yah!"

7. Finally, there are prayers of *joy,* an expressive overflow in which he who prays is, like David, dancing before God, not coming before Him on crutches, as is characteristic of the prayers of petition. "O come, let us sing to God, let us shout for joy!" "Sing to God a new song, sing to God, O all the earth! This is the day God made; rejoice in it and be glad!"

8. Beyond even the prayers of joy are the wordless prayers: the *nigun* or melody of Hassidism, perhaps also what Zen knows as the music of a stringless harp. Here prayer transcends understanding, if only because there is nothing to be understood. Perhaps, after all, prayer in a language we do not know is not always the lowest grade of prayer; it may reach to the highest grade, and thereby close the circle.

85. The Existence of God

Religion is not only a church and a cult; it is also a *creed,* a body of beliefs to which the followers of the religion are presumed to subscribe. Not every point of doctrine is expected to be accepted by every follower, nor are all the beliefs expected to be held with equal fervor. In some religions creed is of far less importance—as compared with church, cult, and faith—than in other religions. Judaism, for instance, enjoins *halakhic* (cultic) observance; the injunction is far less demanding in Reform Judaism than in Orthodox Judaism, Conservative Judaism being intermediate, but in all three there is considerable latitude as to the creed, which in other religions would be expected to explain and justify the cult. The old man, listening to his grandson's exposition of the fallacies underlying the proofs for the existence of God, acknowledges that the objections are quite convincing; "but we must break off the discussion," he concludes, "it's time for evening prayers!" The story is only a slight exaggeration.

The reference to prayers in this connection is especially pointed, for to whom do we pray if there is no God? The difficulty is by no means clear-cut. Prayer may be a central element in every cult, but theism is by no means central to every creed and is even denied in some of them—including doctrines like Mimamsa, which attach great importance to prayer. The question of the existence of God is too often discussed as though the meaning of the concept is quite clear and what is at issue is only whether the concept has an actual instance. When the *roshi* was asked, "Do you believe in God?" he replied "If you do, I don't; if you don't, I do." Thereby he hoped to shift attention from existence to meaning, and ultimately, to the point of the question.

There are many, both among religionists and among philosophers of religion, who regard arguments either for or against the existence of God as beside the point. Not all who enjoy playing or listening to music have an interest in musicology; even those who acknowledge that musical theory might add to their enjoyment would not always admit that it is a precondition to composing or hearing music. A lover might be indifferent to psychological treatises and sex manuals. In all three cases—religion often uses the languages both of art and of love—experience is primary and its conceptualization secondary. The conceptualization presupposes the experience rather than the other way around. As Karl Jaspers put it, God is a premise of religious thought, not a conclusion. Walter Stace, an acute analyst of mysticism and its philosophy, observed that if God is not to be found at the end of a telescope, neither does He appear at the conclusion of a syllogism. Empirical and rational approaches are, in his view, equally irrelevant.

Others take the position that, relevant or not, arguments for the existence of God are impossible. On the empirical side there is no room for argument: God is not something *in* the world, a constituent force or power. If God transcends the world, He thereby also transcends the powers of human reason to grasp Him—the position taken by Kant, by Kapila (the founder of the *Samkhya* school), and by many other philosophers. Apologists for religion are fond of quoting Bacon's aphorism that a little philosophy inclines a man's mind to atheism, but depth in philosophy brings men's minds about to religion. If so, it is doubtful whether they are brought about by arguments for the existence of God.

Surveying such arguments in his *History of Western Philosophy*, Russell concludes: "In order to make their proofs seem valid, philosophers have had to falsify logic, to make mathematics mystical, and to pretend that deep-seated prejudices were heaven-sent intuitions." Here, for instance, is Plato, arguing in such a transparently vicious circle that this passage in the *Timaeus* must have been written with tongue in cheek: "As to the existence of the gods, we must accept the traditions of the men of old time who affirm themselves to be the offspring of the gods, and they must surely have known the truth about their own ancestors. How can we doubt the word of the children of the gods?" An example of making mathematics mystical is provided by Leibniz, who used binary arithmetic—which expresses numbers to the base 2 rather than the base 10—for theological purposes. In this arithmetic, only the numerals 0 and 1 appear, 2 being represented by "10" (since it is the base), 3 by "11" 4 by "100," 5 by "101," and so on; thus, Leibniz argued, Unity, acting on Nothing, produces the whole of finite creation. This is not much different from the story told by De Morgan of how the atheist Encyclopedist, Diderot, was overcome by the mathematician Euler, when both were visiting at the court of Catherine the Great, with an algebraic argument for the existence of God: "Sir, a + b = x, hence God exists." Euler was deeply religious, but not, we may be sure, on the basis of algebraic mumbo-jumbo.

Whether arguments for the existence of God are irrelevant, impossible, or illogical, at best an argument proves the existence only of a God conceived in accord with the premises of the argument. The most widespread fallacy in these arguments is equivocation: using the word "God" in one sense for the sake of the argument, then supposing that the conclusion establishes something about "God" in the sense in which that term is used in quite other contexts—for instance, in prayer. This is the point of the distinction emphasized by Judah Halevi between "the God of Aristotle" and "the God of Abraham"—the bloodless, philosophic abstraction (as Halevi understood it) and the living God of history and prophetic experience. If it is sound, each argument proves the existence of God only in a distinctive sense, whose appropriateness to various religious and philosophical contexts must be separately established. Once Mordecai Kaplan, the distinguished religious leader and educator, in a lecture at the Jewish Theological Seminary, developed the theme that "God" is to be understood as a human concept—of enormous importance, but a human concept nevertheless. At the lunch which followed, one of the seminarians, asked to recite Grace, began, "Our Concept and the Concept of our fathers. . . ."

Among the most widespread of the arguments purporting to prove the existence of God is the *teleological argument* or *argument from design*. The world does not consist of random aggregations but of orderly patterns; it must therefore have been put in order, by a Mind great enough to conceive a cosmic order and powerful enough to establish it. Newton writes in his *Principia*, "This most beautiful system of the sun, planets, and comets could only proceed from the counsel and dominion of an intelligent and powerful Being." Such a Being is not in the strict sense a Creator of the world, for, so far as the argument is concerned, the matter of the world preexists. He is, rather, the Architect of nature—the Engineer, the Mechanic, the Mathematician who designed it, and set all things in motion. The image evoked is Blake's representation of God holding a set of drawing compasses. This conception of God is known as *deist;* it was particularly popular among intellectuals of the Age of Enlightenment, since it appeared to be so consonant with a belief in a rational, natural order.

In more traditional religious perspectives, the argument from design took another form—that the world exhibits not only *orderliness* but also *purposiveness.* Moreover, this purposiveness relates to human goals and aspirations; the world is so designed as to serve man's needs and interests. In a word, it is the work of a divine *Providence.* "In the whole realm of nature," Maimonides declared, "there is nothing purposeless, trivial, or unnecessary." Even noxious creatures—poisonous snakes and vermin—Augustine urged, have their uses: to punish, discipline, and terrify sinners and would-be wrongdoers. All things fit into a pattern intelligible only in the light of human nature and destiny; the pattern therefore demonstrates the existence of a Being which, though cosmic in its powers, is concerned with human purposes; such a Being is God.

The teleological argument has been widely criticized with regard both to its premises and to whether the conclusion follows from them.

The world seems to be designed as a human habitation only when viewed in the most parochial perspectives, and with a vision grossly distorted by egocentrism. Our globe, even our whole solar system, occupies an almost indescribably tiny portion of the cosmos, the whole of human history has lasted less than one-thousandth of one percent of the history even of the earth, and on this earth almost everything is indifferent to, even hostile to, human purposes. To think otherwise is to deceive ourselves with question-begging illogic. It is true that if the earth were somewhat nearer to or farther from the sun, if the sun were hotter or colder, if the earth were more or less massive than it is, if countless other conditions were otherwise, human life would have been impossible. But in that case it would also have been impossible for the whole question to arise—as on countless billions of heavenly bodies, to the best of our knowledge, it *is* impossible. As well conclude, the objection runs, that it is a mark of divine Providence that the skin has openings in it precisely at the place where it fits over the eyes.

At the beginning of his essay on *A Free Man's Worship* Russell presents a version of the story of Creation, which runs, in part:

> Man said: "There is hidden purpose, could we but fathom it, and the purpose is good; for we must reverence something, and in the visible world there is nothing worthy of reverence." And man stood aside from the struggle, resolving that God intended harmony to come out of chaos by human efforts. . . . God smiled; and when he saw that Man had become perfect in renunciation and worship, he sent another sun through the sky, which crashed into Man's sun; and all returned again to nebula. "Yes," he murmured, "it was a good play; I will have it performed again." Such, in outline, but even more purposeless, more void of meaning, is the world which science presents for our belief.

That the cosmos, with all man's struggles, failures, and achievements, presents only a spectacle for Deity may itself appear to be only an amusing fancy. But it may be no less fanciful to imagine that an infinite and perfect

God can have any purposes whatever to be fulfilled. This is the argument Spinoza makes: God or Nature does nothing for the sake of an end, lacking nothing, and acting always only by necessity. Here we come upon a basic problem for traditional theism, the *problem of creation:* why did God create the world to start with?

There are, undeniably, *some* purposes in nature—indeed, throughout the whole domain of life. How are they to be accounted for without invoking a purposive agent on a cosmic scale, which would be nothing other than a species of Providence? Kant struggled with this problem in his *Critique of Judgment* but arrived only at the conclusion that purposes do not in truth exist in nature; they are useful fictions to suit the human mind. Not until the next century could purposes be incorporated into a purely scientific approach. This was the fundamental significance of Darwin's achievement. Darwin could not understand the opposition of religionists to his ideas, writing, at the end of his *Origin of Species,* "I see no good reason why the views given in this volume should shock the religious feelings of anyone," and going on to mention, with some satisfaction, Leibniz's groundless attack on the theory of gravitation as subversive of natural and, inferentially, of revealed religion. Darwin did not shake established creeds because he gave an account of human origins different from the story in Genesis, which had long ago received metaphorical and allegorical interpretations. His impact was more basic: he accounted for design—not just orderliness but also purposiveness—without invoking any agencies outside nature.

The logic of the situation is revealed in the surprising support given by nineteenth-century materialists to the theory of spontaneous generation (as against Pasteur, for instance), so that no God would need to be invoked to account for the origin of life. Only in our own day have there been the beginnings of a scientific account of the origin of life.

Purposiveness was given a natural foundation in the last century by invoking natural selection. Polar bears are white and others brown, not by the grace of divine Providence but because dark bears in the polar regions are more easily seen by potential prey and so are less fit to survive—that is, they leave fewer offspring. The adaptation of organisms to their environment, and the mutual adaptation of parts and processes within the organism, cannot always be so simply accounted for. Here, too, it is only in the present century that a beginning has been made, in cybernetics and related disciplines, to account for purposiveness in terms previously thought to be "mechanistic."

It is ironic that the eighteenth century viewed the world as a clockwork and acknowledged God as its designer; even the skeptical Voltaire admitted, "I cannot think that this watch exists and has no watchmaker." The irony is that clockworks are telic mechanisms of such a low order as scarcely to qualify for the classification at all. The argument from design would have been better grounded if the world could have been seen as a giant computer—but this is further than the most determined and eristic apologist is willing to go.

A second major argument for the existence of God is the *cosmological argument,* especially urged by Aristotle. Everything has its beginning and a cause for its coming to be. The series of causes cannot stretch back forever; God is the *First Cause.* In another locution, all motions are produced by other motions; there must be, at the beginning of motion, an *Unmoved Mover;* this is God. Leibniz makes a similar argument on the basis of his *principle of sufficient reason,* that nothing happens unless there is sufficient reason for *that* to happen rather than something else. Everything in the world is contingent—that is, it might have been otherwise and so needs a reason. The series of reasons can only end with something which cannot be otherwise, that is, something necessary; this *Necessary Being* is God.

The cosmological argument has often been rejected on purely religious grounds—by Philo of Alexandria, for instance, who says that to rely on astronomy (the origin of the universe and its motions) is no other than atheism. A teleological God, by definition, has purposes in which man is directly implicated, and so has religious significance from the outset. It is far from clear, however, why anyone should worship a First Cause or pray to an Unmoved Mover.

From the standpoint of philosophic reflection as distinct from religious thought, the cosmological argument has also been severely criticized. Spinoza points out that whenever we speak of a cause we are speaking of some part of the world in relation to another part; how, then, can we speak of the cause of the whole, there being nothing other than itself to serve as cause? Spinoza concludes that it is this whole, Nature, which stands in the place of "God." In another form, the objection to the cosmological argument is that God, standing outside the causal series (being uncaused), cannot at the same time act as cause; Creation is not causal agency, save by an analogy which breaks down just where it is needed.

"Who made the world?" the child asks. "God." "Who made God?" "No one; He was always there." But if causes can be dispensed with here, why not to start with? The usual answer is the Leibnizian one already given: God is a necessary being, and so needs no cause, while the world is merely contingent. Stated so baldly, this seems to beg the question. The rejoinder might be that while every particular in the world is contingent, the world as a whole is necessary. There are causes *in* the world, but not *of* the world. (That God is uniquely a necessary being forms the substance of the ontological argument, which I shall consider in a moment.)

The cosmological argument rests on another assumption, which Russell has criticized, that the series of causes cannot be infinite but must stop somewhere. Aristotle supposed an infinite regress to be logically unacceptable. Kant argued that if the history of the world stretched backward forever, we could never have arrived at the present moment, for an infinite length of time would have had to be already traversed, and a "completed infinite," as it came to be called, is contradictory. Russell pointed out that not every infinite regress is a vicious regress, and that an infinite series can very well be traversed if there is an infinite time to do it in. Some infinite series have no beginning (like the series of negative integers in order of size, −2 being larger than −3), some have no end (the positive integers), some have neither, and some both (the rational numbers between 0 and 1 exclusive or inclusive, respectively). The premises of the cosmological argument are as problematic as the conclusion it tries to demonstrate. Contemporary theories of the "age of the universe" do not refer to a beginning in the sense of the cosmological argument but only to a beginning of the present structure or pattern (such as the expansion of the galaxies).

The subtlest and most dubious argument for the existence of God is the *ontological argument.* In this argument, the very concept of God ascribes to Him an attribute from which His existence follows. There are two forms of the argument according to the attribute in question.

In one form of the argument propounded by religious thinkers as diverse as St. Anselm and Patanjali, the founder of Yoga, God is defined as a perfect being. Were He lacking existence, He would fall short of perfection: if something is bad, it would be better that it did not exist; but if something is good, it is all the better for being real. God is the limit of the scale of perfection; the very idea of this limit is of something existing. What is contained in our idea of something must, by all the force of logic, belong to whatever our idea is of—triangles *must* have three sides, siblings *must* have brothers or sisters. A perfect being, by the same logic, must exist—and that is God.

To this Kant replied that "existence" does not designate an attribute of things: my idea of a table, say, and my idea of an existing table do not differ in any respect, though of course there is a difference between thinking of a table and believing that a table exists. The difference here is between a concept and a judgment, not between a concept which lacks and a concept which includes a supposed attribute of existence. The existence of a table would not follow from my thinking of an existing table. In Anselm's day, centuries earlier, the objection had already been made that the ontological argument would just as validly prove the existence of a perfect island, or a perfect anything else, if existence were contained in the very idea of perfection.

Here the second form of the argument comes to the fore. In all these other cases we are thinking of something contingent, something which could either exist or not, so far as logic is concerned. God, however, is thought of as a *necessary* being. It is true that from our thought of a contingent existent its actual existence does not follow, for this depends on the existence of whatever it is contingent upon. But such a qualification does not apply to necessary existence. Plants bear witness to the reality of roots, Maimonides pointed out; it would be absurd to suppose that roots themselves need roots. That God is thought of as a necessary existent Spinoza states in the doctrine that the existence and the essence of God are one and the same. Leibniz formulates the doctrine this way: in God it is sufficient to be possible in order to be actual; for contingent existence, however, not only its actuality but its very possibility depends on God.

In Descartes and Leibniz there is also to be found an argument compounded of both the cosmological and the ontological arguments. The fact that men have the idea of God means that there must be something adequate to produce the idea; it cannot be something in this finite and imperfect world, and *a fortiori* not something in men's minds. It can be nothing other than God Himself, whose existence is therefore proved by our having an idea of Him.

The fundamental difficulty with the argument for the existence of God based on the conception of God as a necessary being is its confusing causal and logical necessity. Something *must* come to be only in the sense that its cause has already occurred; something *must* already exist only because it is the sole cause of an existing effect. Darwin stated that there must exist in South America a butterfly with an unbelievably long proboscis because he had found flowers there so deep that they could not otherwise be fertilized; astronomers knew that a planet must exist beyond Uranus to account for the observed perturbations in its orbit. Logical necessity, by contrast, does not relate to existence but to the entailment between one proposition and another—a relation which is always hypothetical: *if* the one proposition is true, then the other must also be true. Necessary truth which is not hypothetical applies only to tautologies (§17), and these pay for their necessity by being void of factual content. The ontological argument sooner or later rests on the claim that God (or the concept of God) is exceptional in some relevant respect. But if exceptional logic is to be employed, there is no point in propounding arguments to start with.

The arguments so far considered are interrelated; what they have in common is an objective thrust, a claim to a truth independent of our wanting to believe it. There is another line of argument which takes a different tack, holding that we may be well advised to believe in the existence of God because of what such a belief means to us; this is the *pragmatic argument*.

One version of this argument is *Pascal's Wager*. Pascal argued that to wager that God exists is a good bet, for if you gain, you gain all; if you lose, you lose nothing. To this it may be objected that, for a good bet, the probability of winning must be greater than 0; it is unclear what reason there is for supposing that this condition has been met. Moreover, there is surely a significant difference between religious faith and playing the odds.

Kant gives the pragmatic argument another form. Virtue does not always make for happiness in this world; we must therefore postulate (assume) the existence of God, as well as of an immortal soul, for the sake of morality. The sense of duty would otherwise be left without leverage on action. But first, morality may not demand that happiness be proportional to virtue, especially if virtue is its own reward. Second, morality may be a prerequisite to religion rather than the other way around (§90)—we may need to postulate an objective difference between right and wrong in order to give substance to a sense of the divine. Or, both the sense of duty and the sense of the divine might be without objective validation; the pragmatic argument would then amount to no more than an encouragement to believe what we choose. "It is expedient that there should be gods," Ovid wrote (in a book called, of all things, *The Art of Love*), "and since it is expedient, let us believe that gods exist."

The pragmatic argument is not necessarily a matter of expediency in the pejorative sense—that is the position taken by William James. What he called *the will to believe* he defended as a logical right to believe even though "our merely logical intellect may not have been coerced." When logic is called "mere" whatever argument follows may well be viewed with suspicion. James urged that if there is no more reason to reject a proposition than to accept it, we have a right to accept it if doing so is advantageous for any reason, even if not because of the preponderance of evidence in its favor. But the psychological consequences of believing a proposition are not to be confused with the logical consequences of the proposition itself. We do not have a right to believe anything merely because doing so would be desirable, unless the desirability is grounded in the usefulness of accepting the logical consequences of the belief; whether this is true in the case of a belief in the existence of God is a question not to be begged, or we may as well beg the fundamental question to start with. If there is no preponderance of evidence in either direction—and certainly if the evidence either way is zero—our right is not to believe what we choose but only to suspend judgment. Even if we must act on one assumption or the other, action does not presuppose belief, as Pascal already saw. Religion can hardly rest on the outcome of tossing a coin, even if "In God We Trust" were inscribed on both sides of the coin.

86. The Nature of God

I set aside the question of the existence of God to consider, rather, the meaning of the term; what is it whose existence is being argued? In the history of religion, warring creeds have typically not denied the existence of other gods; instead, they have reinterpreted these others so as to derogate their qualities—for instance, by making them manifestations or ministers of the true Deity, or by reducing them to the status of demons and other such lesser and malignant beings.

The qualities reserved for one's own God are as likely to reflect the worshipper as what he worships. *Anthropomorphism* in religion was attacked as long ago as the pre-Socratic philosopher Xenophanes, who remarked that if horses believed in a god he would have four legs. Fifteen centuries later Maimonides set himself the task of interpreting every anthropomorphic expression in Scripture—and there are many—as analogical and metaphorical, thereby retracing, in part, a road already traveled by Philo of Alexandria. It is not easy and in principle it may be impossible to explicate religious language, when it invokes the name of God, without recourse to analogy and metaphor. Among the world's major religions there is an extraordinary degree of commonality of conceptions of deity, even of the idioms and allegories by which the conceptions are expressed.

Theistic religion conceives God in unrestricted terms. He is the Creator of matter, the necessary Ground of contingent being. He is the Fountainhead of world energy, the supreme Power, Lord of Hosts and Voice in the Whirlwind. He is the Source of world order, Author of nature, the

Lawgiver Who transforms chaos to cosmos. God is the seat of a familiar set of *cosmic attributes:* He is infinite, eternal, omnipresent; the Supreme Being and Ultimate Reality; almighty, one (or else His power would be limited by the power of other gods), the first and the last; all-knowing, the Sovereign of the world, King of Kings, majestic and sublime.

Magical practices and superstitious beliefs give way to religious cult and creed when cosmic powers are moralized. The gods are neither controlled nor propitiated but imitated and worshipped as the locus of our highest ideals and values. This differentiates the story of Noah from the epic of Gilgamesh from which it derives or with which it has common sources: Gilgamesh was saved while others were destroyed in a flood only as a mark of arbitrary favor or displeasure, while Noah was a righteous man in a wicked generation. God promulgates a moral Law, and is the Judge of all the world according to whether men live by His Law. God is also Guardian and Shepherd, a loving Father, especially to the poor and oppressed, the helpless and lowly. He is the summit of all man's aspirations, the source of our deepest joys; wisdom lies in seeking Him and living in His fellowship. God is thus also the seat of a set of *moral attributes:* He is righteous, upright, and altogether just; benevolent and compassionate, giving comfort and consolation; patient, long-suffering, merciful, and forgiving; a Being of consummate purity and goodness, perfect in all His ways.

Traces of the synthesis of the cosmic with the moral functions of deity, and a corresponding synthesis of the cosmic and moral attributes, can sometimes be identified in the earlier stages of religions. The Vedas focus on Prajapati, the king of the gods, the cosmic divinity, and on Varuna, god of the gentle rain which falls on the just and the unjust alike, a deity which becomes in due course the locus of care and compassion. Elohim is often interpreted (for instance, by Judah Halevi) as the cosmic deity, the First Cause, discernible by reason, while Yahweh is the personal deity, the locus of moral attributes, encountered in prophetic vision.

The cosmic divine manifests itself as the *sacred;* dedicating a person, thing, or action as the locus or occasion for this manifestation is its *sanctification.* The moral divine is manifested as the *holy;* the dedication is known as *purification.* Corresponding religious feelings or attitudes (§91) can also be distinguished, the cosmic divine evoking awe (usually miscalled "fear") and a sense of *humility,* while the moral divine evokes love and a sense of *gratitude.*

Concomitant with this moralization of cosmic forces, there has usually been a movement from primitive polytheism to the *monotheism* of the major theistic religions. The plural ending of the word "Elohim," and various plural locutions ("Let us make man . . .") in Scripture, may point to an earlier polytheism (these plurals are interpreted by fundamentalists as referring to various aspects or emanations of Deity). An intermediate stage has been called *henotheism, kathenotheism,* or "opportunist monotheism," giving ascendancy to one god in special times, places, or circumstances; it is *monolatry* rather than monotheism—the worship of one god while not denying the existence of others. Judaeo-Christian monotheism is an affirmation of cosmic unity and of a unity of the moral order, as against the idea of the existence of a locus of cosmic Evil as well as of Good, a duality between Satan and God, a Power of Darkness and a Power of Light. This was the creed of the Manichaean heresy attacked by Augustine (who had at one time subscribed to it) and of the Albigensian heresy in the late Middle Ages. Residual polytheistic and henotheistic cults and creeds are generally accommodated by some form of the Hindu idea of "avatars"—personifications, manifestations, emanations, theophanies in various forms—of the one true God.

In some religious philosophies, notably Vedanta, monotheism in turn gives way to metaphysical *monism*. God is not the Supreme Reality but the sole Reality; conversely, the whole of reality is God. If this reality is identified with nature, the world of our experience, the doctrine is known as *pantheism*. It was the position of the Stoics and found expression in the nature worship of romanticism, as in these lines from Wordsworth:

All things in nature are . . .
The workings of one mind, the features
Of the same face, blossoms upon one tree;
Characters of the great apocalypse,
The types and symbols of eternity,
The first and the last and midst and without end.

Such locutions are reminiscent of mysticism, with which, however, pantheism is not to be confused (§89).

If God is not exhausted in the world process but transcends it so that the world, though divine, is only a part of God, the doctrine is known as *panentheism*—the position of Sankara, Spinoza, Whitehead, and many other philosophers. Spinoza, a century after his death aptly described (by the romanticist Novalis) as the "God-intoxicated" philosopher, was said to aim at seeing all things in God and God in all things. In Judaism, God is often called, even in prayer, the Place *(ha-Makom);* as the Talmud explains, the world is not the place of God, God is the place of the world. The Master, when a boy, was challenged by a visitor, "I will give you a ducat if you tell me where God is." The boy at once replied, "I will give you a thousand if you tell me where He is not." All this relates to cosmic rather than to moral divinity. In terms of the moral functions of deity, more to the point is another dictum of the Master's: "Where is God? Everywhere? No. God is wherever He is allowed to be."

God conceived as being in the world is known as *immanent;* what lies beyond is *transcendent*. That God is both immanent and transcendent was most simply put in a poem by Judah Halevi (who was more distinguished as a poet than as a philosopher):

Where shall I find You?
High and hidden is Your place.
Where shall I not find You?
The world is full of Your glory!

The word *Adonai,* usually translated as "Lord," is sometimes interpreted as meaning the transcendent God, and *Yahweh* the immanent God. The one is unrevealed deity; the other, the divine as it reveals Itself. As transcendent, God eludes attributes, for these are to be found in the world, or else they are extensions, generalization, idealizations of what is to be found here. Vedanta accordingly distinguishes between Nirguna Brahman (without guna: attributes, or strands of being—§38) and Saguna Brahman (having attributes). (The "N" and "S" are the negative and affirmative prefixes which reappear in the words "no" and "yes"—English being an Indo-European language.) Nirguna Brahman, being without characteristics, is virtually identical with the *Makom* or Place of Judaism and *Sunyata* or the Void of Mahayana Buddhism. It is what Meister Eckhart, the fourteenth-century German mystic, spoke of as "the still waste wherein is no distinction." Whitehead correspondingly contrasts the "antecedent" or "primordial" nature of God with God's "consequent" nature, the reaction on God of the temporal world.

A similar distinction is often drawn between God as He is in Himself and God in relation to man, as an object of worship. The word "God" is sometimes used only for the second, the first being designated the *Absolute;* in Hinduism the names are, respectively, *Brahman* and *Isvara.* Such pairs of names are assumed to have the same denotation, differing only in their connotation, like a woman's married and maiden name. Eckhart wrote, "In Himself He is not God, in the creature only does He become God." As a mystic, Eckhart aspired to overcome even the ultimate barrier imposed by this distinction: "I ask to be rid of God, that is, that God by His grace would bring me into the Essence, that Essence which is above God and above distinction." At the opposite pole of religious devotion is the ritualism of the Mimamsa, which concerns itself with God only in relation to man, and even that relation only as constituted by the rituals. For them, God is defined as "that which is signified, in a sacrificial injunction, by the fourth case ending"—the case used with the name of Him to Whom the offering is being made.

In many theologies, notably that of the Kabbala, there is a doctrine of *sefirot,* aspects or emanations of the divine. In various systems, some ten or so emanations are distinguished; since each is identified by several names, it is not easy to establish correspondences among different theologies, although there is a considerable degree of commonality. Among the most widespread conceptions are the following. The wholly transcendent aspect of deity is the *En Sof,* the Infinite; other designations (or else distinct entities) are the "Simple Point" and "Nothing." *Adonai* is interpreted in some systems as the Creator, the First Cause. Particular philosophic interest attaches to what is known as *El* (the singular form of the same root which appears in the plural in *Elohim*). *El* is the foundation, the ground of stability, of natural law, the root of all existence; it is the reproductive element in nature, potency. Like its Hindu analogue, *sakti,* it is often associated with phallic symbolism. The sum of the immanent activity of the divine is known as the *Shechinah* or Presence.

The *sefirot,* as well as less personalized or reified aspects of the divine, are commonly subsumed under the two major moral attributes of justice and mercy, corresponding to Elohim and Yahweh, Kyrios and Theos, Prajapati and Varuna. The first in each pair is closer to the cosmic deity, but both belong to the moral aspect. Compassion is often identified with a particular one of the emanations (*Rachamim*); each religion has its own divinities serving especially as the locus of this attribute—Mary; Vishnu the Preserver, and his avatar, Krishna; Avalokitesvara; and Kwan-yin. Another common grouping is of masculine and feminine aspects: the *yang* and *yin* of abstract cosmology; the god and his consort when divinity is personalized as in Siva and Parvati (or combined, in the bisexual figures of Shiva Ardha-Nari); God and the Shechinah, especially as dealt with in the *Zohar,* the Shechinah being the divine Bride and Queen.

The willingness to ascribe to God attributes which, if not anthropomorphic, at any rate relate to the affairs of this world makes possible a distinctive treatment of the problem of creation, why God made the world. The extraordinary answer offered is that God needs us. It is only in His creatures that He becomes God, as we saw with Eckhart. God, as immanent deity, is not only Lawgiver and Judge but is Himself a participant in the cosmic process, not only the umpire but also one of the players. Human actions determine more than man's fate; they also effect cosmic destinies. "Why was man created?" the Master asked. "In order to perfect his soul? No. Man was created to raise up the heavens."

There is a familiar moral sense in which man is given cosmic responsibility. The Talmud remarks that a judge who even for one hour passes judgment in accord with the principles of justice is credited as if he had become a partner of God in the creation of the world. This partnership is taken literally in the view of which I am now speaking, that of the sixteenth-century Kabbalist Isaac Luria. The creation of the world is the result of God's contraction into Himself, a withdrawal which leaves sparks of the divine fire encased in embers we experience as the physical world. It is man's task to shatter the outer shells, releasing the sparks within to rise to their Source. The Shechinah, God's Presence in the world, shares with the world the longing for the Divine which has departed, as for Her Beloved. In the political idioms more suited to our times, there is a cosmic government-in-exile. It is man's task to restore the divine rule or, in other metaphors, to unite the heavenly lovers, to put an end to the exile of both man and God.

This man can accomplish because each of his actions, notably those prescribed in the cult, has cosmic as well as earthly consequences, in accord with a familiar metaphysics of correspondences between the upper and the lower worlds (§39). Where you stand, said Moses Cordovero, Luria's teacher, there stand all the worlds. The idea is elaborated in S. Ansky's *The Dybbuk,* a dramatization of the kabbalistic world of hassidism; says the Rabbi:

> And once a year, at the appointed hour on the Day of Atonement, the High Priest entered the Holy of Holies and there revealed aloud the Divine Name. And as this

hour was holy, so was it terrible and dangerous beyond words. If, in that hour, which God forbid, a sinful or a wayward thought had entered the mind of the High Priest, it would have brought on the destruction of the world. Every spot whereon a man stands to lift his eyes to heaven, that place is a Holy of Holies. Every human being created by God in His own image and likeness is a High Priest. Each day of a man's life is the Day of Atonement; and every word he speaks from his heart is the name of the Lord.

I find this doctrine moving and even compelling, but there is something unreal about it. The distinctions drawn are dangerously near to providing only a closed system of ideas (§23); it is far from clear how their meanings might be more objectively specified. Indeed, there is something selr-defeating about attempts at such specifications; most theologians would agree with Maimonides that we understand God in the measure in which we grasp His incomprehensibility. Buber has spoken to the same effect: "Woe to the man so possessed that he thinks he possesses God."

Even if the conceptualizations of God's nature were clear, if someone were suddenly to ask, "How do you know that God is thus and not otherwise?" I, for one, would be at a loss. Corresponding to what Maimonides said about understanding God is Augustine's dictum about the knowledge of God: He is best known in not knowing Him. This is the standpoint of *negative theology*—we can know what God is not, but not what He is. It is the position taken by many philosophies of religion; in the Upanishads it is called the *neti neti* teaching: "not this, not this."

Language seems to be altogether inadequate to what a religious person might know and understand. "When we have found the Father and Maker of all this universe," Plato asks in the *Timaeus,* "how shall we be able to speak of Him to all men?" Plotinus afterwards pointed out that Its nature is that nothing can be affirmed of It, for It transcends all the catagories presupposed in our affirmations. Years ago, a fellow student of philosophy, filling out an admission form, protested against an item asking for his religion by identifying himself as a Taoist. To the inevitable question of clarification he replied coldly with the opening sentence of the Tao Te Ching: "The *Tao* which can be spoken is not the true *Tao*." Yet he did speak, after all. The Zen monk, no longer a novice, knew that Zen, too, is not to be spoken, and so appealed to the *roshi*, "Show me the Way without using words." The rejoinder was, "Ask me without using words!" Here philosophy stops short.

87. The Problem of Evil

All religions claim for themselves the most important place in people's lives. In return, they assign to man the most important place in the scheme of things. The scheme is God's, and in most religions He has worked it out for the sake of man. Saadya Gaon, the tenth-century Jewish theologian who founded the scientific exegesis of Scripture, characterizes man as the axle of the world, the point around which all else turns. Most religionists would agree, while philosophers of religion are likely to be less hominocentric. For all religion, life is meaningful and purposive, and the governance of the world is suited to human purposes. The working of the divine plans and powers, from the standpoint of this suitability, is known as *Providence.* It is conceived in ways as varying as are the conceptions of God.

The most primitive is *anthropomorphic* Providence, little more than a potentate whose purposes can be deflected or modified by bribery and persuasion—sacrifice and prayer. Although the locutions of anthropomorphic Providence abound in the major religions, they need not be taken more literally than any other anthropomorphic idioms (§88).

The concept of a *hidden* Providence does not provide for controlling the divine will but for predicting it and thereby taking steps to avert it. The prediction is assumed to be possible on the basis of omens preceding or accompanying the actualization of the divine will. Here we have all the devices of what is significantly called divination which, in *prophecy* in the narrow sense, may be accomplished by the communication of God's will or its direct apprehension by the soothsayer. More commonly, it is achieved by augury, the interpretation of what appear to be random events—patterns of tea leaves, spilled flour, entrails of sacrificial animals, the flight of birds, dropped sticks, and various devices for casting lots. Orderly and even fixed patterns are also capable of projective interpretation, as in astrology and palmistry. Or recourse might be had to circumstances in which the supposed gifts of the soothsayer can come into play, as in crystal-gazing or communion with the spirits of the dead. In all this, religious practice merges with superstition, as the concept of an anthropomorphic Providence brings religion to the verge of magic, in which Powers are compelled to do our bidding by the recitation of appropriate formulas and the performance of appropriate rituals.

The concept of *watchful* Providence is a way of emphasizing the meaning and purpose of even apparently insignificant and trivial events. "Not a sparrow will fall to the ground without your Father's will," say the Gospels; the Talmud writes, "No one on earth bruises his fingers unless it is decreed from above." It may very well happen that what man proposes God disposes; *our* purposes do not always accord with His. The prayer is not that God's will be done, for that is sure to happen; it is that our will coincide with His. It coincides when we walk only in His Way, living by His Law. David said to the Philistine, "You come to me with a sword and spear and javelin, but I come to you in the name of God." It is for this reason that David triumphed over Goliath; so it was that as Psalmist he wrote, "Unless God keep the city, the watchman wakens in vain."

It is easy to fall into tautology here and conclude only after the event what the intention of divine Providence was. Spinoza clearly saw that when it comes to explaining events, the will of God is "the sanctuary of ignorance." Man's freedom is easily compromised or even willingly sacrificed, if we believe—in what is miscalled faith—that God will act on our behalf instead. There is magnificent self-reliance without any diminution of faith in the cry of Bar Kochba, the heroic leader of a Jewish revolt against the Romans, "God, don't help us, but don't spoil it for us!"

The concept of a *telic* Providence does not relate to particular individuals or events but to the embodiment of purpose in the very nature of things. Here religion is absorbed into a metaphysics of *immanent teleology* (§40): The end to which each thing moves is prefigured in its kind, as an innate potentiality belonging to the kind whose actualization, what Aristotle called an entelechy, gives form to otherwise featureless matter. The end may, however, fail to be attained; we then speak of something "unnatural" or "perverted." The question what is truly "natural" in such contexts is easily begged; on the other hand, the answer is not altogether arbitrary—there *are* perversions (§55). A closely related concept is the Jewish *tachlit,* which means, significantly enough, both outcome and result, goal and purpose, as though these were equivalent. Here the danger of egocentrism is especially great: the *tachlit* of the horse is said to be to carry loads, but that is because we have made of him a beast of burden and broken his spirit in order to do so. Men have destroyed whole species and enslaved one another with the satanic excuse that it is God who has so ordained.

There is a concept of *natural* Providence which invokes only natural law and an all-embracing system of nature. What is providential is that the world allows for human values, that goals can be attained and purposes fulfilled if we have the wisdom to know what is worth pursuing among the real possibilities nature provides, and the courage to embark on the pursuit. These are the perspectives of Confucius and Buddha, the Stoics and Spinoza, and of some religious philosophies in the Judaeo-Christian tradition, although such interpretations are controversial. What is called for by this concept is "natural piety"—the readiness to obey nature, in order to command her—rather than the acceptance of an arbitrary and incomprehensible will, externally imposed.

In all theisms, however they conceive of Providence, the world is seen as being in accord with human standards of value. God has made everything beautiful, says the Preacher; the midrashic legend is that God went on creating worlds and destroying them till at last He created this world and said of it, "It is very good." How, then, are we to account for the existence of evil in the world? How can we continue to believe in a good God of an evil world? This is one of the most pressing and perplexing difficulties theistic religious philosophies face; it is known as *the problem of evil.*

The problem is traditionally formulated as an inconsistent triad, a set of three propositions, each of which seems undeniable, while, apparently, not all three can simultaneously be true. These are (1) there is evil in the world, (2) God has the power to have made the world otherwise if He chose, and (3) being good, He does so choose. If any of these three propositions is denied, the remaining two can easily be accepted. But how is any of them to be denied? The problem is in the question put by Gideon to the Angel: "If God be with us, why has all this happened to us? Where are all His wondrous works which our fathers told us of?" The question is raised more than a thousand years later by Boethius: "If there be a God, where do so many evils come from? If there be no God, where does any good come from?" A thousand years later still, the question of how to assert eternal Providence and justify the ways of God to man is made vivid by Milton. The question is asked in our day by countless victims of cruelty and injustice and by countless others whose faith in a good God is shaken by what they see in His world.

Unlike other difficulties in the philosophy of religion, such as criticisms of the arguments for the existence of God, the problem of evil is felt most keenly by those who have faith. The Preacher recognizes that a righteous man may die in his righteousness while a wicked one lives a long life in his wrongdoing. The Psalmist confesses his envy of the prosperity of the wicked, who are not plagued like other men and say only, "How will God know?" Job declares with the eloquence of simplicity, "I cry aloud, but there is no justice!"

God could surely have things otherwise if he chose. In the *Timaeus*, Plato writes that God desired that all things should be good and nothing bad, adding the remarkable qualification, "as far as this could be accomplished." Are there, then, limits to what God can accomplish? Would divinity so limited be worthy of man's worship? Platonism held that, in general, matter is the seat of evil; did God then not create matter, like all else, or is He but the locus of a superhuman technology which bends matter to His will, but only up to a point? It is the thrust of monotheism that there are no countervailing powers to limit God's will. Job therefore asks rhetorically "If it is not He [Who is the source of injustice], then who is it?"

Anatole France formulates a witty hypothesis in his *Revolt of the Angels:* There was indeed a conflict between God and Satan, as tradition recounts, but the outcome was that Satan was triumphant; it is only to be expected that the deposed Sovereign is described as diabolical and those still loyal to Him are said to be demons. Any doubt that this is what happened is dispelled by reflecting on the present state of things, from which it is surely clear that it is Satan who is now ruling the world, whatever he calls himself.

This is only to abandon faith. Yet what Abraham asked when God declared His intention of destroying the cities of the plain whatever innocents might remain in them, is an insistent question: Shall not the Judge of all the earth do justly? If God Himself does not shrink from injustice, where is the path of righteousness in which man can walk? Where, indeed, is God Himself in my hour of need? asks the Psalmist. Why do you hide yourself in times of trouble? God has forgotten. Why? Why have You forsaken me? I call by day but You do not answer, at night and there is no rest for me. Why are You silent?

Once there was brought before the Master a man accused of impiety in his prayers. "Yes," he admitted, "I said to God: It is true that I am a sinner, guilty of wrongdoing. But what about You, O God? How many are the innocents you allow to suffer and die, victims of injustice who had none but You to help them? What of the disease and famine and flood with which You overwhelm us? What of the poverty and misery there is yet in Your world? I'll tell you what, God: You forgive me, and I'll forgive You!" At which the Master exclaimed, "Ah, you let Him off too easy! You could have held out for the redemption of all the world!"

The traditional treatment of the problem of evil takes three tacks.

1. First is simply the *denial* that there is any evil. The *ontological defense*—found, for instance, in Augustine and Maimonides—is that only good is real, all evil being a privation of a good, as blindness is not something in itself but only the absence of the capacity of sight. Such metaphysics provides no more than comfortless verbalism. Cold is only the absence of heat which alone really exists; yet men may freeze for all that. The *psychological defense* urges that what seems to be evil is no longer such if seen in a larger perspective which includes the long-range consequences: God writes straight with crooked lines, said Augustine. This is an instance of the "for all you know" fallacy, deriving conclusions from ignorance and hope. Such derivations cut both ways: if what seems to be evil may be good in a larger perspective, what seems to be good may turn out to be evil. What perspective is large enough? And why should man suffer, in his limited perspectives, from the limitations with which he was created? A purportedly *logical defense* argues that good has meaning only in contrast with evil, as music can be heard only in silence, and bright colors need a dark background. The universe, Leibniz maintained, could not be made better than it is. To the shallow optimism which holds that this is the best of all possible worlds, the reply has been made that if so, it is only because everything in it is a necessary evil. That evil is necessary makes it all the worse for God, the ground of all necessity.

2. The second tack assigns to evil certain ethical and religious *functions*. Evil teaches a moral lesson, serving as a warning and correction of our sinful ways. But it is elementary pedagogy that people learn better from rewards than from punishments; in any case, God could surely instruct His creatures less painfully. The pain, the argument goes on, is a test for the righteous, and will be followed by a proper reward. God creates the cure with the disease, and suffering is temporary: "Tears may tarry for the night but joy comes in the morning." But how if we do not live to see the dawn? "O that You would hide me in hell," Job cries, "that You would keep me hidden until Your anger is past, that you would set me a time and remember me." But men serve a life sentence, and there is no afterlife in which injustice will be redressed: "Till the heavens be no more they shall not awake nor be roused out of their sleep."

3. The third line of argument is that the evil which man suffers is a just *retribution* for sin. As Tennyson has it,

> *The world is dark with griefs and graves,*
> *So dark that men cry out against the heavens.*
> *Who knows but that the darkness is in man?*

There is in man an innate depravity. In the Book of Job, the Voice asks: "Shall mortal man be just in the eyes of God? Even His angels He charges with folly. How much more those who live in houses of clay, whose foundation is in the dust!" Our human frailties are the inheritance by the sons of Adam of man's original rebellion against God. But Who is it Who has created us with these frailties? Where is the justice in punishing the sons for the sins of their fathers, as Ezekiel and other prophets demanded to know? Why should any person be punished for what are not his sins but the sins of the nation? The soldier who dies in an unjust war dies all the more unjustly for having done his duty. To tell every person who suffers that he deserves his suffering only adds insult to his injuries and begs all the basic questions. This is the significance of the prologue to the Book of Job, in which we are told explicitly that Job was not a sinful man. Does religious faith rest on the morally monstrous denial that there are ever any innocent victims?

Three sorts of evil are to be distinguished. *Moral evil* is what man himself produces. Traditional apologists account for moral evil as a necessary consequence of human free will. I would say, rather, with Spinoza, that it is a consequence of human bondage—of ignorance, folly, and hatred. Our predicament is that while only the free man pursues what is truly good, only what is good can nurture freedom. There is no help for it but to use such good as we have attained to cope with moral evil.

Natural evil is the consequence of no man's action but of the world as it is. Here we face not a predicament but an endless succession of problems. Just as religion does not negate moral evil or it could not define moral aspiration, so also does it not negate natural evil or it could not distinguish earth from heaven. That life always leaves something to be desired is not a shortcoming but the very ground of living.

It is *cosmic evil* which poses the problem of evil: that neither man nor nature but God Himself is the source of evil. Cosmic evil is the negation of value as such, the absence of any real difference between good and bad, right and wrong, since the Perfect Being, righteous in all His ways, is nevertheless responsible for evil. The challenge to faith is not in the circumstance that there are injustices in the world but in the possibility that justice has no meaning, either in the world or transcending it.

Here we encounter not a problem to be solved but a puzzle to be resolved. The puzzle stems from the groundless assumption that the virtuous man has entered into a contract with God; cosmic evil is God's failure to live up to His part of the bargain. Satan asks, "Does Job fear God for nothing? Have You not made a hedge around him, around his house, and all that he has on every side?" Leave the contract unfulfilled, and see what becomes of Job's faith. But Eliphaz asks, "Can even a wise man be profitable to God? Is it any advantage to God that you are righteous? What does He gain when your ways are blameless?" Elihu adds, "If you sin even many times over what do you take from Him? Whether you are righteous or wicked is for you, in your humanity." The notion of a contract underlying the sense of cosmic injustice is tossed aside by the Voice out of the Whirlwind: "Who has given Me anything beforehand that I should repay him? All that is under the whole heavens is Mine."

So far as man's relations with God are concerned, we do get what we have bargained for—because there has been no bargain to start with. True, moral action springs from certain expectations. But what differentiates morality from sheer prudence, and virtue from strategic skill, is that the expectations relate to the *intrinsic* consequences of moral action, not to extrinsic outcomes (§52). The intrinsic consequences are indeed what morality expects them to be. "But, one says, I see the noble and good perishing of hunger and cold," Epictetus writes. "Well, and do you not see those who are not noble and good perishing of luxury and ostentation?" It is these, the intrinsic consequence, which are the conditions of cosmic justice, and these conditions are met.

Win or lose, the game we are playing is not crooked. That there are rules for the game is only to say that principles of morality are not arbitrary and groundless, that meaning and value are not subjective illusions. The child will not continue the game if he is not winning, and older infantilisms also make losing unbearable. For the most part, as Spinoza saw, we judge good and evil not *sub specie aeternitatis* but in the light of our personal undertakings. Maimonides wrote in his *Guide for the Perplexed* that the man lacking in wisdom imagines that the whole universe exists only for him. If *his* desires are not fulfilled, therefore, he accuses God.

The Preacher enjoins, "In the day of prosperity be joyful, in the day of adversity consider: God has made the one as well as the other." Here, Job's faith finds expression: "What! Shall I accept good at the hand of God and shall I not accept evil?" Both are equally undeserved, because morality is not a matter of deserts. What the man of faith has established with God is not a contract but a *covenant,* which does not demand payment but makes a free gift of love. The disavowal of demands is a consequence of the humility and gratitude which embody a sense of the divine. Job's conclusion, when all is said, is stated in the very first chapter of the book: "God gave and God has taken away; blessed be the Name of God!" Kierkegaard was right: it is because Job said "God gave" before he said "God has taken away" that he was able to conclude with a blessing.

88. Religious Doctrines

Religion is not only church and cult but also *creed,* a set of distinctive beliefs. In general, belief is related, directly or indirectly, to action (§11). Religious beliefs are likely to be so far removed from the concreta of daily experience and so involved with symbolic functions in the cult that connections with action are often difficult to trace—except for the actions of expressing and communicating the creed. This is giving lip service to the creed, if no more significant actions are undertaken. We may look first, instead, at a person's actions, then infer the set of beliefs which find expression in his actions. In the religious context, such a set of beliefs is a *credo:* the difference between creed and credo is a special instance of the difference between professed and lived philosophy (§5). Religions differ from one another not only in the importance they attach to creed but also in the ease with which the creed can be made to serve as credo—how closely the creed relates to the concerns of men outside the context of the cult.

Creeds can set people against one another just as churches can be divisive. Such divisiveness may be most marked within the church; the rejected creed is then identified as a *heresy*. Controversy seems to play as much of a part in religion as in politics, often because of divergencies in the practices of the cult; the Mishnah, which codifies the Judaic cult, consists of 523 chapters, of which 517 record disagreements. Most religious controversies focus on elements of creed, even if the disagreements also contain institutional or ritualistic components. Creeds are notoriously fallible; Plato says with good reason that on such subjects we must be content with a likely story. What chiefly signifies in a creed, however, is not its semantics but its pragmatics: not what it says about purported matters of fact, transcendent or no, but how it serves to give coherence and strength to our most basic commitments. Emile Durkheim, in his treatise on the *Elementary Forms of the Religious Life,* declares that no religions are false, since "all answer, though in different ways, to the given conditions of human existence."

Such a functionalist viewpoint of creeds is far more common among outside observers of religion than among the religionists. Those who subscribe to a creed seem inclined to make a *dogma* of it in the strict sense introduced earlier (§14): neither a bare assertion nor merely a proposition tenaciously adhered to but one held to be improper to question or even to examine. Hobbes compares "the mysteries of our religion" to pills which can cure if swallowed whole, but are thrown up without effect if they are chewed. Rejection of both experience and reason, evidence and argument, in order to cling to a traditional creed has gone to such lengths as even subjectivist and irrationalist philosophies find hard to justify. The Mimamsa has taken the position that the fact that the Vedas are at various points contradicted by ordinary experience only shows their superior authority. Western apologists have been guilty of similar absurdities. In defense of the date of the creation of the world computed in the seventeenth century by Archbishop James Ussher as being 4004 B.C. (a chronology then used for years in many editions of the Authorized Version of the Bible), the argument was put forward as late as Darwin's day that fossils plainly calling for a vastly longer history had been put into the rocks with that appearance only to test man's faith. That can scarcely be the reason why man was endowed with good sense.

Orthodoxy—adherence to the established creed—does not necessarily demand *fundamentalism:* a literalist interpretation of the Scriptures accepted by the church as authoritative and used as the foundation of the creed. Reinterpretations of doctrine are recurrent features of the history of all religions, as is resistance to the new interpretations by those whose vested interests commit them to the older creed—the endless conflict between prophet and priest. There are great differences among religions in the degree to which they are dogmatic or even doctrinaire; the Asian religions are admirable for the comparative absence in them of religious tyranny over free thought. Unchanging creeds cannot always continue to be appropriate to changing contexts. Commentators have noted that God told Moses to make new tablets "for those which you have broken," implying divine approval of this act; it may be as meritorious to break the old law as to promulgate a new one.

Doctrines as to the existence and nature of God and His relations to the world do not exhaust religious creeds. Whether or not there are *miracles* and, if so, how they are to be construed raises another set of issues which have occupied philosophers of religion. In some doctrines, belief in miracles is taken to be entailed by acceptance of the relevant scriptures. Other doctrines proceed in the converse direction, holding that the authority of the scriptures and the truth of the religion is established by the miracles. Hume supposed that religion without miracles cannot be believed by any reasonable person, so that religion stands or falls on the issue of whether miracles have indeed occurred.

What is a miracle? To define it as an event transcending the order of nature presupposes that we know what constitutes the natural order. The argument might be made that if the supposed miracle did in fact occur, it thereby disclosed itself to be a part of the order of nature. What was transcended by it was not nature but our prior ideas, now shown to be mistaken, of the limits of the natural order. Supposedly supernatural yogic powers, for instance, whether or not it is believed that anyone has such powers, are not seen as supernatural in their own cultural setting, just as we usually construe great artistic achievements as the result of native genius and prolonged discipline and not, as in Thomas Mann's *Doctor Faustus* and in the stories circulated about Paganini, the result of a pact with the Devil. The existence of apparently supernatural powers is today investigated, in what purports to be a naturalistic framework, by parapsychology, as it was a generation or two ago by the hard-headed British and American Societies for Psychical Research.

A miracle might be conceived as a providential irregularity in the order of nature, but its being an irregularity does not establish it as a consequence of any act of faith, especially a purely cultic act, a ritual or prayer. If it were such a consequence, a new regularity might be looked for in the perspectives of magic, not religion. A prayer which is always answered, though it asks for departure from the usual order of nature, is indistinguishable from a magic formula. Maimonides, an uncompromising critic of both magic and superstition, avoided the difficulty by holding that miracles were fitted into the order of nature from the beginning. In that case, it is not easy to state what differentiates them from other events, especially if grotesque deviations from the usual order of things—such as the power of speech displayed by Eve's serpent and Balaam's ass—are interpreted allogorically, as they were by Maimonides.

The occurrence of supposed irregularities, however interpreted, is doubtful in the extreme. The most compelling objection is that formulated by Hume. The evidence offered for such an occurrence must overcome the crushing weight of contrary evidence, without which the supposed event would not be an irregularity as required. No testimony is sufficient, therefore, to establish a miracle unless, as he says, its falsehood would be more miraculous than the fact which it endeavors to establish. Of course, the source of the evidence might be held to be unimpeachable, and the affirmation of the miracle to be infallible; this position, however, would simply beg the whole question.

Rejection or disparagement of miracles is not necessarily irreligious and may even stem from devoutly religious attitudes. Alleged miracles are often trivial. Ramakrishna, the nineteenth-century founder of the Hindu order bearing his name, was once crossing the countryside in the company of a monk. As they approached a ferry, for which they lacked the two-anna fee, the monk declared that his former teacher had practiced such austerities that he was able to walk across the river; at which Ramakrishna remarked, "His austerities are worth two annas."

If the events are undeniably significant and not to be duplicated by even a moderately advanced technology—as television replaces the clairvoyant or seer, antibiotics the laying on of hands, and the aircraft or spaceship the chariot of the gods—there are still strictly religious objections. The conception of a miracle as divine intervention suggests that God is not active in the ordinary course of things. The notion of a divine Providence limited to occasional miracles, or even revealing Itself only through such occasions, might well be repudiated by the person of faith.

In these perspectives belief in miracles is replaced by a sense of the *miraculous,* which is nourished by the continuing order of things rather than by supposed occasional departures from that order. Nature, the Master said, contains all the miracles of the six days of Creation. "I shall give you rains in their season," God declares; the season is as much His doing as is the rain. Miracles may be rare and special events, but the miraculous is of daily occurrence. The Judaic liturgy contains a prayer in which God is thanked for the miracles which He performs every evening, every morning, every afternoon. At the home of my Master, said the *hassid,* we waded in miracles, and scooped them up by the bucketful.

Comparable issues arise in connection with another frequent component of creeds: a doctrine of *immortality.*

An *empirical* conception of immortality cuts across religion and a number of other domains of belief, sophisticated as well as primitive. On this conception, we may continue to experience an individual after his death, by communication or by other marks of his literal presence, so that, presumably, he himself experiences his own survival. Such a belief characterizes *spiritualism* (sometimes called *spiritism,* so that the former term can be reserved for the opposite of metaphysical materialism). What the belief amounts to is not unfairly conveyed in Noel Coward's comedy, *Blithe Spirit.* Evidence in its favor is scanty and dubious at best; the empirical doctrine belongs rather to the occult sciences (that is, superstitions) than to religion.

The traditional doctrine is not empirical but *metaphysical:* that man has a soul, a simple, spiritual substance, which is incorruptible and thus immortal (§44).

Immortality can also be conceived *naturalistically.* In this view, a person survives by way of his continuing effect on the world. When good people die, says the Talmud, they are not truly dead, for their example lives. Bad examples also survive; Antony was not unduly cynical: the evil that men do lives after them, the good is oft interred with their bones. This is only to say that Hell has the same reality as Heaven. The objection might be raised that the survival of a person's name is not the same as *his* survival; his reputation, whether for good or for ill, might be undeserved, so that it is not truly his effects which persist. Perhaps the conclusion to be drawn is that in that case he is only thought to be surviving, or that he survives in his effects even though they are not recognized as being his.

The locus of an individual's identity is in his doings, not in some elusive metaphysical essence (§47). Walt Whitman rightly says of his *Leaves of Grass,* who touches this book touches a man; if so, the man did not come to a stop with Whitman's death. More accurately, the man died, but personal identity does not end so abruptly; it ends only as an inscription is at long last so eroded that it can no longer be read. The members of the French Academy are called "Immortals"—quite properly so far as concerns what is intended by the recognition. Whether the recognition is deserved—that is, whether the prediction is accurate—is another matter.

Here is survival rather than immortality in a strict sense: on this conception, eternity is out of the question. Moreover, though a person's name may survive and with it his identity, his awareness of himself and of his survival does not persist. These objections do not apply to a *religious* conception of immortality: eternal life is a life devoted to eternal things—a conception to be found in philosophers as diverse as Spinoza, Russell, Plato, and Peirce. He lives eternally who lives in the present, it has been said (by Wittgenstein among others). Nowadays the doctrine is misconstrued as the romantic myth of the eternal moment. What is involved, however, is absorption, not in momentary feelings but in timeless meanings. Buddha says: Those who are in earnest do not die; those who are thoughtless are as if dead already.

Contrary to common misconception or prejudice, there is a widespread emphasis in religion on the consummation of the religious endeavor in this very life. One who has attained such a consummation—a living saint—is known in India as *jivanmukti;* the concept is to be found not only in Samkhya and Vedanta but also in such non-Hindu creeds as the Jain and Buddhist. Apropos, no Asian religion propounds a doctrine of personal immortality in an afterlife (rebirth being another earthly existence and so providing a variant of the empirical conception of immortality touched on above and in §44). Nor is the metaphysical doctrine as important in Western religions as is often assumed; it is more emphasized in philosophies of religion than in the religions themselves, and perhaps most of all in popular mythologies and their literary expression—Dante, Milton, and the rest. The man of faith is likely to declare, with the Psalmist, "I shall see the goodness of God in the land of the living." Questioned about life after death, Confucius replied, "While you do not understand life, what can you understand of death?" The monk who asked the *roshi* how to be assured of life after death was bluntly told, "Leave that to Buddha; it is no business of ours."

Closely related to doctrines of immortality are conceptions of messianism. Two main lines of thought are to be distinguished. In one, best known through Christianity, the creed looks to the coming or the return of a messiah as one who saves or redeems mankind, mediating between man and God, interceding on man's behalf. Many religions, notably Judaism and Buddhism, while identifying distinguished or even unique individuals by a distinctive religious role, conceive of this role as that of a teacher rather than savior, one who enlightens, guides, and inspires rather than one who redeems. No man can ransom another from the death of the spirit, says the Psalmist; in the words of Buddha, the pure and the impure stand and fall by themselves.

In the second conception, the Messiah is the anointed one (the literal meaning of the word), chosen as herald to proclaim the messianic era. In this era, as in the political utopias derived from the conception, all noble human aspirations are to find fulfillment. In earlier versions the religious conception itself was defined politically. In the Talmud is written that there is no difference between this world and the days of the Messiah except in freedom from oppression by governments; the idea is restated in Maimonides. Many creeds formulate detailed doctrines of *eschatology*—"first and last things," the last Judgment, resurrection, and the like. In virtually all of them, however, those who live by the creed are enjoined to a life in which redemption is continuous rather than being reserved for a final apocalyptic moment.

Eschatology, far from being a necessary component of all creeds, is deliberately eschewed by a number of them. Buddha explicitly refused to deal with four questions: whether the world is eternal, whether it is infinite, whether there is a soul and, if so, whether it is immortal. The Apocryphal book of the *Wisdom of Sira* as well as the Talmud caution against occupying oneself with mysteries, with what has gone before and what will be hereafter. The *samsara* and *moksha* of Hindu thought, like the Buddhist *dukkha* and *Nirvana*, do not name any transcendent Hell and Heaven but the condition of man as he is and as he might be in this world. The fires of Hell, says the *aggada*, come from the wicked themselves. In the Midrash we are told that God inflicts on the wicked no more than an awareness of their shame and loss; when they are wholly aware, we might suppose, Paradise will be regained.

The conflict between science and religion which has loomed so large in the West is not intrinsic to religious doctrine, even of the Western religions. The world view of religion, considered in sufficiently fundamental terms, is basic both logically and historically to the scientific outlook, whose underlying conception is the religious one that this is an orderly and unified world, governed by a single set of universal and objectively grounded principles. In men like Copernicus, Kepler, Newton, and Einstein, such religious ideas entered into explicit awareness. Religionists have incorporated both into their creeds and into the philosophic doctrines explaining and justifying them, the conception of a natural order within which man must look to the fulfillment of his destiny. God sends rain; the commentator explains that He says to earth, "Bring Me your clouds and you will get rain." It was an understanding priest who, on being asked by his neighbor at a baseball game, "What does it mean that the batter made the sign of the cross when he stepped up to the plate?" replied, "Not a damned thing, if he can't hit!"

Natural piety, a respect for the ways of nature, a scale of values which takes the simple and natural as its ideal is a widely recognizable feature of the religious life—characteristic of Taoist, Stoic, Zen Buddhist, Quaker, *hassid,* and many others. In Chuang-tzu there is no anxiety about an afterlife or rituals preparing for it: "With heaven and earth for my coffin; with the sun, moon, and stars as my shroud; and with all creation to escort me to my grave—is not everything for my funeral ready?" "Call it Nature, Fate or Fortune," says Seneca; "all are names of the one and selfsame God." "What is the most wonderful Word?" asked the monk—the one true Word, the ultimate Teaching? To which the *roshi* rejoined, "What did you say?" What do you say, what are you saying? If the truth is not in our everyday speech, then there is no truth in us at all.

Science itself can be a *sadhana,* one of the paths to the fulfillment of religious aspiration, coordinate with the paths of moral action and of artistic expression. In the Talmud is written that one who has a scientific mind and refuses to apply himself is to be condemned for indifference to the wonders of God. For Spinoza, the study of nature leads to more than an appreciation of God's wonders; it leads to a direct apprehension of something of the mind of God. The more we understand things, he says, the more we understand God. A succession of philosophers from Plato and Aristotle to Maimonides and Spinoza conceive the outcome of the religious life to be, in Spinoza's terms, "the intellectual love of God"—a nearness to the divine in which the powers of the human mind play a central part.

In such philosophies, religious doctrines must satisfy the human mind. Scripture, even if thought to be directly revealed, must be harmonized with reason, for this also is God-given. Such rationality does not entail that only one religious doctrine can be true, as there is only one logic and only one arithmetic. There are analogous demands that the principles of art harmonize with reason, yet a multiplicity of artistic styles can be acknowledged. In our time, many people, repelled by the divisiveness stemming from doctrinal differences, misconstrue the ecumenical spirit as precluding any element of creed that is not to be found in all creeds, thereby allowing little more than an artificial and empty universalism. The underlying confusion is that already discussed (§6) between accepting others and agreeing with them. A doctrine which harmonizes with reason is not on that account demonstrated by reason; reasonable people may differ with one another even on much simpler matters than those dealt with in our creeds.

The demand which reason makes on religion can better be put negatively: that creeds should not be *un*reasonable. (I will consider in the next section whether faith can accommodate irrationality.) Doctrine is constantly reinterpreted in accord with prevailing standards of reasonableness, as the cult is reinterpreted by moral standards, and church organization by political standards. The key to rational interpretation of the sacred writings of religion is the idea of *allegory,* in a sufficiently broad sense to comprise various modes of symbolism. Philo of Alexandria and Maimonides are among the philosophers who especially elaborated an allegorical interpretation of Scripture, in a Platonist and an Aristotelian perspective, respectively. Allegories are construed as naturalistic—the flaming sword of the cherubim stands for the sun; as psychological—Adam stands for the rational soul, Eve for sense-perception, the serpent for pleasure; or as historical—the sun stands for the kingdom of David, the moon for the Sanhedria. Similar allegorical interpretations are made by Christian religionists and philosophers, as, for instance, Paul takes Sarah to stand for the Church. Doctrinal allegories easily merge into cultic symbolism.

Where reason makes its most undeniable contribution to religious doctrine is in purifying religion of superstition, especially when the doctrine is called upon to provide a basis for various features of the cult, such as the wearing of amulets, recitation of prayers at ancient graves, and the like. In words of striking modernity, Maimonides scores superstition as consisting of "false and fradulent notions with which old idolators used to mislead the ignorant masses in order to exploit them." Whatever its motives or functions, superstition is interwoven in the history of all the religions and is often given a religious sanction.

This sanction is tragically exemplified by the persecutions on charges of witchcraft. According to the laws of Charlemagne, in the ninth century, executing an alleged witch was to be accounted as murder. But in the fifteenth century, formal religious sanction was given to the belief in the evil power of witches; during the next two hundred years over 700,000 human beings were executed on the basis of that belief. Nor was the belief confined to the ignorant masses; William Harvey, the founder of modern medicine who demonstrated the circulation of the blood, was among the many devout and supposedly enlightened men who assisted at the examination of witches. Spinoza, who died fifteen years before the Salem witchcraft trials, might well be speaking for our time as well as his: "How blessed would our age be if it could witness a religion freed from all the shackles of superstition."

89. Religious Experience

The most basic component of religion is *faith*—the complex of feelings, attitudes, values, and commitments symbolized in the cult, organized in the church, and given doctrinal expression in the creed. A number of issues in the philosophy of religion turn on the relation of faith to reason.

At one extreme is the position that faith and reason stand *opposed* to one another. Reason is the greatest enemy faith has, said Luther. While reason insists that belief must be grounded on evidence and argument, faith, in this conception, is belief in defiance of the standards set by reason. The operative principle is that formulated by one of the Church Fathers in the third century and known as Tertullian's "rule of faith": *credo quia absurdum*—I believe because it is absurd, impossible. Such faith may be called *credulity* (§39). It testifies to a willingness to believe and a subsequent strength of conviction, but it does not have any objective reference, for this is what the standards of rational belief are meant to attain. Childhood's faith of which the poets speak is credulity, for the child has not yet learned to shape his beliefs in accord with realities rather than wish-fulfilling fantasies. The child has also not yet learned distrust and despair, so that he may also exemplify faith in another conception, to be considered in a moment.

Faith may be *distinguished* from reason without being counterposed to reason. Augustine defines faith as believing, on the word of God, what we do not see. The content of faith is not absurd but simply something not demonstrated by reason or experience—except religious experience and what our minds, illumined by God's grace, can make of it. We believe many things on the basis of testimony, Augustine points out, like the hearsay on which must rest a man's assurance of who his parents were. The testimony of Scripture, of prophet and saint, is not contrary to reason but only beyond what can be attained by reason alone. "Seek not to understand that you may believe," he therefore enjoins, "but believe that you may understand." What we understand provides a basis only for such beliefs as rest on reason.

Faith, Pascal said in the same vein, is God felt by the heart, not by reason; and the heart has its reasons which reason does not know. We may call this *romantic faith*, the reliance on feeling and will conceived in contradistinction to thought. The most thoroughgoing development of this point of view was carried out by Kant, who undertook, as he put it, to limit reason in order to make room for faith. In Kant's philosophy what we cannot possibly know we are nevertheless asked to believe in order to do justice to our moral sensibilities. The subjective reference characteristic of credulity thus applies to romantic faith as well.

A third conception of faith insists that what we believe must always be *consonant* with reason. John Locke put the requirement explicitly: "Nothing that is contrary to and inconsistent with the clear and self-evident dictates of reason has a right to be urged or assented to as a matter of faith." Here we may speak of *rational faith*, espoused, contrary to popular misconception, by many medieval thinkers—for instance, the eleventh-century philosopher Bahya ibn Pakuda: "You are obligated to use your own faculties to gain clear and definite knowledge of the truth, so that your faith and conduct may rest on a foundation of tradition, reason, and personal understanding." Maimonides, Aquinas, and Sankara are distinguished exponents of rational faith. Whether essential elements of religious doctrine can be established on a rational foundation is controversial. It is denied both by antireligionists and by proponents of credulity and of romantic faith. But reason does not easily submit to limitations, even on behalf of faith. "I would rather be with the wise in Hell than among fools in Paradise," said the Master—adding, however, "but in Paradise, there are no fools."

In all three conceptions so far considered, faith is taken to be a matter of belief, the conceptions differing only in how they justify the belief. There is another conception in which faith is the substance of things hoped for, not the evidence of things unseen. If we are still to speak of belief, belief *in* something is to be distinguished from the belief *that* something is the case. We are speaking of trust, of hope, of aspiration. To believe *in* something is to cherish it, prize it, aspire to it. In this sense, lack of faith is nihilism—having nothing at all to believe in. True faith is believing in what is worthy of aspiration; idol worship is faith which lacks an objective ground, as when men whore after the false gods of the state, or of wealth, pleasure, or power.

This conception is *existentialist faith;* it is a matter of committment, involvement, dedication. Kierkegaard said of faith that it is not a school of numskulls or an asylum for the feebleminded, not because it is grounded in reason but because it concerns what we do rather than what we think, and thinking loosely adds nothing to the significance of our doings. Faith is not the acceptance on some distinctive ground of a body of special propositions —the creed; it is, rather, throwing ourselves into the actions entailed by the propositions to which otherwise we would be giving only lip service. We keep faith or break it not by believing or disbelieving but by living one life or another; to have faith is to be faithful—dependable, trustworthy. Lack of faith is not skepticism but betrayal or despair. The man of faith bears the mark of having wrestled with the angel while his spirit remains unconquered, going even to a martyr's death with the hymn, "God is with me, I shall not fear!"

Life demands faith because man is born into trouble, in the words of that model of faith, Job. "Man has few days and they are full of trouble; he withers like a flower and flees like a shadow; between the morning and the evening of one day he is shattered; he vanishes forever and no one remembers; he dies without wisdom." Each person has his own tribulations, suffers his own sorrows. In the dark night of the soul the Psalmist laments, "There is no man who knows me; I have no way to run; there is none who cares." Alienation and loneliness is not of our time alone (§63, §64), and the dark night is known to all faiths. Life is *dukkha, samsara;* "As a cowherd drives his cows into the stable," says Buddha, "so do age and death drive the life of men." "No man has dominion over the wind, or power over the day of death, and there is no discharge in war"—this is how the Preacher acknowledges the limits imposed upon us by nature, by our bodies, and by society (§3). The Koran notes that when trouble befalls him man is quickly cast down, and he is puffed up with pride when fortune smiles. Pride must give way when the Voice asks, "Where were you when I laid the foundations of the earth? Who determined its measures, stretched the line upon it, and set the cornerstone, when the morning-stars sang together and all the sons of God shouted for joy!" Not only pain but understanding teaches humility.

Faith is not demanded only by extreme situations, the hours of despair. It relates to all our ultimate concerns, as Paul Tillich called them, birth and marriage as well as sickness and death, occasions of joy as well as of sorrow. The Word is in my heart whether I am sitting in my house or walking by the way, when I lie down and when I rise up. To have faith is to cherish life as neither empty nor trivial, earnest though not grim, allowing joy but not frivolity; lack of faith cheapens existence, making of life only a measure of time given us to kill if it does not kill us instead. "It is pleasant to die if there be gods," said Marcus Aurelius, "and sad to live if not"; William James echoes him in seeing sadness at the heart of every "merely positivistic, agnostic, or naturalistic scheme of philosophy." Whatever its underlying philosophy, theistic or no, transcendent or naturalistic, every religion holds out a vision of the good. Faith is the conduct of life in the light of that vision, however our eyes are dimmed in gladness or in grief.

The vision is of good, but we are sunk in evil, encompassed by the dark. The Psalmist's "Out of the depths I cry to You" is the theme of all religious aspiration. "My soul waits for God more than watchmen for the morning" is the theme of every religious hope. Both together make up faith.

In the religious experience the wait is rewarded and there is an answer to the cry. Religions agree that whether faith bears fruit depends only on the faithful—believe and you shall be saved. Faith is self-sufficient, not because it belongs to the domain of the subjective where thinking so is enough to make it so but just the contrary, because it is objectively grounded. The Fact is always there, ready to be believed, and he who believes has thereby taken hold of the Truth. "God is near to all who call upon Him," says the Psalmist; the Book of Proverbs records the assurance, "Those who seek Me earnestly shall find Me."

Religious experience differs from aesthetic experience in requiring no special object for its evocation. Nothing relates to the religious experience as art does to the aesthetic; a presumed religious experience evoked by the work of human hands is only the worship of idols. The experience may be triggered or facilitated by various means, provided we do not mistake them for the end we seek. Spiritual exercises are not meant to bring God closer to us but to bring us closer to Him, for as Buber put it, "He who is not present perceives no Presence." Someone said to Pascal, "I wish I had your faith so I could lead a life like yours," to which he replied, "Lead my life, and you will acquire my faith."

Religious experiences can be looked at as progressive stages of encounter with Ultimates which are differently defined in the symbols and doctrines of different religions, although they are functionally equivalent as the focus of faith.

The lowest stage of encounter, an awareness that there is something to *be* encountered, the sheer sense of Presence, may be called *exaltation.* It is close to the aesthetic experience, especially the experience of the sublime and the tragic. It is the religious feeling, a sensitivity to the objective correlate of what appears subjectively as piety. Exaltation is the experience articulated as seeing the glory of God in the cosmos or in the triumphant achievements of the human spirit. It is said of a great Talmudist that for him the paths of heaven were as bright and familiar as the streets of his native town; for the Master, it was just the other way around. To see the town we live in as the heavenly city—that is exaltation. In Wittgenstein's analysis, "How the world is, is completely indifferent for what is higher.

God does not reveal Himself in the world." This may well be so (in contrast to all but the naturalistic conception of Providence [§87]), so far as concerns the facts which make up the world. The significance of the facts, their meaning and value, is another matter. One could equally say that the beauty of a painting does not reveal itself in the configuration of the paint, and in a sense this is true; but if the beauty is not revealed there it is nowhere. Exaltation is, as it were, the sense of beauty.

Inspiration is the next stage of encounter, to which the aesthetic is linked. By it, what would otherwise be a figment of imagination becomes a fragment of an objective truth. Inspiration allows man to create what brings man to the state of exaltation, as he who received the inspiration was himself exalted. Inspiration, Plato says in his *Timaeus*, is given not to man's wisdom but to his foolishness, when "his intelligence is enthralled in sleep or he is demented by some distemper"; it is a "sober intoxication of the mind" in the words of the Neoplatonist, Philo. It therefore needs subsequent interpretation by those capable of explicating visions and dark sayings. Here a priesthood begins to come to the fore, in both art and religion, as guides to the proper response to the products of inspiration, so that we too may be exalted.

Prophecy is inspiration which illuminates its own meaning, an encounter which knows itself for what it is, and declares itself in such a way that all who hear will also know. There are different modes of knowing; priest and prophet differ in how they know. What Bergson identifies as the two sources of morality and religion (in a book by that name) were traditionally distinguished as *da'at Adonai* and *yirat Adonai*, creed and conscience, discursive knowledge and direct experience, intellectual apprehension and the perspectives of piety, of reverence, and of awe. For the prophet, says Maimonides, the dark is lit up as by a flash of lightning; he communicates to others, as best he can, what he has seen in its light. Prophecy is renewed in every soul encountering God. Inspiration is the receptivity to encounter, while prophecy is the impulse to share the encounter with others, as the lover turns to music and poetry to express his love.

Encounter of more immediacy is known as *revelation*. Inspiration sees; the prophet sees and tells; in revelation, we see because something has been revealed *to* us. Communion has descended to communication. In revelation God speaks to man in dreams, in visions of the night, when deep sleep falls upon us as we lie still in the night; from the burning bush; in a Voice atop the holy mountain; and in the sound of silence. The Hindu word for revelation is *sruti*, from a root meaning to hear (with the inevitable association, "Hear, O Israel!"). It is testimony recorded in scriptures, but owing its validity to the encounter to which the writing is only a witness. Revelation is exaltation given tongue, speaking in a voice not its own, in accents so compelling that to hear is to obey. The faith of the people is shown in that they say first "We shall do it" and only afterwards "We hear it!"

The last stage of encounter is *Presence*, where communication rises once more to communion. The pure in heart shall see God—they will come into the Presence. To be in the Presence is to experience the *numinous*, the uncanny and sacred. It is the experience expressed by the Psalmist: "O God,

You are very great; You are clothed with glory and majesty. You cover Yourself with light as with a garment, stretch out the heavens like a curtain, lay the beams of Your chambers in the waters, make the clouds Your chariot. You walk on the wings of the wind, make the winds Your messengers, fire and flame Your ministers." All this pertains to the cosmic God (§86); the Presence is also of the moral divinity, the holy as well as the sacred. It is here that faith brings comfort and joy, which the Psalmist knows as intimately as reverence and awe: "Where shall I fly from Your presence? If I go up into Heaven You are there, if I make my bed in Hell You are there. If I take the wings of the morning and live in the outermost parts of the sea, even there Your hand shall lead me, Your right hand shall hold me."

To be in the Presence is known as a *mystic* experience; *mysticism* is the aspiration to live in the Presence, the creed expressing the content of such an experience, or the doctrine explicating both the experience and the creed. Mysticism is often confused with the mysterious, the esoteric, and the occult, which were distinguished earlier (§36). The mysterious is what is not yet known or understood. The mystical is not localized in the mysterious or in any way dependent on it; on the contrary, it is more likely to be sustained by what we do know and understand than by ignorance and perplexity. A scientific temper of mind, especially when it is of an abstract and theoretical bent, often finds mysticism congenial.

The *esoteric* restricts a teaching to a privileged group, often a priesthood, or those who have accomplished certain supposedly spiritual disciplines; what is conveyed may be any element of cult or creed, and has no more to do with mysticism than with any other doctrine.

The *occult,* which has had a shameful resurgence in our time, consists of doctrines claiming to be capable of empirical verification, but through data and procedures cut off from the main body of empirical knowledge. Usually, the occult purports to explain what science at that time finds to be mysterious, and the details of its explanations are often esoteric. The occult includes astrology and other types of augury; spiritism, with its related trines of rebirth, clairvoyance, astral bodies, and the like; health fads and spurious "psychotherapies"; and pseudoscientific theories of such matters as the solar system, lost continents, and space travelers. None of these has anything to do with mysticism. Equally irrelevant are witchcraft, diabolism, exorcism, and similar ideas. Systems of occult metaphysics, like theosophy and Kabbala, are related to mysticism, but only peripherally, and chiefly because Presence is a central category of virtually all religious philosophies.

William James, in common with many other observers, has noted the following characteristics of the mystic experience. It manifests a passive receptivity, being felt to come from without, often unexpectedly, and even unwillingly. It has a poetic aspect, giving a sense of insight, illumination, and understanding. It is transient and elusive, hard to maintain and to remember. Its quality and content are felt to be ineffable, perhaps altogether inexpressible. Self-contradictory phrases are often used: "dazzling obscurity," "whispering silence," "teeming desert." The Upanishads say, "It moves; It does not move. It is far; It is near. It is within all this; It is outside all this." Instead of words, other media may be resorted to "Music," James notes, "is the element through which we are best spoken to by mystical truth. Many mystical scriptures are little more than musical compositions." The Master said, "With melody man can open the gates of Heaven"; and on another occasion, in prayer, "If only I were a musician, I could compel You to come!"

A common type of mystical doctrine explicates a *shadow mysticism,* the notion that there is a transcendent parallelism between some higher realm and the domain of ordinary experience (§39), the higher being made vaguely known to us by way of the shadow it casts in the light of the Reality which we experience in the Presence. The world becomes a structure of symbols, to be interpreted by a system of hermeneutics whose key is provided in the mystic experience. Together with the Duke in *As You Like It,* we are to find

Tongues in trees, books in the running brooks,
Sermons in stones, and good in every thing.

As in this instance, shadow mysticism is often associated with a romantic, sentimental approach to nature. Quite different is the *metaphysical mysticism* of, say, Vedanta, for which the world is an appearance of the Reality, but not a system of symbolic correspondences. Different still is the *naturalistic mysticism* of Zen and (in some interpretations) of Hassidism, for which there are not two realms of being but only one, for we stand already and always in the Presence.

If mysticism is more than a pose, it is likely to be patterned in a cult and associated with a creed. Only rarely is it *antinomian*–rejecting law and ritual as irrelevancies and even interferences with coming into the Presence. The popularity in the West of Asian mysticisms—such as Sufism, Yoga, and Zen—may be due to the misconception that they rationalize moral irresponsibility. The mystic, like other religionists, engages in worship and service. Only, he construes his doings as leading to an encounter in which servant and Served meet, and merge at the point of their meeting. "The eye with which I look on God," said Eckhart, "is that with which He sees me." In Hinduism, God is the cosmic magician; the mystic is one who sees through the trick, sharing the illusion while not being deceived by it.

He may be a victim of self-deception. James tells of the great experience of illumination he had after taking nitrous oxide; with enormous difficulty he wrote down at the moment what he had come to understand—and afterwards found the message: "The universe is pervaded by a smell of petroleum!" (I resist the temptation to give this revelation significance after all, in terms of the politics of our own day.) Freud has analyzed what he called "the oceanic feeling"—the infantile state, to which the mystic is charged with regressing, in which the boundaries of the ego have not been formed, or remain fluid and permeable. The erotic symbolism often used to express the content of mystic experience, the merging of two into one, also suggests the workings of earthly impulses disguising themselves as spiritual aspirations. Many of the great mystics have been conspicuous rather for their mental health and maturity, so far as this can be judged by their practical good sense, organizing ability, and ethical realism—I mean men such as Guatama Buddha, Rabbi Akiba, St. Francis Xavier, and Swami Vivekenanda.

The close connection between mysticism and psychopathology, commented on by James in his *Varieties of Religious Experience* and by many psychoanalysts since, cannot be disregarded. That the mystic experience is individual makes it a challenge to religion, which is always socially structured. That the content of the experience is ineffable poses dangers to the intellectual life as well. The Talmud records that of four who entered *Pardes*—the domain of the mystical—one lost his life, one his reason, and one his faith; only Akiba escaped unscathed. Yet as a quality in experience, rather than as a distinctive type of experience, the mystical may be more widely known than is acknowledged in professed philosophies, especially if we include the less developed stages of encounter. If we are not aware that we are in the Presence, we may yet know and cherish a half-understood exaltation.

90. The Religious Life

The religious life consists of membership in a church, practice of a cult, acceptance of a creed, and expression of a faith. For many philosophers of religion, especially in the West, this is thought to constitute nothing other than the moral life: religion is either identified with morality or regarded as its essential foundation. The essence of the divine will is for love and justice among men; having these, we need nothing else. When Satan accused men of turning away from God, God replied, "Let them forget Me altogether, if only they live by My Law." Without religion, it is supposed (§51), there is no ground for moral distinctions, no source of moral knowledge, and no motiviation for moral action. This is the thrust of Dostoevski's dictum cited earlier, that if there is no God everything is permitted. The same position underlies the remark of the skeptical and anticlerical Voltaire that if God did not exist, it would be necessary to invent Him.

Such a standpoint is not universally shared even among religionists. The more orthodox may put as much emphasis on the practice of the cult as on moral action; both cult and morality define spheres of religious obligations and of corresponding religious attainment by fulfilling the obligations. There is undeniably more to the religious life than morality. In the Asian religions moral achievement is prerequisite to religious attainment rather than already constituting such attainment or being a consequence of it. For the Jain and Mimamsa, morality rests on a principle—the law of karma—which needs no God for its workings; yet the religious obligations they acknowledge are even more exacting than those of other cults. The Western pragmatic argument for the existence of God (§85) takes as its *premises* the significance of moral distinctions and the objectivity of moral obligation.

Since Nietzsche, both moral and religious philosophies have attempted to come to terms with the doctrine that God is dead. Existentialism, a philosophy not uncommonly associated with moral heroism, has been characterized by Sartre as "nothing else than an attempt to draw all the consequences of a coherent atheistic position." The view that religion is a presupposition of morality is seriously questioned within the religious camp as well as outside it.

Religion has been attacked for undermining morality let alone not providing a basis for morality. Mimaṁsa criticizes the belief in God because it hinders acceptance of the law of karma and weakens the authority of the Vedas. In Western mythology, the first murder took place after an act of worship, and because the worship was not accepted. The mark of Cain is a religious identification, and only after he received it did Cain depart from the presence of God. Voltaire's assessment is well-known: "For seventeen hundred years the Christian sect has done nothing but harm." Russell is even more extreme: "I say quite deliberately that the Christian religion, as organized by its churches, has been and still is, the principal enemy of moral progress in the world." Christianity is not always singled out in such attacks; the literature of anti-Semitism is extensive, though often Judaism is condemned precisely because it gave rise to Christianity.

Philosophers of religion have noted one threat to morality in the theistic doctrines. It is that God's foreknowledge of man's actions, as well as the divine plan of human destiny, denies human freedom or weakens the impulse to attain and exercise freedom. Some theologies, notably those of Augustine and Calvin, propound a doctrine of predestination: it is decided beforehand who is to be saved. Moral action is given a secondary significance after-the-fact. Behaving virtuously is a sign of something already decided; the behavior is not the basis of the decision. The predominant view in the Judaeo-Christian tradition is that everything is in the power of Heaven save the fear of Heaven, that is, save the religious commitment and the moral choices it entails, so that though all is foreseen, yet man is free. The whole issue relates to the metaphysics of free will rather than to the actualities of human freedom (§48).

Broader issues are raised by the question whether religion is a necessary motivation for moral conduct. Religion does promulgate a moral law—an Israeli wit has proposed that before withdrawing from Sinai we should take advantage of the opportunity to return the Ten Commandments. A preoccupation with the obligations of the cult and with religious attainment at least deflects from moral temptation: the Master said, "I abstain from sin, not because I have no evil urge, but simply for lack of time!" Religious convictions might also interfere with moral action—if, for instance, we rely on God to carry out what remains man's responsibility to his fellowmen. This is why the Master found occasion to say, "Act as if there were no God: you yourself must give the help you pray for." Coleridge remarked that to be an atheist requires a strength of mind and goodness of heart found in not one man in a thousand; the proportion is not much different with regard to the qualities required by a living faith.

On balance, I do not know that religion is significantly better or worse, from a moral standpoint, than the corresponding components of politics, which also has its rituals and loyalties, its institutions and ideologies. The sinner who, after a rousing sermon on the Ten Commandments, consoled himself with the reflection, "Well, anyway, I've never made any graven images!" was probably doing himself an injustice, and certainly his religion. In the history of the West, religion was responsible not only for sectarian bloodshed but also for putting an end to human sacrifices and gladiatorial games; though it espoused special privileges for the clergy, it was also in the forefront of movements for the abolition of slavery and for social equality; though it fought as the Church Militant it also perpetuated and recurrently revitalized the ideal of peace; though it acquired power and wealth it remained concerned for the weak and poor, maintaining schools and hospitals, and refuge for the homeless. The religious life, at its best, embodies the highest ideals of any morality; at its worst, it is no worse, as I perceive, than wholly secular political depravity.

What religion adds to the moral life remains obscure. If ethics purports to answer the question how a person should live, perhaps religion purports to provide a faith in living. The moral choice is the best that can be made; religion may address itself to the doubt whether making the best of things is good enough. In coping with this doubt, religion faces a dilemma. If it focuses on what transcends the moral issues it is likely to be empty and ineffective; if it focuses on moral action, it is likely to lack a distinctively religious content and to lose itself in reformist politics and psychiatric social work. Where it must choose, religion comes down on the side of man rather than God; it is there that its divine mission is most apparent.

The question raised by Confucius confronts every religion: "While you cannot serve men, how can you serve the gods?" The one is more than a preparation for the other; it is its substance. If you want a charm for loving God, said the Master, love man. God has plenty of angels to worship Him; it is good men that He lacks. Their goodness lies in their relationship to other men. The man who, without regard to the needs of his fellows, offers himself to God is doing so at their expense. Every religion has its ideal of the *bodhisattva,* the loving saint dedicated to the welfare of others. Though God rules over the cosmos, He identifies Himself not as the Creator of the world but as the God "Who brought you forth from the land of Egypt." His being is in His meaning for man; what He means to man is the ground of human freedom.

All men matter to Him, not only the members of the community of the faithful. The major religions have a universalist thrust. Like art, religion is culture-saturated but not culture-bound. The message is always that of Isaiah, "Ho! everyone who thirsts, come to the waters!" The Voice at Sinai spoke in all tongues, and prayers may be recited in any language (though the angels are said, in a charming *aggada,* to understand only Hebrew). The turban may be wound differently, the Hindu proverb runs, but unwound it is seen to be of the same cloth. Each religion assigns a special role to the community of the faithful, or else membership in the church would have no religious significance, but the distinction is not necessarily an invidious one. The principle is, rather, that to whom much is given, of him shall much be required. The dance of the righteous is in a closed circle of equal links, but opening always to embrace another in the dance.

The role of the prophet is to infuse the priestly cult with human content. Works contrast with faith only as the fruit differs from the stem by which it is nourished. "What to Me is the multitude of your sacrifices? says God. Learn to do well: seek justice, relieve the oppressed." Thus Isaiah. Amos declares, "I despise your burnt offerings, take away your hymns, but let justice roll down as waters, righteousness as a mighty stream!" And Micah: "What does God require of you but to do justice, love mercy, and walk humbly with your God?" The cult symbolizes and expresses a moral commitment.

As one whose people have suffered every cruelty, inflicted on them in the name of religion, I will not gloss over the inhumanities which couch at the door of every desire, including religious passion. Yet there runs through the religious life in all cultures a strand of human-heartedness as well, kindness and tenderness, as in St. Francis or Levi Yitzhak the Compassionate. If I could only love the greatest saint, the Master said, as God loves the worst sinner! In the legend of the Buddha there is a touching episode of his taking leave of his wife and infant son as he departs to seek enlightenment, wordlessly in the night, lest the tug of family feeling weaken his resolve. A similar episode is reenacted centuries later in a very different social setting by Hillel; both later return with an encompassing love, to be acknowledged as Teachers by those they had left.

The Master said, If anyone is thrust aside with the cry, Make way for the Messiah! he who comes is no Messiah. The dreamer asking to be admitted to Paradise is shown only the *tannaim,* the sages of the Talmud, engaged in studying the Law, while an angel explains to him that the *tannaim* are not in Paradise; Paradise is in the *tannaim.* The kingdom of God is within you because it means righteousness and peace and joy, and these lie within man and between man and man.

The religious life is, above all, a life of aspiration. The religious man worships the God who is not yet; he feels keenly that the world of daily life is not yet the Kingdom of God, and that he himself is not yet godly. He distinguishes the secular from the sacred in order that the secular may be sanctified, the profane from the holy in order that the profane may be purified. In the religious perspective every person is a pilgrim, a wayfaring stranger, walking the Path as he moves through the stages on life's way, but ever and ever again straying from the Path, perhaps losing the way altogether. The word translated as "repentance," *tchuvah,* means literally "the return." The Path remains where it is; though those who find it may be few, it is not hid. In the theistic idiom, God waits with open arms. Faith like Judah Halevi's evokes an even more heartening image: "Going out to meet You, I found You coming toward me." The religious life is a search, but to search for God is already to walk with Him.

The search cannot be carried on within the framework of cult and creed alone. The significance of Job, Kierkegaard pointed out, does not lie in what he said, but in the fact that he acted in accord with his declarations, at whatever cost; religious significance is in the style of life. The style, in turn, is made up of all a man's doings; what signifies is not just what lies within a domain marked out as religious. The spiritual is not another species of value, coordinate with moral, aesthetic, intellectual values; it is the genus of all value, manifested whenever a value is sufficiently intense, comprehensive, and integrative. Even mysticism recognizes the need to provide in our human pursuits a dwelling place for the Presence.

These pursuits, seen in religious perspective, are commonly subsumed under a threefold classification, described by Plotinus as the three roads of spiritual apprehension: the love of beauty, the ascent by way of science, and the path of moral purity. These correspond to the three *yogas* of Hinduism: *bhakti-*, *jnana-*, and *karma-yoga*. *Bhakti-yoga* is the way of feeling, devotion, love, artistic expression—the way of David, Fra Angelico, Rabindranath Tagore, St. Francis. *Jnana-yoga* is spiritual attainment through intellectual activity, science, philosophy—the way of Maimonides, St. Thomas, Sankaracharya, Spinoza. *Karma-yoga* is a life which is religious in quality even though the elements of church, cult, and creed may be inconsiderable, a life attaining its quality through dedicated moral action—the paths of Lincoln, Gandhi, Albert Schweitzer, and Martin Luther King.

Each path ascends the mountain from another side; all lead to the same peak. In Judaism and other Western religions what motivates the ascent is formulated in the injunction, You shall love your God with all your heart, with all your soul, with all your might (the three *yogas* again?). There are religions—as in Hinduism, the school of Yoga itself—in which God is not the Creator or Judge of the world, yet the Object most worthy of contemplation, the Teacher and Inspiration, in a word, the Model for man. That we are to become like the divine, or be guided by that aspiration, is a doctrine also to be found in Plato (the *Theatetus*). In short, you shall be perfect as your Heavenly Father is perfect; "Be you holy, for I your God am holy!"

To love what is less than God is religious insofar as it is love, but it falls short of the true faith insofar as it is directed to a lesser object. In Spinoza's locution, love of the finite puts us in bondage. Everything finite is imperfect, and so foredooms us to disappointment and sorrow; it is mutable and transient, condemning us to anxiety and greed; being finite, it can be possessed only by one person or another, and thus induces rivalry, conflict, envy and hatred; it is beyond man's control, inevitably bringing him to frustration and despair. Since man himself is finite, one who truly loved God, Spinoza pointed out, could not wish God to love him in return. God, too, has His cross to bear, Nietzsche said; it is His love for man. There is unexpected depth beneath the sentimentality of the blessing, "I wish Him joy in His children!"

That the Infinite is nevertheless within reach is the most fundamental religious presupposition. In reaching for It man has no choice but to use the words and images of his own making; the religious life is always threatened by degradation to the worship of idols. Not our gods but our idols are fashioned in our own image—this is what makes them idols. We become like what we worship; the worship of idols is faithless because in place of aspiration it condemns us to no more than what we are—indeed, to that fragment of ourselves we have put into the idols. In the words of the Psalmist, they have mouths which are silent, eyes without sight, ears that hear not, hands that take hold of nothing, feet which can bring them nowhere—and those who fashion them shall become like them. A people which worships a muderous state becomes a nation of murderers, and so for the other idols of our time. Yet it is not enough, as the Master said, to overthrow idols; one must discover and liberate the divine which was sought by their makers.

But what if it is not the divine which is being sought, if there is no divine to be sought, and the religious life is only acting out a psychopathology? The psychological critique of religion is formidable, cutting much deeper than the sociological or political attack. In this critique religion is held to be the product of neurosis or immaturity. "The whole religious complexion of the modern world," an early medical psychologist, Havelock Ellis, declared, "is due to the absence from Jerusalem of a lunatic asylum." He was referring to ancient times; today, no doubt, the absence—not just in Jerusalem—would be desperately felt with regard to the political complexion of the modern world even more than its religious one. In the United States clergymen outnumber psychiatrists by about thirty to one; though the practice of pastoral psychology is an important part of a clergymen's duties, the question might be raised whether this division of labor is to the best interest either of mental health or of religion. Freud, in his *Civilization and Its Discontents*, flatly characterizes religion as a "mass-delusion"; another of his books focusing on religion is called *The Future of an Illusion*. Is religion a subdivision of psychopathology?

Religious symbolism and imagery is so often erotic that the expression "bridal mysticism" has been coined for a widespread species of religious expression. Plotinus is more restrained than many writers on the subject when he characterizes the mystic union as that of which the union of earthly lovers who wish to bind their being with each other is a copy. In the *Zohar*, the great compendium of Kabbalistic materials, the bond of union between the male and female (construed as occult entities) is identified as the secret of true faith; in Tantrism and other sects the bond is taken in a literal sense.

Diagnosis of "bridal mysticism" in terms of repressed sexuality is so obvious as to invite the countercharge of superficiality. Dewey once repudiated the misrepresentation of pragmatism as "the philosophy of the American businessman" with the remark that Cartesian dualism could as reasonably be attributed to the French pattern of keeping a mistress as well as a wife. Many dualisms do in fact use sexual metaphors, as in the Chinese *yin-yang* cosmology. Empedocles spoke of all things as moved by "love" and "hate"; is his metaphysics to be interpreted in terms of repressed hostility? Would it have mattered so very much if instead he had used abstract categories such as "attraction" and "repulsion"?

The criticism goes beyond a mode of expression to underlying ideas. These ideas led Freud to the conclusion that religion is a product of infantile dependency: "The derivation of a need for religion from the child's feeling of helplessness and the longing it evokes for a father seems to me incontrovertible." Freud's position is that as the child matures he learns that the world is not a nursery, and he thereby outgrows religion with his childhood dependency. The imagery of the Father in religion is even more widespread than the idioms of "bridal mysticism," especially in the Gospels: the *sefirot* also include such designations as "the Aged One," "the Ancient of Days," "the White Head." What is to be said about nontheistic religion? Where is the exhortation to dependency in Buddha's injunction, "Be you lamps to yourselves!" Even with regard to the theisms, personal aspiration may be as important as reliance on the Other. Whitehead says, "The worship of God is not a rule of safety—it is an adventure of the spirit, a flight after the unattainable."

If not dependency, the critique continues, it is fear from which religion springs—fear of the gods, fear of death, fear of ghosts. This is a stand taken by philosophers from the time of Epicurus to the nineteenth-century positivists such as Ernst Mach. The Marxist characterization of religion as an opiate originally had a similar content; the contemporary word might be "tranquilizer." There is no doubt that many doctrines play on fears, with their creeds of eternal damnation and the like, and many cults are unquestionably fearsome—the worship of Kali and Durga, for instance, and the demonism in Tibetan Buddhism. There is no doubt, too, that creed may spell out procedures of propitiation, and cult may intensify fear so that it can be exorcised in a ritualized catharsis. But balance of terror is far from a universal religious strategy.

There is undeniably infantilism in religion—the exploitation of dependency, anxiety, guilt, and wish-fulfilling fantasies. But that there are immaturities in some religious experiences and practices does not mean that this is the essence of the matter always and everywhere. There are similar immaturities in politics, even psychopathologies, and the domains of art, law, morality, and interpersonal relations are not exempt. James has characterized religion as a monumental chapter in the history of human egotism; it would be easy to suggest other chapters for the same history. Religionists have the merit of recognizing the elements of immaturity and aspiring to rise above them. Paul, contrasting the religious significance of love with speaking in tongues, having prophetic powers, and understanding mysteries, sums up: "When I was a child I spoke like a child, I felt like a child, I thought like a child; now that I have become a man, I have put away childish things." Maimonides explicitly states the aim of his *Guide for the Perplexed* to be "to put an end to the fantasies that come from the age of infancy."

Countless skeptics have shared Montaigne's assessment: "Man is certainly stark mad; he cannot make a flea, and yet he will be making gods by dozens." Is there any less madness in man's worship of his political leaders, and his expectation of an earthly Paradise to be won after the Revolution or the War of Liberation? In both politics and religion is it not also a tribute to the human spirit that hope and faith survive the bitterest disappointments and defeats?

The genetic fallacy lurks dangerously in the psychological critique of religion: the infantile or neurotic needs which may provide the initial impulse to the religious life do not predetermine the quality of life eventually attained, any more than in the case of similar needs which find expression in lives devoted to intellectual, aesthetic, or social pursuits. Religion is affected by neurosis no less than is art, science, or politics; in all of them, however, what is achieved is owing to health rather than to pathology. In mature religion dependency gives way to humility, anxiety to earnestness of purpose, guilt to moral responsibility, egoistic demands to love and gratitude, fantasies of a future heaven to joy in the present world. For anyone to pretend that all this is exactly the substance of his own religion would be—childish. The achievement of age, as the comedian explains in the Prelude to *Faust*, is to learn at last what children we remain.

91. The Pursuit of Wisdom

Religion characteristically speaks in parables, uniting the homely and concrete with elusive meanings which hint of transcendence. Years ago I was granted an interview with the spiritual leader of South India, known as the Sankaracharya (the name of the medieval philosopher now used as a title) of Kamakotipeetam. The meeting took place outdoors, at night, by torchlight; he was brought in on a palanquin, carried by eight Brahmans naked to the waist (one of them my intermediary, a professor of philosophy in a nearby university), while literally thousands of the faithful, hoping for a glimpse of the holy man, clustered around the neighboring fences and trees. Said I to start with, "I have no specific questions; I want to hear whatever you have to say to me." And he: "It is enough, sometimes, when two souls meet one another in peace." "Sometimes one travels far, only to find his own soul." He countered with, "If a man travels far enough, he returns home at last." Then we began to talk freely.

Not long after, I found myself in New York on the occasion of my mother's death anniversary, and hunted for a hassidic place of worship to join in a memorial service. When I arrived, the rabbi greeted me; the following exchange took place: Said he: "Shalom—peace!" To which I gave the conventional reply, "And to you be peace!" "Who are you?" "A Jew." "From where does a Jew come?" "From some distance." "And why from afar have you come here?" I answered, "I have come to pray." "In that case," said he, "indeed, peace be unto you!" Only then could we speak of my name and city, the purpose of my visit to New York, and other such ordinary matters.

In both dialogues the theme is the Great Journey, in which man finds and fulfills himself. That is the religious idiom for the pursuit of wisdom. All formulations, religious or secular, agree that if the Way is not hard to find, it is very hard to follow; the utmost efforts of an earthbound life may not suffice. A monk, walking with the *roshi* in the temple garden, implored, "Teach me to hear the music of a stringless harp." The *roshi* stopped short, paused a moment, then said, "There! Did you hear it?" "Alas, no, master." Came the reply, "Why didn't you ask me louder?" If having ears we hear not, it is because we are not listening, and look unseeing at the all-encompassing Presence. Perhaps the worship of idols is nothing other than idle worship. The Midrash records the promise, "If you open your heart but the thickness of a needle I shall open it wide as a gate"; the master added, "But you must open it through and through; a mere scratch is not enough."

The parables continue. When the Master's grandson was visiting him the child dashed into the house and burst into tears. "I was playing hide-and-seek with my friends," he explained; "when it was my turn I hid and waited and waited, but they had all gone away." The Master held him close and comforted him; "God says the same thing—I hide and no one seeks Me." A more common imagery is that the Messiah stands ready just outside the city gate, prepared to enter; he is waiting only for you. He is not content to wait passively; in various religious philosophies, wisdom is also in pursuit of man. Daisetz Suzuki was once asked, "Are you a follower of Zen?" "No," he answered, "Zen follows me." One who covered his eyes with his hands so as to avoid seeing the Buddha found that the Buddha reappeared between his fingers. Francis Thompson's "Hound of Heaven" follows those who flee Him

With unhurrying chase,
And unperturbed pace,
Deliberate speed, majestic instancy.

Kant formulated an abstract and secular version of this insistence: the ultimate questions, which reason pronounces to be unanswerable, are not thereby silenced, but over and over again rise up to confront us.

The questions are unanswerable not because of any limits to reason, as Kant argued, or because of reason's weakness within an admittedly universal domain but because the questions arise from predicaments rather than from problems. There are solutions to problems, and whoever solved the problems to start with, their solutions can be applied by everyone who faces the same problems; our problems can even be solved for us by others. When it comes to predicaments, others can only make us more keenly aware of them, strengthen the courage and resolve with which we face them, point the direction in which we can bend our energies to cope with them; all the rest must be our own doing. "Our teaching," says Plotinus—his words are true of both philosophy and religion—"reaches so far only as to indicate the way in which men should go, but the vision itself must be their own achievement."

Nothing at all will be achieved without their own effort; wisdom is attained only in its pursuit. Buber's interpretation of the opening words of Genesis, though unconventional, is not unorthodox. Not *in* the beginning

God created, he suggests, but for the sake of the beginning, *your* beginning. That is why God made His covenant with Abraham rather than with Adam, the first man: when God called to Adam, Adam ran and hid, but when He called to Abraham, Abraham answered, Here I am! In announcing his presence, in being there, with all his being, he brought himself into the Presence. There is in all religion a sense of an opportunity not to be wasted, an enterprise to be undertaken without delay and without reservations. The *Ethics of the Fathers* sums up the situation: "The day is short, the task is great, the workers are indolent, the reward is immense, the Master is urgent."

The task is certainly one which has engaged man's mind: in all the major cultures the literature of philosophy and religion is vast. But if only the mind is engaged, the achievement is little. The besetting sin of intellectuals is, naturally, the intellectualist fallacy (§6), the notion that merely by taking thought we can raise our stature to whatever heights our eyes are raised. "All who worship what is not knowledge enter into blind darkness," says the Upanishad; then it adds, "those who delight in knowledge enter into greater darkness." For religion, that darkness is greatest in theology; absorption in gnosis—the focus on knowledge of presumed spiritual truths—is one of the four great dangers to the religious life which Buber pointed to (the others being magic, subjectivity, and formalism). Whitehead, though his philosophy is decidedly religious, described Christian theology as one of the great disasters of the human race. If other theologies are any less to be condemned, it may be because they have had less impact rather than because their doctrines are any less involuted, abstract, or fanciful.

Wisdom stands apart from knowledge, but we do not necessarily come closer to the one by taking leave of the other. The "fool of God" may be wise, but it would be foolishness to cultivate folly in the expectation of thereby becoming wise. Philosophy commits itself to quite the opposite course, seeking to know in order that it might mount from knowledge to wisdom. Knowledge can be misused here just as it can be misused anywhere else. Philosophy can succumb to linguistic hair-splitting, just as art can degenerate to academic exercise, and political aspiration can be perverted by ideological dogmas. We need not in any of these domains abandon our critical faculties.

The refusal to abandon them may even be a measure of our faith. While I have breath, Job said, I will not let go my integrity; I will argue my ways and this will be my salvation—that I do not come before Him as a hypocrite. For as he says again, in words echoed by Matthew, what can a man hope, whatever his gain, if he loses his own soul? Faith owes more to self-respect than to self-abasement. The Master said, If we bow too low too often, we may forget how to lift our heads to Heaven. Humility is an essential component of the religious attitude and of the pursuit of wisdom in any perspective. But humility is only a pretense if we are fearful of using the faculties we know we have.

Humility is both cause and effect of a man's recognition that he is not

God. Nietzsche says that it is the belly which forces us to this recognition, but our satisfactions as well as our hungers are no more than human. One who has no faith is content to drift, thinking nothing—not even wisdom—worthy of pursuit. One who believes only in himself has a faith of sorts, but it is less faith than credulity, resting either on ignorance or on self-deception. In Buber's terms, for the first man the world consists only of It; for the second, "I" is continually being mistaken for "Thou." Neither man reaches outside himself in either communion or communication.

A sense of the divine is repeatedly said to be the beginning of wisdom. Equivalently, wisdom begins with a sense of the human or a feeling for nature. God, man, and nature are so interlocked that wisdom can encompass all of them by entering deeply enough into any of them. The Way leads into them, through them, but not away from any. "How shall we escape from summer and winter?" asked the monk. "Why not go to the place where there are no seasons?" the *roshi* rejoined. "Where is such a place to be found?" said the monk eagerly. The answer was, "When winter comes we shiver, when summer comes we sweat." In another encounter, the monk complained, "We have to dress and eat daily; how can we escape from all that?" Said the *roshi*, "We dress, we eat." "I don't understand, sir." "If you don't understand," came the sharp reply, "get dressed and eat!" The pursuit of wisdom is not a path of escape.

If there is something from which we are to turn away it is anxiety and guilt. "I know God will forgive me," said Heine on his deathbed; "that is how He makes a living." The irony may conceal the same piety as in the Stoic acceptance of all that Nature brings in her own time and season. When the monk pleaded to have his soul pacified he was told, "Bring me your soul and I will pacify it." "Alas, master, I cannot find it." "There, it is already pacified." The desperate search for a cure is itself the disease. Take no thought for the morrow, the Gospels enjoin, for the morrow will take care of itself.

These expressions of Judaic trust, Stoic acceptance, Buddhist detachment, and Christian faith, taken in isolation, are more negative in tone than wisdom might approve. Spinoza concludes that the person who has properly understood that everything follows from the necessity of the divine nature will discover nothing worthy of hatred, laughter, contempt, or pity. Is the price of wisdom the loss of human feeling? "Come to Me all you who are heavy-laden and I will give you rest." Is the pursuit of wisdom, in the end, but a longing for death? "He who needs others is forever shackled," said Chuang-tzu; "he who is needed by others is forever sad. Drop these shackles, put away your sadness, and wander alone with Tao in the kingdom of the great Void." Is there, then, no place in the Void for friendship and for love?

All this resignation and renunciation may be admirable, but there is in wisdom another strand, less noble perhaps and also less demanding of greatness of soul. Life is not something from which to turn away or to which we must resign ourselves; wisdom lies, rather, in the appreciative recognition of all that life affords. Every man is to recite daily one hundred benedictions; if, on seeing bread, a man said only, How nice this loaf is! that, says the Talmud, is to be considered as its blessing. This is what it means not to live by bread alone; what is to be added is the Word which we ourselves speak.

The Word expresses the transformation of mere acceptance into joy. The truth is not that the sinner suffers; the suffering which we impose upon ourselves, upon one another—that is the sin. The most basic predicament of the pursuit of wisdom is that while sustaining aspiration wisdom also celebrates fulfillment. Says the Preacher, Eat your bread with joy and drink your wine with a merry heart, for God has already accepted your works. To turn your back on joy is to forget God; sin knows no joy—it cannot sing. There is nothing better for man than that he should rejoice; it is in the joy of his heart that God answers man.

The heart alone is not enough; without the discipline of man's mind the answer cannot be understood. For some that is how the answer is most plainly heard. They are the philosophers.

Further Readings

Dates and publishers are not given for works published before 1940, since they are generally available in a variety of editions. Listings are not repeated even though a work may be relevant to more than one topic.

Chapter One: Philosophy

Carnap, Rudolf. *Philosophy and Logical Syntax.*
Chan, Wing-tsit. *Sourcebook in Chinese Philosophy.* Princeton: Princeton University Press, 1961.
De Bary, William T. *Sources of Chinese Tradition.* New York: Columbia University Press, 1960.
———. *Sources of Indian Tradition.* New York: Columbia University Press, 1960.
———. *Sources of Japanese Tradition.* New York: Columbia University Press, 1960.
Dewey, John. *Reconstruction in Philosophy.*
Fung, Yu-Lan. *History of Chinese Philosophy.*
Husserl, Edmund. *Phenomenology and the Crisis of Philosophy.* New York: Harper & Row, 1965.
Jaspers, Karl. *Perennial Scope of Philosophy.* New York: Philosophical Library, 1949.
Kaplan, Abraham. *The New World of Philosophy.* New York: Vintage, 1961.
Langer, Susanne. *Philosophy in a New Key.* Cambridge: Harvard University Press, 1942.
Marcel, Gabriel. *Philosophy of Existentialism.* New York: Citadel, 1961.
Plato. *The Apology.*
Radhakrishnan, Sarvapelli. *History of Indian Philosophy.*

———, and Moore, Charles A. *Sourcebook in Indian Philosophy*. Princeton: Princeton University Press, 1957.
Reichenbach, Hans. *The Rise of Scientific Philosophy*. Berkeley, Calif.: University of California Press, 1951.
Russell, Bertrand. *History of Western Philosophy*. New York: Simon & Schuster, 1945.
Sartre, Jean-Paul. *Existentialism*. New York: Philosophical Library, 1947.
Suzuki, Daisetz T. *Zen and Japanese Culture*. New York: Phaidon Press, 1959.
Urmson, J. O. *Philosophical Analysis*. Oxford: Clarendon, 1958.
Wisdom, John. *Philosophy and Psychoanalysis*. Oxford: Blackwell, 1953.

Chapter Two: Semantics

Ayer, Alfred J. *Language, Truth and Logic*. New York: Dover, 1950.
Black, Max. *Language and Philosophy*. Ithaca, N.Y.: Cornell University Press, 1949.
Bloomfield, Leonard. *Language*.
Carnap, Rudolf. *Meaning and Necessity*. Chicago: University of Chicago Press, 1956.
———. *The Logical Syntax of Language*.
Cassirer, Ernst. *Language and Myth*. New York: Harper & Row, 1946.
———. *Philosophy of Symbolic Forms*. New Haven: Yale University Press, 1957.
Empson, William. *Seven Types of Ambiguity*.
Frege, Gottlob. *Philosophical Writings*. New York: Oxford University Press, 1952.
Gellner, E. A. *Words and Things*. London, 1959.
Jesperson, Otto. *Philosophy of Grammar*.
Morris, Charles W. *Signs, Language and Behavior*. New York: Prentice-Hall, 1946.
Quine, W. V. *From a Logical Point of View*. Cambridge: Harvard University Press, 1961.
———. *Word and Object*. New York: Wiley, 1960.
Russell, Bertrand. *Inquiry into Meaning and Truth*. New York: Norton, 1940.
Sapir, Edward. *Language*.
Shannon, Claude, and Weaver, Warren. *Mathematical Theory of Communication*. Urbana: University of Illinois Press, 1949.
Whitehead, Alfred North. *Symbolism: Its Meaning and Effect*.
Whorf, Benjamin Lee. *Language, Thought and Reality*. New York: Wiley, 1956.
Wittgenstein, Ludwig. *The Blue and Brown Books*. Oxford: Blackwell, 1958.

Chapter Three: Logic

Bacon, Francis. *Novum Organum*.
Carnap, Rudolf. *Introduction to Symbolic Logic*. New York: Dover, 1958.
Church, Alonzo. *Mathematical Logic*. Princeton: Princeton University Press, 1956.
Cohen, Morris R., and Nagel, Ernst. *Introduction to Logic and Scientific Method*.

Copi, Irving M. *Introduction to Logic.* 4th ed. New York: Macmillan, 1972.
Dewey, John. *Logic: The Theory of Inquiry.*
Frege, Gottlob. *Foundations of Arithmetic.*
Hilbert, D., and Ackermann, W. *Mathematical Logic.* New York: Chelsea Publications, 1950.
Mill, John Stuart. *A System of Logic.*
Nagel, Ernst. *Logic without Metaphysics.* New York: Free Press, 1956.
Reichenbach, Hans. *Elements of Symbolic Logic.* New York: Macmillan, 1947.
Russell, Bertrand. *Introduction to Mathematical Philosophy.*
———. *Principles of Mathematics.*
Strawson, P. F. *Introduction to Logical Theory.* New York: Wiley, 1952.
Tarski, Alfred. *Introduction to Logic.*
———. *Logic, Semantics and Metamathematics.* New York: Oxford University Press, 1956.
Weyl, Hermann. *Philosophy of Mathematics.* Princeton: Princeton University Press, 1949.
Wittgenstein, Ludwig. *Tractatus Logico-Philosophicus.*

Chapter Four: Theory of Knowledge

Descartes, René. *Discourse on Method.*
Dewey, John. *Quest for Certainty.*
Hume, David. *Enquiry Concerning Human Understanding.*
———. *Treatise of Human Nature.*
James, William, *Pragmatism.*
Kant, Immanuel. *Critique of Pure Reason.*
Lewis, C. I. *Mind and the World Order.*
Locke, John *Essay Concerning Human Understanding.*
Merleau-Ponty, Maurice. *Phenomenology of Perception.* New York: Humanities Press, 1962.
Moore, G. E. *Philosophical Studies.*
Peirce, Charles S. *Collected Papers.*
Plato, *Theaetetus* and *Sophist.*
Reichenbach, Hans. *Experience and Prediction.*
Russell, Bertrand. *Human Knowledge.* New York: Simon & Schuster, 1948.
———. *Our Knowledge of the External World.*
Santayana, George. *Scepticism and Animal Faith.*
Widsom, John. *Other Minds.* Oxford: Blackwell, 1952.
Wittgenstein, Ludwig. *Philosophical Investigations.* New York: Macmillan, 1953.

Chapter Five: Philosophy of Science

Bridgman, P. W. *Logic of Modern Physics.*
Bronowski, J. *Science and Human Values.* New York: Harper & Row, 1958.
Burtt, Edwin A. *Metaphysical Foundations of Modern Physical Science.*
Carnap, Rudolf. *Logical Foundations of Probability.* Chicago: University of Chicago Press, 1962.
———. *Philosophical Foundations of Physics.* New York: Basic Books, 1966.

Eddington, Arthur S. *Nature of the Physical World.*
Einstein, Albert, and Infeld, L. *Evolution of Physics.*
Galileo. *Dialogues Concerning Two New Sciences.*
Hayek, F. A. *The Counter-Revolution of Science.* New York: Free Press, 1952.
Hempel, Carl G. *Aspects of Scientific Explanation.* New York: Free Press, 1970.
———. *Philosophy of Natural Science.* Engelwood Cliffs, N.J.: Prentice-Hall, 1966.
Kaplan, Abraham. *Conduct of Inquiry.* San Francisco: Chandler, 1964.
Kuhn, Thomas S. *Structure of Scientific Revolutions.* Chicago: University of Chicago Press, 1962.
Nagel, Ernst. *Structure of Science.* New York: Harcourt Brace Jovanovich, 1961.
Poincaré, Henri. *Foundations of Science.*
Popper, Karl. *Logic of Scientific Discovery.* New York: Basic Books, 1959.
Reichenbach, Hans. *Philosophy of Space and Time.* New York: Dover, 1958.
———. *Theory of Probability.* Berkeley, Calif.: University of California Press, 1949.
Weber, Max. *Methodology of the Social Sciences.*
Whitehead, Alfred North. *Science and the Modern World.*

Chapter Six: Metaphysics

Alexander, Samuel. *Space, Time and Deity.*
Aristotle. *Metaphysics.*
Bergson, Henri. *Creative Evolution.*
———. *Introduction to Metaphysics.*
Bradley, Francis H. *Appearance and Reality.*
Descartes, René. *Meditations.*
Dewey, John. *Experience and Nature.*
Heidegger, Martin. *Being and Time.* New York: Harper & Row, 1963.
———. *Existence and Being.* Chicago: Henry Regnery, 1949.
———. *Introduction to Metaphysics.*
Kant, Immanuel. *Prolegomena to any Future Metaphysics.*
Leibniz. *Monadology.*
Lucretius. *Nature of Things.*
Mead, George H. *Philosophy of the Act.*
———. *Philosophy of the Present.*
Plato. *Parmenides* and *Timaeus.*
Plotinus. *Enneads.*
Sartre, Jean-Paul. *Being and Nothingness.* New York: Philosophical Library, 1956.
Schopenhauer, Arthur. *World as Will and Idea.*
Strawson, P. F. *Individuals.* London: Methuen, 1959.
Whitehead, Alfred North. *Process and Reality.*
Wiener, Norbert. *Cybernetics.* New York: Wiley, 1948.

Chapter Seven: Philosophical Anthropology

Bergson, Henri. *Time and Free Will.*

Broad, C. D. *Mind and Its Place in Nature.*
Cassirer, Ernst. *Essay on Man.* New Haven: Yale University Press, 1944.
Dewey, John. *Human Nature and Conduct.*
Erikson, Erik H. *Childhood and Society.* New York: Norton, 1950.
Freud, Sigmund. *General Introduction to Psychoanalysis.*
———. *New Introductory Lectures on Psychoanalysis.*
———. *Psychopathology of Everyday Life.*
Hampshire, Stuart. *Thought and Action.* New York: Viking, 1959.
Hegel, G. W. F. *Phenomenology of Mind.*
Huxley, Thomas H. *Man's Place in Nature.*
James, William. *Psychology.*
Mead, George H. *Mind, Self and Society.*
Neumann, John von, and Morgenstern, Oskar. *Theory of Games.* Princeton: Princeton University Press, 1947.
Piaget, Jean. *Logic and Psychology.* New York: Basic Books, 1957.
Ryle, Gilbert. *Concept of Mind.* London: Hutchinson, 1949.
Skinner, B. F. *Science and Human Behavior.* New York: Macmillan, 1953.
Teilhard de Chardin, Pierre. *Phenomenon of Man.* New York: Harper & Row, 1959.

Chapter Eight: Theory of Value

Aristotle. *Nicomachean Ethics.*
Bentham, Jeremy. *Principles of Morals and Legislation.*
Dewey, John. *Theory of Valuation.*
Hare, R. M. *Language of Morals.* Oxford: Clarendon, 1952.
Hartmann, H. *Psychoanalysis and Moral Values.* New York: International University Press, 1960.
Hartmann, Nikolai. *Ethics.*
Kant, Immanuel. *Critique of Practical Reason.*
———. *Fundamental Principles of the Metaphysics of Morals.*
Lewis, C. I. *Analysis of Knowledge and Valuation.* La Salle, Ill.: Open Court, 1946.
Mill, John Stuart. *Utilitarianism.*
Moore, G. E. *Ethics.*
———. *Principia Ethica.*
Myrdal, Gunnar. *Value in Social Theory.* London: Routledge, 1958.
Nietzsche, Friedrich. *Beyond Good and Evil.*
———. *Genealogy of Morals.*
Plato. *Phaedo* and *Phaedrus.*
Spinoza, Benedict. *Ethics.*
Stevenson, Charles L. *Ethics and Language.* New Haven: Yale University Press, 1944.
———. *Facts and Values.* New Haven: Yale University Press, 1953.
Toulmin, Stephen. *Place of Reason in Ethics.* Cambridge: Cambridge University Press, 1953.

Chapter Nine: Normative Ethics

Bible. Deuteronomy, Proverbs, Ecclesiastes, and Matthew.

Boethius. *Consolation of Philosophy.*
Buddha. *The Dhammapada.*
Camus, Albert. *Myth of Sisyphus.*
Chuang-tzu. *Writings.*
Confucius. *The Analects.*
Conze, Edward. *Buddhist Texts.*
Dostoevski, Fëdor. *Notes from the Underground.*
Epictetus. *Discourses.*
Kautšky, Karl. *Ethics and the Materialist Conception of History.*
Lao-tzu. *Tao Te Ching.*
Legge, James. *Texts of Taoism.*
Marcus Aurelius. *Meditations.*
Mencius. *Writings.*
Morris, Charles W. *Varieties of Human Value.* Chicago: University of Chicago Press, 1956.
Nietzsche, Friedrich. *Thus Spake Zarathustra.*
Schopenhauer, Arthur. *Studies in Pessimism.*
Thoreau, Henry David. *Walden.*
Warren, Henry C. *Buddhism in Translations.*

Chapter Ten: Social Philosophy

Arrow, Kenneth, *Social Choice and Individual Value.* 2d Ed. New Haven: Yale University Press, 1951.
Bukharin, Nikolai. *Historical Materialism.*
Collingwood, R. G. *The Idea of History.* Oxford: Clarendon, 1946.
Engels, Friedrich. *Socialism: Utopian and Scientific.*
Freud, Sigmund. *Civilization and Its Discontents*
Hayek, F. A. *Road to Serfdom.* Chicago: University of Chicago Press, 1944.
Hegel, G. W. F. *Philosophy of History.*
Marcel, Gabriel, *Man against Mass Society.* Chicago: Henry Regnery, 1962.
Marcuse, Herbert. *One-Dimensional Man.* Boston: Beacon Press, 1964.
Marx, Karl, and Engels, Friedrich. *Communist Manifesto.*
Mumford, Lewis. *Technics and Civilization.*
Ortega y Gasset, Jose. *Revolt of the Masses.*
Pareto, Vilfredo. *Mind and Society.*
Popper, Karl. *Poverty of Historicism.* New York: Harper & Row, 1961.
———. *The Open Society and Its Enemies.* London: Routledge, 1945.
Riesman, David, et al. *The Lonely Crowd.* New Haven: Yale University Press, 1950.
Rousseau, Jean Jacques. &*Emile.*
Schumpeter, J. *Capitalism, Socialism and Democracy.* New York: Harper & Row, 1950.
Tawney, R. H. *Equality.*
———. *Religion and the Rise of Capitalism.*
Veblen, Thorstein. *Theory of the Leisure Class.*
Weber, Max. *The Protestant Ethic and the Spirit of Capitalism.*
Whitehead, Alfred North. *Aims of Education.* New York: Mentor, 1960.

Chapter Eleven: Political Philosophy

Aristotle. *Politics.*
Fromm, Erich. *Escape from Freedom.* New York: Holt, Rinehart & Winston, 1941.
Hart, H. L. A. *Concept of Law.* Oxford: Clarendon, 1961.
Hegel, G. W. F. *Philosophy of Right.*
Hobbes, Thomas. *Leviathan.*
Jefferson, Thomas. *On Democracy.*
Kaplan, Abraham. *American Ethics and Public Policy.* New York: Oxford University Press, 1963.
Lasswell, Harold D., and Kaplan, Abraham. *Power and Society.* New Haven: Yale University Press, 1950.
Lenin, Nikolai. *State and Revolution.*
Locke, John. *Civil Government.*
Machiavelli, Niccolò. *The Prince.*
Madison, James, and Hamilton, Alexander. *Federalist Papers.*
Michels, Robert. *Political Parties.*
Mill, John Stuart. *On Liberty.*
Milton, John. *Areopagitica.*
Montesquieu, Charles. *Spirit of the Laws.*
Plato. *The Republic.*
Rawls, John. *Theory of Justice.* Cambridge: Harvard University Press, 1971.
Rousseau, Jean Jacques. *Social Contract.*
Sorels, Georges. *Reflections on Violence.*
Spinoza, Benedict. *Theologico-Political Treatise.*
Tocqueville, Alexis de. *Democracy in America.*

Chapter Twelve: Aesthetics

Aristotle. *Poetics.*
Bergson, Henri. *Laughter.*
Collingwood, R. G. *Principles of Art.*
Croce, Benedetto. *Aesthetic.*
Dewey, John. *Art as Experience.*
Gombrich, Ernst H. *Art and Illusion.* New York: Phaedon, 1962.
Hegel, G. W. F. *Philosophy of Fine Art.*
Hospers, John. *Meaning and Truth in the Arts.* Chapel Hill, N.C.: University of North Carolina Press, 1946.
Hume, David. *Standard of Taste.*
Kant, Immanuel. *Critique of Judgment.*
Langer, Susanne K. *Feeling and Form.* New York: Scribner, 1953.
Lessing, Gotthold. *Laoco;on.*
Longinus. *The Sublime.*
Nietzsche, Friedrich. *Birth of Tragedy.*
Plato. *Symposium.*
Plekhanov, George V. *Art and Society.*
Santayana, George. *Sense of Beauty.*

Sartre, Jean-Paul. *Literature and Existentialism.* New York: Citadel, 1966.
Shelley, Percy B. *Defense of Poetry.*
Tolstoy, Leo. *What Is Art.*
Trotsky, Leon. *Literature and Revolution.*

Chapter Thirteen: Philosophy of Religion

Aquinas. *Basic Writings.*
Augustine. *City of God.*
———. *Confessions.*
Bergson, Henri. *Two Sources of Morality and Religion.*
Bible. Psalms and Job.
Buber, Martin. *I and Thou.*
———. *Tales of the Hassidim.* New York: Schocken Books, 1947.
Dewey, John. *Common Faith.*
Durkheim, Emile. *Elementary Forms of the Religious Life.*
Freud, Sigmund. *Moses and Monotheism.*
———. *The Future of an Illusion.*
Hume, David. *Dialogues Concerning Natural Religion.*
James, William. *The Will to Believe.*
———. *Varieties of Religious Experience.*
Kierkegaard, Sören. *Concluding Unscientific Postscript.*
———. *Fear and Trembling.*
Maimonides, Moses. *Guide for the Perplexed.*
Pascal, Blaise. *Pens' ees.*
Philo Judaeus. *Basic Works.*
Scholem, Gershom. *Major Trends in Jewish Mysticism.* New York: Schocken Books, 1946.
Suzuki, Daisetz T. *Essentials of Zen Buddhism.* New York: Dutton, 1962.
Tillich, Paul. *Dynamics of Faith.* New York: Harper & Row, 1957.
White, A. D. *History of the Warfare of Science with Theology.*

Index

B

C

D

E

H

K

N

O

Q

R

S

U

V

Kaplan, Abraham
In Pursuit of Wisdom